P9-CQC-019

# HISTORICAL ATLAS OF
# CHRISTIANITY

# HISTORICAL ATLAS OF
# CHRISTIANITY

by

FRANKLIN H. LITTELL

CONTINUUM
New York • London

2001

The Continuum Publishing Group Inc
370 Lexington Avenue, New York, NY 10017

The Continuum Publishing Group Ltd
The Tower Building, 11 York Road, London SE1 7NX

# HISTORICAL ATLAS OF CHRISTIANITY

Second revised and expanded edition

Portions of this volume have been published previously as
*The Macmillan Atlas History of Christianity*

*Managing editor:* Barbara Laurel Ball
*Cartography:* Carta, Jerusalem

Library of Congress Cataloging-in-Publication Data

Littell, Franklin Hamlin.
　Historical atlas of Christianity / Franklin H. Littell.
　　p. cm.
　Includes bibliographical references and index.
　ISBN 0-8264-1303-X (hardcover)
　1. Ecclesiastical geography–Maps.　2. Historical geography–Maps.
3. Church history.　4. Civilization, Christian.　I. Title.
　G1046.E4 L5 2001
　270'.022'3–dc21
　　　　　　　　　2001018236

Printed in Israel

# TABLE OF CONTENTS

Foreword ...................................................................................... xi

I.   **EARLY CHRISTIANITY IN ITS SETTING** ........................................ 1
A.   **The World of the Jews** ............................................................ 5
    Lands of the Bible Before Jesus: Palestine, the Crossroads of the Nations.... 8
    The Holy Land Under Roman Rule (1st cent. BCE–1st cent. CE) .............. 10
    The Jerusalem of Jesus ..................................................... 12
    The Jewish Matrix of Christianity ............................................. 13
    The Contribution of Archaeology ............................................. 16
    The Dead Sea Sect ............................................................ 17
B.   **The World of the Greeks** ......................................................... 18
    The Greek Background ....................................................... 19
    The Rise of Hellenism ....................................................... 20
    The Athens of Paul .......................................................... 22
C.   **The Graeco-Roman World** ....................................................... 23
    Christianity Under the Roman Heel (to 325 CE) ............................... 23
    Flight of the Gods to Rome ................................................... 23
    The Roman Conquest of Britain (54 BCE–82 CE) ............................. 26
    The Twelve Apostles in Tradition ............................................. 28
    Christological Debates and Early Councils (2nd–3rd cent.) .................... 31
    Teachers and Persecutions (2nd–3rd cent.) ................................... 33
    Christianity and Gnosticism (2nd–3rd cent.) ................................. 36
    Manichaeism (3rd cent. ff.) ................................................... 38

II.   **THE CHRISTIAN ROMAN EMPIRE** ............................................ 40
A.   **Christianity Becomes Official** ................................................... 42
    The Empire of Constantine and His Successors (f. 313, 325) ................. 42
    Constantinople—A New Capital (f. 330) ..................................... 45
    Byzantine Jerusalem ......................................................... 46
B.   **Division of the Christian Imperium** ............................................. 49
    Resistance to Orthodox Theology and Roman Administration ................ 49
    Council of Chalcedon (451) ................................................... 52
    Decline of Roman Authority (5th–6th cent.) ................................. 54
    Christianity in Byzantium (c 787) ............................................ 56
    Monasticism (2nd cent. ff.) ................................................... 59
        Egypt and Palestine ..................................................... 59
        Cappadocia ............................................................. 61
        Italy and France ......................................................... 62
        Britain and Ireland ..................................................... 63
        Ethiopia ................................................................. 64

Nestorian Christianity (431 ff.) ............................................................ 65

The Kingdom of the Khazars (c 700–1000) ...................................... 66

Mohammed's Struggles ...................................................................... 67

The Rise of Islam (7th cent. ff.) ........................................................ 68

C.  **The Empire of Charlemagne and His Successors** ................................ 70

The Christian Empire of Charlemagne (742–814) ............................ 70

Aachen—A New Capital ...................................................................... 74

Missionary Activities in the North (7th–9th cent.) .......................... 75

Cluny (f. 910) and Monastic Reform .................................................. 76

The Holy Roman Empire of Otto the Great (962–73) and

His Successors .................................................................................... 78

Britain at the Time of Alfred the Great (849–99) ............................ 80

East Versus West—The Omayyads and Abbasids (8th–9th cent.) .............. 81

D.  **Disintegration of the Carolingian Empire** .......................................... 86

Shadows over the Holy Roman Empire (mid-11th cent.) .................. 86

Italy and the Papal States (11th cent.) ............................................ 88

Norsemen and the New World (8th–15th cent.) ................................ 90

England and the Norman Conquest (1066–72) .................................. 92

E.  **Papal Efforts at Reintegration** .......................................................... 94

The Holy Crusades (11th–12th cent.) ................................................ 94

The Capture of Jerusalem by the Crusaders (1099) ........................ 97

The Empire of Frederick Barbarossa (c 1123–90) ............................ 98

Crusader Kingdoms (11th–15th cent.) .............................................. 101

Cistercian Reform Movement (12th cent.) ........................................ 103

Christendom at the Time of the Fourth Lateran Council (c 1215) .............. 105

Teutonic Knights in the Baltic (13th–15th cent.) ............................ 107

Medieval Travelers to the Orient (13th–14th cent.) ........................ 109

Ramon Lull (c 1236–1315) and the Muslims .................................... 110

Medieval Theologians and Mystics (11th–14th cent.) ...................... 112

The Mongol Attack on Islam (12th–15th cent.) ................................ 116

The Black Death (14th cent.) ............................................................ 118

The Jews of Ashkenaz (9th–17th cent.) ............................................ 120

Jewish Messianism: Hopes and Disappointments (13th–18th cent.) .......... 122

The Unification of Spain (13th–early 16th cent.) ............................ 124

Expulsion of the Jews from the Iberian Peninsula (1492 ff.) .............. 126

F.  **Disintegration of Papal Authority** .................................................... 128

Rise of the Cities (12th cent. ff.) ...................................................... 128

Rise of the Universities (11th cent.–1528) ...................................... 130

"Babylonian Captivity"—The Papacy at Avignon (1309–77) .............. 132

The Great Schism (1378–1409) ........................................................ 134

Divisions After the Council of Pisa (1409) ...................................... 134

Reunion of East and West (1438–39) ................................................ 136

Louis of Bavaria and the Pope (14th cent.) ...................................... 137

    Eastern Orthodoxy (1453)...................................................................138

    The Fall of Constantinople (1453).....................................................139

    The Italian Renaissance (15th–17th cent.)........................................140

    The Northern ("Christian") Renaissance (15th–16th cent.)...............142

**G.   Rebellion in Latin Christendom**...............................................144

    German Knights' War (1522–23) ......................................................144

    German Peasants' Wars (1524–26) ...................................................146

    The Radical Reformation (16th cent.)...............................................147

    Hutterite Colonies in Central Europe (16th–17th cent.) ..................150

**H.   The Magisterial Reformation and Reformers**...........................151

    Papal Politics: Alexander VI (Pope 1492–1503) and His Successors ..........151

    The Reformers ...................................................................................153

        Martin Luther (1483–1546) .........................................................153

        Philipp Melanchthon (1497–1560) ..............................................154

        Martin Butzer (1491–1551)..........................................................155

        Ulrich Zwingli (1484–1531) ........................................................156

        John Calvin (1509–64)..................................................................157

    The Index of Forbidden Books..........................................................157

    The Marburg Colloquy (1529)..........................................................158

    The Reformation in Switzerland (16th cent.).....................................160

    The Reformation in Scandinavia (16th cent.) ....................................163

    The Reformation in England (16th cent.) ..........................................165

    New Alignments of Christian Europe (later 16th cent.) .....................170

**I.   Wars of Religion**......................................................................173

    Civil War in France (16th cent.) .......................................................175

    The Flight of the Huguenots (16th–18th cent.)..................................176

    Civil War in the Netherlands (16th cent.).........................................178

    Civil War in England (16th–17th cent.).............................................181

    John Knox and the Civil War in Scotland (16th–17th cent.)..............184

    Thirty Years' War in Germany (1618–48)..........................................187

    Repression of Jews in Europe (16th–17th cent.)................................189

**J.   Imperial and National Efforts at Reintegration of Latin Christendom** .........192

    The Empire of Charles V (Emperor 1519–56) ..................................192

    Portuguese and Spanish Voyages of Discovery (15th–16th cent.).............195

    North European Voyages of Discovery (16th–18th cent.)....................198

    The Realm of Francis I (King of France 1515–47).............................200

    Spain Under Philip II (King 1556–98) ..............................................203

    The Destruction of the Armada (1588) .............................................205

    Latin America (16th–18th cent.) .......................................................207

    Ignatius Loyola (c. 1491–1556) .......................................................208

    The Rise of the Jesuits (16th–18th cent.) ..........................................209

    The Jesuits in the Americas (16th–18th cent.)...................................214

        South America ...............................................................................214

    North America (East) ................................................215

    North America (West).............................................215

   The Council of Trent (1545–63)...................................216

    Period I 1545–47 Sessions I–VIII ...............................216

    Period II 1551–52 Sessions IX–XIV.............................217

    Period III 1562–63 Sessions XV–XXV .........................218

   The Muslim Offensive in Europe (15th –17th cent.) ............219

   Russia Under the Tsars (1547–1725)..............................222

**K.**   **European Christendom in the Age of Colonialism**...............225

   English Colonies in America (17th–18th cent.) ..................225

   Pennsylvania—A Religious Refuge (17th–18th cent.)...........227

   India (c 1706) ......................................................228

   Pietism (17th–18th cent.) ..........................................230

    Pietism in Germany ..............................................231

    Experimental Religion in England and America ...............232

    Romanticism, Nationalism and Religious Revival.............233

   The Enlightenment .................................................234

   The Impact of the French Revolution (1789–1814) .............237

   The Holy Alliance in Europe (1815–1825) .......................241

    Prussia............................................................242

    Russia ............................................................245

    Austria-Hungary .................................................248

   Mennonites and Hutterites in Russia..............................251

   Doukhobors in Southern Russia ...................................252

   The Papal States (1815–70) ........................................252

   The Old Catholic Secession (1870 ff.) ............................256

   Scientific Method and Religion.....................................259

   Latin America from Colonies to Nationhood (19th cent.).......260

   American Expansion and Religion (19th cent.)...................262

   The Aglipayan Church of the Philippines (c 1900) ..............267

   Africa Before European Colonialism (16th cent.)................267

   South African Migrations (19th cent.) ............................270

   Africa Under Colonial Rule........................................272

   Colonial Holdings in Asia (19th–20th cent.) .....................274

   Colonial South Pacific.............................................277

   Imperial England (19th cent.)......................................279

   The Holy Muslim Empire (broken up 1918) .....................281

   The Baha'i Movement..............................................283

   Armenia.............................................................284

**L**   **Initiatives by the Rank and File ("Laity")** .....................286

   New Religious Orders in France (19th cent.) .....................288

   Renewal Movements in Germany (19th cent.)....................289

   Revivals of Religion in England (19th cent.)......................291

| | | |
|---|---|---|
| **III.** | **THE AGE OF PERSONAL DECISION** | 294 |
| **A.** | **Christianity and Ideology** | 296 |
| | Karl Marx (1818–83) | 296 |
| | The European World of Marxism | 298 |
| | The Fascist Empire (1922–45) | 302 |
| | The Spanish Civil War (1936–39) | 304 |
| | The Nazi Empire (c 1942) | 306 |
| | The Two Chinas | 310 |
| | The Arab League (1945 ff.) | 312 |
| | The Two Irelands | 314 |
| | State Religions and Ideologies | 315 |
| **B.** | **Religions in America** | 322 |
| | American Revivals of Religion | 322 |
| | Early Activities of the ABCFM | 324 |
| |   The ABC in the Middle East | 325 |
| |   The ABC in Hawaii | 326 |
| | American Religious Communities and Communes (19th cent.) | 326 |
| | American Universities and Colleges (to 1860) | 329 |
| | The American Civil War (1861–65) | 331 |
| | Negro Higher Education After the Civil War | 334 |
| | The Growth of Roman Catholicism in the USA | 336 |
| | Anti-Evolution Laws in the USA | 339 |
| | Christianity Outside the Ecumenical Sphere | 340 |
| |   The Lutheran Church, Missouri Synod | 340 |
| |   The Southern Baptist Convention | 340 |
| |   The Church of Christ, Scientist | 341 |
| |   Jehovah's Witnesses | 341 |
| |   The Church of Jesus Christ of Latterday Saints (Mormons) | 342 |
| | Black Religion in America | 342 |
| | Major Jewish Communities in the USA | 345 |
| | National Council of the Churches of Christ (f. 1950) | 348 |
| **C.** | **The Great Century of Christian Missions** | 350 |
| | New American Churches | 350 |
| | The Rise of Modern Missions | 352 |
| |   Missionary Awakening in Europe | 354 |
| |   Missionary Awakening in America | 356 |
| |   Missions in Latin America | 358 |
| |   Missions in Asia | 359 |
| |   Missions in the South Pacific | 360 |
| |   Missions in Africa | 362 |
| **D.** | **The Ecumenical Movement** | 364 |
| | The YMCA and YWCA | 364 |
| |   Europe | 365 |

America ............................................................................................ 365

The Work of John R. Mott (1865–1955) ............................................ 366

Mott's Travels in Asia ................................................................... 368

The World's Student Christian Federation (f. 1895) .......................... 368

Ecumenics in the 19th and 20th Centuries ........................................ 370

Vatican II (1962–65) .................................................................... 372

The Harare Assembly of the World Council of Churches (1998) ........... 373

Christian Renewal Movements ........................................................ 375

Post-War Germany ...................................................................... 375

Europe ........................................................................................ 377

USA ............................................................................................ 379

Africa ......................................................................................... 382

Asia and the South Pacific ............................................................ 384

Latin America .............................................................................. 385

Service Committees ...................................................................... 387

Brethren ..................................................................................... 387

Mennonites ................................................................................. 387

Quakers ...................................................................................... 387

E.    **New Perspectives** ........................................................................ 390

Unusual Religious Movements: USA ................................................ 390

Unusual Religious Movements: Germany .......................................... 392

Religious Ferment in Japan ............................................................ 394

Christian Churches and Groups ..................................................... 394

Shinto Centers ............................................................................. 395

Buddhist Groups .......................................................................... 395

Independent African Christian Movements ....................................... 396

"Third Force" in Missionary Action ................................................ 398

Mega-Churches ........................................................................... 400

Centers of Interfaith Dialogue ....................................................... 401

German Councils of Christians and Jews ......................................... 403

F.    **Destruction and Renewal** ............................................................. 404

Christendom and the Holocaust ...................................................... 404

Memory Work After the Holocaust ................................................. 407

A Restored Israel ......................................................................... 411

APPENDICES

A.    Countries Recently Limiting Religious Liberty ................................. 413

B     Members of the International Council of Christians and Jews ............. 414

C.    Stockholm Forum on Holocaust Education ...................................... 414

D.    Members of the World Council of Churches ..................................... 415

SELECTED PERSONS AND CONCEPTS ............................................ 421

INDEX ........................................................................................... 425

# FOREWORD

IN an illustrated survey of an area as large as the history of the Christian movement, many different emphases are available. In any review of the past the ocean of facts is infinite. Most previous surveys, like the monographs which flow weekly from the presses, reflect the interest of the professionals in ideas and institutions. The impression thereby arises that Christian history may be understood in terms of the history of ideas or in terms of the development of institutions. And, since concepts tend to settle into a static state, the Christian faith itself is thereby falsely defined as assent to a set of propositions or obedience to an ecclesiastical power-structure.

The Christian faith is not an ideology. Neither is Christianity contained in institutional structures. Having proved capable of producing many dynamic impulses, Christianity may be surveyed in any one of a number of ways—provided both writer and reader are wise enough to remember that each way that is taken involves a certain arbitrariness of selection and incompleteness of portrayal. An "illustrated tour through church history" might take the path of the development of the liturgy, following in the wake of a great study like Gregory Dix: *The Shape of the Liturgy* (Westminster, Eng.: Dacre Press, 1949). Or it might feature the development of education and educational institutions, since one of the major works of Christians—in the process of civilizing baptized peoples—has been everywhere the founding of schools and (later) universities and colleges. Or, in line with the renewed perception of the nature of the church as a whole people rather than an elite, it would be appropriate to illustrate the highway staked out by Neill and Weber (eds.): *The Layman in Christian History* (London: SCM Press, 1963). Similarly, the path might be the development of music and musical forms—from Gregorian chant through plainsong, chorales, Negro spirituals and gospel songs to the new hymns of today's youth encampments. These, and many more, are possible options, and through any of these approaches the course of Christian history might be opened up for the reader's reflections.

Most atlases, "religious" as well as "secular," are limited to sketching areas of political hegemony. Ethnic and/or national lines provide the basic context within which important concepts are optically presented. And, in the history of religions, much can be conveyed by graphics which are primarily geographical. Christianity, which for centuries followed the political and military fortunes of baptized conquerors of pagan peoples, owes much of its singular worldwide scope to the alliance of church and state which obtained from Constantine the Great's time to the modern period. The fine volume published by Herder— Jedin/Latourette/Martin: *Atlas zur Kirchengeschichte* (Freiburg, 1970)— shows how successful an interplay of geographical and schematic portrayals may be. The same is true of the superb volume done by Edwin S. Gaustad: *Historical Atlas of Religion in America* (San Francisco: Harper & Row, 1976).

Yet as we approach the modern period the dependence upon the creedal preferences of rulers and governments becomes more and more frustrating to cartographer and student. In earlier times it could be assumed that loyal subjects obeyed the chieftain in matters religious as well as political and military: e.g., when Clovis I of the Salian Franks (c 466–511) was baptized in 496 or Ranavalona II of Madagascar was baptized in 1869, each was followed into Christianity by thousands of loyal tribesmen. In post-Enlightenment religion, however, a pluralism of creedal communities marks every advanced society. Even in the political sphere, the most arbitrary of rulers feels compelled to claim a "silent majority" in his support. Totalitarian governments have developed a veritable science of turning out overwhelming statistical "mandates." In religion, the hidden commitment cannot be successfully coerced. Only outward conformity can be. Thus the conscience of the ordinary believer has become important for the first time in history. With this fact has come a dissolution of the old ethnic religions and of such established Christianity as had sunk to the level of mere ethnic loyalty. The reform movements in Hinduism, Buddhism and Islam have "missions" in all of the major cities of North America and Europe, just as the Christian modern missionary movement had begun to abandon the old tribal and national base of "Christendom" a few generations back.

This development, welcome as it is to those who love Religious Liberty, renders the whole geographical portrayal of religions increasingly problematical. We run immediately into two of the most besetting problems in the study of religions. First, how can intensity of religious (or ideological) commitment be measured, if at all? How many Orthodox Christians are left in Russia and other states of the former USSR, now that the previous anti-religious ideological establishment generally has lost its coercive power? How many Protestants are left in the very heartland of the Reformation, now that the anti-religious regime of the Communist DDR has collapsed and the seven provinces of East Germany have reunited with the Federal Republic of Germany?

How shall we reckon the number and life of Christians persecuted in Indonesia, the largest Muslim nation (c 215 million) in the world?...in mainland

China (c. 1.3 billion), officially atheist and in fact persecutory? ...in India (c 1 billion), predominantly Hindu, with Christians subject to sporadic regional persecution? ...in the Sudan, the largest country in Africa (967,493 square miles, c 34 million population), with a fundamentalist Muslim regime and perhaps 1 million Christian martyrs during the last two decades?

Persecution and martyrdom are somber notes that sound throughout large sectors of contemporary Christian history. In brute numbers, more Christians have been martyred in the twentieth century than in all previous centuries put together.

How shall we optically portray "Lutheran" Sweden or "Catholic" Spain, where 98 percent of the population is claimed in each case but internal studies show but 3.6 percent and 15 percent, respectively, in effective connection? Second, how reliable are religious statistics? Very few countries have careful scientific surveys like those available in Israel and the USA, and in the latter situation the reports from the larger denominations—such as the Southern Baptist Convention or the United Methodist Church—contain considerable inflation. In the areas of a once coercive Christendom the statistics are notoriously unreliable. Only in the younger churches of the mission fields of Africa, Latin America, Asia and the islands of the South Pacific is it possible to get highly accurate reports.

The point is that the traditional conceptualizations of religion are open to serious challenge today, and the student who uses an atlas—of necessity largely dependent upon territorial visualization—must keep in mind the ambiguities of that method of portrayal. In the modern period of totalitarian ideologies and parties and governments—symbolized by the Holocaust, by church struggles of varying intensity—Orthodox and Roman Catholic and Protestant Christianity have under pressure and temptation yielded high percentages of disloyalty and apostasy from the Christian faith.

Recognizing the limitations imposed by the method, this book undertakes to present the Christian movement by emphasizing three foci: 1) intellectual discipline (doctrine, dogma, theology, confessions of faith); 2) moral and ethical discipline (church discipline, social teachings, "Christianization" of society, internal style of life, relations with "secular" structures such as government); 3) expansion to a global religion from beginnings in the Roman province of Palestine (missions and ecumenics). The basic conception is perhaps best conveyed by the term "confrontation." The scheme is to highlight those times and places of crisis and decision—either internal or external or both—in which the shape and direction of the Christian movement was determined. In this connection, special attention is given to the interaction of the Christian churches and the Jewish people and to the encounter of Christianity and Islam.

The Jewish people have a special and continuing role in any effort to "fix" Christianity and its condition at a specific point in history. Failure to regard this role in our own time resulted in wholesale murder of Jews by "Christians," a matter as serious for the salvation of the baptized as it has been for the survival of the circumcised. The encounter with Islam has been of very great importance to the development of Christianity, both positively and negatively. Negatively, the centuries of crusades and military adventures developed in Christian thought the mindset of the beleaguered fortress and virtually buried the openness of the Logos Fathers to Truth wherever found. Positively, a then superior Muslim civilization once contributed a great deal to Western Christendom in the way of mathematics, engineering, philosophy, medicine, education. Today, the Muslim awareness of the importance of oral tradition and group loyalty has much to offer a Christianity atomized by the negative aspects of the triumph of technology.

Any scheme of periodization reveals the historian's presuppositions, and this is true of the present work. These presuppositions cannot be argued here, as they have been in other writings, but they can be stated honestly for the reader's awareness and reflection. The somewhat unconventional periodization adopted here has many reasons behind it, but the chief arguments run as follows. First, the language of the spoken and written word controls the articulation of dogma, theology, worldview. In the early period that language was Greek, and that fact had far more to do with shaping Christianity than the details of the reigns of Caracalla, Heliogabalus and Alexander Severus while Christianity was still illicit. Hence the first period of Christian history is organized by the impact of Greek language and culture rather than by reading back into it the later importance of the Roman imperium. Second, the vision of a Christian empire—shaped in large part by Roman law and the Byzantine administrative procedures which the emperors adopted and later nation-states appropriated—was normative as long as "Christendom" remained a viable concept. The break in western Christianity came not with the Reformation but with the Enlightenment. The magisterial Refor-

mation was closer to the world of Thomas Aquinas and Louis of Bavaria than it was to the world of René Descartes and William Penn. And of course the Younger Churches have been closer to early Christianity than to European Christendom. Hence the second period of Christian history is continued to the time when the shape and content of Christian life changed radically, at the opening of the modern age. Third, the chief characteristic of the modern period—both politically and in religious matters—has become individual freedom of choice. This must not be taken to imply a theological bias: the meaning is sociological rather than theological. The rubric is "voluntaryism" rather than "voluntarism" of association. It may seem strange to stress the importance of personal choice in an age when ideological governments and anachronistic police states control large sections of the global land mass. But even they must claim popular support. And in the development of a Christianity fit for resistance to spiritual slavery and capable of dialogue with the other high religions and systems of being, the personal choice of the ordinary believer has taken the place of definitive decision once occupied solely by baptized monarchs and consecrated hierarchs.

It is no longer enough to know the creedal commitments of the earthmovers and -shakers. The responses of believers in Rangpur, Wukari, Hungnam, Gatico, Untsk, Nha Trang and Keokuk must be identified and respected if the present picture is to make sense. This makes the cartographer's work more difficult, but the study of religion becomes far more challenging.

Franklin H. Littell

# ACKNOWLEDGEMENTS

THIS Historical Atlas grew out of the years of teaching the History of Christianity, and in preparing it I was continually conscious of my indebtedness to my teachers (William Walker Rockwell, Robert Hastings Nichols and Cyril Richardson at Union Theological Seminary, Roland H. Bainton, Kenneth Scott Latourette and Luther A. Weigle at Yale University), and to my colleagues and students in survey courses at Candler School of Theology/Emory University, Perkins School of Theology/Southern Methodist University and Chicago Theological Seminary. I am also grateful to my former student and present colleague, Prof. Dr. Erich Geldbach of the Ruhr University of Bochum, for his work in publishing a revised German edition and for useful insights that improve this volume.

Its preparation has occupied specialists and editors in Jerusalem, New York, Philadelphia and London. The basic interpretations are to the credit or fault of the author, but on a multitude of details the willing assistance of team members was a constant psychological and practical support. I want to thank especially Emanuel and Shay Hausman and members of their staff at CARTA, not only for technical assistance but also general helpfulness during my many stays in Jerusalem. I am particularly grateful to Lorraine Kessel, Beni Edden and Shoshana Zioni, as well as to Tsahi Ben-Ami and Vladimir Shestakovsky who added to and improved this new edition. F.H.L.

# I

# EARLY CHRISTIANITY IN ITS SETTING

CHRISTIAN history does not begin with a cosmological myth. Neither does it begin with the creation of man. It begins, like Jewish history, with a specific and unique event in human time and space. This formative event, remembered and re-enacted by men of faith across centuries, is related in the first book of the Pentateuch (Gen. 12:1–25:10). According to the story, a man—Abram—was called out of his natural life of idolatry and polytheism into worship and service of God. The new relationship is described in terms of a compact between God and this particular man:

> Behold, my covenant is with thee and thou shalt be a father of many nations.
>
> Neither shall thy name any more be called Abram but thy name shall be Abraham; for a father of many nations have I made thee.
>
> And I will make thee exceeding fruitful and I will make nations of thee and kings shall come out of thee.
>
> And I will establish my covenant between me and thee and thy seed after thee in their generations, for an everlasting covenant, to be a God unto thee and to thy seed after thee.
>
> And I will give unto thee and to thy seed after thee the land wherein thou art a stranger, all the land of Canaan, for an everlasting possession and I will be their God.
>
> Genesis 17:4–8*

The Israelites were not the first people of earth. They did not call themselves the people, as have so many primitive tribes; neither did they instill that assumption in their teachings, as do so many modern nation-states. They could claim no preeminence in wealth, military equipment, political hegemony: as the first glance at the map on page 9 immediately suggests, they became a small people on a land ridge across which, throughout recorded time, the surge and ebb of mightier empires would move. Their single claim to a place in human affairs was based upon a covenant community's relationship to the God whom they understood to be the Author and Judge of history.

The early Christians also understood themselves to have been called out of pre-history into history as fellow heirs of the same promises declared through apostles and prophets to the Jews. It was the mysterious work of Christ to have grafted them into an older tree of history, to have built their house upon a foundation already laid (Eph. 2:19–20, 3:56). Indeed, the truth itself had been known and proclaimed in Israel before the earthly ministry of Jesus of Nazareth. Later, when most of the Christians were gentiles, the imagery of the covenant which opened the door into history was still retained:

---

* Since this is no exegetical or textual tool, but rather an historical tool portraying the importance of events in the oral tradition and written records, Bible quotations are taken from the King James ("Authorized") Version.

*1*

Ye are a chosen generation, a royal priesthood, a holy nation, a peculiar people; that ye should shew forth the praises of him who hath called you out of darkness into his marvellous light:

Which in times past were not a people but are now the people of God: which had not obtained mercy but now have obtained mercy.

I Peter 2:9–10

Once the historical self-understandings of the Jewish people and the Christian church have been affirmed—against the nineteenth-century misunderstanding of "scholarly objectivity" and the "post-modern" indifference to truth claims, such effort is again respectable—two continuing, unresolved problems can be stated:

First, for Christians who were born Jews (practically all of the first generation of Christian believers), how was the personal event of Christian conversion to be related to the "root experiences" and "epoch-making events" of Israelite history? (The self-understanding of the gentile believers who now had access to these events was less complicated, although from Marcion of Sinope to the *Deutsche Christen* in the Third Reich, there have been numbers of the gentiles baptized who, under pressure and temptation, took flight from history into the non-being of their pre-covenantal existence.)

Second, how is the "everlasting covenant" with the Jewish people to be related to the New Covenant which the Christian church professed? For many centuries and with desperately tragic results in the twentieth century, much of the churches' teaching has sadly waffled this issue. The apostle Paul, who loved the people of his birth and education, wrestled valiantly with the problem (Rom. 9–11), affirming to gentile fellow-believers their share in the promises and at the same time professing that in the end all Israel shall be saved (Rom. 11:26a). In our own time, men like Franz Rosenzweig and Martin Buber have struggled to explicate the interaction by reference to two parallel divine covenants, one with the Jewish people and the other with believing gentiles.

Because of the importance of this interaction between the Jewish people and the Christian church, in both negative and positive aspects, this survey will from time to time graphically present developments of import to both Jews and Christians as well as their impact on each other.

At this juncture the important matter is that the student be aware of the particular, indeed peculiar, way in which Jews and Christians understood history and its meanings.

Since the Enlightenment it has been common for university people to seek speculative and abstract propositions, universal truths good for all times and places. The work of Immanuel Kant (1724–1804) marked the beginning of a series of grandly conceived systems. His categorical imperative—"Act as if the maxim of thy will were to become by thy adopting it a universal law of nature"—has been a two-edged sword: it has in practice led to the rejection of special truths that could not be universalized, and to the flattening out of unique events into further examples of general truth principles.

By such method, in our own time the Holocaust (Hitler's *Endlösung der Judenfrage*, the murder of 6,000,000 European Jews) becomes merely another example of "man's inhumanity to man." In the first years of a "religion" called "Christianity," the death of Jesus—like the death of Socrates—

becomes another example of the fate of those who threaten the establishment. But to the communities involved such abstractions miss the point entirely. The successful program of the Death Camps in Christendom raises specific issues, the most critical being whether Christianity is still credible. And the death of Jesus was, according to the most ancient and central of Christian stories, followed by his resurrection and coming triumph over the powers of darkness. At the very least, the conscientious student must take seriously the lessons of the Social Psychologists: a) no dialogue is possible unless each position is stated in a way acceptable to its adherents; b) no answers can be given unless the right questions are asked, even in the laboratory. Truth-claims are aimed at specific persons facing specific choices at specific times, not at armchair philosophers or visitors from outer space.

Events—epoch-making, formative, archetypal, unique—to which the Christians laid claim in the history and world of the Jews were many. They remembered them, re-enacted them, made them a central part of the Oral Tradition passed from generation to generation. They are still embedded in the creeds and liturgies. Until the fashionable flight from history in the modern period, they were part of that wisdom learned in childhood on which a person's mind and soul are nurtured for the rest of his life.

A minimal list of such events, identified graphically in the first four maps, must include these:

1. the Covenant of Abraham (Gen. 17:4--8);
2. the Exodus (esp. Exod. 14:19--31);
3. the Giving of the Commandments (Exod. 20:1--17);
4. the Dedication of Solomon's Temple (I Kings 8:21--61);
5. Exile and Return (Psalm 137, Isaiah 44:28, Nehemiah).

To these the Christian church has added several:

1. the Birth of a Savior/Messiah (Mt. 1:18--2:23);
2. his Recognition (Mk. 8:27--30);
3. the Last Supper (Mt. 20:20--28);
4. his Death and Resurrection (Mk. 15:16--39, 16:5--14);
5. Pentecost (Acts 2:1ff.).*

In the developing lines of Jewish and Christian histories, several additional epoch-making events may be noted. Some, especially in the modern period, are still subject to debate as to their meaning. Others have become the material for new periodizations of history (e.g., radical Protestantism's use of the idea of "the Fall of the Church" at the time of Constantine the Great). They serve to strengthen the self-understanding of the community, to compete with alternative systems of being; they also provide additional keys to unlock and disclose the essential nature of the faith-communities to the scientific and critical mind.

In Jewish history, such events have been—among others: a) the Fall of the Second Temple, b) the Crusades, external and internal to Christendom, c) the Emancipation. In Christian history, we might single out several by way of illustration: a) the founding of

---

* Again, the purpose of this tool does not require a technical discussion of the distinctions between "history" and "meta-history," *Historie and Geschichte*, and so on. The fact is that these events have been remembered, internalized, and that without them Christian self-identity is unintelligible.

Christendom, b) the Crusades, c) the sixteenth-century Reformation, d) the rise of modern missions, e) the achievement of Religious Liberty, f) the church struggle with anti-Christian worldviews (Marxism, Nazism and their imitators).

As the lines of Jewish and Christian history again converge, there are two epoch-making events which bring the Jewish people and the Christian church together in tragedy and triumph: first, the Holocaust; second, the re-founding of Israel (and the implementation of the Law of Return).

Every student, whatever his persuasion, has conscious or undeclared events in the back of his mind as he remembers and interprets history. Muslims have the Hegira (622 CE), on which they base a new calendar. Marxists had the October 1917 Revolution. Nazis had the twelve years of the millennial Third Reich (1933–45). Secular humanists generally prefer to emphasize the Renaissance and to interpret the Reformation in the light of that intellectual explosion, and to stress the Enlightenment as the dividing line between the medieval and modern periods. The present writer has chosen to identify certain events (inevitably involving a scheme of periodization) and to present them openly for critical appraisal. He will not attempt the (false) "objectivity" of disengagement and indifference, but rather assay the fair presentation of materials for scholarly dialogue.

The important matter is that the student be aware that choices must be made, that the scientific discourse requires that they be identified rather than uncritically taken for granted. The primary issue is this: that the self-understanding of the Christian church, with its Jewish and Greek and Roman and other components, be brought into focus. To fasten upon the historical evidence, both oral and written, a modern scheme of indifference to truth-claims and internal integrity of dogma, however fashionable today, is as biased and tendentious as its counterpart speculation: to refuse to submit internal teachings to scientific analysis at all.

Early Christianity was set in the world of the Jews. The first Christians were Jews. The only sacred scriptures they knew were the Jewish Scriptures. Until the so-called Council of Jerusalem (49 CE), they functioned as a Jewish sect competing with other Jewish sects for the soul of the Jewish nation. When the harvest of gentile "God-fearers" from the synagogues of the Diaspora radically changed the church's ethnic composition, two dramatic results followed on: first, the church became *religio illicita* under Roman law, and a period of persecutions ensued; second, the family quarrel ("sibling rivalry") between Christian teaching and rabbinic Judaism set in, with measurable consequences to the present day.

# A. THE WORLD OF THE JEWS

EARLY Jewish history centers in epochal events and massive personalities. Before the Law was known there was a law-giver. Before Holy History was proclaimed there were patriarchs and prophets. Before a unique ethical monotheism was taught there was a people chosen to carry it.

The epoch-making events recalled and re-enacted by the people were considered unique and formative of their identity. The stories about the men who led the people cast them in large molds. But there was no process of apotheosis, by which in many religions men of apparently superhuman gifts became gods. Neither were the events a replay of heavenly occurrences. The human measure was preserved: God remained alone divine, man remained human, and the historical arena of human responsibility and decision was neither confused nor aborted.

Abraham (Gen. 11:26–25:18) was turned from the gods to God, was then called to proceed to Canaan and invest it; he proved his faith by pilgrimage and by risking the sacrifice of Isaac. He was apparently a contemporary of Hammurabi (c 2100–2000 BCE). Isaac's son, Jacob, had twelve sons who were the ancestors of the twelve tribes; his calling was confirmed at Bethel (Gen. 28:10–22) and at Peniel (Gen. 32:24–30), where he received the divinely appointed name "Israel."

Some centuries later, when the people were slaves in Egypt, Moses was sent to lead them out to freedom. His calling at the Burning Bush on Mt. Sinai (Exod. 3:1–4:17), the ten plagues visited on the Egyptians and the institution of the Passover (Exod. 12:1–30), the Exodus and deliverance at the Red Sea (Exod. 14:21–31), the giving of the Ten Commandments at Mt. Sinai (Exod. 20:1–17)—these are formative events in the faith of the Jewish people—and later to Christians as well.

Under the leadership of Joshua and his successors, Canaan was occupied c 1500–1200 BCE. In the transition from nomadic life to agricultural location, intense struggle ensued between the God of history and the gods of place—each with a coterie of prophets. Elijah, by tradition the first and greatest true prophet (9th cent. BCE), is remembered for upholding by fierce measures the worship of the True God (*Yahweh*) against the false prophets of the Canaanite and Phoenician gods (Baal, Baal Moloch—the Minotaur, Asherah) (I Ki. 18:17–40) and for his unyielding stand for social justice (I Ki. 21:1–24). These twin bases of ethical monotheism are the foundation of the faith of Israel as recorded in the Scriptures. They are summarized strikingly by Micah (6:8—"He hath shewed thee, O man, what is good; and what doth the Lord require of thee, but to do justly, and to love mercy, and to walk humbly with thy God?") and by Jesus' quotation (". . . Jesus said unto him, Thou shalt love the Lord thy God with all thy heart, and with all thy soul, and with all thy mind. This is the first and great commandment. And the second is like unto it. Thou shalt love thy neighbor as thyself." Mt. 22:34–40).

During the monarchy, the struggle was evident also in the kings' courts. David (d. c 970 BCE), king of Judaea

*Moses and the burning bush, from a wall-painting in the synagogue at Dura Europos, Syria, 3rd century.*

and then of the northern tribes, was a consistent defender of the true faith, but although the Temple which he planned was built in the next reign, Solomon (d. c 933 BCE) was not immune from dalliance with foreign gods. Upon Solomon's death the north broke away and established a separate kingdom.

The eighth century prophets (Amos, Hosea, Micah, Isaiah), those of the late seventh and early sixth centuries (especially Jeremiah and Habakkuk), those of the Exile (Ezekiel and Deutero-Isaiah), as well as the post-Exilic prophets (including Jonah and Joel), emphasized the notes of ethical judgment which made it possible for Israel to understand her place in a history where the ambitions for military strength and empire had been crushed between the great powers of the Nile and Tigris/Euphrates valleys.

In 586 BCE Jerusalem was captured by Nebuchadnezzar of the Assyrians and most of the leading families were led into captivity. Most of those left in the Northern Kingdom rejected the historical self-understanding which had led to the building of the Temple as part of a grandiose scheme to make Jerusalem a fit center of a world power; later known as Samaritans, they identified Mt. Gerizim as the place of sacred sacrifice rather than the Mt. Moriah of general Jewish tradition.

When the people returned from exile, under a tolerant Persian Empire, the Temple was rebuilt. But their teachers, introducing and interpreting the Deuteronomic Code under the impress of the prophets, interpreted Israel's identity in terms of faithfulness to God's Law—with the Temple a very important but not indispensable factor. At this time clear precepts—at once religious and civil—were set before the people and a high priesthood, the Sanhedrin, attained critical authority. A succession of conquerors—Alexander the Great, the Ptolemies of Egypt, the Seleucid dynasty of Antioch—ruled the Jews as a subject people. The hope of national freedom grew more intense with generations of frustration, and different religious parties emerged with differing interpretations of Holy History and the Jewish role in it.

In 167 BCE, in reaction to the Hellenizing pressures of the Seleucids, came the revolt of the Maccabees—celebrated by faithful Jews for centuries to come, and indeed becoming a part of the Roman Catholic calendar (August 1st—"Holy Maccabees"). Until the Roman conquest, 63 BCE, a precarious national independence was maintained. Under John Hyrcanus (ruler: 135–05 BCE), however, the differing views of peoplehood and history were fixed in the pattern that obtained during the life and work of Jesus of Nazareth. The Sadducees were the high priestly party, strict constructionists, aristocratic and inclined to such accommodations with foreign powers as would protect their wealth and status. The Pharisees were the popular party, emphasizing the Law both given and developed, opposing foreign influence where they noted it. The Zealots were a splinter off the Pharisees, ready to use violence to recover independence when it was again lost. The recent discoveries of records and writings of the Qumran community have brought home to students the great importance of another element among the Jews: the Essenes. The Essenes were so pessimistic about the world that they left the society and established self-contained communities in the desert.

For the history of Christianity, the important point to mark is the splintering of national self-consciousness among the various Jewish sects during the century and a half before Jesus, the six centuries of subjection—with a tenuous and short-lived recovery of freedom under the Maccabees—and especially the fact that Christianity appeared when the Greek language, culture, philosophies and cults had penetrated even the most resistant circles of the literate.

# LANDS OF THE BIBLE BEFORE JESUS:
## PALESTINE, THE CROSSROADS OF THE NATIONS

CANAAN was the narrow land bridge between the great empires of the valley civilizations, and as such it became the battleground across which surged the armies of conquerors. Jewish dreams of status as a world power were crushed after Solomon's death, but popular belief looked toward the coming of a Messiah who should reverse the obtaining power structures, restore Jewish nationhood and independence, and introduce the kingdom of justice and peace.

During the period of the patriarchs, various natural shrines were captured and re-dedicated to the True God: e.g., Gilgal, Shechem, Shiloh. With David, however, and again upon the return from the Exile, Jerusalem was singled out as the unique and holy place. Initially the people who had turned to the one true God simply believed Him their own, as they were His; other tribes had their own gods. Then He showed himself to be superior in power to the lesser gods. Finally, the lesser gods were exposed as idols. During the same process of growing awareness, the difference between a universal God—of the heavens and the earth and all peoples—and the gods bound to tribal sites ("high places") became ever more clear. The prophets made the point by emphasizing the events of pilgrimage during the nomadic period, and the brotherhood ethic of the nomadic band, against the gods of place and luxury. "Blessed be Egypt my people, and Assyria the work of my hands, and Israel mine inheritance." He "bringeth princes to nothing; he maketh the judges of the earth as vanity." "...their molten images are wind and confusion." "I am God and there is none else...." "It is a light thing that thou shouldest be my servant to raise up the tribes of Jacob, and to restore the preserved of Israel: I will also give thee for a light to the Gentiles, that thou mayest be my salvation unto the end of the earth." (Isaiah 19:25b, 40:23, 41:29, 46:9, 49:6).

Under the impact of the prophets, and embodied in the post-Exilic teaching of the Law, there gradually emerged a universalistic understanding of God and His purpose for all mankind. This remained, however—and in contrast to many later syncretistic and gnostic universalisms—dialectically tied to the mission and self-identity of the people Israel. The vocation of Israel was precisely to be the carrier of history, to be the witness to God's plan of human redemption, to be the community which in its teaching and style of life created a model for all peoples. This burden, with the suffering it brought with it, was the other side of the coin from divine election. Chosenness was to service, not to privilege. In the course of time both the natural ethnocentrism of the gentiles (unless tempered by a calling to suffering service) and the humanistic universalism of post-Enlightenment moderns (without the creative tension of that dialectic of particularism/universalism built into the Jewish faith in the immediate pre-Christian era) would find the genius of the Jewish religion offensive. Into that genius went the lessons of Exile and Return as well as the lessons of Exodus.

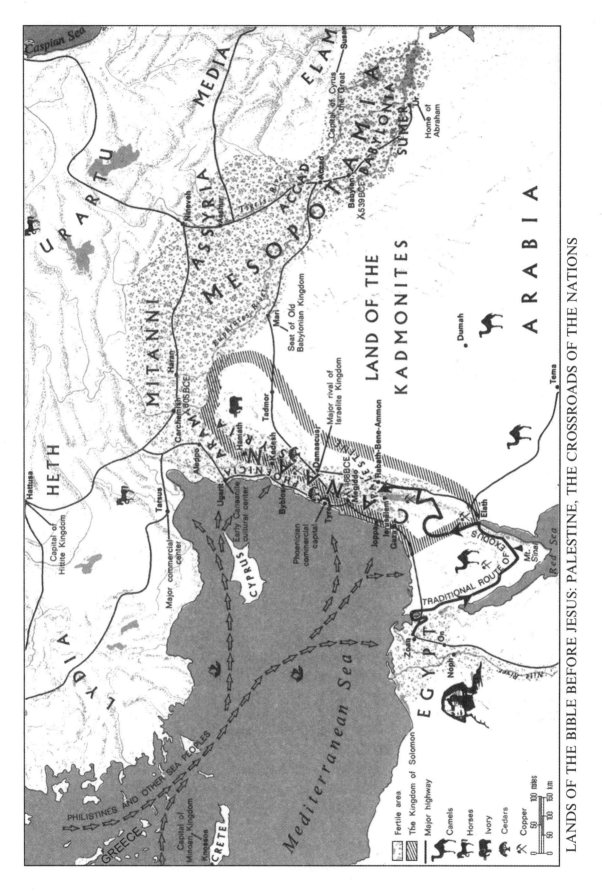

LANDS OF THE BIBLE BEFORE JESUS: PALESTINE, THE CROSSROADS OF THE NATIONS

# THE HOLY LAND UNDER ROMAN RULE
## 1ST CENTURY BCE–1ST CENTURY CE

UNDER Roman administration the conquered peoples enjoyed a considerable measure of autonomy. The particular structures of religious identity—the administration of the Temple in Jerusalem, the interpretation of the Law, the emergence of the synagogue as the Jewish community center of the Diaspora—fitted the exigencies of both Roman imperium and Jewish peoplehood.

Nevertheless, there continued to be a basic conflict between the Jewish understanding of history and the world of Greek learning. An intellectual like Philo of Alexandria (23 BCE?–42 CE?) could develop a highly sophisticated portrayal of the essential agreement of the Old Testament and Greek philosophy, but the ordinary Jew rejected the overt blurring of lines even if he unconsciously assimilated some Greek language and ideas. Even though Herod the Great, the last Hasmonaean ruler (37–4 BCE), erected the grandest building of the Temple complex, he was suspect as a Hellenizer. The Pharisees, who became after the destruction of the Temple (70 CE) the main line of Jewish religion, were the chief party of passive resistance to the Greek philosophies, cults, world-views.

Where Jesus of Nazareth fitted into the competing parties and sects is still keenly disputed. In the current debates

*Philo of Alexandria.*

he is placed on a scale that runs from the Zealots (advocates of violent resistance) to the Essenes (pacifist monastics). The certain thing is that the events of his life and death, and the resurrection which the oldest confession of faith (I Cor. 15:3–8) of his followers celebrated, gave a clear identity and self-knowledge to a company of persuaded Jews. As for the Romans, they gave him the same punishment they meted out to tens of thousands of other slaves and revolutionaries who revolted: crucifixion. This form of punishment, never used by the Jews, the Romans had learned from Carthage.

*Coin of Herod the Great.*

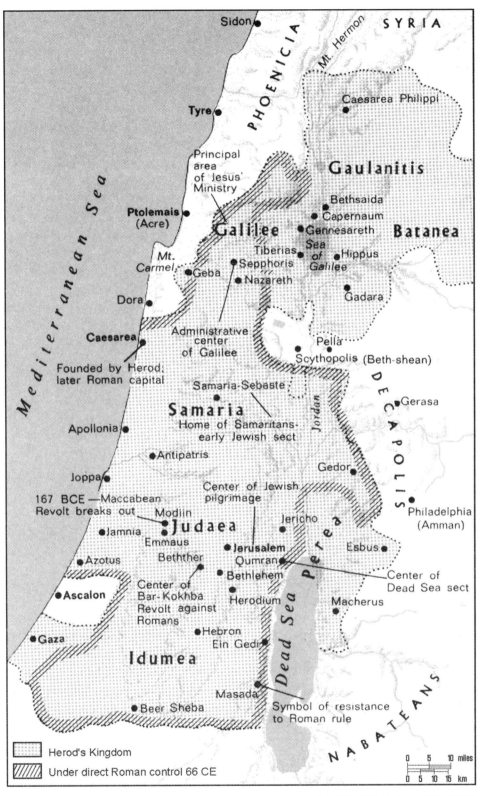

Sidon

SYRIA

PHOENICIA

Mt. Hermon

Caesarea Philippi

Tyre

Mediterranean Sea

Principal
area
of Jesus'
Ministry

Gaulanitis

Ptolemais
(Acre)

Bethsaida

Capernaum

Galilee

Gennesareth

Batanea

Mt.
Carmel

Tiberias

Sea
of
Galilee

Hippus

Geba

Sepphoris

Dora

Nazareth

Gadara

Caesarea

Administrative
center
of Galilee

Pella

Founded by Herod,
later Roman capital

Scythopolis (Beth-shean)

Samaria-Sebaste

DECAPOLIS

Gerasa

Jordan

Samaria

Apollonia

Home of Samaritans-
early Jewish sect

Gedor

Antipatris

Philadelphia
(Amman)

Joppa

Center of Jewish
pilgrimage

167 BCE—Maccabean
Revolt breaks out

Modiin

Jericho

Jamnia

Judaea

Emmaus

Jerusalem

Esbus

Azotus

Bethther

Qumran

Center of
Dead Sea sect

Ascalon

Center of
Bar-Kokhba
Revolt against
Romans

Bethlehem

Herodium

Dead Sea

Perea

Macherus

Gaza

Hebron

Ein Gedi

Idumea

Masada

NABATEANS

Beer Sheba

Symbol of resistance
to Roman rule

Herod's Kingdom

Under direct Roman control 66 CE

0   5   10 miles

0  5  10  15 km

THE HOLY LAND UNDER ROMAN RULE
1ST CENTURY BCE–1ST CENTURY CE

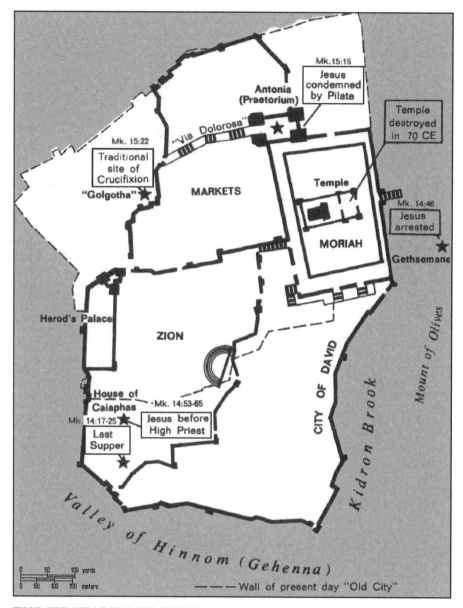

Mk.15:15
Jesus
condemned
by Pilate

Antonia
(Praetorium)

Temple
destroyed
in 70 CE

Mk. 15:22
Traditional
site of
Crucifixion
"Golgotha"

"Via Dolorosa"

MARKETS

Temple

Mk. 14:46
Jesus
arrested

MORIAH

Gethsemane

Herod's Palace

ZION

CITY OF DAVID

Mount of Olives

House of
Caiaphas

Mk. 14:53-65
Jesus before
High Priest

Mk. 14:17-25
Last
Supper

Kidron Brook

Valley of Hinnom (Gehenna)

0  50  100 yards
0  50  100  150 meters

———— Wall of present day "Old City"

THE JERUSALEM OF JESUS

*The Church's Jesus is a gleaming diamond
of a man. So he should be. Two thousand
years of polishing have gone into smooth-
ing out his rough edges.*

  S.G.F. Brandon, *Jesus and the Zealots*

*Crucifixion was a
Roman punishment,
learned from Carthage.*

AT its origin Christianity was one of several Jewish sects. As such it enjoyed the status of a legal religion. When Jesus first taught in the synagogue he found the verses of promise in Isaiah (Lk. 4:16--20) and read them out. When the letter-writers and teachers began to work among his followers after his death, they constantly proved their announcement by reference to Jewish sacred writings: e.g., "to this agree the words of the prophets . . ." (Acts 15:15); ". . . he expounded and testified the kingdom of God, persuading them concerning Jesus, both out of the law of Moses, and out of the prophets, from morning till evening" (Acts 28:23). The early Christians knew no scriptures except the Jewish.

There may be one exception to this generalization about Christian roots in Jewish consensus: Stephen. After the gentile Christians took over, it became commonplace to hail Stephen as a martyr to Jewish particularism, a witness to the universal Christ. Recent studies have suggested that what offended the crowd and led to his death was not his proclamation of salvation to the gentiles but rather his reading of salvation history according to the Samaritan scriptures (Acts 6:8–7:60). The hostility between the Samaritans and the majority of Jews was long-standing.

In any case, there were already large numbers of gentile fellow-travelers of the synagogues and participants in the worship of the true God throughout the Mediterranean basin. The Old Testament had been available to the gentiles for several generations, in a translation into Greek made at Alex-

*Samaritan priest with ancient scroll.*

andria c 285–46 BCE (the Septuagint). Sometimes the gentile worshipers were set aside in a special room. In a few cases, whole tribes converted to the Jewish religion.

The mission to the gentiles was not the offense to traditional Jewish leadership. Neither was the breach of the ceremonial law, although this was serious enough to produce conflict among the Christians themselves and to necessitate a Council of the churches in 49 CE (Acts 15:1–29, Gal. 2:6–9). What gave offense and produced division, far more than the usual conflicts between Jewish sects, was the identification of Jesus as the promised Messiah and the interpretation of Holy History which this profession involved.

Alienation and division between the larger Christian movement, with a growing percentage of gentile members, and the Jewish people came with the destruction of the Temple (70 CE) and the aloofness of the former toward

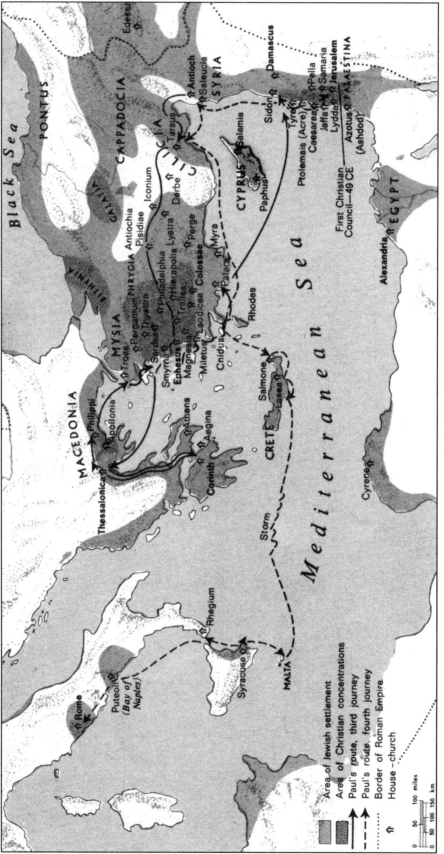

THE JEWISH MATRIX OF CHRISTIANITY

Area of Jewish settlement
Area of Christian concentrations
Paul's route, third journey
Paul's route, fourth journey
Border of Roman Empire
House-church

First Christian
Council—49 CE

0   50        100 miles
0   50  100  150 km

14

Bar Kokhba's desperate revolt (132–35 CE) against Hadrian's plan to erect a temple to Jupiter in a rebuilt Jerusalem (Aelia Capitolina). The Maccabees are remembered by both Jews and Christians; Masada is an indelible event in Jewish history, but no part of Christian self-consciousness.

Students have often marveled at the rapidity with which Christianity spread in the first generations. No credit should be taken from Paul (d. c 65 CE) and Barnabas and other colleagues in the mission to the gentiles. Paul, the best educated of all the Apostles and early Christian teachers, was superbly equipped to reap the harvest that had been prepared. Of the tribe of Benjamin, trained as a Pharisee (including study under Rabbi Gamaliel), he knew both the law and the prophets; moreover he was a Roman citizen and fluent in Greek. His conversion (Acts 9:1–19, 22:5–16, 26:12–18) gave him a clear understanding of his own place in unfolding events, and his subsequent teaching declared the Risen Christ the hinge of history.

The phenomenal success of the mission to the gentiles lies in the fact that tens of thousands of gentile fellow-travelers ("God-fearers") were attached to Jewish worship in the synagogues of the Diaspora. They were ready for just such a word as Paul and his associates carried to them, declaring how in Christ the salvation of the peoples was to be accomplished and the kingdom of God brought near.

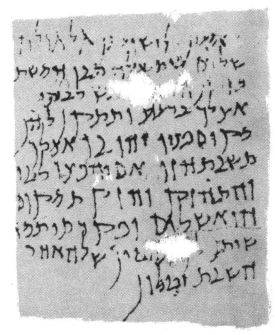

*Letter of Bar Kokhba to a field commander.*

Translation:
"Simeon, son of Kosiba, to Joshua, son of Galgola, and to the men of (Kephar) Habakkuk, greetings. I take heaven as witness against me (that) if anyone of the Galileans who are among you should be ill-treated, I will put fetters on your feet as I did to Ben-Aphlul."

Signed, "Simeon, son of Kosiba"

*Plan of synagogue at Capernaum (note side room for gentile "God-fearers").*

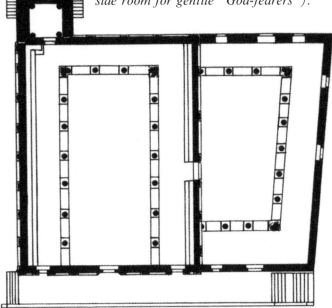

BOTH Renaissance and Reformation pointed scholars to a vigorous pursuit of early sources, classical and Christian. Perhaps the most dramatic scholarly event of importance to church law during the Renaissance was the exposure (by Lorenzo Valla in 1440) of the so-called Donation of Constantine as an eighth- or ninth-century fabrication. The "Donation" invoked the name of the great emperor Constantine to confer both religious primacy and secular authority upon the pope. In the next century archaeological explorations began with the rediscovery (1578) of Christian meeting places and burial grounds in the catacombs of Rome. With the development of the historical and comparative method in the nineteenth century, the emphasis upon primary sources and their authentication (Leopold von Ranke, professor at Berlin 1825–86) became a basic canon of scholarly work. In the location and publication of inscriptions as well as excavation of artifacts and archaeological remains—both classical and Christian—Theodor Mommsen (1817–1903) set a high standard. Of great importance was the discovery of the *Codex Sinaiaticus* by Constantin Tischendorf at the remote monastery of St. Catherine at the foot of Mt. Sinai (1844, 1859). This Codex, dating from the late fourth century, contained the books of the Old and New Testaments plus *Barnabas* and part of *The Shepherd of Hermas*. With the *Codex Vaticanus* it became the principal tool for subsequent biblical translations.

During the twentieth century the harvest of discovery continued to bring in a great wealth of important information on early Christian history. At Dura Europos in Asia Minor (first surveyed by Professor J. H. Breasted in 1921) were unearthed the earliest known synagogue (c 245) and the earliest known Christian church (c 232). The latter was a "house-church," formed by combining two rooms in a dwelling. Far up the Nile River, at Nag Hammadi, there were discovered in c 1946 1,000 pages of sacred writings reflecting Egyptian and Syrian Gnosticism. The most important single item was the so-called Gospel of Thomas. These writings plus texts discovered elsewhere have given a far more complete picture of the encounter of orthodoxy with various systems of semi-Christian accommodation to Platonism, Zoroastrianism, and the mystery religions.

*Theodor Mommsen.*

THE most dramatic modern discovery was the finding of the Dead Sea Scrolls in caves near Qumran (1946–57). In Hebrew and Aramaic, the scrolls have already revealed early texts of most of the Old Testament, apocryphal and pseudepigraphal books, and several items unique and important to the monastic community which apparently hid them during the uncertainties of the First Jewish Revolt (66–70 CE). Since the New Testament gives comparatively little data on the Essenes and others like them who retired from a world of war, violence and civil conflict, the Qumran findings are among the most important in the history of Christianity. They are also important because, like Pharisaic teaching—on which much is known—many teachings and practices in the Qumran community remarkably parallel the Christian.

Qumran (see illustration) was apparently occupied—with a brief interruption at the time of the rebuilding of the Temple—from c 135 BCE to 70 CE (when the Temple was destroyed by the Romans). The people of Qumran thought of themselves as a faithful remnant, awaiting the imminent consummation of history. Theirs was a particularly intense and focused expression of the popular belief in the coming redemption of Israel, heralded by a Teacher of Righteousness. Among their cultic practices were an annual remembrance and celebration of the Covenant, and a regular sacred meal in which bread and wine were the elements. Major writings include Commentaries on the Old Testament, in which the writers demonstrate how Old Testament passages were being fulfilled in their own time, Psalms of Thanksgiving (composed in good part of phrases from the canonical Psalms), an apocalyptic book scholars call "The War of the Sons of Light Against the Sons of Darkness," and a detailed Manual of Discipline rather like the Christian *Didache*.

QUMRAN

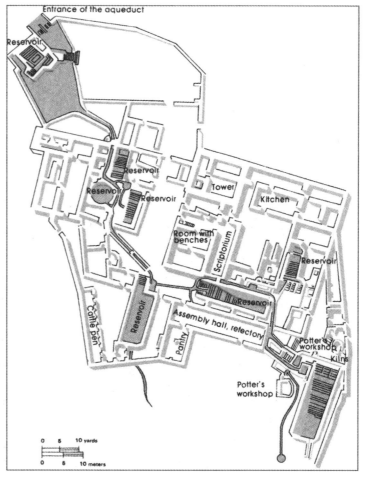

# B. THE WORLD OF THE GREEKS

GREEK language, culture and philosophy dominated literate circles in the Mediterranean basin for more than six centuries. From the time of Alexander the Great (349–23 BCE) through the Council of Nicaea (325 CE), Greek was the language of politics, philosophy and religion. After its first years as a Jewish sect, Christianity developed along the lines of Greek thinking and acting.

Two basic problems were never solved by the Greeks: 1) how to extend the liberty enjoyed by citizens to freedmen and slaves, who in Athens outnumbered the former nineteen to one; 2) how to cement alliances without compelling the unqualified submission of defeated cities as subjects—rather than full and free partners. The city-state (*polis*) remained the basic unit of Greek civilization, with the strengths and weaknesses of such a society.

Under Solon (c 640–599 BCE) the political and economic status of citizens was secured. Pythagoras, the first to call himself "philosopher," flourished c 580–04 BCE. Under Pericles (c 495–29 BCE), who fostered the arts and learning, the city reached its zenith. There developed out of the Dionysian festivals one of the permanent contributions to human civilization: the dramatic tragedy, whose most accomplished creators were Aeschylus (525–456 BCE), Sophocles (495–05 BCE) and Euripides (480–05 BCE). Among others might be singled out Aristophanes (444–388 BCE) and Menander (342–290 BCE), masters of comedy; Hippocrates (c 460–377 BCE), physician; Halicarnassus (c 485–24 BCE), father of history; Pindar (522–422? BCE), lyric poet; Phidias (c 500–432 BCE), master sculptor; and Thucydides (471–395? BCE), historian of the Peloponnesian War. The time of greatest cultural vigor came during the struggle with the Persian Empire; the Persians burned the temple on the Acropolis in 480 BCE, but in 448 BCE peace was negotiated. The Peloponnesian War began in 431 BCE and before this civil strife was ended the political promise and economic substance of the city-states was destroyed.

As Athens peaked and began to decline, however, there appeared two men of massive importance to all subsequent history: Plato (428–348 BCE) and his student Aristotle (384–22 BCE). Unhappily, at the same time

*Socrates.*　　　　*Plato.*　　　　*Aristotle.*　　　　*Seneca.*

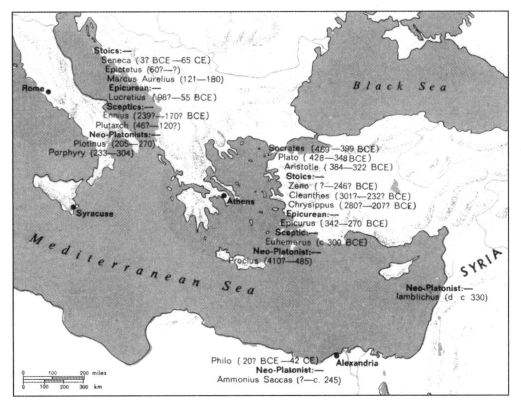

The following text and labels appear on the map:

Stoics:—
Seneca (3? BCE —65 CE.)
Epictetus (60?—?)
Marcus Aurelius (121—180)
Epicurean:—
Lucretius (98?—55 BCE)
Sceptics:—
Ennius (239?—170? BCE)
Plutarch (46?—120?)
Neo-Platonists:—
Plotinus (205—270)
Porphyry (233—304)

Rome

Black Sea

Socrates (469—399 BCE)
Plato (428—348 BCE)
Aristotle (384—322 BCE)
Stoics:—
Zeno (?—246? BCE)
Cleanthes (301?—232? BCE)
Chrysippus (280?—207? BCE)
Epicurean:—
Epicurus (342—270 BCE)
Sceptic:—
Euhemerus (c 300 BCE)
Neo-Platonist:—
Proclus (410?—485)

Syracuse

Athens

Mediterranean Sea

SYRIA

Neo-Platonist:—
Iamblichus (d c 330)

Philo (20? BCE —42 CE)    Alexandria
Neo-Platonist:—
Ammonius Saccas (?—c. 245)

0  100   200 miles
0  100  200  300 km

THE GREEK BACKGROUND

these intellectual giants were perfecting the method of critical dialogue the simple democracy of the assembly was being corrupted by the demagogues— trained in the skills of persuasion but without commitment to truth. The forced suicide of Plato's teacher Socrates (469–399 BCE), for putting the truth ahead of loyalty to the city gods and thereby "corrupting the youth," foreshadowed the end of freedom in dictatorship and militarism.

Alexander too, in his short life of conquest, fostered learning. The superiority of his military formations, especially the development of the phalanx, brought him victory all the way to India and Egypt. Among his associates none was more important to intellectual history than General Ptolemaeus (366–283 BCE), founder of the Egyptian dynasty and patron of poets and scholars. From c 300 BCE Alexandria was the most important center of Hellenism; among the results of the patronage of the Ptolemies was the development of the greatest library of the ancient world (c 400,000 volumes) and the *Museum* (university). Among scholars who flourished there under royal patronage were the mathematicians Euclid (fl. c 300 BCE) and Archimedes (287–12 BCE) and the founder of astronomy as a science, Hipparchus (d. c 125 BCE).

The first rites of Greek religion (of Demeter, Dionysius and Persephone) were introduced at Rome as early as 490 BCE, and the Roman assimilation of Greek culture proceeded rapidly—in spite of the resistance of men like Cato (234–149 BCE). The Greek gods either overpowered their Roman counterparts or appeared intact with Latin names: Zeus/Jupiter, Hera/Juno, Hermes/Mercury, Poseidon/Neptune.

Apollo, later a special favorite of Octavius Augustus (63 BCE–14 CE), the first Roman Emperor, had a temple in Rome by 431 BCE. And in time *Dea Roma* and Augustus had a shrine on the Acropolis.

In certain fields, such as music, the Romans learned almost everything they knew from the Greeks. From 30 BCE to 529 CE, when Justinian closed the schools of philosophy, Greek culture was carried by Roman power. But in that time-span there arose another impulse, Christianity, which both transformed the Greek world of thought, purging it of its origins among the cultic rituals, and was in turn transformed by it.

*Alexander the Great (from a mosaic found at Pompeii).*

## THE RISE OF HELLENISM

THE three great periods of Greek language and culture were the Athenian, the Alexandrian and the Roman. At the time of Christianity's emergence, and during its first generations, the language of intellectuals was Greek. Paul spoke in Greek, making a famous appearance at the Areopagus (Acts 17:19–34), after Solon the center of law in Athens, and Paul's letters to the churches were written in Hellenistic

*Marcus Aurelius.*

Greek. In spite of overt opposition to Greek culture, and especially to the cults of the gods, Jewish thought was infiltrated by Greek philosophy during the intertestamentary period. Many of the modes of accommodation and apologetics developed in this time were later taken over by the intellectual leaders of the early period of church history—especially the "*Logos* Fathers." For the first three centuries of the imperial period Greek language and learning were dominant, and by the time Christianity became the state religion it was thoroughly Hellenized. Tertullian (c 150–c 230) was the first church father to use Latin; Novatian (fl. 251) was the first church leader at Rome to use Latin instead of Greek.

Alexander the Great's dream of a world empire inspired political rulers as late as Charlemagne (742–814). But the chief influence upon early Christianity came through philosophers whose thought-world was adopted, Chris-

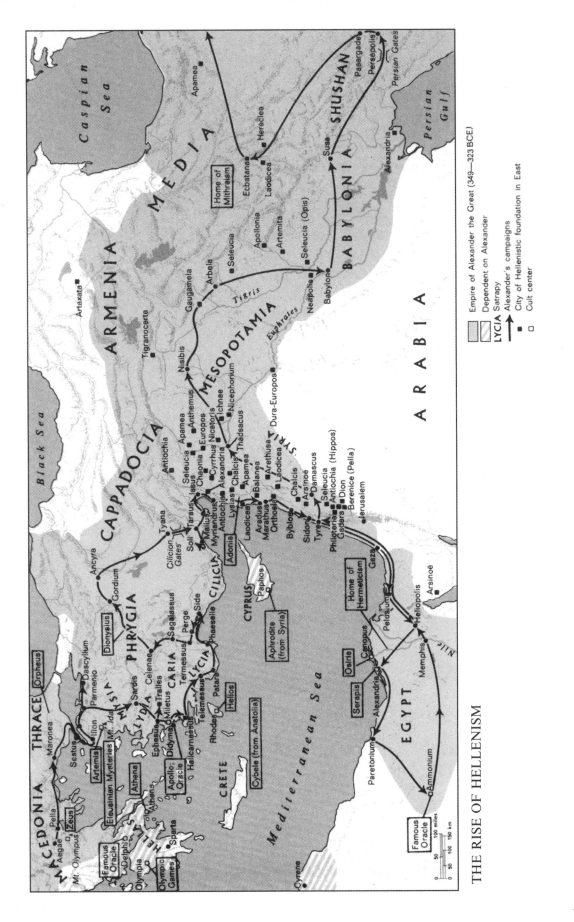

THE RISE OF HELLENISM

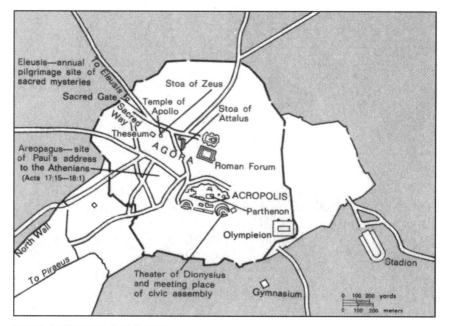

THE ATHENS OF PAUL

tianized and made part of the church's intellectual armory. Chief among these men were:

Plato and Aristotle.

The Stoics, especially Seneca (3? BCE–65 CE) and Marcus Aurelius (121–80).

The Epicureans, especially Epicurus (342–270 BCE) and Lucretius (98?–55 BCE).

The Neo-Platonists, especially Plotinus (205–70), Porphyry (233–304), Iamblichus (d. c 330), and Proclus (410?–85).

Plato and Aristotle are formative forces in Christian thought to the present day. Stoicism has had a lasting influence on Christian ethics, especially on theories of Natural Law. Augustine (354–430) and Synesius (378–430) were among the more important early Christian leaders influenced by Neo-Platonism, a style of thinking which flowed again in the Renaissance and in radical Protestantism.

*

Hebrew is a language of action. Latin is a language of command, administration and legal precision. Greek is a language of feeling, meditation and subtle nuances. With the triumph of gentile Christianity the basic themes of the faith changed. Among ordinary believers, the idea of immortality gained in popularity—supplementary to or even replacing hope in the resurrection. Among the learned, speculation tended to supersede the language of events. The sure grasp of history which marked the Jewish mood yielded place to concern for universal truths and values (which were, however, culturally formed and articulated).

*Epicurus.*

# C. THE GRAECO-ROMAN WORLD

## CHRISTIANITY UNDER THE ROMAN HEEL TO 325 CE

THE Roman Republic fell into the hands of a military dictator, Julius Caesar (102?–44 BCE). On his death his heir Octavian (63 BCE–14 CE), in alliance with Antony, crushed the republican forces. Octavian then fell out with his allies and established himself as master of the Roman world by defeating Antony and Cleopatra at Actium (31 BCE). Given the title of "Augustus" ("revered") by what was left of the Senate, he introduced widespread use of this and other religious symbols to strengthen his political hand.

With the success and wealth of the Empire there occurred a mass movement of the gods to Rome.

The Roman system was "tolerant,"

*Julius Caesar.*

although the claiming of religious honors for Octavius Augustus and his

FLIGHT OF THE GODS TO ROME

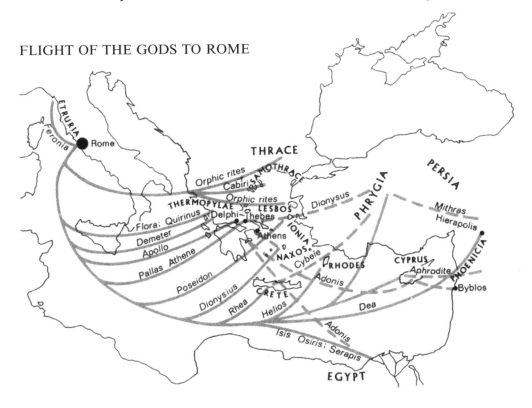

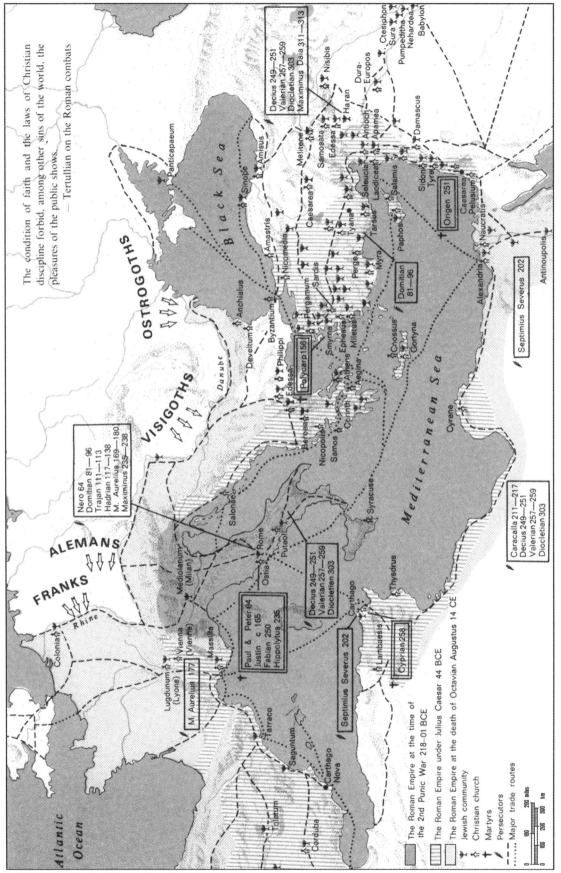

The condition of faith and the laws of Christian discipline forbid, among other sins of the world, the pleasures of the public shows.
— Tertullian on the Roman combats

OSTROGOTHS

VISIGOTHS

ALEMANS

FRANKS

*Atlantic Ocean*

*Black Sea*

*Mediterranean Sea*

Decius 249—251
Valerian 257—259
Diocletian 303
Maximinus Daia 311—313

Origen 251

Domitian 81—96

Septimius Severus 202

Nero 64
Domitian 81—96
Trajan 111—113
Hadrian 117—138
M. Aurelius 169—180
Maximinus 235—238

Polycarp 156

Caracalla 211—217
Decius 249—251
Valerian 257—259
Diocletian 303

Decius 249—251
Valerian 257—259
Diocletian 303

Paul & Peter 64
Justin c 165
Fabian 250
Hippolytus 235

Cyprian 258

Septimius Severus 202

M. Aurelius 177

Panticapaeum
Amisus
Sinope
Amastris
Anchialus
Nicomedia
Caesarea
Byzantium
Sardis
Pergamum
Smyrna
Ephesus
Miletus
Perge
Myra
Tarsus
Nisibis
Samosata
Edessa
Melitene
Tyana
Seleucia
Antioch
Apamea
Laodicea
Sidon
Tyre
Salamis
Paphos
Caesarea
Pelusium
Alexandria
Naucratis
Antinoupolis
Dura-Europos
Damascus
Haran
Ctesiphon
Sura
Pumpeditha
Nehardea
Babylon

Develtum
Philippi
Edessa
Beroea
Thessalonica
Nicopolis
Samos
Athens
Corinth
Aegina
Knossos
Gortyna
Cyrene
Syracuse
Thysdrus
Lambaesis
Carthago
Carthago
Ostia
Rome
Puteoli
Mediolanum (Milan)
Massilia
Vienna (Vienne)
Lugdunum (Lyons)
Coloniae
Tarraco
Saguntum
Carthago Nova
Toletum
Corduba

*Danube*
*Rhine*

The Roman Empire at the time of the 2nd Punic War 218–01 BCE
The Roman Empire under Julius Caesar 44 BCE
The Roman Empire at the death of Octavian Augustus 14 CE
Jewish community
Christian church
Martyrs
Persecutors
Major trade routes

0   100   200 miles
0  100  200  300 km

CHRISTIANITY UNDER THE ROMAN HEEL

24

successors introduced a note that was foreign to Roman republican tradition and dangerous for Jews and Christians. The ablest emperors were the most difficult for the church and became the worst persecutors, for they were the most determined to use a pantheon of equally honored regional gods to strengthen the federal union of the Empire.

Christian historians generally count ten major persecutions, beginning with a local affair under Nero (at Rome, 64 CE) and ending with the most severe of all under Diocletian (303). In the earliest years the Christians appear to have attracted unfavorable attention because they were said to be followers of one crucified as a Jewish rebel and because they refused to bear arms. Later they were despised because of their intolerance toward all other gods. Finally, they worshiped a lord and proclaimed a message which challenged the whole imperial view of history. From the time of the first emperor, Octavian Augustus, events were dated from the founding of Rome (753 BCE according to Varro, 751 BCE according to Cato). The Christians' belief that Christ introduced a new historical era,

*Nero Caesar.*

and their refusal to give the required religious honors to the ruling Augustus (required of all citizens from 249, but used as a test earlier) were signs of a totally different view of man, his nature and destiny.

The devotion of Rome to war and militarism was incompatible with early Christianity. Moreover, as time passed the emperors came to be elected by the legions, to be warlords who established themselves against rival claimants by brute force. The persecuting emperors were often men from the borders, such as Hadrian (b. Spain), Septimius Severus (b. Africa)—who persecuted both Jews and Christians, Decius (b. Pannonia, northwest of Thrace), and Diocletian (b. Dalmatia). And border men who have embraced centrist symbols are notoriously more intensely loyal to them than those who have been born and raised in the midst of them. To the Christians, the bloodthirsty martial symbols and practices were sealed by cruelty toward the church. Such a Rome was another "Babylon the great, the mother of harlots and abominations of the earth...drunken with the blood of the saints, and with the blood of the martyrs of Jesus" (Rev. 17:5–6).

*Roman soldiers, 1st–2nd cent.*

THE map on page 24 shows the dates of conquest of the various territories of the Empire, as well as the pressures of unconquered tribesmen from the east. The chief work of the emperors was to lead troops to pacify conquered peoples, or to defend the fortified *limes* which marked the stable limits of their control, or to carry war to the competing Persian Empire. Marcus Aurelius wrote his classic *Meditations* in a campaigner's tent. Decius fell in battle with the Goths. Valerian was captured and disappeared in war with the Persians. Septimius Severus died at York, and Constantine was at York when proclaimed emperor by his troops (306)—an authority he finally gained after seventeen years of civil struggle.

Britain was the farthest reach of the Empire, and its pacification exercised some of Rome's most talented commanders from the time of Julius Caesar on.

In the early period, the heartland of Christianity outside Palestine was Asia

*Septimius Severus.*

Minor. In the farther reaches of the Empire it followed the trade routes, although there may have been a few secret Christians among the troops. In Britain, a Celtic church was existent at least by the second century, and delegates from it attended the Synod of Arles in 314.

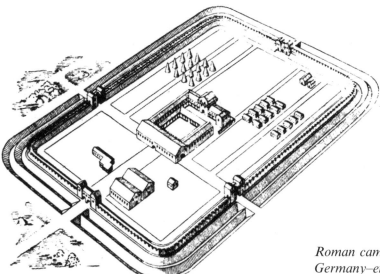

*Roman camp at Saalburg, Germany—engraving.*

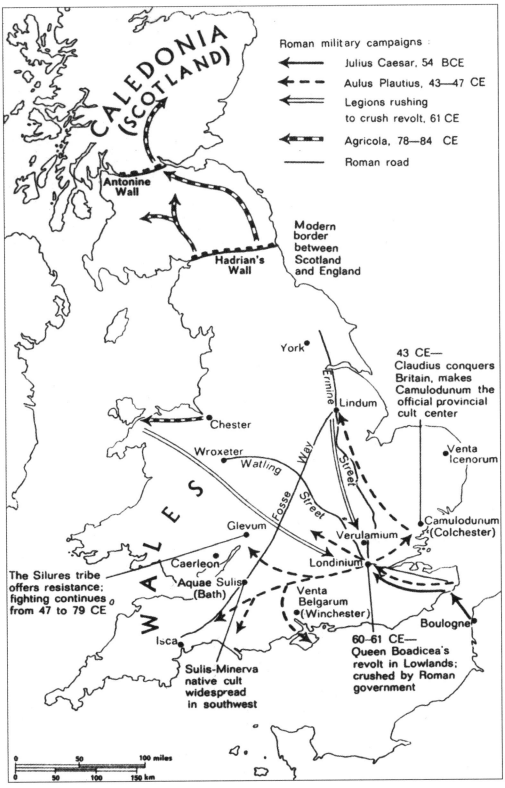

**Roman military campaigns:**

⟵ Julius Caesar, 54 BCE

⟵--- Aulus Plautius, 43—47 CE

⟸ Legions rushing to crush revolt, 61 CE

⟵■■ Agricola, 78—84 CE

— Roman road

CALEDONIA (SCOTLAND)

Antonine Wall

Hadrian's Wall

Modern border between Scotland and England

York

Ermine Street

Lindum

43 CE— Claudius conquers Britain, makes Camulodunum the official provincial cult center

Chester

Wroxeter

Watling Way

Venta Icenorum

W A L E S

Glevum

Fosse Street

Verulamium

Camulodunum (Colchester)

Caerleon

Londinium

The Silures tribe offers resistance; fighting continues from 47 to 79 CE

Aquae Sulis (Bath)

Venta Belgarum (Winchester)

Boulogne

Isca

60–61 CE— Queen Boadicea's revolt in Lowlands; crushed by Roman government

Sulis-Minerva native cult widespread in southwest

0    50    100 miles
0  50  100  150 km

THE ROMAN CONQUEST OF BRITAIN

*We are but of yesterday, and yet we already fill your cities, islands, camps, your palace, senate and forum; we have left to you only your temples.*

— Tertullian to the pagans

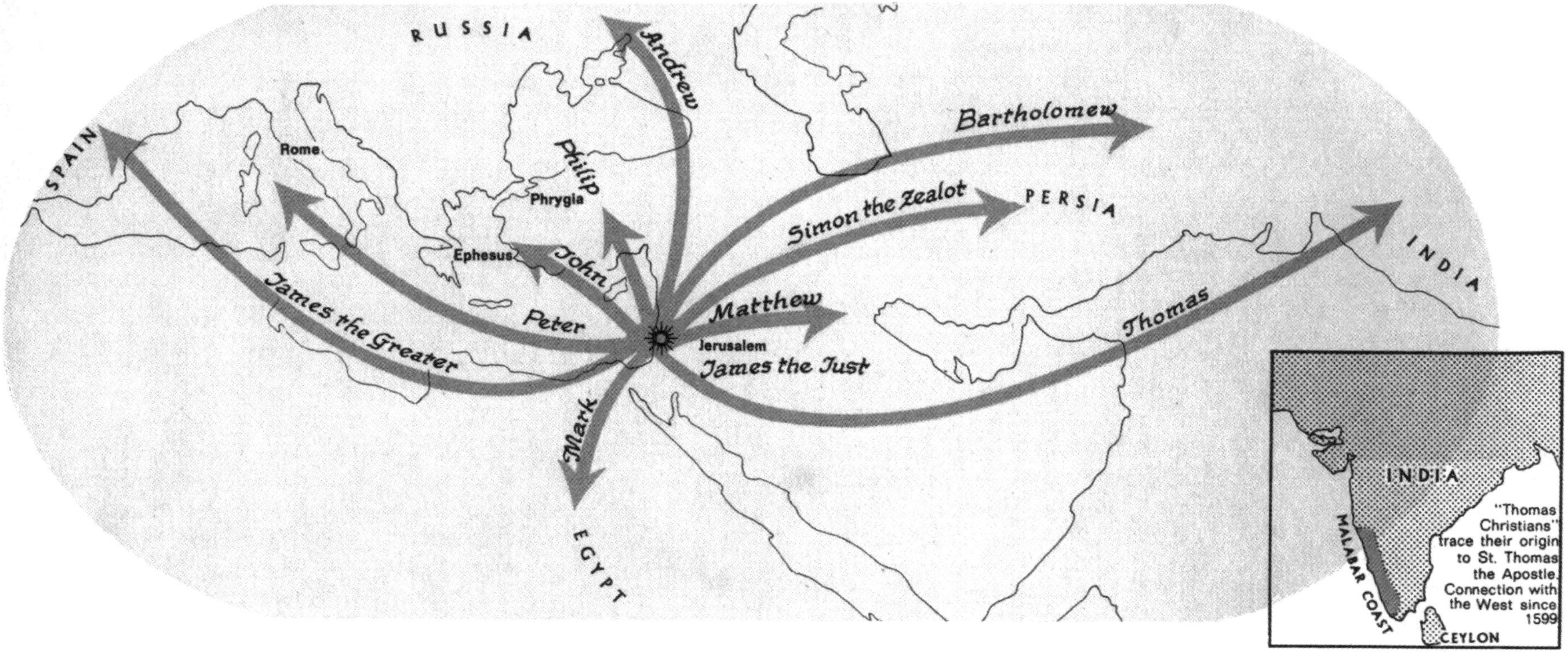

"Thomas Christians" trace their origin to St. Thomas the Apostle. Connection with the West since 1599

THE TWELVE APOSTLES IN TRADITION

28

ONE of the oldest legends of the Christian church is portrayed in the imaginal drawing (opposite). The teaching was that the eleven disciples scattered to the ends of the earth as Jesus commanded them (Mt. 28:16–20, Mk. 16:14–20). One concrete result was that the sixteenth-century Reformers, determined in their controversy with Rome to close off the Apostolic Age from what followed, taught that the Great Commission was exhausted during the early period and no longer operative. The peoples of the earth had had their chance, so to speak.

It was the discovery of America, and the realization that there were large numbers of tribes whom the disciples could not possibly have reached, that cleared away the barrier to organized missions in the established Protestant churches. To Adrianus Saravia (1531–1613), a Dutch Calvinist, goes the credit for first stressing the claims of missions. But he was immediately attacked by Theodore Beza (1519–1605), a Swiss Calvinist, who insisted that the Apostles had fulfilled the missionary mandate. The Anabaptists and radical Puritans, like the Roman Catholics for different reasons, were determined to keep the genius of the Apostolic Age alive.

For gentile Christians of later generations, the sending of the "Twelve" and the "Seventy" was highly significant. But while the gentile churches were breaking from Jewish cultic and ceremonial law, and drinking freely of the wells of Greek culture, the church at Jerusalem continued along a different course. Under James, Jesus' brother (Mk. 6:3), a kind of caliphate obtained. Among Jewish Christians,

the patriarchal model was more acceptable, while among the Hellenistic Christians the procedures of the popular assembly (*ecclesia*) set the pattern of election to governance. With the founding of Aelia Capitolina, a pagan city with a pagan temple in the ruins of a ravaged Jerusalem, under Hadrian (135), all Jews were banished from the region. Not until the pious visits of Helena, mother of Constantine the Great, and the establishment of sacred shrines, at various "holy places," did Jerusalem regain importance as a Christian site—and then it was a gentile church under the supervision of the bishop of Caesarea.

The Christian movement was split between the large number that welcomed the gentile "fellow-travelers" as full members and a minority that kept the food and ritual laws and thought of themselves as Christian Jews, different only from other Jewish sects. There were Christian synagogues in the Galilee until the Persians (then Zoroastrians, although soon thereafter forcibly converted to Islam) came through and slaughtered the Christians wherever they could identify them.

A Jewish Christian element also lingered for a time east of the Jordan River. Known as "Ebionites," this Christian sect—termed "heresy" by Epiphanius (c 315–403) in his *Panarion* (our chief source of information)— stressed the binding character of the Mosaic Law and guarded a strict monotheism by an Adoptionist Christology.

Adoptionism—the teaching that Jesus was born of Joseph and Mary and his adoption by God signalized by the lighting of the dove at his baptism by

*Julian "the Apostate."*

John the Baptist in the Jordan (Mt. 3:13–17)—was but one of the proposed solutions to the mystery of how the Jesus of human history could be the Christ of Christian holy history. Right through to the debates attending the work of Rudolf Bultmann (1884–1976), the church has wrestled with the answer to the question of Jesus: "Who do men say that I am?" (Mk. 8:27). Jewish converts, especially those who had been attracted to the synagogue by its strict monotheism in an age of rampant polytheism, found it difficult to identify him with God. Gentile converts, with their own familial and tribal histories, found it difficult to accept the centrality of Jewish salvation history and

Jesus' particular place in its Christianized version.

The spread of Christianity among the gentile tribes of the Empire raised intellectual problems of tolerating emperors as well as practical problems for persecutors. A tolerant emperor like Alexander Severus (emp.: 222–35) was willing to have in his chapel a statue of Jesus along with figures of Orpheus, Abraham, Alexander the Great and several of his predecessors revered as "Augustus." An equally tolerant emperor, Julian (emp.: 361–63), educated by quarreling Christians, turned against the intolerance of the new religion, was initiated into the Eleusinian mysteries, and sought to degrade Christianity's exclusive claims and revitalize the pagan gods. Whether we accept the argument of a Zosimus (fl. 2nd half 5th cent.) and an Edward Gibbon (1737–94) that the triumph of Christianity brought about the decline of Rome, or the traditional church view that its Christianization spiritualized and redeemed it, there is no question but that the Christian world-view and interpretation of life's meaning put the Empire to the question. By the time Constantine came to power, and favored the Christians at the expense of the pagan cults (and the Jews), Christianity was the most powerful system of being and the best organized constituency in the world known to literate Romans.

A short review of the alternative views of Jesus Christ and of how the conflicts were resolved will show the way in which Christianity achieved a measure of intellectual coherence within and philosophical credibility without.

THE most dangerous early challenge to Christianity came from a counter-church organized and led by Marcion (d. c 160), a wealthy layman. Marcion, as a gentile of education and substance, found the (Jewish) God of the Old Testament unworthy of Christian worship. He was too bloodthirsty, arbitrary, limited and particularistic for a successful gentleman of Rome. Marcion, excommunicated by the orthodox community in 144, set out to organize congregations devoted solely to Jesus' Gospel of Love; an able administrator, he was successful enough to elicit counter-attacks from writers as varied as Tertullian, Irenaeus and Bardesanes. Since he prepared a mangled edition of the Bible, excluding the Old Testament and excising the Jewish element from the New Testament, the church was compelled to fix its own canon.

Paul of Samosata (fl. c 260–72), Bishop of Antioch, held that Christ differed only in degree from the prophets. Noetus of Smyrna (fl. c 180–200) taught that it was God in the appearance of Jesus who was born, suffered and was crucified. A major result of the ensuing controversy, which threatened to reduce Jesus Christ to a superman, a man, or the mere appearance of a man, was to accentuate the importance of the doctrine of the Virgin Birth (based on Mt. 1:20, Mk. 1:26–38)—symbolic guarantee that he was "very God of very God; begotten, not made," as the emerging consensus put it.

The orthodox argument that Jesus Christ was fully divine and fully human was articulated most effectively at that time by Irenaeus (fl. c 200). Bishop of

*Clement of Rome.*

Lyons, he appealed especially to the authority of tradition and to the reliability of those who had faithfully transmitted the truth—the apostles and bishops—in an unbroken line of faithfulness. He also strengthened the tendency of the church to develop separate ranks. Since the argument that because our fathers believed it we confess it is not first-order religious language, the center of authority in the church is shifted from Spirit-conceived charisma to the office which represents tradition.

In the second century the Christian church, in spite of the energy required for mere survival, produced a number of men of power in both theology and church government.

Among those called "Apostolic Fathers" was Clement of Rome (fl. c 93–97), who contributed substantially to procedures in church government.

CHRISTOLOGICAL DEBATES AND EARLY COUNCILS

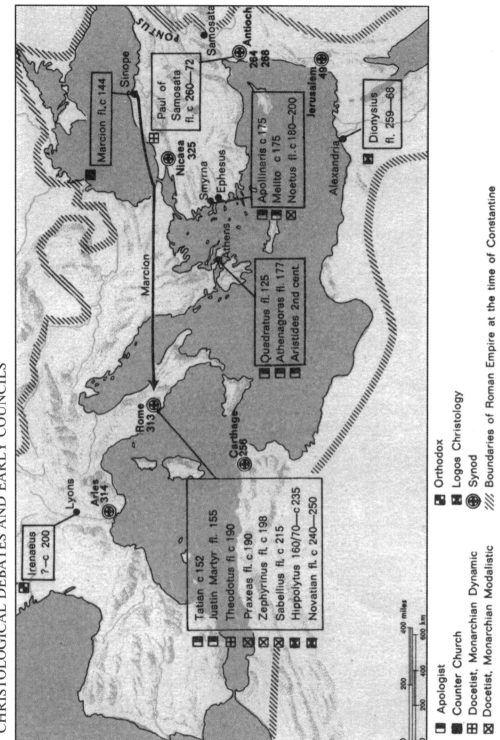

Marcion fl.c 144

Paul of Samosata fl.c 260—72

Apollinaris c 175
Melito c 175
Noetus fl.c 180—200

Dionysius fl. 259—68

Quadratus fl.125
Athenagoras fl. 177
Aristides 2nd cent.

Irenaeus ?—c 200

Tatian c 152
Justin Martyr fl. 155
Theodotus fl c 190
Praxeas fl.c 198
Zephyrinus fl.c 215
Sabellius fl.c 215
Hippolytus 160/70—c 235
Novatian fl.c 240—250

Sinope
Samosata
Antioch
264
268
Jerusalem
Nicaea
325
Smyrna
Ephesus
Alexandria
Athens
Marcion
Rome
313
Carthage
256
Lyons
Arles
314
PONTUS

Orthodox
Apologist
Counter Church
Docetist, Monarchian Dynamic
Docetist, Monarchian Modalistic
Logos Christology
Synod
Boundaries of Roman Empire at the time of Constantine

400 miles
600 km
200
400
200

His First Epistle, referring to bishops and presbyters as equals, gives important evidence on the nature and function of the early ministry. Ignatius of Antioch (c 35–c 107), martyr, strongly defended the authority of the bishop. Polycarp of Smyrna (c 69–c 155), martyr, reached a statesmanlike agreement with the Bishop of Rome that different churches should observe Easter according to their local customs. (At this time many gentile churches were moving from the Jewish calendar, with Easter fixed by the Passover dates, to the time of the pagan spring festival.) The *Didache* (c 130–160) is an important book of discipline of this period.

The "Apologists" argued persuasively to literate pagans. The most prominent was Justin Martyr (c 100–c 165), the first Christian thinker to attempt to reconcile the faith and the rationalism of pagan thinkers. In his *Dialogue with Trypho* he wrote bitterly against the Jews, relegating the Old Testament and its precepts to an earlier dispensation and claiming the church was called to supersede the "old" Israel. His pupil Tatian (c 160), however, moved to the opposite position: he wrote the *Diatessaron*, a life of Jesus compiled from the Four Gospels, and then authored a passionate attack on Greek civilization, portraying its incompatibility with the (Jewish) antiquity and purity of Christianity.

The process of explaining Jesus Christ in terms intelligible to gentile intellectuals reached its early peak in the teachings of the "*Logos* Fathers." In the introduction to the *Gospel of John*, the *Logos* is described as present with God from eternity, the creative Word incarnate in Jesus of Nazareth. Clement of Alexandria (c 150–c 215)— predecessor of Origen as head of the famous Catechetical School—identified Christ with the *Logos* as source of all human reason and revealer of God to mankind.

The use of the *Logos* line of argument preempted the ground taken by earlier Docetics and it made the God-man intelligible to those trained in Greek philosophy. It ran the danger, however, of losing grip on events that happened in human history.

## TEACHERS AND PERSECUTIONS 2ND–3RD CENTURIES

DECIUS (d. 251) undertook as emperor the first systematic persecution of the church throughout the Empire. All citizens were required to furnish proof of having given religious homage to the ruling "Augustus," and thousands of Christians were martyred while many more yielded. The status of those who had accommodated then became an acute issue in the churches for generations, dividing those who readmitted the "lapsed" from strict disciplinarians.

*Mummified figure from excavation at Pompeii.*

33

TEACHERS AND PERSECUTIONS

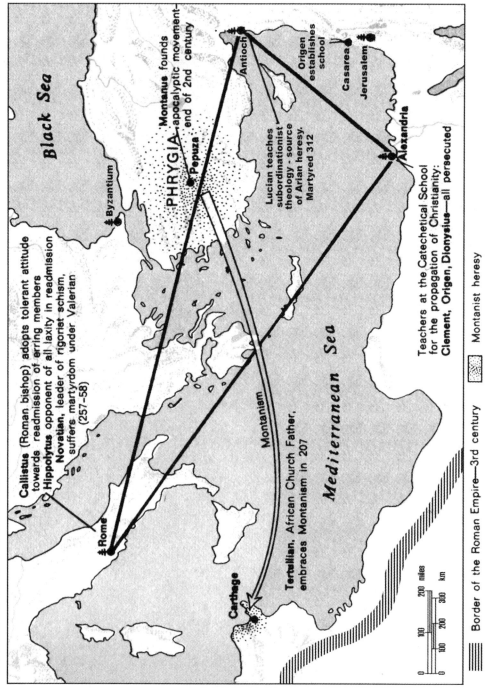

*Go on, rack, torture, grind us to powder: our numbers increase in proportion as you mow us down. The blood of Christians is their harvest seed.*

— Tertullian on persecutions

*It is incredible to see the ardor with which the people of that religion help each other in their wants. They spare nothing. Their first legislator has put into their hearts that they are all brethren.*

— Lucian on the early Christians

Cyprian (d. 258), Bishop of Carthage, who suffered under Decius and was martyred under Valerian, enforced penance and delay in the readmissions, but opposed the rigorism of Novatian (fl. c 251) and the schismatic church which he led in protest against the laxity of the church at Rome. A few years earlier, Bishop Callistus of Rome (bp: 217–22) had set a precedent by readmitting persons guilty of gross immorality—a policy strongly protested by Hippolytus (c 170–c 236). The early church had maintained the strongest discipline against adultery, murder and apostasy. With a greatly expanded membership, church discipline became hard to maintain. Apostates were generally readmitted. The cult of the martyrs provided an ideological control: after the Decian persecution in North Africa, multitudes of lapsed were readmitted by benefit of the merits of the martyrs.

*Diocletian, portrait bust from Nicomedia.*

Under Diocletian (303) came the harshest and most intelligently directed persecution of all. Diocletian, an able administrator who shored up the political structures of the Empire and increased the sacred symbols attached to his person as emperor, began by ordering the destruction of churches and burning of sacred books. Later edicts were aimed especially at the church leaders, followed by a general assault on the leaderless laity. Afterward there occurred a major division in North Africa between those who accepted the relaxed discipline of the church at Rome and those who rejected church officers who were *traditores* (those who handed over the sacred writings; derivative—"traitors").

The rigorist position was condemned by orthodox synods controlled by Rome and also condemned as intolerant and divisive by Constantine and his successors. The power of the bishops, who forgave and received back the lapsed by virtue of office authority, was correspondingly augmented.

During the generations of the persecutions the major teaching centers of the church were Alexandria, Rome and Antioch.

The Catechetical School of Alexandria, in proximity to the famous Hellenistic *Museum*, taught profane studies as well as Christian theology. The aim of the latter effort, which attracted scholars from all over the Christian world, was to prove the faith to the cultured classes of the Empire. Its most famous principals were Clement of Alexandria (c 190–c 202), Origen (c 202–31) and Dionysius (c 233–48). At Antioch, Lucian (d. 312) founded a theological school of considerable influence: among his students were Arius (c 250–c 336) and Eusebius of Nicomedia (d. c 342), advisor and baptizer of Constantine.

At Antioch the more historical and literal understanding of the scriptures was developed. Lucian, for example, was himself a keen student of the written tradition, publishing a text of the Four Gospels which underlay later translations by Erasmus, Beza and the committee which issued the King James Version (AV). At Alexandria, the allegorical style of interpretation was cultivated. Origen (c 185–c 254), a layman, one of the most prolific and creative writers in the history of Christianity, was master of the three levels of insight into Scripture—literal, moral, allegorical—but preferred the allegorical. This approach made it possible to interpret the Old Testament as carrying types and events predictive of Jesus Christ.

Persecution also led some Christians to excited announcements of an imminent Divine intervention in human affairs. Tertullian (c 160–c 220), a layman, took this turn into "heresy." Montanism arose in Phrygia, the old center of the Dionysian cult, combining an emphasis upon inspired prophets and prophecies with an excited expectation of the imminent descent of the Heavenly Jerusalem. It recaptured the early Christian expectation of the *parousia* (Second Coming), and it reflected the heightened sense of the end-time which frequently accompanies the experience of persecution. Tertullian, second only to Augustine as the most important church father of the West, attempted to resist the slide toward moral laxity in the church and the drift from Jewish to Greek modes of thought. This led him into Montanism.

## CHRISTIANITY AND GNOSTICISM
### 2ND–3RD CENTURIES

*The diocetic heresy is the typical heresy of Greek thought. It is pagan thought par excellence. It has one opponent: Jewish thought.* — Dietrich Bonhoeffer

*Medallion showing ancient zodiac symbols.*

THE definition of "Gnosticism" is debated to this day. There is still disagreement among scholars as to whether it was a separate and distinct religious movement or whether it is a term to be applied to the process of accommodating Christian doctrine to a wide variety of alternative cults and philosophies. As polemical writings by major Christian teachers make clear, Gnosticism rose as a powerful challenge to orthodox belief in the second century; if hyphenated religion and Christian accommodation are its distinguishing marks, it obviously threatens Christian integrity from several directions to the present day.

In addition to Marcion, Gnosticism is usually identified by reference to Simon Magus of Samaria (Acts 8:18–

36

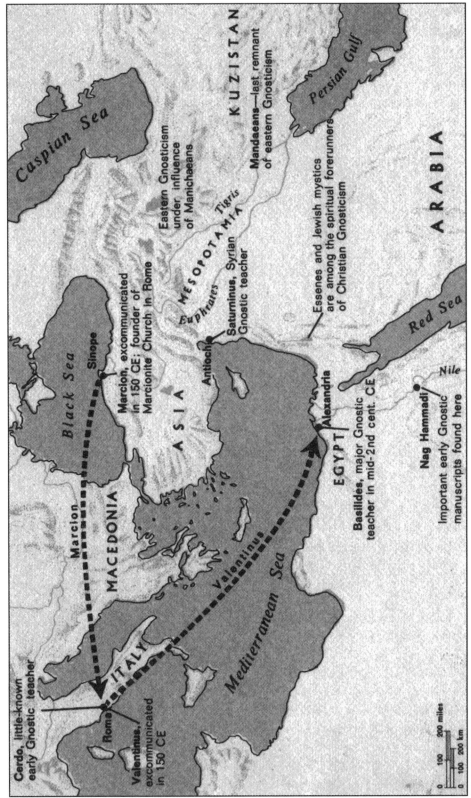

Cerdo, little-known early Gnostic teacher

Valentinus, excommunicated in 150 CE

Marcion

Sinope

Marcion, excommunicated in 150 CE; founder of Marcionite Church in Rome

Eastern Gnosticism under influence of Manichaeans

Mandaeans—last remnant of eastern Gnosticism

Essenes and Jewish mystics are among the spiritual forerunners of Christian Gnosticism

Saturninus, Syrian Gnostic teacher

Antioch

Alexandria

Basilides, major Gnostic teacher in mid-2nd cent. CE

Nag Hammadi

Important early Gnostic manuscripts found here

Valentinus

Rome

ITALY

MACEDONIA

Black Sea

ASIA

MESOPOTAMIA

KUZISTAN

Caspian Sea

Persian Gulf

ARABIA

Red Sea

Nile

Tigris

Euphrates

Mediterranean Sea

EGYPT

0   100   200 miles
0   100   200 km

CHRISTIANITY AND GNOSTICISM

37

*First page of the Gospel of Thomas, from the Nag Hammadi Library, Egypt.*

23), Valentinus (fl. c 136–65), who taught at Rome, Basilides of Alexandria (second century), Saturninus of Antioch (second century) and to revealing writings such as *Pistis Sophia* and *The Gospel of Thomas*. Gnosticism as a philosophy consists of a variety of systems featuring secret wisdom known only to the elect few, depreciation of the "Jewish" God and His authorship of history, enhancement of the salvific function of an impersonal principle of enlightenment (*Gnosis*) at the cost of a personal Redeemer, rejection of a real human history by sharply dividing the spiritual world of ideas from the material world of phenomena. Gnosticism as a vulgar cult involves a hyphenation of Christian standards with non-Christian or anti-Christian religions or world-views.

## MANICHAEISM 3RD CENTURY FF.

As Christian thought became Hellenized and church organization became Romanized, the Persian Empire became the chief base of refuge for Christian dissenters and the most dependable center of anti-Christian world-views.

One such refugee community is the Mandaeans, a Gnostic cult dating from the early second century which still survives south of Baghdad. Because John the Baptist plays a large part in their writings, it has been suggested that they derive from disciples of John who did not accept Jesus as the Messiah.

The Manichaeans, of greater importance to the history of Christianity, share the Mandaean asceticism and radical dualism of soul and body. Mani (c 215–75) grew up at Seleucia-Ctesiphon, capital of the Persian Empire, and opened his epistles with "Mani, Apostle of Jesus Christ." But the ideas of the religion he founded seem more like those of Zoroastrianism, which began in about the sixth century BCE and under the Sassanian dynasty (211–640 CE) was the official state religion of Persia. Man's predicament is traced to a primordial struggle between Light and Darkness, and believers were divided into classes reflecting different degrees of ascent from bondage to the dark and earthy. The religion spread widely in Asia and in parts of the Roman Empire; Augustine was an adherent for some years. During the Middle Ages the opprobrium of "Manichaeism" was laid to the Paulicians, Bogomili and Albigensi.

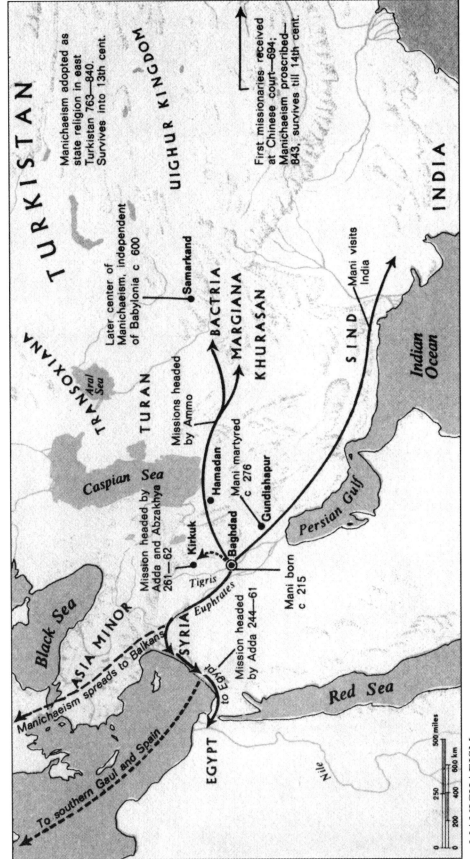

Turkistan

Manichaeism adopted as
state religion in east
Turkistan 763—840.
Survives into 13th cent.

UIGHUR KINGDOM

First missionaries received
at Chinese court—694;
Manichaeism proscribed—
843, survives till 14th cent.

INDIA

Later center of
Manichaeism, independent
of Babylonia c 600

Samarkand

TRANSOXIANA

Aral
Sea

BACTRIA

MARGIANA

KHURASAN

Mani visits
India

TURAN

SIND

Missions headed
by Ammo

Caspian Sea

Hamadan

Mani martyred
c 276

Gundishapur

Persian Gulf

Indian
Ocean

Mission headed by
Adda and Abzakhya
261—62

Kirkuk

Baghdad

Tigris

Mani born
c 215

Euphrates

ASIA MINOR

Black Sea

Manichaeism spreads to Balkans

SYRIA

to Egypt

Mission headed
by Adda 244—61

Red Sea

EGYPT

Nile

To southern Gaul and Spain

500 miles

250

200

400

800 km

0

0

MANICHAEISM

39

# II

## THE CHRISTIAN ROMAN EMPIRE

THE idea that Christianity might act as the cement of Roman civilization arose ten generations after the death of Jesus. The first ruler to conceive of such a thing was Constantine the Great (emp.: 312–37). His every action indicated that he thought the Christian religion and its sacred symbols should simply supersede the old gods of tribe and place which evidently were no longer able to guarantee the success of Roman arms and the well-being of the Roman Empire. The first Christian writer to give systematic and powerful treatment to a political philosophy that would fit the needs of both church and empire was Augustine of Hippo (bishop: 396–430).

The idea of a society pervaded by Christian values and shored up by Christian institutions continued into the modern period, long after the "Holy Roman Empire" ceased to exist (1806) even as a fiction.*

In all later development of a theory of Christendom, the writings of Augustine have remained formative. It was the Donatist controversy (312 ff.) which, by its negative impact on Latin ecclesiastical and Roman administrative powers in North Africa, caused Augustine to develop an apologetic for established religion. The revolt of Punic Christians against Roman control (and laxity of church discipline) moved Augustine to justify intervention by the government to suppress heresy; to develop the idea that the valid administration of church rites is quite separate from the moral quality of the celebrant; to define the church as a holy community not because of the caliber of its members but because of her purposes; to define ecumenical Christianity in terms of fellowship with the chief centers of prestige rather than identity with the church of the New Testament. His arguments were used for centuries to justify Christian persecution of dissent, the presence of unworthy men in sacramental offices, and the neglect of church discipline—none of which was allowed in the Early Church.

The twenty-two books of *The City of God* were written (413–26) to answer

---

* In 1901 Albert Schweitzer published his *Messianitäts- und Leidensgeheimnis*, and in 1906 his *Von Reimarus zu Wrede*. What Schweitzer did for those who study his evidence and follow his reasoning was to destroy the foundations of Christendom as a political and religious unity. Even without the massive evidence now available from the Qumran scrolls, he was led by his studies to conclude that Jesus expected this world to end soon. Jesus' teachings were shaped by that expectation, and his earliest followers reflect the same spirit. The emergence of a theology of expecta- tion (under the persecutions) and of world-denying asceticism (in monasticism) expresses not just a different set of values from the dominant cult but in some sense the continuance of an earlier and central motif in Christianity. That world-view was different from and in conflict with that which came to dominance in Theodosius and Justinian and governed churchly thought and action through Charlemagne to rulers like Charles V, Louis XIV and Wilhelm II (*summus episcopus* of the Old Prussian Union).

the widespread charge that Rome fell to the barbarians (410) because of neglect of the pagan gods. During the republican period, attention to the city shrines and family gods had been the guarantee of virtue and victory. During the imperial period, the ablest emperors had tried to strengthen the civic cult—which after Julius Caesar included religious homage to the emperor as "Augustus"—and suppress the disintegrating effect of Christianity. The fall of Rome came, according to defenders of the old order, because the gods had abandoned a people which neglected their altars. Augustine set out to provide the contrary: that the fall of the city was not only timely but long prophesied, that it was both deserved and providential. To do so he elaborated the fundamental contrast between Christianity and the world, between the City of God and the city of man, between salvation history and pagan existence. He created a model which shaped the vision of Christian rulers for more than 1,500 years.

The early Christians, with their foreshortened view of history, refused to bear arms in worldly strife. The day was to come when many professedly Christian governments would allow only the baptized to hold officers' ranks, in many cases even Jews being excluded. The early Christians practiced a radical sharing of goods, in some cases religious communism. The day came when Roman laws of property, primogeniture and obedience to higher classes would be enforced by "Christian" rulers of "Christian" lands. The early Christians were excited about the prospects for the future. The day came when synods and councils, with their decisions often reinforced by political decrees, looked backward to earlier councils and confessions of faith

for binding decisions as to Christian thought and action. The imagery of the early Christians was that of pilgrimage, of the exodus from civilizations into the life of preparation for the consummation of Holy History. That self-understanding was not to be recovered until the modern period, under the impact of modern science, secularism and totalitarianism.

From Constantine to Charles V, Europe was a mission field. The story of the fourth to the sixth centuries is the story of the gradual Christianization and civilization of the tribes which settled in the old Roman Empire as it disintegrated. In the process, many of the ideas and practices which still carried power were carried over, baptized, and incorporated into the vision of a Christian Empire.

After Augustine, the most powerful synthesizing mind at work in Christendom was that of Thomas Aquinas (c 1225–74). Aquinas wrote as the effect of the Crusades was reaching its maximum. He also wrote as monastic reform movements were sweeping across the church. The system of thought which he built, relying heavily upon the newly available metaphysical writings of Aristotle, is considered by many scholars the supreme intellectual achievement of the Latin Church. His system has been declared authoritative for the Roman Catholic Church in various papal pronouncements. Aquinas' thought is carefully fitted and mortised at all points, like a fortress: once the general design is accepted, the various parts support and buttress each other with admirable dependability. In this it was appropriate to a Christendom which still saw itself threatened from south, east and north but was beginning to be strong enough to impose a unitary order within.

A few generations later, Europe was on the threshold of a supreme push to expand globally and to impose European thought and life-styles upon the most distant peoples. The final stage of Christendom was imperial expansion across the world map. Since we are so close to this series of events, with the final effective period of European colonialism spanning the years from the Congress of Vienna (1815) to World War I (1914–18), it is difficult to discern when Christendom ends and a third period—THE AGE OF PERSONAL DECISION—may be defined. In the meantime we may mark it down that what is left of the old monistic vision of Christendom is fighting a rearguard action. Rulers of "Christian" nations have in recent generations rarely turned to Augustine's *City of God* or Aquinas' *Summa contra Gentiles* to justify their decisions.

# A. CHRISTIANITY BECOMES OFFICIAL

## THE EMPIRE OF CONSTANTINE AND HIS SUCCESSORS
### F. 313, 325

*The Church by its connection with Christian princes gained in power and riches, but lost in virtues.*

— Jerome

THE empire in which Constantine the Great (274–337) finally won power was already coming apart at the seams. Despotism, constant warfare and civil strife had long since destroyed the fiber of republican virtue. Most of the emperors for two centuries had been either tough barbarians or public degenerates, kept in power for a few years by the legions. Brutal spectacles entertained the Roman mob, fed at public expense, while military adventurers and tax-collectors exploited the subject peoples for personal profit. The independent farmers were squeezed out by the *latifundia*—larger and ever larger farms worked by slaves. Moreover, as the political and economic and military and religious situation deteriorated the invasions of tribes from the east became more and more successful.

*Constantine with subdued panther (paganism).*

Constantine set out to stem the downward slide. During his fight for power (306–23) he took a number of steps to rally Christian support. Although he was tolerant of the old faiths, accepted the title of "Augustus," and was called *pontifex maximus* as chief priest of the pagan state cult to the end of his life, his joint grant of toleration with Licinius at Milan in 313 seemed like the dawning of a new era to the long-persecuted Christians. For the

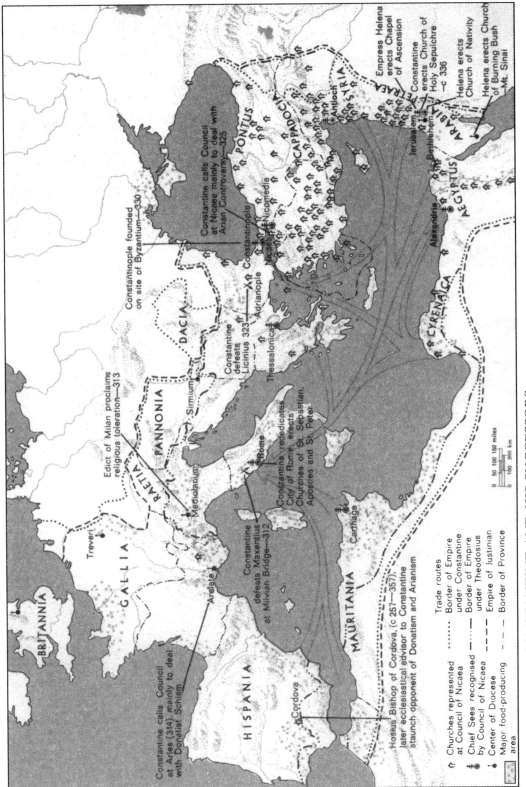

Empress Helena erects Chapel of Ascension

Constantine erects Church of Holy Sepulchre —c 336

Helena erects Church of Nativity

Helena erects Church of Burning Bush —Mt. Sinai

Constantine calls Council at Nicaea mainly to deal with Arian Controversy—325

Constantinople founded on site of Byzantium—330

Constantine defeats Licinius 323

Edict of Milan proclaims religious toleration—313

Constantine rededicates City of Rome, erects Churches of St. Sebastian, Apostles and St. Peter.

Constantine defeats Maxentius at Milvian Bridge—312

Constantine calls Council at Arles (314), mainly to deal with Donatist Schism

Hosius Bishop of Cordova, (c 257—357), later ecclesiastical advisor to Constantine staunch opponent of Donatism and Arianism

Trade routes
•••••• Border of Empire under Constantine
——— Border of Empire under Theodosius
– – – Empire of Justinian
– – – Border of Province

⚑ Churches represented at Council of Nicaea
🏛 Chief Sees recognised by Council of Nicaea
• Center of Diocese
Major food-producing area

0  50  100  150 miles
0  100  200 km

THE EMPIRE OF CONSTANTINE AND HIS SUCCESSORS

43

*Coin of Constantine (top) and the Empress Helena.*

first time they could function in public, receive bequests and build buildings. When Constantine moved his capital to Byzantium, renamed it Constantinople and enlarged it greatly, a number of the new buildings erected at public expense were churches.

Constantine's mother Helena, a zealous Christian, used her position to establish a number of chapels and shrines—including those celebrating the Ascension at the Mount of Olives (Lk. 24:50–53), the Nativity at Bethlehem, and the Burning Bush at Mount Sinai.

Constantine's hope that Christianity would serve as an integrating force, of which the old gods were apparently no longer capable, was not without disappointments. The theological disputes continued to rage, and to these were added the schisms which arose on the treatment of the lapsed. A rigorist split led by Melitius, Bishop of Lycopolis in Egypt, started c 306 and continued with separate clergy and congregations into the eighth century. Another and even more important split was that of the Donatists, who became a major Punic Christian schism—also disappearing only when the Saracen Muslims swept across North Africa. Most dangerous of all was the dispute between Arius (c 250–c 336) and his bishop, Alexander, in Alexandria—a rejuvenation of the debate concerning the nature of Jesus Christ which divided the churches into conflicting factions for several centuries. The controversy embedded itself so deeply among Constantine's successors that Eastern and Western office-holders saw fit to identify themselves as Arians (Constantius, Valens) or Orthodox (Constans, Valentinian), respectively. With the rise of the Gothic, Visigothic, Frankish and Vandal kingdoms, Arianism became even more a matter of political and ethnic loyalty and opposition to Rome and Constantinople.

Arianism taught that Jesus Christ was not eternal but made by the Father to do His creative work. Some taught he was elevated to the position of Son of God because of his great virtue. The teaching appealed to both strict monotheists and to tribesmen who knew all about great men who were elected to be gods. The chief theological champion of what finally became official was Athanasius (c 296–373), exiled five times as the tides of political influence and controversy in church synods ebbed away or flowed toward his defense of the true deity of God the Son.

THE final victory over Arianism was formally achieved under Emperor Theodosius at the First Council of Constantinople (381), but Arianism continued long after that among the tribesmen—first evangelized by Ulfilas (c 311–83), a missionary and Bible translator whose patron and consecrator was Eusebius of Nicomedia (d. c 342). Eusebius had studied under Lucian at Antioch, was a fellow student of Arius, and he had a very great influence at court.

When Constantine called a general synod—subsequently called the First Ecumenical Council—at Nicaea in 325, he had no idea of the subtleties of the issue which was dividing the churches —and certainly no inkling of the staying power of unitarian Christianity. When he wanted wars fought he instructed his commanders; when he wanted cities built he called together his architects and engineers; when he wanted religious concord he ordered out his bishops. Of the more than three hundred who assembled at Nicaea, only six came from the western half of the Empire.

As the Council opened, Eusebius of Caesarea (c 260–c 340)—called "the Father of Church History"—delivered an unrestrained eulogy which acclaimed Constantine as the long-awaited divine ruler whose reign would begin the final triumph of true religion on earth. The emperor, like his predecessors accustomed to the ecstatic greetings of religious sycophants, saw no reason to disagree with the interpretation. Through his able ecclesiastical advisor, Hosius of Cordova (c 257–357), Constantine got what he wanted: various schismatic heresies were condemned and a formula of doctrinal agreement was subscribed by all but two bishops—who were immediately deposed and banished. Constantine himself accepted deathbed baptism from Eusebius of Nicomedia, the Arian cleric whose creed submitted at Nicaea was the first to be rejected.

Whatever skepticism may be owed to the depth of Constantine's devotion to Jesus Christ, there is little argument about his ability as emperor. His reign marks the clear beginning of imperial control of the church, a tradition perpetuated for centuries in Eastern Orthodoxy—where he is revered as "the 13th Apostle" and as "saint."

Constantine's move of the capital to the east left the Bishop of Rome as the chief figure, religious or secular, in the

*Transverse section of Hagia Sophia, Constantinople, 532–37.*

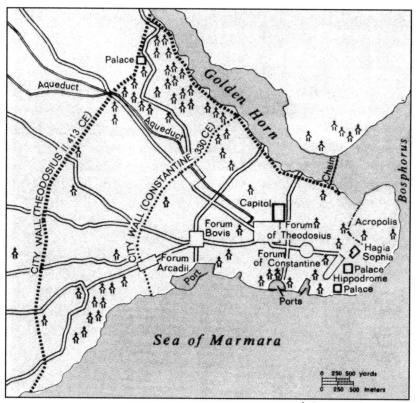

CONSTANTINOPLE

🛉 Church or Monastery

west. From the founding of Constantinople (330) dates the emergence of the papacy to superior power, although later Ecumenical Councils still referred to Rome as co-equal with the sees of Antioch, Alexandria, Jerusalem and Constantinople. The last named city, except for a brief period as center of a Crusader kingdom in the thirteenth century, remained the eastern capital until captured by the Muslim Turks in 1453.

## BYZANTINE JERUSALEM

WHEN Emperor Hadrian rebuilt Jerusalem (135) as a pagan city with a pagan temple, all the resident Jews—including the Jewish Christians—were expelled from the region. Only under Emperor Julian (ruled 361–63) were the Jews permitted a brief toleration and a short-lived effort at rebuilding the Holy City and the Temple. The Christian church that later grew up there was gentile. With Helena's visit, which set the fashion for venerating the Holy Places, the see regained some of its historic eminence. But veneration of the shrines and the Holy City did not lessen the savagery of gentile attacks on Judaism and the Jews. Antisemitic decrees were passed at Nicaea and built into the Codes of Theodosius and Justinian. Under the supervision of the Bishop of Caesarea until the Council of Chalcedon (451), Jerusalem was then placed formally on a par with the other four patriarchates. But the economic and popular base was gone.

The see of Jerusalem remained weak,

although the patriarch played some role in the doctrinal decisions which continued to consume the time of synods and councils—disputes in which the political interests of the Bishop of Rome and the Emperor in Constantinople had as much influence as dogma. In every section, too, bands of monks had begun to play a potent and often disorderly part in the fratricidal dogmatic disputes which were rending Christendom.

The teachings of Athanasius had formally triumphed over Arianism at Constantinople (381). The exposition of the Nicene formula by the Cappadocians—Basil (c 330–79), Gregory of Nazianzus (329–84) and Gregory of Nyssa (c 330–c 390)—had prepared the way for the official resolution of the doctrinal and linguistic difficulties. But the kingdoms of Genseric (c 390–477) in North Africa and Theodoric (c 454–526) in North Italy were still Arian strongholds. In the meantime, in the chief centers of the church the Christological debates took on new forms.

The first great Christological heresy was that of Apollinaris (c 310–c 390), Bishop of Laodicea and friend of Athanasius. Against Arianism he advanced the thesis that in man there exist body, soul and spirit, while in Jesus Christ the spirit was replaced by the divine *Logos*. Fully divine, but lacking complete humanity, Jesus was thereby deprived of exemplary meaning for Christians. Apollinaris's teaching

*What fellowship is there between Athens and Jerusalem, the academy and the church, heretics and Christians?*

— Tertullian vs. Hellenism

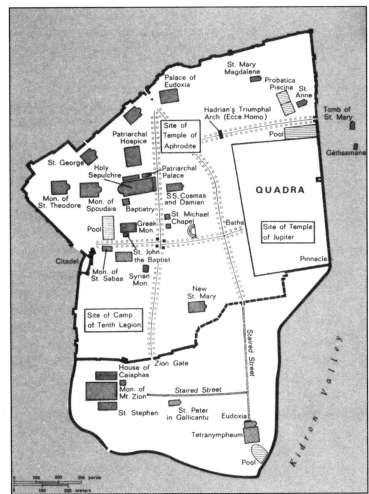

BYZANTINE
JERUSALEM

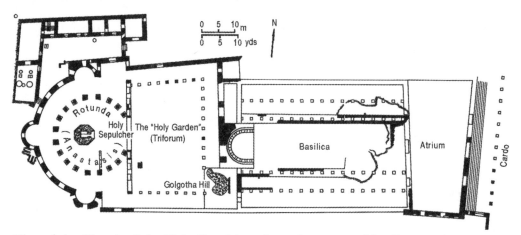

*Plan of the Church of the Holy Sepulchre, Jerusalem, erected by Constantine.*

was condemned at Constantinople (381); he had already seceded and was leading separated churches.

Nestorius (d. c 451), a native of Syria and student of Antioch, came to Constantinople by imperial invitation in 428. As a popular preacher and reformer, in the patriarchal office he set out to defend the full humanity of Jesus and to end the rising cult of Mary, symbolized by the word current in monastic and popular devotion: *Theotokos* ("Mother of God"). His solution was to affirm two separate persons in the Incarnate Christ, one divine and the other human. In his condemnation and banishment at the Council of Ephesus (431), the orthodox re-affirmed the unity of the Second Person of the Holy Trinity—at once human and divine. Eastern bishops who refused to submit to the decision then proceeded to form a Nestorian Church, based in Persia.

Bitterly opposed to Nestorianism was Eutyches (c 378–454), leader of a large monastery in Constantinople. He denied the humanity of Christ was the same as ours, thereby jeopardizing the work of Christ to human salvation. Deposed by the archbishop, he was acquitted at the 449 Council of Ephesus, only to be repudiated by Pope Leo's *Tome* and then condemned at Chalcedon (451). In spite of this action, Eutychian doctrine was favored at Alexandria and gained strong following also in Syria and Armenia. In the seventh century the Eastern emperors, with the patriarch of Jerusalem very active in the debate, attempted to unite the Orthodox and the Monophysites with a new form of words which avoided both monothelete and dyothelete solutions. When the Council of Constantinople of 680 declared the orthodox dogma to be the existence of two wills in Christ, divine and human, the Monophysites separated permanently into three large churches which embraced most of the oldest centers of Christianity: 1) Copts (Egyptian and Ethiopian), 2) Syrian Jacobites, 3) Armenians. The Monophysites stressed the divine nature in Christ to the extent that it transformed the human nature, leaving the historical Jesus a shadow.

Ravaged by generations of sectarian strife, the churches of North Africa and Asia Minor were ripe for Muslim conquest. And with the heartland of early Christianity fell Jerusalem the Holy City itself, already largely robbed of the Jewish presence and soon to be de-Christianized.

# B. DIVISION OF THE CHRISTIAN IMPERIUM

## RESISTANCE TO ORTHODOX THEOLOGY AND ROMAN ADMINISTRATION

*The Church of God in the Scriptures should be proclaimed everywhere holy and without spot.*
— the Donatists' chief affirmation

IN the third and fourth centuries, in spite of the apparent triumph of Christianity as the state religion of the Empire—or perhaps in good part because of it—the churches were rent by dogmatic and ecclesiastical strife. Large sections broke off permanently from fellowship with Rome and Constantinople. In these painful developments, the importance of non-theological factors must be given due weight—even though many Christian theologians, trained in philosophy rather than the social sciences, have interpreted developments almost exclusively in terms of the history of dogma.

*Theodosius and son with halo, staff and globe.*

Donatism had as its immediate occasion the irregular consecration of a bishop of Carthage at the hands of a *traditor* (whence "traitor"), one who had handed over the scriptures to the pagans during the Diocletian persecution. The stricter party elected another bishop and appealed; church synods (including Arles, 314) and emperors decided against them. Since the real strength of Donatism—which persisted in spite of persecution until the Muslim conquest—was its expression of Punic linguistic and administrative resentments of Latin and Roman domination, some of the protestors became partisans (*Circumcelliones*). The con-troversy led to a clarification of the church stand on a number of issues, especially by Augustine: e.g., rejection of re-baptism, affirmation of the validity of sacraments without reference to the personal qualities of the celebrationist, validation of the use of state power to suppress heresy.

Arianism also drew considerable strength from the resistance of the Goths, Visigoths, Burgundians, Lombards, Vandals and other tribes to the established creeds and administration. As the Roman imperium declined, Rome was sacked by the Arian Alaric (c 340–410), King of the Visigoths; Theodosius II (emp.: 408–50) was paying tribute to Attila to prevent a parallel disaster to Constantinople;

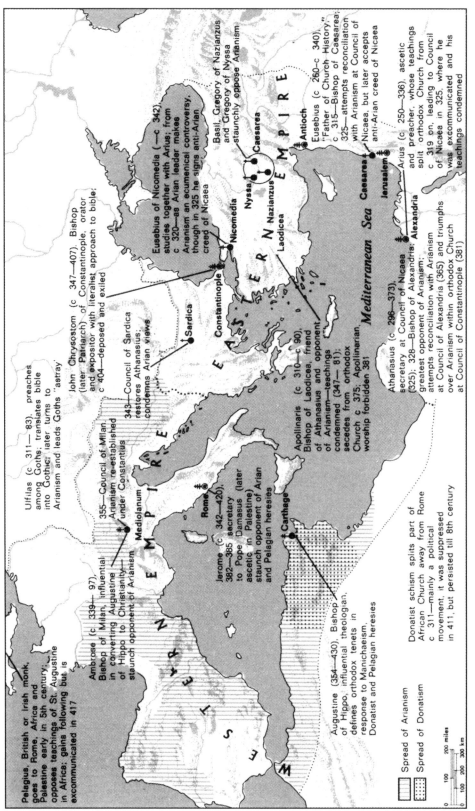

Pelagius, British or Irish monk, goes to Rome, Africa and Palestine early in 5th century; opposes teachings of St. Augustine in Africa; gains following but is excommunicated in 417

Ulfilas (c. 311—83), preaches among Goths; translates bible into Gothic; later turns to Arianism and leads Goths "astray"

John Chrysostom (c. 347—407), Bishop (later Patriarch) of Constantinople, orator and expositor with literalist approach to bible; c. 404—deposed and exiled

Eusebius of Nicomedia (—c 342), studies together with Arius; from c. 320—88 Arian leader makes Arianism an ecumenical controversy, though in 325 he signs anti-Arian creed of Nicaea

Basil, Gregory of Nazianzus and Gregory of Nyssa staunchly oppose Arianism

Eusebius (c. 260–c 340), "Father of Church History," c 315—Bishop of Caesarea; 325—attempts reconciliation with Arianism at Council of Nicaea, but later accepts anti-Arian creed of Nicaea

Arius (c. 250—336), ascetic and preacher, whose teachings split orthodox Church from c 319 on, leading to Council of Nicaea in 325, where he was excommunicated and his teachings condemned

343—Council of Sardica restores Athanasius; condemns Arian views

355—Council of Milan Arianism re-established under Constantius

Ambrose (c. 339—97), Bishop of Milan, influential in converting Augustine of Hippo to Christianity; staunch opponent of Arianism

Jerome (c. 342—420), secretary to Pope Damasus (later ascetic in Palestine) staunch opponent of Arian and Pelagian heresies

Augustine (354—430), Bishop of Hippo, influential theologian, defines orthodox tenets in response to Manichaeism, Donatist and Pelagian heresies

Apollinaris (c. 310—c 90), Bishop of Laodicea, friend of Athanasius and opponent of Arianism—teachings condemned (347—81); secedes from orthodox Church c 375; Apollinarian worship forbidden 381

Athanasius (c. 296–373), secretary at Council of Nicaea (325); 328—Bishop of Alexandria; greatest opponent of Arianism; attempts reconciliation with Arianism at Council of Alexandria (365) and triumphs over Arianism within orthodox Church at Council of Constantinople (381)

Donatist schism splits part of African Church away from Rome c 311—mainly a political movement, it was suppressed in 411, but persisted till 8th century

*Mediterranean Sea*

**E A S T E R N   E M P I R E**

**W E S T E R N   E M P I R E**

Mediolanum

Rome

Carthage

Sardica

Constantinople

Nicomedia

Caesarea

Nyssa

Nazianzus

Laodicea

Antioch

Alexandria

Caesarea

Ierusalem

☐ Spread of Arianism

▦ Spread of Donatism

0    100    200 miles
0  100  200  300 km

RESISTANCE TO ORTHODOX THEOLOGY AND ROMAN ADMINISTRATION

50

powerful Arian kingdoms developed in North Italy, Spain and North Africa. From 439, the Vandal kingdom centered in Carthage controlled most of North Africa and the Western Mediterranean (including Sicily, Corsica, Sardinia). Not until 496, when Clovis of the Franks accepted Catholic baptism, did the tide begin to swing back toward orthodoxy.

In the meantime the eastern churches split badly, with major churches—the most important being Nestorian or Monophysite—breaking away from the imperial state-church and establishing their chief centers on the borders or outside the Empire (reaching as far as Ethiopia, India and the Caucasus).

Resistance to the imperial religion produced two types of protest against accommodation to ecclesiastical administration of the procedures of the political bureaucracy. First was the breaking away of the oldest sections of the church. Parallel to this resistance to Roman centripetal force was a vigorous internal protest, against the style of church life imperial influence was developing: Monasticism. The rigors of monastic discipline also provided for those in earnest a substitute for the function of martyrdom as a social control factor.

There were three major components in the development of the imperial bureaucracy: 1) the development of a systematic levy against the tribes for the army; 2) the development of a system of taxation; 3) the development of a food supply system for Rome. As the birthplaces and "elections" of later emperors indicate, the tribesmen learned how to play the imperial game—and finally to use military formations to effect internal conquests of power. Equally important was the shift of the breadbasket area from the Nile Valley to Dalmatia, enhancing the importance of Rome and Ravenna and reducing the power of Alexandria.

That the church never came to be as totally incorporated into the imperial power system as the Christian emperors intended was partly due to monasticism, partly due to the distance between the Bishop of Rome and the Emperor in Byzantium (a distance that increased markedly with the barbarian invasions), and in part due to the genius of the great Latin Fathers: Ambrose, Jerome and Augustine. These succeeded in defining a style of Christianity which fitted the thrust of the imperial vision but was not identical with it.

Each of them made a significant

*Ambrose.*

*Jerome.*

*Augustine.*

contribution to the rise of monasticism. Ambrose (c 340–397) was a civil administrator in upper Italy, made Bishop of Milan by popular demand, who became a great church administrator, teacher of doctrine, and hymn writer. On a famous occasion he even humbled an emperor, but in the process justified the burning of synagogues. Jerome (c 347–419?), who wore the dress and followed the monastic discipline even while engaged in major diplomatic tasks for the church, was a man of enormous learning whose translation of the Bible (*Vulgate*) was standard for centuries in the Latin Church. Augustine (354–430) was the most influential theologian of all, and his writings of Christian devotion and against various heresies (e.g., Donatism and Pelagianism) still form Christian self-identity. His *City of God* made it possible for Christians to accept the trauma of the fall of Rome (410)— much as the prophets had prepared the Jews for the fall of Jerusalem—without losing faith in the purposes of God in history. Also, encouraged by his friend and patron Augustine, Orosius (c 385–420) at this time wrote his *Seven Books of History Against the Pagans*, which introduced a new periodization of holy history.

Contemporary in the east to the three great Latin Fathers was John Chrysostom (c 347–407), who was a monk, preacher, patriarch and exile. Chrysostom, trained at Antioch, was a master expositor of the literal meaning of the scriptures. Made Patriarch of Constantinople (398), he won the enmity of a dissolute clergy by his powerful demands for moral reform. In his preaching he was bitter in attacks on the Jews as well as the pagan cults. His unpopularity with the court and the intrigue of the Patriarch of Alexandria combined to effect his deposition, exile and death—in spite of unsuccessful intervention on his behalf by the pope and other leaders of the western churches.

## COUNCIL OF CHALCEDON 451

*The Son has a beginning but . . . God is without beginning.*        — Arius

THE ostensible function of councils in the early centuries of Christianity was to subdue heresies and schismatic movements and (hopefully) to achieve a consensus of belief among the baptized. These goals were achieved only partially. Nicaea (325) and Constantinople I (381) were called to deal with Arianism. Ephesus (431) condemned Nestorianism. Chalcedon (451) condemned the views of Apollinaris, Eu-

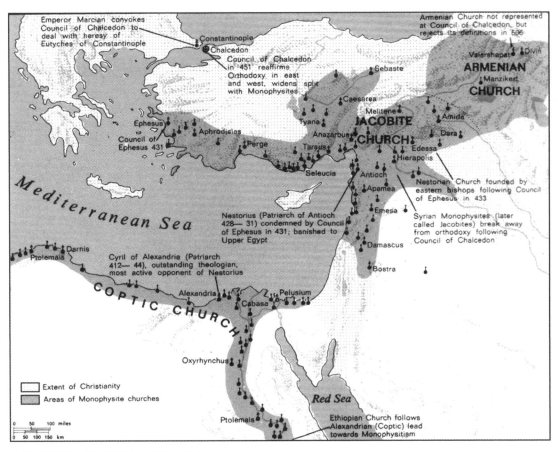

Emperor Marcian convokes Council of Chalcedon to deal with heresy of Eutyches of Constantinople

Constantinople

Chalcedon

Council of Chalcedon in 451 reaffirms Orthodoxy in east and west, widens split with Monophysites

Armenian Church not represented at Council of Chalcedon, but rejects its definitions in 506

Valarshapat  Divin

ARMENIAN

Manzikert

CHURCH

Sebaste

Caesarea

Melitene

Amida

JACOBITE

Tyana

Anazarbus

Dara

Ephesus

Aphrodisias

CHURCH

Council of Ephesus 431

Perge

Tarsus

Edessa

Hierapolis

Seleucia

Antioch

Apamea

Nestorian Church founded by eastern bishops following Council of Ephesus in 433

Mediterranean Sea

Nestorius (Patriarch of Antioch 428—31) condemned by Council of Ephesus in 431; banished to Upper Egypt

Emesa

Syrian Monophysites (later called Jacobites) break away from orthodoxy following Council of Chalcedon

Damascus

Darnis

Ptolemais

Cyril of Alexandria (Patriarch 412—44), outstanding theologian, most active opponent of Nestorius

Bostra

Alexandria

Cabasa

Pelusium

C O P T I C   C H U R C H

Oxyrhynchus

Red Sea

Extent of Christianity

Areas of Monophysite churches

0  50  100 miles
0  50  100  150 km

Ptolemais

Ethiopian Church follows Alexandrian (Coptic) lead towards Monophysitism

COUNCIL OF CHALCEDON

tyches and Nestorius. Constantinople II (553) condemned Montanism, still persisting in Phrygia, and many of the teachings of Origen, the greatest philosopher-theologian of Hellenistic Christianity. Constantinople III (680–81) reaffirmed the condemnation of Monophysite/Monothelete Christianity. Nicaea II (787) dealt more conclusively with Iconoclasm. Behind the scenes, deliberations in council were often dictated by power struggles between the Bishop of Rome and the Emperor, the rival claims of the five major patriarchates, and the desperate desire of the imperial administration to present a united ideological front against the Persian Empire, Attila's empire, and the tribal kingdoms pressing in from the north.

Chalcedon (451), which brought together more bishops than any previous synod (about 600, almost all from the eastern half of the Empire), achieved a formula which quieted the Christological controversy among many of the Greek and Latin congregations, a formula widely accepted to this day among Orthodox, Roman Catholic and Protestant churches. In a creed which was adopted there occur the words still basic to confessions of faith throughout most of world Christianity: "our lord Jesus Christ...truly god and truly man...of the same substance with the Father." This creed was as important for the views it rejected (e.g., Adoptionist, Gnostic, Arian, Nestorian, Monophysite) as for its statement of what had come to be widely believed.

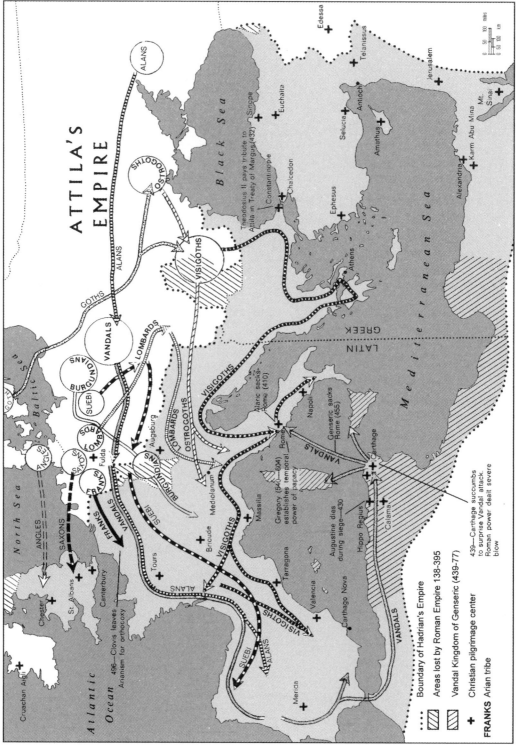

ATTILA'S EMPIRE

DECLINE OF ROMAN AUTHORITY 5TH–6TH CENTURIES

Boundary of Hadrian's Empire

Areas lost by Roman Empire 138–395

Vandal Kingdom of Genseric (439–77)

Christian pilgrimage center

FRANKS  Arian tribe

496—Clovis leaves Arianism for orthodoxy

439—Carthage succumbs to surprise Vandal attack. Roman power dealt severe blow

430—Augustine dies during siege

Gregory (540–604) establishes temporal power of papacy

Theodosius II pays tribute to Attila in Treaty of Margus (432)

Genseric sacks Rome (455)

Alaric sacks Rome (410)

North Sea

Baltic Sea

Atlantic Ocean

Black Sea

Mediterranean Sea

LATIN

GREEK

Craochan Aigli

Chester

St. Albans

Canterbury

Tours

Brioude

Massilia

Tarragona

Valencia

Carthago Nova

Merida

Hippo Regius

Calama

Carthage

Mediolanum

Napoli

Rome

Fulda

Augsburg

Athens

Ephesus

Chalcedon

Constantinople

Sinope

Euchaita

Edessa

Telanissus

Jerusalem

Antioch

Selucia

Amathus

Alexandria

Karm Abu Mina

Mt. Sinai

ALANS

OSTROGOTHS

GOTHS

ALANS

VISIGOTHS

VANDALS

BURGUNDIANS

SUEBI

LOMBARDS

ANGLES

SAXONS

FRANKS

LOMBARDS

OSTROGOTHS

VISIGOTHS

BURGUNDIANS

SUEBI

VANDALS

ALANS

VISIGOTHS

SUEBI

ALANS

VANDALS

VISIGOTHS

VANDALS

BY the time of Theodosius I (346?–95) the tensions between the eastern and western halves of the Empire were clearly evident in politics and religion. The Emperor was required twice to invade Italy to secure the rule of his "Co-Augustus"; the division of the realm became permanent under his sons. Under Theodosius II (401–50), Emperor in the East, the Theodosian Code was issued (438). But his rule was unstable and heavy tribute had to be paid Attila, King of the Huns (fl. 433–53). Under Justinian (Byzantine emp.: 527–65), there was a resurgence of imperial power. Control of Italy was reclaimed from the Ostrogoths and North Africa was regained from the Vandals. Justinian issued a codification of Roman law (*Corpus Juris Civilis*), expounded the doctrine of caesaro-papism, and built the great church of Hagia Sophia. His authority was severely checked, however, by the rise of the Monophysite churches.

In the West, the "wandering of the

*Leo the Great.*

tribes" and the emergence of tribal kingdoms continued. Such continuity and stability as could be identified centered in the Bishops of Rome, of which Leo the Great (pope: 440–61) was a representative type. By skillful diplomacy he extended the power of the Roman see throughout the West, and at the Council of Chalcedon his legates played a conclusive role in the settlements. He resisted the Huns and succeeded in getting their forces to withdraw beyond the Danube (452). Symbolic of the division in Christendom, as well as of the changed cultural base in the western churches, is the fact that Leo the Great wrote extensively in Latin but had no use of Greek.

In Gregory the Great (pope: 590–604), who laid the foundations for the papacy of the Middle Ages, the western half of the Empire found one of its greatest leaders. Raised in privilege, he sold his property and distributed his wealth to the poor. He was a monk before joining the papal staff, and he

*Attila the Hun.*

remained a strong patron of monasticism and the works of charity. As pope he proved a gifted administrator of the extensive church lands and a skillful political leader. He resisted the imperial power and the claims of the Patriarch of Constantinople, made a separate peace treaty with the invading Lombards, eliminated the power of the Byzantine exarch at Ravenna, and launched the Latin missions to Britain (596) with Augustine of Canterbury. Among Gregory's extensive writings on Christian thought and practice were a book on the work of the bishop which became the textbook of the medieval episcopate, and commentaries on the Scripture. He also laid the foundations of the "Gregorian chant." He contributed greatly to the rise of shrines expressing popular religious devotion, to the veneration of relics, and to the popular cult of miracles attributed to the martyrs and confessors.

In spite of a few leaders of ability, however, the numbers and cultural condition of Christianity—rent by internal divisions and suffering from the political instability of the times—declined generally from c 500 to c 950.

## CHRISTIANITY IN BYZANTIUM c 787

IN the Byzantine Empire, theological and ecclesiastical disputes were fought out in the shadow of a resident emperor with more than passing power. Some of the rulers were laymen of considerable theological competence, and all of them thought of themselves as successors to Constantine and his style of religious intervention.

The Seventh Ecumenical Council (Nicaea II, 787) took place in the midst of a bitter fight over the use of images in the church. Emperor Leo III of Syria (c 675–740), who saved the Eastern Empire by victories over Muslim armies in 718 and again in 740, set out to destroy the icons which he believed to be the primary obstacle to the conversion of Jews and Muslims. Leo is said also to have been influenced by Paulician doctrines; of the Paulicians little is known except that they were an offshoot of Manichaeism, stern monotheists, and that colonies of them were transported from Asia Minor and settled in the Balkans during the seventh century.

*Empress Theodora, c 547 from mosaic in San Vitale, Ravenna.*

In the decades of controversy, which bridged several reigns and many synods, western church representatives intervened in favor of visual aids to

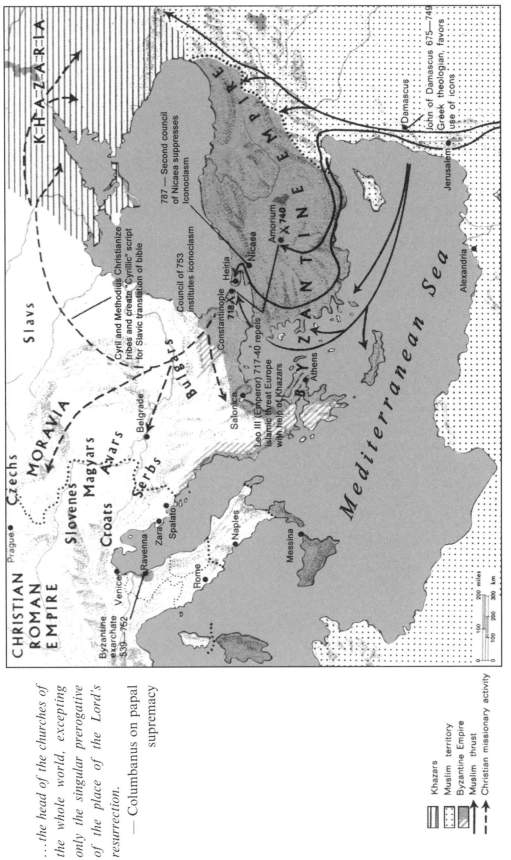

... the head of the churches of the whole world, excepting only the singular prerogative of the place of the Lord's resurrection.
— Columbanus on papal supremacy

CHRISTIAN ROMAN EMPIRE

Byzantine exarchate 539—752

Prague

Czechs

Slavs

MORAVIA

Slovenes

Magyars

Avars

Croats

Serbs

Bulgars

Cyril and Methodius Christianize tribes and create "Cyrillic" script for Slavic translation of bible

787 — Second council of Nicaea suppresses Iconoclasm

Council of 753 institutes iconoclasm

Amorium X 740

Nicaea

Heiria

Constantinople

718 X

Leo III (Emperor) 717-40 repels Islamic threat Europe with help of Khazars

Salonica

Athens

BYZANTINE EMPIRE

KHAZARIA

Damascus

John of Damascus 675—749 Greek theologian, favors use of icons

Jerusalem

Alexandria

Mediterranean Sea

Venice

Ravenna

Zara

Spalato

Rome

Naples

Messina

Belgrade

100    200 miles
100  200  300 km

CHRISTIANITY IN BYZANTIUM c 787

Khazars
Muslim territory
Byzantine Empire
Muslim thrust
Christian missionary activity

*Gregory the Great.*

with philosophy, heresies, and Christian doctrine. He also prepared an extensive volume of scriptural proofs on morality and ascetics. With the Orthodox emphasis upon tradition fixed in the Apostolic Age and confirmed by the Seven Ecumenical Councils, his writings have marked the high tide of Eastern Orthodox thought into the modern period.

The most important expansion of Christianity in the East is associated with the work of the brothers Cyril (826–69) and Methodius (c 815–85) of Thessalonica. In their work among the Slavs they invented the Cyrillic alphabet for translation of the liturgy and the Bible, thus becoming founders of Slavonic literature.

devotion—"the books of the poor," as Gregory the Great called them. In the East the chief defenders of icons were the monks. Nicaea II decided in favor of their use, a decision enforced by imperial decree then and again in 843.

Among the chief defenders of the use of icons was John of Damascus (c 675–c 749), a monk and theologian who grew up under Muslim suzerainty. His "Fount of Wisdom" deals at length

As Christianity pushed northward among the Slavs it received a great impulse with the conversion of Vladimir (956–1015), Prince of the Kievan Rus. Seven decades later the split between the Latin Church and Eastern Orthodoxy was formalized (1054). When the center shifted from Kiev to Moscow, the latter was already the chief city of a Christian empire, a "Third Rome."

*Warrior horseman, from 7th–8th centuries.*

MONASTICISM is one of the most fascinating fields of study in the history of religions, especially in an age which is seeing a resurgence of communes. By no means limited to one religion, and in the judgment of many, more fitted to the world-denying ethos of a religion like Buddhism than to a world- and history-affirming faith like Judaism or Christianity, it has as a matter of fact made a major impact in all dimensions of Christian life and thought.

Although monastic communities have commonly espoused apostolic

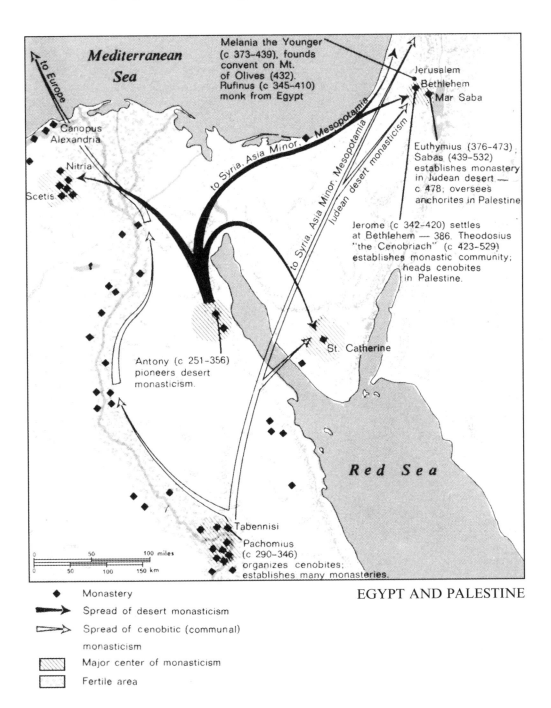

Melania the Younger (c 373–439), founds convent on Mt. of Olives (432). Rufinus (c 345–410) monk from Egypt

Euthymius (376–473), Sabas (439–532) establishes monastery in Judean desert — c 478; oversees anchorites in Palestine

Jerome (c 342–420) settles at Bethlehem — 386. Theodosius "the Cenobriach" (c 423–529) establishes monastic community; heads cenobites in Palestine.

Antony (c 251–356) pioneers desert monasticism.

Pachomius (c 290–346) organizes cenobites; establishes many monasteries.

EGYPT AND PALESTINE

- ◆ Monastery
- ➤ Spread of desert monasticism
- ▷ Spread of cenobitic (communal) monasticism
- ▨ Major center of monasticism
- ▢ Fertile area

non-resistance (Mt. 5:38–44) as well as celibacy, three of the strongest orders important to Christian history—the Templars, Hospitalers and Teutonic Knights—were noted for their military accomplishments. Although they have sworn apostolic poverty, certain orders have drawn enormous income from land, banking and commerce and have earned the enmity of revolutionary movements. Although many orders have been suspicious of human learning, others have been founders of distinguished schools and universities, and monasticism itself is credited with preserving culture during the dark ages. Although sponsored by some of the greatest church fathers and bishops, monasticism has been a continuing protest against the worldliness and power-consciousness of the establishment.

The founders of the monastic community seem to have been Antony of Egypt (c 251–356) and Pachomius (c 290–346). Both lived and worked in the Nile Valley. About 305, Antony gathered hermits under a common rule. He was active in support of the worship of Mary and opposed to Nestorius. About 320, Pachomius built a community at Tabennisi; by the time of his death there were nine communities for men and two for women under his rule. The major teachings were virginity, poverty and obedience; great stress was laid on realization of the rule of the Early Church (Acts 4:32ff.) in contrast to the worldliness of institutional Christianity.

With the union of church and state under Constantine and his successors, and with the disappearance of martyrdom as a social control factor in the church, the appeal of monastic discipline increased. The self-denial of the monastics, who had rejected the ambitions of the world for the favor of

*Mar Saba monastery in the Judean Desert.*

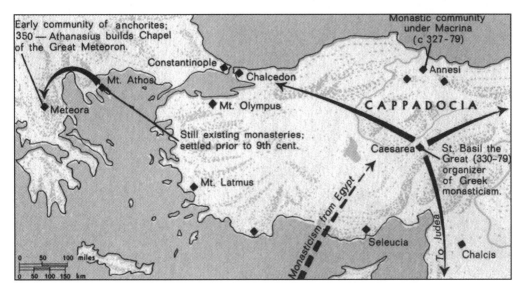

CAPPADOCIA

Christ in the world to come, provided psychological compensation for the loss of martyrdom; it also built the esteem in which the monastics were held by Christians whose own lives were spent in war and violence.

Basil the Great (c 330–79), noted for his theological contributions to resolution of the Christological disputes, erected at Caesarea a great complex of buildings for monks, care of the poor, nursing the sick. The rule which he put forward in 358–64—with hours for prayer and hours for physical labor—remains the core of Orthodox monasticism to the present day. Centers such as Athos, Ochrid and Kiev have been focal points of both learning and devotion.

In the West, Martin (335?–97), Bishop of Tours (and later patron saint of France), was a leader in founding monastic communities, including the first in Gaul (Legugé, f. 361). John Cassian (c 360–435) should also be mentioned; having spent some years studying monastic life in Egypt, he wrote two books reporting his conversations with the leaders of these communities and setting forth the basic rules of community life. He founded two centers near Marseilles.

Although Athanasius, Ambrose, Augustine, Jerome, and other key leaders strongly supported monasticism, the major institutional foundation in the West came from Benedict of Nursia (c 480–c 550). Disillusioned by the corruption at Rome, where he grew up, Benedict withdrew for a time as a hermit and then c 525 founded a community at Monte Cassino where he remained until his death. In Benedict's Rule, which has continued with various reforms to the present day, stability was added as a mark of monastic life. Government is patriarchal, with the abbot elected by vote of the membership.

From Egypt, the monastic model spread to Palestine and Asia Minor, catching up there the response of Christians who remembered the golden years of early Christianity and were repelled by the doctrinal and political strife which seemed to arise with prosperity and patronage. A fact symbolic of the appeal of monasticism: Jerome spent the last 34 years of his life in a commune at Bethlehem.

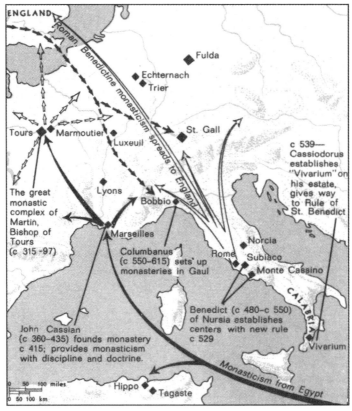

Legend:
- Celtic monasticism
- Egyptian monasticism
- Roman monasticism
- Evangelists from Marmoutier
- Chief center of monastic learning

Map labels:
ENGLAND
Roman, Benedictine monasticism spreads to England
Fulda
Echternach
Trier
Tours
Marmoutier
Luxeuil
St. Gall
The great monastic complex of Martin, Bishop of Tours (c 315–97)
Lyons
Bobbio
Marseilles
Columbanus (c 550–615) sets up monasteries in Gaul
Rome
Norcia
Subiaco
Monte Cassino
CALABRIA
John Cassian (c 360–435) founds monastery c 415; provides monasticism with discipline and doctrine.
Benedict (c 480–c 550) of Nursia establishes centers with new rule c 529
c 539—Cassiodorus establishes "Vivarium" on his estate, gives way to Rule of St. Benedict
Vivarium
Monasticism from Egypt
0    50    100 miles
0   50  100 km
Hippo
Tagaste

ITALY AND FRANCE

before the islands were reduced almost to barbarism by Viking and Saxon raids, also produced vigorous missionary activity. Columba (c 521–97), founder of the monastery on Iona, and Columbanus (c 500–615), also abbot there, were both active in missions. The latter founded the great centers at Luxeuil (France) and Bobbio (Italy).

MONASTICISM attracted persons of sensitive spirit and intellectual bent, including many of the nobility who were not willing to devote their lives to war and intrigue in an age of disintegration. Such a man was Cassiodorus (c 485–c 580), a member of the Roman nobility and a successful diplomat, who founded two Benedictine monasteries at Vivarium. Retiring from public affairs, he introduced into the monastery the work of copying manuscripts—both classical and Christian—and thus added a discipline of greatest importance to the preservation of learning in the dark ages.

Much of the work of Christian missions was carried out by monks. Among them were Boniface and Willibrord, who worked among the tribes across the Rhine.

Celtic Christianity, in its high period

*Columbanus.*

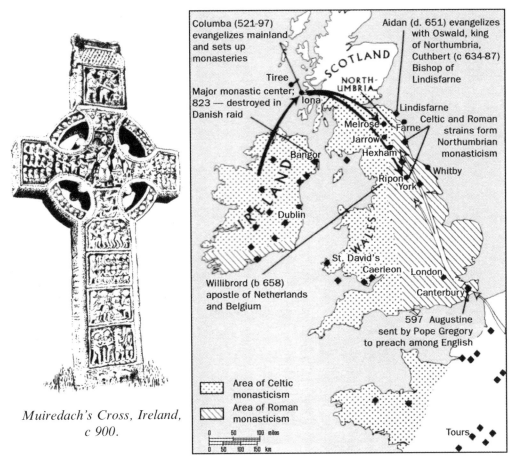

Columba (521-97) evangelizes mainland and sets up monasteries

Aidan (d. 651) evangelizes with Oswald, king of Northumbria, Cuthbert (c 634-87) Bishop of Lindisfarne

Tiree

SCOTLAND

NORTH-UMBRIA

Major monastic center; 823 — destroyed in Danish raid

Iona

Lindisfarne

Celtic and Roman strains form Northumbrian monasticism

Melrose

Farne

Jarrow

Bangor

Hexham

Whitby

IRELAND

Ripon

York

Dublin

WALES

St. David's

Caerleon

London

Willibrord (b 658) apostle of Netherlands and Belgium

Canterbury

597 Augustine sent by Pope Gregory to preach among English

Area of Celtic monasticism

Area of Roman monasticism

0   50   100 miles
0   50   100   150 km

Tours

BRITAIN AND IRELAND

*Muiredach's Cross, Ireland, c 900.*

THE Celtic monks established important monasteries and centers of learning in Gaul. Focus of attention on the Continent was natural, as the Celts had covered a large part of Europe—and far enough into the Balkans to have a great encampment at Ochrid (now in Yugoslavia, near the Albanian border)—until driven out in tribal wars during the fourth century BCE. These monks, often traveling in groups of twelve or making missionary trips two by two in imitation of the Twelve and the Seventy of the New Testament, were brought into conflict with the Roman rite and calendar. It was the Synod of Whitby (664) in England that settled this dispute in favor of the latter tradition. One of the practices which

the Celtic Christians developed which was generally adopted throughout the Western church was use of the private confessional, along with an elaborate system of penitential discipline.

During the late fifth century Saxon invasions destroyed many of the old centers of Christianity in England, and it was not until Alfred the Great (849–99) defeated the Danes and fostered a religious and educational renaissance, in the year 897, that the tide turned again significantly away from the tribal gods and their priests. In the substantial writings of Bede the Venerable (c 673–735)—exegetical, historical and practical—we have evidence of the continuing vigor of the church in Britain even in adversity.

# ETHIOPIA

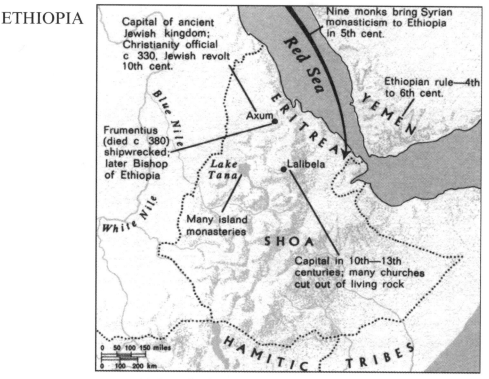

Capital of ancient Jewish kingdom; Christianity official c 330, Jewish revolt 10th cent.

Nine monks bring Syrian monasticism to Ethiopia in 5th cent.

Ethiopian rule—4th to 6th cent.

Red Sea

ERITREA

YEMEN

Axum

Frumentius (died c 380) shipwrecked; later Bishop of Ethiopia

Blue Nile

Lake Tana

Lalibela

White Nile

Many island monasteries

SHOA

Capital in 10th—13th centuries; many churches cut out of living rock

0  50 100 150 miles
0   100  200 km

HAMITIC TRIBES

·········· Modern Border

ETHIOPIA traces its connection with biblical events and Holy History as far back as the visit of the Queen of Sheba to King Solomon's court (II Chron. 9:1–12). Jewish influence has remained substantial across centuries, and to this day the church observes several Jewish customs (e.g., circumcision, Sabbath observance, avoidance of unclean meats), while the Falasha people count themselves adherents of Judaism. In recent years tens of thousands have been brought to Israel.

Christianity of record was brought to Ethiopia by Frumentius (c 300–c 380), who was consecrated as a missionary bishop by Athanasius. Monasticism came with the faith, therefore, and is important yet today. During the Christological disputes the Church of Abyssinia followed the leadership of Alexandria, after the rise of Islam developing its own patriarchate (*Abuna*).

Many Ethiopian monasteries and churches are architecturally striking, with fronts carved in a rock wall and the rooms behind cut out of solid rock. Similar structures, also indicating a continuing experience of attack and need for tight defense, are found in other centers of Eastern Christianity (e.g., Ochrid and Kiev).

*Monolithic church at Lalibela, Ethiopia.*

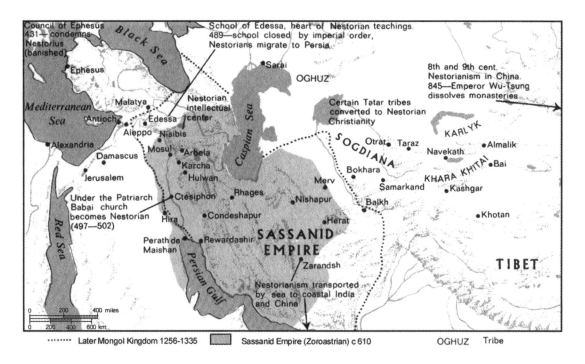

Council of Ephesus 431— condemns Nestorius (banished)

School of Edessa, heart of Nestorian teachings. 489—school closed by imperial order, Nestorians migrate to Persia.

8th and 9th cent. Nestorianism in China. 845—Emperor Wu-Tsung dissolves monasteries

Certain Tatar tribes converted to Nestorian Christianity

Nestorian intellectual center

Under the Patriarch Babai church becomes Nestorian (497—502)

Nestorianism transported by sea to coastal India and China

Black Sea · Ephesus · Mediterranean Sea · Alexandria · Antioch · Malatya · Edessa · Aleppo · Nisibis · Damascus · Mosul · Arbela · Jerusalem · Karcha · Hulwan · Ctesiphon · Rhages · Hira · Condeshapur · Perath de Maishan · Rewardashir · Persian Gulf · Red Sea · SASSANID EMPIRE · Zarandsh · Caspian Sea · Sarai · OGHUZ · Merv · Nishapur · Balkh · Herat · SOGDIANA · Bokhara · Samarkand · Otrat · Taraz · Navekath · Kashgar · KARLYK · KHARA KHITAI · Almalik · Bai · Khotan · TIBET

······· Later Mongol Kingdom 1256-1335　　　　Sassanid Empire (Zoroastrian) c 610　　　　OGHUZ　Tribe

DOCTRINAL and political factors in the rise of Nestorianism have been discussed previously. For a time Edessa was a strong Nestorian center. According to an old tradition, King Abgar V corresponded with Jesus, was healed by one of the Seventy, and converted. In any case, Abgar IX (179–214) did convert—bringing his people with him in one of the earliest mass conversions to Christianity. For a time (435–89) Nestorianism found a haven in Edessa, but under Byzantine and Monophysite persecution many migrated to Persia after Chalcedon. A school with several hundred students was developed at Nisibis. The see of the patriarch (*Catholicos*) was fixed at Seleucia-Ctesiphon, the capital of the Persian Empire. It was moved to Baghdad c 775.

By the sixth century Nestorian missionaries were active in Arabia, India and Turkestan. Under the early Sassanids they suffered severely: Zoroastrianism was the favored religion and

persecution was severe. After the Muslim conquest of Persia (651) they were alternately tolerated and persecuted. Over the centuries they lost ground to Islam, but the scattering of refugees helped to spread Nestorian beliefs into new areas. In 1625 a large stone slab was found in Northwest China (*Sigan-Fu* Stone), which recorded the history of a Nestorian mission of considerable success for the years 635–783. A replica of this early evidence of Christianity in the Far East may be found in the Metropolitan Museum of Art, New York.

The invasion of Tamerlane (c 1336–1405) and the wars of the Mongols and Ottoman Turks reduced the home base to ruins. The Nestorian churches disappeared in China. Only a small community of "Assyrian Christians" still survives near the northernmost border of Iran.

According to tradition, Christianity was carried to India by the Apostle

Thomas. Travelers from Europe at the beginning of the modern period found thoroughly established churches on the coasts of southern India and Ceylon. Inscriptions were found—dating from the seventh to ninth centuries—in Middle Persian and their liturgical language was Syriac. Their closest church connection was with the Nestorians of Mesopotamia; in 1440 they received new bishops from the Catholicos at Baghdad.

In the modern period sections of the "Malabar Christians" reunited with Rome (1599, 1662, 1930). Another group joined the Church of Syria ("Jacobites"). Another, the Mar Thoma Church, has since 1889 been organized along presbyterian lines and doctrine and is a member of the World Council of Churches.

Across the centuries both Nestorian and Monophysite churches have—influenced by powerful forces which tend to blur or eliminate the details of ancient doctrinal disputes—"normalized." Several have joined the World Council of Churches (f. 1948) and for a term one of the Presidents of the WCC was from the Malabar Christians.

## THE KINGDOM OF THE KHAZARS c 700–1000

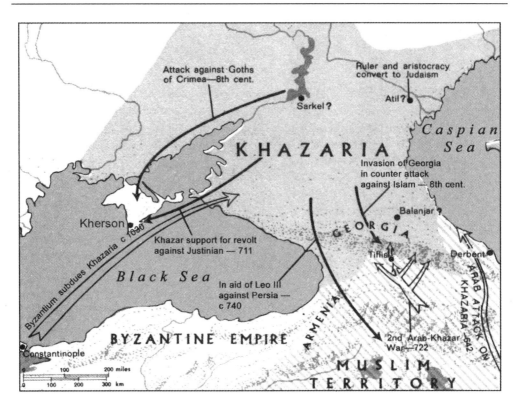

THE most powerful people between the Don and the Volga rivers after the fifth century were the Khazars, former nomads of Turkic origin. They controlled the Crimea and exacted tribute from the Eastern Slavs. They built a kingdom substantial enough for them to be coveted as allies against the Muslims by the Byzantine emperor.

The royal house and a majority converted to Judaism (c 740); toward religious minorities they practiced toleration.

Until defeated by the Duke of Kiev

in 969 they were the most important political and military force preventing Muslim conquest in South Russia. This defeat, coupled in 1030 with Khazar submission to Byzantium, came just before Duke Vladimir (956–1015) tied his fortunes to Constantinople and set out—often forcibly—to convert his subjects to Greek Orthodoxy.

With the fall of Khazaria came the end of the last massive experiment in missions by Judaism, although individual conversions occur up to the present day wherever the laws permit.

## MOHAMMED'S STRUGGLES

*The sword is the key of heaven and hell. A drop of blood shed in the cause of Allah, a night spent in arms, is of more avail than two months of fasting and prayer.* — Mohammed

*Mohammed bringing offerings to the Kaaba, from 16th cent. manuscript.*

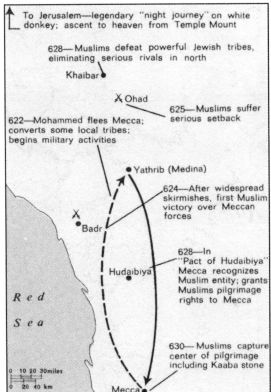

To Jerusalem—legendary "night journey" on white donkey; ascent to heaven from Temple Mount

628—Muslims defeat powerful Jewish tribes, eliminating serious rivals in north

Khaibar

X Ohad

622—Mohammed flees Mecca; converts some local tribes; begins military activities

625—Muslims suffer serious setback

Yathrib (Medina)

624—After widespread skirmishes, first Muslim victory over Meccan forces

X Badr

628—In "Pact of Hudaibiya" Mecca recognizes Muslim entity; grants Muslims pilgrimage rights to Mecca

Hudaibiya

Red Sea

630—Muslims capture center of pilgrimage including Kaaba stone

0 10 20 30 miles
0 20 40 km

Mecca

MOHAMMED (570–632) grew up in Mecca and there achieved commercial success. After a time of inner unrest, resolved during prayer and meditation in the desert, he felt the call to turn his neighbors to the One God and preparation for His coming Judgment. Persecuted for his unpopular message, he fled with a few followers to Medina (622—*Hegira* = flight, the beginning of the Muslim calendar). At Medina he founded a strongly theocratic society, which as a prophet he strengthened by able leadership and reinforced by revelations.

In 630 Mohammed's forces defeated Mecca in battle. The central cultic rites were established at the Kaaba (with reverence for the Black Stone, anteceding Islam). The duty of pilgrimage was fixed, and the forces launched which in short decades brought the most serious threat to Christianity until the rise of totalitarian ideologies in the twentieth century.

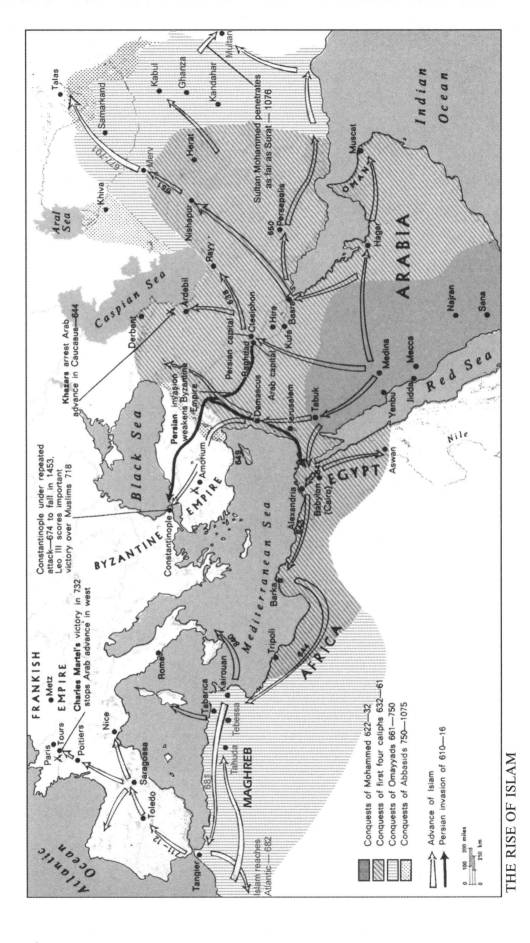

THE RISE OF ISLAM

Conquests of Mohammed 622—32
Conquests of first four caliphs 632—61
Conquests of Omayyads 661—750
Conquests of Abbasids 750—1075

⟹ Advance of Islam
━➤ Persian invasion of 610—16

0   100   200 miles
0   250 km

Charles Martel's victory in 732
stops Arab advance in west

Constantinople under repeated
attack—674 to fall in 1453.
Leo III scores important
victory over Muslims 718

Khazars arrest Arab
advance in Caucasus—644

Persian invasion
weakens Byzantine
Empire

Sultan Mohammed penetrates
as far as Surat—1076

Atlantic
Ocean

FRANKISH
EMPIRE
Metz
Paris
Tours
Poitiers
Nice
Rome
Saragossa
Toledo
Tangier
Tabarca
Kairouan
Tebessa
Tahuda
Tripoli
Barka

MAGHREB

AFRICA

Mediterranean Sea

Black Sea

Constantinople
BYZANTINE
EMPIRE
Amorium

Caspian Sea
Derbent
Ardebil
Rayy
Nishapur
Herat

Aral
Sea
Khiva
Samarkand
Talas

Kabul
Ghanza
Kandahar
Multan

Baghdad
Ctesiphon
Persian capital
Arab capital
Hira
Kufa
Basra
Damascus
Jerusalem
Tabuk

Babylon
(Cairo)
Alexandria
EGYPT
Aswan

Nile

Red Sea

Medina
Mecca
Jidda
Yenbu

ARABIA
OMAN
Muscat
Hager
Najran
Sena

Indian
Ocean

Persepolis

68

ALTHOUGH Emperor Justinian I suppressed the ancient pagan schools of philosophy in 529, an act formally signalizing the triumph of Christianity over its Hellenistic adversaries, in fact Christianity was in decline from c 500 to c 950.

The contribution of fratricidal strife among Christians to the developing crisis can scarcely be exaggerated. The loss of the ancient churches in the region of the Middle East has been noted. To this must be added the battles in North Africa between the Orthodox and the Montanists, Donatists and Arians. Hundreds of thousands of Christians in the oldest centers of the faith went over to Islam with its simple statement of faith and clear call of brotherhood, presumably with a sigh of relief. With the fall of over half of Christendom to Islam—and the most civilized and traditional areas at that—the task of Christianity was fixed for centuries: to survive in a beleaguered Europe.

Islam professed to be a new dispensation superseding both Judaism and Christianity, and at the same time claimed to be the original universal faith of mankind before sectarian division set in. It swept across the civilized world with astonishing speed. By the time of Mohammed's death (632), Arabia was largely won—although small Jewish or Christian tribes resisted briefly. There followed the conquests of Syria, Palestine and Egypt. Within one century the religion was dominant in North Africa, Spain, Iraq, Persia, Cyprus, Crete, Sicily, and was stopped only by Khazar and Byzantine forces (718) and by the Frankish king at Tours (732) from overrunning both eastern and western Christian empires.

Islam is based upon the Koran, said to be God's own word in the Arabic language; unlike the holy books of the Jews and Christians, the Koran is inerrant (utterly without error). Mohammed is believed to be the last of a line of prophets which includes many biblical persons, his role being that of warning mankind of the impending Last Judgment.

For centuries Christian controversialists followed the path of John of Damascus in interpreting Islam as a Christian heresy. With the Crusades, a stance of more implacable hostility was adopted and defined.

*Dome of the Rock, Jerusalem.*

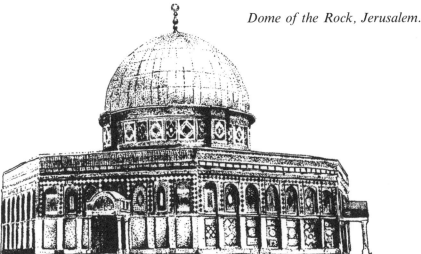

# C. THE EMPIRE OF CHARLEMAGNE AND HIS SUCCESSORS

## THE CHRISTIAN EMPIRE OF CHARLEMAGNE 742–814

THE break in the Arian tribal front came in 496, when Clovis of the Franks accepted Catholic baptism. Having defeated the Romans, the Alemanni, the Burgundians and the Visigoths in battle, Clovis laid the foundations of what was to become France. The alliance of the papacy and France continued into the sixteenth century. Pepin the Short (c 714–68), father of Charlemagne, ended the Merovingian line; he consolidated the relations with the papacy by defeating the Lombards and ceding the areas to the pope which became the Papal States.

Charlemagne (c 742–814) re-established with papal blessing the office of the Emperor (800) of what was widely called the "Holy Roman Empire," and in his long reign proved to be one of the ablest rulers in western history. In a series of campaigns he conquered the Saxons, the Wends, the Avars and other tribes to the east, for the first time carrying the claims of Orthodox Christianity and imperial interests east of the Rhine. In 21 CE Hermann, German chieftain, had defeated the Roman legions; Roman advance beyond the Rhine was stopped for centuries. Charlemagne conducted eighteen campaigns against the Saxons (770–84); they and other tribes he defeated were baptized at the point of a sword. He also sent five expeditions against the Saracens in Italy and seven against the Arabs in Spain. In the first of the latter series Roland was killed, under circumstances long celebrated as

*Charlemagne.*

symbolic of the heroism and faithfulness of the Christian knight and the virtue of chivalry. In consolidating his expanding realm the Emperor introduced several major institutions, including military frontier marches and regular regional inspections carried out by his personal administrative representatives.

Charlemagne thought of himself as heir to the Byzantine tradition, and he reorganized the church by setting up twenty-two new metropolitan sees; these posts supervised the bishops and also created a barrier between them and papal intervention. He intervened in doctrinal matters through the Synod of Frankfurt's support of icons (794), the Synod of Aachen's adding *filioque* (809) to the Creed, and elsewhere.

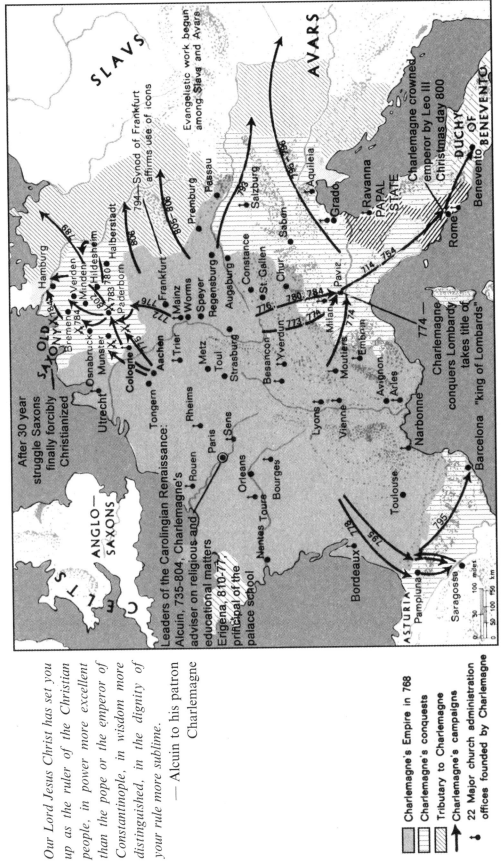

*Our Lord Jesus Christ has set you up as the ruler of the Christian people, in power more excellent than the pope or the emperor of Constantinople, in wisdom more distinguished, in the dignity of your rule more sublime.*

— Alcuin to his patron Charlemagne

After 30 year struggle Saxons finally forcibly Christianized

Evangelistic work begun among Slavs and Avars

794—Synod of Frankfurt affirms use of icons

Charlemagne crowned emperor by Leo III Christmas day 800

SLAVS

AVARS

ANGLO-SAXONS

CELTS

OLD SAXONY

Leaders of the Carolingian Renaissance: Alcuin, 735-804, Charlemagne's adviser on religious and educational matters Erigena, 810-77, principal of the palace school

Charlemagne conquers Lombardy takes title of "king of Lombards"

Barcelona    Benevento

DUCHY OF BENEVENTO

PAPAL STATE

Ravenna

Aquileia

Grado

Salzburg

Saben

Chur

St. Gallen

Constance

Augsburg

Regensburg

Speyer

Worms

Mainz

Frankfurt

Paderborn

Hildesheim

Halberstadt

Minden

Verden

Bremen

Hamburg

Osnabruck

Munster

Cologne

Tongern

Aachen

Trier

Metz

Toul

Strasburg

Besancon

Yverdun

Moutiers

Embrun

Avignon

Arles

Narbonne

Toulouse

Lyons

Vienne

Bourges

Tours

Nantes

Orleans

Bourges

Paris

Rouen

Rheims

Sens

Utrecht

Pavia

Milan

Rome

Bordeaux

Pampluna

Saragossa

ASTURIA

Premburg

Passau

THE CHRISTIAN EMPIRE OF CHARLEMAGNE 742–814

Charlemagne's Empire in 768

Charlemagne's conquests

Tributary to Charlemagne

Charlemagne's campaigns

22 Major church administration offices founded by Charlemagne

During the Carolingian renaissance several theological controversies developed, indicating that the church of the area had developed a literate culture. Two of the issues were rather stale: adoptionism was revived by Felix of Urgel, and Gottschalk elaborated a hardline doctrine of double predestination already condemned by the Synod of Orange (529). More important was Radbertus of Corbie's treatise on the Eucharist (c 831), which argued that by a miracle the actual flesh and blood of Christ are present in the bread and wine; this dogma was to become official in the Latin Church five centuries later. After his death Charlemagne was beatified and is honored as a "saint" in some locales.

At the time of Charlemagne's coronation as Emperor, Alcuin—his chief religious and educational advisor—explained that there were three highest powers in the world: the papacy in Rome, the Emperor in the Second Rome (Constantinople), and the royal dignity of Charles. Of these three, the last was the most important.

But Charlemagne's effort to establish an efficient administration ran counter to the customs of the tribes, where society was familial and authority was personal. When his own personal authority disappeared with his death, the structures he had fashioned began to fall apart. At the Treaty of Verdun (843), his sons divided his empire into parts recognizable to this day: Lothair received the title of Emperor and the middle kingdom (Burgundy, Alsace-Lorraine), Louis was given the region east of the Rhine (Germany), and Charles the Bald retained most of what is now France. As political and military power declined at the center, heavy raids came from all directions. The Scandinavian Normans plundered and

*Christus Pantocrator "King of kings," painted with the presumed crown of Charlemagne.*

burned and finally settled permanently (Normandy). Italy was raided by the Saracens, on one occasion St. Peter's itself being pillaged (841). From the east the Hungarians carried extensive forays into Germany and Italy. The standards of common life and the cultural levels sank steadily before the overbearing demands of mere survival.

In this crisis, feudalism developed rapidly. Based upon personal loyalty to a military leader, with land tenure tied to military service, it seemed the necessary solution to the imperative need of defense. In fact, the loss of dependable and objective procedures at law made the subjects totally dependent upon the personal virtues or vices of the warlords. For the church, an immediate result was that each lord functioned much as had the great emperors—where possible hiring and firing churchmen at will and using the church as a support of personal politics. But whereas the ecclesiastical interventions of a Charlemagne had integrated church and culture, the same conduct attempted by a host of minor lords seriously damaged the church and brought a series of conflicts between secular rulers and princes of the church ("investiture controversy").

Under Charles the Bald there was a brief burst of intellectual energy. John Scotus (?–877?), one of the great theologians of the Middle Ages, carried on a remarkable work as a solitary. But with the disintegration of imperial authority, the chief initiative in Christianity returned to Rome. The enhancement of papal power was often supported by the lower clergy as a foil against the concentrated power wielded by great secular and religious lords.

The Roman see had at this time some of its ablest incumbents, contrasting in intellectual and political stature—and sometimes even military—with most of the warlords of Europe. Leo IV (pope: 847–55) led forces that fought off the Saracens. Nicholas I (pope: 858–67) asserted the superior right of the pope over all worldly rulers, and he made his claims stick by defending the rights of the Queen of Lorraine against her husband's effort to divorce her and of a deposed bishop against arbitrary action by the Archbishop of Rheims.

Charlemagne's assumption of the title and crown of Emperor, and his deliberate appropriation of the Byzantine and Constantinian symbols (evident even in the architecture at Aachen), not to mention his ecclesiastical interventions, exacerbated tensions between east and west. Orthodox Christianity had triumphed over Arianism, but the relations between the heads of the Latin Church and the Greek Church had not improved. At this time occurred the quarrel between Pope Nicholas I and his successors and Patriarch Photius of Constantinople (patr.: 858–67, 878–86) which foreshadowed the terminal break of 1054. The Greek Church still held to the tradition of five nearly equal patriarchs; the popes asserted Roman preeminence. The Council of Constantinople (869–70), which condemned Photius (a decision reversed in council in 879–80), is counted an ecumenical council (eighth) by Roman Catholics; the Eastern Orthodox stop with seven Councils, and revere Photius as a saint.

The competition of Rome and Constantinople for the control of the religion of the Bulgar Kingdom highlighted the confrontation. The territory of ancient Thrace and Moesia, which had supplied mercenaries for centuries to the armies of Greece and then Rome, was conquered in the seventh century by Bulgar tribesmen. Building up a strong kingdom, for a time they exacted tribute of Byzantium. Boris I, ruling as *khan* from 853 to 888, accepted baptism from Greek clergy sent out by Photius. Missionaries came from the Franks and Bavarians, and the pope sent two bishops. Boris hoped to play Rome and Constantinople off against each other and have his own church and metropolitan, but eventually the confrontation in his realm forced a decision. Under his son Simeon (tsar: 893–927) the conversion of the people was largely completed. In good part due to the influence of the work of Cyril and Methodius, the literary language of the Bulgarians was Slavonic and the church was Eastern Orthodox. A great center of monasticism and education was established at Lake Ochrid.

Within three generations after Charlemagne's death the pope had become again the chief political as well as religious figure in the west. In the same period the pattern of caesaro-papism was fully established in the east. To this pattern only the monks provided from time to time a measure of resistance.

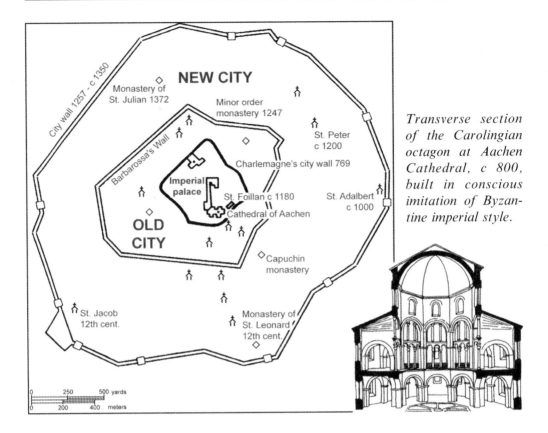

NEW CITY

City wall 1257 - c 1350

Monastery of
St. Julian 1372

Minor order
monastery 1247

St. Peter
c 1200

Barbarossa's Wall

Charlemagne's city wall 769

Imperial
palace

St. Foillan c 1180

St. Adalbert
c 1000

Cathedral of Aachen

OLD
CITY

Capuchin
monastery

St. Jacob
12th cent.

Monastery of
St. Leonard
12th cent.

0   250   500 yards
0   200   400   meters

*Transverse section of the Carolingian octagon at Aachen Cathedral, c 800, built in conscious imitation of Byzantine imperial style.*

LIKE Constantine before him, Charlemagne set out to build up a great capital which should symbolize his program and vision. The cathedral which he erected at Aachen was modeled on San Vitale of Ravenna, site for many years of the Byzantine exarchate in the west and itself modeled on Santa Sophia of Constantinople. Although illiterate, Charlemagne liked to be read to: his favorite book was Augustine's *City of God*, which provided him with a Christian political philosophy.

Charlemagne gathered scholars in his court from all over Europe. For the leadership of his educational reform he turned to Alcuin (c 735–804), trained by a student of Bede the Venerable— master of the cathedral school at York in Britain and a relative of the great missionary statesman Willibrord (658– 739). Alcuin was both friend and advisor of the Emperor, taught in his palace school, and fostered both missions and monasticism (neither of which interested Charlemagne greatly). When Charlemagne defeated a tribe he exacted baptism as part of the price of peace; he founded a few monasteries, but more as centers of learning than as refuges for practice of the Christian life. His own style neither began nor ended in retreat from the world.

Alcuin wrote a number of educational manuals. He encouraged questions of his pupils, of whom several were later famous, rather than being content with memorization. In material content, he made Augustine basic. For method, he featured the Latin grammarians. Most of his public work was, of course, a fight simply for literacy in an ocean of barbarism.

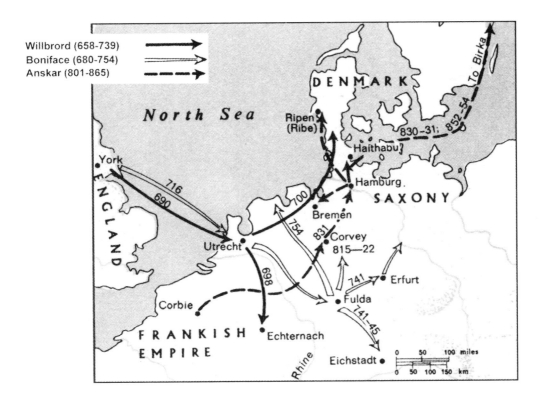

THE pattern of Christian conversion for most of Christian history has been familial and tribal rather than individual. Whether as a result of military defeat or political submission, tribal chieftains accepted baptism and their peoples followed suit. Missionary work was dangerous, especially since the tribal religions frequently involved ritual human sacrifice; doubly so, because the missionaries were identified with the expansionist programs of the Christian empires of East and West.

Willibrord (658–739), "Apostle of Frisia," founded the monastery of Echternach, which developed into a missionary center, and built his cathedral at Utrecht.

Boniface (680–754), "Apostle of Germany," c 743 established the abbey of Fulda. His courage in felling Thor's Oak at Geismar greatly impressed the tribesmen.

Anskar (801–65), "Apostle of the North," traveled widely among the Scandinavians but found them still resistant to conversion.

*Boniface.*

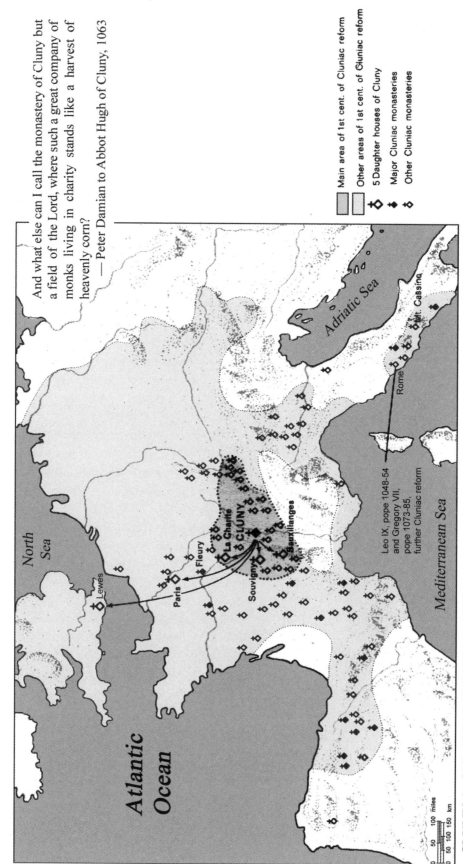

And what else can I call the monastery of Cluny but a field of the Lord, where such a great company of monks living in charity stands like a harvest of heavenly corn?
— Peter Damian to Abbot Hugh of Cluny, 1063

Main area of 1st cent. of Cluniac reform
Other areas of 1st cent. of Cluniac reform
5 Daughter houses of Cluny
Major Cluniac monasteries
Other Cluniac monasteries

North Sea

Atlantic Ocean

Adriatic Sea

Mediterranean Sea

Lewes
Paris
Fleury
La Charité
CLUNY
Souvigny
Sauxillanges
Rome
Mt. Cassino

Leo IX, pope 1048-54 and Gregory VII, pope 1073-85, further Cluniac reform

0  50       100  miles
0  50  100  150  km

CLUNY (F. 910) AND MONASTIC REFORM

DURING centuries of great violence and disorder, the monastic life came to represent something quite different from the original thrust of self-denial and discipline. The monasteries were the chief libraries and centers of learning, and their prestige came to be based on accomplishment rather than simple piety. Spiritual discipline became lax. Large properties were acquired through the donations of the pious. The identification of the monastic life with the Christian way tended to divide Christians between those who practiced the rules of the Christian life and those who admired them for doing it.

The monastery of Cluny was founded to reestablish the original impulse and to control with strict ascetic discipline the lassitude which had crept into the Benedictine centers. A series of gifted leaders, especially Odo (abbot 927–42) and Odilo (abbot 994–1048), led the reform movement. The personal spiritual life was stressed, along with common worship and manual labor.

Because the cause of Christendom was so vividly represented by certain great personalities, the illusion sometimes is created that the period from Charlemagne to Hildebrand represented a high point of Christian civilization. Almost the reverse is true: the continuing and sometimes desperate proclamations of church authority and independence clearly indicate that such were challenged from every side.

Christendom was in retreat before outside attacks and internal chaos. Islam was a much more cultured area. So was the China of the Sung Dynasty (960–1279). Most of the warlords were illiterate, polygamous barbarians, and the life of the common people was nasty, brutish and short. Slavery was widespread, and so were wasting diseases like leprosy as well as epidemic plagues. In many places church offices were bought and sold; secular lords appointed bishops and bishops led armies; in the Celtic church the religious sachems of the tribal bands passed down the office from father to son, just as the chieftains passed on political power when they could. In Rome, the papacy was for decades the plaything of wealthy families: between 897 and 955 seventeen popes followed each other in rapid succession, the products and then the victims of intrigue.

Two great forces opened up the West to civilization: the monastic reform movements and the Crusades. Strangely, as we shall see, the two impulses were intimately connected.

*Cluniac monastery on Reichenau, an island in Bodensee.*

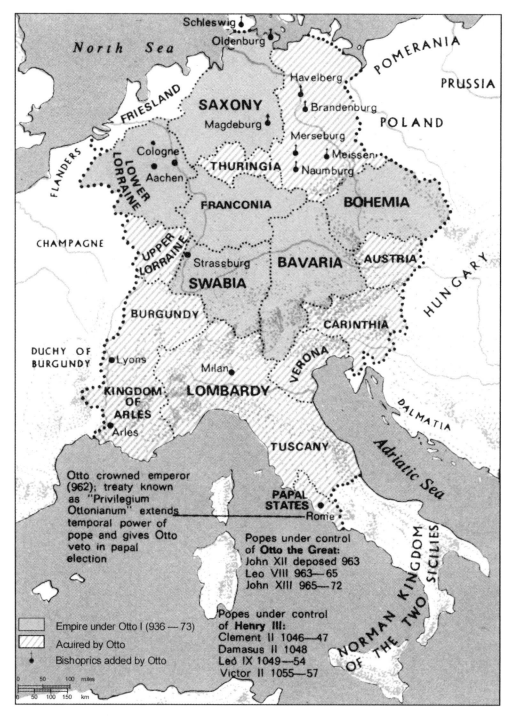

North Sea

Schleswig
Oldenburg

POMERANIA

PRUSSIA

FRIESLAND

Havelberg

Brandenburg

POLAND

SAXONY

Magdeburg

Merseburg

Meissen

Cologne

THURINGIA

Naumburg

Aachen

LOWER LORRAINE

FLANDERS

CHAMPAGNE

FRANCONIA

BOHEMIA

UPPER LORRAINE

Strassburg

BAVARIA

AUSTRIA

SWABIA

HUNGARY

BURGUNDY

CARINTHIA

DUCHY OF BURGUNDY

Lyons

Milan

VERONA

KINGDOM OF ARLES

LOMBARDY

Arles

TUSCANY

Adriatic Sea

DALMATIA

Otto crowned emperor (962); treaty known as "Privilegium Ottonianum" extends temporal power of pope and gives Otto veto in papal election

PAPAL STATES

Rome

Popes under control of **Otto the Great:**
John XII deposed 963
Leo VIII 963—65
John XIII 965—72

NORMAN KINGDOM OF THE TWO SICILIES

Popes under control of **Henry III:**
Clement II 1046—47
Damasus II 1048
Leo IX 1049—54
Victor II 1055—57

Empire under Otto I (936—73)

Acuired by Otto

Bishoprics added by Otto

0    50    100  miles

0  50  100  150   km

THE HOLY ROMAN EMPIRE OF OTTO THE GREAT (962–73)
AND HIS SUCCESSORS

# THE HOLY ROMAN EMPIRE OF OTTO THE GREAT (962–73) AND HIS SUCCESSORS

UNDER Otto the Great (king of the Germans: 936–73) there came a resurgence of imperial power and a parallel decrease of papal authority. In 962 he was crowned Holy Roman Emperor of the German Nation, a post that lasted until Napoleon ended it in 1806. Otto appointed his own bishops and used them to offset the power of the hereditary nobility, and he also controlled the papacy. He repelled Danish marauding bands, defeated the Magyars, and reestablished areas of military control on the eastern borders. He also collected scholars at his court and financed monasticism and missions.

*Otto the Great.*

Otto's successors, notably Henry II (emp.: 1002–24), Henry III (emp.: 1035–56) and Henry IV (emp.: 1065–1106) carried on the tradition of meddling in church disputes and wasting strength in transalpine military interventions. The critical issue was control of the major episcopal and arch-episcopal posts, since the church was the wealthiest landowner. The emerging national rulers could not consolidate their regimes without controlling the clerical nobility. Western Emperor and Pope fought this issue for generations, but the rising tide of Cluniac reform strengthened the papal hand. In 1077 Gregory VII compelled Henry IV to do penance at Canossa; the first substantial settlement of the investiture controversy was achieved in the Concordat of Worms (1122). Nevertheless, the issue whether bishops and abbots might be appointed and controlled by laymen ("lay investiture") arose again and again to trouble relations between the pope and secular rulers.

In spite of confusion in the Western Empire and the severe losses to Islam by Byzantium, Christianity continued to gain ground. Tribes to the east and north were baptized. The rulers of the Bulgars, Slavs, Moravians, Bohemians, Poles, Magyars and Verangians were won over, and usually in one or two generations the mass baptism of their peoples followed. In the second half of the tenth century Christianity spread rapidly by the same process among the Danes, Norwegians and Swedes.

Although the records are sparse, it is of some interest to Americans that the first Christian to reach the new world was a Viking convert, Leif Erikson (c 1001).

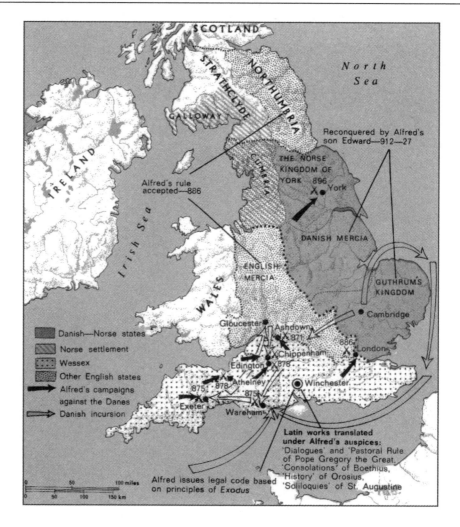

SCOTLAND

STRATHCLYDE

NORTHUMBRIA

North Sea

GALLOWAY

IRELAND

CUMBRIA

Reconquered by Alfred's son Edward—912—27

THE NORSE KINGDOM OF YORK 896
X York

Alfred's rule accepted—886
X

DANISH MERCIA

Irish Sea

ENGLISH MERCIA

GUTHRUM'S KINGDOM

WALES

Gloucester ● Ashdown
X 871

Cambridge ●

886
X London

Chippenham
X

Edington X 878

875 X
878 Athelney
Exeter X
Wareham
X 875

Winchester ◉

Danish—Norse states
Norse settlement
Wessex
Other English states
Alfred's campaigns against the Danes
Danish incursion

Latin works translated under Alfred's auspices: 'Dialogues' and 'Pastoral Rule of Pope Gregory the Great, 'Consolations' of Boethius, 'History' of Orosius, 'Soliloquies' of St. Augustine

Alfred issues legal code based on principles of *Exodus*

0    50    100 miles
0    50   100   150 km

FOR generations England had been plundered and then settled by marauding tribes from Scandinavia and Germany. The descendants of the original inhabitants who survived were pressed into the outlying areas. Celtic Christianity, at its height one of the most cultured and productive flowerings of Christianity, survived in mountain retreats and on fortified islands.

In Alfred the Great (849–99), King of Wessex, there appeared a ruler who reversed the tide and established a regime that invites comparison with Charlemagne's rule. He fought off the Vikings, conquered much of England, and promoted education and church reform. Gathering about him a company of scholars, he translated a number of Latin standard books—including Boethius' *Consolations*, Orosius' *History*, and Augustine's *Soliloquies*. With his encouragement a team of recorders compiled the major section of the important records of the English called the *Anglo-Saxon Chronicle*.

The leading English churchman of the era came two generations later. Dunstan (c 909–88), Archbishop of Canterbury, was a strict ascetic who enforced the Benedictine Rule as abbot and as advisor to the king reformed both secular and religious administrations.

IN less than three centuries Islam conquered the ancient strongholds of Christianity in Asia Minor and North Africa, subdued most of the Iberian peninsula and pressed hard against the Byzantine Empire. By a century after Mohammed's death the faith already extended over a larger area than the Roman Empire at the height of its power. Combining religious and political factors in its concept of the faithful community, Islam was early rent by protest movements reflecting the forces operative in the newly subjugated peoples.

In Damascus a dynasty of Meccan caliphs replaced the earlier caliphate based upon popular election. Their adherents, the largest sector of Islam, were called Sunnis—followers of the general community practice. Opposed to the Sunnis were the Shiites, who held to a dynastic succession of the family of Mohammed. Another sect, the Kharijites, declared the right of the community to choose its own head and to depose him for wrongdoing.

Because of the emphasis upon community structure, ethics and jurisprudence took precedence over theology in the theoretical development of Islam. The Koran was supplemented by a body of traditional teachings handed down from first-generation companions of Mohammed. Within each of the major sects, schools of interpretation developed which were hostile to each other. This was especially marked between Sunnis and Shiites, the latter accepting only those traditions derived from Ali, Mohammed's son-in-law, or his descendants.

The legalism of the teachers was balanced by the emergence of Sufism, the pursuit of spiritual experience by use of ascetic discipline and mystical intuition. In its very nature defying systematic exposition, Sufism fell into the common practice of monastic movements of dividing the community between the spiritual elite and the mass of believers. By the twelfth and thirteenth centuries great religious societies—"orders of practitioners"—had spread across Islam. In the various regions they imbedded themselves by assimilating into Muslim teaching many of the earlier tribal religious practices and customs. Holy men were revered as saints and intercessors, and their miracles were noted and related among the followers. By assimilating Platonic and Gnostic concepts of emanation and light-mysticism, Sufism moved far from the Koranic teachings of the One God and submission to His Law in history.

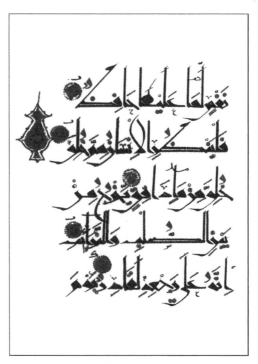

*Page from the Koran.*

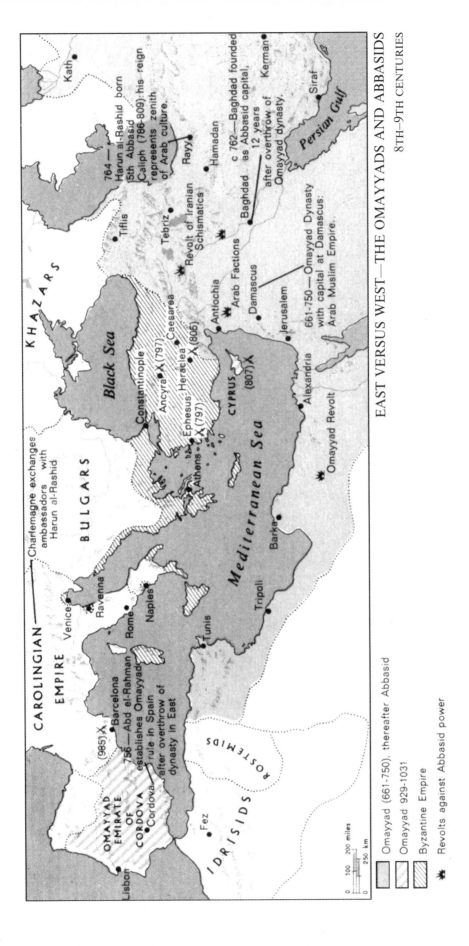

82

Kath

764 —
Harun al-Rashid born
[5th Abbasid
Caliph (786-809):his
reign
represents zenith
of Arab culture.

Kerman

Siraf

*Persian Gulf*

c 762 — Baghdad founded
as Abbasid capital,
12 years
after overthrow of
Omayyad dynasty.

Hamadan

Rayy

Baghdad

Tiflis

Tebriz

Revolt of Iranian
Schismatics

*KHAZARS*

*Black Sea*

Constantinople

Ancyra X(797)

Heraclea
X (806)

Ephesus
X (797)

Caesarea

Antiochia

Arab Factions

Damascus

Jerusalem

661-750 — Omayyad Dynasty
with capital at Damascus;
Arab Muslim Empire.

*BULGARS*

CAROLINGIAN
EMPIRE

Charlemagne exchanges
ambassadors  with
Harun al-Rashid

Venice

Ravenna

Rome

Naples

Tunis

Athens

CYPRUS
(807)X

Alexandria

*Mediterranean Sea*

Barka

Tripoli

Omayyad Revolt

*IDRISIDS*

*ROSTEMIDS*

Fez

Lisbon

OMAYYAD
EMIRATE
OF
CORDOVA

(985)X

Barcelona

756 —
Abd el-Rahman
establishes Omayyad
rule in Spain
after overthrow of
dynasty in East

Cordova

0   100   200 miles
0        250 km

Omayyad (661-750), thereafter Abbasid

Omayyad 929-1031

Byzantine Empire

Revolts against Abbasid power

EAST VERSUS WEST—THE OMAYYADS AND ABBASIDS

8TH–9TH CENTURIES

Since Muslim thought interacted with the political and even military necessities of various times and places, and popular belief was blended with different tribal cultic practices, Islam early developed geographical divisions as distinctive as the lines of the differing sects. The strongest of the Muslim states was that of the Abbasids, ruled by caliphs in Baghdad who were descended from Abbas, uncle of Mohammed.

Under the Abbasid caliphs there were Nestorian, Melchite and Jewish communities—all three enjoying greater toleration than under the Byzantine state-church, and all three with important ecclesiastical leaders in residence.

For various reasons the condition of Christians under the Omayyad rulers was less fortunate. Many thousands fled the western Mediterranean areas, carrying the customs and literature of Hellenistic Christianity to Italy and southern France.

A caliphate was in time established at Cordova. During the Fatimid dynasty, 909–1171, which claimed descent from Mohammed's daughter Fatima, a third caliphate was founded in Cairo.

Although Muslims and Christians were officially—and often in fact—at each other's throats, political and economic divisions often cut along other than faith lines. Western Christian rulers like Charlemagne not seldom aligned themselves with the Muslim rulers at Baghdad, creating a counter force against both Christian Byzantium and Muslim dynasties at Cairo and Cordova. Similarly, the ancient cultural and commercial connections between Constantinople and Alexandria were sometimes expressed in alliances which crossed the lines of faith and theology.

Not until the Crusades did a some-

*Mosque at Samarra, Mesopotamia, Abbasid, 9th century.*

what united Christendom face a somewhat united Islam, and even there the western Christians pillaged the capital of Eastern Orthodoxy and the rulers of the crusader kingdoms speedily sought alliances with different Muslim emirs to strengthen their hand against each other.

In most fields of knowledge the Muslim civilization was far more advanced than Christendom. The oldest existing university in the world was founded in 988 in Cairo, mandated by the caliph in the mosque of el-Azhar which was converted to that purpose. In translations of Greek classics, commentaries, mathematics and algebra, alchemy and chemistry, optical instruments, geography, medicine, astronomy and other fields, Islam surpassed Christendom until the rise of the modern universities which followed the Crusades.

In the Iberian peninsula the encounter and interaction of Islam and Christianity reached a high point. Two

*Traditional portrait of Maimonides.*

writers in Arabic who profoundly influenced later Christian thought were Averroës (1126–98) and Moses Maimonides (1135–1204).

Averroës (a Muslim) held high public positions in Cordova until driven into exile by religious zealots and wrote in philosophy, theology, jurisprudence, astronomy and medicine. His commentaries on Aristotle were basic to the rediscovery of "the Philosopher" in the west, although in time many points of Averroism were condemned by the church. Among the "errors" condemned were his doctrine of the eternity of the world and matter, denial of freedom of the will, denial of the immortality of the soul.

Maimonides, considered the greatest Jewish philosopher of the Middle Ages, was educated by Muslim teachers in Cordova. His family was also forced out of Spain by the Almohade religious zealots and found refuge in Egypt. His *Mishneh Torah* was an exhaustive presentation and exposition of that body of Jewish teaching. In one section of his *Commentary on the Mishnah* he laid down thirteen basic articles of Jewish belief, and in the process he drew boundaries against both Christianity and Islam. In his *Guide for the Perplexed* he treated the major philosophical questions in a rational and critical way; the work, in Latin translation, profoundly influenced the rising Christian Scholasticism, although it was condemned and burned by the Inquisition in 1233.

At the same time Islam was providing the chief intellectual stimulus to the west it was spreading rapidly through the Indian sub-continent, Russia, China and Indonesia. United by the holy language, Arabic, and by the five simple precepts which are observed by true believers, it proved capable of adjusting its political and cultural forms to the most diverse tribes and peoples. No other religion—even Christianity when it harvested the gentile fellow-travelers of the synagogues of the diaspora—has ever spread so rapidly and gained so many adherents as Islam in its first two centuries.

Over and above the simplicity and directness of its message, which among common folk contrasted favorably with elaborate theological or philosophical systems controlled by a small caste of intellectuals, Islam has three major appeals. First, it taught and practiced brotherhood among believers—regardless of race. Second, it proclaimed an original religion—a body of truth which was said to be general among the peoples of the earth before sectarian division and party rancor introduced faction and confusion. Third, its mood was one of urgency, with an acute awareness of the imminence of the Last Judgment. Mohammed was the last prophet of a series. Islam was the superseding and final message in human history.

During the reign of Harun al-Rashid (c 764–809) the Byzantines were defeated and the caliphate consolidated administrative and legal processes. Harun al-Rashid was also the first to introduce the requirement that Jews wear the yellow badge in public. Under Mamun the Great (caliph: 813–33) the capital was transferred to Baghdad and intellectual and cultural life strongly supported. At an academy, established with a great library near the Baghdad Observatory, extensive literary work was carried on—including translating of literary, scientific and philosophical works from Greek, Persian and Sanskrit.

Thus Islam managed to combine both popular appeal and the highest level of cultural creativity.

*El Aksa Mosque, Jerusalem.*

*Floor plan of the El Aksa Mosque.*

# D. Disintegration
# of the Carolingian Empire

## SHADOWS OVER THE HOLY ROMAN EMPIRE MID-11TH CENTURY

*Leo IX.*

AFTER Charlemagne, the Western empire disintegrated into warring principalities. Conflicts between rulers and popes increased, particularly when a reforming pope like Leo IX (pope 1049–54) attempted to reestablish the dignity of his office and the integrity of the church's conduct of its affairs.

A strong supporter of the Cluniac reform movement, Leo IX led a fight against simony and for clerical celibacy (Easter Synod, 1049). He suffered military defeat by Norman armies and saw the permanent division between the Latin Church of the west and Eastern (Greek) Orthodoxy. The latter misfortune had been long in coming and was foreshadowed by the break at the time of Patriarch Photius of Constantinople (863). By this time, however, Byzantium no longer enjoyed intellectual preeminence. Patriarch Michael Cerularius (patriarch: 1043–58) was spiritual head of an eastern kingdom riven by internal intrigue and cramped between the powerful empire of the Bulgars and the constantly expanding Muslim empire of the Turks. During the period 1025 to 1080 Orthodox Christianity suffered severe setbacks in Asia Minor, and in the latter year the Turks captured Nicaea (less than 100 miles from Constantinople).

Economic disintegration accompanied political division and subdivision in the Holy Roman Empire. Between 970 and 1048 no less than forty-eight famine years brought the peoples of the west to the level of a bare struggle for survival. Commerce declined. Communications broke down. Travel was dangerous. Robber barons ruling small areas and commanding marauding bands preyed on travelers and terrorized an illiterate and brutish peasantry.

Only in the church, and particularly in the monastic communities, were the fruits of civilization tended—and it was to be some decades before the reform movement in these centers would again successfully shape society as a whole and attempt its reintegration.

As government disintegrated, and the administrative structures created by the Roman emperors and their successors fell apart, the patterns of political power reverted to tribal practices. That is, power was wielded by personal force rather than office, and a style of rule based upon personal loyalty and cohesion which is common practice among primitive peoples again took over. This was the origin of feudalism, a system of political, economic and social relationships grounded in obligations between persons.

In one type of agreement, in return

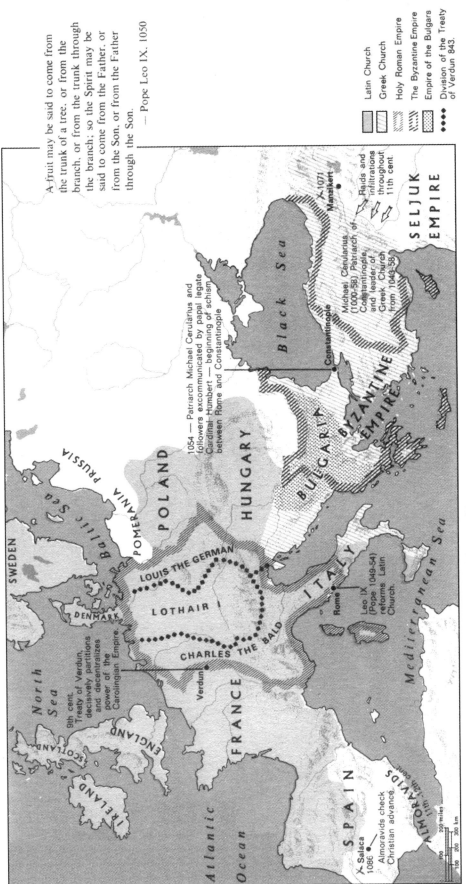

A fruit may be said to come from the trunk of a tree, or from the branch, or from the trunk through the branch; so the Spirit may be said to come from the Father, or from the Son, or from the Father through the Son.

— Pope Leo IX. 1050

Latin Church
Greek Church
Holy Roman Empire
The Byzantine Empire
Empire of the Bulgars
Division of the Treaty of Verdun 843.

SELJUK EMPIRE

Raids and infiltrations throughout 11th cent.

×1071 Manzikert

Michael Cerularius (1000-58) Patriarch of Constantinople, and leader of Greek Church from 1043-58

Constantinople

Black Sea

1054 — Patriarch Michael Cerularius and followers excommunicated by papal legate Cardinal Humbert — beginning of schism between Rome and Constantinople

BYZANTINE EMPIRE

BULGARIA

HUNGARY

POLAND

PRUSSIA

POMERANIA

Baltic Sea

SWEDEN

DENMARK

LOUIS THE GERMAN

LOTHAIR I

CHARLES THE BALD

Verdun

9th cent. Treaty of Verdun, decisively partitions and decentralizes power of the Carolingian Empire.

ITALY

Rome

Leo IX (Pope 1049-54) reforms Latin Church.

Mediterranean Sea

North Sea

SCOTLAND

IRELAND

ENGLAND

Atlantic Ocean

FRANCE

S P A I N

ALMORAVIDS 12th cent.

×Salaca 1086

Almoravids check Christian advance.

11th cent.

100 200 300 km
100 200 miles

SHADOWS OVER THE HOLY ROMAN EMPIRE MID-11TH CENTURY

for the vassal's oath to do military service for his liege, the latter promised him food and protection from others. The Roman emperors had forbade this procedure (called *comitatus* by Tacitus, who had found it among the German tribes), for local and tribal rulers became thereby strong enough to defy the central government. In another case, the owner of a large estate parceled it out among vassals who swore to fight for him in return for protection. In yet another pattern, small landowners gave their lands to a powerful neighbor in return for protec-tion and life use. By these and other arrangements, a highly complex network of mutual obligations was built up. Their common characteristic was that personal authority and rule had replaced office-authority and bureaucracy, and that personal fealty took the place of clearly defined legal status.

The feudal relationships were sanctified by the church. The oath was taken in a religious ceremony in which the vassal did homage to his lord and the Lord placed his hands upon his follower.

## ITALY AND THE PAPAL STATES 11TH CENTURY

THE Middle Ages were defined in good part by the claim of the Emperor to exercise religious authority and the assertion of secular authority by the pope.

At a synod in Rome, in February of 1076, marriage of the clergy was denounced, lay investiture was abolished, simony was condemned. Five of the Emperor's councillors were excommunicated for buying offices in the church. In Henry IV's violent reply, the Emperor asserted that he received his power from God, not from the pope. The pope replied by excommunicating the Emperor and releasing his subjects from their oaths of obligation. Faced by rebellion Henry went to Canossa. He achieved remission and returned home to achieve victory in a civil war and to reestablish his authority. The pope's humbling of the Emperor remained for centuries the symbol of high papal power.

But the winner at Canossa was the secular ruler.

Those who notice only the progress of the reform movement in the church and remember especially Gregory VII ("Hildebrand"; pope: 1073–85) and his temporary victory over Emperor Henry IV at Canossa (1077) are apt to overlook the essential weakness of the Latin Church and the papacy in this age of confusion and near-anarchy. Henry did make a dramatic penance, but in return he regained control of his lesser lords—while Gregory died in exile. The Normans did free Sicily of Muslim rule, but the Christianity they reestablished was largely independent of Rome. The ruler of the Normans did rescue Gregory from northern enemies, but only to

*Henry IV as supplicant (in Canossa Codex, 12th century).*

1076 — Henry IV defies reforms of Gregory VII in German Church matters: convokes assembly at Worms; 1081-84 — attempts to depose Pope and installs anti-Pope: invades Italy and besieges Rome.

MARCH OF VERONA

Henry IV, after being excommunicated, appeals to Pope as penitent: absolved: later re-excommunicated.

KINGDOM OF LOMBARDY

Genoa and Pisa seize Corsica, Sardinia, Balearic Isles and foothold in Spain from 1016 on.

Milan

Venice

Ravenna

Venice begins expansion along Dalmatian coast: later very active throughout Eastern Mediterranean

CROATIA

Genoa  Canossa

Adriatic Sea

Pisa

DUCHY OF TUSCANY

CORSICA

To Pisa 1020

Tyrrhenian Sea

DUCHY OF SPOLETO

Rome

DUCHY OF CAPUA

DUCHY OF BENEVENTO

1084 — Robert Guiscard, Norman vassal, comes to the rescue of Gregory; his troops devastate Rome, Henry forced to withdraw to North after besieging Gregory VII and installing anti-Pope Clement III, who crowned him emperor.

Gaeta  Capua

Naples  Benevento

Gregory VII (c 1025-85), planner of crusade to Holy Land, attempts centralization of Christianity; conflicts with Henry IV, ruler of Holy Roman Empire.

SARDINIA

To Pisa and Genoa 1050

Salerno

DUCHY OF SALERNO

APULIA

1085 — Gregory VII dies in exile.

1059 — Papal recognition of Norman rule in Southern Italy.

Fiore

Joachim of Fiore, Cistercian mystic and writer of apocalyptic works.

CALABRIA

Normans penetrate into Southern Italy from 1027 on.

Mediterranean Sea

Palermo

SICILY

1060 — Normans free Sicily from Muslim rule, restoring Latin Church there, largely independent of Rome.

0    50    100 miles
0    50    100    150 km

Byzantine territories    Venetian territories    Norman territories to 1091
Muslim territories    Papal States    •••••• Border of the Holy Roman Empire

pillage Rome and set up an anti-pope to crown him Emperor when Gregory refused to do it. The Italian peninsula was as confused politically as Germany.

In 1059 an important step was taken to free the papacy from the control of the Roman mob: the election of the pope was assumed by the College of Cardinals. But the economic and political base provided by the Papal States was too small for the office of the pope to be anything but a political football.

In theory, Christendom as a unitary society was sustained by cooperation between the "two swords," secular and spiritual. In practice, for centuries the men who achieved the symbolically important posts of pope or emperor vied with each other for preeminence and domination. The weaponry of the papacy included excommunication and the interdict. The tactics of the Emperor included use of military violence and on occasion creation of puppet popes or anti-popes.

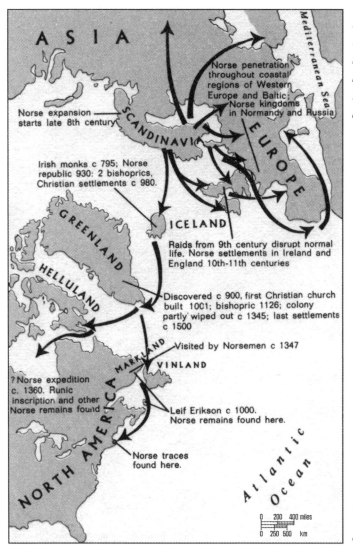

Norse penetration throughout coastal regions of Western Europe and Baltic; Norse kingdoms in Normandy and Russia.

Norse expansion starts late 8th century

Irish monks c 795; Norse republic 930: 2 bishoprics, Christian settlements c 980.

Raids from 9th century disrupt normal life. Norse settlements in Ireland and England 10th-11th centuries

Discovered c 900, first Christian church built 1001; bishopric 1126; colony partly wiped out c 1345; last settlements c 1500

Visited by Norsemen c 1347

? Norse expedition c. 1360. Runic inscription and other Norse remains found

Leif Erikson c 1000. Norse remains found here.

Norse traces found here.

*Erik (the Red) was reluctant to abandon his old religion; his wife Thjohild, however, was converted immediately and she built a church....*

— Erik's Saga

*(below) The Norman Invasion in the Bayeux tapestry.*

FOR centuries western Europe was pressed between Muslim advances from Asia Minor and North Africa and raiders from Scandinavia. Fleets of Viking ships and warriors even appeared before the walls of Constantinople; the city was also attacked by Swedes (Varangians) who came down

from Russia. Western cities like Utrecht, Paris, Nantes, Bordeaux—even Seville—were sacked.

In the period c 850–1050 there began the conversion of the northern tribes which had for so long threatened Christendom. By the middle of the eleventh century Christianity was well established in Denmark, Norway and Sweden. The pattern of conversion was the standard one: chieftains converted and their subjects followed in a generation or two. In each of the three kingdoms royal patronage was achieved, and each of the kings obtained the creation of an archbishopric to head the church in his territories.

Of fateful import for the future, the movement of personnel and supplies to Scandinavian Christianity came not from the ancient missionary see of Hamburg-Bremen but from the church in England.

As the old tribal religions crumbled, Christianity established some of its standard institutions among the Scandinavians. Bishops and archbishops were installed. Churches and cathedrals were built. But indigenous customs also continued. The bards, who had traveled from encampment to encampment carrying the oral culture, spread the new faith in song and story. In Iceland the bishops, although consecrated abroad, were elected by the popular assembly (*Althing*)—the oldest democratic assembly in the world. In Sweden, by exception, the first arch-

*Christ-figure from runic stone, 10th cent.*

bishop installed at Uppsala (1164) in the cathedral—erected on the site of the former head temple of paganism—was a member of the Cistercian reform.

Almost at the same time as Christianity's advance across the seas to the west, the Scandinavian kingdom in Russia was opening up to the new faith. The Viking rulers of Novgorod and Kiev ("Varangians" or "Rus") had, however, adopted the Slavonic language of their subjects. When the mass conversions came, in the reign of Vladimir (956–1015), the ruler deliberately chose Greek Orthodoxy. For generations the Varangians looked to Constantinople to supply missionary and teaching monks. The metropolitan of Kiev was for centuries appointed by the Greek patriarch.

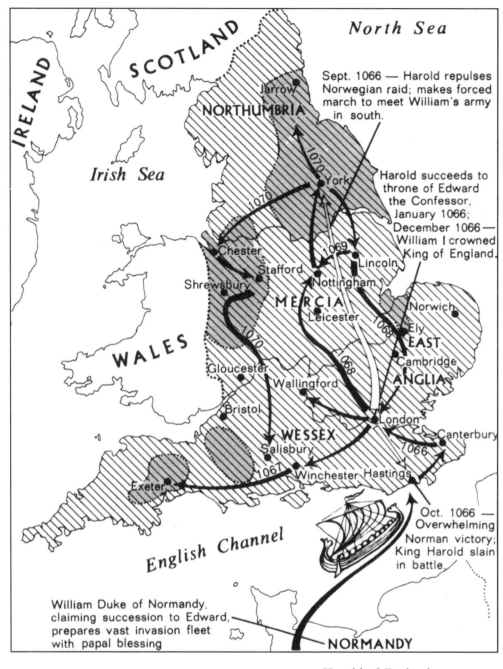

North Sea

SCOTLAND

IRELAND

NORTHUMBRIA

Jarrow

Irish Sea

York

Sept. 1066 — Harold repulses Norwegian raid; makes forced march to meet William's army in south.

Harold succeeds to throne of Edward the Confessor, January 1066; December 1066 — William I crowned King of England.

1070

1070

Chester

Shrewsbury

Stafford

1069

Lincoln

Nottingham

MERCIA

Leicester

Norwich

Ely

Cambridge

EAST
ANGLIA

1068

1068

WALES

Gloucester

Wallingford

Bristol

London

Canterbury

1066

WESSEX

Salisbury

1067

Winchester

Hastings

Exeter

Oct. 1066 — Overwhelming Norman victory; King Harold slain in battle.

English Channel

William Duke of Normandy, claiming succession to Edward, prepares vast invasion fleet with papal blessing

NORMANDY

 Harold's campaigns

⟶ William's routes of conquest 1066-72

▨ Areas of Saxon resistance till 1072

▧ Extent of Norman conquest

*Harold of England —*
*Killed in action defending his*
*country from the invader. 14th*
*October 1066.*
— Annual memorial notice in
*The Times* of London

ENGLAND AND THE NORMAN CONQUEST
1066–72

THE Norman conquest of England (1066) was in a real sense a continuation of the pattern of tribal migration and conquest which had marked the Scandinavian peoples for centuries. Within half a century after the first Norse raid on England (c 787) the islands were flooded by tribesmen escaping the population pressure back home. In 911 Charles III of France, unable to drive the Norse from the lower Seine, gave a huge part of what became Normandy to Hrolf the Genger in return for the latter's homage. For a century the area was flooded by immigrations from Scandinavia.

The Normans began the conquest of South Italy c 1040, encouraged by the papacy. Although ruled by an able emperor, Alexius Comnenus, Byzantium was unable to defeat the Normans in battle during a war which the latter carried to the Greek peninsula (1081–85). In the continuing wars the Seljuk Turks reaped the profit. By 1071 the Byzantine power was virtually destroyed in Asia Minor.

In the first half of the eleventh century both church and government in England were in the process of consolidation. Under Canute (king of both Denmark and England: 1019–35) an impressive northern kingdom was emerging, including also Norway for a time. Great earls held the continuing economic and political power at this time; however, the king was elected by the Witan. The most powerful earl, Godwin of Wessex, succeeded in getting his man elected after Canute's line ran out. Edward the Confessor (king: 1042–66), married to Godwin's daughter, was brought up in Normandy and spoke French. Seeking to Normanize the court he ran headlong into the politics of Godwin and his Saxon supporters. Godwin managed to secure the deposition of the Norman archbishop of Canterbury and his replacement by a Saxon (Stigand). The latter had, however, supported an anti-pope. On the king's death Duke William of Normandy claimed he had Edward's promise of succession. One of Godwin's sons supported his claim. The pope gave his blessing.

Harold was chosen king by the Witan. As William's forces were crossing the channel the king had to lead his army north to repel a Norse invasion. This he did successfully, but his army arrived back in the south so tired and battered that it was defeated and Harold was killed (Battle of Hastings, 14 October 1066).

Constructively, King William achieved a remarkable balance between Norman feudal structures and continuance of the Anglo-Saxon administrative procedures at the local level. The power of the earls was broken. In the church, King William removed Archbishop Stigand and most of the bishops and abbots. Although he brought in a zealous Cluniac reformer, Lanfranc (c 1005–89) as archbishop, William retained control of appointments and drew his administrative staff largely from the church. He retained veto power over synods, and his approval was required for release of papal messages in England, sending of papal legates, and pronouncement of excommunications. In effect, the church became a department of the state.

# E. PAPAL EFFORTS AT REINTEGRATION

## THE HOLY CRUSADES 11TH–12TH CENTURIES

*If you will attack the Muslims on one side while the Crusaders attack them on the other, we shall see an end of their damnable religion for ever. And if you say you are afraid the Latins will attack you while your troops are engaged on your other frontier, the answer is simple: return to the unity of the Roman Church and all fears of this kind can be put aside for ever.*
— Pope Clement IV to Michael VIII Paleologus, 1267

*Urban II.*

A new initiative for the reintegration of Christendom was launched by Urban II (pope: 1088–99) at the Council of Clermont. Formerly Prior of Cluny, Urban was a vigorous enemy of corruption in the church and an opponent of lay investiture. His message to the assembled company was accompanied by an appeal for help against the Seljuk Turks which had come from the Emperor of the East. His message was also informed by convictions for peace popularized by the reform movement and institutionalized in the "Truce of God" and the "Peace of God" (1095). When it proved impossible to tame the warlords, with their romantic code of militarism, and to hold them to rules of conduct which made certain religious seasons off-limits and protected certain classes of persons, the reformers turned them against a common foe. Remission of sins and eternal life were promised those who took up the sword in a mighty brotherhood of common effort to recover the Holy Places.

Urban proposed that the monastic ethic should govern, that all property should be held in common in the brotherhood of crusaders. His idealistic vision of a selfless lay order serving true religion had little to do with reality, however. With the exception of the mutual aid and community of discipline developed by specific crusading orders, like the Knights Hospitaler and Knights Templar, the crusades became a license for ambitious lords to carve out kingdoms and their followers to plunder where they went.

In his message at Clermont, Urban had appealed especially to the Franks. In the First Crusade (1096–99) some 30,000 of them converged on Constantinople under Godfrey of Bouillon (Lorraine), Raymond of Toulouse (Provençal) and Bohemund of Otranto (Norman kingdom in South Italy). The combined Greek and crusading forces scored major victories: Nicaea, the

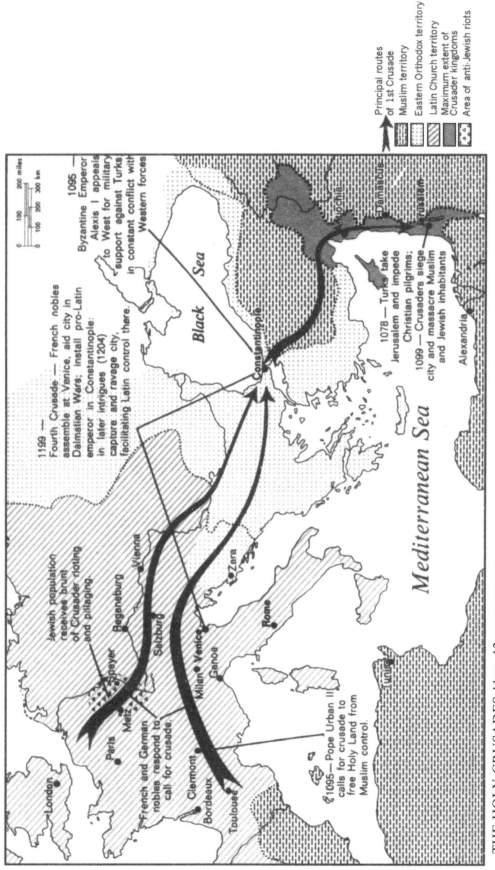

**Principal routes of 1st Crusade**

Muslim territory

Eastern Orthodox territory

Latin Church territory

Maximum extent of Crusader kingdoms

Area of anti-Jewish riots

1199 — Fourth Crusade — French nobles assemble at Venice, aid city in Dalmatian Wars; install pro-Latin emperor in Constantinople: in later intrigues (1204) capture and ravage city, facilitating Latin control there.

1095 — Byzantine Emperor Alexis I appeals to West for military support against Turks in constant conflict with Western forces.

Black Sea

Antioch

Damascus

Jerusalem

1078 — Turks take Jerusalem and impede Christian pilgrims; 1099 — Crusaders siege city and massacre Muslim and Jewish inhabitants.

Alexandria

Mediterranean Sea

Jewish population receives brunt of Crusader rioting and pillaging.

Vienna

Regensburg

Salzburg

Speyer

Metz

Zara

Paris

London

Milan Venice

Genoa

Rome

Clermont

Bordeaux

Toulouse

French and German nobles respond to call for crusade.

1095 — Pope Urban II calls for crusade to free Holy Land from Muslim control.

Tunis

0   100   200 miles
0   100   200   300 km

THE HOLY CRUSADES 11TH–12TH CENTURIES

Seljuk capital in Asia Minor, was taken in 1097, Edessa in 1097, Antioch in 1098, Jerusalem in 1099.

Because of the weakness of Byzantium and divisions among the Muslims, the crusader kingdoms developed as Latin states. After the sack of Jerusalem and murder of the Jewish and Muslim inhabitants, Godfrey was elected king and "Protector of the Holy Sepulchre." The kingdom was feudal in structure, with the chief power held by the king's leading vassals. The Kingdom of Jerusalem was in close alliance with Genoa, Pisa and Venice and controlled commerce through its Mediterranean port and along the Red Sea to the south. Other Latin states were the County of Edessa, established by Godfrey's brother Baldwin; the Principality of Antioch, established by Bohemund; the County of Tripoli, established by Raymond of Toulouse. These three were fiefs of Jerusalem, which was itself divided into four major baronies.

The Second Crusade (1147–49) was preached by Bernard of Clairvaux and led by Emperor Conrad III and King Louis VII of France. The Normans of Sicily took advantage of the event to attack Athens and Corinth and seize certain Greek islands.

The Third Crusade (1189–92) came after Muslim reunification had been accomplished by Saladin, with Syria and Egypt under a single rule. The crusader kingdoms had been reduced to the cities of Antioch, Tripoli and Tyre, and Jerusalem had been recaptured (1187) without being plundered. Leaders of the crusade were Frederick I, "Barbarossa" (emperor: 1155–90), an excommunicate, who drowned; Richard I "the Lion-Hearted" of England (king: 1188–99), who was captured and released on payment of a heavy ran-

som; Philip II of France (king: 1180–1223), who quarreled with Richard and scurried home to plot with Richard's brother John during Richard's captivity (1192–94).

The Fourth Crusade (1202–04) was launched as part of a continuing scheme to erect a Norman empire on the ruins of the Greek. To satisfy Venetian exactions for shipping armies to Egypt, the Christian city of Zara (Dalmatia) was taken and plundered. Pope Innocent III excommunicated the crusaders. In Constantinople (1204) the demands of the crusaders aroused the populace to revolt; the crusaders sacked the city with indescribable savagery and set up a Latin emperor and a Latin patriarch. The papacy proclaimed the reunion of east and west, a fiction which was maintained while the Greek emperors ruled at Nicaea (1204–61) but ended when Constantinople was retaken by Michael VIII in 1261.

In 1212 the so-called Children's Crusade brought thousands of youths to Marseilles, port of embarkation; there ship captains took them aboard and sold them as slaves in Muslim North Africa.

The Fifth Crusade (1218–21) was proclaimed by Innocent at the Fourth Lateran Council, which also introduced the Inquisition and fixed several anti-Jewish decrees. Determined to regain control of the crusades, the papacy replaced the King of Jerusalem with a papal legate. Military action against Egypt ended in defeat.

The Sixth Crusade (1228–29) was led by Frederick II (emperor: 1220–50), King of Jerusalem by marriage and a Sicilian Norman by upbringing. Germany interested him as a source of men and money. While excommunicated, he recaptured Jerusalem; the pope was

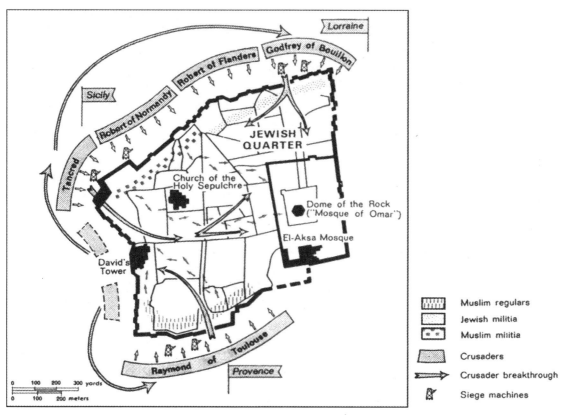

THE CAPTURE OF JERUSALEM BY THE CRUSADERS 1099

forced to accept him as a ruler in the Holy Land.

The Seventh Crusade (1248–54) was launched by Louis IX of France (king: 1236–70), considered the highest type of medieval king and canonized by Boniface VIII in 1297. Although an able administrator at home, as well as an advocate of justice and patron of learning, Louis led a poorly organized campaign and was captured. Ransomed, he spent several years on pilgrimage in Jerusalem.

The Eighth Crusade (1270) was also launched by Louis IX, in league with Edward of England. King Louis died in Tunis and nothing was achieved.

Under Gregory X (1274) and again with papal insistence at the fall of Constantinople (1453) crusades were preached but not launched. The Fourth Crusade, with the spoliation of Con-

stantinople, in fact marked the end of popular respect for the crusading theme and role. Acre, the last of the great fortresses, fell in 1291.

*

For almost two hundred years (1099–1291) the crusader kingdoms persisted on the landbridge between the two great Muslim empires of Syria and Egypt. Even today the pilgrim to the Holy Land is astonished, in visiting great fortresses and churches such as Acre, to see the massive stones with which the crusaders built for eternity.

The most important constructive thing the Crusades accomplished was to put western Europe in touch with a civilization greatly superior to its own. When Islam captured more than half of Christendom in its first surge of energy, it got the best half. During the centuries when the Teutonic and Frankish and

*Seal of Crusader king of Jerusalem.*

Scandinavian tribes kept western Europe in turmoil and the eastern region was in decline, great Muslim empires advanced all areas of human knowledge. The result of two hundred years of conflict and commerce was an intellectual impulse that affected Europe's progress in many ways. The rise of university faculties and the cultural renewal of the Renaissance were two of the more important effects.

The most serious negative effect was to fasten upon theology, which was already fortress-oriented, the mindset of opposition and polarization. Instead of the openness of the Logos Fathers to truth wherever they found it, Christianity became frozen in a posture of hostility to the strange. This posture has carried into the present, and is a particularly fateful orientation in our century of rapid communication, when Christianity has to deal face to face with high religions like Hinduism and Buddhism and sophisticated systems of being like Marxism.

The mindset of the Crusades not only blinded Christian thought to the value of careful study of the "outside" alternatives: it also led to savage repression of the "other" within Christendom. Christian dissenters were dealt with as brutally as was the outside enemy. The internal crusades against the Albigensi in the Provençal, whose prince had been one of the key leaders in the First Crusade, and the Bogomili of Bosnia and Herzegovina, as well as the Waldensians of North Italy, fill some of the most disgraceful pages in the history of Christianity.

For the Jews, even more, the crusades were an unrelieved disaster. Like the Moors, they were the victims of the last great military crusade as well as the first: that crusade (1492) in the Iberian peninsula which made Spain a model of medieval Christendom and began the wanderings of the Sephardic Jews from the land which had once been the scene of a Golden Age of culture and intellectual achievement.

## THE EMPIRE OF FREDERICK BARBAROSSA c 1123–90

FREDERICK I (c 1123–90), called "Redbeard," was a Swabian whose career as Holy Roman Emperor demonstrated the difficulties which confronted the papacy in attempting the reintegration of Christendom. His life also demonstrated the price paid by the German states for centuries because of the determination of the chief German ruler to dominate the papacy and control the Italian peninsula.

Frederick thought of himself as another Charlemagne, when the bishops were imperial agents and the papacy was a creature of the secular arm. At the beginning he had papal approval because of his rescue of the city of Rome from the popular party of the heretic Arnold of Brescia. Five years later he was supporting a counter-pope, Victor IV, splitting the church. Twenty years later his forces were decisively

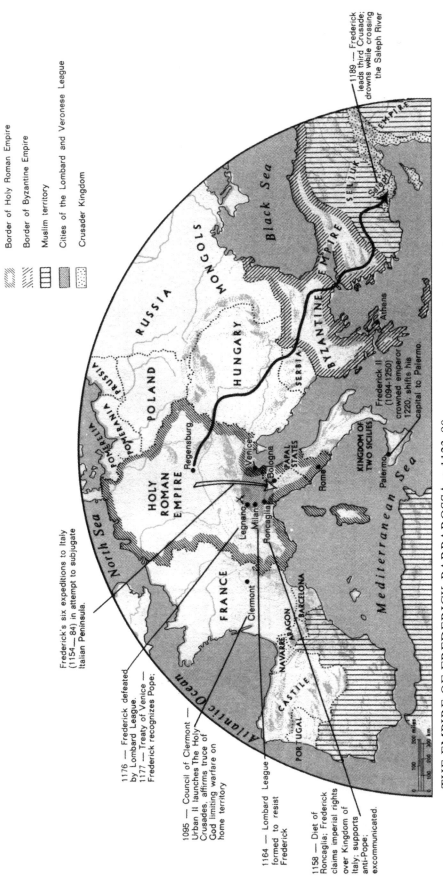

Border of Holy Roman Empire

Border of Byzantine Empire

Muslim territory

Cities of the Lombard and Veronese League

Crusader Kingdom

Frederick's six expeditions to Italy (1154—84) in attempt to subjugate Italian Peninsula.

1176 — Frederick defeated by Lombard League.
1177 — Treaty of Venice — Frederick recognizes Pope;

1095 — Council of Clermont — Urban II launches The Holy Crusades, affirms truce of God limiting warfare on home territory

1164 — Lombard League formed to resist Frederick

1158 — Diet of Roncaglia; Frederick claims imperial rights over Kingdom of Italy; supports anti-Pope; excommunicated.

1189 — Frederick leads third Crusade; drowns while crossing the Saleph River

Frederick II (1094-1250) crowned emperor 1220; shifts his capital to Palermo.

THE EMPIRE OF FREDERICK BARBAROSSA c 1123–90

*Frederick I (Barbarossa).*

There was for long a popular legend in middle Germany that Barbarossa sat waiting in a subterranean cave in the Harz Mountains, to arise in power when the German states finally united to reestablish the empire and to throw off the yoke of the Italian pope.

Frederick II (1194–1250), who was a ward of Innocent III during his minority, demonstrated even as Barbarossa the inexorable conflict between an emperor who thought of himself as walking in the path of Constantine and Charlemagne and a pope whose self-understanding recalled Gregory the Great.

Sicily was then the most fertile and beautiful area of the Empire, and Frederick was by upbringing and inclination a Norman of Sicily. His only interest in the German states, which he governed by legates from afar, was to raise there the military levies and monies for his court and politics in Italy.

Having procrastinated in his pledge to go on a crusade, Frederick was excommunicated by the pope (1227). He then turned the tables by conducting a highly successful crusade, at the end of which he was crowned—while still excommunicated—King of Jerusalem. For the rest of his reign his time and effort were consumed in suppressing revolts in Germany, fighting the Lombards, and trying to control the papacy.

Like his grandfather Frederick I, Frederick II contributed to the growing impatience of the Germans with transalpine rulers and foreign wars. Like his grandfather also, he was remembered by later anti-clericals for patronage of learning and for successful resistance to the papal claim to oversight of Christendom and its secular rulers.

defeated by the armies of the Lombard League of northern Italian cities. With the marriage (1186) of his son and heir to the heiress of the Norman kingdom in Sicily, his policy of containing the papacy reached its highest point. A year later he drowned in Asia Minor while on the Third Crusade.

An excommunicate from 1160, his thirty years of dramatic politics and diplomacy served to undermine the authority of the papacy and to make credible the process of secularization. On the other hand, his long absences from the German states and the pressures put upon them by his transalpine adventures allowed unrest and rebellion to develop.

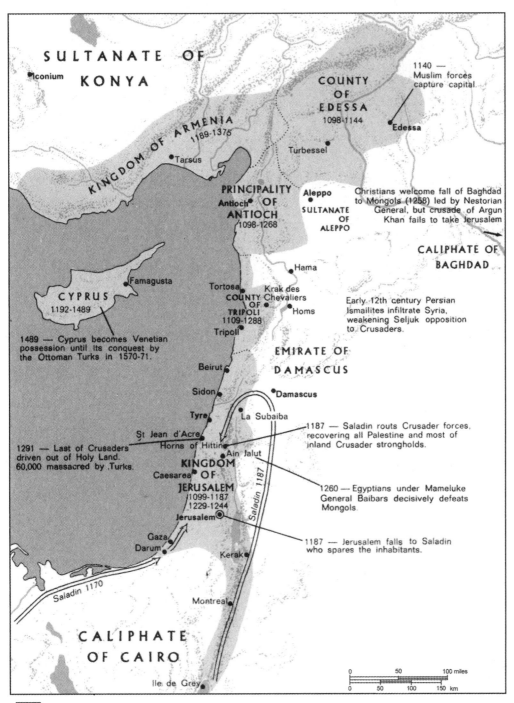

SULTANATE OF KONYA

Iconium

COUNTY OF EDESSA 1098-1144

1140 — Muslim forces capture capital.

Edessa

KINGDOM OF ARMENIA 1189-1375

Tarsus

Turbessel

PRINCIPALITY OF ANTIOCH 1098-1268

Antioch

Aleppo

SULTANATE OF ALEPPO

Christians welcome fall of Baghdad to Mongols (1258) led by Nestorian General, but crusade of Argun Khan fails to take Jerusalem

CALIPHATE OF BAGHDAD

Hama

CYPRUS 1192-1489

Famagusta

Tortosa

COUNTY OF TRIPOLI 1109-1288

Krak des Chevaliers

Tripoli

Homs

Early 12th century Persian Ismailites infiltrate Syria, weakening Seljuk opposition to Crusaders.

1489 — Cyprus becomes Venetian possession until its conquest by the Ottoman Turks in 1570-71.

Beirut

Sidon

EMIRATE OF DAMASCUS

Damascus

Tyre

La Subaiba

St Jean d'Acre

Horns of Hittin

1187 — Saladin routs Crusader forces, recovering all Palestine and most of inland Crusader strongholds.

1291 — Last of Crusaders driven out of Holy Land. 60,000 massacred by Turks.

Ain Jalut

KINGDOM OF JERUSALEM 1099-1187 1229-1244

Caesarea

Saladin 1187

1260 — Egyptians under Mameluke General Baibars decisively defeats Mongols.

Jerusalem

Gaza

Darum

Kerak

1187 — Jerusalem falls to Saladin who spares the inhabitants.

Saladin 1170

Montreal

CALIPHATE OF CAIRO

Ile de Grey

0    50    100 miles
0    50    100    150 km

Maximum extent of Crusader kingdoms

ALTHOUGH the crusader kingdoms lasted but two centuries (1099–1291), to this day the buildings they erected testify to their sense of history. The several rulers who carved out principalities had an eye also for political power: they were quite prepared to enter alliances with the Muslim rulers to secure their holdings against Byzantine or Latin competitors. And for generations the act of going on crusade was a foil well used by kings as far

*Crusader fortress "Kerak des Chevaliers."*

afield as Norway to harness and control the unruly energies of their half-subdued nobles.

Reference has been made to the secondary effects of the Crusades, generally being more impressive than their stated purposes. The indirect political consequences back in the homelands were also great. The commercial prosperity of the city states of Venice, Genoa and Pisa was greatly enhanced. Venice was powerful enough at sea to defeat the Byzantine navy and to extort trading privileges by which she dominated the Greek islands, the Black Sea coasts, and several Syrian seaports. The island of Cyprus was a Venetian possession from 1489 to 1570. Several orders of crusading knights emerged, initially combining the disciplines of monastic order with the style of feudal chivalry, and for centuries were important in the Mediterranean and later in the Baltic.

The Knights of the Temple (Templars) wore a white mantle with a red cross. They were founded in 1120 to protect pilgrims to the Holy Land. Their rule was written by Bernard of Clairvaux, on the Cistercian model. In 1307, having grown very wealthy and sedentary, they were destroyed and pillaged by Philip "the Fair" of France.

The Knights of St. John (Hospitalers) wore a black mantle with a white cross. Beginning in 1070 to care for the Hospital of St. John, they were made a military order in 1130. Only nobles could belong. They later moved to Cyprus, Rhodes, and finally to Malta.

These international orders were paralleled by a number of national or ethnic orders, of which the most important were the Teutonic Knights. They wore a white mantle with a black cross. With the fall of Acre their energies were transferred to the eastern frontier of Germany.

*Crusader knights battle Muslim warriors; stained glass window, Monastery of St. Denis, destroyed during French Revolution.*

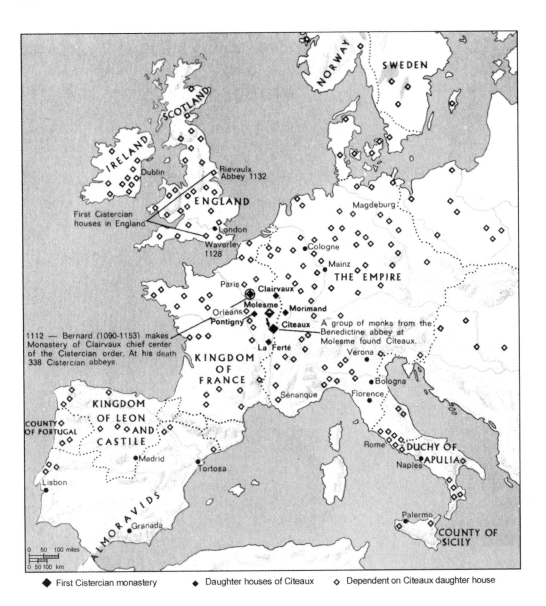

First Cistercian monastery     Daughter houses of Citeaux     Dependent on Citeaux daughter house

Map labels:
- NORWAY
- SWEDEN
- SCOTLAND
- IRELAND
- Dublin
- Rievaulx Abbey 1132
- ENGLAND
- First Cistercian houses in England
- London
- Waverley 1128
- Magdeburg
- Cologne
- Mainz
- THE EMPIRE
- Paris
- Clairvaux
- Molesme
- Morimand
- Orléans
- Pontigny
- Citeaux
- A group of monks from the Benedictine abbey at Molesme found Citeaux.
- La Ferté
- Verona
- 1112 — Bernard (1090-1153) makes Monastery of Clairvaux chief center of the Cistercian order. At his death 338 Cistercian abbeys.
- KINGDOM OF FRANCE
- Sénanque
- Bologna
- Florence
- KINGDOM OF LEON AND CASTILE
- COUNTY OF PORTUGAL
- Madrid
- Tortosa
- Rome
- DUCHY OF APULIA
- Naples
- Lisbon
- ALMORAVIDS
- Granada
- Palermo
- COUNTY OF SICILY
- 0  50  100 miles
- 0  50 100 km

THE Cistercian Order was founded at Cîteaux, near Dijon in France, in 1098. Its initial purpose was to restore a strict and primitive Benedictine rule, and to this end houses were established in remote locations where brothers could worship and work and practice mutual aid without interference from the world. To strict rules of fasting and silence they added a discipline of manual labor.

Because of strictness of life and high purpose for the church, Cistercians soon became the major force for reform within the institution and finally in the papacy itself. By example of selflessness, by the high esteem they enjoyed among the common people, and by skillful use of position they greatly strengthened the continuing fight against simony, nepotism, and lay manipulation of church posts and finances.

Being self-contained and self-sup-

*Bernard of Clairvaux.*

The most famous monk of the Cistercian Order was Bernard of Clairvaux (1090–1153), of Burgundian noble stock. Just two years after he entered Cîteaux he was sent to establish and lead what became Clairvaux, one of the most influential houses of the order.

Because of his rigorous asceticism and great popularity as a preacher, Bernard played a major part in the political and religious life of the age. He successfully defended the pope against a pretender. He fought the heresy of Henry of Lausanne and the heterodoxy of Abelard. He traveled widely preaching the Second Crusade. In Christian thought he was at his best as a mystic and hymn-writer. ("Jesus, thou joy of loving hearts," of which he wrote the Latin original, is still widely sung.) As a man of charity, he was at his best in denouncing the persecution of the Jews.

When Bernard joined the order at the age of twenty-two he brought about thirty friends and relatives with him, including five of his own brothers, who had been won by his charismatic devotion. He founded the fourth house of the order and remained its abbot until his death. When he died, the most famous man of his age, there were 388 Cistercian houses, scattered all over Europe. Members of the order were in key church posts in courts from Castile to Sweden.

porting economies, the Cistercian communes became important agricultural pioneers. They developed the first rudimentary science of selective breeding and are credited with a major role in English sheep raising.

As in the Cluniac reform movement, which had declined by the time the Cistercians came to prominence, two ideas were evident which had explosive potential for the church as a whole—and this in spite of their devotion to the church's order and sacramental life. First, they helped to spread the idea that Christian life in its most prestigious model—monasticism—might need energetic reform. Second, they took as their model for reform a return to primitive Christianity, Christianity of New Testament style.

*Cistercian Abbey of Sénanque.*

THE Fourth Lateran Council (1215) marked the high point of the papal effort to establish and control a unitary Christendom. The highest verbal expression, to be sure, was Boniface VIII's bull *Unam Sanctam* (18 November 1302); but Boniface died from injuries received at the hands of Philip the Fair's soldiers. In 1215, when Innocent III (pope: 1198–1216) was at the height of his powers, the realization of the dream seemed possible.

Innocent thoroughly dominated the politics of Europe. He gained Sicily as a papal fief from Frederick II on accession to the throne of the Empire, and he asserted the right of the pope to examine the selections of emperors and to crown and invest them. Intervening in England, he got King John to recognize him as his feudal overlord. Although the Fourth Crusade, which he sponsored, turned out to be an expedition to loot Constantinople, he turned the misadventure to account by installing a Latin patriarch and announcing the reunion of east and west. He encouraged the new orders, Dominicans and Franciscans, and used the former in his crusade against the Albigensi.

The Albigensi, before being slaugh-

*Innocent III.*

tered and plundered (1206–26), had developed one of the highest cultures of the age.

To the unitary Christian commonwealth purposed by Innocent III, internal crusades against "heretics" were as essential as external crusades against Muslims.

Shortly after the Fourth Lateran Council (1215) a crusade was launched against the Bogomili. The Bogomili were a Christian sect, apparently dating from the early centuries, which was settled on the military frontiers by a series of Byzantine and Bulgarian emperors. Moving northward and westward, they eventually came within the sphere of influence of the Latin church. Now confronted by the threat of coercion and destruction, the Bogomili converted to Islam en masse rather than submit to the pope. They are the progenitors of the Muslims of Bosnia.

Equally cruel were the decrees against the Jews. Repressive legislation issued at the Fourth Lateran Council included the requirement—imported from a Muslim prince's realm—that in public Jews must wear the yellow badge and the Star of David.

*Bogomili tombstone.*

Decree against the Jews, 1245.

"By a decree of this synod, that when in the future a Jew, under any pretext, extort heavy and immoderate usury from a Christian, all relationship with Christians shall therefore be denied him until he shall have made sufficient amends for his exorbitant exactions. The Christians, moreover, if need be, shall be compelled by ecclesiastical punishment without appeal, to abstain from such commerce. We also impose this upon the princes, not to be aroused against the Christians because of this, but rather to try to keep the Jews from this practice."

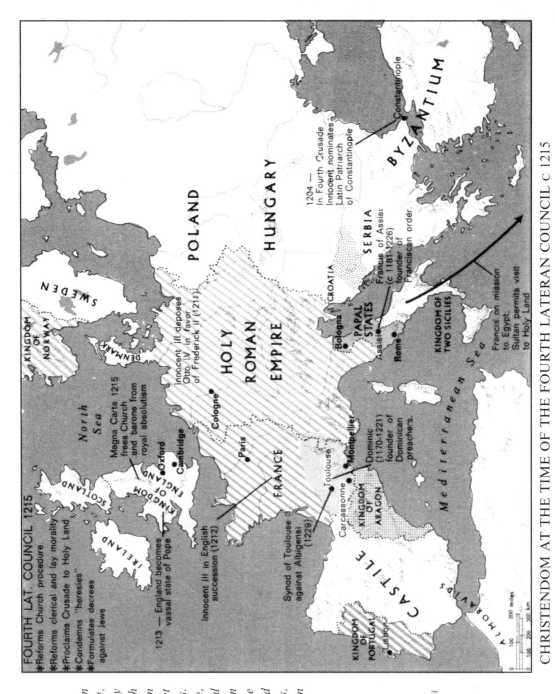

FOURTH LAT. COUNCIL 1215
★Reforms Church procedure
★Reforms clerical and lay morality
★Proclaims Crusade to Holy Land
★Condemns "heresies"
★Formulates decrees against Jews

1213 — England becomes vassal state of Pope

Magna Carta 1215 frees Church and barons from royal absolutism

Innocent III in English succession (1212)

Synod of Toulouse against Albigensi (1229)

Dominic (1170-1221) founder of Dominican preachers.

Innocent III deposes Otto IV in favor of Frederick II (1214)

Francis of Assisi (c 1181-1226) founder of Franciscan order.

1204 — In Fourth Crusade Innocent nominates Latin Patriarch of Constantinople

Francis on mission to Egypt. Sultan permits visit to Holy Land

Papal States under Innocent III
Papal vassal state
Papal intervention
Albigensi
Bogomili

Paris — Main Dominican center

CHRISTENDOM AT THE TIME OF THE FOURTH LATERAN COUNCIL c 1215

CHARLEMAGNE had made the first major campaigns to subdue and Christianize the German tribes to the east of the Rhine. The Cistercian Order did significant work in Mecklenburg, Brandenburg and Scandinavia. The conquest and Christianization of the Baltic area was carried out largely by a combination of two forces: the commercial energy, with rising town life, of the Hanseatic League; second, the transfer of the Teutonic Knights from the Mediterranean to the Baltic. The foundation of Riga in 1201 was a symbolic event: the city soon became a major commercial, crusading and missionary center.

In 1226 Frederick II reorganized the knights, gave the Grand Master a place as a Prince of the Empire, and set them loose against the Prussians. In a diplomatic coup, the knights gave all their acquired and conquered lands to the pope, receiving them back as fiefs of the church; they were thus answerable only to a distant papacy. Latvia and Courland were acquired, and Memel founded in 1252 to hold them. Dozens of fortified towns were established: Thorn (c 1231), Marienwerder (1233), Elbing (c 1237), Königsberg (1254). By the late thirteenth century, the order was enormously wealthy. Its patronage of schools and manuscript collections was famous.

During the fourteenth century, Lithuania and Poland were penetrated. German colonization and town-building moved forward rapidly, especially where the Mongol depredations had created an economic vacuum. In the key cities the new commercial classes

*Castle of the Teutonic Order.*

TEUTONIC KNIGHTS IN THE
BALTIC 13TH–15TH CENTURIES

........... Boundaries 1466

- - - - -Present day Polish-German border

▨ Ecclesiastical lands

▨ Retained by Order as fief of Church

★ Market town

1226 Acquired by German Orders

➤ Advance of Teutonic Order

became German in speech and law. After military defeat, in which the German towns joined with the Poles against the arbitrary rule of the order, the knights opened their ranks to Polish members (Second Peace of Thorn, 1466), and the German eastward march was stayed until the division of Poland (1772–95). In 1525 East Prussia was secularized by the Grand Master and became a fief of the Hohenzollerns.

World War II terminated six centuries of official Teutonic and Christian domination of the Baltic Sea.

*Standard of the Grand Master of the Teutonic Order.*

To many of the Muslim historians, the Mongol conquest marks a faultline of geological proportions between the highly civilized cities and cultures of the Seljuk Turks and the desolation and decline of Islam in Asia Minor which continued into the modern period. The terror which greeted the first Mongol appearance in Europe (capture of Cracow, 1241), with the subsequent devastation of Poland, left a permanent impress also. In subsequent conquests, the Golden Horde defeated the Silesians, Hungarians, Bulgarians, and established a kingdom of two centuries' duration on the lower Volga River in Russia.

In spite of their ruthless military style, the Mongols generally pursued enlightened policies toward subject peoples and their religions. And they opened the roads from the west to China, where the Great Khan had founded his capital at what is now Peiping. Along these roads passed great caravans and trading parties, and both Islam and Christianity became permanently lodged in areas today Russian and Chinese.

The most intrepid Christian missionaries, men of the new Dominican and Franciscan orders, found in the great cities along the trade routes and in China Christians from the time of Nestorian missions many centuries earlier. In 1294 an Italian Franciscan,

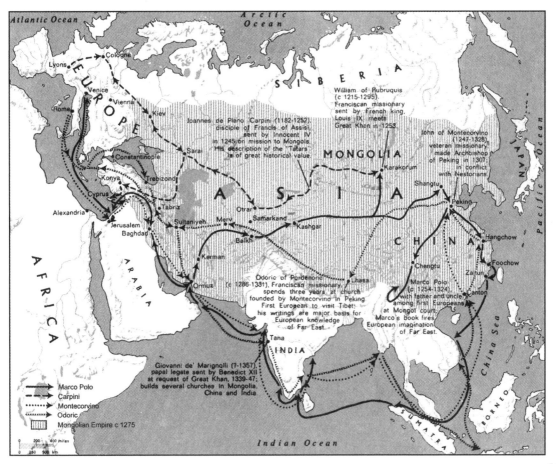

*Marco Polo.*

familiar names in Christian history.

The Polos were merchants. Marco's father and uncle had already made one trip, from which they returned bringing a letter from Khubilai Khan asking for teachers of science and religion. Over the years many friars responded to the Khan's appeal. When the Polos reached the Mongol capital again, they entered the service of the Khan and for seventeen years Marco traveled throughout the empire and as far afield as Burma and India. His *Book of Experiences* was extraordinarily popular and shaped the European picture of the Orient for generations.

In 1368 the Mongols were overthrown and the Ming dynasty closed China again to foreigners. The southern routes were closed a few years later when Tamerlane overran Khorasan, Afghanistan, Azerbaijan, Kurdistan (1380–87) and followed up his conquest of Persia by savaging the Kingdom of Delhi (India).

Nevertheless, Christianity persisted in China. And the adventures of Marco Polo found a permanent place in the romantic literature of the west, the literature by which boys and men have for long understood and misunderstood the distant kingdom of "Cathay."

John of Montecorvino (1247–1328), arrived at the court of the Khan with a letter from the pope. He spent thirty years there, building churches, translating the New Testament, and winning several thousand converts.

The most populous and splendid of lands ruled by the Mongols was China, and Marco Polo (d. 1324), who reported on what he saw there in the years 1271–95, became one of the most

## RAMON LULL (c 1236–1315) AND THE MUSLIMS

*Many knights do I see who go to the Holy Land thinking to conquer it by force of arms. But, when I look at the end thereof, all of them are spent without attaining that which they desire. Wherefore, it appears to me, O Lord, the conquest of that sacred land will not be achieved.*

— Ramon Lull, *Book of Contemplation*

PETER the Venerable (d. 1155) of Cluny had furthered the translation of the Koran into Latin to help missionaries to a better understanding of Islam. In the Iberian peninsula, disputations between Muslims, Jews and Christians were not uncommon. In 1220 Francis of Assisi himself, while visiting the crusader army in Egypt, sought an audience with the Sultan and attempted to persuade him to convert to Christ.

The period's great missionary to Islam was Ramon Lull (c 1236–c 1315), who upon his conversion at thirty devoted himself to that work. He was a prodigious writer—as a mystic (forerunner of Teresa and John of the Cross), as a theologian (adversary of Averroism), as a poet (important to Catalan literature). He bought a slave to teach him Arabic, and mastered it sufficiently to write religious treatises in that language as well as in Latin and Catalan. In 1276 he founded a college at Miramar for the cultivation of Arabic studies. He also taught at Montpellier and Paris.

Lull's missionary journeys took him through Africa and Asia to the frontier of India. He died a martyr's death at the hands of a Muslim mob at Bougie, North Africa.

Ramon Lull's reputation, which in his own time suffered somewhat due to the hostility of the Dominicans, has grown steadily with the rise of modern missions.

The loss of the oldest and best half of Christendom to Islam was a traumatic experience for Christian apologists. From the high Middle Ages to the opening of the Ottoman Empire in the nineteenth century, churchmen and theologians have been polarized between those who regarded Islam as a potentially great mission field and those who viewed in blackest rejection.

The advance of the Mongols, who were generally tolerant in religious matters, seemed to favor Christianity. The old Nestorian communities again flourished, enjoying full protection. A Nestorian archbishopric was created for Peiping in 1275, and communication between the Baghdad patriarchate and China flourished. Genghis Khan and Khubilai Khan were Mongol rulers related to Christian families by marriage diplomacy, and it was said that the ruling Khan of 1251–59 had himself accepted baptism. The Mon-

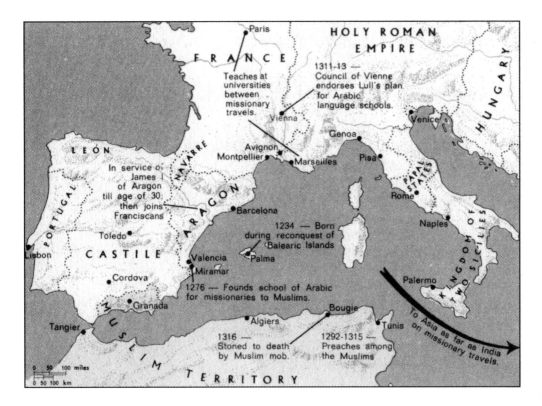

*Ramon Lull, effigy from his tomb.*

ever, they divided in several directions. Most popular was Buddhism. Khubilai Khan accepted a gift of relics of the Buddha from the ruler of Ceylon and gave the chief educational post of his court to a Tibetan lama. In Yunnan province the governor favored Islam and built two mosques. Along the southern tier of central Asia, Persian and Arab traders established growing Muslim communities which vied with the Christians until the fall of Mongol power closed the trade routes.

Under the leadership of Ramon Lull, a fairly sophisticated program of missions to Muslims was developed in the west. Intellectual commerce between Islam and Christendom was already advancing rapidly, especially in the new universities. Controversy yielded slowly to dialogue, but works like the *Summa contra Gentiles* of Thomas Aquinas showed that a philosophy of peaceful coexistence was emerging.

gols were traditionally shamanists, which meant that they were vulnerable to a more advanced religion.

When the Mongols converted, how-

## MEDIEVAL THEOLOGIANS AND MYSTICS 11TH–14TH CENTURIES

*Wisdom is not studied in Paris, but in the sufferings of the Lord. — Johann Tauler*

THE economic and social base for a flowering of Christian culture was provided by the monasteries and the new universities.

At the opening of the age, religious learning was dominated by Peter Lombard (c 1100–60), whose *Sentences* pieced together Christian learning in clearly organized concepts, with a wealth of quotations from Latin and even Greek fathers, in a form suitable for schoolboy memorization.

Anselm (1033–1109), Archbishop of Canterbury, was a vigorous supporter of the Cluniac reforms. He was for

*Anselm.*

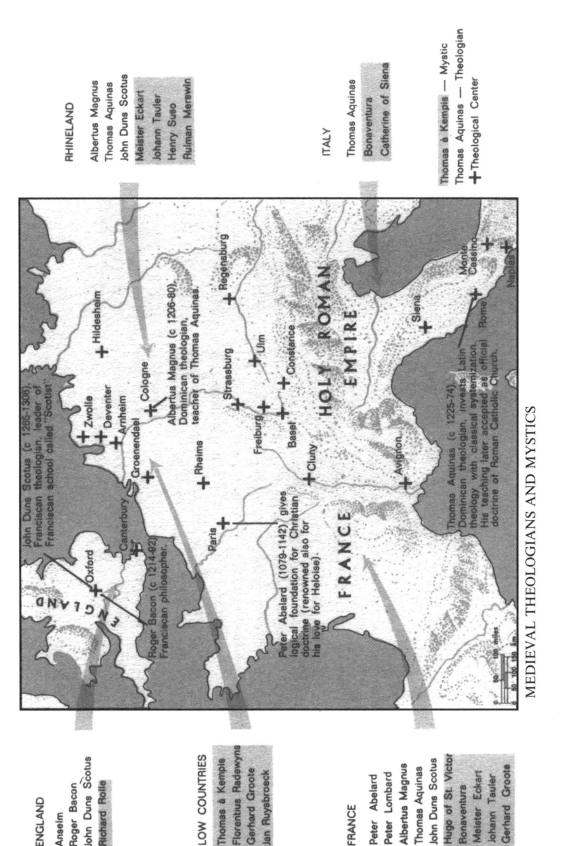

ENGLAND

Anselm
Roger Bacon
John Duns Scotus
Richard Rolle

LOW COUNTRIES

Thomas à Kempis
Florentius Radewyns
Gerhard Groote
Jan Ruysbroeck

FRANCE

Peter Abelard
Peter Lombard
Albertus Magnus
Thomas Aquinas
John Duns Scotus
Hugo of St. Victor
Bonaventura
Meister Eckart
Johann Tauler
Gerhard Groote

RHINELAND

Albertus Magnus
Thomas Aquinas
John Duns Scotus
Meister Eckart
Johann Tauler
Henry Suso
Rulman Merswin

ITALY

Thomas Aquinas
Bonaventura
Catherine of Siena

Thomas à Kempis — Mystic
Thomas Aquinas — Theologian
✝ Theological Center

John Duns Scotus (c 1265-1308), Franciscan theologian, leader of Franciscan school called "Scotist"

Roger Bacon (c 1214-92), Franciscan philosopher.

Albertus Magnus (c 1206-80), Dominican theologian, teacher of Thomas Aquinas.

Peter Abelard (1079-1142) gives logical foundation for Christian doctrine (renowned also for his love for Heloise).

Thomas Aquinas (c 1225-74), Dominican theologian, invests Latin theology with classical systemization. His teaching later accepted as official doctrine of Roman Catholic Church.

ENGLAND

HOLY ROMAN EMPIRE

FRANCE

Oxford
Canterbury
Zwolle
Deventer
Arnheim
Groenendael
Cologne
Hildesheim
Regensburg
Rheims
Paris
Strassburg
Freiburg
Ulm
Basel
Constance
Cluny
Avignon
Siena
Rome
Monte Cassino
Naples

MEDIEVAL THEOLOGIANS AND MYSTICS

*113*

*Roger Bacon.*

*Thomas Aquinas.*

years in bitter conflict with the kings of England over the independence of the church. Anselm's study of the atonement, *Cur Deus Homo*, is one of the "great books" of Christianity.

Peter Abelard (1079–1142) was one of the great Christian thinkers, although outside theological circles he is best remembered for his fateful romance with Heloise. Caught in the powerful intellectual cross-currents of the day, the monk and nun rated their options as follows: 1) virginity (according to the church the highest state); 2) an affair (much praised by the troubadors, through whom Muslim romanticism spread throughout Europe); 3) marriage (the inglorious lesser state, reaching back through Christian sacramentalism to the family covenant of Jewish tradition). Abelard's most brilliant work was *Sic et Non*, a dialectical exposition of contradictory excerpts from Scripture and the church fathers which greatly influenced the use of paradox among later scholastics.

Roger Bacon (c 1214–92) has been considered by some a forerunner of modern science. Probably he did invent

gunpowder, a telescope, a thermometer. His three great *Opera* were an encyclopedia of the knowledge of the day. In advance of his time, his devotion to close observation and laboratory experimentation, and to study of Hebrew and Greek, showed a style of thinking then very rare.

Another Englishman and Franciscan, John Duns Scotus (c 1265–1308), provided the system of thought recognized as authoritative by the Franciscans. In contrast to the Dominicans' Thomism, Scotism gives primacy to love and the will rather than knowledge and reason.

Albertus Magnus (c 1206–80) traveled widely for his order (Dominican) and on assignments for the pope. He also taught in the universities of Paris and Cologne. He made extensive use of Jewish and Muslim writers as well as Aristotle and Augustine.

His pupil, Thomas Aquinas (c 1225–74), was able to provide the order and clarity to go with vast learning which his master never achieved, and his *Summa contra Gentiles* and *Summa Theologica* have never been surpassed as comprehensive statements of Christian thought. In a Europe which lived in daily consciousness of being surrounded by enemies—Muslims and Vikings and Mongols—the appeal of a massive intellectual fortress where every piece fitted neatly into its neighboring and supporting rampart is evident. His teaching was dominant in Roman Catholic circles by the end of the sixteenth-century split with Protestantism. After the European revolutions, official papal instructions again emphasized its authority in the Roman Catholic Church.

*

Parallel to the intellectual renaissance in Christendom came a flowering of mystical devotion.

Hugo of St. Victor (c 1096–1141) shows the influence of Platonism, transmitted through the writings of Augustine and the *Celestial Hierarchy* attributed to "Dionysius the Areopagite."

Bonaventura (1221–74), a Franciscan, championed the divine illumination of the faithful Christian over all the achievements of human reason. As

*Bonaventura.*

General of the Order he strove to overcome the divisions caused by the conflict of the Fraticelli ("Spirituals") with the papacy. His biography of Francis of Assisi was made authoritative within the order and others destroyed.

In Meister Eckart (1260–1327) and his students Johann Tauler (c 1300–61) and Henry Suso (c 1295–1366) we have three Germans famous as mystics, preachers and spiritual directors. They functioned at a time when the Black Plague repeatedly ravaged Europe and the consciousness of death was pronounced. There was a strong tendency to pantheism in their thought. Their writings—of which Suso's *The Book of Eternal Wisdom* was the most widely read book of meditations for two centuries—were popular with later religious individualists and even anticlericals for their stress upon the privacy of religious experience, the indwelling of God in the solitary soul, the divine spark in the individual, the unmediated contact point between God and His creature.

*West front of Notre Dame Cathedral, Paris.*

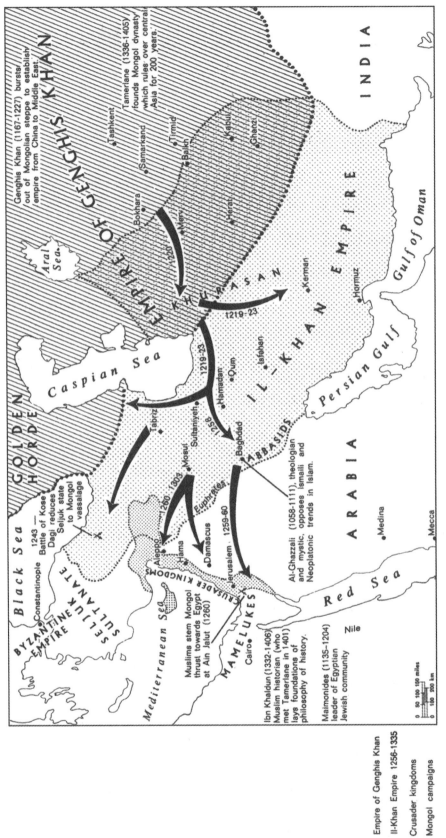

THE MONGOL ATTACK ON ISLAM 12TH–15TH CENTURIES

Genghis Khan (1167-1227) bursts out of Mongolian steppe to establish empire from China to Middle East.

Tamerlane (1336-1405) founds Mongol dynasty which rules over central Asia for 200 years.

INDIA

EMPIRE OF GENGHIS KHAN

Tashkent

Samarkand

Tirmid

Balkh

Kabul

Ghazni

Bokhara

Merv

1220

Herat

Kerman

IL-KHAN EMPIRE

Aral Sea

KHORASAN

1219-23

Gulf of Oman

Hormuz

1219-23

Caspian Sea

Qum

Isfahan

Hamadan

Persian Gulf

GOLDEN HORDE

Tabriz

1258

Mosul

Sultaniyeh

Baghdad

ABBASIDS

Al-Ghazzali (1058-1111), theologian and mystic, opposes Ismaili and Neoplatonic trends in Islam.

ARABIA

Black Sea

1260-1303

Euphrates

Aleppo

Hama

Damascus

1259-60

Jerusalem

Medina

Mecca

1243 — Battle of Kose Dagi reduces Seljuk state to Mongol vassalage

Constantinople

BYZANTINE EMPIRE

SELJUK SULTANATE

Mediterranean Sea

CRUSADER KINGDOMS

MAMELUKES

Cairo

Red Sea

Nile

Muslims stem Mongol thrust towards Egypt at Ain Jalut (1260)

Ibn Khaldun (1332-1406) Muslim historian (who met Tamerlane in 1401) lays foundations of philosophy of history.

Maimonides (1135-1204) leader of Egyptian Jewish community.

0  50  100 150 miles
0   100  200 km

Empire of Genghis Khan

Il-Khan Empire 1256-1335

Crusader kingdoms

Mongol campaigns

ONCE the Mongol conquerors had China in their control, they rapidly rolled over Central Asia, Persia, Mesopotamia, Asia Minor, Russia, and scourged Poland. They established a ruling caste in India. Pillaging and subduing the eastern Muslim empire of Baghdad and Aleppo, they were only stopped at the border of Egypt at Ain Jalut (1260). Egypt thus became the last refuge of Muslim culture except for Moorish Spain.

Following the ejection of Byzantine power from Asia Minor (c 1071), the Seljuk Turks had created an empire of great culture and expanse. Colleges, observatories, libraries, museums were built in the principal cities. At Baghdad the great theologian Al-Ghazzali (1058–1111) systematized the teachings and reduced the appeals of mysticism and visionary leaders.

The crusader kingdoms lasted only for a time, but the Seljuks were unable to regain military and economic strength before the Mongol invasion. Anatolia fell to the Mongols between the Sixth and Seventh Crusades. Persia was ravaged c 1250 and again c 1370.

The Ottoman dynasty was founded as the last outpost of the crusaders (Acre) was abandoned in 1291.

Cultural historians maintain that a civilization builds its most impressive edifices after it has peaked and begun to decline. The most impressive philosophy of history by a Muslim intellectual was that of Ibn Khaldun (1332–1406). Ibn Khaldun's premise is primitivism: the people of virtue and spiritual vigor are the men of the desert, while the people of the cities slide into luxury, ethical and religious corruption. A civilization falls when soft-living urbanites replace the hardy, clear-eyed and physically vigorous men of the open spaces.

Ibn Khaldun used the Mongol hordes, whose great leader Tamerlane he had met, as Tacitus used the blonde and warlike German tribesmen to reproach his effete Roman contemporaries. However useful as a moralist's device, primitivism of this type does not lend itself readily to progressive reform, to improvement of a given situation.

*Mongols besieging Muslims.*

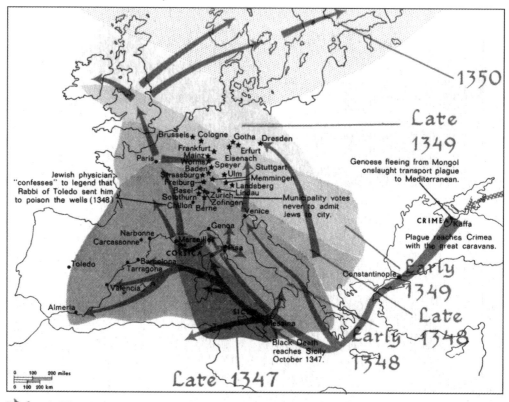

Spread of Black Death     ★ Town where Jews were massacred, 1348-49

*Beginning in the regions of the North and East it advanced over the world and ended with so great a destruction and scarcely half of the people remained. Towns once full of men became destitute of inhabitants, and so violently did the pestilence increase that the living were scarcely able to bury the dead.*

— Rolls Series *History of England* 1:273

THE people of the Middle Ages lived in a world which was inhabited by devils and witches, and they dreamed of a heaven populated by angels. War and violence were rife. Life, such as it was, was brutal and short. Bathing was infrequent and wasting diseases like leprosy were common.

The Crusades, which brought booty to a few and commercial prosperity to some, produced a labor shortage.

Decrees were issued to compel the able-bodied unemployed to work at fixed wages. The nobility began to take over the common lands and forests and to restrict fishing and hunting by the peasants. The freemen, on the other hand, exhilarated by their military adventures in far places, were rife with social unrest.

Into this unrest, evident in such popular pieces as Langland's *Piers Plowman*, came the Black Death. Starting in Constantinople in 1347, it swept across Europe; estimates of losses suffered run as high as 50% of the population. In 1358 a violent peasants' revolt (the *Jacquerie*) arose. In 1381 Wat Tyler's rebellion led to a like burning of manors, tenant records, hanging of landlords and lawyers—and ruthless suppression. Whether in

France or England or in the German states the circumstances were much the same and the explosions and suppressions ran the same course.

The Black Death was spread by rats. In the crowded and filthy cities garbage and refuse were freely thrown out, along with human excrement, into the narrow streets and alleys. Medical care was primitive, and unavailable to any but the wealthy. Germs would not be heard of for another half-millennium. To the illiterate common folk, the plague seemed the consequence of mysterious and indefinable malevolence—to be exorcised or to be located and crushed.

It was a bad time to be known as a witch or—equally mysterious—a Jew.

Unitary Christendom had always bracketed the Jews out, although often the practice did not live down to the theory. During the Crusades they were victimized. With the coming of the Black Death, which ravaged Europe's cities a dozen times during the second half of the fourteenth century, their plight became acute.

"Witches" were tortured and burned, to the number of several hundred thousand. Another victim was ready at hand: the Jews had already been stigmatized by the church fathers and in repeated acts of synods and councils. They were accused of sorcery, alchemy, magic, "the evil eye," "stench and unbelief," deicide, well-poisoning, ritual murder. The cultural antisemitism which was to support the political antisemitism of the twentieth century was already thoroughly imbedded in official church teaching in the Middle Ages.

In earlier times the Jews had enjoyed some protection from kings and prelates, chiefly for financial or political services performed well. They were not allowed to own land or go into the professions in most areas, and so filled in the chinks of feudal society—the high-risk enterprises, like lending money to bishops or princes. A royal exception might be made; but there was no secure base in law or popular opinion for their continued existence. Popular movements tended to express the superstitions of the mob and to be antisemitic.

In the inflation and social unrest that followed the crusades the Jews were particularly vulnerable. New banking houses arose in the Italian cities which loaned money to rulers, thereby rendering a few well-placed Jewish moneylenders—who cast their protection over their people—redundant. Some rulers, like Philip the Fair of France, simply robbed them and expelled them.

Others diverted the restlessness of the peasants and city unemployed against the Jews, distracting attention from the real source of exploitation—thus beginning a practice which was skillfully practiced by the last of the Russian tsars and which continues in some places to the present day.

*Burning of Jews accused of spreading the plague.*

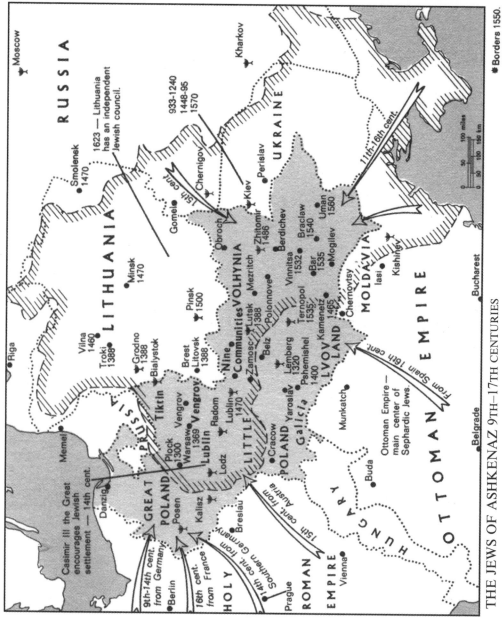

*Because of their sins they are subject to perpetual servitude, and their goods are at the disposition of the ruler; only he must not take from them so much that they are deprived of the means of life.*

Thomas Aquinas on the Jews

THE JEWS OF ASHKENAZ 9TH–17TH CENTURIES

120

DURING the murderous attacks on their communities in western Europe, which became rife during the Black Death and peasants' revolts and continued with the emergence of the first modern nationalisms, the Jews migrated eastward. In spite of the wars and political vicissitudes of the region, in spite of the deep antisemitism imbedded in the Orthodoxy of Russia and the Catholicism of Poland and the Ukraine, in spite of desperate poverty, the Jews of eastern Europe developed a religion and cultural reserve of enormous vitality and great staying power. The tongue was Yiddish, a language where the considerable number of words of German origin clearly indicates the refugees' earlier area of origin. The basic social unit was the *stetl*, defined as "an island of Jewish life surrounded by a gentile sea."

In the early Middle Ages, a high Jewish civilization (Sephardic) developed in the Mediterranean area—especially in Muslim lands. Out of this seedbed came the poetry of a Judah Halevi (b. 1075), the Talmudic expositions of Rashi (1040–1105), the philosophical writings of Maimonides (1135–1204). With the eastward migrations, and especially with the destruction of Spanish Jewry, the traditions of the Ashkenazic—or German—Jewry took the center of the stage in Europe. In the "Pale of Settlement" in the east, in the Jewish quarters of the western cities, the Jewish people developed techniques of survival—of resistance to Christian coercion—which served them well until the Third Reich.

In the *stetl* or the ghetto there was no real opportunity for intellectual commerce with the gentile world, as in the

*Depiction of medieval Jews, 13th century.*

Golden Age in Cairo or Toledo. Within the Ashkenazic settlements Jewish intellectual and spiritual life continued in medieval mold into the nineteenth century.

As has often been the case with attacks on the Jews, the instigators were not seldom renegades. Even today, when students of human nature are familiar with the syndrome of self-hate, the generalization remains true. In the period of persecution which followed the Black Death, the word of a renegade was often enough to condemn a whole community. And whole communities sought refuge outside the Holy Roman Empire.

In Poland, Boleslav V (king: 1227–79) had welcomed Jewish immigrants to help build cities and found industry and commerce, granting them broad charters of self-government. Casimir III, the Great (king: 1333–70) granted extensive privileges to the Jews (1334). A patron of learning and culture, he founded (1364) a school at Cracow which became a university, the foremost intellectual center in eastern Europe. It was natural that Jewish refugees from the German states should look to liberal Poland.

Refuge in eastern Europe was precarious too. The rise of Ukrainian nationalism was accompanied by a period of terrible persecution of the Jews, led by Bogdan Chmielnicki (1595–1657).

It was their misfortune that the Polish constitution contained a disastrous voting system which enfeebled the king and gave the nobles power to block public measures and executive policy. After generations of central weakness and warfare, Poland was gobbled up by Russia, Prussia and Austria (1772–95) and the Jewish settlements found themselves under Catherine the Great (queen: 1762–96); 900,000 Jews fell into her hands, and she had already resolved to keep Jews out of Holy Russia. As a ruler imported from Germany, she had made it a basic practice to cultivate favor with the Orthodox Church.

The Jews were allowed to travel in Poland, Lithuania and the Ukraine, and to inhabit the "Pale of Settlement" along the western border of Russia. Here, in the increasingly hard struggle for survival, the emphasis upon the Law and upon preserving the internal life of the Jewish people became dominant.

# JEWISH MESSIANISM: HOPES AND DISAPPOINTMENTS
## 13TH–18TH CENTURIES

THE Europe of plagues, wars, inflation and civil conflict produced a harvest of revolutionary movements more inspired by dreams of a final judgment against the oppressors than informed by practical political and military reflection.

In the Jewish communities a number of false messiahs arose to plague the faithful. Intolerable conditions of the present combined with a heightened awareness of death produced sometimes a single-minded concentration on the Last Things. The coming of the Messiah was to usher in the righting of ancient wrongs and a return to the time of peace and plenty.

Abraham Abulafia (1240–91) was a student of the mysteries of the Cabbala, son of a rich Spanish Jewish family. On pilgrimage to Jerusalem he heard a voice instructing him to convert the pope. He failed, but he escaped alive.

David Reuveni (fl. 1524–32) and his associate Diojo Pires ("Solomon Molcho") claimed to represent a powerful Jewish king in Arabia, ready to attack from the rear the Turks who again were threatening the invasion of Christendom. The Portuguese king and Roman pope had been enthusiastic, but Emperor Charles V heard them coldly and turned them over to the Inquisition.

There were many other self-styled deliverers of the Jewish people, especially as their conditions deteriorated in eastern Europe. Most important of all

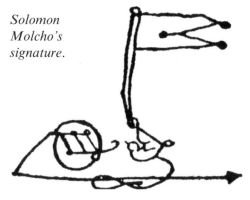

*Solomon Molcho's signature.*

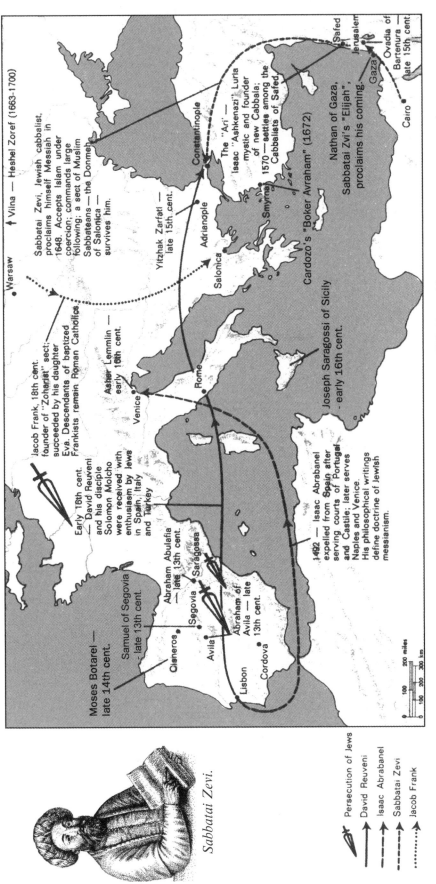

JEWISH MESSIANISM: HOPES AND DISAPPOINTMENTS 13TH–18TH CENTURIES

was Sabbatai Zevi (1626–76), a student of the Cabbala who appeared when Europe was prostrate from the Thirty Years' War. From Turkey to England he was greeted as the long-awaited messiah, although his own work was confined to Turkey, Egypt and Palestine. Converted under coercion to Islam, Sabbatai was survived by a Muslim movement that took his name.

Sabbatai was succeeded by a charming rogue, Jacob Frank (1726–91), who with his daughter Eve (d. 1817) enchanted Polish and Russian and Austrian high society. Having declared himself a prophet, winning the belief and support of a section of the suffering Jews, he lived royally in the gentile society. He was instrumental in leading some numbers of Jews into conversion to Christianity, in a well-staged court ceremony.

Contemporary to Frank was a remarkable teacher who also accented the importance of feeling, of the mysteries, of the wondrous: the Ba'al Shem Tov (1700–60). From this authentic man and his followers there arose Hasidism, a genuinely Jewish way of religious response that was to play a vital role in sustaining the Jewish people in their time of greatest trial.

## THE UNIFICATION OF SPAIN 13TH–EARLY 16TH CENTURIES

THE triumph of the Spanish Christian Empire ended 800 years of Muslim civilization in the Iberian peninsula.

Spain was conquered by the Muslims in 711–15. The defeated rulers were Visigoths, who c 587 had abandoned their Arianism and made religious peace with the Roman see. Under the Omayyad Dynasty (756–1031), Cordova became the greatest intellectual center in Europe. Through scholars like Averroës (c 1126–98) classical learning was transmitted to the west; his commentaries on Plato and Aristotle laid the foundation for Christian Scholasticism. Spanish Christians and Jews enjoyed wide toleration, although—supported by Christian tribes in the north (Asturias, Leon, Castile)—they frequently revolted against their Muslim rulers.

After the fall of the Omayyads, and the defeat of the Almohade forces by Christian chieftains at Las Navas de Tolosa (1212), only provincial Muslim dynasties remained. Christian unification came first, and the expulsion of the Muslims followed.

By the Treaty of Corbeil (1258) France and Aragon traded off their claims on either side of the Pyrenees and stabilized the frontier. James I of Aragon (king: 1213–76) was thereby freed to devote himself to fighting the Muslims and unifying the Iberian peninsula. In the process there were intermittent wars with Portugal, and successful adventures through which the Balearic Islands, Sardinia, Corsica and Sicily were brought under the House of Aragon. In 1340, at the battle of Rio Salado, Alfonso XI of Castile ended the participation of African

*Interior of Mosque of Cordova.*

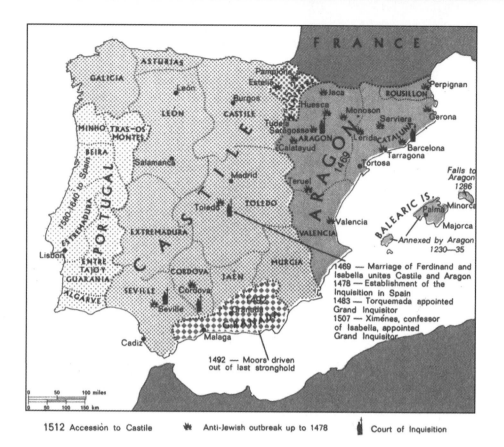

1469 — Marriage of Ferdinand and Isabella unites Castile and Aragon
1478 — Establishment of the Inquisition in Spain
1483 — Torquemada appointed Grand Inquisitor
1507 — Ximénes, confessor of Isabella, appointed Grand Inquisitor

1492 — Moors driven out of last stronghold

Falls to Aragon 1286

Annexed by Aragon 1230—35

1512 Accession to Castile    ✹ Anti-Jewish outbreak up to 1478    Court of Inquisition

Muslim forces in Spanish conflicts until Franco used them in his invasion of July, 1936.

The marriage in 1469 of Ferdinand of Aragon (king: 1479–1516) and Isabella of Castile (queen: 1474–1504) opened the way for the eventual unity of Spain and a triumphantly expanded Christian Empire. The nobility was brought under control by means of a royal-sponsored confederation of towns. Church affairs were skillfully nationalized. The conquest of Granada (1492) ended Moorish power in Spain. The discovery of America in the same year brought a tremendous expansion of overseas empire, divided by the pope in 1493 between Spain and Portugal. Crusades against Islam conquered Oran and Tripoli and laid the foundations of the Spanish North African empire. In 1512 Navarre was annexed to Castile. When the grandson of Ferdinand and Isabella, Charles of Ghent, came to the throne (king: 1516–56, emperor from 1519) he became ruler of the largest area ruled by any European since Charlemagne.

Ferdinand represented the old imperial tradition, in which a single religion provides the emotional and symbolic sanctions of the state. The Jews were driven out as well as the Moors. The Inquisition was called in to suppress all Christian dissent and to compel churchmen and theologians to conform to a unitary system of creed and practice.

At the same time, in part by robbing those driven out and in part on the foundation of riches from America, the period was one of intellectual and spiritual giants: Francisco Suarez (1548–1617), Ignatius Loyola (1491–1556), Bartolomé de Las Casas (1474–1560), Felix Lope de Vega (1562–1635), Miguel de Cervantes (1547–1616), El Greco (1547–1614).

125

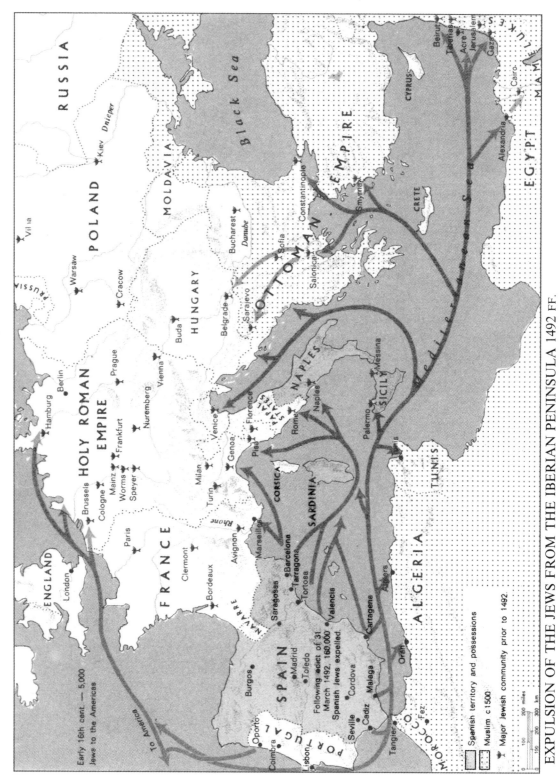

RUSSIA

POLAND

Vilna

Warsaw

Cracow

PRUSSIA

MOLDAVIA

HUNGARY

Buda

Bucharest

Danube

Black Sea

Sofia

Belgrade

Sarajevo

Salonica

OTTOMAN EMPIRE

Constantinople

Smyrna

CYPRUS

CRETE

Beirut

Tiberias

Acre

Jerusalem

Gaza

Cairo

Alexandria

EGYPT

MAME

TURKS

Mediterranean Sea

HOLY ROMAN EMPIRE

Berlin

Hamburg

Brussels

Cologne

Prague

Frankfurt

Mainz

Worms

Speyer

Nuremberg

Vienna

Milan

Turin

Venice

Florence

Pisa

Genoa

PAPAL STATES

Rome

NAPLES

Naples

SICILY

Palermo

Messina

Tunis

CORSICA

SARDINIA

Rhône

Avignon

Marseilles

FRANCE

Paris

Clermont

Bordeaux

London

ENGLAND

NAVARRE

Saragossa

Barcelona

Tarragona

Tortosa

Valencia

SPAIN

Madrid

Toledo

Burgos

Cordova

Malaga

Cartagena

Algiers

Oran

Cadiz

Seville

Tangier

Fez

MOROCCO

ALGERIA

TUNIS

PORTUGAL

Lisbon

Coimbra

Oporto

Following edict of 31
March 1492, 160,000
Spanish Jews expelled

Early 16th cent. — 5,000
Jews to the Americas

to America

Spanish territory and possessions

Muslim c 1500

Major Jewish community prior to 1492.

0   100   200   300 km
0      100      200 miles

EXPULSION OF THE JEWS FROM THE IBERIAN PENINSULA 1492 FF.

THE force of the Spanish Inquisition, whose chief Torquemada (1420–98) has given a name to special cruelty that outlasts the centuries, was felt especially by the Moors and the Jews. More precisely, it was felt especially by those who had accepted baptism but were accused of continuing some of their traditional practices: the Marranos ("secret Jews") and the Moriscos ("secret Muslims"). At this distance it is impossible to determine whether, as ethnic minorities, they were simply trying to keep alive in private some cultural identity or whether they were in fact sham Christians. In an age which made no distinction between religious and political loyalties, whatever they did to resist forced assimila-

*Tomás de Torquemada.*

tion and loss of identity was suspect.

In 1492 some 200,000 Jews were ordered to convert or emigrate. Most fled to Muslim areas, especially to areas which had been ravaged during the Mongol invasions and needed building up. Large communities of refugees grew up in Jerusalem, Damascus and other ancient cities. Under the Ottoman Empire they were granted the same legal status as Christian minorities (the *millet* system), enjoying a provisional toleration and some prosperity for centuries.

Other Jewish refugees sought haven in less intense parts of Christendom. A substantial number settled in Constantinople, from which most of their descendants have since 1948 moved to Israel. A notable group shifted to Rome, where they had a substantial influence on the emergence of Unitarianism among Italian intellectuals of the radical Reformation.

The last effort of Moriscos to resist their fate occurred in 1567–71, in a revolt that was savagely suppressed. By 1609 the last Muslim presence in the peninsula was terminated.

The expulsion from Spain, followed by expulsion from Portugal (1496), also brought the first Jewish settlers to the Americas.

*Spanish woodcut of c 1474, showing the Inquisitory walking with ax and sword and behind him Jews symbolically blindfolded because "they do not see the truth."*

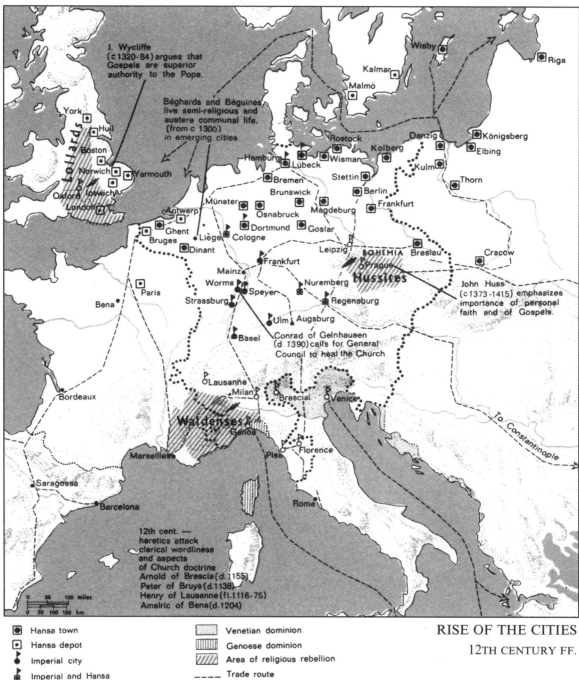

J. Wycliffe (c 1320-84) argues that Gospels are superior authority to the Pope.

Béghards and Béguines live semi-religious and austere communal life. (from c 1300) in emerging cities

John Huss (c 1373-1415) emphasizes importance of personal faith and of Gospels.

Conrad of Gelnhausen (d 1390) calls for General Council to heal the Church

12th cent. — heretics attack clerical wordliness and aspects of Church doctrine Arnold of Brescia (d. 1155) Peter of Bruys (d. 1138) Henry of Lausanne (fl. 1116-75) Amalric of Bena (d. 1204)

York, Hull, Boston, Norwich, Oxford, Ipswich, London, Yarmouth, Lollards

Antwerp, Ghent, Bruges, Dinant, Liège, Cologne, Münster, Osnabruck, Dortmund, Goslar, Bremen, Brunswick

Hamburg, Lübeck, Wismar, Rostock, Kolberg, Danzig, Königsberg, Elbing, Kulm, Thorn, Stettin, Berlin, Magdeburg, Frankfurt

Wisby, Riga, Kalmar, Malmö

Leipzig, BOHEMIA, Breslau, Cracow, Prague, Hussites

Frankfurt, Mainz, Worms, Speyer, Strassburg, Nuremberg, Regensburg, Ulm, Augsburg, Basel

Paris, Bena, Bordeaux

Lausanne, Milan, Brescia, Venice

Waldenses, Genoa, Marseilles, Pisa, Florence, Rome

Saragossa, Barcelona

To Constantinople

| Legend | |
|---|---|
| Hansa town | Venetian dominion |
| Hansa depot | Genoese dominion |
| Imperial city | Area of religious rebellion |
| Imperial and Hansa | - - - - Trade route |
| North Italian city state | •••••• Boundary of Holy Roman Empire |

RISE OF THE CITIES
12TH CENTURY FF.

# RISE OF THE CITIES
## 12TH CENTURY FF.

THE failure of the high medieval effort to create a unitary Christendom was not immediately evident. Ferdinand and Isabella cherished the world-view of the age of Pope Innocent III (1160–1226), as later did Philip II with his Grand Armada (1588). The internal crusade was as much a part of their thinking as the war for Christendom against external enemies. But explosive forces were at work which would render "Christendom" an obvious fiction, and replace more than a millennium of church-state identity with a clear pluralism of religious and political interests. The disintegration of papal authority was accelerated by the rise of the cities, and the rise of the universities.

*Clock of the seasons, from Town Hall of Prague, 15th century.*

To break a closed circle, within which both world-view and lifestyle have become static, there must be political and economic bases outside the control of the ruling powers of the past. The rising cities, which grew so rapidly during and after the crusades, provided those bases ouside the closed circle of Christendom. In the time before conscription, when military forces were hired mercenaries, a prosperous Lombard or imperial city was just as able to defend its interests and advance its claims as any king or bishop.

The major networks were the Hanseatic League, chartered imperial cities in the Holy Roman Empire (65 in number), the cities of the Lombard League, Genoa and Venice and their respective allies.

Although each had its own history and local loyalties, the development of a city north of the Alps followed a course somewhat as follows. Let us assume the city to be situated on the Rhine River, one of the major "highways" of Europe. First, a measure of independence was won from the bishop—whose *Hofrecht* had provided both religious and civil law. Second, precedents and processes which had grown up in the guilds and lower courts became communal law. Third, two assemblies developed, one with representatives of the citizens and the other composed of heads of the old patrician families. During this change the city was confirmed in its right to exact tolls, issue coins, provide police and an army. By the time of the Reformation it was making its own treaties of alliance, sending diplomatic envoys, governing itself by a City Council (the "Small Council," different from the "Great Council" of the assemblies).

The cities which evolved in this fashion played their political game of survival, sometimes in alliance and sometimes at war with bishop and/or pope, king and/or emperor, competing commercial cities. In most of them the commercial and banking and early manufacturing classes were dominant. The city had a new university which was a center of local pride.

Uppsala 1477

Aberdeen 1494

Glasgow 1431

St. Andrews 1412 — First Scottish university

1479 Copenhagen

1209 — Founded by refugees from Oxford; 1511 — Erasmus in Lady Margaret's professorship

Rostock 1419

Greifswald 1456

1168 Oxford

Cambridge

Dominicans make Cologne a seat of learning long before founding of University, 1388.

Frankfurt 1506

Wittenberg 1502

Winchester 1387

Louvain 1425

Cologne

Erfurt 1379

Leipzig 1409.

Marburg 1527

Trier 1454

Mainz 1476

Würzburg 1402

Prague "Studium Generale" in all faculties, chartered 1347

Cracow 1364

Caen 1437

Paris

First Reformation foundation

Heidelberg 1385.

Regensburg 1365

Vienna 1365

Charter of 1219 defines universitas as "a fellowship of teachers and students"

Freiburg 1455

Tübingen 1477

Ingolstadt 1459

Pressburg 1467

Budapest 1465

Angers 1337

Orléans 1305

Besançon Basel 1422 1460

Nantes 1461

Poitiers 1432

Bourges 1464

Vicenza 1204-10

Treviso 1318

Founded 1229 originally to refute Albigenses.

Bordeaux 1441

Grenoble 1339

Valence 1452

Vercelli 1228

Padua 1222

Turin 1405

Pavia 1361

Ferrara 1391

Orange 1365

Cahors 1332

Avignon VAUCLUSE

1248 Reggio 1210

Bologna

Oldest European university, f. 1088

Toulouse

Montpellier 1289

Florence 1349

Aix 1409

Pisa 1343

Arezzo 1215

Valladolid 1346.

Palencia 1208

Perpignan 1379

Siena 1246

Perugia 1308

Salamanca 1243

Huesca 1359

Petrarch (1304-71) first major humanist poet combining both classical and Christian motifs in his work.

Rome 1303

1224 Naples

Saragossa 1474

Sigüenza 1489

Lérida 1300

Salerno 1173

Coimbra 1308

Alcalá de Henares

Barcelona 1450

Dante (1265-1321) renowned Italian poet, wrote "The Divine Comedy", exiled for support of anti-papal faction.

First medical school in Europe, given control of medical practice by Emp. Frederick II in 1221; channel of Muslim scholarship

Lisbon 1290

Founded 1508 by Card. Ximénes de Cisneros, editor of Complutensian Polyglot Bible

Valencia 1500

Palma 1483

Catania 1444

Seville 1254

0 100 200 miles
0 100 200 300 km

1527  Date of founding of University

# RISE OF THE UNIVERSITIES
## 11TH CENTURY–1528

*Seal of the University of Paris, 1292.*

*Crest of Philipps-Universität, Marburg.*

130

MODERN universities owe their origin to the monastic and cathedral schools. To this day, on many campuses the dormitory, the refectory—not to mention the chapel and many classroom procedures—recall the day when young novitiates entered the tutelage and personal supervision of the older brothers.

The great explosion of learning—both in recovery of the classical writings and in the rudimentary beginnings of science—came with the Crusades. From Muslim scholars, and to a certain extent from Greeks who came through Venice and Ravenna, the writings of Plato and Aristotle and others became available again in early texts—rather than through paraphrases or translated snippets.

*

For centuries such learning as could be found was confined to the monasteries, and the educational *cursus honorum* lay within the church. The invention of printing by Johann Gutenberg (1396–1468) had an impact comparable to the arrival of computers, data processing and e-mail in our own time: access to information exploded and could no longer be limited to authorized persons. Both the Protestant Reformation and the rise of democracy would have been impossible without the proliferation of books.

The new commercial classes demanded and got education for their sons outside the religious vocation. Kings and princes looked to the new universities to provide them with accountants and lawyers. Scholars disinterested in theology began to find in the universities a satisfactory replacement of the precarious patronage of eccle-

*Crest of Oxford University.*

siastics or doges. The cities took strong pride in their local universities. Theology was the "Queen of the Sciences," and her faculty led the academic processions; but the teachers in the theological faculties from the beginning were engaged in frequent controversies with their colleagues in the "secular" sciences. They were also not infrequently under investigation by the church authorities as well.

The prestige of the university and its status as a social institution can be judged by the way cities and princes acted. When the leading Protestant ruler, Philipp of Hesse, undertook the reform of his land in 1526–29, he had in mind three practical programs: first, visitation and inspection of local churches, schools and monasteries; second, the organizing of a Protestant league of allies from Zurich to Denmark; third, the founding of a university. The university was Marburg (f. 1527), the first Protestant university and the first in Germany with a princely rather than papal charter.

# "BABYLONIAN CAPTIVITY" — THE PAPACY
## AT AVIGNON 1309–77

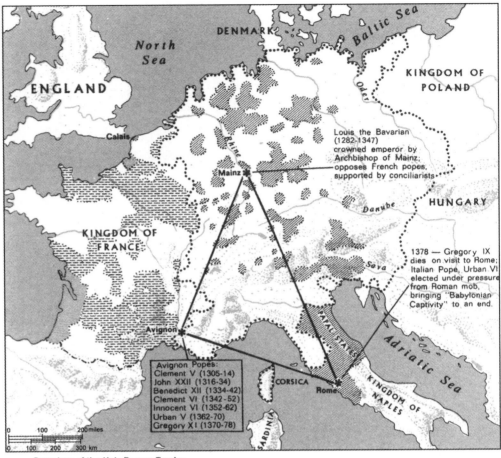

Louis the Bavarian (1282-1347) crowned emperor by Archbishop of Mainz; opposes French popes; supported by conciliarists

1378 — Gregory IX dies on visit to Rome; Italian Pope, Urban VI elected under pressure from Roman mob, bringing "Babylonian Captivity" to an end.

Avignon Popes:
Clement V (1305-14)
John XXII (1316-34)
Benedict XII (1334-42)
Clement VI (1342-52)
Innocent VI (1352-62)
Urban V (1362-70)
Gregory XI (1370-78)

..... Boundary of the Holy Roman Empire
▨ Church land
▨ French royal domain
▨ English domain in France

*...the sink of every vice, the haunt of all iniquities, a third Babylon, the Babylon of the West.* — Petrarch on Rome

FROM the beginnings of the Cluniac reform (910), the great churchmen had tried to resist the manipulation of the church finances and appointments by secular rulers. But the vision of a church independent of worldly power was contradicted by two facts: first, great rulers like Constantine and Charlemagne had always dominated "their" bishops as well as their generals, and the ablest emperors and kings always emulated the old model of close control; second, in the complex of feudal relationships, of which the pope and bishops were a part, it was frequently impossible to sort out "religious" from political or military obligations.

"Lay investiture" of churchmen in church offices was the chief symbol of the struggle for centuries, with simony and nepotism and clerical celibacy related issues. And in fact, in terms of some Concordats in effect to this day, the church has never achieved complete freedom of appointment and control. In the disintegration which followed Innocent III's Council and Crusades, the struggle between the Bavarian and

French kings and the papacy culminated in the French capture and control of the office.

Clement V (pope: 1305–14) moved the papacy from Rome to Avignon, and in his complicity in the destruction of the Templars (1311) and other matters showed himself King Philip IV's faithful servant. Gregory XI (pope: 1370–77) returned to Rome in response to the appeals of Catherine of Siena, to restore order in the Papal States and in Florence. Upon his death the Roman mob demanded an Italian and elected Urban VI (pope: 1378–84).

The Avignon papacy was an open offense to non-Frenchmen. Worse still, the removal of the pope from the income of the Papal States put him in a financial straitjacket, from which he escaped by introducing measures offensive to moralists and humanists. The sale of church offices and indulgences became commonplace.

What followed on the election of Urban VI was even more scandalous, resulting for generations in two and sometimes three "popes": "the Great Schism of the West" (1378–1409). Some said that Urban was mad; he was in any case a disaster. At one point he had six of his cardinals tortured and five put to death. The French elected Clement VII (Robert of Geneva) and continued a papacy at Avignon.

Spain, France, Naples, Scotland and some of the German states supported Clement. Italy, England, Poland, Portugal stayed with Urban. In the emergency, various writers, churchmen and rulers turned to the idea of a General Council as the way to heal a divided western Christendom. Professors at the

*Gregory XI returning to Rome.*

University of Paris had for some time been calling for a General Council to cure the church of her weaknesses and corruptions, and their writings gained persuasiveness.

To be sure, the most radical exponent of Conciliarism, Marsilius of Padua (c 1275–1342), had been excommunicated and his teachings in *Defensor Pacis* condemned. Furthermore, he had worked as advisor to an excommunicated ruler, Louis of Bavaria. His theory of civil and religious affairs was strikingly modern: the emperor derives his authority from the people, who may depose him if he defaults; the papacy derives its authority, limited to spiritual matters, from the state. In all religious matters a General Council, composed of priests and laymen, is supreme.

*Palace of the Avignon popes.*

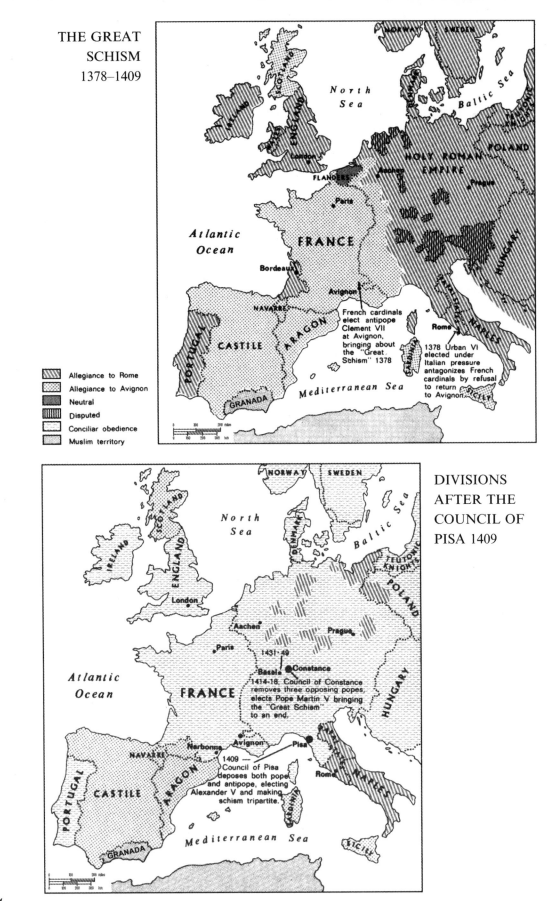

THE GREAT
SCHISM
1378–1409

*North Sea*

*Baltic Sea*

NORWAY  SWEDEN

IRELAND  SCOTLAND

ENGLAND

London

FLANDERS

Paris

HOLY ROMAN EMPIRE

POLAND

Prague

HUNGARY

*Atlantic Ocean*

FRANCE

Bordeaux

Avignon

NAVARRE

French cardinals
elect antipope
Clement VII
at Avignon,
bringing about
the "Great
Schism" 1378

Rome

1378 Urban VI
elected under
Italian pressure
antagonizes French
cardinals by refusal
to return
to Avignon

PORTUGAL  CASTILE  ARAGON

GRANADA

SARDINIA

*Mediterranean Sea*

SICILY

| | |
|---|---|
| ▨ | Allegiance to Rome |
| ▦ | Allegiance to Avignon |
| ■ | Neutral |
| ▥ | Disputed |
| □ | Conciliar obedience |
| ▦ | Muslim territory |

DIVISIONS
AFTER THE
COUNCIL OF
PISA 1409

NORWAY  SWEDEN

IRELAND  SCOTLAND

*North Sea*

*Baltic Sea*

DENMARK

ENGLAND

London

TEUTONIC KNIGHTS

POLAND

Aachen

Prague

Paris

1431–49

Basle  Constance

HUNGARY

1414–18, Council of Constance
removes three opposing popes,
elects Pope Martin V bringing
the "Great Schism"
to an end.

*Atlantic Ocean*

FRANCE

Narbonne

Avignon

Pisa

1409 —
Council of Pisa
deposes both pope
and antipope, electing
Alexander V and making
schism tripartite.

Rome

NAVARRE

PORTUGAL  CASTILE  ARAGON

SARDINIA

GRANADA

*Mediterranean Sea*

SICILY

134

THE existence of two popes threw into open relief the pitiable condition of the organized church and did much to destroy the aura of sacrosanct authority which had surrounded the papacy from the time when it was the only principle of order left in the west.

The Great Schism created a hearing for radical reformers like John Wycliffe (c 1329–84) and his Lollards. Wycliffe challenged papal authority by Scripture, called for a church without property or pomp or worldly power, and spread a translated Bible among the common people that they might judge their faithless church leaders for themselves.

Not to be forgotten too is the teaching of Joachim of Fiore (c 1132–1202), which surfaced with increasing frequency among radical groups. Joachim had introduced a new periodization of history which rendered the very existence of the papacy suspect. He proclaimed a breaking in of the "Age of the Spirit," with a withering away of the church and its sacramental order. Some of the Spiritual Franciscans, in their fight with the papacy, had identified the pope as "the Antichrist"—the chief enemy of the New Age. Wycliffe used this language, and so did Martin Luther—and they were only two among a multitude of critics to whom the papacy was identified with the dying age.

## DIVISIONS AFTER THE COUNCIL OF PISA 1409

EVENTUALLY cardinals in both camps agreed to call a council. At Pisa (1409) both popes were deposed and the cardinals elected another. Now there were three.

Among those who gave a theoretical base for Conciliarism were Pierre d'Ailly (1350–1420) and Jean Gerson (1363–1429), and at the Councils of Pisa (1409), Constance (1414–18) and Basel (1431–49) their thought was dominant. As key figures at the University of Paris, they were free of the taint which attended Marsilius of Padua's career. Neither were they suspected of Joachimite radicalism like William of Occam (c 1300–49), a conciliarist who had sided with the radical Franciscans against John XXII. Their argument was limited to the emergency of the church: only a General Council, by its nature superior to the pope, could end the Schism.

Unfortunately, Pisa complicated matters. And Constance was a mixed blessing. It did heal the Schism. John XXII of the conciliar line and Benedict XIII of Avignon were deposed; the Roman pope, Gregory XII, resigned with honor. The new pope, Martin V (pope: 1417–31), was upright and able. Unhappily, the Council of Constance began by burning two of the chief advocates of reform in the church, John Huss (c 1369–1415) and Jerome of Prague, and thereby considerably tarnished the theology of dialogue and consensus which had been a fundamental part of conciliar theory.

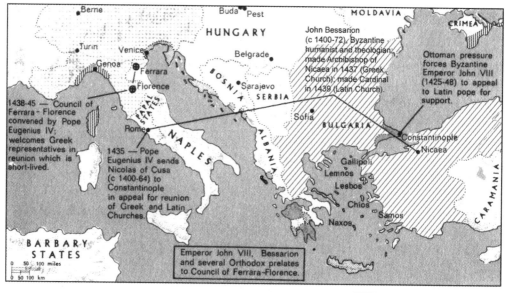

Berne · Buda · Pest · MOLDAVIA · CRIMEA

HUNGARY

Turin · Venice · Belgrade

Genoa · Ferrara · BOSNIA · Sarajevo · SERBIA

Florence · Sofia · BULGARIA

PAPAL STATES · Rome · ALBANIA · Constantinople · Nicaea

NAPLES · Gallipoli · Lemnos · Lesbos · Chios · Samos · Naxos · CARAMANIA

BARBARY STATES
0  50  100 miles
0  50  100 km

1438-45 — Council of Ferrara-Florence convened by Pope Eugenius IV; welcomes Greek representatives in reunion which is short-lived.

1435 — Pope Eugenius IV sends Nicolas of Cusa (c 1400-64) to Constantinople in appeal for reunion of Greek and Latin Churches.

John Bessarion (c 1400-72), Byzantine humanist and theologian, made Archbishop of Nicaea in 1437 (Greek Church); made Cardinal in 1439 (Latin Church).

Ottoman pressure forces Byzantine Emperor John VIII (1425-48) to appeal to Latin pope for support.

Emperor John VIII, Bessarion and several Orthodox prelates to Council of Ferrara-Florence.

□ Holy Roman Empire
▨ Ottoman Empire
■ Byzantine territory
▥ Genoa and Genoese territory
▩ Venice and Venetian territory

VOTING at the Council of Constance followed university practice, with division by nations. After a single pope was chosen, reform was again postponed. Two decrees were issued, one declaring a General Council superior to a pope, and the other providing for regular meetings in council.

At the Council of Basel (1431–49) anti-papal feeling was strong. The Council resisted papal effort to dissolve it and passed some reform measures—including a compromise with the Hussites. The papal strategy, which centered on reestablishing papal supremacy over councils, was built around the hope of reunion of east and west.

The possibility of healing the Schism of 1054 weakened resistance to papal initiative, although part of the Council remained in session when the papal party walked out. They elected an anti-pope. The offensive had passed to Pope Eugenius IV, however, and in 1439—at the Council of Ferrara-Florence, controlled by the papal party—the Greek delegates accepted the terms of union. Their agreement was, however, repudiated in Constantinople.

But the purpose of the reunion effort was achieved: Conciliarism was dead.

Conciliarism went through several stages. First, it was an ideological weapon of the emperor against a French pope. Then it became a tool of church reformers against the papacy. Finally its arguments on popular sovereignty and lay authority were resurrected in democratic political and religious thought in the modern period.

*Great Seal of Louis of Bavaria.*

136

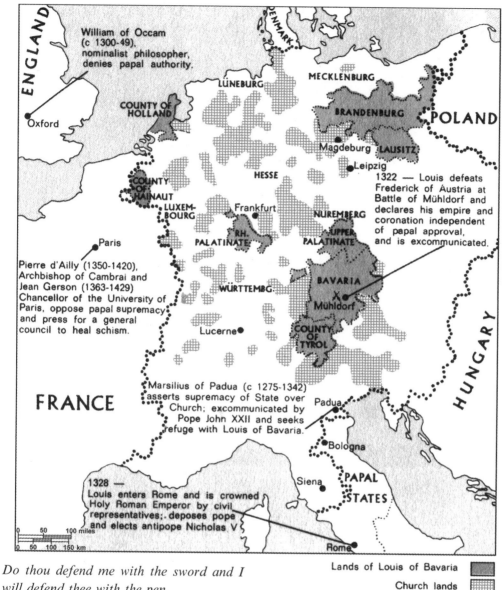

William of Occam (c 1300-49), nominalist philosopher, denies papal authority.

1322 — Louis defeats Frederick of Austria at Battle of Mühldorf and declares his empire and coronation independent of papal approval, and is excommunicated.

Pierre d'Ailly (1350-1420), Archbishop of Cambrai and Jean Gerson (1363-1429) Chancellor of the University of Paris, oppose papal supremacy and press for a general council to heal schism.

Marsilius of Padua (c 1275-1342) asserts supremacy of State over Church; excommunicated by Pope John XXII and seeks refuge with Louis of Bavaria.

1328 — Louis enters Rome and is crowned Holy Roman Emperor by civil representatives;. deposes pope and elects antipope Nicholas V

*Do thou defend me with the sword and I will defend thee with the pen.*
— William of Occam to Louis of Bavaria

Lands of Louis of Bavaria
Church lands
Boundary of Holy Roman Empire

WHEN Louis IV (king: 1314–47) was elected emperor he was refused confirmation of the election by the pope in Avignon. He then became a sponsor of Marsilius of Padua and others who argued the power of the General Council over the pope.

To prevent future dispute, the Golden Bull was issued in 1356 creating seven hereditary Electors of the Empire: the Archbishops of Trier, Mainz and Cologne, the Count of the Palatinate, the Duke of Saxony, the Margrave of Brandenburg and the King of Bohemia.

The imperial succession during this period shifted from the House of Luxembourg to the House of Habsburg. Louis's contemporary, John of Luxembourg (king: 1310–46), had made Bohemia a power in European politics.

Labels on map (reading):
RUSSIA · Novgorod · Suzdal · Moscow · Riga · Vitebsk · Smolensk · Vilna · Mohilev · Königsberg · Novogrudok · Lübeck · Thurn · GRAND DUCHY OF LITHUANIA · UNION 1386 · Warsaw · KINGDOM OF POLAND · Kiev · HOLY ROMAN EMPIRE · Prague · Cracow · Vladimir · Regensburg · Lemberg · Halicz · Tana · Vienna · Pest · Suceava · HUNGARY · Venice · Bologna · Florence · Pisa · Belgrade · WALLACHIA 1462 · BOSNIA 1463 · SERBIA 1389 · BULGARIA 1393 · Sinope · Rome · RUMELIA 1430 · Constantinople · Zonguldak · Bari · Salonica · Taranto · ALBANIA 1479 · MOREA 1460 · Antioch

1453 Mohammed II captures Constantinople after slaughter of Christian inhabitants; Patriarch of Constantinople recognized as head of conquered Orthodox Christians.

Ottoman conquests sever trade routes between Eastern Europe and Mediterranean, and between Venice and Genoa and the Levant.

Legend:
- Ottoman Empire
- - - - Principal trade route
1460 Date of Ottoman conquest
Centers of Orthodoxy

*Be baptized and no prince in the world will be your equal in glory and power. We will call you Emperor of the Greeks and of the Orient....*

– Letter of Pope Pius II to Mohammed II

THE closing of the eastern trade routes by land during the Mongol conquest was nothing compared with the traumatic effect of the fall of Constantinople to the Ottoman Turks in 1453. For more than a thousand years the city had stood as the chief religious and political center of eastern Christianity, recalling to the faithful the triumph of Christianity throughout the Roman Empire and Hellenistic civilization.

With the conquest the inhabitants were slaughtered and the city pillaged.

Classical Christian institutions were transformed into Muslim centers (e.g., Hagia Sophia). After an unsuccessful effort to repopulate the city with Muslims, Mohammed II (sultan: 1451–81) let in Christians again and established legal Greek and Armenian communities on the *millet* system. He then completed the conquest of Albania, Bosnia and Wallachia, and took over most of the outposts of Venice and Genoa.

One effect of the fall of the city was to enhance interest in voyages of exploration and discovery. The Portuguese, who had closed the Red Sea route, were especially active in opening new sea routes. Under Prince Henry the Navigator (1394–1460), carefully planned and conducted expeditions were sent out frequently, with Ethiopia and India the ultimate goals. The coasts and rivers of West Africa were charted; in 1487 the Cape of Good Hope was rounded; in 1498 Vasco da Gama reached India; in 1500 Brazil was reached; in 1519–22, under Castilian auspices, Magellan's ships circumnavigated the globe. As it happened, the pope divided the new world in 1493 in such a way that to the Spanish fell the areas with advanced and wealthy societies (Aztec, Inca), while the Portuguese were given what is now Brazil. In Africa and Asia, however, the Portuguese built and maintained a prosperous colonial trade.

A second effect of the advance of the Ottomans was to end Greek domination of Eastern Orthodoxy and enhance the importance of the Russian church. By the time of Alexander Nevski (d. 1263), Christianity was strong in Kiev and Novgorod, but the energies of the chieftains were still consumed in resisting the advance of the Swedes, dealing with the Mongol overlords, and (more recently) resisting the Teutonic Knights. In 1472 Ivan the Great, the first national ruler of Russia, married Zoë, niece of the last Greek Emperor of Constantinople. From this time dates the claim of the Russian rulers to succeed the Greeks as protectors of Orthodox Christianity and successors to Byzantium. Moscow was called "the Third Rome," the ruler called himself "Tsar" (Caesar).

Eastern Orthodoxy has traditionally conceived itself in static terms, preserving intact the definition of Christianity expounded in the first Seven Councils. Orthodoxy never developed a body of Christian ethics or a philosophy of missions. At least until recently there had been little development of theological thought since John of Damascus (c 675–c 749), who worked under Muslim sovereigns in Damascus and Jerusalem.

Russian Orthodoxy, however, developed a deep liturgical and meditation tradition, with a rich use of vocal music and popular art forms. Its close connection with autocratic rulers was to have disastrous consequences for Christianity in the nineteenth and twentieth centuries.

## THE FALL OF CONSTANTINOPLE (1453)

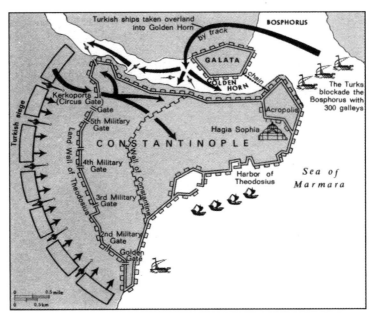

# THE ITALIAN RENAISSANCE
## 15TH–17TH CENTURIES

Dome of Florence Cathedral, from 1420 (designed by Brunelleschi).

Guicciardini — Historian

Milan

Verona
Padua

Bellini — Painter
Giorgione — Painter
Titian — Painter
J. Sansovino — Architect
Palladio — Architect

Venice

Turin    Correggio — Painter
Parma

Ferrara

Ravenna

A. Sansovino — Architect
Brunelleschi — Architect
Ghiberti — Sculptor
Valla — Humanist
Donatello — Sculptor
Alberti — Humanist
Verrocchio — Sculptor, Poet
Lorenzo de Medici — Poet
Ghirlandajo — Painter
Botticelli — Painter
Da Vinci — Painter
Ficino — Philosopher
Machiavelli — Philosopher

Bologna

Pisa    Florence    Urbino
Arezzo
Vasari — Art historian,
Siena               Painter
Perugia

Ancona

Civitavecchia

Rome

Bramante — Architect
Raphael — Painter
Peruzzi — Architect
Michelangelo — Sculptor,
Painter, Architect
Bernini — Sculptor

S. Giorgio Maggiore, Venice, 1560-80 (designed by Palladio)

Dome of St. Peter's, Rome, late 16th cent. (designed by Michelangelo).

*We Italians are more irreligious and corrupt than others…because the Church and its representatives set us the worst example.*
— Machiavelli

THE cities of northern Italy prospered greatly during and after the Crusades. They were strong enough to defeat the Emperor on the battlefield (Legnano, 1176) and to wrest from him virtual independence as city-states. They were engaged in prosperous trade with Byzantium. They were shippers and/or outfitters of the crusaders. They handled the trade that developed between Muslim areas and the west. At a time when major political and economic forces linked northern and western Europe to the Italian peninsula, they were located on the lines of march and commerce.

Milan, dominant in the Lombard League, was too close to the border and suffered from the vicissitudes of French and Spanish politics. But Venice long dominated trade in the Adriatic and possessed many trading posts and colonies in the eastern Mediterranean. The fall of Constantinople (1453) and subsequent Turkish conquest of Greece and Albania weakened her position; her chief contribution to the explosion of learning was in fostering printing presses. Nevertheless, Venice—like Ravenna—was a major channel for introducing Greek learning and lecturers into the west. Florence, where the merchants achieved access to the sea through Pisa and great expansion in banking through connection with the papacy, provided the setting for the most brilliant flowering of Renaissance energies.

Florentine forerunners of the Renaissance included Dante (1265–1321), Petrarch (1302–74), Boccaccio (1313–75) and Giotto (1276–1337). Under the rule of the Medici, humanists and manuscript copyists, musicians, poets and translators flourished. Libraries were established. The Platonic Academy became a center of learning which drew from all over Europe.

Because of the way textbooks are organized in chapters, the common opinion prevails that the Renaissance preceded the Reformations of the sixteenth century. As a matter of fact, they were virtually simultaneous. Leonardo da Vinci died, to be sure, just two years after Luther posted the Ninety Five Theses; but Michelangelo outlived the Saxon reformer by eighteen years and Titian (d. 1576) outlived him by forty years. The basic motifs of Renaissance and Reformation—return to the original sources, discontent with inherited traditions and accruements, hostility to existing power structures, release of explosive truths that break the closed circle of knowledge—make a remarkable overlay.

Artists stopped painting stereotyped figures, beautiful and ethereal, and painted the human person as he really is. Geographers ceased publishing books of imaginary places and mythical beasts and began to publish detail maps. Scholars became discontent with

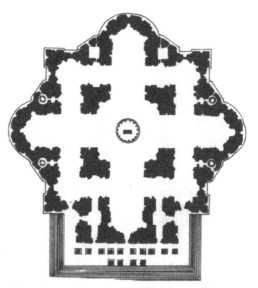

*Michelangelo's plan for St. Peter's. Rebuilt 1546–64.*

paraphrases and rumors and reported opinions and began to collect and study the original texts, in the original languages.

Precise observation and careful analysis destroyed many traditions which had gone unquestioned for centuries. Even a radical like Marsilius of Padua did not think to question the so-called Donation of Constantine; in *Defensor Pacis* (1324) he used it as a model for the state's grant of prerogatives to the church. Leo IX had used it in his correspondence with M. Cerularius in 1054, and it carried great weight during the Middle Ages. In 1440, Lorenzo Valla (1406?–57) proved it a forgery.

It was the methodology that was dangerous: to pit observed evidences against long-standing theoretical propositions. In the beginning, among the men of the renewal movements, there was no "conflict of science and religion." That came when the spirit of exploration waned.

# THE NORTHERN ("CHRISTIAN") RENAISSANCE
## 15TH–16TH CENTURIES

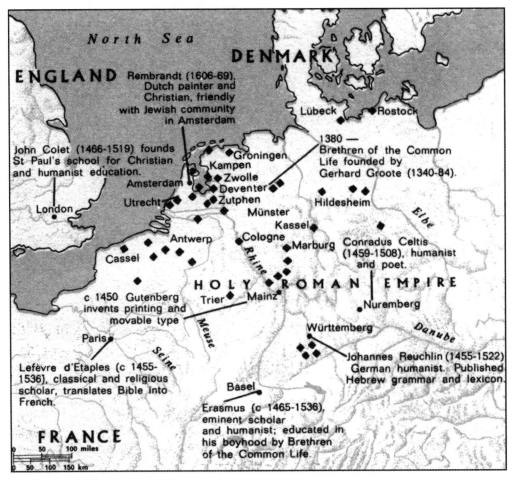

North Sea

DENMARK

ENGLAND  Rembrandt (1606-69),
Dutch painter and
Christian, friendly
with Jewish community
in Amsterdam

Lübeck    Rostock

John Colet (1466-1519) founds
St Paul's school for Christian
and humanist education.

Groningen
Kampen
Zwolle
Amsterdam
Deventer
Utrecht    Zutphen

1380 —
Brethren of the Common
Life founded by
Gerhard Groote (1340-84).

Hildesheim

London

Münster
Kassel

Antwerp    Cologne
Marburg    Conradus Celtis
(1459-1508), humanist
and poet.

Cassel

HOLY    ROMAN    EMPIRE

Elbe

c 1450 Gutenberg
invents printing and
movable type

Trier    Mainz

Nuremberg

Paris

Württemberg

Danube

Lefèvre d'Etaples (c 1455-
1536), classical and religious
scholar, translates Bible into
French.

Johannes Reuchlin (1455-1522)
German humanist. Published
Hebrew grammar and lexicon.

Basel

Meuse

Seine

Rhine

Erasmus (c 1465-1536),
eminent scholar
and humanist; educated in
his boyhood by Brethren
of the Common Life.

FRANCE

0    50    100 miles
0    50    100    150 km

◆ Houses of Brethren of Common Life.

*From midday till one o'clock I work, sometimes singing a hymn to drive away boredom or excite devotion. Then at three o'clock I read vespers and go over the subject-matter of the day's Office. After this I study or prepare parchment till four o'clock when I take up my allotted task [of copying] till supper-time. At supper I behave as I did at dinner [taking no notice of others etc.] and immediately after supper I read compline. After this I examine myself for my failings and sins for some time, and when I have done this I rule or scrape parchment till eight o'clock.*
— Daily life of one of the Brethren of the Common Life, mid-15th cent.

FOR a variety of reasons the Italian Renaissance rarely came into focus in terms of return to the primitive and uncorrupted church. Perhaps the bitter experience of the Waldenses and Spiritual Franciscans, who had sought to practice a simple and unspoiled Christian life, was inhibitive. Perhaps the "capture" of ancient learning by wealthy secular and religious patrons defused its radical implications.

There were, to be sure, some individuals who caught a vision of church reform and renewal, of return to early models—men like Juan Valdés (c 1500–41), Peter Martyr Vermigli (c 1500–61),

Bernardino Ochino (1487–1564). But they came relatively late and seem to have been influenced as much by the Reformation as by earlier models of Christian piety.

In the north, especially under the auspices of the Brethren of the Common Life, there developed an extensive renaissance of Christian Humanism and lay witness which anteceded the sixteenth-century Protestant and Catholic renewal movements. The Brethren were founded by Gerhard Groote (1340–84). They were laymen who, in addition to earning their living in the world, practiced works of charity. Their model was the New Testament church, and they were noted for great devotion and compassion. At Deventer and Zwolle (Netherlands), and then in several dozen other towns in the Lowlands and in the German states, they founded excellent schools—offering an education to poor boys, without fees. Under Florentius Radewyjns (1350–1400), their second head, the common life was introduced and a discipline of living; Radewyjns also founded the monastery at Windesheim (c 1384).

The "Modern Devotion" which the Brethren cultivated had great impact upon men like Pierre d'Ailly (1350–1420), Hadrian VI (pope: 1522–23), Gabriel Biel (c 1420–95), Nicholas of Cusa (c 1400–64), Rudolf Agricola (1443–85), Thomas à Kempis (c 1380–1471)—author of *The Imitation of Christ*, and Desiderius Erasmus (c 1466–1536). The latter was perhaps their most representative alumnus, in the combination of Christian moralism and love of New Testament studies that characterized him.

Christian Humanism had many spokesmen, joining love of the ancient and uncorrupted with a passion for

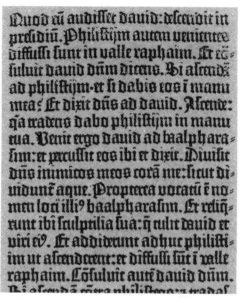

*A column (II Sam. 5:7–24) in Gutenberg's 42-line Bible of 1452–56.*

ethical religion—not all of them products of the Brethren schools, but all of them after 1500 indebted in one way or another to Erasmus's writings.

Johannes Reuchlin (1455–1522) is a case in point. He studied Latin, Greek and Hebrew intensively and published lexicons and grammars. His *De Rudimentis Hebraicis* (1506) and treatise on Hebrew accents (1518) became basic tools for other Humanists who were pursuing Old Testament studies. A renegade Jew, Pfefferkorn, joined with a group of Dominicans at Cologne to demand the destruction of Hebrew books. Reuchlin joined the fray to defend scholarship and the essential materials for scholarly work. Among the pamphlets produced during the fray was the famous *Letters of Obscure Men* (1515–17), in which the Humanists uproariously celebrated the ignorance and corruption of the men of the establishment. Their line of attack combined knowledge of the basic materials with satirical treatment of those whose lifestyle and ignorance fashioned a poor accreditation of Christian truth.

# G. REBELLION IN LATIN CHRISTENDOM

## GERMAN KNIGHTS' WAR 1522–23

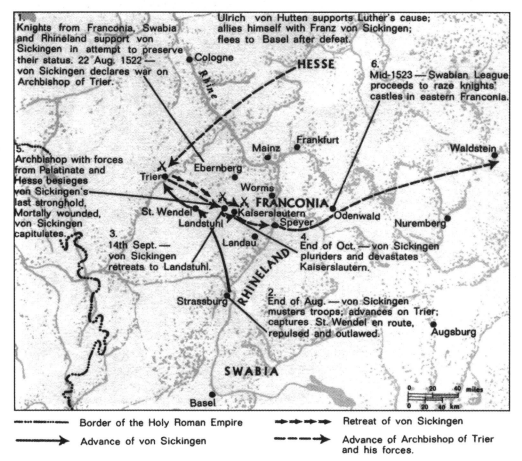

**1.** Knights from Franconia, Swabia and Rhineland support von Sickingen in attempt to preserve their status. 22 Aug. 1522 — von Sickingen declares war on Archbishop of Trier.

Ulrich von Hutten supports Luther's cause; allies himself with Franz von Sickingen; flees to Basel after defeat.

**6.** Mid-1523 — Swabian League proceeds to raze knights' castles in eastern Franconia.

**5.** Archbishop with forces from Palatinate and Hesse besieges von Sickingen's last stronghold. Mortally wounded, von Sickingen capitulates.

**3.** 14th Sept. — von Sickingen retreats to Landstuhl.

**4.** End of Oct. — von Sickingen plunders and devastates Kaiserslautern.

**2.** End of Aug. — von Sickingen musters troops; advances on Trier; captures St. Wendel en route, repulsed and outlawed.

*Map labels:* Cologne · HESSE · Waldstein · Rhine · Mainz · Frankfurt · Trier · Ebernberg · Worms · FRANCONIA · Odenwald · Nuremberg · St. Wendel · Kaiserslautern · Speyer · Landstuhl · Landau · Strassburg · RHINELAND · Augsburg · SWABIA · Basel

- - - - - - - Border of the Holy Roman Empire
→→→→ Retreat of von Sickingen
——→ Advance of von Sickingen
–→–→ Advance of Archbishop of Trier and his forces.

*Three things are most praised and yet most rare in Rome: devotion, faith and innocence.* — von Hutten

IN the dissolution of medieval Christendom, the lesser nobility of the German states found themselves ground between major forces they could neither control nor moderate. Many were dependent upon payments in kind from their lands, and this shortage of cash income was made more acute by the spiraling inflation which followed the discovery and plundering of the new world. The rise of kings, as well as the power and wealth of some princes

*Ulrich von Hutten.*

*The Knights on the march.*

of the church, further jeopardized their status and excited their envy. Their self-image had been inflated by the code of chivalry and by their role in the Crusades; now their economic base and political power were both declining rapidly.

The knights rose in revolt under Franz von Sickingen (1481–1523) and Ulrich von Hutten (1488–1523). Both men were humanistically trained. Both became adherents of the Lutheran cause, seeing in it a chance to recover the deteriorating influence of the Christian nobility of the German nation. Sickingen defended Reuchlin in the controversy with Pfefferkorn, a popular cause among Humanists, and also made his castles available as places of refuge for persecuted evangelicals. He was defeated and slain while waging war against the Archbishop of Trier.

Hutten attended a number of universities and was a major contributor to the famous *Letters of Obscure Men.* Made poet laureate of the empire and receiving a high post with the Elector of Mainz, Archbishop Albert of Brandenburg, he nevertheless gave up his honors to espouse the Lutheran reformation. After Sickingen's defeat he fled to Basel. Shortly before his death he was given an island of refuge by Zwingli.

There were parallel and equally unsuccessful civil wars launched by the lesser nobility in Scandinavia, Poland, France, England and Spain. The Knights' War in Germany is best remembered because of its connection with the Reformation and because it preceded by only a few months the far more desperate revolt(s) of the peasants.

*Johann Reuchlin.*

*Franz von Sickingen.*

*When Adam delv'd and Eve span, Where was then a gentleman?*
— John Ball, c 1382

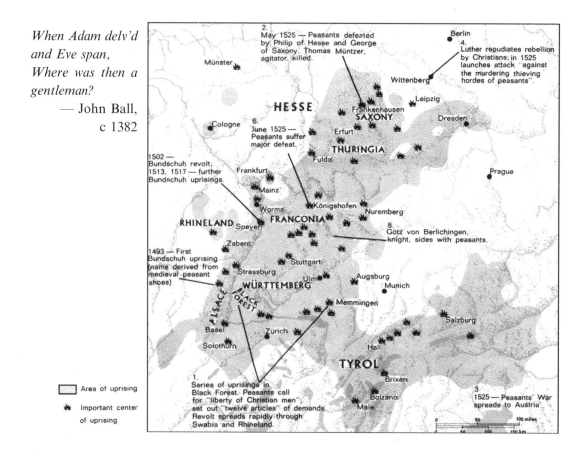

2. May 1525 — Peasants defeated by Philip of Hesse and George of Saxony. Thomas Müntzer, agitator, killed.

4. Luther repudiates rebellion by Christians; in 1525 launches attack "against the murdering thieving hordes of peasants".

6. June 1525 — Peasants suffer major defeat.

1502 — Bundschuh revolt; 1513, 1517 — further Bundschuh uprisings.

1493 — First Bundschuh uprising (name derived from medieval peasant shoes)

5. Götz von Berlichingen, knight, sides with peasants.

1. Series of uprisings in Black Forest. Peasants call for "liberty of Christian men"; set out "twelve articles" of demands. Revolt spreads rapidly through Swabia and Rhineland.

3. 1525 — Peasants' War spreads to Austria

☐ Area of uprising

🗲 Important center of uprising

SERFDOM was chiefly of two kinds: personal ownership of the chattel and legal attachment of the individual and his descendants to the land. During the fourteenth and fifteenth centuries the enforceability of serfdom was lessened. Every social shock, from the Black Death to war, resulted in the flight or disappearance of some serfs. Upon the free peasants, the financial and personal burdens from the lords bore down with growing weight.

Against the Roman laws of property and inheritance, which steadily gained ground in the German states from the early decades of the thirteenth century, the peasant had the group memory of earlier communal rights and dignities. In the many *Bundschuh* revolts of the fifteenth century, as well as in the German Peasants' Wars of 1524–26, the many dozens of (still extant) revolutionary proclamations claimed to assert old rights: e.g., 1) to fish in communal waters; 2) to hunt in communal forests, as well as gather wood; 3) to graze cattle on communal lands; 4) to choose their own priests. The communal waters, forests and land had been sequestered by the nobility.

The great revolts of the peasants in Swabia, Franconia and Thuringia, which the Catholics blamed on the evangelicals (Protestants, German *Evangelisch*) and the evangelicals blamed on the Anabaptists, were suppressed with great brutality. Over 100,000 were killed, contrasting with the c 6,000 killed for participating in the English Peasants' Revolt of 1381.

*To burn a heretic is not to defend a doctrine, but to kill a man.*

     – Castellio, *De Hereticis*, 1554

WHEN Anabaptism arose, denying the medieval parochial and territorial inclusiveness, repudiating infant baptism as unscriptural, and refusing the oath and bearing arms, most churchmen condemned it as revolutionary.

As a matter of fact, the model for Anabaptism was the early church. There were indeed revolutionary impulses in the "Left Wing of the Reformation." But the Anabaptists, the largest sector of radical reformers and the ones who have had the greatest subsequent influence, condemned civil war and revolution as fervently as international war and violence.

In the course of time, four major wings emerged in the Anabaptist movement. (The term "Anabaptist" came from their persecutors, to bring them under the Empire's death penalty for "re-baptizers": they preferred the simple names "Brethren" or "Christians.") They first appeared in the circle which surrounded Ulrich Zwingli at Zürich. In 1525 some of Zwingli's most energetic followers became impatient with his determination to proceed slowly

*Ulrich Zwingli.*

and swing the whole canton to the evangelical course. They denied the authority of the government to decide religious matters, as they had previously agreed with Zwingli in denying the authority of pope and hierarchy to control religious change. They split off from Zwingli to found voluntary house-churches organized according to New Testament principles. They were in truth "restitutionists" rather than "reformers"; they understood "apostolicity" to mean "true to Jesus and the apostles" rather than continuity of ordination (Catholic) or preaching (Lutheran).

The Anabaptist view of the church is, technically speaking, a form of primitivism. That is, history is divided into three periods: Golden Age, Fall, and Restitution. In the case of the Anabaptists, the Golden Age was the early church, the Fall occurred with the union of church and state under Constantine, and the Restitution began with their own break from the state churches. In their eyes the state-church Protestants, who carried on wars and coerced those who disagreed with them, belonged just as much to the "fallen" period of the church as the Roman Catholics.

The leader of the Swiss Brethren was Conrad Grebel (c 1495–1526), scion of a patrician family of Zürich. The movement spread through South Germany by traveling preachers who, rejecting the whole idea of "Christendom," said the "so-called Christians" were just as much in need of conversion as the Turks. In cities like Augsburg, Ulm and Strassburg the South German Brethren gained a large following. Their greatest leader was a layman, Pilgram Marpeck (?–1556).

Further down the Rhine, the great highway of Europe, Anabaptism was the first and for a time the strongest Protestant movement. The key leader became Menno Simons (1496–1561), and in time both the Dutch (*Doopsgezinde*) and those Swiss and South German Brethren who survived savage persecution came to be called "Mennonites." In the Dutch area the question of church discipline became acute, and the most strict congregations of Anabaptists practiced "shunning" (*Meidung*) and "churching" (the Ban, Mt. 18:15–19). A later split among the Swiss (c 1690), the Amish, introduced a parallel initiative for austerity and strictness. Menno and his colleagues shepherded little pacifist (non-resistant, Mt. 5:9, 39, 43–44) congregations and also picked up some of the broken fragments of the movement which experimented with social revolution at Münster and elsewhere.

The fourth wing of Anabaptism was the Hutterite.

Because of the stress they laid upon ethics and morals in a Christian style of life, the Anabaptists were charged by the Lutheran apologists with "monkishness" and "works-righteousness." Because they followed the general theological line of the Reformers, Catholic apologists called the Anabaptists the logical fruit of Protestant radicalism, "enthusiasm," and individualism. Individualists they were not: their practice of a strict covenant enforced by congregational discipline gave them an identity more pronounced than either Roman Catholics or Reformers. "Enthusiasts" they were not: they sought literally to restore the "True Church" of the New Testament in faith and form. Radicals they were: they broke the continuity with the Christendom of the middle ages; they taught that the restitution of the True Church was the preliminary stage to the return of all creation to its original perfection—with the peace, plenty, and communism of Eden in the end replacing the wars, violence and exploitation of a dying world.

The lineal descendants of Anabaptism are the Mennonites, Hutterites, Amish and Brethren. All are today present in strength in America, having found there a religious freedom present in an earlier Europe only in the Netherlands. The Brethren came into being as a result of the renewal impulses of Pietism, adopting the Anabaptist model of a separated and restitutionist church when they came to America (1723–35).

The influence of Anabaptism, in spite of the bad name given the movement by defenders of the established churches, spread far beyond the immediate circle of lineal descent. In the Netherlands, the leaders of refugee churches from England came in contact with them and restitutionist ideas helped shape the radical Puritanism which flowered during the Commonwealth (1649–60), in New England and elsewhere. Moreover, Confirmation was introduced into the Lutheran and Anglican communions (1534 ff.) as an answer to the Anabaptists' believer's baptism, and church discipline was built into the Calvinist church order as the "third mark" of the true church (after sound preaching and sacramental life) as a result of encounters between Martin Butzer and the Anabaptists of Strassburg and Hesse.

The world-view which identifies this breed of Christians is above all a certain periodization of church history. Restitutionist thought is in the end as distinct from state-church Protestantism as it is from Roman Catholicism.

*Menno Simons.*

◇ Hutterite colony

THE Hutterite wing of 16th century Anabaptism began in Moravia in 1529, when a little band of religious refugees from Switzerland, the Tyrol and South Germany adopted the communism of the Church at Jerusalem. Under Jakob Hutter (?–1536) they practiced a communism of consumption; a few years later their able leader Wolfgang Brandhuber reorganized their work pattern to effect a communism of production. They carried on the most active Protestant missions of the sixteenth century on that economic base. During their hightide, before their communities were destroyed by the Counter-Reformation, the Hutterites numbered some 60,000.

In their *Greater Chronicle* and *Lesser Chronicle* the Hutterites recorded their view of history. The only history of which they took note began with the great figures and events of the Bible— Abraham, Moses; the Covenant, the Exodus, Sinai. They relate how Jesus came and called the church into being. Three centuries later the church "fell" when "the cross was welded to the sword" under Constantine. During the dark ages the true Christians wandered in the wilderness like the Hebrews of old. In their own time a restitution of true Christianity set in, not including half-way men like those of Wittenberg and Zürich.

The main principles of the sixteenth century Hutterites were pacifism, communism, voluntary membership (adult baptism), separation of church and state, separation from the world. Their attitude on the authority of the Bible and on the creeds and confessions was thoroughly evangelical, and it remains so today. After generations of persecution and wandering they came a century ago to the great plains of Canada and the United States, and in the new world they have prospered mightily. They now have strong communities in the United States and Canada, totaling c 37,000 members in 400 colonies.

Perhaps the best example of outside Hutterite influence is the *Bruderhof* movement founded by Eberhard Arnold in Germany after World War I (1919). The *Bruderhof* drew its first members from the German Student Christian movement. Persecuted by the Nazis, they migrated to England, then to the USA, where they now have a dozen communities. Some years ago they undertook conversations with the Hutterites of the American western plains, but no organic union emerged.

# H. The Magisterial Reformation and Reformers

## PAPAL POLITICS: ALEXANDER VI (POPE 1492–1503) AND HIS SUCCESSORS

ALONG with the ravages of the Turks and the spread of Lutheranism, the low level of the papacy made miserable Charles V's critical early years. Alexander VI (pope: 1492–1503) was a moral degenerate. He shared responsibility for the expulsion of the Jews and Moors from Spain and Portugal, and for the killing of Savonarola (1452–98) in Florence. Savonarola, a popular Dominican preacher, had attempted to reform the morals of the city and to champion the poor.

Julius II (pope: 1503–13), although a patron of Raphael and Michelangelo, was chiefly noted for military campaigns and aggrandizement of the political claims of the papacy. His warring is memorialized scathingly in Erasmus' *In Praise of Folly*.

Leo X (pope: 1513–21), the second son of Lorenzo de Medici, was a luxury-loving incompetent who had no comprehension of what was involved in the movement surrounding Luther, whom he excommunicated.

The brief reign of Adrian VI (pope: 1522–23), the last non-Italian pope until John Paul II, effected little. A product of the Brethren of the Common Life and a Doctor of Theology from Louvain, he was a worthy man who failed to purge the Curia of corruption. Neither was he able to raise the princes of Christendom to the relief of Rhodes, center of the crusader Order of St. John, which fell to the Turks 24 October 1522.

Clement VII (pope: 1523–34), another de Medici, was vacillating and incompetent. Indecisive in the conflicts between France and Spain, he laid Rome open to the terrible sack of the city by imperial armies (1527). Procrastinating in the divorce case of Henry VIII against Catherine of Aragon, he irritated both parties and lost England.

He was equally incapable of stopping Protestantism on the continent.

*Alexander VI.*

*Julius II.*

*Leo X.*

PAPAL POLITICS: ALEXANDER VI (POPE 1492–1503) AND HIS SUCCESSORS

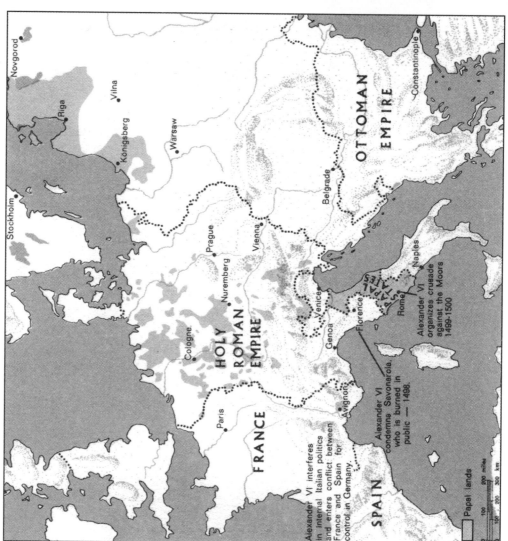

Alexander VI interferes in internal Italian politics and enters conflict between France and Spain for control in Germany.

Alexander VI condemns Savonarola, who is burned in public — 1498.

Alexander VI organizes crusade against the Moors 1499–1500.

Papal lands

*Heresy is a sin which merits not only excommunication but also death, for it is worse to corrupt the Faith which is the life of the soul than to issue counterfeit coins which minister to the secular life.*

— Thomas Aquinas, *Summa Theologica*

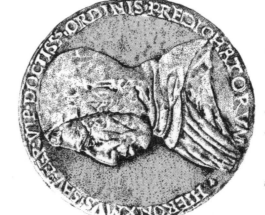

*Savonarola, from a medal.*

THE voyages of discovery brought economic and political upheaval. The universities and the invention of printing brought an intellectual ferment that dissolved medieval Christendom, its culture and power structures. To these forces must be added the slow awakening to awareness of a greatly expanded world and universe. The Protestant Reformers of the established churches used the language and authority of the Bible to attack dogmas and disciplines that had remained substantially unchallenged for centuries.

*Martin Luther.*

*I would not have missed seeing Rome for a hundred thousand florins, for then I might have been afraid of being unjust to the Pope.*
— Luther

Territory of Luther's protector, Frederick the Wise.

## MARTIN LUTHER 1483–1546

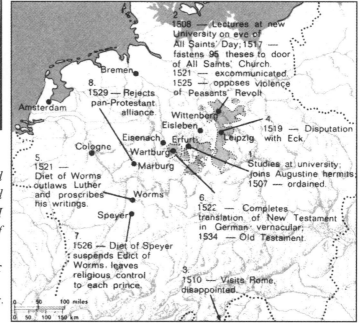

2.
1508 — Lectures at new University on eve of All Saints' Day; 1517 — fastens 95 theses to door of All Saints' Church. 1521 — excommunicated. 1525 — opposes violence of Peasants' Revolt.

8.
1529 — Rejects pan-Protestant alliance.

4.
1519 — Disputation with Eck.

5.
1521 — Diet of Worms outlaws Luther and proscribes his writings.

1.
Studies at university; joins Augustine hermits; 1507 — ordained.

6.
1522 — Completes translation of New Testament in German vernacular; 1534 — Old Testament.

7.
1526 — Diet of Speyer suspends Edict of Worms, leaves religious control to each prince.

3.
1510 — Visits Rome, disappointed.

Bremen · Amsterdam · Wittenberg · Eisleben · Leipzig · Eisenach · Erfurt · Cologne · Wartburg · Marburg · Worms · Speyer

IN an action remembered as symbolic of the breakup of West European Christendom, on 31 October 1517, Luther posted Ninety-Five Theses for debate. The central word was this, that God through Jesus Christ saves the sinner as a gift—without any deference to or dependence upon ritual procedures or even presumed personal virtue.

The place of the posting was the door of the church at the new University of Wittenberg. Luther had given lectures grounded in the Bible, which he was soon in public debate (Leipzig Disputation with Eck, 1519) to declare a higher authority than either popes or councils. In 1520 he published three of his greatest messages: "To the Christian Nobility of the German Nation" (calling on lay nobles to reform the church), "On the Babylonian Captivity of the Church" (criticizing the Roman Mass and sacramental order), and "Concerning the Freedom of a Christian Man" (affirming the precedence of faith over good works). Called to account, he refused to recant and was excommunicated. He also refused to deny his beliefs at the Imperial Diet in Worms (1521) and was for a time thereafter hidden under the protection of his prince.

Trained as a religious before he became an academic, Luther abhorred any blending of violence and war with the Gospel. He condemned the rebellions of the knights and the peasants, both of which made appeal to Christian religion. He was less patient, however, with heretics and Jews: toward both, he justified use of the sword. He looked to the nobility to act as responsible laymen, to carry out the reform of a Latin Christianity grown lazy and corrupt and lacking in clergy leadership of spiritual quality.

The churchly deference to those in political authority was to have pernicious consequences for Christianity for centuries to follow. Not until after the Holocaust did a leading German Lutheran churchman (Bishop Otto Dibelius at Hannover, 1952) distinguish adequately between subservience to "the powers that be" and obedience to "the higher powers" (Rom. 13:1).

## PHILIPP MELANCHTHON 1497–1560

*This is almost the sum of our teaching. It can be seen that nothing in it is discordant with the Scripture, or the teaching of the Catholic Church, or the Roman Church as it is known from ancient writers.*

— Melanchthon,
*Augsburg Confession*

LUTHER was little influenced by Humanism, although he used the tools of higher learning; even in his hymns and exegesis he remained a preacher. Melanchthon, by contrast, had the irenical style of a man of intellectual dialogue and the devotion to education of a teacher. Although he wrote the *Augsburg Confession* (1530) in a way to accent the common ground of Catholics and Protestants, and later participated in reunion efforts (1540, 1541), he was a true friend and supporter of Luther.

To Melanchthon must go much of the credit for consolidating and systematizing the Lutheran movement. His *Loci Communes* was the first book of Protestant dogmatics, going through many editions and revisions. He was called the "Praeceptor Germaniae" because of his extensive writings and practical work to reform and reorganize the school system—from village schools through the universities.

*(opposite) Philipp Melanchthon.*

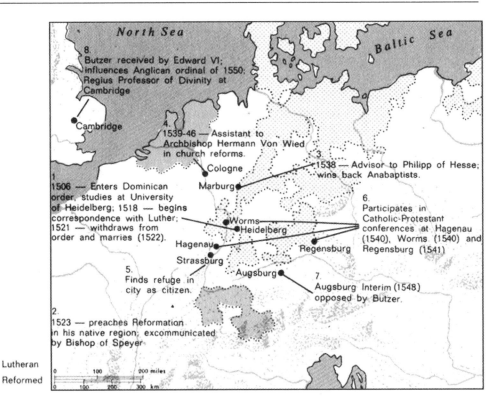

North Sea
Baltic Sea

8.
Butzer received by Edward VI;
influences Anglican ordinal of 1550;
Regius Professor of Divinity at
Cambridge

Cambridge

4.
1539-46 — Assistant to
Archbishop Hermann Von Wied
in church reforms.

Cologne

3.
1538 — Advisor to Philipp of Hesse;
wins back Anabaptists.

Marburg

1.
1506 — Enters Dominican
order, studies at University
of Heidelberg; 1518 — begins
correspondence with Luther;
1521 — withdraws from
order and marries (1522).

Worms
Heidelberg

6.
Participates in
Catholic-Protestant
conferences at Hagenau
(1540), Worms (1540) and
Regensburg (1541)

Hagenau
Strassburg
Regensburg

5.
Finds refuge in
city as citizen.

Augsburg

7.
Augsburg Interim (1548)
opposed by Butzer.

2.
1523 — preaches Reformation
in his native region; excommunicated
by Bishop of Speyer

☐ Lutheran
▨ Reformed

0    100    200 miles
0   100   200   300  km

LEADER of the movement in Strassburg, Butzer also worked as advisor to Philipp the Magnanimous in the reformation of Hesse and to Hermann von Wied in the latter's vain effort as Archbishop Elector of Cologne to effect an internal church reform.

In a vitriolic age, Butzer was remarkable for his devotion to Christian piety and compassion. At Strassburg he conducted many discussions and public debates with radical reformers. He also introduced house-meetings to further a high quality of Christian life among preachers and laymen. In Hesse his open mind and spirit helped win the Anabaptists back into the established church.

Calvin owed much to Butzer's reports and example in developing church discipline as the "third mark" of the true church, after sound biblical preaching and the right administration of the sacraments. Martin Butzer also developed the rite of Confirmation, which spread from Strassburg throughout Swiss and German Protestantism, and he introduced it into the Anglican ordinal while in England near his life's end.

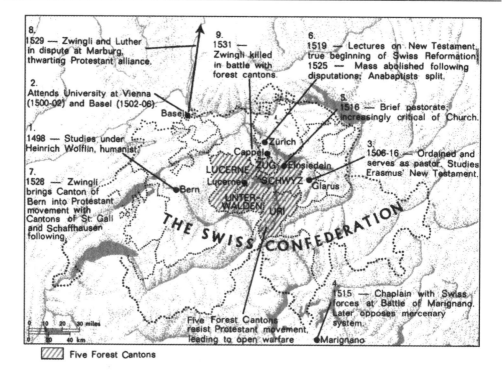

8.
1529 — Zwingli and Luther in dispute at Marburg, thwarting Protestant alliance.

9.
1531 — Zwingli killed in battle with forest cantons.

6.
1519 — Lectures on New Testament, true beginning of Swiss Reformation. 1525 — Mass abolished following disputations; Anabaptists split.

2.
Attends University at Vienna (1500-02) and Basel (1502-06).

5.
1516 — Brief pastorate; increasingly critical of Church.

1.
1498 — Studies under Heinrich Wolflin, humanist.

3.
1506-16 — Ordained and serves as pastor. Studies Erasmus' New Testament.

7.
1528 — Zwingli brings Canton of Bern into Protestant movement with Cantons of St. Gall and Schaffhausen following.

THE SWISS CONFEDERATION

Basel
Zürich
Cappel
LUCERNE ZUG Einsiedeln
Lucerne SCHWYZ
Bern UNTER-WALDEN URI Glarus

4.
1515 — Chaplain with Swiss forces at Battle of Marignano. Later opposes mercenary system.

Five Forest Cantons resist Protestant movement, leading to open warfare

Marignano

0  10  20  30 miles
0  20  40 km

▨ Five Forest Cantons

*We thirst for no man's blood, but we will cut the nerves of the oligarchy.* — Zwingli

ZWINGLI came into his own as the leading preacher of Zürich's cathedral. He was a man of the city, a citizen rather than a feudal subject, and a Humanist—three points distinguishing him from Luther. Yet Luther's writings and courageous example helped convert Zwingli from enlightened criticism of corruptions in the church to passionate reformer. His purpose was to win all Zürich to the evangelical cause, and he deferred to the cantonal government to decide what steps should be taken and when.

Zwingli was a close friend and confidant of Philipp of Hesse—the most important Protestant prince in Germany. With him he conceived of a Protestant federation extending from Switzerland to Denmark, defending the Gospel against pope, emperor, Catholic princes and Turks. This vision died at the Marburg Colloquy (1529), for Luther would not agree to an alliance with the Swiss and Strassburgers: they considered the Lord's Supper a memorial and sign of spiritual community rather than a mysterious event at which Christ was miraculously present in the bread and wine.

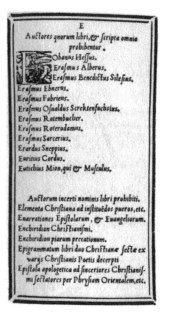

*The Index of Forbidden Books.*

*Even a dog barks if he sees anyone assault his master. How could I be silent if God's truth is assailed?*

– Calvin to Marguerite of Navarre

1. 1533-34 — Breaks with Latin Church; flees to Basel.

5. 1541 — Becomes friendly with Melanchthon at Diet of Regensburg

6. 1541-55 — Consolidates theocratic regime; approves deaths of Servetus and other "heretics"; 1555-64 — worldwide correspondence and counsel on behalf of Reformation. 1559 — Establishes Academy (University).

2. 1536 — Publishes "Institutes."

4. 1538-41 — Butzer's guest; 1540-41 — represents Strassburg at conferences of Hagenau and Worms.

3. 1536-38 — Preacher and professor of theology; publishes "Articuli de Regimine Ecclesiae"

⊞ University where Calvin studied 1522-25

➤ Calvin expelled

CALVIN belonged to the second generation of the Reformation. In *The Institutes of the Christian Religion* he presented the most clear, comprehensive, and consistent system of Christian thought worked out by a Protestant. He made Geneva a city of international importance—a place of refuge for religious persecutees of many countries, and a model of Reformed statecraft.

The austere type of Christian which Calvinism produced fitted well into the leadership of rising commercial and industrial nations. Hard work, frugality, measured decision and iron self-discipline were combined with the utter recklessness of men who were convinced that a right and true course once chosen should be pursued regardless of consequences.

Although Calvin called Luther his father-in-God, his sense of the importance of structures and the majesty of law (including Old Testament Law) led his followers toward a quite different church style and political ethics.

## THE INDEX OF FORBIDDEN BOOKS

THE books of "heretics," as well as pagan materials, were burned by imperial decree after the union of church and state under Constantine. During the middle ages the books of many important thinkers who fell into ill repute were destroyed. With the institution of the Inquisition, books were burned as well as persons.

The invention of printing complicated the problem greatly, but the Council of Trent instituted the Index of Prohibited Books (1559) to protect the minds of the faithful and to suppress criticism of the church. Even the writings of reform-minded Catholic writers were listed. One serious result was that the Roman Catholicism in Spain and Latin America remained thoroughly medieval: not only Protestant books but also the writings of Catholic liberals were prevented from circulation. A special congregation exercised the control until 1917, when its duties were transferred to the Curia.

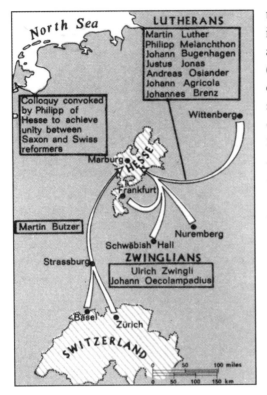

LUTHER had called upon the German princes to carry through a church reform if the pope and bishops were backward in fulfilling their duty. No royal layman took this word more seriously than Philipp of Hesse (Landgrave: 1518–67). Philipp was an avid student of the Bible and other Christian literature, a vigorous defender of the Protestant cause, and as sturdy in church reform as he was on the battlefield. He was unique among the rulers of his generation for his refusal to use the death penalty against "heretics."

Although the plunder of America brought ample specie into the coffers of Catholic Spain (including Charles V's treasury), and some was diverted by freebooters into Dutch and English treasuries, many of the German rulers were still operating in a feudal economy. Payment was made in kind. Since troops were mercenaries, a government tended to be as strong as its cash income. Philipp was fortunately situated on the great highway of Europe (Danube-Rhine river system), and could exact payment from ships passing up and down. At the Imperial Diet of 1530, where the Wittenbergers and Strassburgers and Swiss presented their arguments, the well-equipped cavalry of Philipp and his brother-in-law John of Saxony appeared carrying the same colors. The meaning of this act was not lost to Charles V, whose zeal for the old faith was balanced by his desire to hold his realm together.

The Marburg Colloquy was the high point of Philipp's effort to achieve an evangelical alliance through the theologians. When that failed, he turned to practical political solutions like the Schmalkaldic League (1531). As the most energetic political leader on the side of reformation, Philipp succeeded in bringing to his castle for the Colloquy (1529) the key theologians of the new faith: Luther, Melanchthon, Johann Bugenhagen, Justus Jonas, Andreas Osiander, Johann Agricola, Johannes Brenz, Martin Butzer, Ulrich Zwingli, Johann Oecolampadius. Bugenhagen (1485–1558) was a Wittenberg ally of Luther, who later gave substantial leadership in the reformation of Hamburg, Braunschweig, and other north German cities. He also supervised the reorganization of the Danish church and the University of Copenhagen. Jonas (1493–1555) helped reorganize the University at Wittenberg and led the reformation of Halle. Osiander (1498–1552) was an evangelical preacher at Nuremberg and then professor at Königsberg. Agricola (1494–1566) was a reformer at Frankfurt/Main and Eisleben, and later

*Philipp of Hesse.*

church superintendent in Berlin. Brenz (1499–1570) was the great reformer of Württemberg and reorganizer of the university in Tübingen. Oecolampadius (1482–1531) led the reformation in canton Basel and also won Bern to the cause.

The Marburg participants agreed upon 14 1/2 points, but the Colloquy was shattered on the doctrine of the Lord's Supper. From then on the doctrines and laws in Lutheran territories condemned the "sacramentarians" (Strassburgers and Swiss), who claimed that Christ was truly present in the community celebrating the Eucharist but not uniquely in the elements of bread and wine.

Cooperation between the theologians was only a part, if the most difficult part, of Philipp's general strategy. In the reform of his own territory he pursued a program which was very effective. With the initial help of Francis Lambert (1486–1530), who cultivated contacts at both Zürich and Wittenberg, his Bad Homburg Synod (1526) set up a model for change. First,

the church order was to be restructured on the model of the Early Church. This proved impossible for a land-church, although a plan of church discipline was later put on paper (Ziegenhain Synod, 1539). Parishes throughout Hesse were to be visited regularly by inspection teams and religious and educational reforms carried out. Nuns and monks were encouraged to convert or accept pensions: in any case, the monastic communities were to be liquidated. Second, a university was to be founded on Reformation principles. This was Marburg, the oldest Protestant university in the world (f. 1527).

On the larger map, Philipp was also imaginative and resourceful. When the papal legate formed a league of princes loyal to Rome, Philipp cultivated princes and cities friendly to the reform of the church: e.g., Brandenburg, Mecklenburg, Mansfeld, Magdeburg, Nuremberg, Augsburg, Ulm, Strass-

*The signatures at the Marburg Colloquy.*

burg. Prince Albert of Hohenzollern, Grand Master of the Teutonic Knights —who held a vast Baltic empire in fief to the pope, came over to the Lutheran side and carried East Prussia with him.

The Protestant alliance was not tested right away, for a threatened Turkish invasion produced a truce in 1532 between the Emperor and the Schmalkald League. Then Charles V was out of Germany until 1541, conducting a series of wars with Francis I of France. Among other things that happened during this relaxation of military pressure from the Roman Catholic side, the defeat of the city revolution at Münster (1534–35) may be mentioned. Philipp also intervened in Württemberg to restore the Protestant Duke Ulrich to his throne, compelling the Emperor's brother to relinquish claim to the duchy. Charles in the meantime pressed the papacy to participate in efforts at church reconci-liation (Hagenau, Worms, Regensburg, 1540–41), of which the Curia was as suspicious as the hardline Lutherans, and to call a General Council, which with papal reluctance finally started in 1545.

When Charles V returned to Germany determined to suppress Protestantism, the time was propitious. Philipp had lost heavily in public esteem through a bigamous marriage. Luther died in 1546. By 1547 both Philipp and his brother-in-law John of Saxony were defeated and imprisoned. But within five years an alliance of Moritz of Saxony and Henry II of France led to Charles V's defeat and the resurgence of the Protestant cause. After his release, Philipp gave his chief attention to Hesse. Before his death he saw Lutheranism accorded legal status in Germany, Charles V resign, and England solidly in the Reformation camp.

# THE REFORMATION IN SWITZERLAND
## 16TH CENTURY

THE original nucleus of Switzerland was the three forest cantons of Uri, Schwyz and Unterwalden. By 1513 there were thirteen cantons (six rural and seven urban) represented in a federal diet, along with a number of allied states. The role of the Swiss in European affairs was determined largely by their control of mountain passes vital to the politics of larger states. They were also much sought after as mercenaries.

In the fifteenth century the Swiss defeated Burgundy, Milan and finally the Emperor (1499), and were factually independent. Not until after the Thirty Years' War (1618–48) was that independence legally recognized, so the Swiss participated in the political disputes and church conflicts of the empire during the sixteenth century. In both politics and religion each canton retained a high degree of autonomy. From the battle of Cappel between the Catholic cantons and Zürich, in which Zwingli died while serving as a chaplain (1531), through the religious Villmergen Wars (1656, 1712), to the establishment of the French-sponsored Helvetic Republic (1798), religious divisions immobilized the nation and guaranteed cantonal autonomy. During the War of the Spanish Succession (1701–14), thousands of Swiss mercenaries fought on both sides—from Catholic cantons for

I affirm also that
your magistrate did
right in punishing,
after a regular trial,
this blasphemous
man.

— Melanchthon to
Calvin on Servetus'
death

THE REFORMATION IN SWITZERLAND 16TH CENTURY

Catholic Canton

Zwinglian and
Calvinist Canton

Mixed Canton

### Within the map:

HOLY ROMAN EMPIRE

FRANCHE-COMTÉ

Johann Oecolampadius
(1482-1531)

Mulhouse

Basel
Basel
Aarau
Aargau
Baden
Solothurn
Solothurn

Schaffhausen

Constance
Lake of Constance
Thurgau
St. Gall
St Gall
Appenzell

J. Vadianus
(1484-1551)

Ulrich Zwingli (1474-1531)
Leo Jud (1482-1548)
Heinrich Bullinger (1504-75)

April 1525 — Zürich
accepts Reformation.
1527 — Martyrdom
of Felix Manz.
1549 — Consensus
Tigurinus establishes
influence of Calvin
in Zürich.

Zürich
Zürich

Chur

Graubünden

Bormio

Valtellina

Chia-
venna

Republic of Venice

Glarus
Glarus
Zug
Schwyz
Uri
Unterwalden
1529 —
The five
cantons form the
Christian Union

Ticino

Bellinzona

Lucerne

Duchy
of
Milan

Bern
Bern

Berchtold Haller
(1492-1528)

1528 — Following
public disputation
Bern adopts Protestantism.

Fribourg
Fribourg

1536-59 —
Pierre Viret leads
Reformation in Lausanne.

Sion

Valais

Neuchâtel

Vaud

Lausanne

Lake of Geneva

Chablais

Geneva
Geneva

1530 —
Led to Reformation
by Farel.

Guillaume Farel (1489-1565)
John Calvin (1509-64)
Theodore Beza (1519-1605)

1535 — Reformers forbid
celebration of Mass.
1553 — Martyrdom of Servetus.

24 miles
30 km
12
15
0

France, from Protestant cantons for the Dutch and English. Perpetual neutrality was guaranteed a restored Switzerland at the Congress of Vienna (1815).

Ulrich Zwingli, who was born in St. Gall, served his first church in Glarus, and led the reformation of Zürich, was the most political man among the reformers. He was proud of his citizenship and determined to carry the whole canton into the cause of the Reformation. Public disputations were used to argue the issues before the citizens, although Zürich had a City Council. (In several cantons, political decisions were made in public assembly and the tradition of self-government by free men was strong in most of them.) This meant, however, that Zwingli would not move faster than the political authorities—a fact which turned his most earnest followers against him and led to their launching of what became the Swiss Brethren wing of the Anabaptist movement.

In the First Disputation (January, 1523), Zwingli and allies defeated the representatives sent by the Bishop of Constance and the city moved into reformation of the church calendar and liturgy. In the Second Disputation (October, 1523) the rift between Zwingli and the radicals surfaced. Persecution of the latter soon followed. By 1528 Bern, Basel, St. Gall and Schaffhausen had joined Zürich on the evangelical side. Shortly thereafter Guillaume Farel (1489–1565) introduced the Reformation in Neuchâtel and Geneva.

After Zwingli's premature death, the official leadership in Zürich passed to Heinrich Bullinger (1504–75), who produced the major Swiss confessions of faith: the *Consensus Tigurinus* (1549), co-authored with John Calvin, and the Second Helvetic Confession (1566). Bullinger's influence in Britain was great, for during the reign of Mary the Catholic, important Protestants found refuge in Switzerland.

The finished form of Swiss Protestantism was given largely by John Calvin, who relinquished his plan to live a life of quiet scholarship in response to Farel's appeal. From 1536 until his death, with a brief exile in Strassburg 1538–41, his leadership shaped Geneva toward a godly state (theocracy). From there his influence reached as far as Poland, Scotland, and finally New England and around the world. Calvin's system of thought made dutiful obedience to Almighty God central to the Christian life, rather than love of Christ. The representative form of church government he developed profoundly influenced the rise of republican institutions of civil government. Among his followers and interpreters, especially in France and Holland, Scotland and England, a theory of political legitimacy and of resistance to tyranny was articulated which still distinguishes Reformed from Lutheran Protestantism.

*John Calvin.*

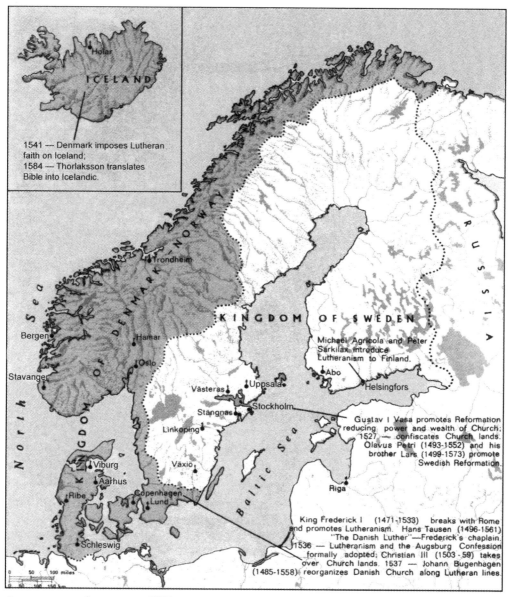

1541 — Denmark imposes Lutheran faith on Iceland;
1584 — Thorlaksson translates Bible into Icelandic.

Michael Agricola and Peter Särkilax introduce Lutheranism to Finland.

Gustav I Vasa promotes Reformation reducing power and wealth of Church; 1527 — confiscates Church lands. Olavus Petri (1493-1552) and his brother Lars (1499-1573) promote Swedish Reformation.

King Frederick I (1471-1533) breaks with Rome and promotes Lutheranism. Hans Tausen (1496-1561) "The Danish Luther"—Frederick's chaplain. 1536 — Lutheranism and the Augsburg Confession formally adopted; Christian III (1503-59) takes over Church lands. 1537 — Johann Bugenhagen (1485-1558) reorganizes Danish Church along Lutheran lines.

♟ Archbishopric　　♟ Bishopric　　▨ Kingdom of Denmark — Norway

SCANDINAVIA was governed, according to the Union of Kalmar (1397), by the monarchs of Denmark. The countries' internal affairs were for generations shaped by conflict between the crown and the nobility, the popular interest and the church, national development and the power of the Hanseatic League. In 1520 the Danish king massacred the leaders of the national Swedish party, whereupon Gustav Vasa organized a successful revolt and became king of an independent Sweden. Under Vasa's dynasty Sweden became the strongest Baltic power, holding Russia in check, defeating

*Exterior and interior of the Cathedral at Uppsala, Sweden.*

cated. Through the hymnal and Bible translation of G. Thorlaksson, the Old Norse tongue was saved and the Reformation became popular.

In Sweden, Gustavus I (Gustav Vasa, king: 1523–60) secularized the church lands and made the bishops dependent on the king. The chief preacher was Olavus Petri (1493–1552), graduate of the newly founded university at Uppsala (f. 1477) and M.A. from Wittenberg. On winning the throne, Gustavus invited Petri to Stockholm as preacher. The church was brought under royal control, the program of reformation was carried out, and most of the bishops and clergy came over to Lutheranism. "Apostolic succession" was thus maintained in Sweden, though not in Denmark.

Under Eric XIV (king: 1560–68) and Charles IX (king: 1604–11), sons of Gustav Vasa, attempts were made to eliminate the bishops and promote Calvinism. Under Sigismund (king: 1592–99, king of Poland from 1587), a devoted Catholic, efforts were made to restore the old religion. Sigismund was deposed, and Sweden persisted in the peculiar combination of old customs and Lutheran religion which obtained until disestablishment in 2000.

Poland, and decisively intervening for the Protestant cause in the German wars of religion.

As the Reformation dawned, the church owned about one third of the land of Denmark. A new university, founded in Copenhagen in 1478, became the center of ferment. Under Christian III (king: 1534–58), who was elected against the bishops' opposition, church property was secularized. A Lutheran national church was established on a plan provided by Johann Bugenhagen, who crowned the king and queen, consecrated seven new bishops, and reorganized the university.

Norway was under the Danish crown (until 1814), and the Reformation was carried through with little popular support. The archbishop, an adversary of the king, fled into exile. Two bishops became Lutherans, the others were expelled and replaced.

Under Christian III, the Roman Catholic bishops in Iceland were turned out and their property confis-

*Sigismund III.*

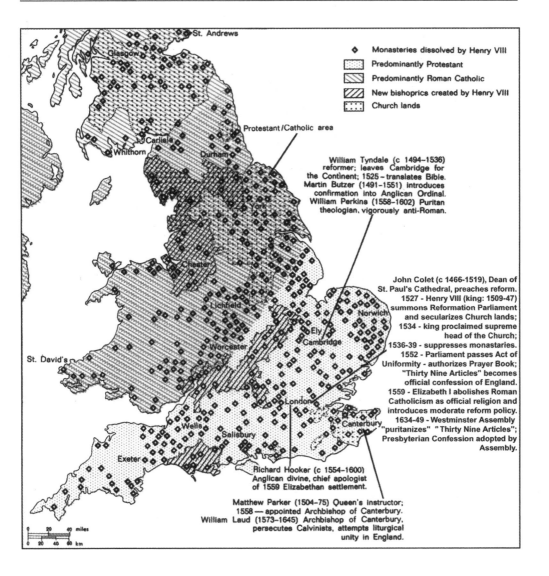

St. Andrews

◆ Monasteries dissolved by Henry VIII

Predominantly Protestant

Predominantly Roman Catholic

New bishoprics created by Henry VIII

Church lands

Glasgow

Carlisle

Whithorn

Durham

Protestant / Catholic area

**William Tyndale (c 1494–1536)** reformer; leaves Cambridge for the Continent; 1525 – translates Bible. **Martin Butzer (1491–1551)** introduces confirmation into Anglican Ordinal. **William Perkins (1558–1602)** Puritan theologian, vigorously anti-Roman.

Chester

Lichfield

Norwich

Ely

Cambridge

Worcester

St. David's

London

Wells

Salisbury

Canterbury

Exeter

**John Colet (c 1466-1519),** Dean of St. Paul's Cathedral, preaches reform. 1527 - Henry VIII (king: 1509-47) summons Reformation Parliament and secularizes Church lands; 1534 - king proclaimed supreme head of the Church; 1536-39 - suppresses monastaries. 1552 - Parliament passes Act of Uniformity - authorizes Prayer Book; "Thirty Nine Articles" becomes official confession of England. 1559 - Elizabeth I abolishes Roman Catholicism as official religion and introduces moderate reform policy. 1634-49 - Westminster Assembly "puritanizes" "Thirty Nine Articles"; Presbyterian Confession adopted by Assembly.

**Richard Hooker (c 1554–1600)** Anglican divine, chief apologist of 1559 Elizabethan settlement.

**Matthew Parker (1504–75)** Queen's instructor; 1558 — appointed Archbishop of Canterbury. **William Laud (1573–1645)** Archbishop of Canterbury, persecutes Calvinists, attempts liturgical unity in England.

0  20  40  miles
0  20  40  60  km

*I take it as a matter of faith, that no man should follow the Pope, or even any of the saints in heaven, except as they follow Christ.* — John Wycliffe

*Be of good comfort, Master Ridley, we shall this day light such a candle by God's grace in England as, I trust shall never be put out.*
— Latimer to Ridley before martyrdom (Oxford, 1555)

THE measures which Henry VIII (king: 1509–47) undertook to control the church in his realm were little different from those taken by many others, including most who remained Catholics. Henry's case attracted rabid attention for two reasons. First, he managed to confuse hopelessly the matter of England's relations to Rome with the sensational series of events in his own marital life. Second, for over a century and a half it remained uncertain which way the balance would tilt in England—to Catholicism or Protestantism, and if to Protestantism what kind it would be.

*The executions of Thomas More and John Fisher.*

Henry VIII started as a prince of rarest promise, a star of the northern Renaissance with its combination of Humanistic learning and Christian ethical concern. In 1521 he won from the pope the title of "Defender of the Faith" (a title still carried by the British monarch) for his refutation of Luther. His troubles began when, having no male heir and only one surviving child (Mary), he sought to put away his first wife. The argument was stronger than usual in such cases: she had been his brother's wife, a marriage for his father's convenience, and a papal dispensation had been necessary to accomplish what many at the time had considered dubious. But the argument was not strong enough: his wife was Catherine of Aragon, aunt to Emperor Charles V, who was closer at hand and much more dangerous for the pope to offend than Henry. So the arrangement of an annulment, a commonplace among persons of high station and sufficient wealth, failed. The other common solution shipwrecked on Anne Boleyn's ambition and Henry's pride. Most of the rulers of the day, not to mention princes of the church, kept a stable of mistresses and concubines. But Anne would be queen and the king would have it so. It took from 1527 to 1533 to accomplish, in the process of which the sovereign was made Head of the Church in England and the tie to Rome was broken.

Elizabeth was born in 1533. The crown confiscation of the monasteries was completed in 1536–39.

Henry VIII left three children. Edward VI (king: 1547–53), son of Jane Seymour, came to the throne at the age of ten. Under the regent a number of changes were made in the church, including the use of English and the giving of communion in both kinds. A new ordinal and the First and Second Books of Common Prayer were introduced, their use enforced by severe penalties. Strong influence from Protestantism on the continent, including work on the Books of Common Prayer by Martin Butzer and Peter Martyr, was felt in both church and university.

Mary Tudor succeeded (queen: 1553–

*Title page of the Great Bible (1539) with foreword by Thomas Cranmer, author of the Book of Common Prayer.*

58) and married Philip II of Spain. The alliance with Spain was unpopular; in a resulting war with France, England lost Calais—the last outpost of a once great continental empire. Mary's efforts to return the country to the old religion produced many hundred martyrdoms —Thomas Cranmer, Hugh Latimer, Nicholas Ridley and John Hooper among them.

With the accession of Elizabeth I (queen: 1558–1603), many prominent Protestant refugees returned from exile in Frankfurt, Zürich, and Geneva. The Roman Catholic position on her legitimacy (all of the bishops rejected the Oath of Allegiance and refused to take part in the coronation) pushed Elizabeth toward Protestantism. With the appointment of Matthew Parker (Archbishop of Canterbury: 1559–75), the chaos in the church was reduced and a middle ground cleared in doctrinal and liturgical matters.

With the relations of church and state still very close, Roman Catholic opposition was considered treasonous as well as heterodox. In 1570 the pope excommunicated Elizabeth (who was not a member of his church) and released her subjects from allegiance. In 1587 the queen ordered the execution of Mary Stuart, a rallying point for Roman Catholic conspiracies. In 1588 Philip II sent the Grand Armada against her; but it was shattered by a great storm at sea. England became the most powerful Protestant power in Europe.

Even within the established church Puritanism was growing. The publication of the bestseller, *Foxe's Book of Martyrs* (1563), strengthened the Puritan cause and view of holy history, as well as further discrediting "Bloody Mary" and her religion.

Disabilities against Roman Catholics

*William Tyndale.*

were law in England until the nineteenth century. Under Paul VI (pope: 1963–78) a number of martyrs under Elizabeth's rule were beatified.

Among "reformers before the reformation," John Wycliffe (c 1329–84) was the most important person in England. Although his longest years were spent as a scholar and lecturer at Oxford, he is best remembered for his efforts toward church reform in the last years of his life. In books on divine and civil dominion he argued that all ownership is God's, and that God grants the use of property only to faithful stewards. Those who misused their holdings, including ecclesiastics, could be removed. A worldly pope was dangerous and should be removed— an explosive doctrine during the decline of papal reputation which attended the Avignon papacy and the Schism. Wycliffe sent out traveling preachers ("Lollards") to distribute the Bible, the supreme authority, in translation.

William Tyndale (c 1494–1536), trained at Oxford, also prepared the way for reformation by his translations of OT and NT into English from the Hebrew and Greek.

Among Humanists, who inveighed against corruption in the church and cultivated learning, John Colet (c 1466–

1519) should be mentioned. He delivered a series of lectures on the NT Epistles at Oxford, notable for their devotion to the order of the primitive church. His friend Thomas More (1478–1535) was also devoted to the classics. More's *Utopia* was a vision of the ideal community. In this and more controversial writings he attacked abuses in the church. Colet and More were friends of Erasmus and longed for the same kind of ethical and reasonable reform.

*Hugh Latimer.*

*Thomas Cranmer.*

Thomas Cranmer (1489–1556) became Archbishop of Canterbury because his views of royal prerogatives ("Erastianism") pleased Henry VIII. He managed the break with Rome and served the king during his marital difficulties. Influential under Edward VI, he died at the stake under Mary Tudor. He made England a haven for continental refugees like Martin Butzer and Peter Martyr.

Nicholas Ridley (c 1500–55) was Cranmer's chaplain, and his ally while Bishop of London. He worked on the 1549 Book of Common Prayer and helped establish Protestantism at Cambridge. He was martyred under Mary Tudor.

Hugh Latimer (c 1485–1555) became one of the king's advisors when Henry VIII broke with the pope. He was famous for his sermons on social justice and school reform. He enjoyed great popularity as court preacher under Edward VI and died a martyr with Ridley at Oxford during Mary's reprisals. Latimer did not believe in unqualified obedience to any ruler, and during one of Henry VIII's pendulum swings toward Catholicism (Statute of the Six Articles, 1539) he resigned his episcopacy rather than submit.

John Hooper (?–1555) was educated at Oxford and spent some years studying with Protestants on the continent (Zwingli, Bullinger, Butzer). As a bishop under Edward he was famous for his espousal of Reformed church views and for his Puritan writings. He too was martyred under Mary.

*Nicholas Ridley.*

Matthew Parker (1504–75) was Archbishop of Canterbury under Elizabeth I. He had identified himself with the cause of church reform while still a student at Cambridge, received preferments under Henry VIII and Edward VI, survived in obscurity under Mary Tudor. The regularity of Parker's episcopal consecration is disputed between Anglicans and Roman Catholics. He was responsible for the issuance of the Thirty-Nine Articles, the "Bishops' Bible," and instructions on the ritual (*Advertisements*, 1566).

*Matthew Parker.*

Richard Hooker (c 1554–1600) developed the foremost apologetic for the Elizabethan settlement: *The Laws of Ecclesiastical Polity*. Against the Puritan reliance upon biblical instructions Hooker elaborated a philosophy of natural law, divine and absolute, under which human laws and institutions must be formed and changed according to circumstance.

For more than a century it was uncertain whether the Church of England, once separated from Rome, should become episcopal or presbyterian—or even congregational—in government. Among conservative Puritans, Thomas Cartwright (1535–1603) was the most gifted spokesman. He suffered exile under both Mary Tudor and Elizabeth, being a Puritan opponent of the inclusive state-church conceived by Parker and Hooker. In 1570 he was hounded out of his professorship at Cambridge. He was associated with *The Admonition to Parliament* (1572), which demanded a non-episcopal constitution for the Church of England and also condemned "papist" practices retained in the ritual. He wrote the *Millenary Petition* presented to James I on his accession (1603).

Among conservative Puritans, William Perkins (1558–1602) was also well-known on the continent as well as popular in England. He taught and lectured at Cambridge, and his writings circulated widely among Calvinists; they later, in translation, considerably influenced German Pietism.

Among radical Puritans, who had no interest in the establishment's hierarchy except to condemn them as signs of the "fallen" church, Robert Browne (c 1550–1633) was an early and important figure. At Cambridge he was influenced by Thomas Cartwright and immediately began to establish independent congregations. Jailed for schism, on release he took his Norwich congregation to the Netherlands and wrote there—among other items—the famous *Treatise of Reformation Without Tarrying for Anie* (1582). Although Browne later made submission, his program of a restored New Testament church without hierarchy was influential in radical Puritanism. John Smyth (c 1554–1612) and Thomas Helwys (c 1550–c 1616) were founders of Baptist congregations, working as refugees in the Netherlands as well as in England. Helwys' *Declaration of the Mystery of Iniquity* (1611), printed in Holland, was the first plea for universal religious toleration and denial of government authority in religious matters to be written by an Englishman.

*

CALVINISM strongly affirmed the fulfillment of God's promises and the attainment of His purposes in human history. A deterministic view may develop, according to which there is no such thing as an accidental or meaningless event, although the sense of things may be hidden from human understanding. The desire to emphasize God's omnipotence leads in strict circles to perceiving in damnation as well as salvation the working of God's foresight and intention.

In Christian life this tends to produce—among those who can give a clear testimony—an assurance of their own salvation. A person who has once known God's grace cannot fall from grace, but perseveres in the path of self-discipline (and perhaps self-sacrifice) set before him.

As to salvation history, Calvinism appropriates for Christians the covenant with Abraham and identification with the unique and archetypal events of Old Testament history. There is but one covenant, without a split between the Old Testament and New Testament. Through Christ, believing gentiles are grafted into a history that is already moving and purposeful, and they worship a God who made Himself known through prophets and apostles before Jesus. By serious study of the record of God's earlier action in human history, the man of faith can see in the events of his own time evidence that He is faithful who has promised and that His hand is outstretched to protect those whose trust is in the Lord.

In English Puritanism this consciousness of reliving biblical history was so fundamental that it became an unconscious assumption. Children were given Old Testament names, and adults assumed them among intimates. Coupled with this was the certainty that history was moving with gathering speed toward its consummation: the return of Christ and the ushering in of the Kingdom of God on earth. The faithful read their prophecies and meditated upon the signs of the times. Many of them—especially when they emerged from hiding during the Commonwealth—gathered as "Christian sabbatarians" into separate communities observing the Jewish law and the Sabbath. Others formed covenanting congregations, restoring the ordinances of the Early Church in eager anticipation of the coming restoration of all things.

## NEW ALIGNMENTS OF CHRISTIAN EUROPE
### LATER 16TH CENTURY

AT the opening of the sixteenth century there were important reform impulses within Spanish and Italian Catholicism, Juan de Valdés (c 1500–41) was a Castilian whose devotional writings became classics. In Naples he was the leader of a group of highborn laymen eager for reform and renewal of the church. Peter Martyr (1500–62), a friend of Valdés, was a leading Augustinian prior who in the course of intense biblical studies came under the influence of Butzer and Zwingli. He became a Reformer. Bernardino Ochino (1487–1564) was another of Valdés's associates. Born in Siena, he rose to be General of the Franciscans and then head of the stricter Capuchins. Converted to the evangelical cause, he was pastor to the Italian Protestant congregation in Augsburg. In his last years he traveled to Poland, where the Minor

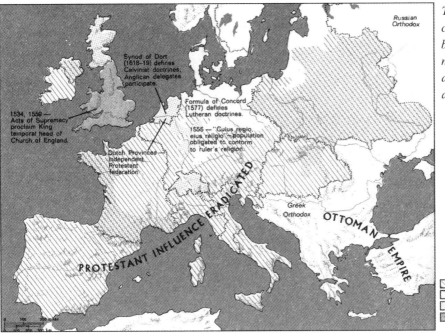

**NEW ALIGNMENTS OF CHRISTIAN EUROPE**

Church was pursuing a radical reformation. There were others. But even Ignatius and the Jesuits fell into disfavor from time to time with the Inquisition; any less obedient mystics, humanists or advocates of renewal were simply driven into exile or killed.

In the process of tightening up discipline and providing a more vigorous church operation, the leaders of the Latin church at the Council of Trent created a new thing: the Roman Catholic Church. Excluded from it were the Lutherans and Calvinists and English Protestants, who were also heirs to the Catholic traditions and teachers of earlier centuries. Only the Radical Reformation, which claimed to have jumped the centuries between the Early Church and the restitution of the True Church, would feel no deprivation.

In 1577 the Lutheran churches drew up in their Formula of Concord a precise and definitive statement of belief. Leaders in the project included Jacob Andreae (1528–90) and Martin Chemnitz (1522–86). Romanism and Calvinism, and also the more irenic

*The Council of Trent.*

*Hugo Grotius, called "the father of international law."*

positions of Melanchthon, were excluded. In addition to the formula, the 1580 Book of Concord published the ancient creeds—and the more recent Lutheran statements. Representatives of many German state-churches signed the Concordia, along with several thousand pastors and teachers.

In 1618–19, at the Synod of Dort, Calvinists from the Netherlands, England, Switzerland, Scotland, the German Palatinate and other states performed a similar work for their sector of Christendom. Here again the decisions were aimed against moderates of their own movement as well as against the Lutherans and Roman Catholics. Moderate Calvinism, whose leading personalities were Jakob Arminius (1560–1609) and Hugo Grotius (1583–1645), was condemned. Hardline statements on election, atonement, total depravity, grace, and the perseverence of the saints were adopted. Dominant in the formulation of Calvinist orthodoxy was Francis Gomar (1563–1641).

There was internal resistance to all three of the confessional positions

defined, but Catholic moderates were suppressed after Trent, Lutheran moderates after the Concordia, Calvinist moderates after Dort. In France the Tridentine formulae were never published. In Denmark the Formula of Concord was never adopted. In the Church of England the Calvinist line later lost out to an inclusive via media between Protestantism and Roman Catholicism. Nevertheless, as divisive as the three polarized positions seemed at first glance, they gave doctrinal and disciplinary uniformity to larger areas of Christendom than had ever before experienced it.

During the Middle Ages the Latin church had adapted to the most varied customs and practices. After Trent, the Concordia and Dort, theological and liturgical and church orders were uniform over large areas. The training of the laity was provided for. Institutions for theological education of the clergy were strengthened and increased in number. The self-consciousness and sense of historical mission of each of the three confessions were greatly augmented.

All three affirmed a continuity of Christian history, beginning with the Church Fathers and early creeds and including teachers and saints of the Middle Ages like Anselm and Francis of Assisi and Bernard of Clairvaux. The major watershed was the Roman Catholic insistence upon the finality of papal authority and the Protestant insistence upon the finality of biblical rule. With rare individual exceptions, none of the three paid much attention to Eastern Orthodoxy. As for the Anabaptists, who repudiated all three for belonging to the "fallen" period of church history, all three establishments agreed they were heretics and should be put to death.

# I. Wars of Religion

Anabaptism, radical Puritanism and Pietism all had radical social and economic consequences, although such derived indirectly from their understanding and practice of the Christian life—not from a direct attack on the problems of the world. Many of their practices were later "secularized" and contributed much to the development of democracy: the style of discussion leading to a consensus; the form of a church meeting into a town meeting (and even House of Commons' discussion procedures); the right of women equally to be heard and to help in decision-making; even recognition of the validity of conscientious objection to participation in war was achieved in societies having respect for freedom of conscience.

Beside the Anabaptists there were three other types of radical reformers deserving mention, and one of them advocated political as well as religious revolution.

Anti-Trinitarianism, of which Michael Servetus (1511–53) and the Sozzinis (Lelio: 1525–62, Fausto: 1539–1604) are the best known spokesmen, appeared in strength among sixteenth-century intellectuals and influenced especially churches in Poland and the Netherlands. Servetus, a native of Navarre, shocked Protestants and Roman Catholics both with his book *Concerning the Errors of the Trinity* (1531). Denounced in the Inquisition, he escaped to Geneva, only to be burned there as a heretic. His death produced some of the finest tracts written on religious liberty up to that time (including Sebastian Castellio's *On Heretics and Those Who Burn*

*Michael Servetus.*

*Them*, 1554). Fausto Sozzini was leader of the Polish "Minor Church" for a quarter of a century.

A third type, after Anabaptism and Anti-Trinitarianism, was the individual spiritualizer. Typical of these men, who rejected doctrinal names and party caucuses and proclaimed a non-sectarian (*unpartheyisches*) Christianity, were Sebastian Franck (c 1499–c 1542) and Caspar Schwenckfeld (1490–1561). The spiritualizers (*Spiritualisten*) were scandalized by the intolerant language of Roman Catholic and Protestant controversialists and concerned for the unity of Christians. Like the Anabaptists, they rejected war and violence and advocated freedom of conscience. Franck's *Weltbuch* (1531) is one of the most impressive volumes of Christian history, noteworthy especially for its careful citation of sources—even the statements of his enemies. Schwenckfeld's letters and tracts contain some of the purest writing in defense of freedom of conscience ever penned.

A fourth type of radical reformer was the social revolutionary. Thomas Müntzer (c 1490–1525), who has enjoyed a revival of reputation due to Marxist attention (Engels, Kautsky, Bax, Block, Smirin, among others), was such a man. Breaking away from Lutheranism, he organized a "Gideon's Band" of Christian revolutionaries and in the name of the gospel called upon the nobility to give up their privileges and share their properties. When this appeal failed he denounced them, sided with the peasants of Thuringia in their unsuccessful revolt, and was captured, tortured, and killed.

Another ex-Lutheran preacher, Bernt Rothmann (c 1495–1535), was agitator in a revolt of artisans and peasants who seized control of Münster in Westphalia (1534–35). Rothmann's most influential books were *The Restitution of True and Sound Christian Teaching*, in which he said that there had been until now no true church for fourteen hundred years, and *The Book of Wrath*, in which he called upon the people to rise up and slay the godless oppressors. Communism was introduced on the model of the Church at Jerusalem. Polygamy was introduced during the siege, following the example of the Old Testament patriarchs. The city was besieged and captured by combined Protestant and Roman Catholic forces; its king and prophet and councillors were tortured and slain. At the time of the 1919 revolution in Germany, iron cages with a few bleached fragments of their bones still hung on the tower of the St. Lambert Church.

Because of the polemical attacks of the Reformers and the Roman Catholics, "Anabaptists" became a term comparable to "Communists" in the twentieth century. Court testimonies show, however, that the authorities were well aware of the difference between Christian communism of the Hutterite type and the violent communism set up at Münster in 1534–35.

*Thomas Müntzer.*

*(below) Thomas Müntzer preaching, woodcut, 1527.*

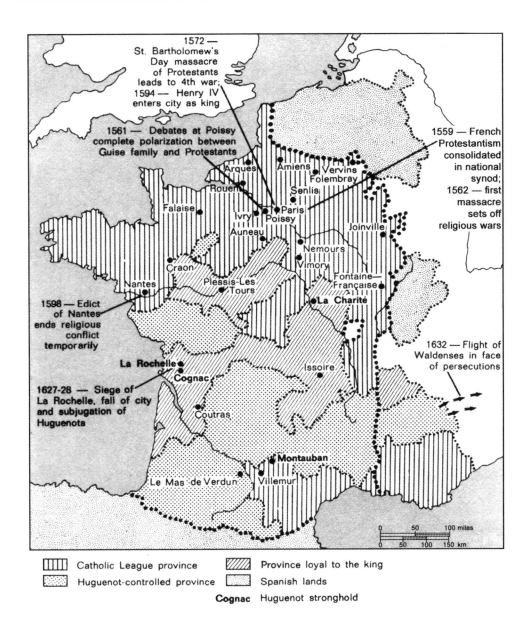

1572 — St. Bartholomew's Day massacre of Protestants leads to 4th war; 1594 — Henry IV enters city as king

1561 — Debates at Poissy complete polarization between Guise family and Protestants

1559 — French Protestantism consolidated in national synod; 1562 — first massacre sets off religious wars

1598 — Edict of Nantes ends religious conflict temporarily

1632 — Flight of Waldenses in face of persecutions

1627-28 — Siege of La Rochelle, fall of city and subjugation of Huguenots

Arques Amiens Vervins Folembray Rouen Senlis Falaise Ivry Poissy Paris Auneau Joinville Craon Nemours Vimory Nantes Plessis-Les-Tours Fontaine-Française La Charité La Rochelle Cognac Issoire Coutras Montauban Le Mas de Verdun Villemur

| | | |
|---|---|---|
| ▥ Catholic League province | ▨ Province loyal to the king | |
| ▦ Huguenot-controlled province | ▢ Spanish lands | |
| **Cognac** Huguenot stronghold | | |

For a time it was not clear whether France would go Roman Catholic or Protestant. Calvinism won a large following among the French nobility (from 40 to 50 percent) and carried the merchant and manufacturing middle class with it. On 15 April 1598 the Edict of Nantes was issued, granting freedom of the Reformed religion to certain high nobles and to citizens of specified cities and towns. In the end the French Protestants, Huguenots, had to choose between forced conversion and exile: following the Revocation of the Edict of Nantes, over 50,000 families left the country.

In 1561 a Disputation was held at Poissy, near Paris, with a confrontation between Roman Catholic leaders headed by Cardinal de Tournon and Calvinists led by Theodore Beza.

The religious wars broke out in 1562.

Many thousands of Protestants were surprise victims of the St. Bartholomew's Day Massacre, 1572. Henry of Navarre (king: 1589–1610) outwitted his competition for the throne by becoming Roman Catholic and defeating them on the diplomatic and military fields of action.

For most of his first three decades as monarch, Louis XIV (king: 1643–1715) was dominated by Cardinal Mazarin; during most of the later years he was totally under the influence of his favorite mistress, Madame de Maintenon, a devout Catholic. His constant wars over a long reign not only weakened France economically but in spite of early victories ended in the loss of major objectives. The Netherlands achieved total independence. The Protestant succession in England was recognized, and the Stuart pretender banished from France. France lost Nova Scotia, Newfoundland and Hudson Bay territory, retaining only Quebec in the new world. The French were excluded from Italy, ending centuries of title and influence there. The Revocation of the Edict of Nantes (1685) was but one of many expensive blunders by a bad king, whose disastrous reign prepared his country for revolution.

## THE FLIGHT OF THE HUGUENOTS 16TH–18TH CENTURIES

THE strength of the Huguenots lay in commerce and industry, in the nobility, and among officers of the army and navy. During the French wars of religion the performance of the Huguenot cavalry was excellent, but close order drill had not yet been introduced among French Calvinist infantry.

After the Revocation of the Edict of Nantes (1685), those who remained in France came under increasingly brutal repressive measures. Quite apart from the dangers of assassination and murder, dangers which increased with each year of Louis XIV's reign, their political and economic life space steadily narrowed. Their children were taken from them for compulsory Roman Catholic education, mounted troops (dragonnades) were sent to attack their homes and churches, no marriage performed by their ministers was accorded legal status. The political rights won and contracted at the accession of Henry IV were withdrawn by an absolutist king who ruled "by divine right."

Before the final break some Huguenot writers developed a sturdy doctrine of the right of resistance to tyranny. Calvin himself had defined a limited right, in which the lesser magistrates might act against a higher magistrate in cases of extremity. In France—as also in Scotland during the same period—his followers pursued the logic of the representative system to a more forceful conclusion: a Christian man has not only the right but the duty to resist, and if necessary to depose, a ruler who breaks the higher law (so Francis Hotman, Samuel Rutherford).

England, the Netherlands, Zürich and Geneva, Prussia and the other Protestant German states opened their doors to the Huguenot refugees.

The Huguenot refugees had been persons of substance and superior education. Their contribution to the spread of republican principles was substantial wherever they sunk new roots.

*St. Bartholomew's Day massacre by François Dubois de Amiens.*

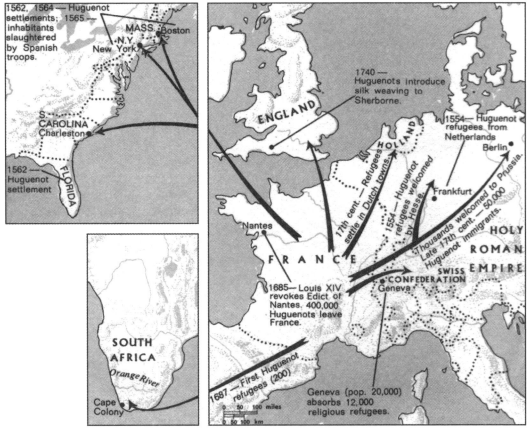

1562, 1564 — Huguenot settlements; 1565 — inhabitants slaughtered by Spanish troops.

MASS. Boston
N.Y.
New York

S. CAROLINA
Charleston

1562 — Huguenot settlement

FLORIDA

SOUTH AFRICA
Orange River

Cape Colony

1740 — Huguenots introduce silk weaving to Sherborne.

1554 — Huguenot refugees from Netherlands
Berlin

ENGLAND

HOLLAND

17th cent. — Refugees settle in Dutch towns.

1554 — Huguenot refugees welcomed by Hesse.

Frankfurt

Thousands welcomed to Prussia. Late 17th cent. — 50,000 Huguenot immigrants.

HOLY ROMAN EMPIRE

Nantes

FRANCE

SWISS CONFEDERATION
Geneva

1685 — Louis XIV revokes Edict of Nantes. 400,000 Huguenots leave France.

1687 — First Huguenot refugees (200)

Geneva (pop. 20,000) absorbs 12,000 religious refugees.

0  50  100 miles
0  50  100 km

## THE FLIGHT OF THE HUGUENOTS
### 16TH–18TH CENTURIES

# CIVIL WAR IN THE NETHERLANDS
## 16TH CENTURY

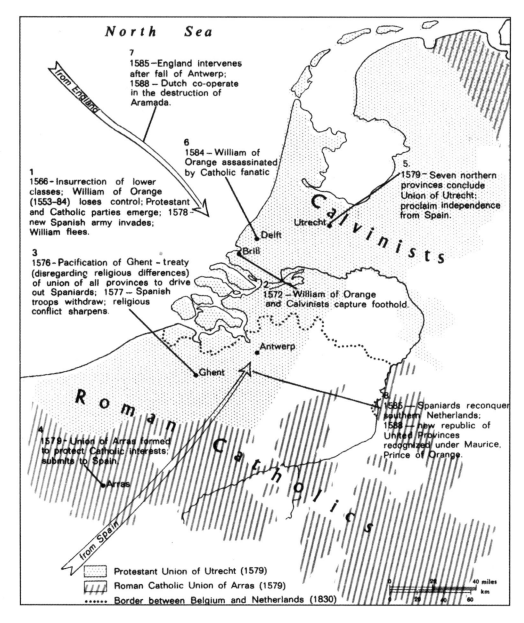

North Sea

**7**
1585 – England intervenes after fall of Antwerp; 1588 – Dutch co-operate in the destruction of Aramada.

from England

**6**
1584 – William of Orange assassinated by Catholic fanatic

**1**
1566 – Insurrection of lower classes; William of Orange (1553–84) loses control; Protestant and Catholic parties emerge; 1578 – new Spanish army invades; William flees.

**5.**
1579 – Seven northern provinces conclude Union of Utrecht; proclaim independence from Spain.

Calvinists

Utrecht

Delft

**3**
1576 – Pacification of Ghent – treaty (disregarding religious differences) of union of all provinces to drive out Spaniards; 1577 – Spanish troops withdraw; religious conflict sharpens.

Brill

**2**
1572 – William of Orange and Calvinists capture foothold.

Antwerp

Ghent

Roman Catholics

**4**
1579 – Union of Arras formed to protect Catholic interests; submits to Spain.

**8**
1585 – Spaniards reconquer southern Netherlands; 1588 – new republic of United Provinces recognized under Maurice, Prince of Orange.

Arras

from Spain

░░░ Protestant Union of Utrecht (1579)
//// Roman Catholic Union of Arras (1579)
••••• Border between Belgium and Netherlands (1830)

0    20    40 miles
km
0    20    40    60

FOR six hundred years the lowlands belonged to a middle kingdom between the Frankish and Germanic powers—after Charlemagne, to Lothringia; later, to Burgundy. In the period of our present concern they were divided linguistically and culturally into Dutch in the north, Flemings in the center, and French-speaking Walloons in the south. By dynastic politics they became part of the inheritance of Charles V, and in 1548 he annexed the seventeen provinces. He had grown up there, although he made Spain his primary base of operations as emperor. The provinces had long enjoyed important legal privileges, and their strategic location at the crossroads of the Rhine

River and the sea routes to England and the new world had produced a considerable growth in cash economy.

During the century before the Reformation the Netherlands became the chief center of a movement of spiritual renewal in the church and in the cultural renaissance among intellectuals. The earliest reform teaching to gain support was Anabaptist, which led some scholars of an older generation to see a peculiar affinity between the Christian humanism of Erasmus and the ethical rigor of Menno Simons. But the Protestant doctrines which most appealed to the rising shipping and industrial and commercial elements were Calvinist. In 1571 Guido de Brès (1522–67) prepared the Belgic Confession, drawing heavily on the *Confessio Gallicana* adopted in the first synod of French Huguenots (Paris, 1559). The Belgic Confession denounced Anabaptism and made a firm statement of Calvinist principle; adopted in synods at Antwerp (1566) and Dort (1619), it committed the Netherlands to the Reformed line. Another important Dutch Calvinist theologian, who also became a leader in the Dutch struggle for independence, was Philip van Marnix (1538–98). Marnix was a personal disciple of Calvin and Beza and a close advisor to William the Silent. In 1547 the University of Leyden was founded to advance Calvinism.

In the meantime, Philip II had come to the Spanish throne and introduced measures for the suppression of Protestantism which soon led to religious and political rebellion in the Netherlands. His attempt to use Roman Catholicism to strengthen his control, notably in the creation of five new bishoprics and elevation of Utrecht to an archbishopric, was a failure. National self-consciousness came first, while the old feudal loyalties to dynasties were fading, and the public appeal which rallied the lowlands to resistance was issued by Lutheran, Roman Catholic and Calvinist members of the nobility.

Withdrawing to Spain, Philip II attempted to rule the lowlands through his illegitimate sister Margaret of Parma and her advisor Bishop Granella, supported by the occupation troops of the Duke of Alva. The south, which later became Belgium (1830), remained Roman Catholic. But in the north the United Provinces declared their independence and after much struggle and suffering—and with the help of their English partners in trade—won their freedom.

The leader in the struggle for independence was William the Silent (1533–84), a convinced Protestant and dedicated patriot. Although Philip next sent the popular hero of Lepanto, his illegitimate brother Don Juan of Austria, as governor, neither Alva's cruelty nor Don Juan's popularity could quiet the country. William was made heredi-

*William the Silent.*

*The "Sea Beggars" capture Brill, 1572.*

tary ruler (*Statthalter*). Philip II put a price on his head, and like Henry IV of France he was assassinated by a Roman Catholic zealot, but this only strengthened the Calvinist provinces in their determination and weakened the Spanish party in Roman Catholic territory. William was far in advance of his age in his appreciation of religious as well as political freedom. Having spent his boyhood in Hesse, where his cousin Philip the Magnanimous had given the only example of royal toleration in the first half of the century, William's first act as ruler was to issue a decree of religious toleration. Following this lead the Netherlands—although the Mennonite and Calvinist churches maintained vigorous internal discipline—became the foremost European nation in respecting the dignity and integrity and freedom of conscience of the human person.

Dutch and English sea power, with foundations already laid in ocean trade, grew rapidly in this period. Their freebooters raided the Spanish convoys from the new world. After the defeat of the Spanish Armada (1588), they began to conquer the Portuguese colonial possessions and even intervened in Portugal itself. In this they were aided by native Portuguese unrest over the poor treatment they received while subject to the Spanish crown and its representatives (1580–1640).

Following the achievement of independence, finally confirmed by the Treaties of Westphalia (1648), the Netherlands enjoyed a period of great prosperity and cultural renewal. The work of Rembrandt (1606–69) was a high mark in this tide of religious and cultural renaissance.

*Rembrandt's* Abraham and the Angels *(left) and* The Anger of Saul.

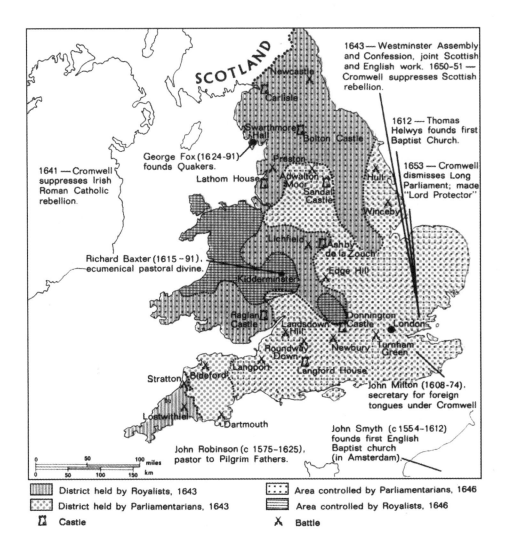

1643 — Westminster Assembly and Confession, joint Scottish and English work. 1650-51 — Cromwell suppresses Scottish rebellion.

1612 — Thomas Helwys founds first Baptist Church.

1653 — Cromwell dismisses Long Parliament; made "Lord Protector"

George Fox (1624-91) founds Quakers.

1641 — Cromwell suppresses Irish Roman Catholic rebellion.

Richard Baxter (1615 - 91), ecumenical pastoral divine.

John Milton (1608-74), secretary for foreign tongues under Cromwell

John Smyth (c 1554-1612) founds first English Baptist church (in Amsterdam).

John Robinson (c 1575-1625), pastor to Pilgrim Fathers.

| | |
|---|---|
| ▦ District held by Royalists, 1643 | ⬚ Area controlled by Parliamentarians, 1646 |
| ▦ District held by Parliamentarians, 1643 | ▤ Area controlled by Royalists, 1646 |
| ⛫ Castle | ✗ Battle |

*The poorest he that is in England hath a life to live as the richest he.*

— Col. Rainborough, Leveller, in the New Model Army debates.

JAMES Stuart (king of Scotland: 1567–1625) succeeded to the throne of England in 1603 as James I. He was immediately presented in London with a Millenary Petition of the Puritans, which begged to be relieved of mere human rites and ceremonies which burdened the church. Committed to a repudiation of all acculturations and accruements which had been added during the "fallen" period of Christianity, they listed a number of objectionable customs—including confirmation, the surplice, desecration of the Sabbath, use of the apocryphal books in the services. A few months later the episcopal and Puritan parties came at the king's call to Hampton Court, and there James gave his support to the episcopal cause in the Church of England: "No bishop, no king." The "Divine Right of Kings" and "Apostolic Succession" were thus joint articles of the royal will. The most permanently useful result of the meet-

*James I.*

ist interests converged. By 1646 the New Model Army had defeated the royal forces. In 1649 Charles I was condemned to death for defying the law of the land.

The man who led the forces of popular sovereignty and untrammeled religion was Oliver Cromwell (1599–1657, Lord Protector from 1653). Cromwell was a member of parliament and a congregationalist leader who turned out to be also a military genius. His psalm-singing foot soldiers not only regularly defeated much larger forces of royalists: they also defeated Scottish and Irish armies and intervened on behalf of the Waldenses in France and Savoy. Although offered the post of king, Cromwell refused it: he exercised power ably, but he did not enjoy it, and he preferred most to be known as the defender of political and religious liberties. As the debates in the army show, he believed that a sound government was grounded in full and responsible discussion, discussion pointing toward a consensus, discussion carried on with the full and unintimidated participation of every loyal citizen. The sense of propriety, of respect for the basic liberties, of concern for due process of law, of the superiority of the law to government itself—all of these owe much to Cromwell. Although those who conspired against Parliament were sometimes harshly put down, even the most despised sect or church or prophet could look to the Protector for defense of their rights of conscience as Englishmen. Cromwell is also noteworthy for initiating the return of the Jews to England, a land from which they had been expelled four centuries earlier.

Among the able men who worked with Cromwell were John Durie (1596–1680) and John Milton (1608–74).

ing was the appointment of a commission which eventually produced the King James Version (AV) of the Bible.

The conservative Puritans, who hoped for an established church governed along presbyterian principles, were thus thrown into the arms of the popular party.

James had an inflated opinion both of his own abilities and the status of a king with disappearing parliamentary support. Charles I (king: 1625–49) added to the offenses of the king against parliament by giving the see of Canterbury to William Laud (archbishop: 1633–45), who used the Star Chamber in brutal suppression of the Puritans. In Scotland the ecclesiastical policy was so coercive that the National Covenant of 1638 was undertaken by the Scots, pledging their land to presbyterianism. As the actions of the king toward parliament grew more arrogant, and civil war ensued (1642 ff.), the parliament entered into a Solemn League and Covenant with the Scots (1643). In both areas the king had treated with contempt the dignities of parliament and the rights of free men, and so ineptly and crassly meddled in the affairs of the church, that Puritan, patriotic, and anti-royal-

Cromwell had not only an acute sense of the importance of liberty of conscience but also—like most radical Puritans—a strong conviction of the original style of the church and its coming restoration. He used Durie as his agent in Scandinavia and on the continent to effect an ecumenical cooperation of Protestants. Milton served for a time as Cromwell's foreign secretary, drafting in his elegant Latin the Protector's correspondence with foreign powers. Milton wrote some of the greatest defenses of personal freedom, including the first defense of divorce by a Christian theologian (in 1643) and a noble statement for freedom of the press (*Areopagitica*, 1644). He also defended the execution of Charles I in his *Tenure of Kings and Magistrates* and other tracts (1648–54).

After the collapse of his religious and political hopes with the Restoration (1660), and in spite of his total blindness (from 1651), Milton wrote three of the noblest epic poems in the English language: *Paradise Lost* (1667), *Paradise Regained* (1671), and *Samson Agonistes* (1671).

Cromwell had refused the kingship, and at his death the coalition collapsed. The Stuarts were returned to the throne. Under Charles II (king: 1660–85) the Puritans were again severely persecuted. Even so irenic a man as Richard Baxter (1615–91), who had played a prominent part in the recall of the Stuarts, was victimized by the King and his Judge Jeffreys when he urged toleration of Presbyterians who could not accept the 1662 Book of Common Prayer. Baxter's *Saints' Everlasting Rest* (1650) and *The Reformed Pastor* (1656) are two of the great classics of Christian devotion.

Charles II was a secret Roman Catholic, James II (king: 1685–88) an open one. When the Archbishop of Canterbury and seven other bishops refused to carry out James's orders in church matters they were sent to the Tower; their acquittal was celebrated by crowds in the streets. William III of Orange was invited to come to England and save the land from "papist tyranny." This call he accepted, with his queen (Mary, daughter of James II), and in spite of abortive attempts by Stuart pretenders over some decades, supported by invasions from abroad, England and Scotland remained Protestant.

*Oliver Cromwell.*

*John Milton.*

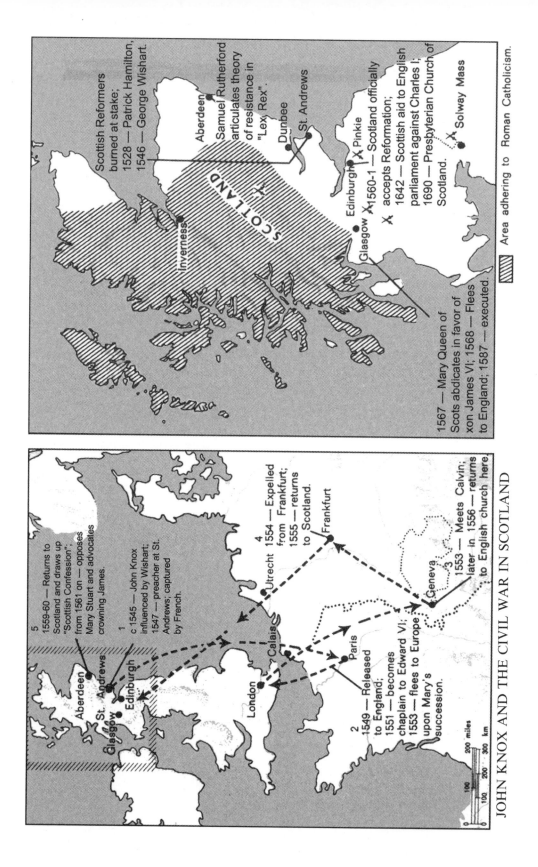

**JOHN KNOX AND THE CIVIL WAR IN SCOTLAND**

**SCOTLAND**

Scottish Reformers burned at stake;
1528 — Patrick Hamilton.
1546 — George Wishart.

Samuel Rutherford articulates theory of resistance in "Lex Rex".

1560-1 — Scotland officially accepts Reformation;
1642 — Scottish aid to English parliament against Charles I;
1690 — Presbyterian Church of Scotland.

1567 — Mary Queen of Scots abdicates in favor of xon James VI; 1568 — Flees to England; 1587 — executed.

Aberdeen
Dunbee
St. Andrews
Edinburgh X Pinkie
Glasgow X
Solway Mass

Area adhering to Roman Catholicism.

5
1559-60 — Returns to Scotland and draws up "Scottish Confession"; from 1561 on — opposes Mary Stuart and advocates crowning James.

1
c 1545 — John Knox influenced by Wishart; 1547 — preacher at St. Andrews; captured by French.

4
1554 — Expelled from Frankfurt; 1555 — returns to Scotland.

3
1553 — Meets Calvin; later in 1556 — returns to English church here.

2
1549 — Released to England; 1551 — becomes chaplain to Edward VI; 1553 — flees to Europe upon Mary's succession.

Aberdeen
St. Andrews
Glasgow
Edinburgh
London
Calais
Paris
Utrecht
Frankfurt
Geneva

184

*"What have you to do with my marriage? Or what are you in this commonwealth?" "A subject born within the same, madam. And albeit I am neither earl, lord, nor baron within it,...to me it appertains no less to forewarn of such things as may hurt it, if I foresee them, than it doth to any of the nobility."*
— John Knox to Mary Queen of Scots

*John Knox.*

SCOTLAND early produced martyrs to the Reformation cause. Of these, Patrick Hamilton (c 1504–28) was noteworthy. As a student at Paris he was attracted to Luther's writings and later attended lectures at both Wittenberg and the new university of Marburg. Charged at home with heresy, he converted the man assigned to him—Alexander Alesius (1500–65), who later held important posts as a professor at Frankfurt/Oder and in England under Edward VI. Hamilton was burned at the stake. George Wishart (c 1513–46) was another early martyr under Cardinal Beaton, who was himself assassinated for his oppression of the young reformers. Wishart's major contribution was his influence upon John Knox, who became the chief leader of the Scottish Reformation.

John Knox (c 1505–72) was educated at Glasgow and converted to the Reformation later (at 42 years of age). For a time he was a slave in the French galleys. On release he played an important part in English reform as chaplain to Edward VI. During Mary Tudor's reign he worked on the continent, where he became acquainted with Calvin. As a preacher in the English church at Geneva, he published his diatribe against the domination of French politics by Mary of Guise: *Against the Monstrous Regiment of Women* (1558). Elizabeth remembered the book when she became Queen of England, and so did Mary Stuart when she came to the throne of Scotland (1561). Knox had in the meantime acquired a considerable following in Scotland, to which he returned in 1559. In the *Scottish Confession* (1560) and *The First Book of Discipline* (1560) he laid the foundations for the Scottish Reformation. The 25 articles of the former were strongly anti-Roman and Calvinist, and it prevailed until superseded by the Westminster Confession in 1647. The latter adapted the Genevan church government to the Scottish scene, although its enforcement was sabotaged by the nobility because Knox proposed a system of national education which threatened loss of revenue to the lords. His *Book of Common Order* (1556–64) became the standard service book.

Knox came into sharp conflict with Mary Stuart because of her having celebration of the Mass at court and

*Mary Stuart.*

also because of her dissolute royal entourage and personal life. For a year before her abdication he preached almost daily against her, and he preached at the coronation of her son James VI. Knox was a harsh man of great courage and power of preaching. His *History of the Reformation in Scotland* has gone through many editions.

Although Scotland embraced presbyterian principles in 1560, for more than a century the church of the land was directly affected by the determination of the Stuarts to enforce episcopacy. Scottish nationalism, resistant to English control, later made Scotland a base of operations for the Stuart pretenders.

After the death of Knox the mantle of leadership passed to Andrew Melville (1545–1622), a man of great intellectual and administrative gifts. After serving in important academic posts at Poitiers and Geneva, he became in 1574 the principal of the University of Glasgow. Here he carried through reorganization. Later he was head of the theological faculty at St. Andrews. Conflict with the king finally led to four years of imprisonment in the Tower of London—from which he was released to go into exile. Twice Moderator of the General Assembly, he worked hard to eliminate all traces of episcopacy in Scotland and to strengthen the presbyterian party in the Church of England.

Under crown pressure pro-episcopal measures were adopted in 1584 but reversed in 1592. In 1612 episcopacy was re-established and in 1618 episcopal usage enjoined. But the effort to enforce Archbishop Laud's Prayer Book brought about an alliance between Scots presbyterians and Charles I's opponents in England: the Solemn League and Covenant (1643). With Scottish support, the English parliament convened the Westminister Assembly to define a Calvinist confession of faith and presbyterian church order for both kingdoms. During the Commonwealth, when congregationalism moved ahead of presbyterianism in England, Scottish disaffection was checked by Cromwell's army. After the Restoration (1660), episcopacy was again introduced by Stuart edict, but after bitter conflict the Church of Scotland became finally presbyterian with the accession of William and Mary (1689).

Mary Stuart (queen: 1543–67) lost Scotland for Roman Catholicism. Her son James VI and his successors lost Scotland for the episcopal cause. But the victory of Calvinism and presbyterianism, which created a church both national and free, was achieved by men like Hamilton, Knox and Melville. In the process, principles of representative government came to the fore in political as well as churchly affairs. *Lex, Rex* (1644), a refutation of absolute monarchy, and *The Divine Right of Church Government* (1646), a defense of presbyterian and church polity, both by Samuel Rutherford (c 1600–61), are two of the most powerful statements of republican principles in the English language.

THE "wars of religion," which shook every country in Europe, were complicated by other volatile forces of the period: especially, the rise of nationalism, the competition of different noble families, the conflict of king and ambitious nobles, the decay of imperial authority. In the German area each of these forces was present, enhanced by the extraordinary number of small states and principalities which still survived from the feudal age. The Thirty Years' War, which reduced Germany to the level of crude barbarism, brought the end of dozens of small political units. The destruction at the hands of several armies, self-justified by religious ideologies, was so thorough that in a whole county only a single broken family might survive out of a population of six thousand. Plague and famine followed the mercenary armies. Cannibalism was reported in several starvation zones. The population of the Germanies was in one generation reduced 80 to 90 percent.

The Thirty Years' War consisted of a series of wars, considered as a unit by historians because the peace settlement—the Treaties of Westphalia (1648)—was comprehensive. The first phase (1618–29) was primarily religious, the final phase (1630–48) was a struggle over the power of the Habsburg dynasty and the influence of Sweden and France in the empire.

War started in Bohemia, a part of Europe long rendered unstable by the alternating forces of Muslim invaders, Reformation and Counter-Reformation, Hungarian and Bohemian and Transylvanian nobilities, Habsburg claims. The immediate occasion was the liquidation of two Hussite churches

*War, famine, conquest and death (Rev. 6:1–10) accompanied the Wars of Religion. Dürer, 16th century woodcut.*

by Roman Catholic rulers, followed by the appointment of Roman Catholic regional governors. The Bohemian Protestants (*Utraquists*) called for help, and the Protestant Union responded with an army that defeated the imperial forces. At Vienna, however, the tide turned the other way. Ferdinand II, made emperor at Frankfurt by six of the seven electors, turned and crushed the Palatine Elector Frederick V, head of the Protestant Union, leading German Calvinist, son-in-law of James I of England, at the Battle of the White Mountain (8 November 1620). Frederick fled to the Netherlands, the Protestant rulers of Anhalt and Brandenburg were put under imperial ban, extreme measures of Counter-Reformation were executed in Bohemia, Austria and Silesia.

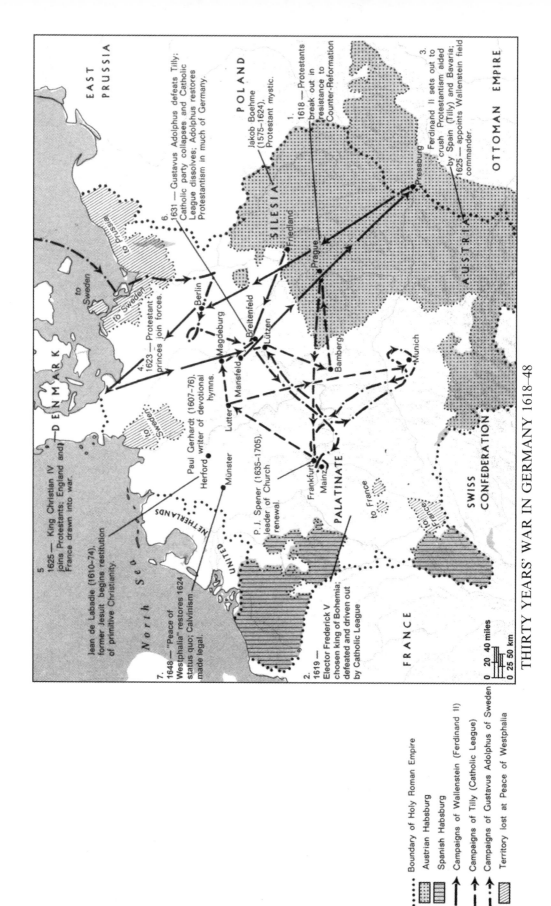

THIRTY YEARS' WAR IN GERMANY 1618–48

5
1625 — King Christian IV
joins Protestants; England and
France drawn into war.

Jean de Labadie (1610–74),
former Jesuit begins restitution
of primitive Christianity.

7.
1648 — "Peace of
Westphalia" restores 1624
status quo; Calvinism
made legal.

6.    1631 — Gustavus Adolphus defeats Tilly;
      Catholic party collapses and Catholic
      League dissolves; Adolphus restores
      Protestantism in much of Germany.

Jakob Boehme
(1575–1624).
Protestant mystic.

1.    1618 — Protestants
      break out in
      resistance to
      Counter-Reformation

3.
Ferdinand II sets out to
crush Protestantism aided
by Spain (Tilly) and Bavaria;
1625 — appoints Wallenstein field
commander.

4.    1623 — Protestant
      princes join forces.

Paul Gerhardt (1607–76),
writer of devotional
hymns.

P. J. Spener (1635–1705),
leader of Church
renewal.

2.
1619 —
Elector Frederick V
chosen king of Bohemia;
defeated and driven out
by Catholic League

EAST PRUSSIA

POLAND

SILESIA

AUSTRIA

OTTOMAN EMPIRE

DENMARK

North Sea

NETHERLANDS

UNITED

SWISS CONFEDERATION

FRANCE

PALATINATE

to Prussia

to Sweden

to Sweden

to Sweden

to France

to France

Friedland

Prague

Pressburg

Berlin

Magdeburg

Mansfeld

Breitenfeld

Lützen

Lutter

Bamberg

Munich

Münster

Herford

Frankfurt

Mainz

0  20  40 miles
0  25  50 km

······  Boundary of Holy Roman Empire
        Austrian Habsburg
        Spanish Habsburg
  →     Campaigns of Wallenstein (Ferdinand II)
  ⇣     Campaigns of Tilly (Catholic League)
  ⇢     Campaigns of Gustavus Adolphus of Sweden
        Territory lost at Peace of Westphalia

The forces of the Roman Catholic League, cooperating with a Spanish army and an Imperial army (Wallenstein, commander), defeated the north German forces led by Christian IV, King of Denmark and Holstein, and set about it to destroy all "sects" not guaranteed by the Peace of Augsburg (1555).

King Gustavus Adolphus of Sweden arrived in Pomerania in July of 1630 at the head of an army committed to the relief of German Protestantism. He won brilliant victories at Leipzig (1631) and Lützen (1632), but the tide of battle ebbed and flowed inconclusively for years. In 1635 French forces entered the struggle, cooperating with the Swedes against Habsburg imperial interests. In the settlement of exhaustion at Westphalia, both Sweden and France came out with important territorial and political gains. Calvinism attained to the same recognized legal status as Roman Catholicism and Lutheranism before 1618, with the choice of legal faith dependent upon the government of each territory. Among other general settlements, Switzerland and the Netherlands were accorded independence.

The religious developments reflected the agony of the peoples who had suffered so greatly from the armies, pestilence and starvation. There was an upsurge of individual mysticism, of which Jakob Boehme (1575–1624) was representative. This world was repudiated, the hope of heaven was accentuated. Boehme's writings reflect a continuing exhilaration in the divine presence in the soul, and they include elaborate and intense speculations concerning the essence of God, man, and nature. Within the established churches, Paul Gerhardt (c 1607–76) represented the highest level of personal piety. His hymns, including "O sacred head, now wounded" (based upon a song attributed to Bernard of Clairvaux), combine Catholic mysticism and Protestant spirituality.

## REPRESSION OF JEWS IN EUROPE 16TH–17TH CENTURIES

*God made him, and therefore let him pass for a man.*
— Shakespeare, *The Merchant of Venice*
I:2

*A Jew or Jewish heart is so wooden/stone/ iron/devil hard, that it can be moved in no way....In sum, it is a young devil, damned to hell.* — Luther

THE vision of a unitary Christendom did not cease with the division of western Christendom into three major blocs (four, finally, when Anglicanism departed the Calvinist camp). Neither did it decline in Eastern Orthodoxy. The very rise of popular participation in the religious life, desirable as it was from a churchly point of view, was disastrous for any who would not conform to the established religious practices.

The close alliance of church and state which characterized all sectors of Christendom in the sixteenth and seventeenth centuries added yet another count to the score against counter-cultures: refusal to support the religion approved by the state was counted not just as unbelief, but treason as well. The principle of the right to emigrate to more friendly territory (*jus emigrandi*) was a distinct advance. This principle was fundamen-

Luther denigrates Jews for not accepting Christ Urges that they either be deported to Palestine or find livelihood in tilling the soil.

Balthasar Hübmaier leads mob against synagogue.

1648-56 — Cossack leader Bogdan Chmielnicki leads Orthodox in revolt against Polish Catholic rulers; more than 100,000 Jews killed; remaining Jews flee

1553 — Cardinal Caraffa has all copies of the Talmud burned. 16th cent — Ghettoes and "Jews'-Street" introduced first in Italy then in Austria.

Saxony 1432, 1450 — Jewish persecutions with date

Principal towns where Jews were massacred

Area of Chmielnicki uprising

tal to the Peace of Augsburg, 1555: Lutherans and Catholics were guaranteed the right to leave—with life, goods and savings—from an area where the prince decided for the other religion. In 1648 the Calvinists received the same right.

The plight of the Jews in a time of surging nationalism and energetic drive toward religious conformity was acute. In Spain they were simply compelled to convert, emigrate, or die, after more than a millennium of residence which included some of the most splendid pages in their history as a people. Some found refuge in the Papal States, for the Inquisition there was less savage than in Spain; there they had some considerable influence upon north Italian Humanists and later upon individual radical reformers, among whom Anti-Trinitarianism was a recurring theme.

In the cities where the free citizens had more to say, a single demagogue might turn the mob against the Jews. Balthasar Hübmaier (c 1485–1528),

later himself an Anabaptist convert and martyr, while a priest at Regensburg preached a series of diatribes against the Jews which led to burning of the synagogue and much suffering. After his conversion he never preached or wrote against "the Jews," but many Anabaptist and Free Church churches have followed Luther in a dangerous polarization between the Old Testament and the New, the age of ceremonial law and the age of grace. In his last years Martin Luther looked back with misgiving upon the partial failure and corruption of the reformation he had led. He had anticipated the conversion of the Jews to accompany the bringing of a purified gospel to light. Among other disappointments, this did not happen, and he turned against the Jews with some of his most vulgar and scurrilous writing. The Nazis were later able to re-issue his tract, *Against the Jews and Their Lies*, which the Lutheran churches had never republished, eighteen times during the Third Reich.

The Counter-Reformation also

brought renewed suffering. Among other things, the papal bull *Vices eius nos* (1 September 1577) required Jews in the Papal States to attend on conversionist sermons, frequently preached by renegade Jews like Vitale de Medici (formerly Jehiel de Pesaro). This degrading custom continued in Italy and France until the French Revolution.

Antisemitism is a distinctly Christian product, although it is endemic also in Islam and in post-Christian ideologies such as Marxism and Nazism. It is certainly false to identify it with the hostilities which have existed between various tribes and peoples since time immemorial. Antisemitism—that is, hatred of the Jews (*Judenfeindschaft*) —arises with an ideology which denies a place in continuing history to the Jewish people. This the church fathers, with few exceptions, did. As Hellenes they resented the Jewish claims of election and uniqueness. Transferring the same to "the New Israel," the Christian Church, they declared that the role of the Jewish people as carriers of history was finished. The Jews were condemned for the crucifixion of Jesus, the martyrdom of Stephen; after Christ, they were to wither away and disappear.

Upon this base of theological antisemitism an overlay of cultural antisemitism was laid. In the twentieth century, among totalitarian parties and ideologies, antisemitism has reached a further development: it has become a political weapon. But behind all antisemitism is the genocidal thrust, whether mouthed by preachers or engineered by Ph.D.s—as at Auschwitz.

In the Middle Ages, while the Jews were allowed by law to survive only in the crevices of Christendom—in the high-risk roles, like moneylenders to princes and sea-going traders—the caricature of the Jew as an extortionist and usurer became a part of cultural antisemitism. In the inflation, the peasants' revolts, the wars of the nobility against kings, the threatened Turkish invasions, the wars of religion, the terrible filth and epidemics of the expanding cities, the frustrations and resentments of the masses during the sixteenth and seventeenth centuries found easy relief in attacks on the Jews.

The explosion of popular religious and political movements which attended the expansion of the European frontier into America, Africa and Asia, along with the rise of modern nation-states enjoying the sanctions of Christian churches, placed the Jewish communities in their greatest jeopardy since the First Crusade (1096).

*Medieval portrayal of a triumphant church and blind synagogue.*

# J. IMPERIAL AND NATIONAL EFFORTS AT REINTEGRATION OF LATIN CHRISTENDOM

## THE EMPIRE OF CHARLES V (EMPEROR 1519–56)

THE grandson of Ferdinand and Isabella, Charles V (1500–58), took charge at the age of nineteen of the largest Christian empire in many centuries. The model of Constantine and Charlemagne rose quite naturally before his eyes, but he was never able to carry through his ambitions.

In Germany, which was supposed to be the core of the Holy Roman Empire, the rise of Lutheranism tormented his days and nights. After various wars and shifting alliances, the Protestant princes succeeded in forcing upon him the Augsburg Peace (1555).

The papacy was again centered in a single man at Rome, but the moral and spiritual quality of the incumbents was low. Not until Paul III (pope: 1534–49) was there an incumbent of administrative vigor. But in private life he was immoral and corrupt. He could not check Lutheranism, and he drove England into religious rebellion. By the time a representative of Catholic reform came to the papacy—Paul IV (pope: 1555–59), founder of the Theatine Order and re-organizer of the Inquisition—Charles V had already given up his hope of reestablishing a renewed Christendom.

The Turks threatened Europe several times during Charles V's reign, forcing him to compromise on internal issues to mobilize resistance. The memory of the fall of Constantinople (1453) was still fresh, and after the capture of Belgrade (1521) the Turks made frequent raids throughout central Europe. The First Siege of Vienna (1529) ended

*Charles V.*

in a stalemate, but a series of wars continued.

It may be counted one of Charles V's greatest misfortunes to have been emperor during the reign of Suleiman the Magnificent (sultan: 1520–66), the greatest of the Turkish rulers, who outperformed and outlasted him.

Under Suleiman and his father before him, Persia was defeated, Syria and Egypt and Tunisia conquered and their governments reorganized under Turkish suzerainty. The Sherif of Mecca surrendered voluntarily and the Ottoman rulers gained control of the Holy Places.

Turkish success in Europe was almost as impressive, although considerable energy had to be devoted to evacuation and resettlement of Moors from Spain and Portugal. Serbia was

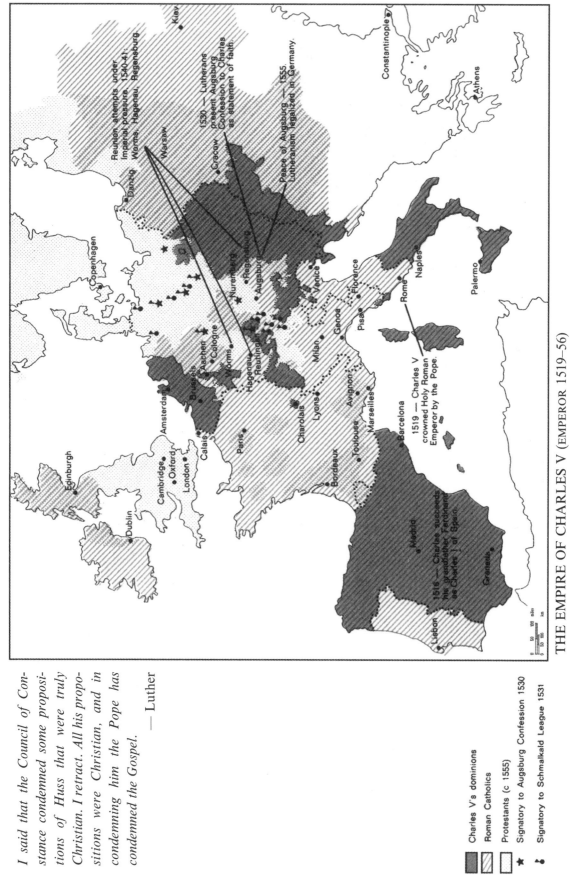

*I said that the Council of Constance condemned some propositions of Huss that were truly Christian. I retract. All his propositions were Christian, and in condemning him the Pope has condemned the Gospel.*

— Luther

THE EMPIRE OF CHARLES V (EMPEROR 1519–56)

Reunion attempts under imperial pressure, 1540-41; Worms, Hagenau, Regensburg.

1530 — Lutherans present Augsburg Confession to Charles as statement of faith.

Peace of Augsburg — 1555; Lutheranism legalized in Germany.

1519 — Charles V crowned Holy Roman Emperor by the Pope.

1516 — Charles succeeds his grandfather, Ferdinand as Charles I of Spain.

Charles V's dominions

Roman Catholics

Protestants (c 1555)

★ Signatory to Augsburg Confession 1530

Signatory to Schmalkald League 1531

193

*Martin Luther preaching.*

already a vassal state, as were Bosnia and Herzegovina and Montenegro. Most of Hungary was under direct control from 1547 to 1606, and the Turkish threat to central Europe did not ebb until the failure of the Second Siege of Vienna (1683).

The Emperor's influence in that section of the domains claimed by the Habsburgs was weakened by the continuing struggle between Catholics and Hussites in Bohemia. Wars raged for generations after the murder of Huss and Jerome at Constance (1415), in spite of recognition granted the Hussites at the Council of Basel (the *Compactata*, 1436). The issue was not settled, with destruction of the Bohemian nobility and incorporation of Bohemia into the Hungarian realm, until the Battle of the White Mountain (1620).

In the meantime, with the rise of cities in Hungary and Bohemia and Transylvania, thousands of German settlers moved into the eastern Habs-burg area. Lutheranism spread with them, so that neither in the east nor in the German states could Charles V realize his dream of a unitary Christian empire. In the heart of the empire, in spite of the efforts of some Protestants (Butzer, Melanchthon) and Catholics (Contarini, Morone), the polarization continued to swell and all efforts to maintain a united but reformed Christendom failed.

Shortly after assuming the imperial crown, Charles V called his vassals to the Diet of Worms. The tide of the "new faith" was running rapidly. The attempt to suppress Luther's rebellion by use of monastic discipline had failed: in the meeting of his chapter at Heidelberg (1518) he not only resisted but actually won over some of his brethren, notably Martin Butzer. The papal bull *Exsurge Domine* condemned his teachings; on his refusal to recant, he was excommunicated (3 January 1521).

The Emperor was unable to stop Luther's work, however. He was thwarted by princes and cities friendly to the Reformation. Philipp of Hesse's scandalous bigamy (1540) and Maurice of Saxony's defection (1547) gravely weakened the League of Protestant Princes, and made it possible for the Emperor to attempt to freeze the status quo until the Council of Trent should settle points in dispute (Augsburg and Leipzig Interims, 1548).

But the Protestants played no role at Trent, the Emperor's forces were defeated in battle and he himself almost captured, and in the Peace of Augsburg (25 September 1555) Lutheranism and Catholicism were both made legal options.

BOTH China and India were important to Europeans of education and commerce in the high Middle Ages, as they had been important to all advanced western societies in the pre-Christian era.

The closing of the old trade routes to the east set off a series of exploratory voyages in the fifteenth century. The fall of the Mongol control of China and southern Asia, with the rise of the Ming Dynasty (1368 ff.), closed off access to much of Asia. The uncertainty of land traffic with India because of the resurgence of Muslim power following the collapse of the crusader kingdoms impelled attempts to reach India by sea. In this enterprise Portugal and Spain took the lead, although Genoa and Venice also participated.

Prince Henry the Navigator (1394–1460) of Portugal was general of an important knightly order and directed its monies and personnel into scientific, commercial, and religious expeditions. Under John II (king: 1481–95) Portugal's eminence in voyages of discovery rose higher yet. Having rounded Cape Bojador after a decade of effort, by 1487 the Portuguese were moving rapidly into Africa from south of the bulge.

In that year they reached Timbuktu, center of the great Mandingo Empire. In 1490 they worked their way far up the great river and converted the King of the Congo Empire. A few years later they established the colony of Mozambique. At the same time the push for a sea route continued. In 1500 Cabral sailed a fleet to India, returning with a load of pepper and spices. Lisbon became the chief trading center with

*Henry the Navigator.*

the Orient—with Goa, acquired in 1510, the Portuguese center in the Indian sub-continent.

The India which the Portuguese found was divided among principalities and minor empires, both Hindu and Muslim. The Mogul Empire consolidated Muslim power in 1526, lasting until the British conquest (1761). The great ruler Akbar (emperor: 1562–1605) added North India and introduced an efficient administration and religious toleration. Public debates on religion were opened to Muslims, Jains, Hindus, Zoroastrians and Christians. Christian missionaries were welcomed (Portuguese Jesuits), but made little headway.

Spain was jealous of Portuguese initiative. In 1492 Queen Isabella took the step which gave Spain the most lucrative colonies of all: she sponsored Christopher Columbus, a Genoese, in his venture to reach the Orient by

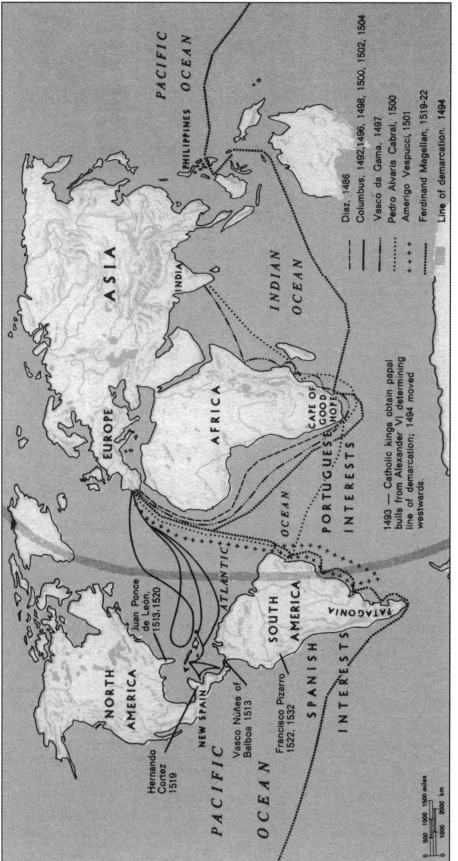

Diaz, 1486
Columbus, 1492, 1496, 1498, 1500, 1502, 1504
Vasco da Gama, 1497
Pedro Alvaris Cabral, 1500
Amerigo Vespucci, 1501
Ferdinand Magellan, 1519-22
Line of demarcation, 1494

1493 — Catholic kings obtain papal bulls from Alexander VI determining line of demarcation; 1494 moved westwards.

PORTUGUESE AND SPANISH VOYAGES OF DISCOVERY 15TH–16TH CENTURIES

*The* Santa Maria, *Columbus' flagship on his voyage to the New World.*

sailing west. He carried letters to the Great Khan, and after encounters with the brown natives of what are now the Bahamas, Cuba and Santo Domingo, he returned to report discovery of the Indies.

The New World thus opened to Spanish conquest, which was divided between Spain and Portugal in 1493, brought untold wealth to Europe. Great shipments of gold and silver bullion flowed toward the homeland, bringing both prosperity for a few and inflation to the masses. Within a few decades all of western Europe was in the throes of civil unrest and occasional revolution.

Negro slavery was introduced in 1501, for the Indians proved quite unsuitable to work the mines and fields as slaves. In several areas their numbers were decimated, in spite of the efforts of some men of conscience—notably Bartolomé de Las Casas (1474–1560)—to protect the natives from cruelty and early death. Las Casas personally argued the cause of the Indians before Charles V and Philip II, but his efforts to check the brutality of the conquistadors and establish Christian Indian colonies were generally thwarted by white reaction to intermittent desperate Indian revolts.

For a time (1529–56), by a grant from Charles V, the Augsburg banking firm of Welser was allowed to exploit the Chibcha Indian Empire of northern South America (Venezuela and New Granada). Francisco Pizarro, under a royal patent, conquered the Inca Empire and founded Lima (Peru). Also by royal patent, several adventurers (including Hernando Cortez) conquered the Aztec Empire, killing the rulers and founding Mexico City after razing the native capital, Tenochtitlan. The papacy and religious orders worked very closely with the Catholic monarchs of Spain and Portugal to guarantee the staffing of missions and education throughout the empires.

The extraordinary wealth traveling in great galleons to Spain naturally aroused the cupidity of Dutch and English freebooters, strengthened as their actions were by national and religious hostility to Spain. A single ship captured by Francis Drake in the name of Queen Elizabeth brought her more wealth than her entire annual crown revenue at home.

*Francisco Pizarro.*

Amerigo Vespucci (1454–1512), the explorer after whom the New World was named.

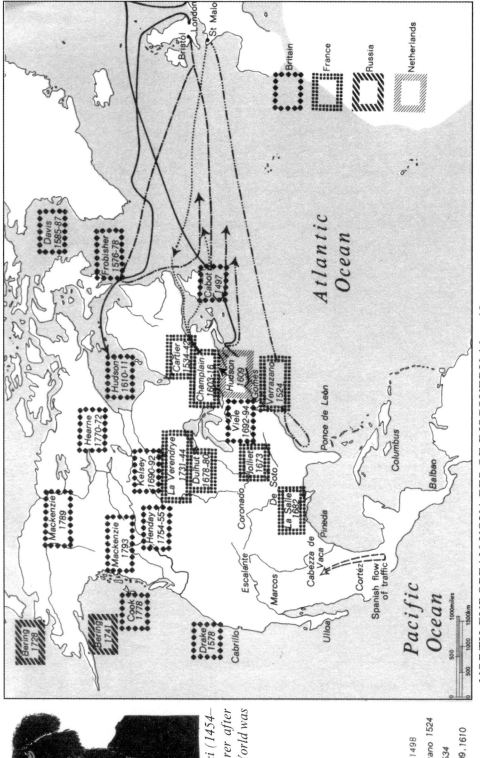

NORTH EUROPEAN VOYAGES OF DISCOVERY 16TH–18TH CENTURIES

Britain
France
Russia
Netherlands

Davis 1585-87
Frobisher 1576-78
Cabot 1497
Hudson 1610-11
Cartier 1534-42
Champlain 1603-16
Hudson 1609
Gomes
Verrazano 1524
Hearne 1770-72
Viele 1692-94
Kelsey 1690-92
La Verendrye 1731-44
Dulhut 1678-80
Jolliet 1673
De Soto
Mackenzie 1789
Mackenzie 1793
Henday 1754-55
La Salle 1682
Coronado
Escalante
Cabezza de Vaca
Cortéz
Bering 1728
Bering 1741
Cook 1778
Marcos
Ulloa
Drake 1578
Cabrillo

London
Bristol
St Malo

Ponce de León
Columbus
Balboa
Pineda

Spanish flow of traffic

Atlantic Ocean
Pacific Ocean

500
1000
1500 km

500
1000miles
0

John Cabot 1497 1498
Giovanni of Verrazano 1524
Jacques Cartier 1534
Henry Hudson 1609 1610

FRANCE and the north European countries were slower to send out voyages of discovery. Their most important efforts at colonization were directed at the northern continent. In North America there were no advanced societies to plunder, of the sort that made the Spanish (but not Portuguese) colonies in America such sensational acquisitions. One result was that a quite different kind of settler crossed the ocean to North America: not the nobleman seeking new wealth nor the adventurer seeking a quick fortune to buy a title, not the highborn settler with slaves and peons impressed to work his hacienda but the farmer or trader accustomed to do his own work. A middle class developed slowly and late in Latin America. In North America the only major attempt to build a society on the plantation system—in the Old South of the United States— was crushed by free labor and independent farmers (Civil War, 1861–65).

The French and British and Dutch, and even the Danes, made some inroads into the Caribbean and Central America. The Spanish made important extensions of their domain into the areas which are now Florida, Texas, Arizona, New Mexico and California. But the above generalization holds in the large.

The explorers carried letters authorizing them to Christianize the natives and subdue them to "civilized" norms, along with their political and commercial grants of authority. During the colonial period, and in some cases long after, the New World was a "peninsula" of Europe and the churches of the colonies were but outposts of the recognized (and predominantly estab-

*Henry Hudson.*

lished) churches of Europe. Not until the successful rebellion of the thirteen British colonies which became the United States of America did a significant section of the New World cease to be religiously as well as politically a dependency of Europe.

The first French explorations were by Jacques Cartier, who explored the St. Lawrence River (1534–41), and Samuel de Champlain, who founded Quebec (1608). Missionary work was started by Recollet Friars (1615) and Jesuits (1625). Montreal was founded in 1642. The Great Lakes area was explored. The Mississippi Valley was discovered by Fathers Marquette and Jolliet (1673), and a decade later La Salle reached the Gulf and claimed the whole valley for the French king. Settlements were founded at the junction of Lake Erie and Lake Huron (Detroit, 1701), along the coast (Mobile, 1710; New Orleans, 1718), as well as forts along the great river to check English and Spanish advances.

In 1497 John Cabot, a wealthy Italian merchant living in England, discovered Newfoundland while searching for Brazil. The following year his second fleet of ships cruised along Greenland, Labrador, Newfoundland, the New England coast and some distance south before returning in disappointment at finding no precious wood or spices. While circumnavigating the globe (1572–80), Sir Francis Drake made the first claim of territory for England—and this along the coast of what is now California. Jamestown was founded in 1607, with the Church of England the official religion. In 1620 a group of Separatists ("Pilgrim Fathers") reached Cape Cod aboard the Mayflower. They had fled from England to Holland to practice their religion, and from Holland to America to preserve their culture and language. A few years later they joined with the larger settlement of conservative Puritans in Massachusetts Bay Colony (f. 1629) in maintaining a state-church and suppressing dissenters of opinions other than their own. Roger Williams (1603?–83), champion of Religious Liberty and friend of the Indians, founded Rhode Island (1636).

In 1632 Lord Baltimore established Maryland under a charter which allowed Roman Catholicism, and a number of gentlemen of that persuasion became settlers.

Henry Hudson, an Englishman employed by the Dutch East India Company, explored much of the northern coastline—including the estuary which bears his name—in 1609. Fur trade with the Indians was begun. By 1626 Manhattan Island had been purchased and New Amsterdam (later "New York") founded. Along the great river, men of standing, called patroons, were given huge tracts of land in return for bringing over bands of settlers. The Dutch Reformed Church (*Hervormde Kerk*) was privileged, as at home.

## THE REALM OF FRANCIS I
### (KING OF FRANCE 1515–47)

*Francis I on horseback.*

DURING most of the fourteenth century, the French kings dominated the papacy. The great university at Paris was the chief center of learning and of proposals for reform in Christendom. But the continuance of English rule in large and prosperous French provinces was a constant aggravation. When the leaders of the Flanders communes saluted Edward III (king of England: 1327–77) as King of France too, the Hundred Years' War was launched. English forces, making skillful use of archers, frequently defeated armies which much outnumbered them (Crécy 1346, Agincourt 1415), and by 1420 the whole of France was under English rule.

An astonishing deliverance was wrought by Joan of Arc (1412–31), whose inspired leadership relieved Orléans and commended Charles VII—whose coronation she blessed—and his cause to the people. Betrayed and

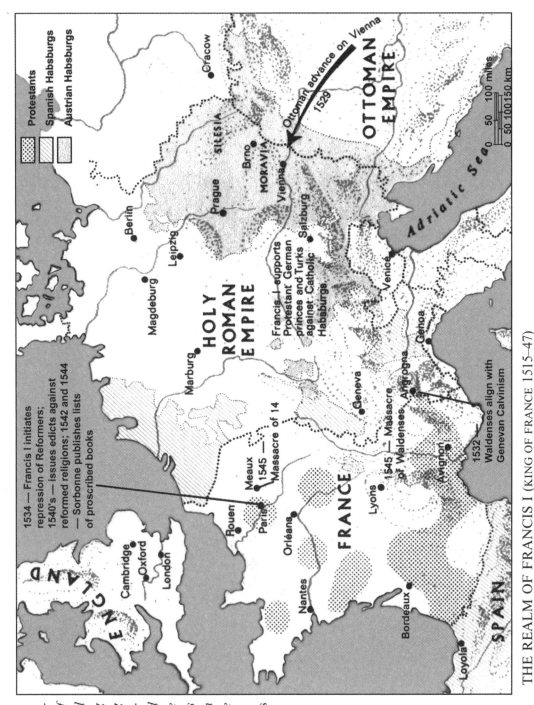

THE REALM OF FRANCIS I (KING OF FRANCE 1515–47)

Protestants

Spanish Habsburgs

Austrian Habsburgs

Ottoman advance on Vienna

1529

OTTOMAN EMPIRE

Cracow

SILESIA

Berlin

Leipzig

Prague

MORAVIA

Brno

Vienna

Salzburg

HOLY ROMAN EMPIRE

Magdeburg

Marburg

Francis I supports Protestant German princes and Turks against Catholic Habsburgs.

Venice

Adriatic Sea

Genoa

ENGLAND

Cambridge

Oxford

London

Meaux

Rouen

Paris

Orléans

1545 — Massacre of 14

Geneva

Lyons

1545 — Massacre of Waldenses, Angrogna

Avignon

1532 — Waldenses align with Genevan Calvinism

FRANCE

Nantes

Bordeaux

SPAIN

Loyola

0   50   100 miles
0  50 100 150 km

1534 — Francis I initiates repression of Reformers; 1540's — issues edicts against reformed religions; 1542 and 1544 — Sorbonne publishes lists of proscribed books

*The signs of the times announce that a reformation of the Church is near at hand and, while God is opening new paths for the preaching of the Gospel by the discoveries of the Portuguese and the Spaniards, we must hope that He will also visit His Church and raise her from the abasement into which she has now fallen.*

— Lefèvre d'Étaples

201

burned for witchcraft, she was rehabilitated by the church twenty-five years after her martyrdom. By 1453 English power in France was checked and reduced, to be tied up then for thirty years in the Wars of the Roses. French nationalism was surging upward, identified with the cause of Christianity. From this time the French king was addressed as "Most Christian King" (*Rex Christianissimus*).

Under the able leadership of Louis XI (king: 1461–83), France broke the power of Burgundy. Swiss mercenaries were employed in the victory (Nancy, 1477), and it was Swiss mercenaries employed by France's enemies a few years later that drove the French out of Italy (Novarra, 1513).

The first important act of Francis I on coming to power (king: 1515–47) was to conclude a treaty of perpetual peace between France and Switzerland. The treaty was kept until Napoleon's time. Equally important: the French king secured the right to recruit Swiss soldiers for his battles elsewhere. The second thing Francis I accomplished immediately after his accession was a Concordat with the papacy which brought the church in France under his control: in return for guaranteed annates the pope gave the king the choice of bishops and abbots. His third act of statesmanship was an agreement with Henry VIII of England which freed Francis for a series of wars with the Emperor, Charles V.

Francis I never became a Protestant, but the service which he did Protestantism in distracting the time and energies of the Emperor, was immense.

Although the Sorbonne became a major center of anti-Protestant effort, the Humanist background to church reform was not absent in France. Both Guillaume Farel (1489–1565) and John Calvin (1509–64) studied at Paris, the former being influenced by a man of the type of Erasmus: Jacques Lefèvre d'Étaples (c 1455–1536). Because of two New Testament essays, "Stapulensis" was condemned by the faculty for heresy and fled to Strassburg, later coming under the protection of Navarre. His critical textual work and his translations of the Old and New Testament into French were important, but he never subscribed to Reformation views on matters such as grace, predestination, justification.

Stapulensis' friend Guillaume Briçonnet, Bishop of Meaux, used his post to further devotion and renewal. He was the chaplain to Margaret d'Angoulême (1492–1549), sister of Francis I and by marriage Queen of Navarre. Margaret was herself a lay theologian and much devoted to Humanistic, mystical and Reformation writings.

Among those over whom the bishop and queen threw their protecting mantles was Clément Marot (c 1497–1544), hymn-writer and psalmist. Marot became a Huguenot and was forced to flee France, ending at Geneva. Theodore Beza used 150 of Marot's works to issue the first Protestant Psalter (1562). Others associated with the circle at Meaux lost their lives, as Protestantism—or even internal reform efforts—came under condemnation of kings and parliaments.

None were more pitiful victims than the Waldenses, New Testament Christians who lived in rural villages in southern France, French-speaking Switzerland and Lombardy. They had been refused recognition as lay communities in 1179 and placed under the ban; Innocent III had declared one of his crusades against them; they had survived, in spite of repeated persecutions, by fleeing into the mountain fastnesses. With the coming of the Reformation the Waldenses sought contact with various teachers and in a synod in 1532 decided to unite with the Swiss reformed. Delegates included Guillaume Farel and Olivetan (c 1506–38); the latter was Calvin's cousin, a refugee in Strassburg.

Henry II (king: 1547–59), son of Francis I, was a sworn enemy of Protestantism—dominated by his mistress and subservient to advisors from the Guise family. Nevertheless, he was unable to crush the movement. By 1559 there were 2,000 Calvinist congregations in France, and in that year a national synod was convened at Paris which adopted a confession of faith and set a presbyterian form of church organization.

# SPAIN UNDER PHILIP II (KING 1556–98)

WHEN Charles V resigned, the office of emperor and the eastern Habsburg lands were turned over to his brother Ferdinand (emp.: 1556–64). Spain— with the colonies, Naples, Sardinia, Sicily, Milan, Franche-Comté and the Netherlands—went to his son Philip. Ferdinand's chief problem was the pressure of the Turks: he had to abandon most of Hungary. Philip's fleet more than equalled the Turks, but he found the Dutch and English raiders a constant irritation.

Philip failed in the Netherlands, where William of Orange led his people to independence. He failed in his efforts to reclaim England. He failed to prevent Henry of Navarre's gaining the French throne. Under his son and successor Spain, seriously depopulated by wars and emigrations, entered a long period of decline.

In the unitary Christian empire which Ferdinand of Castile, Charles V and Philip II all envisioned, churchmen played important public roles. Tomás de Torquemada (1420–98) was Grand Inquisitor, executor of the policy to eliminate the Muslims and Jews by forced conversion, emigration or death. He controlled what amounted to a state within a state.

*Philip II.*

Francisco Ximénez de Cisneros (1436–1517), cardinal archbishop of Toledo, was a great patron of learning and founder of the university of Alcalá (1508). He was regent during the minority of Charles V.

Among monastics, Teresa of Avila (1515–82) and John of the Cross (1542–1605) of the Reformed Carmelites contributed testimonies of importance to the development of mystical devotion.

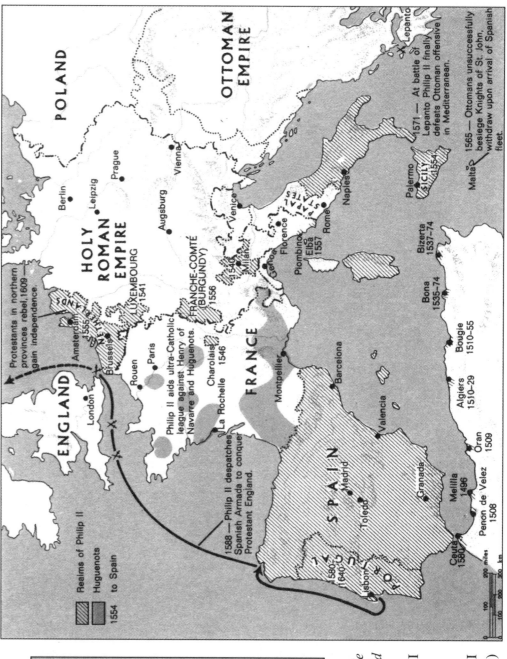

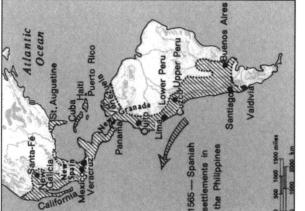

*If you only knew with how little*
*application of understanding the world*
*is governed, you would be amazed!*

— Pope Julius III

SPAIN UNDER PHILIP II
(KING 1556–98)

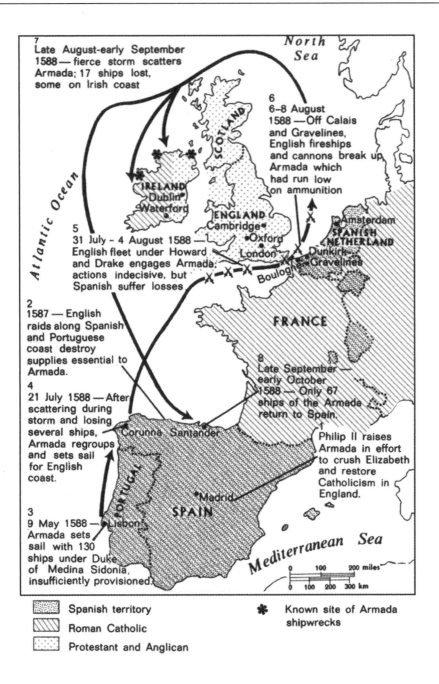

**7**
Late August–early September 1588—fierce storm scatters Armada; 17 ships lost, some on Irish coast

*North Sea*

**6**
6–8 August 1588—Off Calais and Gravelines, English fireships and cannons break up Armada which had run low on ammunition

*Atlantic Ocean*

SCOTLAND

IRELAND
Dublin
Waterford

ENGLAND
Cambridge
Oxford
London

Amsterdam
SPANISH NETHERLAND
Dunkirk
Gravelines
Boulogne

**5**
31 July – 4 August 1588—English fleet under Howard and Drake engages Armada; actions indecisive, but Spanish suffer losses

**2**
1587 — English raids along Spanish and Portuguese coast destroy supplies essential to Armada.

**4**
21 July 1588—After scattering during storm and losing several ships, Armada regroups and sets sail for English coast.

**3**
9 May 1588—Armada sets sail with 130 ships under Duke of Medina Sidonia, insufficiently provisioned.

FRANCE

**8**
Late September— early October 1588 — Only 67 ships of the Armada return to Spain.

**1**
Philip II raises Armada in effort to crush Elizabeth and restore Catholicism in England.

Corunna Santander

PORTUGAL
Lisbon
Madrid
SPAIN

*Mediterranean Sea*

0    100    200 miles
0  100  200  300 km

Spanish territory
Roman Catholic
Protestant and Anglican

✳ Known site of Armada shipwrecks

PHILIP II formed his Grand Armada to answer a number of grievous challenges to his Roman Catholic faith and his dignity as King of Spain and Naples (1556) and Portugal (1580). He was a religious zealot, sure of his personal mission to reestablish Catholic Chris-tendom. He put down a last desperate revolt of the Moriscos—secret Moorish Muslims, who had outwardly con-formed to the established religion—with ruthless severity (1569–71). On 7 October 1571 the long naval duel with the Turks culminated in the Battle of

*Commemorative medal showing Elizabeth I of England, struck after the defeat of the Spanish Armada, 1588.*

Lepanto. In the greatest naval action since Octavian defeated Antony and Cleopatra at Actium (31 BCE), eighty Turkish galleys were sunk and 130 captured. Philip ruled over half the Habsburg interests and the fabulously rich Spanish empire in the New World, and he did not think of himself as a man to be trifled with.

The English were a constant irritation. They sympathized with the Dutch and gave them assistance. Their freebooters raided the convoys from New Spain. They defied the pope and persisted in loyalty to a bastard, excommunicate queen. They reversed the return to Catholicism which Philip's wife Mary Tudor had initiated while she was queen. Finally, they acquiesced in the death of the Catholic

Mary Stuart, Queen of Scots, who had been forced out of her realm by John Knox and the Protestant chiefs and then—after a long imprisonment—was executed by order of Queen Elizabeth I.

The Grand Armada was the most awesome force sent against England for half a millennium, and it was supported and equipped by the most wealthy and powerful ruler on the continent. Anxiety ran high.

The Armada (132 vessels and 3,165 cannons) was harassed by the small, fast British ships under Drake, Hawkins and Howard. Its ruin was completed by great storms, which drove the unwieldy galleons on shore. In this great deliverance the devout perceived the hand of God, and poets and preachers made the most of it.

After the defeat of the Armada, the British and Dutch began to attack Portuguese possessions. Portugal was under Philip's rule from 1580 until his death. By 1640 many of the Portuguese colonies had fallen to the combined attack.

*A Spanish ship of the Armada.*

*I have come to win gold, not to plow the fields like a peasant!* — Cortez

## LATIN AMERICA 16TH–18TH CENTURIES

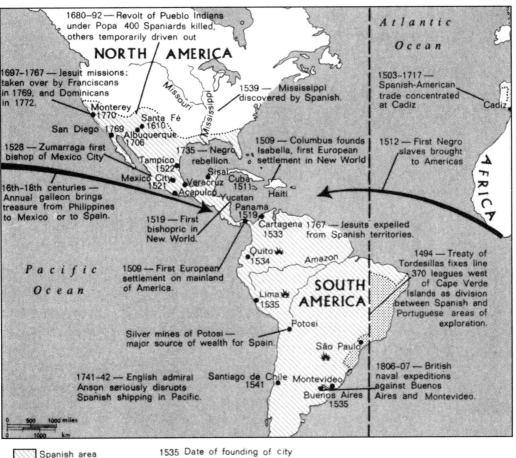

1680–92 — Revolt of Pueblo Indians under Popa 400 Spaniards killed, others temporarily driven out

**NORTH AMERICA**

1697–1767 — Jesuit missions; taken over by Franciscans in 1769, and Dominicans in 1772.

1539 — Mississippi discovered by Spanish.

*Atlantic Ocean*

1503–1717 — Spanish-American trade concentrated at Cadiz

Cadiz

Monterey 1770

Santa Fé 1610

San Diego 1769

Albuquerque 1706

1528 — Zumarraga first bishop of Mexico City

1735 — Negro rebellion.

Tampico 1522

Mexico City 1521

Veracruz

Sisal

Cuba 1511

1509 — Columbus founds Isabella, first European settlement in New World

1512 — First Negro slaves brought to Americas

16th–18th centuries — Annual galleon brings treasure from Philippines to Mexico or to Spain.

Acapulco

Yucatan

Haiti

1519 — First bishopric in New World.

Panama 1519

Cartagena 1533

1767 — Jesuits expelled from Spanish territories.

1509 — First European settlement on mainland of America.

Quito 1534

Amazon

1494 — Treaty of Tordesillas fixes line 370 leagues west of Cape Verde Islands as division between Spanish and Portuguese areas of exploration.

*Pacific Ocean*

**SOUTH AMERICA**

Lima 1535

Potosi

São Paulo

Silver mines of Potosi — major source of wealth for Spain.

1741–42 — English admiral Anson seriously disrupts Spanish shipping in Pacific.

Santiago de Chile 1541

Montevideo

Buenos Aires 1535

1806–07 — British naval expeditions against Buenos Aires and Montevideo.

AFRICA

0  500  1000 miles
0  1000  km

▨ Spanish area
▦ Portuguese area

1535 Date of founding of city
❦ Major 18th cent. Indian revolt

MANY of the great Spanish conquests were achieved in the New World by adventurers, who paid their own costs of expedition in return for letters patent to control and exploit the new area (*adelantado* system).

By 1542 there existed a Viceroyalty of Peru (capital: Lima) which included Panama and all of South America except Venezuela, and a Viceroyalty of New Spain (capital: Mexico City), including all claims north of Panama, the West Indies, Venezuela and the Philippines. Under the new legal code of 1542–43 admonition was issued to end the enslavement of the Indians and to guarantee that the settlers provide the natives who worked for them with protection and instruction in Christianity. In fact, however, hundreds of thousands of Indians were slaughtered in the Spanish conquests of the Aztec and Inca empires, and the remainder were decimated by disease and slavery.

Papal bulls regulated the conduct of church affairs in Spanish America. The church had its own court system governing the clergy and spiritual affairs. The Inquisition was introduced in 1569. Within a century there were seven archbishoprics and thirty-five dioceses.

*207*

5.
1528–30 — Begs among Spanish in Flanders and England.

DENMARK

IRELAND

ENGLAND

Hamburg

Cologne

*Atlantic Ocean*

HOLY ROMAN EMPIRE

Paris

FRANCE

Vienna

6.
1528–35 — Studies in Paris (M.A. 1535); 1534 — takes vows along with disciples.

1.
1521–22 — During convalescence after being wounded seriously in battle, Ignatius gains deep interest in religion.

2.
1522–23 — Lives as beggar, begins formulation of concepts leading to Jesuit movement.

Milan

Venice

GUIPÚZCOA

SPAIN

Manresa

7.
1535 — To Spain, then Italy; joined by disciples; 1537 — ordained; 1539 — Loyola and disciples form new order; 1540 — approved by Pope Paul III.

PAPAL STATES

Rome

Salamanca

Alcalá

Barcelona

NAPLES

Naples

PORTUGAL

4.
1524–26 — Studies at Barcelona, Alcalá, Salamanca; gains following; persecuted for teachings.

3.
1523–24 — Pilgrimage to Holy Land.

*Mediterranean Sea*

0   100   200 miles
100   200   300 km

IGNATIUS Loyola (c 1491–1556) was one of the most remarkable persons in Christian history: he combined the spiritual strains of the crusades and monasticism, the crusaders' tradition of public heroism with a strongly disciplined program for the individual soul and mind. In addition, he had a genius for charismatic and yet clear-headed leadership.

Painfully wounded while a professional soldier, he resolved to become a faithful follower of Jesus. He went to the Montserrat Monastery and there took the monastic vows and hung up his arms in the chapel of the "Black Madonna." After temptations and agonies of soul that paralleled Luther's, he was given his Christian assurance in visions and trances. He worked out the first form of the manual of self-discipline, *Spiritual Exercises*, and then made a pilgrimage to Palestine.

Returning home, he won his M.A. at Paris and gathered his nucleus of a new order. On 15 August 1534 Ignatius and six others took vows of poverty, chastity and obedience and celebrated communion together.

The first plan of the group was to

*The "Black Madonna" of Montserrat.*

secure papal blessing and go to Palestine. The trip was not feasible, for the emperor, pope and Venice were all involved in a series of diplomatic and military actions to break up the alliance of Francis I and Suleiman I. Suleiman (sultan: 1520–66) had opened his long reign by conquering Belgrade, capturing the island of Rhodes from the Knights of St. John, invading Hungary, and mounting the First Siege of Vienna. By the time Suleiman died the Jesuit missionary passion, which remained constant, had reached thousands of miles further than Jerusalem.

In 1540 the order received written authorization from Paul III and set out to accomplish its mission: the internal reform of the church, the carrying of the gospel to the peoples of the newly discovered continents, and fighting heresy.

# THE RISE OF THE JESUITS
## 16TH–18TH CENTURIES

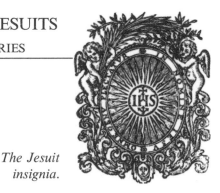

*The Jesuit insignia.*

THE Jesuits grew very rapidly, attracting especially the younger sons of noble families—many of whom had grown up in the atmosphere of knightly customs and with the education of a Christian prince, but who found no vacancies to fill at court. Because of their excellent contacts they were able to make the Society a power very early: it was the strongest force in the Counter-Reformation, including the final sessions of the Council of Trent. During the first hundred years the Society developed a number of the most important Roman Catholic leaders. They also wielded great influence among the laity by supervising the education of princes and by serving as advisors to kings. The order was military and authoritarian in structure, with absolute obedience to the "General" confirmed by vow.

Francis Xavier (1506–52) was a member of the original group. At the invitation of the King of Portugal he left Lisbon as a missionary to India, and in the last ten years of his life he baptized tens of thousands in India, Ceylon and Japan.

Matteo Ricci (1552–1610) began a great work in China, providing Chris-

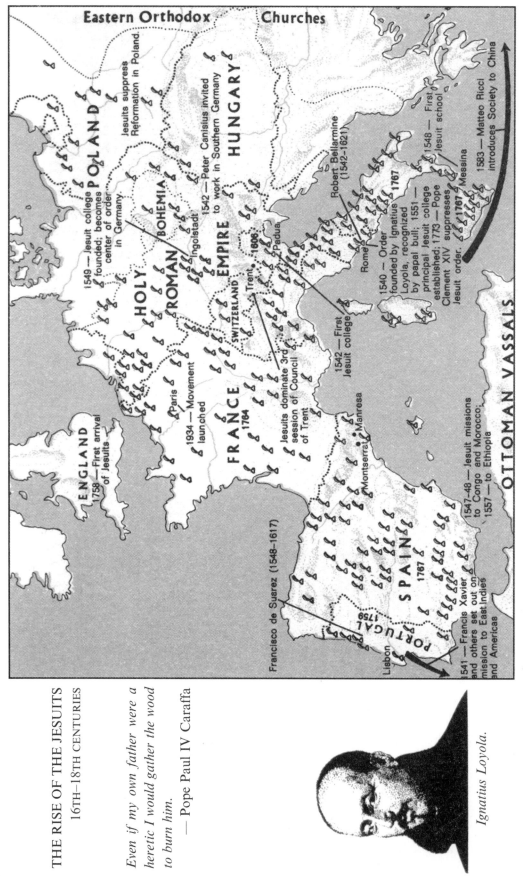

# THE RISE OF THE JESUITS
16TH–18TH CENTURIES

*Even if my own father were a heretic I would gather the wood to burn him.*

— Pope Paul IV Caraffa

Eastern Orthodox Churches

1549 — Jesuit college founded; becomes center of order in Germany.

Jesuits suppress Reformation in Poland.

POLAND

HUNGARY

1542 — Peter Canisius invited to work in Southern Germany

BOHEMIA

Ingolstadt

HOLY ROMAN EMPIRE

Trent 1606

Padua

SWITZERLAND

Robert Bellarmine (1542–1621)

Rome

1540 — Order founded by Ignatius Loyola, recognized by papal bull; 1551 — principal Jesuit college established; 1773 — Pope Clement XIV suppresses Jesuit order.

1767

1548 — First Jesuit school

1583 — Matteo Ricci introduces Society to China

Messina

1767

Jesuits dominate 3rd session of Council of Trent

1542 — First Jesuit college

ENGLAND
1758 — First arrival of Jesuits

Paris

1934 — Movement launched

FRANCE
1764

Montserrat

Manresa

OTTOMAN VASSALS

1547–48 — Jesuit missions to Congo and Morocco; 1557 — to Ethiopia

Francisco de Suarez (1548–1617)

SPAIN
1767

PORTUGAL 1759

Lisbon

1541 — Francis Xavier and others set out on mission to East Indies and Americas

𝄞 Jesuit college          1767 Date of expulsion of Jesuits

*Ignatius Loyola.*

210

*Jesuit convent in Macao, China, 19th century engraving.*

tian literature in Chinese. He adapted Christian concepts and ceremonies to traditional Chinese forms with a freedom that later produced considerable controversy. A century after his death some of his adaptations were officially condemned. Robert De Nobili (1577–1656) performed a similar service among the Brahmins for India.

James Laynez (1512–65) succeeded Ignatius as General and was a leader of the hardline caucus at Trent. By this time there were over a thousand members. Peter Canisius (1521–97) was an able preacher, apologist and diplomat—the most influential adversary of the Reformation in Germany and Poland. He founded colleges at Augsburg, Munich and Innsbruck. Francis Borgia (1510–72) was the third General. He reorganized and improved all phases of the Society's work. He gave special attention to missions in the Americas.

Robert Bellarmine (1542–1621), later a cardinal, was an erudite scholar who published an able refutation of Protestantism. Although in a long series of controversies with Protestants he also defended papal authority, his views on that subject were minimalist—which long delayed his canonization.

Francisco de Suarez (1548–1617) taught at several Jesuit colleges and at Alcalá and Coimbra. He published massive treatments of the thought of Thomas Aquinas, organized and brought up to date to appeal to contemporary thinkers, and thereby contributed to the revival of Thomism which attended the Counter-Reformation.

The Jesuits had a new understanding of discipleship, one that combined vision and planning on a large map with ascetic self-denial and resolute obedience. A representative case of selflessness and loyalty to the order, one that could be multiplied many times over, was Peter Canisius' rejection of the bishopric of Vienna. Because of his opposition to the reforms attempted by Hermann von Wied in the Cologne area, he attracted the sponsorship of Charles V's brother Ferdinand. When Ferdinand succeeded

*Pope Paul IV Caraffa.*

to the Empire, he offered Peter Canisius the key post in Vienna. Canisius refused the offer on instructions from the Jesuit General. In fact the Jesuits regularly refused preferment in the church, relenting only on papal demand.

The term "Counter-Reformation" has been used for centuries by Protestant and secular historians to refer to those measures successfully undertaken to check the evangelical movement in Spain, Italy, France, South Germany, Bohemia, Moravia and Poland. Because of its association with the Index and the Inquisition, and because of the polarization of opinion and politics which accompanied the wars of religion in France, the Netherlands and Germany, the Jesuit order was for long the special bête noire of lovers of political and religious liberty. Today it is clear that the roots of the reform movement within the entity that became the Roman Catholic Church at the Council of Trent (1545–63) lie deep in religious energies inspired by more than mere anti-Protestantism.

Although the Jesuits became the spearhead of reform within the church, as well as leaders of the fight against "heresy," several other orders preceded them in seeking a return to vigorous, selfless Christian service. The Theatines were founded at Rome in 1524 by Cajetan and Caraffa. Cajetan (1480–1547) was an advocate of internal church reform. Caraffa became Paul IV (pope: 1555–59), the first of the Counter-Reformation popes. The Capuchins were an offshoot of the Franciscans. In a rule drawn up in 1529 they sought to return to the austerity and primitive simplicity of the early years of the order. They survived the defection of their third General, Bernardino Ochino (1487–1564), to Protestantism, and became respected as preachers and men of action. The Barnabites were founded at Milan in 1530, with stress on educational and missionary work.

The internal reforms which these movements advocated were virtually the same as those advocated by the Protestants: elimination of simony, nepotism, immorality, etc. In doctrine they took another path, and they held to obedience to the pope in a way that brooked no compromise with those who pursued national, republican or democratic principles of church government.

While South Germany was being held to Roman obedience, the Catholic cantons of the Swiss confederation were also given support and leadership. Milan was still a major political force, whose treaties or wars with emperor, Spain, France and Naples were important in the history of the period. Milan's relations with Switzerland were both politically and militarily very active. Under Charles Borromeo (1538–84), who was prominent at Trent, a thoroughgoing reformation of Milan was carried out with reorganization of education, discipline of immorality in the clergy, and expansion of the works of charity. The archbishop also established a Jesuit seminary in Lucerne in 1577. Francis de Sales (1567–1622) was bishop and leader of the Counter-Reformation forces in Geneva. He was also spiritual director of Jane Francis de Chantal, founder of the Order of the Visitation (Annecy, 1610).

The greatest victory of the Counter-Reformation was probably scored in Poland, where a heterogeneous Protestantism—Lutheran, Calvinist, Anabaptist and Anti-Trinitarian—was predominant until the coming of the Jesuits and the Inquisition. Here Copernicus (1473–1543) had upset the official teaching about the sun and the planets, with revolutionary impact on the men of the universities. Here John à Lasco (1499–1560), a scholar and preacher of international reputation, was the foremost spokesman for conservative reformation (Calvinist).

In the immediate pre-Reformation and Reformation periods Poland was politically weak. Russia, Sweden and Denmark all had claims. Pressure from the Teutonic Knights was constant. Turkish invasions were not unknown. The elected king was dependent upon a national diet composed of noble delegates, among whom unanimous decisions were required on important issues. Under Sigismund II (king: 1548–72) both learning and the new faith flourished. His successor promised religious freedom for all parties. With Sigismund III (king: 1587–1632), a Vasa who had been educated by the Jesuits came to the throne. His long reign brought grave damage to Protestantism, and his constant wars shattered Poland economically.

The most significant intellectual scores against the Jesuits were made by Blaise Pascal (1623–62), the great mathematician and theologian of Port-Royal. His *Lettres provinciales* (1656–57) became a famous attack on Jesuit casuistry: he charged them with betraying the discipline and simplicity of the early church.

In the age of the "enlightened despots" the Society—charged with political reaction, ardent loyalty to an international power, and hostility to liberty and progress—was expelled from a number of countries and for a generation suppressed by the pope (1773–1814).

*Copernicus.*

*Blaise Pascal.*

MISSIONARIES to the American Indians often went out with a thoroughly romantic notion of the natives, their life unspoiled by the corruptions of European society. When the Swiss Brethren of Zürich were imprisoned for their beliefs (c 1525), they spoke of escaping their persecutors by "going to the red Indians across the sea." Some of the Jesuit fathers entertained the same illusions, but they found the natives capricious and cruel.

To the natural suspicions of the Indians against the intruder must also be reckoned the effect of European morals, wars and other customs upon a less aggressive society. By and large the French colonists and traders were allied with the Algonquin tribes, the English with the Iroquois. Fathers Brébeuf and Jogues were indeed martyred by the Iroquois—but whether as Christian missionaries or as Frenchmen is uncertain. Nor does it make too much difference, perhaps, when neither Indians nor white men distinguished between political and religious purposes.

Indian wars were a kind of game, rough but not genocidal. Even scalping, a supposedly typical Indian unpleasantness, seems to have gotten its big impulse when the British started paying bounties to allied Indians for enemy scalps. The Indians gave Europe many things, including the pumpkin, squash, potato (which made the Prussian military establishment possible), tobacco, corn (maize); the Europeans gave the Indians many things, including smallpox, whooping cough, whiskey, broken treaties, syphilis, and Christianity. In both Spanish and English empires, the natives who survived ended up near the bottom of the economic ladder: only the African slaves and their descendants were worse off. The French treated the Indians better.

Some of the missionaries faced not

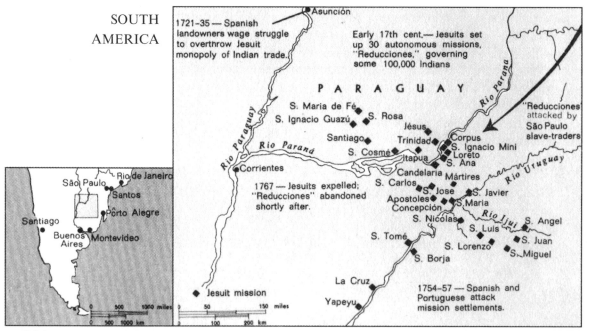

SOUTH AMERICA

1721–35 — Spanish landowners wage struggle to overthrow Jesuit monopoly of Indian trade.

Asunción

Early 17th cent.— Jesuits set up 30 autonomous missions, "Reducciones," governing some 100,000 Indians

PARAGUAY

Rio Paraná

"Reducciones" attacked by São Paulo slave-traders

S. Maria de Fé
S. Ignacio Guazú
S. Rosa
Jésus
Santiago
Trinidad
Corpus
S. Ignacio Mini
Loreto
S. Cosmé
Itapua
S. Ana
Corrientes
Candelaria
Mártires
Rio Uruguay

1767 — Jesuits expelled; "Reducciones" abandoned shortly after.

S. Carlos
Apostoles
Concepción
S. Nicolás
S. Tomé
S. José
S. Javier
S. Maria
Rio Ijui
S. Angel
S. Luis
S. Juan
S. Lorenzo
S. Miguel
S. Borja

Rio Paraguay

Rio Paraná

La Cruz
Yapeyu

1754–57 — Spanish and Portuguese attack mission settlements.

♦ Jesuit mission

0    500    1000 miles
0  500  1000 km

0    50    150 miles
0   100   200 km

Rio de Janeiro
São Paulo
Santos
Pôrto Alegre
Santiago
Buenos Aires
Montevideo

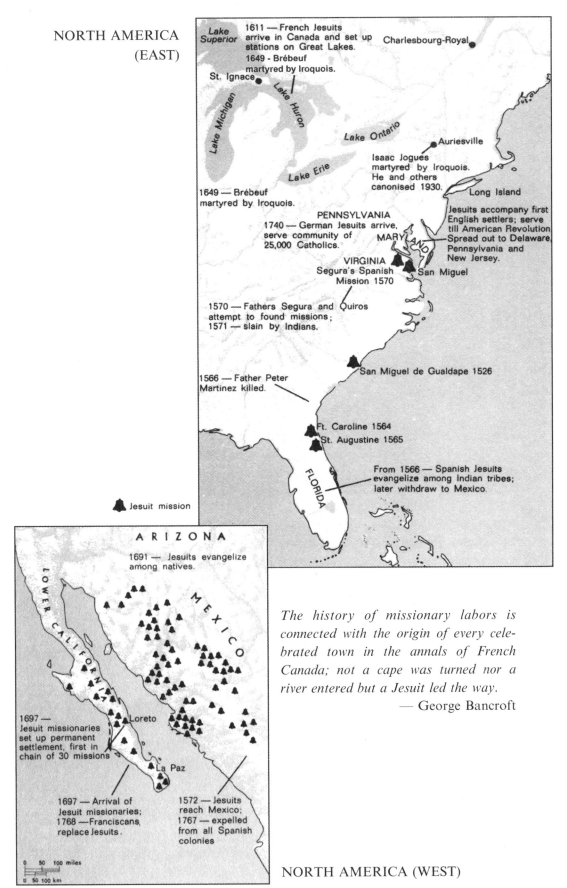

NORTH AMERICA
(EAST)

1611 — French Jesuits arrive in Canada and set up stations on Great Lakes.
1649 - Brébeuf martyred by Iroquois.

Charlesbourg-Royal

Lake Superior

St. Ignace

Lake Michigan

Lake Huron

Lake Ontario

Lake Erie

Auriesville

Isaac Jogues martyred by Iroquois. He and others canonised 1930.

1649 — Brébeuf martyred by Iroquois.

Long Island

PENNSYLVANIA
1740 — German Jesuits arrive, serve community of 25,000 Catholics.

Jesuits accompany first English settlers; serve till American Revolution. Spread out to Delaware, Pennsylvania and New Jersey.

MARYLAND

San Miguel

VIRGINIA
Segura's Spanish Mission 1570

1570 — Fathers Segura and Quiros attempt to found missions; 1571 — slain by Indians.

1566 — Father Peter Martinez killed.

San Miguel de Gualdape 1526

Ft. Caroline 1564
St. Augustine 1565

FLORIDA

From 1566 — Spanish Jesuits evangelize among Indian tribes; later withdraw to Mexico.

△ Jesuit mission

ARIZONA
1691 — Jesuits evangelize among natives.

LOWER CALIFORNIA

MEXICO

1697 —
Jesuit missionaries set up permanent settlement, first in chain of 30 missions

Loreto

La Paz

1697 — Arrival of Jesuit missionaries; 1768 — Franciscans replace Jesuits.

1572 — Jesuits reach Mexico; 1767 — expelled from all Spanish colonies

*The history of missionary labors is connected with the origin of every celebrated town in the annals of French Canada; not a cape was turned nor a river entered but a Jesuit led the way.*
— George Bancroft

0   50   100 miles
0   50  100 km

NORTH AMERICA (WEST)

215

only the natives but also their exploiters with exemplary courage. Bartolomé de Las Casas (1474–1560) and Domingo de Salazar (1513–94) were outstanding; the latter was later Bishop of Manila and champion of the natives' interests in the Philippines.

One of the most famous efforts to protect the natives from the destructive effect of contact with the Europeans ran from 1618 to 1767 in Paraguay. To accomplish their purpose the Jesuits secured a patent of monopoly in the Indian trade and proceeded to gather them into communes in an area remote from both slavers and white gentry. Here the Indians received careful instruction, practical training in farming and the manual arts. Each commune was built about a church, which was the center for singing and religious dances. A militia was organized and drilled in self-defense. At one time this Jesuit experiment in Christian community life numbered some thirty communes and between 100,000 and 150,000 members.

## THE COUNCIL OF TRENT 1545–63

PERIOD I
1545–47
SESSIONS
I–VIII

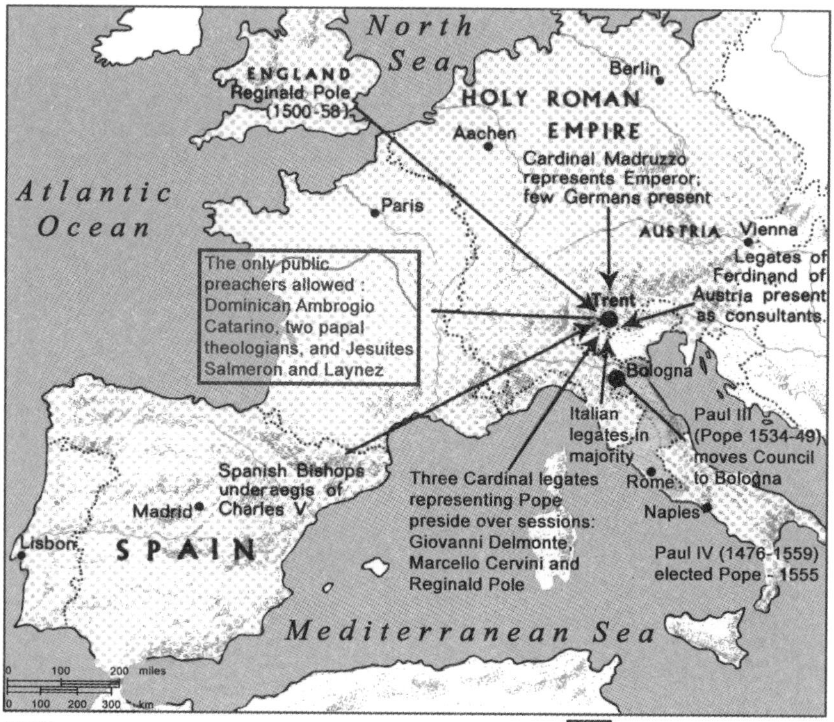

Key also to maps on p. 217, 218.
Countries with major representation at Council
Countries represented at Council
German Protestants
Borders 1550

In the judgment of some historians the call for a General Council came too late: instead of bringing about a reunion of the *corpus christianum* on a reform program, it could only shore up and define the polarization on the Catholic side.

The delay, however, arose from several causes besides the disinterest of Martin Luther and the pope. It was

216

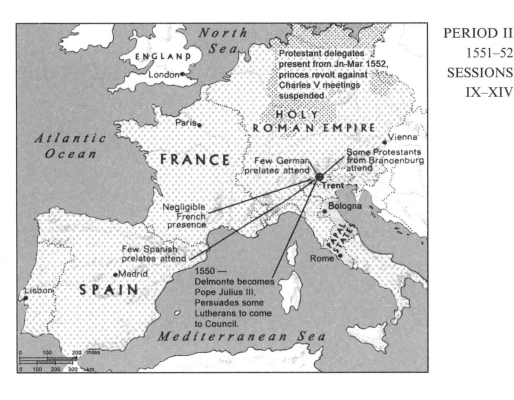

Map labels:
North Sea
ENGLAND
London
Atlantic Ocean
Paris
FRANCE
HOLY ROMAN EMPIRE
Vienna
Protestant delegates present from Jn–Mar 1552, princes revolt against Charles V meetings suspended
Some Protestants from Brandenburg attend
Few German prelates attend
Trent
Negligible French presence
Bologna
PAPAL STATES
Few Spanish prelates attend
Rome
Madrid
SPAIN
Lisbon
1550 — Delmonte becomes Pope Julius III, Persuades some Lutherans to come to Council.
Mediterranean Sea

the continuing conflict of Spain (Charles V) and France (Francis I) that was most responsible for the delay. By the time the Council finally convened, Lutheranism was an organized body of doctrine, Strassburg and Hesse were set in their religious ways, and Calvin was well into his second administration at Geneva.

The first sitting was small, and it consisted of churchmen rather than the lay princes to whom the Reformers looked for leadership. There were present some Catholic reformers of the Humanist tradition, with whom Protestants like Butzer and Melanchthon had cultural affinity and with whom they had worked in reunion meetings in 1540–41. Prominent among them was Reginald Pole (1500–58), Archbishop of Canterbury under Mary Tudor, a correspondent of More and Erasmus who missed election to the papacy in 1549 by one vote. But the method of voting which had been used at Constance (1414–18) was changed to individual balloting, which gave the pro-papal Italian bloc control. And only members of the papal caucus, including two Jesuits, were allowed to preach at the public meetings.

The first important decision was to treat doctrinal and disciplinary matters alternately. On 8 April 1546 it was decided that the Bible and tradition are equally valid sources of the truth, that the church alone may interpret the Bible authoritatively, that Jerome's translation (the *Vulgate*) was normative. This meant that no reconciliation with the Protestants was intended, for all present knew well the Reformers' assertion of the primacy of the Bible and of the preacher's responsibility to study out the Word from the original texts. The decrees on justification, original sin and the sacraments (seven of them fixed for the first time at the Council of Florence in 1439 and here reaffirmed) simply reinforced the wall between the churches.

The second setting was attended for a

time by some Protestants, who called unsuccessfully for a reopening of debate on earlier decisions. They also tried to get the council to reaffirm the doctrine which had governed the reform council of Basel (1431–49), namely the supremacy of a General Council over the pope. With little participation from France or Spain, the council proceeded under Italian domination to several important decisions: e.g., the Eucharist was defined in terms of transubstantiation and Calvinist, Zwinglian and Lutheran views were condemned.

No meeting took place under the violently anti-Protestant Paul IV (pope: 1555–59). When the final sitting was held the Jesuits were in control. Most of the Humanists of the Erasmian tradition had died out and their works were already on the Index. Substantial delegations from Spain and France appeared, the latter sometimes at cross-purposes with the Italians. Important reforming measures were

passed on education, providing for greatly improved training of priests and control of their conduct. The appointment of bishops was regularized. Provision was made for synods at provincial and diocesan levels. An initiative undertaken by the Emperor (Ferdinand II) working through the Cardinal of Lorraine, calling for a thoroughgoing reorganization and reform of the Latin church, was thwarted. The Council was kept on its predetermined course in good part through the able chairmanship of Cardinal Giovanni Morone (1509–80), the last remaining high churchman who had once enjoyed the confidence of Erasmians, Reformers and secular rulers.

After the Council adjourned its actions were confirmed and issued by Pius IV (26 January 1564), along with his revisions and decisions on several issues which the Council had left unsettled. The Roman Catholic Church was set on its course.

PERIOD III
1562–63
SESSIONS
XV–XXV

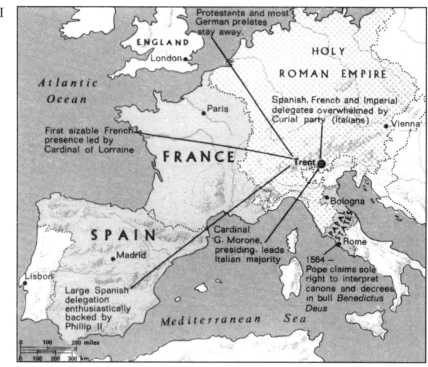

Protestants and most German prelates stay away.

ENGLAND
London

Atlantic Ocean

Paris

First sizable French presence led by Cardinal of Lorraine

FRANCE

SPAIN
Madrid

Lisbon

Large Spanish delegation enthusiastically backed by Phillip II

Mediterranean Sea

HOLY ROMAN EMPIRE

Spanish, French and Imperial delegates overwhelmed by Curial party (Italians)
Vienna

Trent

Bologna

Cardinal G. Morone, presiding, leads Italian majority

PAPAL STATES

Rome

1564 — Pope claims sole right to interpret canons and decrees in bull *Benedictus Deus*

100    200 miles
100  200  300 km

WITH the fall of Constantinople (1453) the Ottoman Turks became the masters of the eastern Mediterranean. Their mastery of the sea was not challenged until Lepanto (1571), nor their surge up the Balkans into central Europe checked until John Sobieski (king of Poland: 1674–96) saved Vienna (1683). During the entire period of the Reformation and Counter-Reformation, therefore, the Turks were a powerful factor in European politics. Their military might was indeed substantial: during the Second Siege of Vienna, Belgrade (captured in 1521) was used as the staging area, and caravans numbering some 70,000 camels hauled supplies for the assault.

*Turkish soldier with two captured peasants.*

The Venetian republic, which had dominated eastern trade after the decline of Byzantium, was checked and reduced (wars between Venice and the Turks: 1463–79, 1499–1503, 1537–40, 1645–64, 1718). The Habsburg domains in eastern Europe were under constant attack after the Balkans were overrun, and even sections of Poland, the Ukraine and western Russia were for long periods of time under Turkish control or tribute. In 1571 the pope organized a Holy League against the Turks, which resulted in the victory of Lepanto under Don Juan of Austria; but Spain and Venice fell out and let the immediate benefits run through their fingers.

The Ottomans had first crossed into Europe in 1345, intervening in a dynastic quarrel in Byzantium. From that time on they controlled the eastern emperors. A few years later the Janissary corps was organized, consisting of Christian children kidnapped, re-educated and trained as elite Muslim fighters. Turkish dominion was extended over Bulgaria, Serbia, Wallachia, Albania and Bosnia even before Constantinople fell. As a result of the battle of Mohács (1526), Hungary came under Turkish dominion, although Lutheranism was well established in the cities. Transylvania, where the majority of both nobility and middle class embraced Calvinism, and religious toleration was decreed in 1560, paid tribute to the Turks from c 1540.

In terms of the kind of Christianity that survived in the Balkans it is worth remembering that Greece was under Muslim control until 1831 and Serbia until 1856.

Dynastic struggles divided Islam as well as Christendom, and even during the most earnest military engagements between one Muslim ruler and another Christian prince the adversaries of both might form an alliance. Francis I of

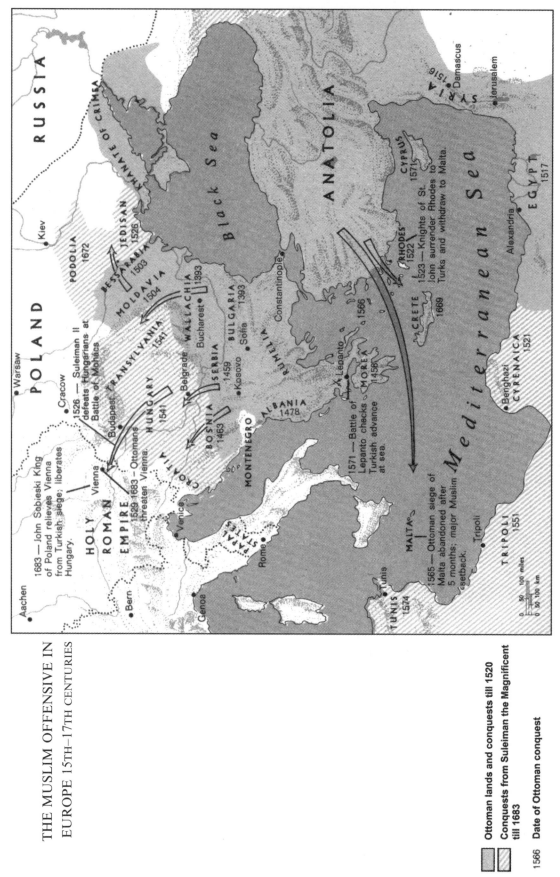

THE MUSLIM OFFENSIVE IN
EUROPE 15TH–17TH CENTURIES

Ottoman lands and conquests till 1520

Conquests from Suleiman the Magnificent
till 1683

1566   Date of Ottoman conquest

1683 — John Sobieski King of Poland relieves Vienna from Turkish siege; liberates Hungary.

1529-1683 – Ottomans threaten Vienna.

1526 — Suleiman II defeats Hungarians at Battle of Mohács

1565 — Ottoman siege of Malta abandoned after 5 months; major Muslim setback.

1571 — Battle of Lepanto checks Turkish advance at sea.

1523 — Knights of St. John surrender Rhodes to Turks and withdraw to Malta.

France cultivated Suleiman and their joint fleets bombarded Nice during his fourth war with Charles V (1542–44). During Selim I's 1516 campaign against Persia, the Mameluke Sultan of Egypt entered into an alliance with Persia; Selim defeated him and sacked Cairo.

Under Selim II (Ottoman sultan: 1566–74), an interesting experiment in resettlement was undertaken. Among the thousands of Spanish Jews who arrived in and around Constantinople during the expulsion of Muslims and Jews from Spain and Naples, one Don Joseph Nasi became a friend and confidant of Selim. Selim gave him the region around the Sea of Galilee to settle Jewish refugees from Italy.

*Selim II.*

Except for occasional outbursts of fanaticism under zealots like the Almohades (10th–11th centuries) or Wahhabis (18th century), Islam—until the resurgence of Arab nationalism in the modern period—has frequently shown itself more tolerant than Christendom. In Egypt and Asia Minor small Christian communities wintered through for more than a millennium, although in rather fossilized conditions. When the Jews were forced out of the Iberian peninsula, most of them found haven in North Africa and Asia Minor. During their rule in eastern Europe, Turkish administrators protected Christian minorities. In the Balkans, substantial Christian churches emerged at the end of the nineteenth century with their liturgies and dogmas intact—although without any corpus of Christian ethics or idea of missions.

The Muslim policy of toleration never involved full equality for non-Muslim subjects. The *millet* system, an administrative device to define the status and handle the affairs of minorities that goes back to the Roman Empire ("isopolity"), regulated the status of Christians and Jews under Islam. Muslim hostility toward its own "heresies" has been far more ruthless, as—for example—toward the Druses, followers of the prophet Al-Hakim (Egyptian caliph: 996–1020), or in Selim II's slaughter of some 40,000 of his own Shi'ite subjects (1514).

*Suleiman the Magnificent.*

Archangel — Closed to shipping 6 months a year.

1721 — "Great Northern War" with Sweden ended by Treaty of Nystadt. Russia acquires "window" on the Baltic.

1703 — Peter founds St. Petersburg; later capital.

1666 — "Old Believers" excommunicated; and savagely persecuted.

1652-67 — Reforms of Nikon, Patriarch of Moscow, (1652-66), lead to schism of "Old Believers"

1695 — Peter attacks Turks, captures Azov, sets up Taganrog naval base; 1711 — surrenders all gains.

1722-23 — Russia invades Persia.

1637 — Cyril Lucaris (1572-1638) Patriarch of Constantinople, in contact with Western Calvinists. 1642 — his doctrines repudiated at Synod of Jerusalem.

White Sea

Gulf of Bothnia

CARELIA
Petrozavodsk

Baltic Sea

Vyburg
Helsingfors

Dagö Is.

ESTONIA
INGRIA St. Petersburg
Narva

Osel Is.

LIVONIA
Riga

Novgorod

Vilna

Minsk

Smolensk

Gomel

Chernigov

Kiev

Lemberg

Kursk

Poltava

Kharkov

Kaluga

Orel

Voronezh

Yaroslavl
Rostov
Suzdal
Vladimir
Moscow

Ryazan

Nizhni Novgorod

Kazan

Penza

Samara

Sartov

Yaitsk

Tsaritsyn

Guryev

Astrakhan

RUSSIA

Pelym

Solikamsk

Taganrog
Azov

Azov Sea

Herch

Balaklava

Black Sea

CAUCASUS

Caspian Sea

Tarki
Derbent

Baku

Constantinople

OTTOMAN EMPIRE

Resht

PERSIA

0   100   200 miles
0   100   200   300 km

Russia before Peter the Great
Territory added by Peter the Great

RUSSIA UNDER THE TSARS
1547–1725

BEFORE the Schism of 1054 the Latin Church and the Eastern Orthodox churches were already going separate ways. The Orthodox rejected all doctrinal change after the last of the first Seven Ecumenical Councils (Nicaea II, 787). Unlike western Europe, where for centuries the pope was the only leader of power and authority both religious and political, in eastern Europe the Orthodox churches used the languages of their peoples and developed church orders within the nations, under an Ecumenical Patriarchate at Constantinople.

In 1547 Ivan IV (ruler: 1533–84) was the first to take the title of Tsar. He gained an outlet to the Baltic after a war with the Teutonic Knights. In 1589 Moscow was given an independent patriarchate, and the vision of the city as "the Third Rome" came to the fore in the Russian church.

In the religious ferment of the period, Russian Orthodoxy withstood strong shocks from without and within. From Poland, where able kings were supporting the Jesuits, came pressure for a union with Rome. Following a synod in 1596, considerable numbers of Orthodox in Poland and Lithuania because Uniates (in communion with Rome but retaining their own rites). At the same time, Cyril Lucaris (1572–1638), who represented the Patriarch at the 1596 synod against union with Rome and was himself made Patriarch of Constantinople in 1620, was cultivating relations with Geneva and with the Church of England. In response to the Uniates and to Lucaris, Peter Mogila (1597–1646), Metropolitan of Kiev, prepared a full and authoritative survey of Orthodox teaching.

*Ivan IV.*

Under Michael Romanov (tsar: 1613–45), political order was restored after a "time of troubles." Shortly thereafter occurred one of the most important and lasting schisms in Orthodoxy. Nikon (patriarch: 1652–66), one of the ablest and most zealous men in Russian church history, undertook a reform of the service books according to old texts. He was opposed by another reform group that took the more traditional Russian ways of prayer and fasting. The resistance accused Nikon of corrupting the familiar texts, of using the hierarchy to undermine the rights of ordinary priests, of arbitrary exercise of power. He was deposed when he lost the support of the tsar, Alexis. But the synod which deposed him adopted many of his reforms, and the Old Believers refused to obey. Since their cause rallied many of the lower classes, and was even linked to a revolt of the Moscow garrison (*Streltzy*), the autho-

*Nikon, Patriarch of Moscow.*

*Statue of Peter the Great, St. Petersburg.*

rities set out to crush them. Tens of thousands were buried alive, many more had their right hands chopped off (for using two fingers instead of three in the blessing)—but they have persisted to the present day.

Under Peter the Great (tsar: 1689–1725), the Russian church was brought so completely under state control that the patriarchate lapsed for two centuries. In its place the Holy Synod emerged (1721), and the government's Monastic Office was reconstituted to control the wealth of the church. Peter's energies were directed toward the modernization of his realm and the strengthening of the monarch's authority against centrifugal forces—nobles (*boyars*) and church. During this era occurred the last great intervention of the Swedes, with the wars of Charles XII against Russia (1700–21), which ended with the cession by Sweden to Russia of Livonia, Estonia, Ingermanland and other territories. Russia became a European power.

# K. EUROPEAN CHRISTENDOM IN THE AGE OF COLONIALISM

## ENGLISH COLONIES IN AMERICA 17TH–18TH CENTURIES

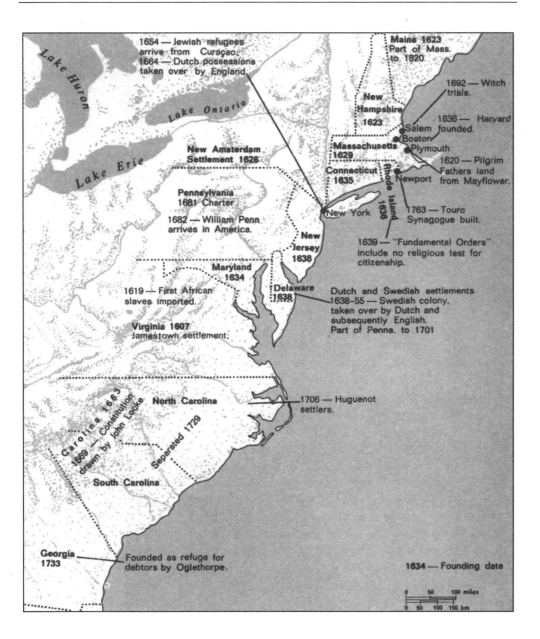

1654 — Jewish refugees arrive from Curaçao.
1664 — Dutch possessions taken over by England.

Maine 1623 Part of Mass. to 1820.

1692 — Witch trials.

New Hampshire 1623

1636 — Harvard founded.

Salem
Boston
Plymouth

Massachusetts 1629

New Amsterdam Settlement 1626

Connecticut 1635

Rhode Island 1636
Newport

1620 — Pilgrim Fathers land from Mayflower.

Pennsylvania 1681 Charter

1682 — William Penn arrives in America.

New York

1763 — Touro Synagogue built.

New Jersey 1638

1639 — "Fundamental Orders" include no religious test for citizenship.

Maryland 1634

Delaware 1638

Dutch and Swedish settlements 1638-55 — Swedish colony, taken over by Dutch and subsequently English. Part of Penna. to 1701

1619 — First African slaves imported.

Virginia 1607 Jamestown settlement.

Carolina 1663 Constitution 1669 drawn by John Locke

North Carolina

1706 — Huguenot settlers.

Separated 1729

South Carolina

Georgia 1733

Founded as refuge for debtors by Oglethorpe.

1634 — Founding date

0    50    100 miles
0  50  100  150 km

*No person within the said Colony, at any time hereafter, shall be in any wise molested, punished, disquieted or called in question, for any differences in opinions in matters of religion.*

— Rhode Island petition for a charter

ALTHOUGH several European nations undertook settlements in North America, only English and French exploration and colonization were extensive enough to make a bid for control of the continent. The Spanish settlements,

*Penn makes the Charter Oak Treaty with the Indians.*

important for a time in what are now Florida and Louisiana, left permanent impress upon the Southwest and West (now Texas, New Mexico, Arizona and California). This was an extension northward, however, of the earlier empire of New Spain. The question whether England or France would control the continent was not settled until the Seven Years' War (in America the "French and Indian War," 1756–63).

New Amsterdam was founded in 1626, after Dutch traders had for more than a decade carried on a profitable fur trade along the Hudson River; in 1664 it fell to English forces and was renamed New York. In 1638, Swedish settlements were made along the Delaware, but the Dutch captured Fort Christiana and took control of New Sweden from 1655 until the English victories.

English fishing and trading posts operated along the coast for some years before permanently chartered colonies were founded. Of these, the first was Jamestown Colony (1607) in Virginia. The Church of England was established. In 1612 the cultivation of tobacco was started. In 1619 the first African slaves arrived aboard a Dutch ship. The rule of the colony was aristocratic and authoritarian, producing continual conflict between independent farmers and artisans and the governing element which was fostering a plantation economy.

In 1620 there arrived on the "Mayflower," landing in the dead of winter at Cape Cod, a company of English separatists. Making landfall south of the territory which had been granted the London Company with which they had dealt, they drew up the first democratic charter in the new world. By the Mayflower Compact they translated into a political agreement the understanding of the voluntary base of human associations which had already made them radical Puritans in church matters, exiles in the Netherlands from King James' England. Further settlements were made in areas which became New Hampshire and Maine, and then in 1629 and 1630 major expeditions of some twenty-two ships and 1,400 settlers arrived under the auspices of Massachusetts Bay. Although these latter were more conservative Puritans, they brought their charter with them along with their own governor (John Winthrop). Over the next decade or so more than 16,000 additional settlers came from the mother country. By 1636 a college was established (Harvard).

Plymouth Colony remained more democratic, and one of its major institutions—the congregational covenant—spread throughout the Bay Colony also. Massachusetts, with early villages at Salem, Boston, Dorchester, Watertown, established a state church and a representative assembly ("General Court") to replace the earlier open assembly of free citizens. Conflicts early arose between the establishment and dissenters like Anne Hutchinson and Roger Williams, and movements to the frontiers (Providence, Hartford) began which combined the quest for religious freedom, political democracy and economic opportunity.

To the south of Virginia, in the Carolinas and Georgia, the mixed tradition prevailed. Religiously, these colonies were officially Anglican; eco-nomically, the power rested with gentlemen plantation owners who worked slaves. Over against them were small farmers and artisans, largely Puritan, who tended to move westward from the tidewater region into the foothills of the Appalachian mountains.

## PENNSYLVANIA—A RELIGIOUS REFUGE 17TH–18TH CENTURIES

*I ever understand an impartial liberty of conscience to be the natural right of all men, and that he that had a religion without it, his religion was none of his own. For what is not the religion of a man's choice is the religion of him that imposes it: so that liberty of conscience is the first step to have a religion.*

— William Penn

WILLIAM Penn (1644–1718) was the largest landowner of his day, and because of his Quaker conviction he turned his holdings into a place of refuge for the persecuted "sects" of Christendom. He received the grant of Pennsylvania in payment of a debt owed his father by the Stuarts, with whom he remained on personal terms—although the connection did not save him from occasional imprisonment as a "sectarian."

The Society of Friends, commonly called "Quakers," had been pulled together by George Fox (1624–91) out of a number of individual "seekers" and mystical groups that flourished in radical Puritanism. Fox's extensive missionary journeys included the West Indies and North America. In 1682, Penn acquired letters patent to East Jersey and Pennsylvania. The Frank-

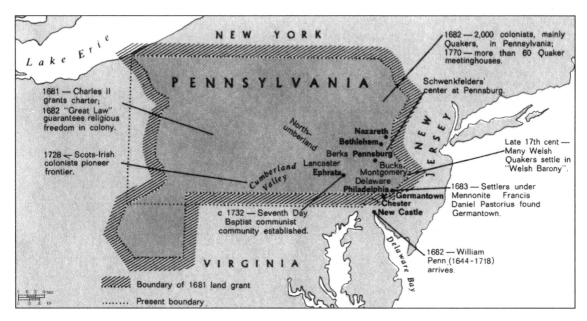

*The oldest Mennonite church in America, Germantown.*

German Mennonites, "Dunkers" (Brethren), Schwenkfelders, Baptists and others were immigrating and taking up land for communal settlements or individual farms. Many of the immigrants, too, were German Lutherans or Calvinists who made use of the *jus emigrandi* when the government of their home states chose other official religions than their own.

Pennsylvania thus became quite early the only large American colony with complete religious liberty (distinct from toleration, where an established church refrains from persecuting other churches), although under his sons and successors Penn's high standard was not maintained. Penn's own dealings with the Indians were also a model of fairness (Charter Oak Treaty, 1683), but here again his successors were unworthy and alienated the tribes by cheating them in land and trading deals.

furt Land Company which he founded became the instrument whereby many thousands of religious refugees escaped religious persecution in the old world. Thirty years after the colony was established on a platform of religious liberty there were more Friends in America than left in England, and

## INDIA c 1706

IN the eighteenth century the Indian sub-continent became a prime object of the ambitions of European trading and colonial interests, with the British finally establishing dominance (1761–1947). The way for colonial control was cleared by a century of religious wars and persecution between Moguls, Hindus and Sikhs. The victory of England over France was attained in a series of global conflicts which also involved North America (French and Indian Wars, 1756–63).

The earlier missionary work of the Jesuits is described elsewhere (see p. 209). The first Protestant missions came in 1706, under the sponsorship of the (Lutheran) King of Denmark; staffing was undertaken by the Pietist Missionary Center under August Hermann Francke (1663–1723) at Halle. B. Ziegenbalg (1683–1719) translated the New Testament and part of the Old Testament into Tamil. Part of his support came from missionary societies in Germany, part from the Society for Promoting Christian Knowledge (SPCK) in England. Another Lutheran missionary who made substantial contributions to the growth of Christianity in India was C. F. Schwarz, who worked there from 1750 until his death in 1798.

One of the major effects of Pietism was the growth of missionary awareness in Lutheran and Calvinist

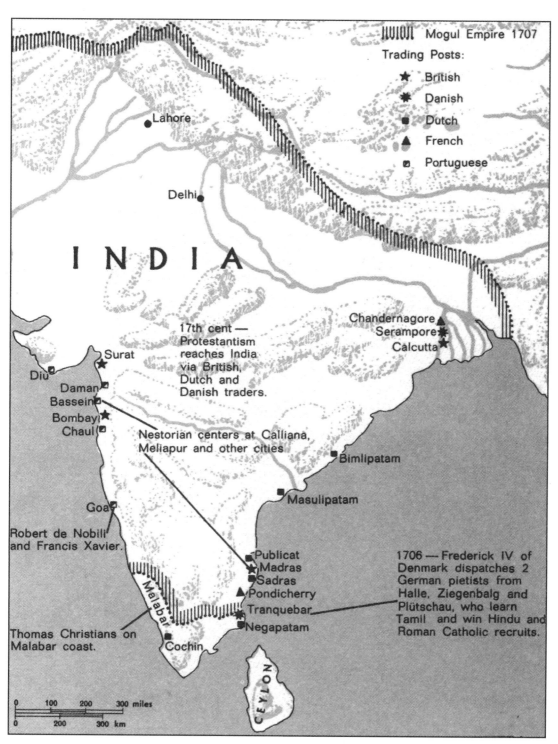

Mogul Empire 1707

Trading Posts:
- ★ British
- ✳ Danish
- ■ Dutch
- ▲ French
- ▣ Portuguese

Lahore

Delhi

INDIA

17th cent —
Protestantism
reaches India
via British,
Dutch and
Danish traders.

Chandernagore
Serampore
Calcutta

Surat
Diu
Daman
Bassein
Bombay
Chaul

Nestorian centers at Calliana,
Meliapur and other cities

Bimlipatam

Masulipatam

Goa

Robert de Nobili
and Francis Xavier.

Publicat
Madras
Sadras
Pondicherry
Tranquebar
Negapatam

1706 — Frederick IV of
Denmark dispatches 2
German pietists from
Halle, Ziegenbalg and
Plütschau, who learn
Tamil and win Hindu and
Roman Catholic recruits.

Malabar

Thomas Christians on
Malabar coast.

Cochin

CEYLON

0  100  200  300 miles
0  200  300 km

INDIA c 1706

229

*The Pietist Missionary Center at Halle, with portrait of August Hermann Francke in medallion, 18th century copperplate.*

churches. Admiring the early church, they stressed the authority of the Great Commission (Mt. 28:28–20, Mk. 16:15–16) and the model of Paul's journeys and epistles to young congregations. Francke, influenced by Philipp Jakob Spener, founded at Halle—where he was a professor from 1692— a number of institutes which reflected the Pietist concern of social service and missions. His educational practices later influenced the Prussian system and his missionary strategy opened the modern expansion of Protestant Christianity around the world.

## PIETISM 17TH–18TH CENTURIES

PIETISM is to be understood in part as a recovery of the eschatological dimension of primitive Christianity, re-emerging in a time of great suffering and despair of the prevailing conditions of Christendom. The hope of an imminent end of the old age of war and violence and brutal self-seeking was heightened. The marks of the last times included the reunion of the churches and the carrying of the Christian gospel to the most distant tribes and peoples. Some of the more intense Pietist groups established pacifist and communist communes in anticipation of the speedy return of the Lord to earth, in preparation for life in the coming kingdom.

Pietism was also in part a defense against the loss of whole sections of thought and culture to rationalism and secularization. Traditional orthodoxy, sustained by a coercive state-church system, was simply incapable of resisting the onslaught of the Enlightenment.

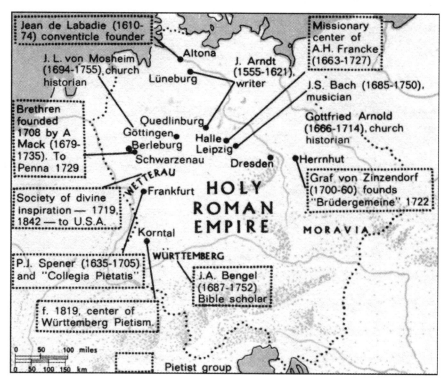

PIETISM IN GERMANY

The response of Pietism was to concentrate upon the internal history of the individual soul, upon evangelism and missions. Pietist historians like Gottfried Arnold (1666–1714) and Johann Lorenz von Mosheim (1694–1755) popularized the view of church history which made their own movement the culmination of the hope of the ages.

For centuries Christianity had spread by military conquest and political expansion, with whole tribes accepting baptism from dominant powers. With Pietism, individual conversion became the model. Nikolaus Ludwig, Count Zinzendorf (1700–60), founder of the Herrnhuter fellowship of brethren, explicitly repudiated mass conversions. At the same time he founded a number of communities of converted Christians in Europe and America, being opposed to both rationalist individualism and orthodox state-church coercion of a whole territory. Moravian work among the American Indians of Pennsylvania and Ohio was especially significant, although it ended as tragically as the earlier efforts of John Eliot in New England. In New England, after King Philip's War the Christian Indians were sold into slavery in the West Indies along with their warring family members. From 1763 to 1782 a series of semi-official sorties by mobs and militia wiped out the colonies of pacifist Christian Indians in Pennsylvania.

Men like John Wesley (1703–91), the founder of Methodism, and Jonathan Edwards (1703–58), theologian of the Great Awakening (the first of the great revivals of religion to produce masses of Christian volunteers in America), applied to evidences of religious renewal the powers of observation and reporting that others directed to the natural world.

As a student and teacher at Oxford,

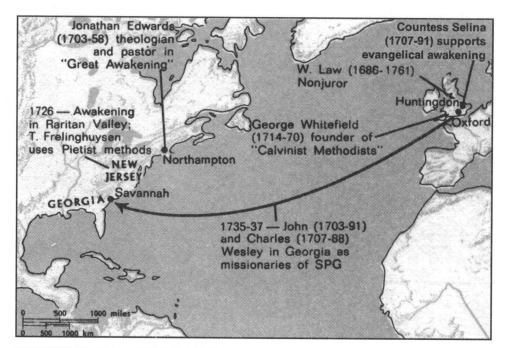

Wesley gathered about him a small group of earnest Christians living under a strict discipline of life. After brief missionary work in Georgia, during which he alienated his parishioners by condemning slavery and hard

*John Wesley.*

liquor and by an ill-conceived attempt to apply church discipline, he returned to England. Profoundly influenced by the Moravians, both on the continent and in England, he was converted to a live personal faith and became a wonderfully effective field preacher and organizer. With his brother Charles (1707–88), gifted hymn-writer, and George Whitefield (1714–70), John Wesley was founder of the Evangelical movement both within and outside the Church of England.

Jonathan Edwards, whose long pastorate at Northfield (Mass.) was cut off when he tried to introduce church discipline according to the New Testament model, like Wesley made keen and careful observations of the revival phenomena. His reports on the effects of the Great Awakening in New England (1734 ff.) are still valued by psychologists and educators. In principle a defender of orthodox Calvinism and New England's standing order, he found the evidence of the revivals to demonstrate the importance of the human response to the divine initiative, and the needs of the new converts to point toward voluntary religious activity and support not provided by the old parish system. Open to innovative "science," he died of an inoculation for smallpox, shortly after becoming president of the new "log college" set up by Presbyterian revivalists at Princeton.

The effect of Pietism was generally to carve out an area of personal and small group religion that was little affected by the Enlightenment's impact upon the orthodox religious establishments. Accepting the New Testament model as normative, it also had the effect of reducing the authority of Old Testament teachings and events and bringing the Jews under individual conversionist efforts.

There was another less consciously Christian response to the breakdown of the orthodox establishment: Romanticism. Already at work in J. G. Herder's thought, Romanticism stressed feeling, spirituality, poetic and artistic sensibility as innate human qualities. The "inwardness" which in George Fox and P. J. Spener had been clearly Christocentric was in Jean-Jacques Rousseau (1712–78), Johann Wolfgang von Goethe (1749–1832) and others abstracted in a way which combined indifference to historic Christianity with affirmation of natural human gifts—capable of either good or demonic consequences.

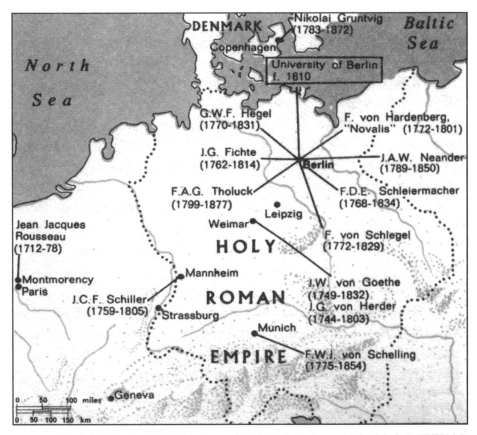

ROMANTICISM, NATIONALISM AND RELIGIOUS REVIVAL

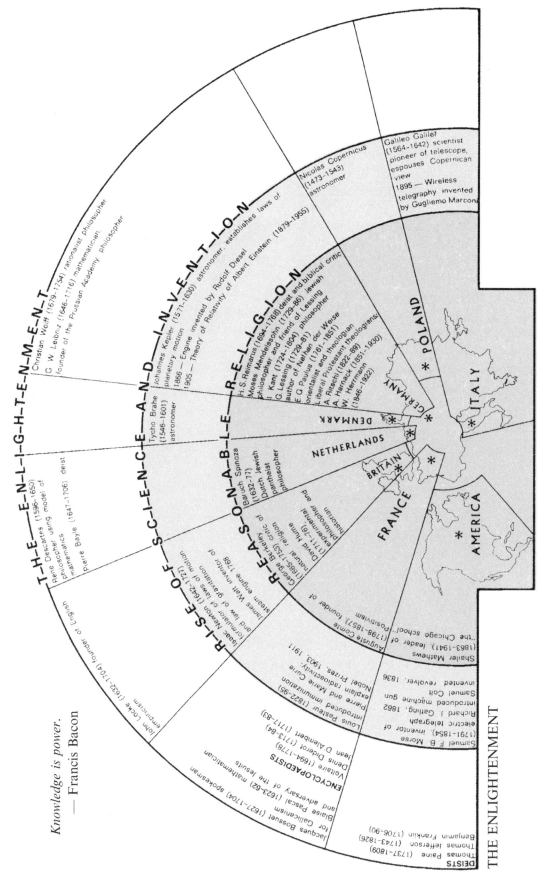

*Knowledge is power.*
— Francis Bacon

T-H-E---E-N-L-I-G-H-T-E-N-M-E-N-T

Christian Wolff (1679–1754) rationalist philosopher
G. W. Leibniz (1646–1716) mathematician, founder of the Prussian Academy philosopher

Rene Descartes using model of philosopher mathematics (1596–1650)

Pierre Bayle (1647–1706) deist

John Locke (1632–1704) founder of English empiricism

R-I-S-E---O-F---S-C-I-E-N-C-E---A-N-D---I-N-V-E-N-T-I-O-N

Nicolas Copernicus (1473–1543) astronomer

Galileo Galilei (1564–1642) scientist, pioneer of telescope, espouses Copernican view

1895 — Wireless telegraphy invented by Gugliemo Marconi

Johannes Kepler (1571–1630) astronomer, establishes laws of planetary motion

1866 — Engine invented by Rudolf Diesel
1905 — Theory of Relativity of Albert Einstein (1879–1955)

Tycho Brahe (1546–1601) astronomer

Isaac Newton (1642–1727) formulator of laws of motion and law of gravitation

James Watt inventor of steam engine 1788

R-E-A-S-O-N-A-B-L-E---R-E-L-I-G-I-O-N

H.S. Reimarus (1694–1768) deist and biblical critic
Moses Mendelssohn (1729–86) Jewish philosopher and friend of Lessing
G. Lessing (1724–1804) philosopher author of Nathan der Weise
E.G. Paulus (1761–1851) orientalist and theologian
A. Ritschl (1822–89) Liberal Protestant theologians;
A. Harnack (1851–1930)
W. Herrmann (1846–1922)

Baruch Spinoza (1632–77) Dutch Jewish pantheist philosopher

George Berkeley critic of natural religion (1685–1753)

David Hume (1711–76) experimental philosopher and historian

Auguste Comte (1798–1857) founder of "the Chicago school" positivism

Shailer Mathews (1863–1941), leader of

Samuel Colt invented revolver, 1836

Richard J. Gatling, 1862 introduced machine gun

Samuel F B Morse (1791–1854), inventor of electric telegraph

Louis Pasteur (1822–95) introduced immunization

Pierre and Marie Curie explain radioactivity; Nobel Prizes, 1903, 1911

Jean D'Alembert (1713–84)
Denis Diderot (1694–1778)
ENCYCLOPAEDISTS
Voltaire (1694–1778)

Blaise Pascal (1623–62) mathematician

Jacques Bossuet (1627–1704) spokesman for Gallicanism and adversary of the Jesuits

Benjamin Franklin (1706–90)
Thomas Jefferson (1743–1826)
Thomas Paine (1737–1809)
DEISTS

POLAND *
ITALY *
GERMANY *
DENMARK *
NETHERLANDS
BRITAIN *
FRANCE *
AMERICA *

THE ENLIGHTENMENT

THE Enlightenment marks in many ways the transition from medieval ways of life and thought to modernity. During the Renaissance and Reformation, the closed circle of unitary Christendom was shaken but not shattered. Martin Luther remained a medieval mind in his views on social and economic affairs. Leonardo da Vinci, in spite of his extraordinary imagination as a scientist and inventor, remained a pensioner of popes and executor of ecclesiastical commissions. Moreover, the devotion of the most creative minds of the period 1450–1550 to careful and critical observation of the evidence—whether physical or textual—had not yet produced the deep divisions between "science" and religious ideology, between "natural" evidence and "supernatural" faith, between technology and wisdom, which mark the world of post-Enlightenment men.

In the process of establishing a monolithic and comprehensive system of thought and controls, medieval Christianity had committed itself to a number of teachings about the natural world which could not stand the test of experimentation and careful observation. Nicholas Copernicus (1473–1543), Tycho Brahe (1546–1601) and Johannes Kepler (1571–1630) destroyed the model of an earth-centered universe which made possible traditional views of hell, earth and heaven. Kepler expounded "laws" of planetary motion which overpowered the apologetics of the churchmen, defended the Gregorian reform of the calendar against traditionalists both Roman Catholic and Protestant, and made a calculation concerning the "star of the Magi" (a conjunction of Mars, Saturn and Ju-

*John Locke.*

piter) which shifted the probable birth date of Jesus to 6 BCE. Isaac Newton (1642–1727), like Kepler deeply religious, nevertheless elaborated "laws" of motion and "laws" of gravitation which superseded the traditional churchly views of a static universe held together or transformed by divine intervention. The language of Mathematics began to replace the language of Myth.

The effect of the critical and skeptical approach soon made itself felt in religion, as well as in science and invention. Blaise Pascal (1623–62), a pioneer in calculus and hydrodynamics, was also a powerful champion of Jansenism against the Jesuits and the papacy. Gottfried Wilhelm Leibniz (1646–1716), the inventor of differential calculus, advanced a new theory of the divine nature of the universe. John Locke (1632–1704), a religious man but free of ecclesiastical discipline and dogma, developed a political theory which included reasonable religion and toleration.

The dominant figure in the German *Aufklärung* was Immanual Kant (1724–1804), Professor of Logic at Königsberg (East Prussia). He provided a system of philosophical thought which was moral but non-mysterious, of religious ideas consonant with Newtonian physics and mathematical formulae. His *Critique of Pure Reason and Religion Within the Limits of Reason Alone* repudiated the traditional Christian supernaturalism and left no place for a personal redeemer, no need for miracles, no room for mystical experiences. Religious events were of the same order as natural events, reasonable and understandable. Every event has an intelligible cause, and all knowledge is dependent on nature. His followers—men like H. S. Reimarus (1694–1768), Gotthold E. Lessing (1729–81), J. G. Herder (1744–1803)—rejected miracles, saints and relics, clerical celibacy, and were skeptical of organized religion generally. Lessing's friend Moses Mendelssohn (1729–86),

*Immanuel Kant.*

who was probably the model for his *Nathan der Weise*, furthered the spread of reasonable religion among educated Jews.

In the French Enlightenment, the leading figures—Denis Diderot (1713–84) of the *Encyclopédie*, Jean d'Alembert (1717–83) the Jansenist and mathematician, François-Marie Arouet/"Voltaire" (1694–1778)—were even more strongly opposed to the mysterious and traditional in religion. Opposed to the mythical and "irrational," they were both anti-Christian and antisemitic.

In the development of the science of religion (*Religionswissenschaft*) and scientific theology, later university men undertook to apply the canons of reasonable religion to Christian scriptures, doctrines, and church order. Toward the latter they were emancipated. Toward scriptures and doctrines, they pursued the rule that the mysterious and obscure teachings are less authoritative (or even authentic) than those that are clear and amenable to common sense.

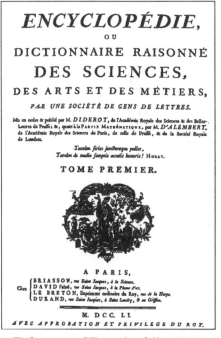

*Title page of* Encyclopédie, *1751.*

THE folly of Louis XIV, in destroying the French middle class (Huguenots) out of religious bigotry, and in impoverishing the peasantry to support his personal extravagances and constant warring, discredited the *ancien regime*. The brightest of the intellectuals, like the *Encyclopédistes*, were bitterly anti-clerical; they also challenged the viability of the absolute monarchy which had brought the country to disaster. They advocated the cause of the Third Estate (commons). As evident in *L'Esprit des Lois*, the great treatise on the separation of powers in a just government written by Montesquieu (Charles Louis Joseph de Secondat: 1684–1755), the example of England—which had just soundly defeated France in America and Asia—was potent. So also was the dramatic success of the American Revolution, where in the New World a grand experiment in popular sovereignty and civic liberty had just been launched.

As things developed, however, the French Revolution went another way from the American Revolution and the earlier English Commonwealth. The American and English revolutions were essentially conservative, aimed at re-establishing the historic rights of Englishmen; the French Revolution was heavily ideological, with futuristic phrases about "the Rights of Man." The American and English revolutions were in no sense anti-clerical, in spite of the inclination of Benjamin Franklin, Thomas Paine and Thomas Jefferson toward Deism; the French Revolution was bitter against the Roman Catholic establishment, in the Law of Associations (1792) crippled its international contacts, and in the following year attempted to substitute an official Cult of Reason. The American and English revolutions were aimed at creating a public consensus, a "national town meeting" with participation by all free citizens of whatever status; the French Revolution tried to destroy the privileged classes and enthrone the common man. The American and English revolutions had limited and specific objec-

*The "Little Corporal" introduced the modern system of conscription.*

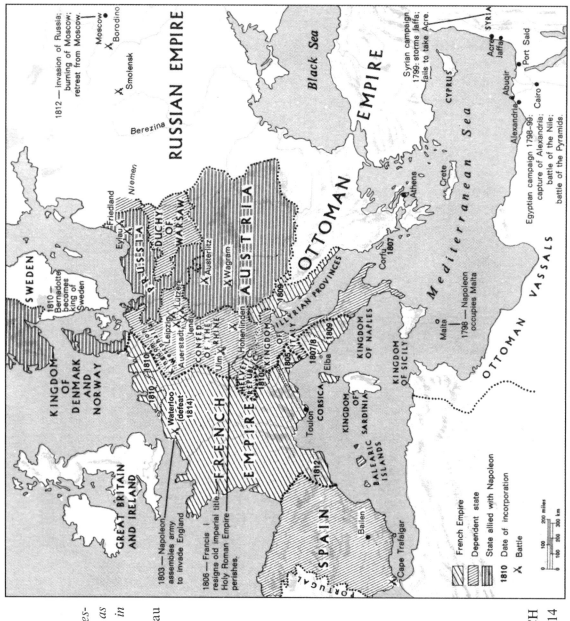

*The general will achieves its purest expression when all citizens confront the state as individuals and are not bound together in lesser associations.*

— Jean-Jacques Rousseau

THE IMPACT OF THE FRENCH
REVOLUTION 1789–1814

1803 — Napoleon assembles army to invade England

1806 — Francis I resigns old imperial title; Holy Roman Empire perishes.

1812 — invasion of Russia; burning of Moscow; retreat from Moscow.

Syrian campaign 1799: storms Jaffa; fails to take Acre.

Egyptian campaign 1798–99: capture of Alexandria; battle of the Nile; battle of the Pyramids.

1810 — Bernadotte becomes king of Sweden

1798 — Napoleon occupies Malta

RUSSIAN EMPIRE

Black Sea

OTTOMAN EMPIRE

OTTOMAN VASSALS

Mediterranean Sea

SWEDEN

KINGDOM OF DENMARK AND NORWAY

GREAT BRITAIN AND IRELAND

PRUSSIA

DUCHY OF WARSAW

AUSTERIA

CONFED. OF THE RHINE

FRENCH EMPIRE

ILLYRIAN PROVINCES

SPAIN

PORTUGAL

KINGDOM OF SARDINIA

CORSICA

KINGDOM OF NAPLES

KINGDOM OF SICILY

BALEARIC ISLANDS

CYPRUS

SYRIA

Moscow
Borodino
Smolensk
Berezina
Niemen
Friedland
Eylau
Austerlitz
Wagram
Lützen
Leipzig
Jena
Auerstadt
Hohenlinden
Ulm
Waterloo (defeat) (1814)
Toulon
Elba
Bailén
Cape Trafalgar
Corfu 1807
Athens
Crete
Malta
Acre
Jaffa
Abuqir
Alexandria
Cairo
Port Said

Key:
French Empire
Dependent state
State allied with Napoleon
1810 Date of incorporation
X Battle

0  100  200 miles
0  100  200  300 km

tives, to be obtained with a minimum of upheaval and bloodshed; the French Revolution was aimed at ultimates, and ended in tyranny and a dynamic drive to conquer the world.

In the Estates-General (1789), National Assembly (1789–91), Legislative Assembly (1791–92), National Convention (1792–95), and the Directory (1795–99), an unstable and shifting alliance of parties and caucuses ended the monarchy, tolerated the Reign of Terror, and introduced military conscription. By fiscal irresponsibility and infatuation with parliamentarian and ideological debates (enlivened by assassinations), they also destroyed their own credibility. After Napoleon's considerable successes on the battlefield against combined European armies, he was made First Consul (1799) and then Emperor (1804–14).

In the years of his rule Napoleon made a number of permanent contributions to European law and customs, some of them representative of the revolutionary slogan, "Liberty, Equality, and Fraternity." A simple illustration is the custom of seating national delegates at international meetings alphabetically rather than according to presumed eminence. Another symbolic event was the official termination of the Holy Roman Empire (1806), in part to prevent Napoleon from taking the title. Another is the practical expression of "the nation in arms," universal conscription; since Napoleon's dictatorship, this has been a common institutionalization of the negative aspect of popular sovereignty.

Of the artificial political creations, such as the Batavian Republic (Kingdom of Holland), the Cisalpine Republic (Kingdom of Italy), the Ligurian Republic (Genoa), the Roman Republic (Kingdom of Rome), the Partheno-

*Napoleon in 1798, painted by David.*

pean Republic (Kingdom of Naples), the Helvetic Republic (Switzerland), the Kingdom of Westphalia, little remained. The secularization of church lands, which among other things brought the German universities under government control, had permanent consequences. So also did the Code Napoléon, a body of law and legal institutions which continues over wide areas of the world to this day. The reorganization of the French university system, the National Academies, and the foundation of the Legion of Honor, are permanent monuments to his memory.

For America, two of the most important actions were French support during the War of 1812 with the British, and the Louisiana Purchase (1803), which gave the new republic the drainage area of the Mississippi River throughout the great plains. Napoleon's intervention in Haiti was less felicitous.

At the height of his power, Napoleon controlled most of the German states through the Confederation of the Rhine. He had already eliminated most of the old imperial cities and secularized the ecclesiastical estates. He humiliated Prussia. Berlin was occupied. Prussia was cut almost to half its former size, saddled with a heavy indemnity, and obliged to support 150,000 French occupation troops until payment was made. The defeat of the Austrians at Austerlitz (2 December 1805) and the Prussians at Jena (14 October 1806) became symbols, however, for nationalist revivals in those two realms. Austria's reaction was premature and military, and brought considerable loss of territory: France organized the Illyrian provinces under the "Duke of Ragusa" (Dubrovnik) as her direct gain, and Napoleon made gifts of Austrian land to Russia, the Grand Duchy of Warsaw, the Kingdom of Italy (which acquired the southern Tyrol).

The Prussian reaction was more measured. Of fateful consequence, the Germans thereafter misunderstood "democracy" to mean the rule of the mob—as Plato had indeed defined it. Watching the excesses of the French Revolution, they confused parliamentarianism with the spirit of representative government. They failed to perceive that Edmund Burke (1729–97)—for example—condemned the French Revolution's misunderstanding and abuse of popular sovereignty, while at the same time preserving its essential spirit and style. During the nationalist revival, under Karl Freiherr von Stein (1757–1831), Prussia carried out a thorough reorganization of civil and military administration. The University of Berlin was founded (1810), and under Alexander von Humboldt it was organized along the lines that made the German university preeminent in the nineteenth century. Specialized research fields were defined, the research degree, the Ph.D., superseded the M.A., a humanistic degree. J. G. Fichte's *Addresses to the German Nation* and Ernst Moritz Arndt's poems (as well as his polemic against Napoleon, *Vom Geist der Zeit*) added to the intellectual and emotional revival of nationalism. They also helped to fill out the authoritarian and anti-democratic motifs which retarded the development of German representative institutions well into the twentieth century.

F.D.E. Schleiermacher (1768–1834) became the Christian preacher and theologian of the German revival. He developed a religious philosophy based on intuition and feeling which blended well into the upsurge of popular sentiment, and his influence upon subsequent religious thought (e.g., Albrecht Ritschl, Adolf von Harnack, Ernst Troeltsch) was very great.

Napoleon's imperialism thus helped to create a fatal polarization of opinion among Europeans, retarding the development of democratic institutions and helping to produce in other lands a connection of legitimacy and established religion which was not to be overcome for generations.

*Friedrich Daniel Ernst Schleiermacher.*

# THE HOLY ALLIANCE IN EUROPE
## 1815–1825

1822 — Great Britain refuses to accede to Holy Alliance.

1818 — Congress of Aix-la-Chapelle

1819 — Conference at Carlsbad — "Carlsbad decrees"

Sept. 26, 1815 — Holy Alliance between Alexander I (Russia), Francis I (Austria), Frederick William III (Prussia) formed to repress "liberalism".

1820 — Congress of Troppau

Nov. 19, 1815 — France secretly admitted to Holy Alliance.

Military revolt

1821 — Congress of Laibach

1823 — French intervention in Spain

1822 — Congress of Verona

1820 — Widespread revolt

1821 — Austrian intervention in Naples and Piedmont

Popular revolt — Carbonari

1821 — Greek revolt supported by the Tsar

Congress of the Holy Alliance

National uprising

Member of the Holy Alliance

ALTHOUGH the work of the Congress of Vienna was interrupted by Napoleon's escape and return from Elba ("The Hundred Days"), his defeat at Waterloo prepared the way for the Holy Alliance (26 September 1815) and the Quadruple Alliance (20 November 1815). By the latter, England, Austria, Prussia and Russia guaranteed to support each other in implementing the terms of the treaty of peace. They also agreed to continuing consultations to maintain European stability through a series of international congresses.

The Holy Alliance cast the mantle of religion over a program of suppressing not only popular revolution but all popular and democratic developments. Prepared by Alexander I (Russian tsar: 1801–25) under the influence of the Pietist Barbara von Krüdener (1764–1824), it pledged the signatories to conduct their relations on the basis of "the sublime truth which the holy religion of our savior teaches." It was eventually signed by all European powers except the Sultan, the English Regent, and the Pope. Although Lord Castlereagh of England called it "a piece of sublime mysticism and nonsense," there is no doubt but that it placed the religious establishments

*Barbara von Krüdener, Pietist who inspired the Holy Alliance.*

treaties the Austrian monarchy added Lombardy, Venetia, Illyria, Dalmatia, the Tyrol, Galicia. The Grand Duchy of Warsaw became the Kingdom of Poland, under the Russian tsar but with its own official language and constitution. Prussia added Posen and Danzig, most of Saxony, a large part of Westphalia, Swedish Pomerania. Sweden retained Norway, the latter given a separate constitution. The Kingdom of the Netherlands was formed of Holland and Belgium, to divide again in 1830. A Germanic Confederation of thirty-nine states was formed, which functioned only loosely.

In the shadow of the Congress of Vienna, Jews in the Papal States were again forced to attend conversionist sermons. At subsequent congresses, the suppression of popular revolutions in Spain and Italy was approved. Liberal opinion forced England's representatives to withhold support from the pan-European reactionary policies of the Alliance, and the congress system of international cooperation collapsed.

squarely on the side of reaction and further alienated the swelling masses of the industrial proletariat as well as the articulate bourgeoisie.

As against government based on popular sovereignty, the keynote of the age was "legitimacy." In the

## THE HOLY ALLIANCE—PRUSSIA

*We shall not go to Canossa.*
— Bismarck in a Reichstag speech, 1872

FOLLOWING the Congress of Vienna, the German states were dominated by Austria. The system of censorship, espionage, secret police and close control of the universities introduced by Prince Metternich retarded movements toward national identity and representation. A German Diet of sovereign states met at Frankfurt/Main under the chairmanship of the Austrian delegate. In the German universities, students organized liberal and nationalist political societies (*Burschenschaften*), but

after the assassination of the journalist August F. F. von Kotzebue in 1819 the Diet issued the Carlsbad Decrees—tightening control of the universities, with stringent measures against student organizations. Nevertheless, the progressive movement flourished underground. In the 1830 revolutions, the rulers of Hessen-Kassel, Braunschweig and Saxony were forced to abdicate and new constitutions were adopted in these and other states. Additional repressive measures were adopted in the Hannover domain and seven eminent professors ("the Göttingen Seven") refused to take an oath of loyalty

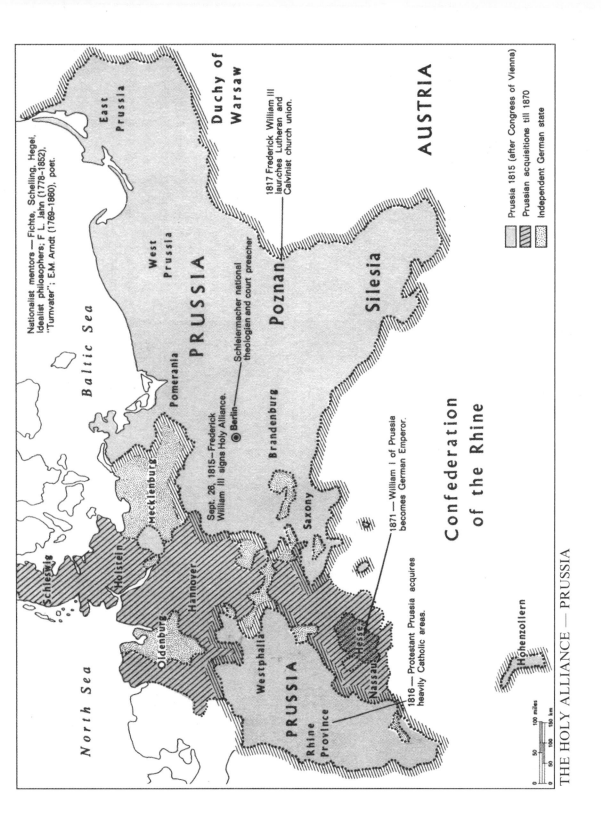

Nationalist mentors — Fichte, Schelling, Hegel, Idealist philosophers; F. L. Jahn (1778–1852), "Turnvater"; E.M. Arndt (1769–1860), poet.

1817 Frederick William III launches Lutheran and Calvinist church union.

Schleiermacher national theologian and court preacher

Sept. 26, 1815—Frederick William III signs Holy Alliance.

1871 — William I of Prussia becomes German Emperor.

1816 — Protestant Prussia acquires heavily Catholic areas.

East Prussia

West Prussia

PRUSSIA

Pomerania

Berlin

Brandenburg

Baltic Sea

Mecklenburg

Schleswig

Holstein

Oldenburg

Hannover

North Sea

Westphalia

PRUSSIA

Rhine Province

Saxony

Hesse

Nassau

Hohenzollern

Duchy of Warsaw

Poznan

Silesia

AUSTRIA

Confederation of the Rhine

Prussia 1815 (after Congress of Vienna)

Prussian acquisitions till 1870

Independent German state

0    50    100 miles
0  50  100  150 km

THE HOLY ALLIANCE — PRUSSIA

(1837) after a new king overthrew the constitution of 1830.

In 1848 an attempt was made to unite the German states under parliamentary institutions. As in 1830, it was the revolution in France that inspired the German effort to achieve democratic government. The Frankfurt National Assembly was anything but a popular meeting, however, consisting of lawyers, professors, businessmen and other middle-class professionals. The meeting was split between those who wanted a loose confederation of sovereign states, those who wanted a sovereign federal government based on universal suffrage, those who wanted a constitutional monarchy, and those who wanted a central monarchy to which all the German states would be subject. While the Assembly debated, the various existing governments regained their control. The Frankfurt Constitution of 1849 created a constitutional monarchy and a system of parliamentary and judicial independence; the Prussian king was then elected Emperor of the Germans. Friedrich Wilhelm IV (king of Prussia: 1840–61) now informed the assembly that a king "by divine right" could not accept a mandate from an elected body, and the popular initiative collapsed.

Prussia was able in the meantime to achieve the leadership position among the German states and to reduce the previous dominance of Austria, by a series of tariff and trade agreements which by 1853 included all of non-Austrian Germany. The major political leadership was given by Otto von Bismarck (1815–98), who from 1862 to 1890 guided Prussian affairs. He capitalized upon the national sentiment by skillfully directing wars against Denmark (securing Schleswig and Holstein, 1864) and Austria (acquiring Hannover, Hessen-Nassau) and France (acquiring Alsace-Lorraine). On 18 January 1871 Wilhelm I became German Emperor.

The King of Prussia, now German Emperor as well, was also the head (*summus episcopus*) of the Church of the Old Prussian Union. This ecclesiastical unit had been formed in 1817 of Lutheran and Calvinist churches, not without considerable resistance from confessional Lutherans. Although Bismark's effort (*Kulturkampf*, 1871–83) to reduce the power of the papacy after the declaration of papal infallibility (8 December 1869) was not too successful, resulting in fact in the organization of a Roman Catholic Party (the *Zentrum*), Germany was in fact launched as a Protestant nation. Roman Catholics were placed psychologically in the position of having to prove their patriotism as Germans.

During the century between the Congress of Vienna (1815) and the outbreak of the First World War (1914), the interaction between France and an emerging German nation was fateful. The insurrection of the workers of Lyons (1831), in Paris (June 1848), in the Paris Commune (1871), frightened royalists all over Europe and reinforced their belief that every trend toward popular sovereignty must be resisted. Johann Hinrich Wichern (1808–81) was able to bring a considerable section of German Protestantism to support social welfare and relief, as Wilhelm E. Ketteler (1811–77) accomplished also in Roman Catholicism in Germany; but in the matter of political power both churches remained conservative to reactionary.

*We stopped the first revolution by means of Jewish pogroms.*

— Member of Russian Duma, 1906

RUSSIAN Orthodoxy was defective in missionary vision and lacking in ethical theory. Its strength lay in liturgical splendor and in the quiet devotion of its monks. The masses of the baptized were left virtually untrained. The leaders of the church were identified with the tsar, whose political authority was bolstered by the religious mystique. Inevitably, any movements toward modernization and social progress were anti-clerical. The greatest theological minds of nineteenth-century Russia, Feodor M. Dostoevski (1821–81) and Leo Tolstoy (1828–1910), were both declared enemies of the religious establishment.

Dostoevski endured four years of forced labor in Siberia. The literary review which he founded with his brother to promote democratic ideas was suppressed. His novels—including *Crime and Punishment* and *The Brothers Karamazov*—are among the most profound interpretations of the human predicament and Christian salvation ever penned, and they had a great influence on the Theology of Crisis in the twentieth century. Tolstoy's *War and Peace* and *Anna Karenina* are also of front rank. His later years were devoted to an effort to develop a model of the Christian life based on the Sermon on the Mount, discarding the mysteries and the mystical in favor of practical expressions of an ethic of love. He was excommunicated in 1901.

The Romanov tsars of the late nineteenth century were feeble leaders, dominated by reactionary political and clerical advisors. Democratic movements among the students and intelligentsia were savagely suppressed. Secret police, internal espionage, absolutism of rule were substituted for economic justice and political progress. The end of serfdom came very late (3 March 1861) and was carried out in

*Dostoevski.*

*Tolstoy.*

THE HOLY ALLIANCE—RUSSIA

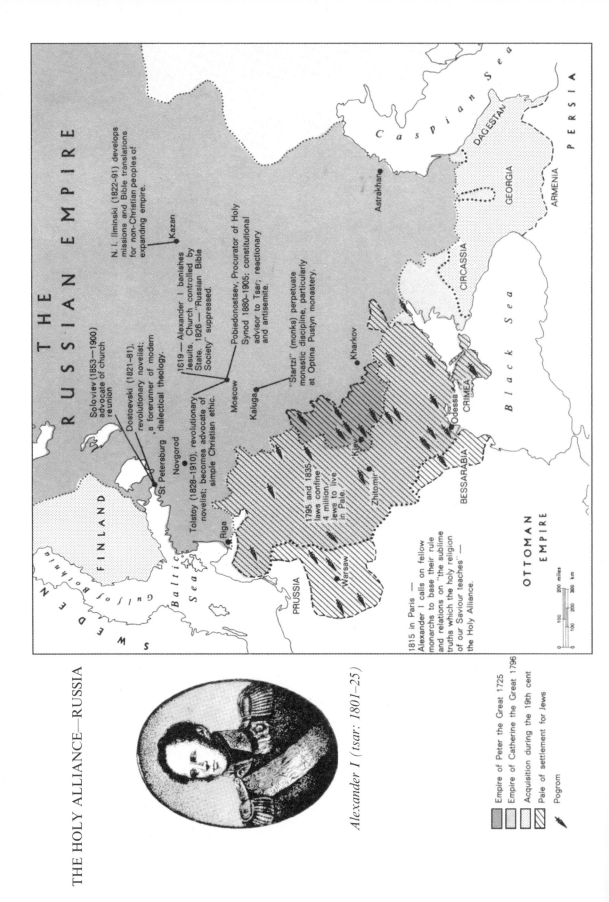

*Alexander I (tsar: 1801–25)*

### THE RUSSIAN EMPIRE

N. I. Ilminski (1822–91) develops missions and Bible translations for non-Christian peoples of expanding empire.

Soloviev (1853–1900), advocate of church reunion

Dostoevski (1821–81), revolutionary novelist; a forerunner of modern dialectical theology.

1819 — Alexander I banishes Jesuits. Church controlled by State. 1826 —"Russian Bible Society" suppressed.

Pobiedonostsev, Procurator of Holy Synod 1880–1905; constitutional advisor to Tsar; reactionary and antisemite.

Tolstoy (1828–1910), revolutionary novelist; becomes advocate of simple Christian ethic.

"Startzi" (monks) perpetuate monastic discipline, particularly at Optina Pustyn monastery.

1795 and 1835 laws confine 4 million Jews to live in Pale.

Kazan
Astrakhan
Kharkov
Moscow
Kaluga
Novgorod
St Petersburg
Riga
Kiev
Zhitomir
Odessa
Warsaw

CRIMEA
BESSARABIA
PRUSSIA
FINLAND
SWEDEN
Gulf of Bothnia
Baltic Sea
Black Sea
Caspian Sea
DAGESTAN
GEORGIA
ARMENIA
CIRCASSIA
PERSIA
OTTOMAN EMPIRE

1815 in Paris — Alexander I calls on fellow monarchs to base their rule and relations on "the sublime truths which the holy religion of our Saviour teaches" — the Holy Alliance.

miles
km
0 100 200
0 100 200 300

Empire of Peter the Great 1725
Empire of Catherine the Great 1796
Acquisition during the 19th cent
Pale of settlement for Jews
Pogrom

such a way as to flood the cities with homeless and unemployed proletarians. In foreign affairs, Russian interests were equally mismanaged: Polish independence movements were severely crushed, in the Crimean War and Russo-Japanese War humiliating defeats were sustained, and in the Balkan Wars and First World War both Russian diplomacy and military offensives were expensive and inept. In the Crimean War the western powers (Austria, England, France) took away from Russia her traditional role as Orthodox guarantor of Christians in Turkish areas; they forced upon the Sultan the important edict, Hatt-i Humeyun (18 February 1856), which defined the protected status of Christian minorities in the Holy Muslim Empire.

In the last decades of its disintegration, the tsarist absolutist government attempted to divert popular attention from real political and economic problems by encouraging antisemitic propaganda (including the famous forgery, *The Protocols of the Elders of Zion*) and active pogroms against the Jews.

Since the time of Peter the Great, the state had controlled the church through the Holy Synod. In the surge of religiosity which accompanied the first years of the Holy Alliance, a Russian Bible Society was founded and other efforts were also made to advance religious education among the literate. But the masses remained illiterate, untended. In 1826 the Bible Society was suppressed. A Slavophile reaction against Roman Catholic "tyranny" and Protestant "individualism" proclaimed for Holy Orthodox Russia a special mission among the nations.

The assassination of Alexander II in 1881 opened a time of increased repression. The dominant figure from

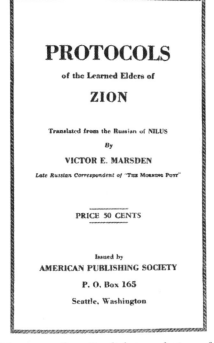

*Title page of an English translation of the fictitious* Protocols of the Elders of Zion.

1880 to 1905 was C. P. Pobedonostsev (1827–1907), who as head of the Holy Synod and chief advisor to the tsar opposed trial by jury, parliaments, and public education. He also maintained a strict censorship of all books and newspapers and magazines, along with a system of terror by secret police. He was a vicious antisemite.

The vitality of Orthodoxy was maintained by the *startzi*, monks whose disciplined practice of ancient monastic rules and quality of spiritual life made them counselors much sought after. Among theologians, perhaps the greatest was Vladimir S. Soloviev (1853–1900), who developed a philosophical base for the regeneration of humanity. He longed for peace among men, opposed the Slavophiles, and cultivated friendship with Roman Catholics and Protestants. His influence upon later ecumenical thought was important, but Russian Orthodoxy largely ignored his message.

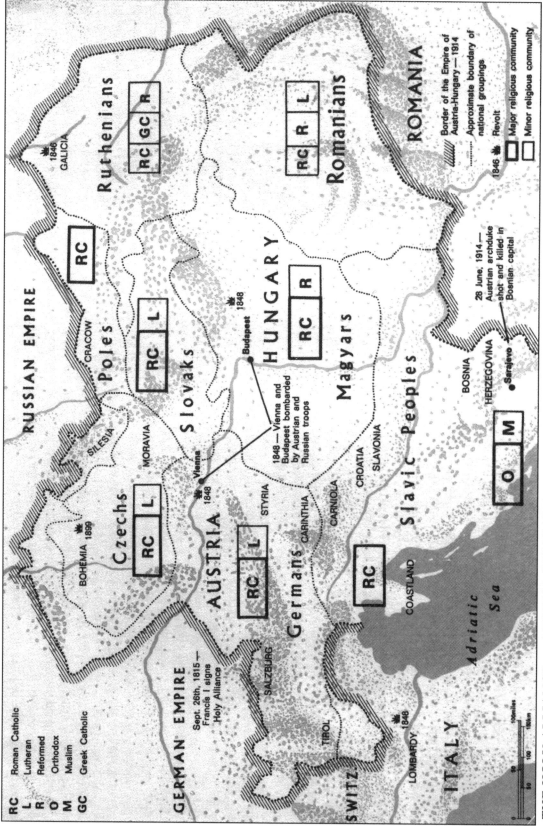

THE HOLY ALLIANCE — AUSTRIA-HUNGARY

Border of the Empire of Austria-Hungary — 1914

Approximate boundary of national groupings

Revolt

Major religious community

Minor religious community

RC   Roman Catholic
L    Lutheran
R    Reformed
O    Orthodox
M    Muslim
GC   Greek Catholic

RUSSIAN EMPIRE

GERMAN EMPIRE
Sept. 26th, 1815 — Francis I signs Holy Alliance

Ruthenians

| RC | GC | R |

Romanians

| RC | R | L |

ROMANIA

Poles

RC

Slovaks

| RC | L |

HUNGARY

Magyars

| RC | R |

Czechs

| RC | L |

Germans

| RC | L |

Slavic Peoples

RC

| O | M |

AUSTRIA

1846
GALICIA

CRACOW

SILESIA

MORAVIA

BOHEMIA 1899

SALZBURG

TIROL

SWITZ.

LOMBARDY 1848

ITALY

Vienna 1848

STYRIA

CARINTHIA

CARNIOLA

CROATIA

SLAVONIA

COASTLAND

Adriatic Sea

Budapest

1848

1848 — Vienna and Budapest bombarded by Austrian and Russian troops

BOSNIA

HERZEGOVINA

Sarajevo

28 June, 1914 — Austrian archduke shot and killed in Bosnian capital

1846

100 miles
100 km

# THE HOLY ALLIANCE—AUSTRIA-HUNGARY
## 18TH–19TH CENTURIES

FOLLOWING the defeat of Napoleon, Austria was dominant on the continent and "the Metternich system" (named for Austrian diplomat von Metternich, 1773–1859, reactionary enemy of all democratic ideas and movements) of repression and reaction was followed by most ruling monarchs. In the second half of the nineteenth century, Prussia and her German allies surpassed the Austro-Hungarian Empire in power and prestige.

Many of the peoples which adhered to the Habsburgs in 1815—when the peace treaties, Holy Alliance, military alliances and system of international congresses set out to freeze the status quo against nationalism, democracy and liberty—were themselves the remains of once great nations. Through others a fresh wind was blowing, due to the French Revolution or to pan-Slavism or to secularist antipathy to sacral governments (the Papal States, the Holy Muslim Empire of the Ottomans) and those allied with them. Some were hereditary holdings, such as Austria and Slovenia, while others came by virtue of Habsburg acquisition of the crown of Hungary and Bohemia. Many were a result of war and military conquest: e.g., Bohemia, Hungary, Moravia, Galicia, Transylvania, Croatia, Dalmatia, Italy, Venetia, Lombardy. Hungary was the source of a double unrest, since the national movement was pushing for a separate constitution and program of development and use of the Magyar tongue—and at the same time favored maintenance of Magyar domination over other minorities.

In 1848, inspired by news from Paris, revolts occurred in several territories.

*Franz Josef I of Austria (emperor: 1848–1916).*

Hungary started off, led by Louis Kossuth (1802–94). The Emperor and the Empress fled Vienna. Czech rebellion, led by Francis Palácky (1798–1876), produced the first great Pan-Slav Congress (aimed against German language and culture), but Prague was bombarded and a military dictatorship established over Bohemia. The people of Vienna went to the barricades to support the Hungarian revolution. The imperial forces shelled the city and hanged the popular leaders. Hungary, where a republic had been declared, was crushed by an Austrian army supported by Russian forces sent by the tsar. In spite of ceasefire pledges, a dozen Hungarian generals were hanged or shot.

In December, Franz Josef ascended the throne (emperor: 1848–1916), beginning one of the longest and most unfortunate reigns in western history. Although Prussia was steadily gaining ascendancy among the German states, the Austrian constitution was suspended and a policy of Germanization forced upon the subject peoples. An 1855 Concordat with the pope gave the Roman Catholic Church broad powers, especially in education. In 1867, after wars with Russia, France, the Germanic Confederation and Piedmont, a compromise was reached which established a dual monarchy of Austria and Hungary—with each allowed to rule its own minorities at will.

The volatile popular movements within the empire constantly reflected the condition of related ethnic groups in the Ottoman Empire, which was slowly losing control of the Balkans. With Russian, French and British assistance the Greeks won independence (1821–31). The Serbians, who won autonomy—including religious toleration—in 1817, took the lead in organizing a Balkan Confederation in 1867. But Austria occupied Bosnia and Herzegovina, the Serbian goals in the war against Turkey. Montenegro regained its independence in 1878. Bulgaria achieved an Orthodox exarchate in 1870, and independence came a decade later with Russian assistance. In 1862 Romania achieved some autonomy for a union of Moldavia and Wallachia. Expropriation of the monasteries and land reform on behalf of the peasants led to a reactionary revolt. Independence for a native monarchy was recognized in 1878, but Romania did not keep the pledge to protect the Jewish communities then given the Sultan.

In the First and Second Balkan Wars nationalist interests predominated, but in the background the imperialistic designs of Russia, Austria-Hungary and the Ottomans frequently collided. The latter power was fading, and in 1878 the Berlin Congress opened the way for British and French expansion in the Middle East. The Habsburgs were not drawn into the general pattern of colonial and imperial expansion, being too involved in keeping a balance in the Balkans and meeting the challenge of successive internal revolts. The immediate occasion of the First World War was the assassination of Austrian Archduke Ferdinand at Sarajevo (28 June 1914), by an agent of the Serbian "Black Hand."

To the confused ethnic and national picture of Austria-Hungary and the neighboring Balkan states must be added religious antipathies. Serbia was Orthodox, tied to Russia by Pan-Slavic romanticism and religion. Albania and much of the ruling element of Bosnia were Muslim. Bohemia, Hungary and Transylvania had strong Lutheran or Calvinist churches. Franz Josef and his court were devotedly Roman Catholic, even contributing money and personnel to missions overseas. The best that any of the several state-churches had learned was a provisional toleration of legal religious minorities. Of religious liberty, which might have made a federal system more workable, there was no understanding. The tragic relations in recent decades between Croatian Roman Catholics, Serbian Orthodox and Bosnian and Kosovar Muslims show how little has been learned in that area during the last century.

# MENNONITES AND HUTTERITES IN RUSSIA

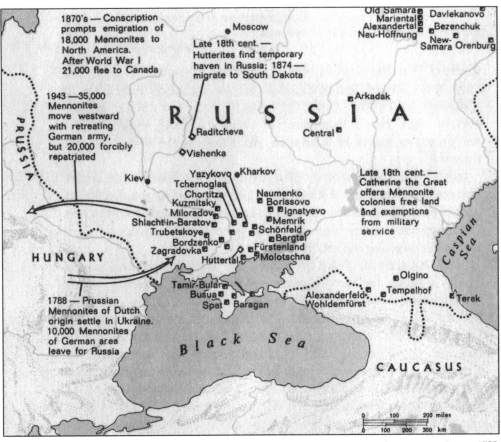

1870's — Conscription prompts emigration of 18,000 Mennonites to North America. After World War I 21,000 flee to Canada

Late 18th cent. — Hutterites find temporary haven in Russia; 1874 — migrate to South Dakota

1943 —35,000 Mennonites move westward with retreating German army, but 20,000 forcibly repatriated

Late 18th cent. — Catherine the Great offers Mennonite colonies free land and exemptions from military service

1788 — Prussian Mennonites of Dutch origin settle in Ukraine. 10,000 Mennonites of German area leave for Russia

Moscow

Old Samara · Davlekanovo
Mariental · Bezenchuk
Alexandertal · New-
Neu-Hoffnung · Samara Orenburg

Arkadak

R U S S I A

Raditcheva
Vishenka
Central

Kiev
Yazykovo · Kharkov
Tchernoglas
Chortitza
Kuzmitsky
Miloradov
Shlacht'in-Baratov
Trubetskoye
Bordzenko
Zagradovka
Huttertal

Naumenko
Borissovo
Ignatyevo
Memrik
Schönfeld
Bergtal
Fürstenland
Molotschna

PRUSSIA

HUNGARY

Tamir-Bular
Busua
Spat · Baragan

Alexanderfeld
Wohldemfürst

Olgino
Tempelhof
Terek

Caspian Sea

Black Sea

CAUCASUS

0  100  200 miles
0  100  200  300 km

☑ Center of Mennonite farms   ◇ Hutterite Bruderhof   •••••• Boundary of Catherine's Empire 1796

CATHERINE II "the Great" of Russia (ruler: 1762–96) ardently cultivated her public image as a supporter of the Orthodox and noble establishment, but in her self-image she was a ruler of the Enlightenment stamp. Like Joseph II of Austria and Frederick II "the Great" of Prussia, she patronized Voltaire and other French spokesmen for education and progress. As an "enlightened despot" she invited Mennonite and Hutterite settlers to immigrate from the German area, where they still suffered from religious discrimination and persecution. Besides, she very much needed able farmers.

They were promised freedom from military duty, a promise kept by the Russian rulers until Alexander II introduced universal conscription in 1874. At this point many of the two Anabaptist "peace churches" emigrated to the great plains of the United States and Canada.

The Hutterites had been, right from their beginning, committed to a tight practice of mutual aid and counter-culture. In the Russian area, the Mennonites also developed intact agricultural communities quite separate from the Russian society—in faith, language, and style of life.

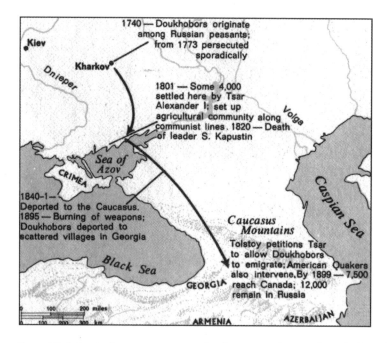

Within map:

Kiev

Kharkov

Dnieper

1740 — Doukhobors originate among Russian peasants; from 1773 persecuted sporadically

1801 — Some 4,000 settled here by Tsar Alexander I; set up agricultural community along communist lines. 1820 — Death of leader S. Kapustin

Volga

Sea of Azov

CRIMEA

Caspian Sea

1840-1 — Deported to the Caucasus. 1895 — Burning of weapons; Doukhobors deported to scattered villages in Georgia

Caucasus Mountains

Tolstoy petitions Tsar to allow Doukhobors to emigrate; American Quakers also intervene. By 1899 — 7,500 reach Canada; 12,000 remain in Russia

Black Sea

GEORGIA

ARMENIA

AZERBAIJAN

0 100 200 miles / 100 200 300 km

LEO Tolstoy's last great novel, *Resurrection* (1899), was written in defense of the persecuted Doukhobors ("spirit-wrestlers"). This, plus the extraordinary work of the American Friends' Service Committee in resettling some 7,500 of them in Canada, attracted public attention to one of the most unusual of modern Christian movements.

The origin of this movement is much disputed. Arising among the peasants in the early eighteenth century, it combined a simple Sermon-on-the-Mount ethic with strong expectation of the early end of the age. A series of individual prophets, recognized as inspired and accorded blind obedience, led the Doukhobors. After enduring severe persecution from the Orthodox clergy for their religion, and from the tsarist government for their pacifism, many emigrated.

As children of the last times, they have caused a tolerant Canada considerable difficulty by refusing to observe minimal legal requirements—including registration of land titles, births, deaths, marriages—and by occasional outbursts of group prophecy and violence against "the world."

## THE PAPAL STATES 1815–70

ALTHOUGH the pope was not a signatory of the Holy Alliance, until late in the nineteenth century every weight of the office was thrown against liberalism and democracy.

Napoleon followed up the Concordat of 1801 with the "Organic Articles," which provided state regulation of church activities in France. The government assumed power over papal documents entering the country and over decisions of councils and synods; over public processions and dress, rents and parish boundaries; over theological education. The Gallican Articles of 1682 had to be taught, which among other things denied the temporal authority of the pope and affirmed the supremacy of councils. In 1809 the Papal States were incorporated into the

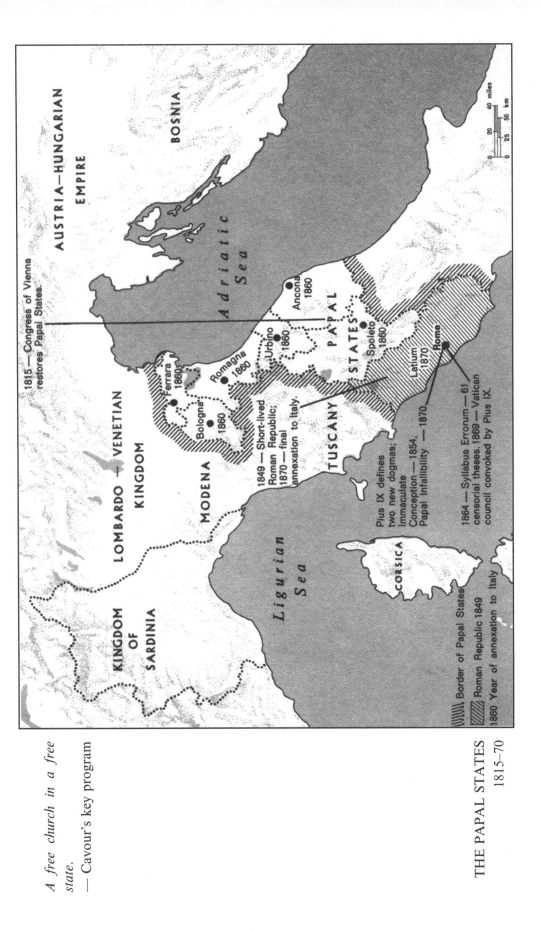

*A free church in a free state.*

— Cavour's key program

AUSTRIA—HUNGARIAN EMPIRE

BOSNIA

1815 — Congress of Vienna restores Papal States.

*Adriatic Sea*

LOMBARDO — VENETIAN KINGDOM

KINGDOM OF SARDINIA

MODENA

Ferrara 1860

Bologna 1860

Romagna 1860

Urbino 1860

Ancona 1860

PAPAL STATES

Spoleto 1860

1849 — Short-lived Roman Republic; 1870 — final annexation to Italy.

TUSCANY

Latium 1870

Rome

*Ligurian Sea*

Pius IX defines two new dogmas; Immaculate Conception — 1854, Papal Infallibility — 1870

1864 — Syllabus Errorum — 61 censorial theses; 1869 — Vatican council convoked by Pius IX.

CORSICA

0 20 40 miles
0 25 50 km

Border of Papal States
Roman Republic 1849
1860 Year of annexation to Italy

THE PAPAL STATES
1815–70

*Garibaldi (1807–82), leader of Italian national unification.*

French Empire and Pius VII (pope: 1800–23) was carried away to Paris and compelled to agree to extensive grants of authority to Napoleon over the church in France. With the defeat of Napoleon, Ultramontanism combined with reaction returned in strength. Even among Protestant and Orthodox rulers a friendliness toward Rome was evident, based upon the axiom that the union of throne and altar was the best bulwark against popular movements.

Upon return to Rome, Pius VII immediately reestablished the Jesuit order and the Inquisition. The Congress of Vienna reestablished the Papal States. The pope condemned the Carbonari for their democratic revolution in Naples (1821). A system of Concordats was worked out between the papacy and various European governments.

Under Leo XII (pope: 1823–29) the Concordat system was extended throughout South America, guaranteeing the Roman Catholic Church special privileges at law. His internal policies were extremely reactionary: he condemned the Bible Societies, religious dissent, and persecuted the Jews. In spite of this, during these years the English parliament passed the liberal Catholic Emancipation Act—removing the civil disabilities which had been borne by English Roman Catholics for 150 years.

Gregory XVI (pope: 1831–46) was a reactionary. In the Papal States all popular aspirations were rebuked and movements crushed. In the encyclical *Mirari vos* (15 August 1832), liberty of conscience, freedom of the press, and popular revolt against established government for any cause were all flatly condemned.

Pius IX (pope: 1846–76) had the longest—and in many ways one of the most unfortunate—incumbencies of

*Pius VII.*

*Pius IX.*

any pope. During the revolution of 1848 he fled from Rome; upon his return he issued a series of encyclicals calculated to strengthen traditional authority. The bull *Ineffabilis Deus* (8 December 1854), released without benefit of council, proclaimed the dogma of the Immaculate Conception of Mary. In the encyclical *Quanta cura*, with an appended Syllabus of Errors (8 December 1864), he turned his face squarely against modern civilization. While the statement that "it is an error to believe that the Roman pontiff can and ought to reconcile himself to, and agree with, progress, liberalism, and contemporary civilization" is undoubtedly true, the notion that the conflict between the church and the world can be equated with a conflict between the middle ages and modernity is not. After a sweeping condemnation of various modern moods and movements, he explicitly condemned liberty of conscience and worship, tolerance, universal suffrage and public education. In 1869 he called the first Vatican Council, which on 18 July 1870 proclaimed

the dogma of Papal Infallibility. Even Roman Catholic Austria immediately annulled its Concordat. In Prussia, the *Kulturkampf* broke out. In France, the polarization process produced by the revolution was accentuated—with a sequence of events from the Dreyfus Case (1894–1906) to the moral collapse of the Pétain regime to document the price to be paid when a church withdraws itself from genuine dialogue with the world.

The first shift away from reactionary politics came with *Rerum Novarum* (15 May 1891), the social encyclical of Leo XIII (pope: 1878–1903).

Writers who helped to justify the reactionary role of the popes in this critical period included René de Chateaubriand (1768–1848), Joseph De Maistre (1753–1821), Charles René Montalembert (1810–70) and Robert de Lamennais (1782–1854). Lamennais left the Roman Catholics, however, when the papacy repudiated the ideal of a utopian society informed by a reasonable Christianity which he had called upon the pope to help create.

*René de Chateaubriand.*

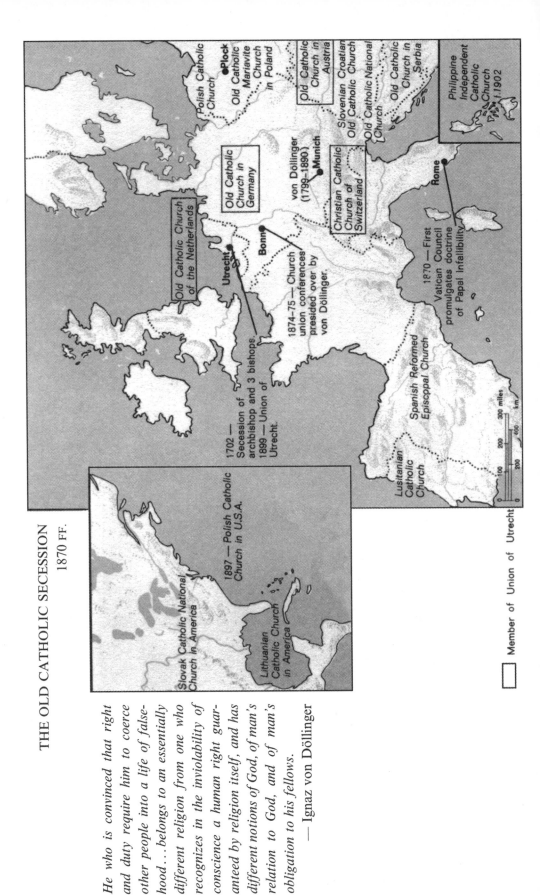

## THE OLD CATHOLIC SECESSION
### 1870 FF.

*He who is convinced that right and duty require him to coerce other people into a life of falsehood...belongs to an essentially different religion from one who recognizes in the inviolability of conscience a human right guaranteed by religion itself, and has different notions of God, of man's relation to God, and of man's obligation to his fellows.*
— Ignaz von Döllinger

### Map labels

Polish Catholic Church

Plock — Old Catholic Mariavite Church in Poland

Old Catholic Church in Austria

Slovenian Croatian Old Catholic Church

Old Catholic National Church

Old Catholic Church in Serbia

Philippine Independent Catholic Church f.1902

Old Catholic Church in Germany

von Döllinger (1799–1890)

Munich

Christian Catholic Church of Switzerland

Rome

Old Catholic Church of the Netherlands

Utrecht

Bonn

1874–75 — Church union conferences presided over by von Döllinger.

1870 — First Vatican Council promulgates doctrine of Papal Infallibility

1702 — Secession of archbishop and 3 bishops.
1899 — Union of Utrecht.

Spanish Reformed Episcopal Church

Lusitanian Catholic Church

Slovak Catholic National Church in America

1897 — Polish Catholic Church in U.S.A.

Lithuanian Catholic Church in America

300 miles
400 km
200
200
100
100
0
0

☐ Member of Union of Utrecht

FOR those of the Catholic tradition, the doctrine of "apostolic succession" is very important. In most Protestant circles, "apostolicity" is understood to mean "true to the example of the apostles." For those who stress "apostolic succession," the key idea is a succession of episcopal consecrations running back through the centuries in unbroken continuity to Peter and the others with Jesus.

The Old Catholic claim to succession rests upon a schism which occurred in the Netherlands at the time of the Spanish occupation and the Jansenist controversy in France. From 1580 to 1853 the Roman Catholic Church in the Netherlands was without resident bishops, being governed by papal legates. In 1702 Petrus Codde (1648–1710), Roman representative and titular archbishop, was censured for sympathy with the hard Augustinianism of Cornelius Jansen (1585–1638), the Abbé de Saint-Cyran (1581–1643) and their followers at the convent of Port-Royal (including Blaise Pascal).

The Jansenist positions had been condemned by Innocent X in *Cum Occasione* (31 May 1653) and Clement XI in *Unigenitus* (8 September 1713). The basic teachings are, first, that because of man's sin he cannot perform God's commandments without a special gift of grace, and second, that the operation of grace cannot be resisted. The effect of Jansenism was to destroy the basis of any natural theology, including the Thomistic system then gaining increasing authority in Roman Catholic circles. Its message and mood is to the Protestant strongly reminiscent of Calvinism.

In 1724 the archbishopric of Utrecht with three bishops separated from Rome. After the declaration of Papal Infallibility, considerable numbers of Catholics in Switzerland, Austria and Germany split from the Roman Church—which they considered now a "sect" for making a peculiar teaching normative.

At the Council itself, business was speeded by use of cloture to terminate debate and by use of voting by standing. Its sessions were suspended for the Franco-Prussian War, and one of the interesting questions which arose in connection with the council announced by John XXIII in 1959 was whether it would be a continuance or a new meeting. That later council is appropriately called "Vatican II" today, being of another spirit and another age. At Vatican I, leading Roman Catholic churchmen and scholars like J. J. Ignaz von Döllinger (1799–1890) and F.A.P. Dupanloup (1802–78) were in favor of updating the church and the form of its message, but they were overridden. The Old Catholic separation ensued.

The leading mind of the opposition to Papal Infallibility was Ignaz von Döllinger, whose articles in the *Augsburger Allgemeine Zeitung* and book *The Pope and the Council* (1869) exercised a wide influence. Döllinger was the leading Catholic church historian of his age. John Henry Newman (1801–90), a key figure in the Oxford Movement before his change from Anglicanism to Rome, had defended the idea of Christian development in his writings, but he submitted to the decree. So did Lord Acton (1834–1902), whose essays on liberty and other historical studies were a monumental contribution to religious and political theory. Dupanloup, in spite of his educational leadership and counsel to the minority, also submitted. Döllinger became the consistent champion of the historical and critical method, also applied to church institutions—and was excommunicated (1871).

Döllinger's writings were voluminous and still deserve careful study. At the National Assembly in Frankfurt he had defended the idea of a Catholicism in Germany free from state control and in communion with Rome. In his books *The Reformation* and *Luther* he showed a scholarship and a spirit which came into its own a century later. Professor of Church History at Munich from 1826 to 1873, he was a great teacher, a prolific scholar, and a formidable opponent of papal infallibility. He was Chairman of the Bonn Reunion Conferences of 1874 and 1875, which drew together leading scholars and churchmen from Germany (both Catholic and Protestant), America, England, the Netherlands and Eastern Orthodoxy. The ideal was a church which was ecumenical, united, and obedient to the apostolic rule of government by the Holy Spirit.

The first Old Catholic bishop of the newer movement was consecrated in 1874 with see at Bonn, and a Swiss bishop followed in 1876 with headquarters at Bern. Later, bishops were consecrated in Bohemia and Austria. The Old Catholics recognize the first seven Ecumenical Councils, teach the classical Christian doctrines, and hold services in the vernacular. Bishops and other clergy are allowed to marry.

In later times, national Catholic movements have developed in the United States ("Polish National Catholic Church"), in Poland, in Czechoslovakia, in Yugoslavia, as well as in the Philippines. The development of Roman Catholic Bible study, ecumenism and social concern in connection with Vatican II (1962–65) has created a quite new situation for the Old Catholics, as it has also for the Anglo-Catholic movement in the Church of England.

*Ignaz von Döllinger.*

*John Henry Newman.*

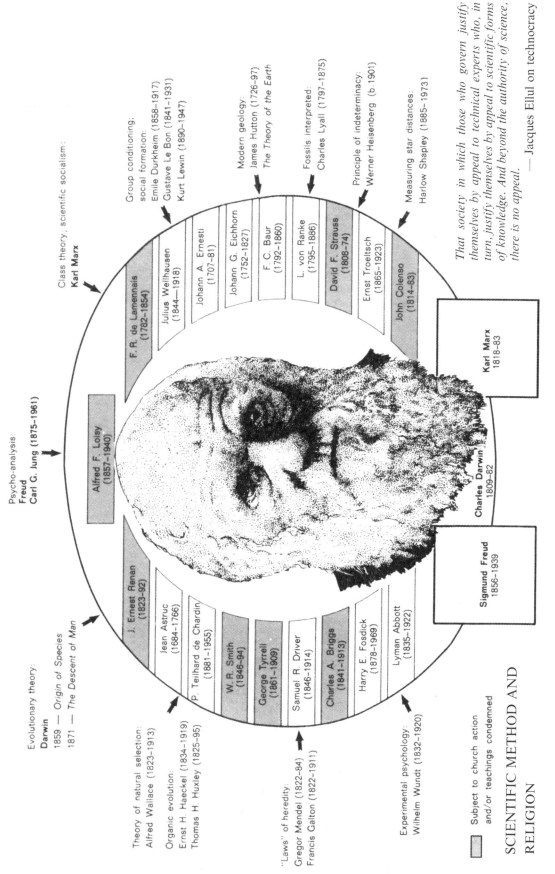

Psycho-analysis:
**Freud**
**Carl G. Jung (1875–1961)**

Class theory, scientific socialism :
**Karl Marx**

Group conditioning:
social formation:
Emile Durkheim (1858–1917)
Gustave Le Bon (1841–1931)
Kurt Lewin (1890–1947)

Modern geology:
James Hutton (1726–97)
*The Theory of the Earth*

Fossils interpreted:
Charles Lyall (1797–1875)

Principle of indeterminacy:
Werner Heisenberg (b.1901)

Measuring star distances:
Harlow Shapley (1885–1973)

*That society in which those who govern justify themselves by appeal to technical experts who, in turn, justify themselves by appeal to scientific forms of knowledge. And beyond the authority of science, there is no appeal.*

— Jacques Ellul on technocracy

F. R. de Lamennais
(1782–1854)

Julius Wellhausen
(1844–1918)

Johann A. Ernesti
(1707–81)

Johann G. Eichhorn
(1752–1827)

F. C. Baur
(1792–1860)

L. von Ranke
(1795–1886)

David F. Strauss
(1808–74)

Ernst Troeltsch
(1865–1923)

John Colenso
(1814–83)

Alfred F. Loisy
(1857–1940)

**Karl Marx**
1818–83

**Charles Darwin**
1809–82

**Sigmund Freud**
1856–1939

Evolutionary theory:
**Darwin**

1859 — *Origin of Species*
1871 — *The Descent of Man*

Theory of natural selection:
Alfred Wallace (1823–1913)

Organic evolution:
Ernst H. Haeckel (1834–1919)
Thomas H. Huxley (1825–95)

J. Ernest Renan
(1823–92)

Jean Astruc
(1684–1766)

P. Teilhard de Chardin
(1881–1955)

W. R. Smith
(1846–94)

George Tyrrell
(1861–1909)

Samuel R. Driver
(1846–1914)

Charles A. Briggs
(1841–1913)

Harry E. Fosdick
(1878–1969)

Lyman Abbott
(1835–1922)

"Laws" of heredity:
Gregor Mendel (1822–84)
Francis Galton (1822–1911)

Experimental psychology:
Wilhelm Wundt (1832–1920)

☐ Subject to church action
and/or teachings condemned

SCIENTIFIC METHOD AND
RELIGION

259

THE impact of Charles Darwin (1809–82) upon the development of modern philosophical thought has reached far beyond the biological sciences. In *The Origin of the Species* (1859) and *The Descent of Man* (1871) he correlated a multitude of reports and observations on living creatures. He proposed that natural selection governs the evolution of forms of life, with the fittest surviving. The later proposition became the basis of several schools of politics and social philosophy, including both laissez-faire economics and Nazism. Evolutionary theory displaced the view of man as a fallen angel and replaced it with man conceived as a risen animal. Most important was the introduction of a developmental theory that, by analogy, profoundly affected understandings of social institutions and even theology.

The developmental theory led as naturally to reductionist philosophies, to efforts to define the primitive situation, as to portrayal of the growth of complex systems. An illustration of this method was Ernest Renan's *La Vie de Jésus*, which created a sensation in European intellectual circles. Renan 1823–92) cast aside all supernatural and mysterious elements with which piety had presumably surrounded Jesus and pictured him as a simple teacher of Galilee. George Tyrrell (1861–1909) faced the other way, portraying Christianity as a stage along the way toward a final universal religion.

Applied to study of the Bible and to Christian doctrinal positions, the developmental view relativized the authority of the received tradition, leading to a selective process as to which books and which teachings were to be accorded greater attention and which might be cast aside.

# LATIN AMERICA FROM COLONIES TO NATIONHOOD
## 19TH CENTURY

SPANISH and Portuguese America was settled a full century before the English colonies. The University of Lima antedated Harvard by more than a century. Nevertheless, national consciousness and movements for representative government emerged much later in Central and South America, in good part because the role of the church in those areas was consistently reactionary. Another basic reason was that in Latin America the Indian population was much larger and a far greater effort was required to accomplish Europeanization and modernization. Most important, perhaps, was the fact that the economy was from the beginning organized about great plantations, with slaves and serfs at the base and a middle class very late in developing.

During the nineteenth century most of Latin America freed itself from colonial control, but not from the plantation system and not from the curse of militarism. Characteristic of the plantation economy, whether in Latin America or the Antebellum South (USA) or old Prussia, is the dominance of romantic militarism among younger sons and others raised to command—but themselves lacking the base on the land.

As for the Roman Catholic Church, practice varied: in Paraguay, the dictator made himself the head of the church (1816); in Bolivia, public worship other than Roman Catholic was permitted in 1908; in Ecuador, the extraordinary power of the church (Concordat of 1862) was later sharply reduced by a liberal government (Constitution of 1906); Colombia was rent for decades by conflict between clerical Conservatives and secular-minded Liberals, and also by the loss of Panama (1903); in Brazil, a federal republic was established and church and state separated (1891).

After the loss of Texas and other territories to the United States (1836–48), a Mexican republic under Benito Juárez (1806–72) separated church and state, secularized the church lands, and suppressed religious orders.

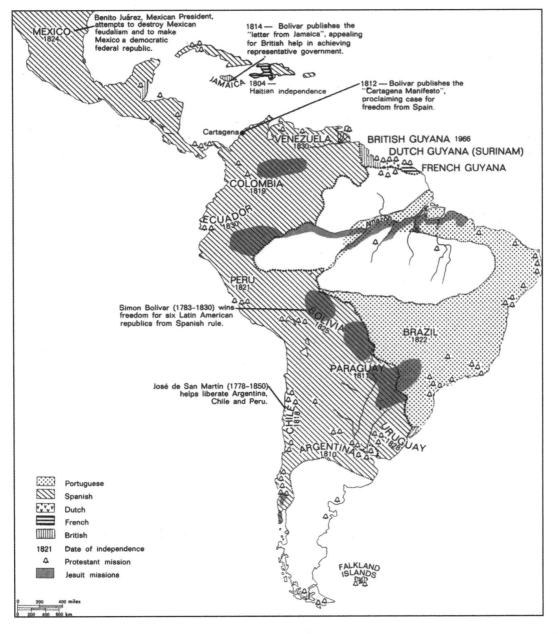

MEXICO 1824

Benito Juárez, Mexican President, attempts to destroy Mexican feudalism and to make Mexico a democratic federal republic.

1814 — Bolívar publishes the "letter from Jamaica", appealing for British help in achieving representative government.

JAMAICA 1804 — Haitian independence

1812 — Bolívar publishes the "Cartagena Manifesto", proclaiming case for freedom from Spain.

Cartagena

VENEZUELA 1830

BRITISH GUYANA 1966
DUTCH GUYANA (SURINAM)
FRENCH GUYANA

COLOMBIA 1819

ECUADOR 1830

Amazon

PERU 1821

Simon Bolívar (1783–1830) wins freedom for six Latin American republics from Spanish rule.

BOLIVIA 1825

BRAZIL 1822

PARAGUAY 1811

José de San Martín (1778–1850) helps liberate Argentina, Chile and Peru.

CHILE 1818

URUGUAY 1828

ARGENTINA 1810

Portuguese
Spanish
Dutch
French
British
1821    Date of independence
△       Protestant mission
        Jesuit missions

0    200    400 miles
0   200  400  600 km

FALKLAND ISLANDS

*261*

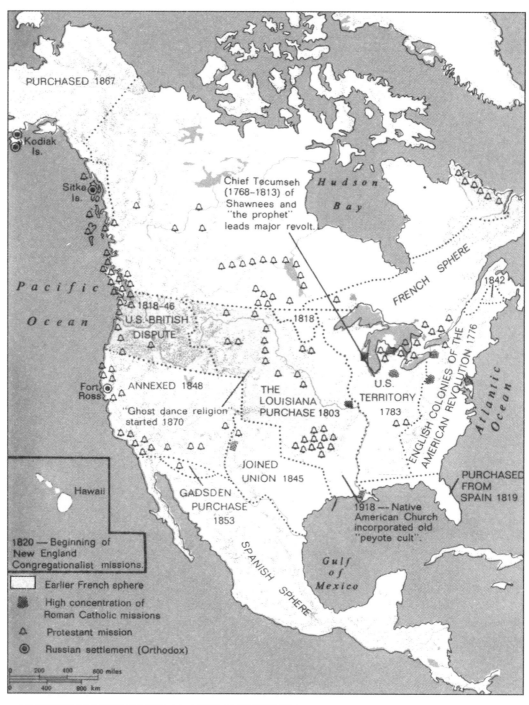

PURCHASED 1867

Kodiak Is.

Sitka Is.

Chief Tecumseh (1768–1813) of Shawnees and "the prophet" leads major revolt.

*Hudson Bay*

FRENCH SPHERE

1842

*Pacific Ocean*

1818–46 U.S. BRITISH DISPUTE

1818

U.S. TERRITORY 1783

ENGLISH COLONIES OF THE AMERICAN REVOLUTION 1776

*Atlantic Ocean*

Fort Ross

ANNEXED 1848

"Ghost dance religion" started 1870

THE LOUISIANA PURCHASE 1803

PURCHASED FROM SPAIN 1819

JOINED UNION 1845

1918 — Native American Church incorporated old "peyote cult".

Hawaii

GADSDEN PURCHASE 1853

SPANISH SPHERE

*Gulf of Mexico*

1820 — Beginning of New England Congregationalist missions.

Earlier French sphere

High concentration of Roman Catholic missions

△ Protestant mission

◎ Russian settlement (Orthodox)

0  200  400  600 miles
0  400  800 km

# AMERICAN EXPANSION AND RELIGION
19TH CENTURY

*The tribal relations should be broken up,
socialism destroyed, and the family and the
autonomy of the individual substituted.*
— Report of the Commissioner of
Indian Affairs, 1889

# AMERICAN EXPANSION AND RELIGION
## 19TH CENTURY

IN the English colonies (1607–1776), established churches of the European type dominated the scene. In New England, a modified form of Congregationalism was privileged until 1817 in New Hampshire, 1819 in Connecticut, and 1834 in Massachusetts. From the beginning there was a basic inconsistency between the parish system (with tax support) and the gathering of congregations of believers by church covenant (voluntaryism). During the Great Awakening (1734 ff.) and Second Great Awakening (1798–1810), nearly a hundred congregations broke away from state control, eventually to become Baptist. In the period 1806–19, the split between Unitarian Congregationalists and Trinitarian Congregationalists exposed the incoherence between the parish and covenantal patterns, and forced the orthodox into an alliance with revivalism.

*Thomas Jefferson.*

In the southern colonies, the Church of England enjoyed special privileges. In South Carolina, the political government was even organized by "parishes." The lack of a resident bishop, however, resulted in a democratization of church control: 1) no episcopal visitations could be carried out, and the leading laymen were often not even confirmed; 2) lay vestries developed to provide agencies for land ownership, and even for calling and dismissing clergy; 3) many clergy were educated in New England colleges, which strengthened the natural bent of the farmers and artisans toward Puritanism.

In the middle colonies, the picture was blurred. The Church of England was most important and enjoyed the most privileges for the longest periods of time. In Pennsylvania, on the other hand, during William Penn's lifetime a free and voluntary style of religion obtained. After his death the colony returned to the practice which prevailed even where there was no single state-church in a colony: religious oaths were required which disenfranchised Unitarians, Jews, and Roman Catholics.

Only Rhode Island from the beginning guaranteed religious liberty, having been founded by Roger Williams, himself a refugee from intolerance. In the other New England colonies, the dissenting Quakers and Baptists suffered civil penalties. The breakthrough to a new style of religion began in Virginia, with the adoption of the Great Bill of Religious Freedom (1784–86). This model of separation, of which James Madison (1751–1836) and Thomas Jefferson (1743–1826) were the chief architects, was followed in the First Amendment to the Federal Constitution (1789–91). By these ac-

*Slaughter of Indians at the Christian mission town of Gnadenhütten.*

tions, governments for the first time in history gave up the claim to use a preferred religion for political sanction, and guaranteed the churches their "natural right" to pursue their own self-definition and self-identity. By a subsequent series of court decisions the voluntary principle was made to apply to state and local governments as well.

During the nineteenth century, those churches best equipped to follow the frontier and to address the ordinary settlers came to the fore. Revivals of religion, using "new methods" of persuasion, became the chief agency of winning the people to voluntary participation and support. In the Second Great Awakening in New England, President Timothy Dwight (1752–1817) of Yale and Lyman Beecher (1775–1863) were important leaders. A number of missionary societies resulted, including the American Board of Commissioners for Foreign Missions (f. 1810). In the west, the Cane Ridge Revival (1801) and later "camp meetings" reached the people. Francis Asbury (1745–1816), Barton W. Stone (1772–1844), Alexander Campbell (1788–1866) and Charles G. Finney (1792–1875) were leading personalities,

Campbell and Finney making major contributions also in founding and leading Christian colleges. The Methodists, Baptists, and Disciples of Christ (or "Christians") proved to be the denominations best able to employ the new techniques and win the largest number of adherents. In the year of John Wesley's death (1791) the Methodists numbered 43,265 members in America; by 1900, the number was more than 5.5 million. In 1800 the Baptists counted slightly more than 160,000; in 1900 they were more than 4.5 million. The Disciples or Christians started in the period 1820–30; in 1900 they numbered at least 900,000, but this and subsequent growth figures are unreliable because the more conservative Christian congregations refuse to report statistics for religious reasons.

For the Indians of North America, history faced eastward and not westward. The churches tried from time to time to carve out an area of sanctuary and settlement, but the destruction of John Eliot's Christian Indian villages and the Moravians' Gnadenhütten was symbolic of the general program of white civilization: pacification, expropriation of Indian lands, destruction of

Indian society. From time to time, as in the Revolt of Tecumseh in the Ohio Territory, in the spread of the Ghost Dance Religion on the great plains, or the modern growth of the Native American Church of North America ("Peyote Cult"), the Indians have found a religious ideology to strengthen their resistance to the westward march of white civilization and inspire hope of a return to the freedom and dignity of their fathers. But the general record has been one of disintegration and despair.

Among black Americans, by contrast, a distinctive institution—the Negro church—became the successful center of survival and identity. The percentage of black Christians is as high as that of white Christians, and following Emancipation (1863, 1865) black religion became a more powerful force among that minority than Christianity in the life and thought of the whites. Not until the rise of "the Nation of Islam" in recent decades has the place of Christianity in the culture of Afro-Americans been seriously challenged.

During the nineteenth century there also occurred great immigrations of Roman Catholic, Lutheran and Jewish peoples, but by and large they entered the mainstream of American religious consciousness in the twentieth century.

By the purchase of Alaska (1867), the United States acquired a number of Russian Orthodox churches in addition to those already gained by the conquest of California. In 1872 the Orthodox bishopric was moved to San Francisco (and later to New York). But the greatest acquisitions during the century of expansion were Spanish and Roman Catholic.

When the Congress took over the western lands from the states (1798–1804) following federal union, and the Louisiana Purchase added the whole western drainage area of the Mississippi River (1803), a considerable number of French and Spanish missions and settlements were added. In Louisiana the "parish" has remained the basic political unit to this day, with the southern part of the state still over 90 percent Roman Catholic.

By the Treaty of Guadalupe Hidalgo at the close of the Mexican War (1848) Mexico gave up claims to Texas, New Mexico and California. By the Gadsden Purchase of 1853 the territory south of the Gila River was added. From these actions land was acquired which later formed the states of Texas, New Mexico, Arizona, California, Nevada, Utah, and parts of Wyoming and Colorado. In California and New Mexico there were Spanish settlements of considerable importance; along the Rio Grande River the Texas counties are to this day over 90 percent Roman Catholic.

In the nineteenth century the United States was still self-consciously Protestant, and constitutional commentators as well as the public liturgy showed it. In the education of the American Indians and the black Freedmen, churches as radically separationist as the Quakers and Baptists and Methodists still accepted tax grants to achieve the Christianization of the wards of the state. Puritan New England, which had inspired the founding of missionary and Christian education societies, and which had produced abolition, still provided the chief religious and political ideology. Roman Catholicism, which the "founding fathers" had considered the religion most inimical to true Christianity and democratic institutions, was still despised. Pius IX's encyclicals attacking most of the rights and liberties which Americans held sacred simply reinforced the prevailing anti-Roman mindset.

It was one of the great achievements of church statesmen like Archbishop John Hughes (1797–1864) and James Cardinal Gibbons (1834–1921) that they persuaded the more reasonable of their fellow-citizens that Roman Catholics could be good and loyal citizens; the latter also won breathing space for American Catholics against reactionary papal pronouncements on liberalism, labor unions, even "Americanism." But the popular prejudice against Roman Catholicism continued, and Nativism remained a potent political force through the 1928 election. The Americans of Spanish ancestry and Roman Catholic religion suffered from social and economic discrimination. Neither did they have in the nineteenth century the leadership and political militancy which soon made the Irish Catholics a factor in the politics of the eastern states.

*Our Country* (1885), by Josiah Strong, expresses the characteristic combination of confidence in human progress through the American world mission. The Anglo-Saxon race, Protestantism and republican institutions were to be carried by America across the world map. Strong was a leader in home missions, in the Evangelical Alliance, and in the Federal Council of Churches. When William Randolph Hearst, Theodore Roosevelt and other imperialists succeeded in maneuvering an enthusiastic America and a reluctant Spain into the Spanish-American War (1898), Protestants saw a chance to strike a blow for missions and against absolutism. The United States acquired Puerto Rico and the Philippines, and Cuba became independent.

In Puerto Rico two important move-

*José Rizal (1861–96), Filipino leader.*

ments for self-government had been brutally suppressed in 1868 and 1887. The national movement in the Philippines was articulate and well led.

The conquest of the Philippines was accomplished in a burst of piety. Actually, it took three years for American troops to subdue the islands (1899–1902), for the natives were no more partial to American conquest than they had been to the Spanish control which they had just helped the Americans to overthrow.

The rising national movement brought an end to three hundred years of Roman Catholic dominance, during which other Christian churches were forbidden to work. Because of the close ties between the church hierarchy and the Spanish imperial interest, an *Iglesia Filipina Independente* ("Aglipayan Church") broke off (1890–1902), with its own hierarchy, priesthood and schools. Although its growth was severely hampered by the fact that the American occupation sided with the traditional church in matters of property settlement, the Aglipayan Church is today the second largest Christian body in the islands.

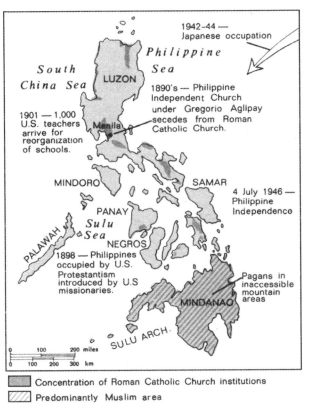

THE AGLIPAYAN
CHURCH OF THE
PHILIPPINES
c 1900

1942-44 —
Japanese occupation

*Philippine
Sea*

*South
China Sea*

LUZON

1890's — Philippine
Independent Church
under Gregorio Aglipay
secedes from Roman
Catholic Church.

1901 — 1,000
U.S. teachers
arrive for
reorganization
of schools.

Manila

MINDORO

SAMAR

4 July 1946 —
Philippine
Independence

PANAY

*Sulu
Sea*

NEGROS

1898 — Philippines
occupied by U.S.
Protestantism
introduced by U.S
missionaries.

PALAWAN

Pagans in
inaccessible
mountain
areas

MINDANAO

SULU ARCH.

0   100   200 miles
0   100   200   300 km

Concentration of Roman Catholic Church institutions

Predominantly Muslim area

*There was nothing left for us to do but to take them all and to educate the Filipinos and uplift and civilize and Christianize them and by God's grace do the very best we could by them, as our fellow men for whom Christ also died.*

— President McKinley on the
Spanish-American War

With American occupation, a host of Protestant missions began work—Bible Societies, Presbyterians, Methodists, Disciples, Episcopalians, Congregationalists, etc. A number of good colleges and universities have grown up, along with seminaries and publishing projects. Independence was attained after World War II, during which the Americans and Filipinos again fought side by side against another empire (Japan). Puerto Ricans acquired American citizenship in 1917 and voted for Commonwealth status in 1952.

# AFRICA BEFORE EUROPEAN COLONIALISM
## 16TH CENTURY

THE spread of Islam across Asia Minor and Africa north of the Sahara cut the continent off from all but occasional contacts with Christendom until the great Portuguese and Spanish voyages of exploration. Substantial Christian minorities, exclusively of ancient churches which had resisted Byzantine and Roman control (Copts, Jacobites, Nestorians), persisted in spite of Muslim conquest and pressure.

Islam spread among the tribes south of the Sahara through traders and slave-dealers. Black slaves had been important to the economy of the ancient world, and they were known to all sections of the Muslim empire. Gelded, they served a certain function in the harems; in a few cases they achieved eminence in government.

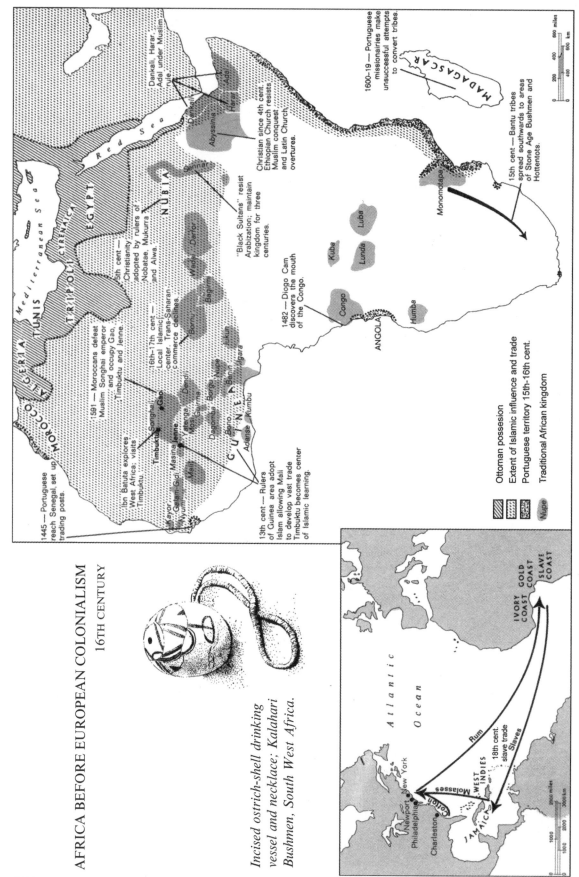

AFRICA BEFORE EUROPEAN COLONIALISM
16TH CENTURY

*Incised ostrich-shell drinking vessel and necklace; Kalahari Bushmen, South West Africa.*

1445 — Portuguese reach Senegal, set up trading posts.

Ibn Batuta explores West Africa; visits Timbuktu.

1591 — Moroccans defeat Muslim Songhai emperor and occupy Gao, Timbuktu and Jenne.

16th-17th cent — Local Islamic center. Trans-Saharan commerce declines.

5th cent — Christianity adopted by rulers of Nobatae, Mukurra and Alwa.

13th cent — Rulers of Guinea area adopt Islam allowing Mali to develop vast trade Timbuktu becomes center of Islamic learning.

"Black Sultans" resist Arabization; maintain kingdom for three centuries.

Christian since 4th cent. Ethiopian Church resists Muslim conquest and Latin Church overtures.

Dankali, Harar, Adal under Muslim rule.

1482 — Diogo Cam discovers the mouth of the Congo.

15th cent — Bantu tribes spread southwards to areas of Stone Age Bushmen and Hottentots.

1600-19 — Portuguese missionaires make unsuccessful attempts to convert tribes.

Ottoman possesion
Extent of Islamic influence and trade
Portuguese territory 15th-16th cent.
Traditional African kingdom

18th cent. slave trade
Rum
Slaves
Molasses
Cotton

IVORY COAST  GOLD COAST  SLAVE COAST

268

When the European powers began their colonial expansion into the area they found the slave trade a well organized Arab monopoly.

During the period before European contact was established there were a few native kingdoms of considerable size; in a few cases architectural remains can be studied, but there were no written records. Such include the great stone ruins of Zimbabwe (Rhodesia). In the thirteenth century a native convert to Islam put together a great empire (Soso and Mandingo) at the bend of the Niger River; at the beginning of the following century the Songhai Empire was subjugated, and Timbuktu became the center of an advanced culture. At this time both Christian and Jewish merchants were engaged in a vigorous trans-Sahara trade, chiefly in gold and ivory. In 1487 the Portuguese reached Timbuktu by overland route from the coast.

Timbuktu was visited by the great Arab traveler, Ibn Batuta, on a route which took him across the Sahara through Tuareg territory in 1349. He had already spent some years in India, Ceylon and China. He reported extensive trade down the east coast from Egypt, and also across the Sahara from Morocco.

In 1402 an Ethiopian embassy reached Venice. In 1441–42 Ethiopian delegates participated in the Council of Florence. Other embassies from "the land of Prester John" reached Lisbon in 1452 and Rome in 1481. Although nothing came of their immediate purpose, which was to establish an alliance against the Muslim powers in Cairo and Baghdad, their visits served to arouse western interest in the dark continent.

Christianity, with an extensive network of monastic communities, was

*The Afo-a-Kom, sacred figure of the Kom tribe.*

present in Ethiopia from very early times. Before that, Jewish influence was great, and the Ethiopian Church to this day makes extensive use of Jewish religious festivals and symbols. There is also a large tribe (Felashas) which considers itself Jewish in faith and practice. In recent decades large numbers have immigrated to Israel. In the middle of the thirteenth century a flowering of Christian work began under an able patriarch ("Abuna"). His successors were made advisors to the throne. Several popes sent embassies to bring the Coptic church of Ethiopia into communion with Rome, but they all failed. A Dominican mission sent for this purpose in the late thirteenth century was slaughtered.

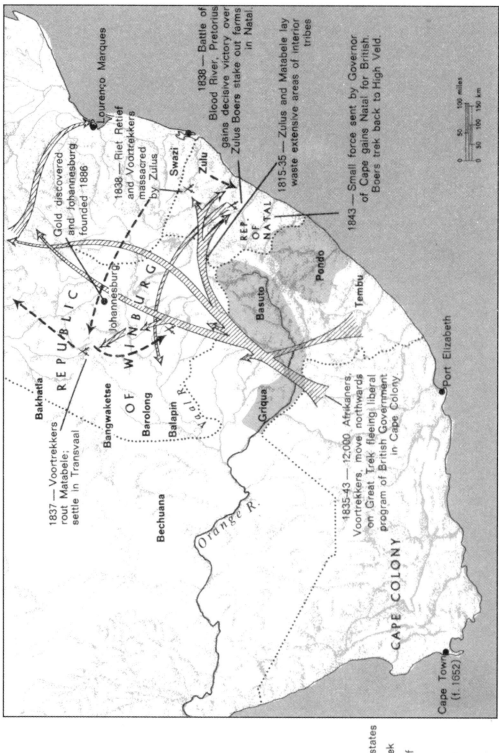

SOUTH AFRICAN MIGRATIONS 19TH CENTURY

Lourenço Marques

1838 — Battle of
Blood River, Pretorius
gains decisive victory over
Zulus Boers stake out farms
in Natal.

1838 — Riet Retief
and Voortrekkers
massacred
by Zulus

Swazi

Zulu

1815-35 — Zulus and Matabele lay
waste extensive areas of interior
tribes

1843 — Small force sent by Governor
of Cape gains Natal for British.
Boers trek back to High Veld.

Gold discovered
and Johannesburg
founded 1886

REP.
OF
NATAL

Pondo

Johannesburg

W I N B U R G

Basuto

Tembu

R E P U B L I C

Port Elizabeth

1837 — Voortrekkers
rout Matabele;
settle in Transvaal

Bakhatla

Bangwaketse

O F

Barolong

Balapin

Vaal R.

Griqua

1835-43 — 12,000 Afrikaners,
Voortrekkers, move northwards
on Great Trek fleeing liberal
program of British Government
in Cape Colony.

Bechuana

Orange R.

CAPE COLONY

Cape Town
(f. 1652)

Tribal treaty states

The Great Trek

Movements of
Bantu Tribes

X    Major battles

Swazi    Tribe

100 miles
50
150 km
100
0    50

AFRICA was opened to extensive European settlement in the nineteenth century, although considerable trade developed before that.

In 1517 Charles V chartered the African slave trade. Timbuktu was conquered by a force from Morocco using firearms, in 1591. In 1626 the first French settlements were made on Madagascar, and in 1686 Louis XIV annexed the territory. In 1652 Cape Town was founded by the Dutch. By the Assiento Treaty (1713) the British acquired the right to import slaves into Spanish America, launching an extensive and lucrative trade. In 1787 the British acquired Sierra Leone and began to use it for resettling freed slaves. In 1833 they suppressed the slave trade throughout their empire. In 1865 slavery was prohibited in the United States. In 1928 a commission of inquiry under the League of Nations found slavery still common in parts of Africa and Asia, chiefly where Islam is dominant.

Christian missionary interest was inspired by reports of the expeditions of the Scottish Christian, David Livingstone (1813–71). Livingstone first spent years as a missionary of the London Missionary Society, in association with Robert Moffat (1795–1883), in Bechuanaland. Thereafter his explorations, reported to the Royal Geographic Society and in popular books and articles, crossed Africa. He was buried in Westminster Abbey.

The earliest settlements in the Cape were Dutch and Huguenot. After the fall of Napoleon Bonaparte, Britain took control, and many missionary societies began work. Administrative and legal institutions were anglicized,

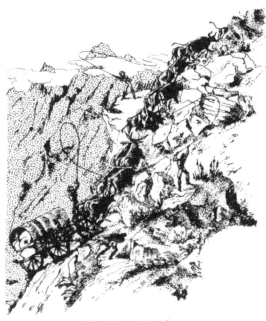

*The Great Trek.*

replacing the former Dutch system.

In 1833 slavery was abolished in the Cape and about 35,000 slaves set free. From 1835 to 1837 the Dutch farmers (Boers), dissatisfied with abolition and the friendly English policy toward the natives, began the Great Trek into the Transvaal, Zululand and Natal. A few decades before this a series of bloody tribal wars had led to mass migrations of Bantus into the same area. In 1842 a war was fought between the Boers and the British, and Natal came under British control; many Boer families moved across the Vaal River. In 1852 the independence of the Transvaal was recognized. The next year the Cape Colony received a republican constitution, with the franchise extended to both blacks and whites who could satisfy property requirements. The following year the Orange Free State (Boer) was constituted, and by 1860 close cooperation between it and the South African Republic (Transvaal) was established.

In 1856 two-thirds of the Kaffirs died of starvation, after a prolonged war with the white settlers. Ten years later the Basutos were defeated by the Orange Free State and compelled to cede large tracts for white settlement; the British intervened and returned the land to the tribe. After a Second Kaffir War in 1877–78 the British extended the Cape control into the Pondo area and annexed the South African Republic in violation of earlier treaties. Following the Zulu War, the Boers revolted against the British, whose moderate policy seemed to them to invite native rebellions (1880–81), and secured again the independence of the Transvaal. After another series of wars with the tribes and abortive efforts to achieve peaceful federal union, the British determined upon war.

The Boer War (1899–1902), in which the British had finally to bring in 300,000 troops to deal with 60,000 Boer farmers and to hold some 120,000 Boer women and children in concentration camps (where 20,000 died of disease and starvation), was opposed in England by many Christian groups. It turned the natural Boer nationalism into the hard line of totalitarian ideology (including racism) and organization which subsequently marked it off.

In 1867 diamonds were discovered in the Orange River, and in 1886 extensive gold deposits were located in the Witwatersrand. In the exploitation of these resources, the imperialist Cecil Rhodes (1853–1902) was a key figure. He managed to corner a large share of the gold mining (Consolidated Goldfields), and to achieve a virtual monopoly of the diamond interests (De Beers Corporation). For his British South Africa Company he received almost unlimited powers north of the Transvaal and west of Mozambique. In 1892 a railroad was opened from the Cape to Johannesburg (f. 1886 on the Rand); by 1897 it was built to Bulawayo, southern Rhodesia. Rhodes intended to extend it the length of the continent to Cairo (in British Egypt). The Boer War intervened.

In a foreshadowing of future encounters, Transvaal legislation against Asiatics was opposed by a campaign of passive resistance (1907) led by Mohandas K. Gandhi (1869–1948), who returned to India after Jan Christian Smuts (1870–1950) pledged that the laws would be enforced in a just and equitable manner.

## AFRICA UNDER COLONIAL RULE

THE European raid on Africa was completed during the decades between the Congress of Vienna and the First World War. By 1914 the only independent African countries were Liberia, founded in 1823 as a place of resettlement for freed American slaves, and Ethiopia, the ancient Christian kingdom on the east coast. The colonizing projects were conceived in a marriage between business and missionary interests.

In 1883 the British occupied Egypt; in 1906 the Sinai was taken from Turkey and given to Egypt. In 1914 a British protectorate over Egypt was established. An Anglo-Egyptian Condominium had already been established over the Sudan (1899). In 1830 the French began the conquest of Algeria;

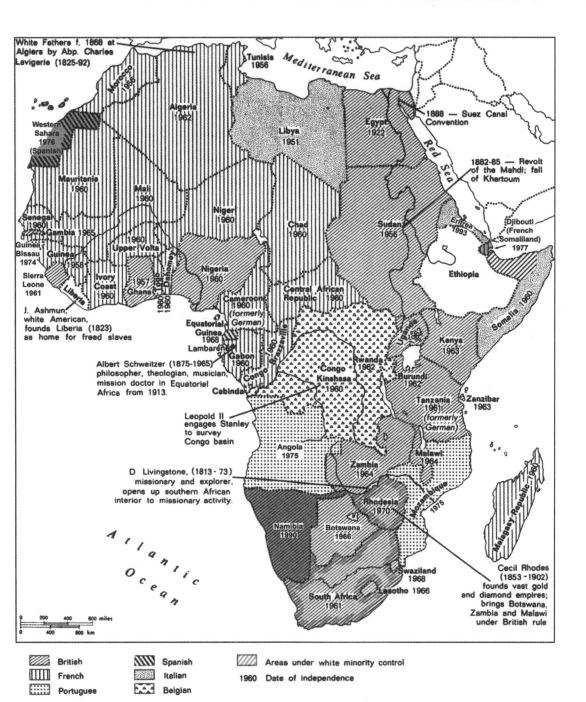

White Fathers f. 1868 at Algiers by Abp. Charles Lavigerie (1825-92)

Mediterranean Sea

Tunisia 1956

Morocco 1956

Algeria 1962

Libya 1951

Egypt 1922

1888 — Suez Canal Convention

Red Sea

1882-85 — Revolt of the Mahdi; fall of Khartoum

Western Sahara 1976 (Spanish)

Mauritania 1960

Mali 1960

Niger 1960

Chad 1960

Sudan 1956

Eritrea 1993

Djibouti (French Somaliland) 1977

Senegal 1960

Gambia 1965

Upper Volta 1960

Nigeria 1960

Central African Republic 1960

Ethiopia

Guinea Bissau 1974

Guinea 1958

Ivory Coast 1960

Ghana 1957

Dahomey 1960

Cameroon 1960 (formerly German)

Somalia 1960

Sierra Leone 1961

Liberia

J. Ashmun, white American, founds Liberia (1823) as home for freed slaves

Equatorial Guinea 1968

Lambaréné

Gabon 1960

Congo Brazzaville 1960

Congo Kinshasa 1960

Rwanda 1962

Uganda 1962

Kenya 1963

Burundi 1962

Albert Schweitzer (1875-1965) philosopher, theologian, musician, mission doctor in Equatorial Africa from 1913.

Cabinda

Leopold II engages Stanley to survey Congo basin

Tanzania 1961 (formerly German)

Zanzibar 1963

D Livingstone, (1813 - 73) missionary and explorer, opens up southern African interior to missionary activity.

Angola 1975

Zambia 1964

Malawi 1964

Mozambique 1975

Madagasy Republic 1960

Rhodesia 1970

Namibia 1990

Botswana 1966

Atlantic Ocean

Swaziland 1968

Lesotho 1966

South Africa 1961

Cecil Rhodes (1853 -1902) founds vast gold and diamond empires; brings Botswana, Zambia and Malawi under British rule

0  200  400  600 miles
0  400  800 km

| | British | | Spanish | | Areas under white minority control |
| | French | | Italian | 1960 | Date of independence |
| | Portugues | | Belgian | | |

in 1881 Tunisia became a French protectorate; by 1904 they were in control of Morocco. The Italians completed the subjugation of Tripoli (Libya) in 1913.

To the south, native chieftains were also unable to defend their lands against the superior firepower of European troops. Among the conquests: Gold Coast (Britain, 1850), Senegal (France, 1890), Togoland (Germany, 1884), Cameroons (Germany, 1884), Dahomey (France, 1890), Nigeria (Britain, 1899). French West Africa was set up in 1904. In 1885 King Leopold II of Belgium took the central Congo as a personal possession and organized exploration of the great copper resources in Katanga so ruthlessly that an international scandal

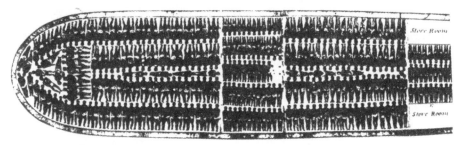

*Plan of slave ship. The horrors of the "Middle Passage."*

broke. Following this period of forced labor and great loss of native life, the Belgian state took over (1908) and conditions improved; an official program of "Christianization" was undertaken.

Southwest Africa was divided between the Germans and Portuguese (Angola) in 1886. To the east, the Germans established substantial holdings. The British set up a protectorate over Zanzibar and the French over Madagascar. Nyasaland became a British colony. After a series of conflicts between Muslim, Protestant and Roman Catholic factions in Uganda, a British protectorate was established in 1894 and an uneasy peace maintained. In most of these areas there were repeated tribal revolts, unsuccessful. The German colonies fell to allied forces with the First World War.

Missionary work accompanied colonialism. The Church Missionary Society carried out considerable work in British West Africa. The Basel Mission (Swiss and German) was active. In 1878 the White Fathers were assigned by the pope to mission work in Africa. Christianity expanded rapidly in Uganda, in the Congo, in Nigeria, and among the native population of South Africa.

## COLONIAL HOLDINGS IN ASIA 19TH–20TH CENTURIES

THE European conquest of Asia was less complete than the conquest of Africa. Two of the greatest nations, China and Japan, never submitted—although China was compelled to accept trade and extraterritorial agreements. Japan herself, opened to the west in 1857, speedily became a colonial power in imitation of the west. Japan took over Korea, a Chinese tributary since 1637, after handing China a series of humiliating defeats in the war of 1894–95. Siam also maintained a measure of independence, by playing off French, British and American trading interests against each other.

Persia was alternately dominated by Russia or England. Afghanistan was also a center of friction between Russia and England, with the latter winning out (1907 treaty). The British established their power over the many principalities and kingdoms of the Indian sub-continent, ending the Mogul (Muslim) dynasty after the Sepoy Rebellion (1857–58); in 1877, Queen Victoria was proclaimed Empress of India. In 1886 the India National Congress was formed; it became the

# COLONIAL HOLDINGS IN ASIA
## 19TH–20TH CENTURIES

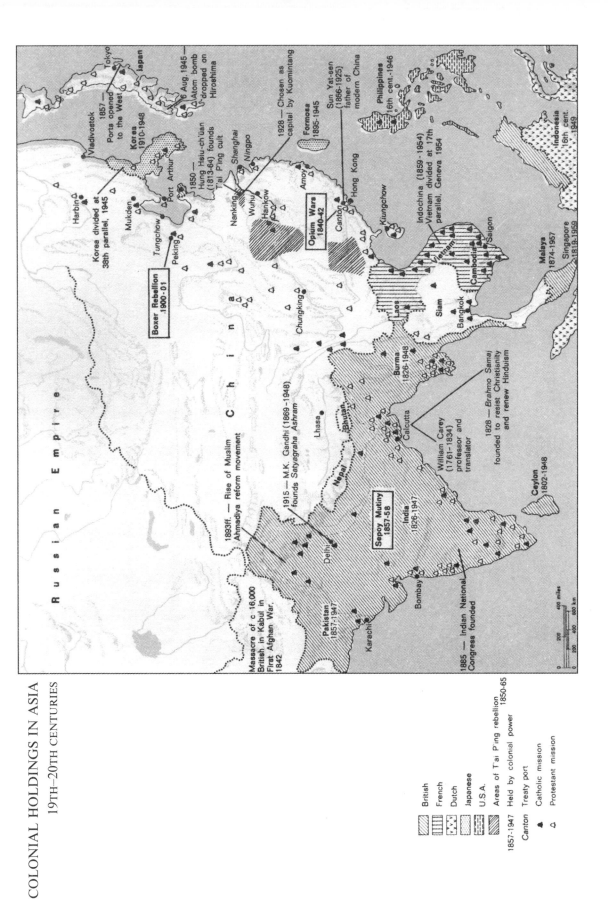

**Legend:**

- British
- French
- Dutch
- Japanese
- U.S.A.
- Areas of T'ai P'ing rebellion 1850-65
- 1857-1947 Held by colonial power
- *Canton* Treaty port
- Catholic mission
- Protestant mission

**Map labels:**

- Russian Empire
- China
- Tokyo
- Japan
- Vladivostok
- 1857 — Ports opened to the West
- 6 Aug. 1945 — Atom bomb dropped on Hiroshima
- Philippines 16th cent. -1946
- Korea 1910-1948
- Korea divided at 38th parallel, 1945
- Harbin
- Mukden
- Port Arthur
- Peking
- *Tungchow*
- Boxer Rebellion 1900-01
- 1850 — Hung Hsiu-ch'uan (1813-64) founds T'ai P'ing cult
- Nanking
- Wuhu
- Hankow
- Shanghai
- Ningpo
- 1928 — Chosen as capital by Kuomintang
- Formosa 1895-1945
- Sun Yat-sen (1866-1925) father of modern China
- Amoy
- Canton
- Hong Kong
- Opium Wars 1840-42
- Chungking
- Kiungchow
- Indonesia 16th cent. -1949
- Indochina (1859-1954) Vietnam divided at 17th parallel, Geneva 1954
- Vietnam
- Saigon
- Cambodia
- Laos
- Siam
- Bangkok
- Malaya 1874-1957
- Singapore 1819-1959
- Burma 1826-1948
- Lhasa
- Bhutan
- Nepal
- Calcutta
- 1828 — *Brahmo Samaj* founded to resist Christianity and renew Hinduism
- William Carey (1761-1834) professor and translator
- 1893ff. — Rise of Muslim Ahmadiyya reform movement
- 1915 — M.K. Gandhi (1869-1948) founds *Satyagraha Ashram*
- India 1826-1947
- Sepoy Mutiny 1857-58
- Delhi
- Massacre of c 16,000 British in Kabul in First Afghan War, 1842
- Pakistan 1857-1947
- Karachi
- Bombay
- 1885 — Indian National Congress founded
- Ceylon 1802-1948

400 miles
200
600 km
400
200
0

275

rallying point of the nationalist movement and under Mohandas K. Gandhi (1869–1948) finally attained its objectives. Extensive Christian missions led to the founding of major colleges and universities. Organized Hindu resistance at the religious level began with the Brahmo Samaj (f. 1828). After several wars the British achieved control of Burma (1885). France, with Roman Catholic missionary interests playing an active part, established a protectorate over Indo-China. Britain took over the Malay Peninsula, dominated for a century before by the Dutch. The Dutch and the British divided Indonesia.

Before treaties with the west had been accepted, and while there was still a proscript against Christian literature and missions, Robert Morrison (1782–1834) arrived in Canton. He translated the Bible and edited the first Chinese-English dictionary. After the Opium Wars, trade agreements were negotiated by the British and the French which also guaranteed toleration of Christianity. The T'ai P'ing Rebellion of 1851–64 combined political and religious motifs of anti-foreignism, and the Boxer Rebellion of 1900–01 was another desperate effort to throw off the concessions and controls seized by European nations. Although missionary work from Europe and America made substantial contributions in advancing education and medicine and other subjects, the patriotic movements tended to be anti-Christian, anti-Manchu (pro-republican), and anti-foreign.

In Korea too the Christian missionaries stole into the country before legal proscriptions were lifted, and in 1865–70 a number were martyred. After some years of jockeying between Russia and Japan, the latter annexed the country (1910). American Presbyterian missions continued to be important, and native Christians were chief leaders in the fight for independence.

Japan modernized rapidly after 1857. The feudal political structures (*shogunate*) were dismantled: universal education was undertaken in 1871, a modernized army based on conscription in 1872, a bicameral national legislature in 1889. Expansion into Korea, China, and finally Mongolia followed. Religion in Japan was a fairly vigorous complex of Buddhist and Shinto cults and subdivisions, but Christianity made steady advances.

Among the great men of the missions were William Carey (1761–1834), a self-taught man of enormous gifts as a linguist and translator (Burma and India), and J. Hudson Taylor (1832–1905), founder of the interdenominational China Inland Mission (f. 1865). The CIM was not only the largest mission in China: it set a model of self-supporting mission work copied all over Africa and Asia.

*William Carey.*

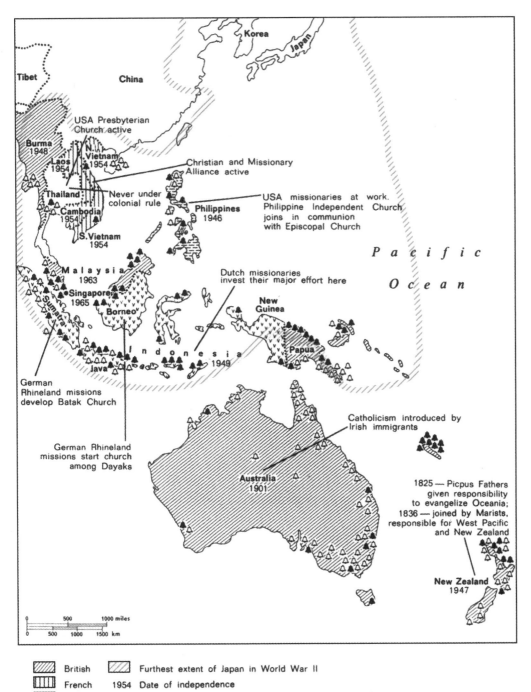

Korea

Japan

Tibet    China

USA Presbyterian
Church active

Burma
1948    N.
Laos    Vietnam
1954    1954
                Christian and Missionary
                Alliance active

Thailand:    Never under
             colonial rule
Cambodia                Philippines
1954                    1946
                                USA missionaries at work.
                                Philippine Independent Church
S.Vietnam                       joins in communion
1954                            with Episcopal Church

M a l a y s i a                         P a c i f i c
1963
    Singapore                                O c e a n
    1965    Borneo        Dutch missionaries
                          invest their major effort here

                              New
                              Guinea

German        I n d o n e s i a
Rhineland                    1949    Papua
missions
develop Batak Church    Java

German Rhineland
missions start church
among Dayaks
                                Catholicism introduced by
                                Irish immigrants

                    Australia
                    1901
                                    1825 — Picpus Fathers
                                    given responsibility
                                    to evangelize Oceania;
                                    1836 — joined by Marists,
                                    responsible for West Pacific
                                    and New Zealand

                                    New Zealand
                                    1947

0    500    1000 miles
0    500    1000    1500 km

| ▨ British | ▨ Furthest extent of Japan in World War II |
| ▥ French | 1954 Date of independence |
| ▤ U.S.A | ▲ Catholic mission |
| ⩊ Dutch | △ Protestant mission |

THE impact of modern civilization upon the peoples of the South Pacific islands has been disastrous, in some areas genocidal. In Hawaii, of a population of c 800,000, only c 12,000 pure-blood descendants of the original population remain. In Tahiti, the population was decimated by diseases carried by the white man. Sailors on some of the early ships shot the natives

*The Khmer shrine of Angkor Wat, Cambodia, 12th century.*

for sport. World War II victimized the peoples of numerous islands in the crushing struggle between the Allied and Japanese Imperial forces. French atomic tests later showered the islands with deadly fallout. Of the colorful earthly paradise immortalized by Robert Louis Stevenson and Gauguin and sought by a century of tourists ever since, little but the fantastic scenery remains.

Australia, the largest island and a continent in its own right, is thoroughly Europeanized. By exclusion acts it long resisted settlement by Asia's teeming millions. It was first settled as an English penal colony. Chaplains and missionaries followed for prisoners and their guards. Only in the modern period have some of the original native population, few and scattered from the start, become prominent public figures.

In New Zealand, 1,600 miles to the south, the native population was much more advanced in social and economic affairs than the original inhabitants of Australia. The Maoris now enjoy equal rights with the whites in a welfare state.

Missions to other islands have also generally followed the lines of colonial administration. The first missions in Polynesia were established under the London Missionary Society, founded in 1795 by members of the Free Churches and Evangelicals in the Church of England. When the French took over the area, the LMS transferred its work to the Paris Evangelical Missionary Society. Roman Catholic work in Tahiti began also at this time.

The Methodist work in Fiji began in 1835. In 1879 laborers were brought in from India. Today their descendants comprise the majority, many of them still adhering to Hinduism.

World War II brought modern violence to the islands. The Japanese occupied the Philippines and spread out through the smaller islands to the south. Some of the heaviest battles of the war were fought on and around the Marshalls and the Marquesas.

In spite of the negative aspects of the modern impingement upon their life, the natives took rapidly to Christianity and participated in its expansion. Christianity was carried to Paumotu by native Protestants from Tahiti, just twenty years after missionaries arrived at the larger island. The Christianization of Samoa, the Navigator Islands, was begun in 1830 by native Methodists from Tonga. Rotuma, Fiji, New Hebrides and the Loyalty Islands were all first approached by native Christians.

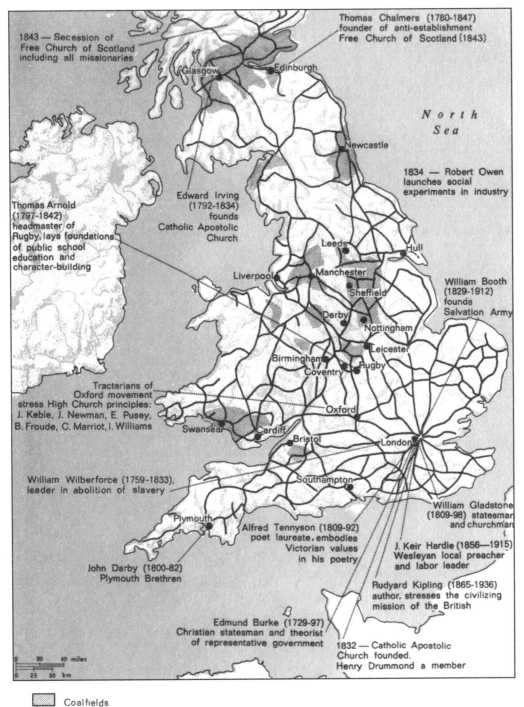

1843 — Secession of
Free Church of Scotland
including all missionaries

Thomas Chalmers (1780-1847)
founder of anti-establishment
Free Church of Scotland (1843)

*North
Sea*

1834 — Robert Owen
launches social
experiments in industry

Thomas Arnold
(1797-1842)
headmaster of
Rugby, lays foundations
of public school
education and
character-building

Edward Irving
(1792-1834)
founds
Catholic Apostolic
Church

William Booth
(1829-1912)
founds
Salvation Army

Tractarians of
Oxford movement
stress High Church principles:
J. Keble, J. Newman, E. Pusey,
B. Froude, C. Marriot, I. Williams

William Wilberforce (1759-1833),
leader in abolition of slavery

William Gladstone
(1809-98) statesman
and churchman

Alfred Tennyson (1809-92)
poet laureate, embodies
Victorian values
in his poetry

J. Keir Hardie (1856—1915)
Wesleyan local preacher
and labor leader

John Darby (1800-82)
Plymouth Brethren

Rudyard Kipling (1865-1936)
author, stresses the civilizing
mission of the British

Edmund Burke (1729-97)
Christian statesman and theorist
of representative government

1832 — Catholic Apostolic
Church founded.
Henry Drummond a member

Glasgow · Edinburgh · Newcastle · Leeds · Hull · Liverpool · Manchester · Sheffield · Derby · Nottingham · Leicester · Birmingham · Coventry · Rugby · Oxford · Swansea · Cardiff · Bristol · London · Southampton · Plymouth

0  20  40 miles
0  25  50 km

▨ Coalfields

—— Railways built by 1870

ALTHOUGH English statesmen criticized the excesses of the French Revolution and the people participated decisively in the defeat of Napoleon's despotism, Britain did not swing far away from her commitment to liberty and self-government. The Holy Alliance on the continent, with its reactionary and

*"Gin Lane," after Hogarth.*

repressive policies, collapsed for lack of British cooperation.

Parliament had been kept in frequent defiance of the public purpose by corruption in the House of Commons and blockage of social legislation by the House of Lords. In the Great Reform Bill (1832), the "pocket boroughs" (where the patron appointed representation) and "rotten boroughs" (where bribery controlled the few voters in a rural area) were sharply reduced. The House of Lords was also put in a position where it was unable permanently to check popular legislation. The commercial and industrial middle class thus came to power, but the majority of the population remained disenfranchised until the Second Reform Bill (1867) and the Franchise Bill (1884) and Redistribution Bill (1885).

The major social force of the century was the rapid expansion of industry, fed by raw materials from the colonies, and the consequent expansion of the great cities. As in many countries with rapid urbanization and industrialization, the lot of the poor was desperate. As it was said at the time, a bottle of gin was the fastest road out of London. Political liberty and social legislation followed but slowly the shifts of population. The first era of trade-unionism was unproductive, since the movement for collective bargaining was heavily influenced—and its objectives blunted or diverted—by the Utopian Socialist ideas of Robert Owen (1783–1833). After 1845 the union movement was reorganized with more pragmatic objectives. In its rise of influence the local preachers of the Wesleyans and other Free Churches played a major role. J. Keir Hardie (1856–1915), founder of the Labour Party, was a local preacher.

In the latter part of the century the governments, both Liberal and Tory, with William E. Gladstone (1809–98) and Benjamin Disraeli (1804–81) the most famous party leaders, passed social legislation which provided considerable benefits for the working people. Disabilities against Jews were removed (1858). The last religious tests for taking university degrees were lifted (1871).

Monarch during most of this period of internal change and colonial expansion was Victoria (queen: 1837–1901), during whose reign the population of the United Kingdom more than doubled. The increase was in spite of massive emigrations of Irish, Scots and Welsh.

The churches of Britain participated fully in the growth of Christian missions, as well as in movements for social reform at home. It was also a time of remarkable energy in Christian renewal movements, from the Tractarians of John Henry Newman (1801–90) to the Plymouth Brethren (f. John Nelson Darby, 1800–82) and Salvation Army (f. 1865 by William Booth, 1829–1912).

THE nineteenth century brought the steady dissolution of the "Holy Muslim Empire." The separatist movement in Egypt under Mohammed Ali (1832 ff.) and the nationalist movements of the Balkans (beginning with Greece, 1830) gradually convinced the European powers that the Ottoman Empire was incapable of maintaining itself. In 1853 a general European war resulted, with France and England and Austria stepping in to guarantee the Ottomans against Russian encroachment. Russian Orthodoxy, which had incorporated the Byzantine tradition, considered this action of the western powers a wretched betrayal of Christianity. (It was during this war that Florence Nightingale [1820–1910] made a major contribution to the quality, appeal, and status of nursing.)

The status of the "holy places" was frequently the excuse for foreign intervention. In the Hatt-i Humeyun (18 February 1856) the Turkish government was forced to make substantial guarantees of the property and rights of Christian minorities. In 1876, however, the presentation of a new and liberal constitution, which combined minority rights with extensive provisions for basic liberties and parliamentary government, led to the overthrow of the reformer Midhat Pasha (1822–84). Repeated revolts by Christian peoples (e.g., Crete, 1866–68, 1878, 1889, 1896–97; Armenia, 1890–97, 1909, 1914) received little assistance from the "Christian" powers. These powers did, however, invest many lives and much money to take over Ottoman territories such as Egypt, Tunis, Algeria, Morocco, and to secure commercial

*Mohammed VI of Turkey, the last Ottoman emperor.*

advantages (e.g., construction and opening—1869—of the Suez Canal).

From the beginning of the century, efforts to reform the administration of the empire and to make it fit for resistance to the imperial intentions of the large European powers ran up against the reactionary self-interest of the religious leaders and the self-serving and corrupt control of the army by the elite janissaries. In 1826 Mahmud II (ruler: 1808–39) succeeded in splitting the two and getting the religious leaders to agree to liquidation of the janissaries. When the Young Turk movement arose (1896 ff.), chiefly among exiles in Europe, it was nationalist, liberal and anti-clerical. In 1913, shortly after the Albanian proclamation of independence, the Young Turks staged a successful coup d'état, but the opening of the First World War delayed execution of internal reforms.

The Ottoman Empire was opened to

# THE HOLY MUSLIM EMPIRE
## (BROKEN UP 1918)

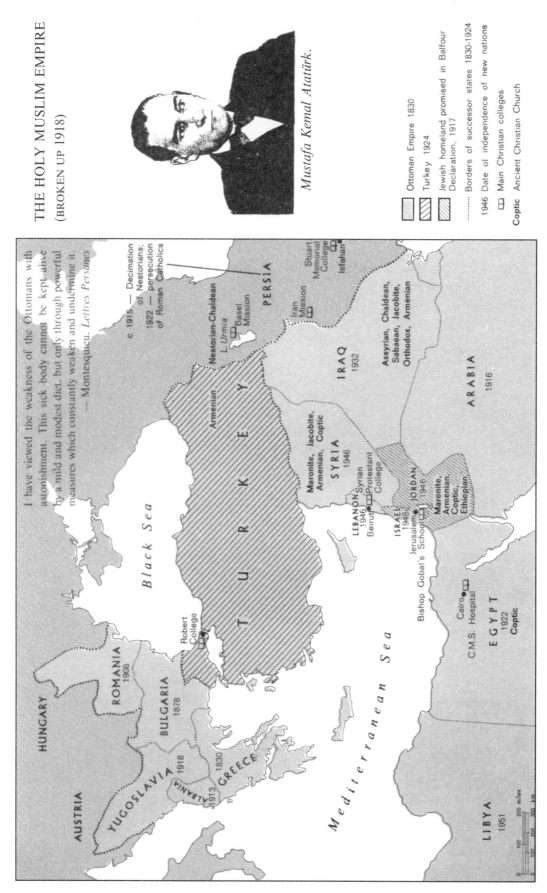

*Mustafa Kemal Atatürk.*

I have viewed the weakness of the Ottomans with astonishment. This sick body cannot be kept alive by a mild and modest diet, but only through powerful measures which constantly weaken and undermine it.
— Montesquieu, *Lettres Persanes*

c 1915 — Decimation of Nestorians:
1922 — persecution of Roman Catholics

HUNGARY

AUSTRIA

ROMANIA
1908

YUGOSLAVIA
1918

BULGARIA
1878

ALBANIA
1913 1830

GREECE

*Black Sea*

Robert College

*Mediterranean Sea*

LIBYA
1951

T U R K E Y

Armenian

Nestorian-Chaldean
L. Urmia
Basel Mission

PERSIA

Stuart Memorial College
Isfahan

Iran Mission

IRAQ
1932

Assyrian, Chaldean,
Sabaean, Jacobite,
Orthodox, Armenian

ARABIA
1916

SYRIA
1946

Maronite, Jacobite,
Armenian, Coptic

LEBANON
1946
Beirut
Syrian Protestant College

ISRAEL
1948
Jerusalem
Bishop Gobat's School

JORDAN
1946

Maronite,
Armenian,
Coptic,
Ethiopian

EGYPT
1922
Coptic

Cairo
C.M.S. Hospital

Ottoman Empire 1830

Turkey 1924

Jewish homeland promised in Balfour Declaration, 1917

Borders of successor states 1830-1924

1946 Date of independence of new nations

Main Christian colleges

**Coptic** Ancient Christian Church

0 100 200 miles
0 100 200 300 km

282

Christian missionary work in the 1820s. In Lebanon, where the ancient Maronite Church and the Greek Orthodox Church had long existed, work by the Congregationalists and the Presbyterians resulted among other things in the founding of the Syrian Protestant College, later the American University. In Egypt, where an ancient Coptic church yet survived, after several martyrdoms the missionaries persisted and eventually founded colleges. The most important achievement in the section that became the Turkish Republic in 1923 was the founding of Robert College (1860).

At the beginning the republic was committed to the practices of a liberal and secular state. In 1928 Islam ceased to be accorded constitutional privileges as a state religion. In recent years military professionals with modern education have vied for political power with Fundamentalist Muslims from the villages. The expulsion of old Greek settlements and the persecution of the Kurds in recent decades indicate that neither the moderns nor the traditionalists have been able to conceive of a nationalism and patriotism freed from ethnic definition.

## THE BAHA'I MOVEMENT

WHILE the reactionary Muslim establishment was producing holy wars and massacres, among the Shi'ites in Persia there was born one of the most remarkable of universal religions: Baha'i.

The movement originated with the Bab, "Gateway" (Mirza Ali Mohammed, 1819–50). He was martyred in 1850, having announced the coming of a greater messenger of God, who would usher in an age of peace for all humanity. In 1863 Mirza Husayn-Ali (1817–92), Baha'u'llah, "the Splendor of God," declared himself to be the one prophesied by the Bab.

Many of the Bab's followers were slaughtered, and others fled into the Turkish Empire. Driven into exile, Baha'u'llah spent his last forty years there—a prisoner at Acre, 1868–92. In his will he appointed his eldest son, Abdul Baha (d. 1921), to lead the Baha'i community and interpret the writings.

Baha was succeeded by his eldest grandson, Shoghi Effendi (d. 1937). Thereafter governance passed to an elected council, the Universal House of Justice.

The central principles of the Baha'i faith are the oneness of God, the oneness of religion, and the oneness of mankind. Beautiful gardens and buildings today house the central administration of the faith on Mount Carmel, Haifa. There is a shrine of great beauty on each of the continents, with architectural design noting the presence of the nine living religions which the Baha'i faith supersedes.

Although a savage persecution of the Baha'is remaining in Iran is a recurring phenomenon even in the 1990s, since the breakup of the Turkish Empire the movement has found peace in *Eretz Israel*.

## ARMENIA

IN its death throes the "Holy Muslim Empire" produced one of the first cases of attempted genocide in the twentieth century: the wholesale massacre of the Christians of Armenia. Here, as so often with genocide, the policy of persecution was a product of a combination of lowgrade religion and a rising national identity defined by ethnicity.

The Armenians had been the first nation converted to Christianity (c 301). With the Muslim conquest they were granted a provisional toleration, although Islam claimed to supersede both Judaism and Christianity and expected both to wither away and disappear.

In the late nineteenth century the Armenian minority imbibed the current national and liberal political ideas and attempted to get the "Christian" na-

tions to intervene on their behalf. Neither the Hatt-i Humeyun (1856) nor the Treaty of Berlin (1878) provided sound guarantees, and there had been no reform of provincial administration. A series of massacres ensued: in 1894 around Sassun, in 1895 throughout Anatolia, in 1896–97 the most extensive of all—with tens of thousands slaughtered. In 1909 the massacres were resumed at Adana and elsewhere, and in 1914–15 c 750,000 were murdered and nearly a million driven into exile—chiefly to America and Australia. Some made the trek over the land bridge to Russia, and built a republic around the old trade center of Yerevan. No Armenian lives today near Mount Ararat, none in the ancient heartland of the people.

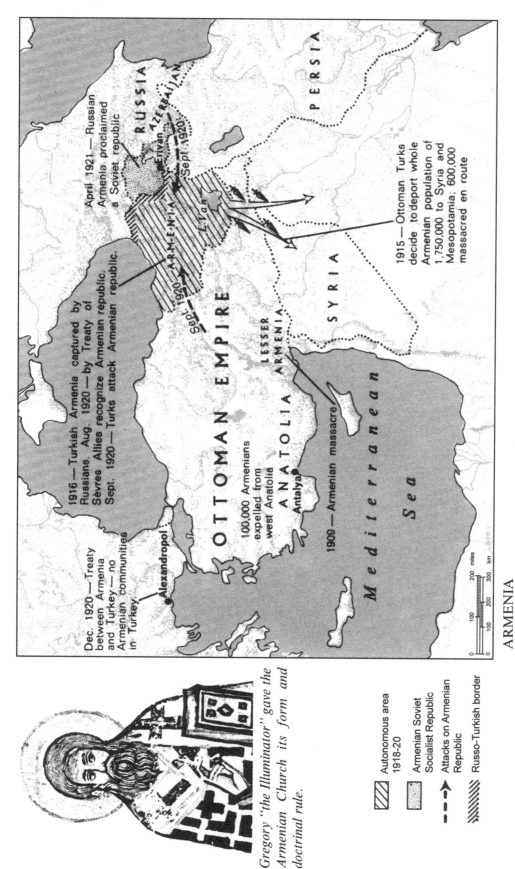

ARMENIA

April 1921—Russian Armenia proclaimed a Soviet republic.

1915—Ottoman Turks decide to deport whole Armenian population of 1,750,000 to Syria and Mesopotamia; 600,000 massacred en route

1916—Turkish Armenia captured by Russians. Aug. 1920—by Treaty of Sèvres Allies recognize Armenian republic. Sept. 1920—Turks attack Armenian republic.

Dec. 1920—Treaty between Armenia and Turkey—no Armenian communities in Turkey.

100,000 Armenians expelled from west Anatolia

1909—Armenian massacre

RUSSIA

AZERBAIJAN

Erivan

PERSIA

Sept. 1920

A-R-M-E-N-I-A

Sept. 1920

L. Van

OTTOMAN EMPIRE

SYRIA

LESSER ARMENIA

ANATOLIA

Antalya

Alexandropol

Mediterranean Sea

0  100  200 miles
0  100  200  300 km

Gregory "the Illuminator" gave the Armenian Church its form and doctrinal rule.

⬚ Autonomous area 1918-20
▦ Armenian Soviet Socialist Republic
⇢ Attacks on Armenian Republic
▨ Russo-Turkish border

285

# L. INITIATIVES BY THE RANK AND FILE ("LAITY")

THE nineteenth century opened with massive assaults on European Christendom by avowedly anti-religious movements. During the Middle Ages, Renaissance and Reformation periods, the establishments were dominated by princes of the church and by kings who ruled "by divine right." The forces of modernity—an emerging nationalism, a growing public literacy, an expanding map of intellectual and economic commerce, military conscription ("the nation in arms")—undermined the monopolies of power claimed by religious and political regimes, not seldom united in one person.

The French Revolution released popular energies that remained the major horror of religious and political conservatives in Europe until, more than a century later, the Bolshevik Revolution brought Russia to the fore as a center of militant atheism and ideological hostility to traditional religions.

In the early nineteenth century, with the French Revolution and the Napoleonic Wars spreading subversive republican and democratic ideas among the common people of Western Europe, the leaders of the religious and political establishments on the Continent—both Roman Catholic and Protestant—responded with great anxiety. The decisions of the Congress of Vienna (1815), which attempted to put things right again after the military defeat of Napoleon Bonaparte (1769–1821), were followed by harsh suppression of popular movements. Interfaith cooperation by rulers (Protestant, Roman Catholic and Orthodox) was expressed in the verbal pieties of the Holy Alliance and by concrete measures such as the control of student groups through the Carlsbad Decrees.

In 1848 the attempt was made in several European states, more in the line of the American Revolution than the French, to secure a share in government for the emerging middle-class elites of several German states, Hungary, Austria, France.... This too was thwarted. Some thousands moved to America, while *The Communist Manifesto* of Karl Marx (1818–83) began its slow penetration of the cultures of European intellectuals and proletarians disaffected from organized religion.

A creative and peaceful story of wrestling with the problems of the nineteenth century established churches can be read in the record of Lutheran Denmark. The two great Christian thinkers and teachers were N.F.S. Grundtvig (1783–1872) and Søren Kierkegaard (1813–55).

Grundtvig believed in a close connection between national life and culture and Christian faith, and was—rather late in life—elected a bishop in the established Church of Denmark. He opposed both the arid dogmatism of traditional Lutheran orthodoxy and the rationalism of the intellectuals. He championed the "folk school" movement, the cooperative movement, and other agencies that bettered the life of the people. Believing in a singing church, he also authored several hundred hymns.

Kierkegaard moved beyond student

days of dissipation and smart cynicism to study Theology and write prodigiously on religious subjects. Out of agonizing personal relationships in his family and an unsuccessful love affair, haunted by guilt and sin, he developed a dialectical interpretation of Christian belief in which only God in Christ can overcome the contradictions and incoherences. One of his more powerful books is an attack on Christendom, which he thought false to the New Testament, and on his deathbed he refused to accept the sacrament from "the king's officials." In the twentieth century, in the Europe of two world wars, with the ravages caused by two dictatorships inspired by anti-Christian ideologies, in the ruins of a pretentious "Christian" civilization, Kierkegaard's message became very popular.

*Søren Kierkegaard.*

A signal Protestant reaction to modern trends were the institutions and political party founded in the Netherlands by Abraham Kuyper (1837–1920) after Marxism was making strong gains in Western Europe. Kuyper's 1879 book, *Our Program*, led to the founding of the Anti-Revolutionary Party, the Calvinist Free University in Amsterdam, and the secession of the strictly Calvinist Reformed Churches (*Gereformeerde Kerken*) from the larger Netherlands Reformed Church (*Hervormde Kerk*). He was strongly opposed to Liberal Protestantism and its social and economic views. While Minister of the Interior, he used government power to crush a strike by railway workers. His successor as leader of the Anti-Revolutionary Party, Hendrikus Colijn (1869–1944), served five times as Prime Minister, the last time in collaboration with the Nazi occupation.

The reaction of the Vatican to republican and democratic ideas was anxious but unambiguous. On the one hand, such popular principles as liberty of conscience, toleration, universal suffrage and public education were severely condemned. Pius IX's *Syllabus of Errors* (1864) listed eighty headings on "errors of the day." On the other hand, a process of bureaucratic centralization was developed in the Roman Catholic Church, culminating in the dogma of papal infallibility (1871). With some splintering and substantial losses in Europe and South America, it has come through to the present day as the most enduring absolute monarchy in Christendom. On this autocratic principle of church government, there has been a tightening line in Rome— from Pius IX through Pius XII to John Paul II.

There is another face to Roman Catholicism in the modern period, however, and that is primarily due to a surge of devotion among working priests and ordinary believers ("laity"). Lay initiative and energy has given a face of faith and hope, creating an astonishing number of new orders and opening up dozens of new fields of work at home and abroad.

DURING the French Revolution, church lands were nationalized (1789), religious orders were suppressed (1790), and the attempt was made to enforce an oath of clergy submission to civil government. Among other experiments, establishment of public devotion to a Cult of Reason was attempted. For twelve years (November 1793 to 31 December 1805) records were kept according to an anti-clerical Revolutionary Calendar, with new names for the twelve months and a new way to calculate their length.

The anti-Christian campaign, often accompanied by antisemitic outbursts, failed. In the year 1815, two new societies of Christian service were founded by Catholics disturbed by the de-Christianization of the French masses. One was the Society of the Missionaries of France, founded to revive devotion in the parishes. Another was the Marianists, who maintained boarding schools and workshops. Also in 1815, Pius VII—having returned to Rome from several years as a prisoner of Napoleon—gave his support to the work among the disaffected populace of the Congregation of the Most Precious Blood. The Congregation had been founded by a man of humble origins, Gaspare del Bufalo (1786–1837), to missionize the masses, eventually spreading throughout Italy and also to North America.

The following year, 1816, saw the founding of the Oblates of the Immaculate Virgin Mary, designed to provide home missionaries among the population de-Christianized by the Revolution. The Marist Brothers also started in 1816, eventually spreading their work among the de-Christianized of France to the unreached peoples of North America and the South Pacific.

In later decades, great impetus was given to foreign missions by initiatives begun among the aroused Catholics of France. Among them:

1822—the Society for the Propagation of the Faith, which organized the devout to pray daily for missions and contribute one centime a week;

1843—the Association of the Holy Infancy, enlisting children to pray daily for missions and give a centime a week for missions among children;

1866—a community of women instituted for foreign missions: the Franciscan Missionaries of Mary;

1868—the Society of Missionaries of Our Lady of Africa ("White Fathers"), founded by Charles Martial Lavigerie (1825–92).

## RENEWAL MOVEMENTS IN GERMANY 19TH CENTURY

CHURCHMEN and theologians in the German states strongly rejected the message and mode of the French Revolution, although a few Free Church Protestants, a few Jews, and a few men of the universities sympathized with the revolutionaries' hatred of Christendom's coercive union of church and state.

The Germanies were not united until after the Franco-Prussian War (1870–71), and until then Austria dominated the German-speaking areas. Among significant Catholic initiatives were the Ludwig-Missionsverein of Bavaria, founded 1828 in response to an appeal from the see of Cincinnati for help in holding German immigrants to their hereditary faith, and the Society of the Divine Word—founded 1875 to recruit and train missionaries for China.

With the rise of Prussia to a position of political, military and cultural dominance, Roman Catholics fell into a role as second-class citizens. The churches of the Old Prussian Union, established and privileged, were comfortable with a Kaiser who was both Emperor and lay *summus episcopus*.

During the nineteenth century the German universities came to be recognized as preeminent in the Western world. Protestant theology worldwide carried the stamp of Friedrich D. E. Schleiermacher (1768–1834), Albrecht Ritschl (1822–89), Julius Wellhausen (1844–1918), Ernst Troeltsch (1865–1923) and Adolf von Harnack (1851–1930).

In the parishes, German Protestantism experienced several movements of spiritual energy and practical devotion.

THE HOLY ROMAN EMPIRE BEGINNING OF 19TH CENTURY

At one level, a rising spirit of nationalism was blended with religious piety and coupled with hostility to the French Revolution—evident in J. G. Fichte's "Address to the German Nation" and E. M. Arndt's polemic against Napoleon, "On the Spirit of the Times."

At a more popular level of piety, the older work of the Pietist Herrnhuter, widespread in Germany, found partnership and support from new lay movements of awakening. Centers of renewal and devotional training were established in Swabia, in Korntal and Bad Boll, and in the Rheinland. The first institute for training missionaries was founded, and achieved a considerable following and support among the landed families of Saxony and Pomerania. A break from the established churches led to the founding of an "Old Lutheran Church," with centers in Kiel, Neuendettelsau and Hermannsburg. Free Churches such as the Baptists and the Methodists and the Evangelical Association grew steadily, although most of their members continued to pay church taxes rather than join militant atheists and anticlericals in public opposition to the established churches that dated back to the sixteenth-century Reformation.

Especially important in evangelization, with groups for prayer and Bible study in the homes, was the *Gemeinschaftsbewegung*, which also drew from the older Pietism and the more recent movements of lay awakening. With industrialization, country parishes with a tax-supported clergy might have only a handful of families left on the land, while new cities might struggle with a proportion of one clergyman to 30,000 souls—many of them ardently courted by Marxists and other anti-Christian organizers. In spite of the best efforts of creative Christian statesmen like Johann Hinrich Wichern (1808–81) and the Roman Catholic Wilhelm Emanuel von Ketteler (1811–77), however, the proletariat wandered from the churches.

As geographical horizons expanded, awakened German laymen were drawn into the work of the Evangelical Alliance, the YMCA, Christian Endeavor, the German Student Christian Movement and the World's Student Christian Federation. Many of these creative associations of Germans with active Christians of other countries were, however, impeded by World War I and the "peace" of Versailles, slowed by the internal struggles of the Weimar period, and choked off by the dictatorship of the Third Reich.

## REVIVALS OF RELIGION IN ENGLAND 19TH CENTURY

ENGLAND escaped most of the civil strife and spiritual anguish associated with the impact of the French Revolution and the later rise of Marxism on the Continent. This was in good measure due to the peaceful changes wrought on the political front. The functions of the royal house became increasingly symbolic, while the authority of the House of Commons was purified by the Reform Bill of 1832, the Reform Act of 1867, and acts in 1884 and 1885 that provided virtually universal suffrage.

Within the Church of England, an Evangelical party developed over against the Tractarian caucus. The Tractarians, so called because of the series of pamphlets ("Tracts for the Times") published to advance their cause, furthered the cause of Christian spirituality through study of the Church Fathers. Their greatest leader was John Henry Newman (1801–90), who converted to Roman Catholicism and later became a Cardinal. His *Idea of a University* (1852) is still worth study, and his *Apologia pro vita sua* (1864) is a classic among Christian autobiographies.

Another important figure in the Oxford movement and convert from Anglicanism to Rome was Henry Edward Manning (1808–92), who served at Westminster Cathedral, which he founded. He staunchly supported papal infallibility at the Vatican Council (1869–70) and was made a Cardinal in 1875.

The Evangelicals, or "Low Church" wing of the Church of England, were influenced by the Wesleyans and followed their examples by staying within the Church of England. (Later, the British Methodists founded a separate Wesleyan Conference, and the American Methodists founded an independent church, reluctantly and due only to practical necessity.)

The churches also avoided the easy

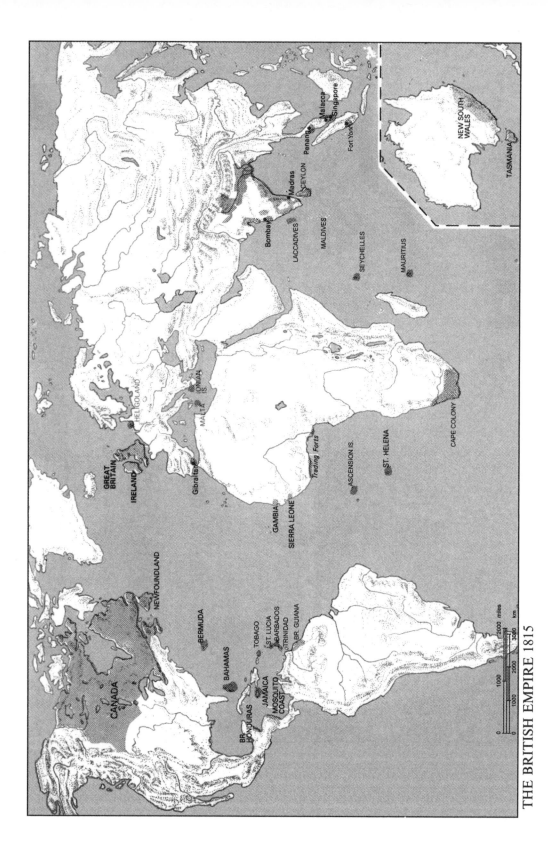

THE BRITISH EMPIRE 1815

way, so familiar on the Continent, of uncritical championship of the interests of the privileged classes. Many of the early leaders in the labor union locals were Methodist local preachers, and the Labour Party itself showed its origins in Christian idealism.

A great figure among the Evangelicals was William Wilberforce (1759–1833), a layman and for much of his life a member of the House of Commons. His residence at Clapham became the meeting place of a company of earnest Christians. Among the causes he championed were the founding of the Church Missionary Society (1798) and the Bible Society (1803), and especially the abolition of slavery. The Emancipation Act of 1833 put the power of the British Navy, by then the most powerful in the world, at the service of stopping the slave trade.

Among other significant figures in nineteenth-century Anglicanism, who left their marks upon the society as well as in the church, were Samuel Taylor Coleridge (1772–1834), Thomas Arnold (1795–1842), Frederick D. Maurice (1805–72), Frederick W. Robertson (1816–53) and Charles Kingsley (1819–75). Coleridge's little classics—"Aids to Reflection" and "Confessions of an Inquiring Spirit" —greatly influenced younger men. Arnold was famous for his intellectual and spiritual leadership of the school at Rugby. Maurice, a prominent theologian and professor, founded Queen's College (1848) to provide higher education for women and headed the Workingmen's College in London. Robertson was one of the greatest preachers of the age, and also attracted a following among servants and laborers for his lectures in a working-

men's center he founded. Kingsley was a prominent novelist, also numbered with Maurice as a leader of "Christian Socialism."

The nineteenth century in England is also remembered as the time when the British Empire spanned the globe, celebrated at home in such rollicking comic operas as *H.M.S. Pinafore, The Pirates of Penzance, The Mikado, The Yeoman of the Guard* and *The Gondoliers.* William S. Gilbert (1836–1911), playwright, wrote the words. The music was written by Arthur S. Sullivan (1842–1900), who also wrote the militant hymn "Onward, Christian Soldiers!" and the song that was once considered the greatest religious poem ever written: "The Lost Chord."

During the nineteenth century steam power made ocean travel easier, postal communication faster, and telegraph messages possible. Leading religious personalities traveled back and forth between England and the United States with facility. Among prominent travelers to England were the evangelists Charles G. Finney (1792–1875), Dwight L. Moody (1837–99) and Ira D. Sankey (1840–1908), and Student Christian Movement leaders John R. Mott (1865–1955) and Robert P. Wilder (1863–1938). Among those coming to America from England, none was more influential than John Nelson Darby (1800–82). His overt memorial is the life and work of the Plymouth Brethren, but his larger influence is through his reading of the periods of history: "dispensationalism." Millions of Americans who have never heard the name of Darby have embraced his view of the end-time, history's preparation for it, and the quiet preparation of the faithful in anticipation.

# III

# THE AGE OF PERSONAL DECISION

  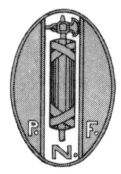

FOLLOWING the Enlightenment it became customary for social writers to avoid the mysterious and miraculous and to advance hypotheses which might reasonably explain human behavior. The analogs of the "laws of gravitation" and "the laws of stellar motion" and "the laws of human descent" governed writings about human affairs and finally the study of religion. Men became supremely conscious that they were "modern," and that modernity involved the rejection of superstition in favor of education, miracles in favor of rational explanation, social statics in favor of progress. Supernatural interventions were replaced by laws of human conduct, unique events were replaced by general patterns of human behavior: the universe expanded and man grew small.

Among the writers who expounded laws of human behavior were Adam Smith in *The Wealth of Nations* (1776), T. R. Malthus in *The Essay on Population* (1798), David Ricardo *On the Principles of Political Economy and Taxation* (1817), August Comte in *The System of Positive Politics* (1822), and John Stuart Mill in *Principles of Political Economy* (1848). From perception of the "laws" of human conduct to social engineering is but a step. Although there have been significant contributions to the systematic interpretation of social conduct since 1848—notably Georges Sorel's *Refléxions sur la Violence* (1908), V. Pareto's *Treatise of General Sociology* (1916), and Kurt Lewin's foundation of the academic discipline of Social Psychology, the critical event occurred in that year: the issuance of *The Communist Manifesto* by Karl Marx and Friedrich Engels, which marked the advent of "scientific socialism."

By a course of events both ironical and tragic, the development of theories of ironclad rules governing human affairs came at the same time as the widening of areas of liberty and decision among some previously mute sections of humankind. While at one level—with expanding empires, military conscription, and assembly line procedures—freedom was being reduced and active dehumanization augmented, on another level the dignity and integrity of the human person was recognized as never before.

To the radical Puritans and Pietists, Quakers and Moravians especially, goes the credit for first making central to Christianity the worth of every human person—whether Hottentot, Esquimaux, African, or European peasant. Before their time, even well-meaning Christians had found no great fault in slavery, and the use of government to enforce religious conformity was questioned by very few. Thus, while the economic conditions which might provide a base for freedom of choice were worsening, and the economic theorists were embracing one or another systematic statement of determinism, in Christianity an awareness of the importance of freedom of choice and personal decision was coming to the fore.

Across most of its history, Christianity has expanded by political and military conquest, by alliance with powerful economic and cultural forces. Most peoples who became Christian swung over en masse, in a matter of two or three generations, with rulers leading the way. In the ranks of the Radical Reformation, especially important in America in the first generations of the American republic, the emphasis shifted to individual persuasion and decision. Many churches shifted to adult baptism, with each person to make up his/her own mind at the "age of understanding" (i.e., post-puberty). And such ideas spread in both the religious and the political spheres.

Modern missions developed largely on the voluntary principle. The competition for the minds and souls of common people has broken the old pattern of ethnic religions and also changed the nature of politics. Even dictators must today claim popular support, whether they in fact enjoy it or not.

# A. CHRISTIANITY AND IDEOLOGY

## KARL MARX 1818–83

*...religion, or the duty which we owe to our creator, and the manner of discharging it, can be directed only by reason and conviction, not by force or violence.*

— James Madison, 1784

BUILDING upon the political tradition of the French Revolution and the philosophical tradition of German Idealism, Karl Marx developed the most powerful of post-Christian systems of being.

Marx, whose father was a Prussian civil servant who converted to Protestantism from Judaism, became the declared enemy of all religions and religious interpretations of events. His close friend and supporter was Friedrich Engels (1820–95), whose parents were well-to-do supporters of Krummacher, Jung-Stilling and other leaders of Christian renewal along Pietist lines.

Marx rejected the approach of earlier Socialists, especially those who recruited voluntary communities to establish "models" for social progress. Calling them "Utopians," he elaborated an interpretation of political power as an expression of economic reality. He also rejected the assumption of philosophical idealism that truths carry history and that change can be effected by teaching new value systems. He held that values and systems of thought arise from the conflict of classes which is basic in the historical process.

*Karl Marx, founder of "scientific socialism."*

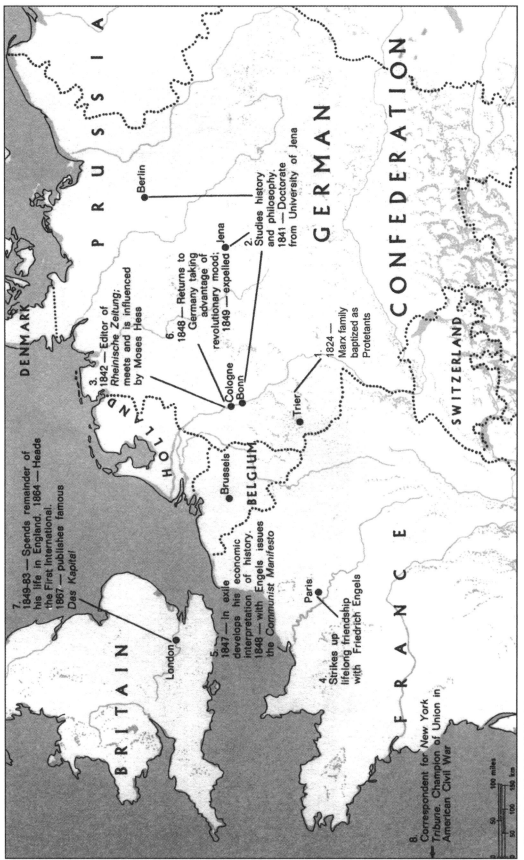

1. 1824 — Marx family baptized as Protetants

2. Studies history and philosophy. 1841 — Doctorate from University of Jena

3. 1842 — Editor of *Rheinische Zeitung*; meets and is influenced by Moses Hess

4. Strikes up lifelong friendship with Friedrich Engels

5. 1847 — In exile develops his economic interpretation of history. 1848 — with Engels issues the *Communist Manifesto*

6. 1848 — Returns to Germany taking advantage of revolutionary mood; 1849 — expelled

7. 1849-83 — Spends remainder of his life in England. 1864 — Heads the First International. 1867 — publishes famous *Das Kapital*

8. Correspondent for New York Tribune. Champion of Union in American Civil War

KARL MARX 1818–83

DENMARK

P R U S S I A

Berlin

G E R M A N

Jena

Cologne
Bonn

Trier

C O N F E D E R A T I O N

HOLLAND

BELGIUM

Brussels

SWITZERLAND

F R A N C E

Paris

B R I T A I N

London

100 miles
150 km

*Religion is a personal matter.*
— Gotha Program of the German Social
Democrats, 1875

MARXISM provided both an interpretation and a practice. *The Communist Manifesto* was published by Marx and Engels in 1848, a year of revolutions throughout Europe. The fundamentals of the belief were elaborated in depth in *Capital* (1867–94), but the style of Marx's politics can best be seen in writings directed at concrete decisions—such as *The Holy Family* (a refutation of philosophical idealism), *Anti-Dühring* and *The Critique of the Gotha Program* (repudiation of Socialist gradualism).

Marxism has been termed "an elaborate misunderstanding of the French Revolution." For Marx, at least, the first year of the French Republic (1792) was the first year of the modern epoch—of the period in which the proletariat would wrest power from the bourgeoisie, to be followed by the emergence of the classless society. The model of revolutionary action was the Paris Commune, in which during the French Revolution and the revolts of 1830, 1848 and 1871 the urban proletariat carried the torch of human progress. Instead of proving to be the next and inevitable step in industrially advanced societies, however, Marxism won its way in a marginal situation: Russia. Here a society passed, practically, from feudalism to Bolshevism—with only six months of "bourgeois" (i.e., liberal democratic) government in between (March–October, 1917).

The guiding genius of the Marxist revolution in Russia, which developed after the overthrow of the Romanov dynasty and the fall of the Menshevik

*Title page of the first edition of* The Communist Manifesto.

(moderate) government of Aleksandr Kerenski, was N. Lenin (pseudonym of Vladimir Ilyich Ulyanov, 1870–1924). He carried Marxist theory further, particularly in advancing the application of theory to the seizure and exercise of power. Lenin developed the theory of the role of a trained revolutionary cadre—"professional revolutionaries"—in the conquest of power: without such a vanguard the revolutionary moment may be abortive.

In the Bolshevik seizure of power (November 1917), the revolutionaries were able to capitalize on the political bankruptcy of a regime which spent too much time in theoretical debate. More important, the Soviets in the army and on the land channeled the disenchantment of the soldiers and peasants with continuance of the war.

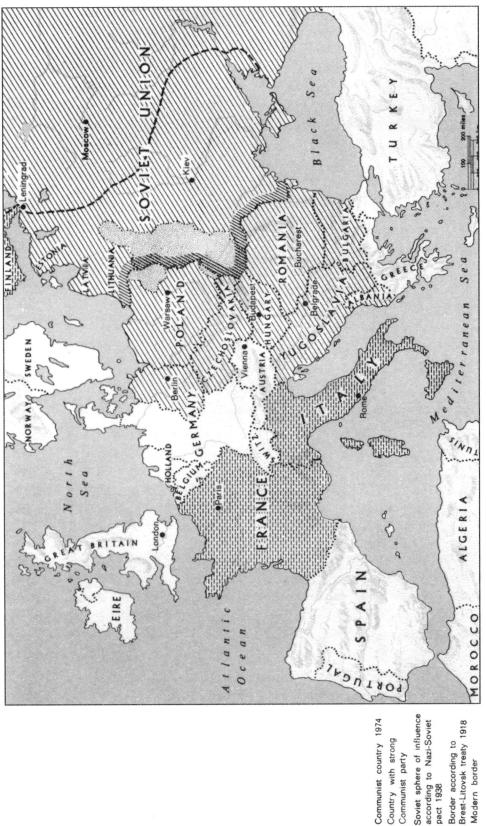

THE EUROPEAN WORLD OF MARXISM BEFORE 1989

Communist country 1974

Country with strong
Communist party

Soviet sphere of influence
according to Nazi-Soviet
pact 1938

Border according to
Brest-Litovsk treaty 1918

Modern border

*Lenin, leader of the Russian Revolution (1917).*

Russia pulled out of the war. Finland and the Baltic states declared their independence.

With the collapse of the eastern front against the Kaiser's Germany, peace was fixed in the Treaty of Brest-Litovsk (3 March 1918). Although they lost heavily in that settlement, the new Russian government acquired singular gains a few years later in agreements with the revolutionary government in Turkey. The revolutionary Russian government alienated Allied governments by publishing the secret treaties by which England and France and Italy planned to attain political and economic advantages by the war.

During the 1920s, when Soviet Russia was quarantined by the western countries, a defeated Germany worked out advantageous military and economic relations with Russia. In exchange for industrial equipment, German military forces were equipped and trained in Russia; revolutionary Russia had not been a signatory of the Versailles Treaty.

Lenin was succeeded in 1924 by Josef Stalin (1879–1953), who two years later won an internal fight with Leon Trotsky (Bronstein, 1879–1940). The Russian Orthodox Church, which had opposed the Revolution and allied itself with counter-revolutionary forces during the civil war, was subjected to harsh and repressive measures. The government nationalized all church property. About forty bishops and a thousand priests perished in the civil war. The public activities of the church (publication, social welfare, education, etc.) were severely curtailed. Many of the ablest theologians (e.g., Nicholas Berdyaev, 1874–1948; Georges Florovsky, 1893–1979) went into exile.

With the rise of Adolf Hitler to power in Germany (1933), Marxism suffered a certain ideological trauma. On the one hand, Stalin admired Hitler and enjoyed his attacks on the degenerate bourgeois governments of the west. He had himself murdered millions who stood in the way of his planned political and economic utopia. On the other hand, the orthodox Marxist dogma declared that Nazism was the last spasm of middle-class prejudice and capitalist struggle for existence and would fall of its own weight. On this ideological basis the German communists were ordered in 1933 to withhold their resistance, and Hitler gained and consolidated his power by the Enabling Act of March 24th.

On 23 August 1939 the Soviet-Nazi Pact was signed. A few days later Poland was invaded and divided. In June of 1941, after successfully overrunning the Netherlands, Belgium and most of France, Hitler invaded Russia. Russia joined the western Allies in a crushing defeat of the Third Reich. In 1945 delegates of fifty nations met at San Francisco to set up the United

Nations. Russia was a major force in the peace settlements, expanding its hegemony over eastern Europe, the Baltics, and into the Mediterranean.

After Stalin's death (1953), Nikita Kruschev, General Secretary of the Communist Party, opened discussion of the genocidal crimes of Stalin, but continued Soviet suppression of dissenting movements in the satellites and Soviet support of revolutionary proxies around the world. In 1989 the front of the "Cold War" broke, with the collapse of the hardline Communist government of East Germany. In this collapse the initiative of the churches (*Kerzenrevolution*) was important.

Following Mikhail Gorbachev's election as General Secretary (1985), steps were taken in cooperation with the USA to reduce the proliferation of nuclear weapons. His internal reform program met resistance, several nations in the USSR declared their independence, and the USSR officially broke up in 1991, one day after Gorbachev resigned. Boris Yeltsin took the helm in Russia, a confederation was declared (CIS), and amidst political and economic confusion the Russian Orthodox Church regained its public profile and many of its former privileges. His successor, Vladimir Putin, has not changed religious affairs policies of post-Soviet Russia.

As the century came to an end, the leadership in Moscow was beset by Muslim Fundamentalist revolts in former dependencies, by hardline Communist resistance in some cities and states, and by a restless military establishment which long functioned as a state within a state. Antisemitism is still widespread in cultural circles and the status of minor churches and religions is precarious.

Outside Russia and its sphere, the story of Marxism in China is noteworthy. In 1949 Mao Tse-tung (1893–1976) won a victory over Chiang Kai-shek and brought a new and major force into the Marxist camp. Chiang Kai-shek fled with some of his forces to Taiwan. Here religion, including the Christian form, has flourished. The People's Republic was proclaimed for the mainland at Beijing (1 October 1949). With one-fifth of the world's population, mainland China has large Christian, Muslim and Buddhist communities. The policy toward religion is suppressive and sporadically persecutory. In the military conquest of Tibet, expulsion of indigenous Buddhist natives, and settlement of ethnic Chinese, Beijing's policies have been genocidal.

Lin Piao—the chief theoretician of Maoist Marxism—introduced a new model of revolutionary action. Instead of the urban proletariat (Paris Commune), the rural peoples are to be carriers of history. Lin Piao developed the theory of the revolt of the countryside against the world metropolis. Asia, Latin America, the "Arab nation" and Africa ("The Third World") thus became carriers of a world revolution directed against the "World City" (an axis from Moscow to Washington). By definition, Israel (f. 1948) belonged to the colonial and imperialist powers.

---

**Lenin**
(1870–1924) founder of Bolshevism and driving force behind Russian Revolution
**Stalin**
(1879–1953) leader of Soviet Union and Communist world
**Trotsky**
(1879–1940) revolutionary leader and chief organizer of the Red Army. Eliminated in 1924–26 power struggle

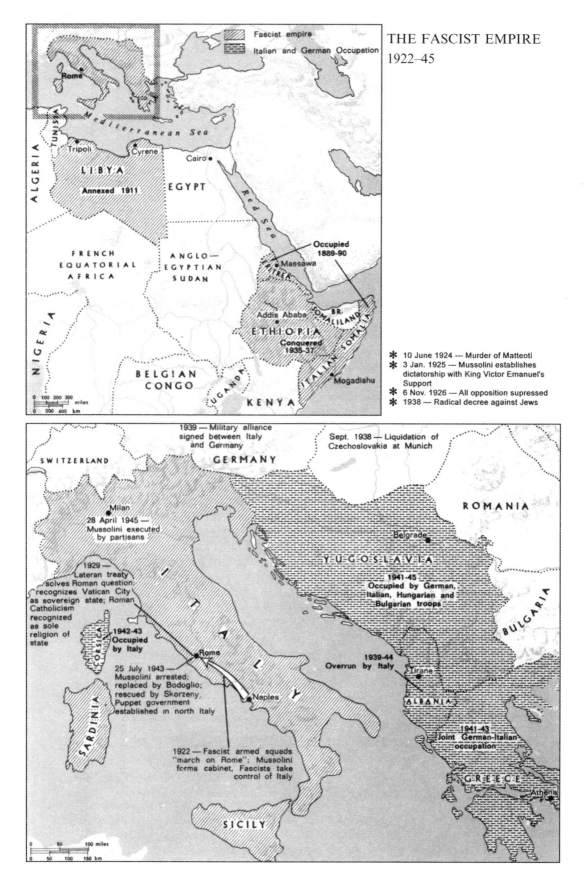

THE FASCIST EMPIRE
1922–45

Fascist empire

Italian and German Occupation

Rome

ALGERIA

TUNISIA

Tripoli  Cyrene

Cairo

Mediterranean Sea

LIBYA

Annexed 1911

EGYPT

Red Sea

FRENCH
EQUATORIAL
AFRICA

ANGLO—
EGYPTIAN
SUDAN

NIGERIA

Occupied
1889-90

Massawa

ERITREA

SOMALILAND

BR.
SOMALILAND

ITALIAN SOMALILAND

Addis Ababa

ETHIOPIA

Conquered
1935-37

Mogadishu

BELGIAN
CONGO

UGANDA

KENYA

0  100 200 300  miles
0    200  400  km

* 10 June 1924 — Murder of Matteoti
* 3 Jan. 1925 — Mussolini establishes
  dictatorship with King Victor Emanuel's
  Support
* 6 Nov. 1926 — All opposition supressed
* 1938 — Radical decree against Jews

1939 — Military alliance
signed between Italy
and Germany

Sept. 1938 — Liquidation of
Czechoslovakia at Munich

SWITZERLAND

GERMANY

ROMANIA

Milan

28 April 1945 —
Mussolini executed
by partisans

Belgrade

YUGOSLAVIA

1941-45
Occupied by German,
Italian, Hungarian and
Bulgarian troops

1929 —
Lateran treaty
solves Roman question;
recognizes Vatican City
as sovereign state; Roman
Catholicism
recognized
as sole
religion of
state

CORSICA

1942-43
Occupied
by Italy

I
T
A
L
Y

Rome

BULGARIA

1939-44
Overrun by Italy

Tirane

25 July 1943 —
Mussolini arrested;
replaced by Bodoglio;
rescued by Skorzeny.
Puppet government
established in north Italy

Naples

ALBANIA

SARDINIA

1941-43
Joint German-Italian
occupation

1922 — Fascist armed squads
"march on Rome"; Mussolini
forms cabinet, Fascists take
control of Italy

GREECE

Athens

SICILY

0    50    100 miles
0   50   100  150 km

302

*Incapable of understanding modern social organization, he has a nostalgia for periods of crisis in which the primitive community will suddenly reappear and attain its temperature of fusion. He wants his personality to melt suddenly into the group and be carried away by the collective torrent.*

— Jean-Paul Sartre on the Antisemite

*Mussolini in a favorite pose.*

THE initial experiment in fascist government was instituted in Italy by Benito Mussolini (1883–1944). Mussolini, a former Socialist, gained power in October of 1922 after a skillful play of public violence and verbal devotion to "law and order." When Giacomo Matteotti—author of *The Fascisti Exposed*—was murdered by fascists (10 June 1924), Mussolini's power was sufficient to secure release of the criminals. His authority was greatly strengthened in February of 1929 by the Lateran Treaties with the papacy, which created Vatican City and regularized Italian state relations with the papacy. They had been suspended in 1871.

In 1935 Mussolini invaded Ethiopia, and the Roman Catholic Church rang the church bells of Rome and seized the opportunity to launch extensive efforts to bring the Copts under Roman control. In the Spanish Civil War (1936–39), Mussolini maintained 75,000 "volunteers" on the side of the rebels. By the end of 1938 he had concluded a military alliance with the Third Reich and was beginning to persecute the Italian Jews.

Mussolini's theory of politics was much influenced by the *Refléxions sur la Violence* of Georges Sorel (1847–1922), which combined Marxist thought with a penchant for violent acts against the state (syndicalism). After he gained power, Mussolini's style of conducting international relations showed the same bent toward "the politics of the deed." He was shot by partisans (28 April 1945) at the end of Italian participation in World War II, and his body exposed to public disgrace with that of his mistress.

With the help of allies in the Curia, Mussolini was able to crush democratic opposition to his dictatorship. Count Carlo Sforza (1873–1952), a liberal Roman Catholic, was forced out of politics, just as the movement headed by Don Luigi Sturzo (1871–1959) had been sacrificed (1923) to please the dictator.

*303*

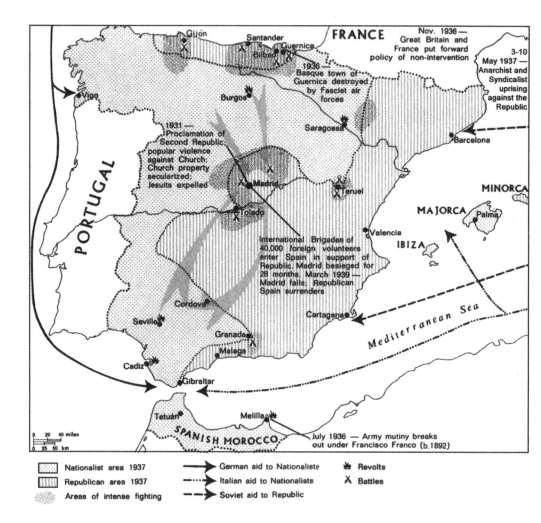

The map contains the following labels and notes:

Gijón, Santander, Guernica, Bilbao

FRANCE

Nov. 1936 — Great Britain and France put forward policy of non-intervention

3-10 May 1937 — Anarchist and Syndicalist uprising against the Republic

1936 Basque town of Guernica destroyed by Fascist air forces

Vigo, Burgos

Saragossa

Barcelona

1931 — Proclamation of Second Republic popular violence against Church; Church property secularized; Jesuits expelled

PORTUGAL

Madrid

Teruel

MINORCA

MAJORCA — Palma

International Brigades of 40,000 foreign volunteers enter Spain in support of Republic. Madrid besieged for 28 months. March 1939 — Madrid falls; Republican Spain surrenders

Toledo

Valencia

IBIZA

Cordova

Seville

Cartagena

Mediterranean Sea

Granada

Malaga

Cadiz

Gibraltar

Tetuán

Melilla

SPANISH MOROCCO

July 1936 — Army mutiny breaks out under Francisco Franco (b.1892)

0  20  40 miles
0  25  50 km

**Legend:**
- Nationalist area 1937
- Republican area 1937
- Areas of intense fighting
- German aid to Nationalists
- Italian aid to Nationalists
- Soviet aid to Republic
- Revolts
- Battles

---

*Mercenary Armies have at one time or another subverted the liberties of almost all the Countries they have been raised to defend.* — George Washington

THE Spanish Civil War was the first great watershed dividing for decades the political preferences of churchmen throughout Europe and America. Spain, although spared the immediate effects of World War I, did not escape the winds of political ideologies and revolution. Separatist movements were strong (especially among the Basques and Catalonians) and military disaffection was pronounced. From 1923 to 1930, Primo de Rivera ruled as a dictator—suspending parliament, rigidly censoring the press, crippling the courts, and administering by martial law. Leading intellectuals like Miguel de Unamuno (1864–1936) and Blasco Ibáñez (1867–1928) were driven into exile.

In 1931, after overwhelming electoral victories by the republican forces, Alfonso XIII was deposed and royal properties confiscated. The government successfully repressed a military revolt from the right (Seville) and a rebellion of anarchists and syndicalists on the left (Barcelona), as well as an independent movement in Catalonia. After measures were taken to dispossess the church of its extensive lands and establish a secular government with separation of church and state, several generals in Spanish Morocco set out to invade the homeland and overthrow the republic. Most of the army and air force defected to the rebels, along with large numbers of Muslim mercenaries. They received the blessing of Roman Catholic prelates; only among the Basques were churchmen loyal to the republic. Franco was assisted in his invasion of Spain by a policy of "non-intervention" on the part of France and Britain. The republic was dependent upon untrained and poorly equipped civilians, although eventually some thousands of volunteers came from America, England, France and other countries to fight for the republic in the International Brigades.

In the end, Mussolini had c 75,000 in the field, Hitler had c 10,000 specialists in tank and air warfare, and Stalin had sent some hundreds of agents and commanders—plus limited matériel—to strengthen the Communist drive to capture and control the republican government. The greatest difficulty faced by a series of prime ministers was in fact the sectarian in-fighting of the anarchists, syndicalists, socialists and communists—with their several splinters and subdivisions. The parties of the middle were unable to keep them in tandem: revolts and withdrawal of support occurred from time to time and political assassinations became a commonplace within the parties and the popular militia. The Spanish Civil War was in that sense a trial run for the ideological confrontations of World War II. One of its most fateful and long-lasting "lessons"—a false one

embraced by considerable sectors of the church hierarchy, industrialists, and ruling classes throughout the West—was the notion that fascism was the only answer to communism.

Franco's forces moved steadily forward, their victories prepared by awesome use of scorched-earth tactics by their air forces—immortalized by Picasso's painting of *Guernica.* In March 1938 came the fall of Madrid; 750,000 had perished (c 30,000 by assassination or execution during sectarian political struggles); Franco immediately set out to kill or imprison hundreds of republican leaders who had survived. England and France recognized Franco's fascist government on 27 February 1938, the United States on April 1st.

Contrary to the expectation of his allies, Franco kept Spain out of direct participation in World War II, although thousands of Spanish volunteers fought for the Nazis in Russia. Spain served as a useful escape route for many thousands of Jews and other potential victims of Nazism. After the war it became a place of refuge for Nazi officials and a pipeline of escape for war criminals on their way to Latin America.

*"The Valley of the Fallen,"* Spanish *Nationalist monument.*

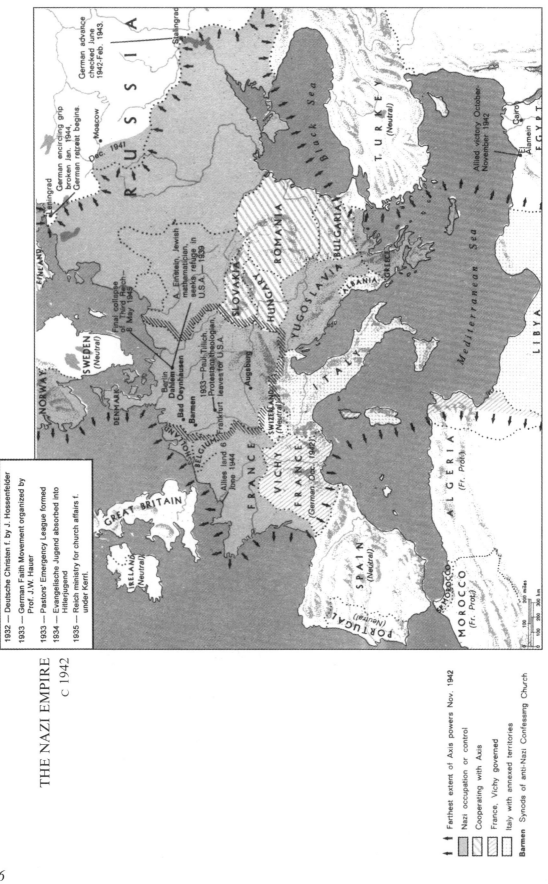

THE NAZI EMPIRE
c 1942

1932 — Deutsche Christen f. by J. Hossenfelder
1933 — German Faith Movement organized by
Prof. J.W. Hauer
1933 — Pastors' Emergency League formed
1934 — Evangelische Jugend absorbed into
Hitlerjugend
1935 — Reich ministry for church affairs f.
under Kerrl.

German advance
checked June
1942-Feb. 1943.

Stalingrad

German encircling grip
broken Jan. 1944.
German retreat begins.

Moscow

Dec. 1941

Leningrad

R U S S I A

Black Sea

T U R K E Y
(Neutral)

Cairo

Allied victory October-
November 1942

El Alamein

E G Y P T

FINLAND

SWEDEN
(Neutral)

NORWAY

DENMARK

ROMANIA

SLOVAKIA

HUNGARY

BULGARIA

YUGOSLAVIA

GREECE

ALBANIA

Mediterranean Sea

LIBYA

A. Einstein, Jewish
mathematician,
seeks refuge in
U.S.A. — 1939

Final collapse
of Third Reich—
8 May 1945

Berlin
Dahlem

Bad Oeynhausen

Barmen

1933—Paul Tillich,
Protestant theologian,
leaves for U.S.A.

Augsburg

Frankfurt

SWITZERLAND
(Neutral)

ITALY

HOLLAND

BELGIUM

Allies land 6
June 1944

F R A N C E

VICHY
FRANCE
(German Oct. 1942)

GREAT BRITAIN

IRELAND
(Neutral)

SPAIN
(Neutral)

PORTUGAL
(Neutral)

MOROCCO
(Fr. Prot.)

Sp. MOROCCO

A L G E R I A
(Fr. Prot.)

100        200 miles
0   100   200   300 km

→ ← Farthest extent of Axis powers Nov. 1942

Nazi occupation or control

Cooperating with Axis

France, Vichy governed

Italy with annexed territories

Barmen  Synods of anti-Nazi Confessing Church

*Let it be said that though we have been
sentenced to death and know it, we have
not lost our human features.*

    — E. Ringelblum in Warsaw Ghetto

THE chief architect of the Third Reich
(1933–45) was Adolf Hitler (1889–
1945), a semi-literate demagogue from
the political underworld of Vienna and
Munich. His public notice was won at
the "Beer Hall Putsch" in Munich (8–
11 November 1923), in which his tiny
National Socialist Party was allied with
radical right forces led by General
Erich Ludendorff. The attempted coup
failed, and Hitler ostensibly turned to
parliamentary means to power. The
NSDAP remained a terrorist movement, however, as assassinations and
street-fighting attested. Hitler served
less than a year of a five-year sentence,
using the time—with Rudolf Hess as
his amanuensis—to write *Mein Kampf*.
This book became the bible of his
movement, being an intensely wrought
combination of primitive ideology (including violent antisemitism), statist
political program, and autobiographi-
cal reflections inspired by a messianic
sense of vocation.

The German people, having emerged
particularly late as a nation, were ripe
for a psychological rehabilitation that
stressed the Teutonic genius. They still
smarted from the (false) charge laid
against them in the Versailles Treaty,
that they were solely guilty for World
War I, and from the post-Armistice
blockade of eight months during which
hundreds of thousands died of hunger.
It proved to be an unrelieved burden
upon the Weimar Republic that it was
founded by men who had signed a
treaty including the "war guilt" clause.

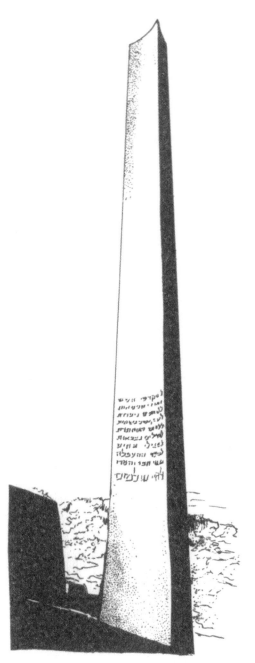

*The Pillar of Heroism at Yad Vashem,
Jerusalem. The inscription reads, "Now
and forever in memory of those who
rebelled in the camps and the ghettoes,
who fought in the woods, in the underground and with the Allied forces, of those
who braved their way to the land of Israel
and those who died sanctifying the name of
God."*

307

Many traditional elements in the military and church establishments never accepted the legitimacy of the republic, remaining monarchists.

The Weimar Republic, suffering from a poor start and a weak self-image, was burdened by economic exactions as well as internal political polarization. The Allies demanded 132,000,000,000 gold marks in reparations and French and Belgian troops occupied the Ruhr when Germany defaulted. A Rhineland republic was proclaimed at Aachen in October 1923, but it lasted only a few months. A communist uprising in Saxony and a monarchist conspiracy in Bavaria were also thwarted. But the wild inflation of 1922–23 wiped out all savings and threw pensioners on relief. The Dawes Plan (1924), accompanied by massive injections of U.S. credit, produced a stabilization of the new economy. The Young Plan (1929) provided a milder schedule of reparations and would have made a permanent solution to the German economic crisis but for the world depression which ensued in October of that year.

Since the French Revolution, German religious and intellectual leaders had understood "democracy" in French parliamentarian terms. They were suspicious of the mechanical procedures which seemed to deny genuine community and consensus, and they did not perceive that English and American self-government had a different center of gravity from the French. The drive to achieve a community of purpose tended therefore to develop in extramural ways, leading to a harsh polarization between ideological blocs of right and left. When Hitler came to power (30 January 1933; Enabling Act, 23 March), he did so according to the rules of the parliamentary game, but a genuine national consensus was lacking and thereafter impossible.

Claiming to restore "law and order" after a period of political and economic crisis, Hitler also appealed to the conservative elements of the population by presenting Nazism as a "bulwark against atheistic Bolshevism." His most important coup, arranged with Papal Nuncio Pacelli (from 1939 Pope Pius XII), was the Concordat of 10 July 1933: this gave him a gentility which painted over years of thuggery.

Hitler asserted that his most important contribution to the Germans would be the creation of a true national identity (*Volksgemeinschaft*), and he immediately demonstrated that the ethos of street-fighting and assassination which had accompanied his rise would continue to inform his actions as dictator. The Communists (outlawed after the Reichstag fire of 27 February), the Social Democrats (who cast all of the votes against the Enabling Act that made Hitler dictator, 23 March 1933), the trade unions, and finally all independent centers of discussion and action, were attacked and destroyed as functioning entities (policy of *Gleichschaltung*). Even a dissident element in the ranks of his own followers, one that was more socialist and revolutionary than his industrialist financiers could tolerate, was wiped out in a blood purge ("The Night of the Long Knives," 30 June 1934).

The crimes of Hitler and the Nazi Party were multifold, even without the assault on the Jewish people. The racist program involved the murder of several hundred thousand Roma and Sinti ("Gypsies"), as well as tens of thousands of Polish intellectuals and nearly three million Russian prisoners of war.

The same "politics of the deed" was

pursued in international affairs. Germany, which even under the Weimar Republic had been rearming secretly with Soviet assistance, withdrew from the League of Nations in October of 1933. The Rhineland was occupied without effective protest (7 March 1936); Hitler had given secret instructions to his commanders to withdraw if the French occupying army resisted, but the French politicians waffled and the French generals were overruled. No resistance to the aggression was encountered. Alliances were firmed up with Italy and Japan. Austria was invaded and annexed (12–13 March 1938), and Chamberlain, Daladier and Bonnet (later a leader in the post-World War II fascist O.A.S. conspiracy against De Gaulle) surrendered Czechoslovakia to dismemberment. The Munich Agreement (29 September 1938) marked the high point of western appeasement. What was left of Czechoslovakia, undermined by fascist forces led by Monsignor Tiso in Slovakia, was occupied by Germany in March of 1939. This event was a landmark, for it indicated that Hitler was interested in imperial expansion—and not merely in achieving a Greater Germany defined along racial lines. In August of 1939, after conclusion of a Soviet-Nazi Pact between Stalin and Hitler, Poland was attacked and divided. England and France declared war against Germany.

The Nazi Party Platform had since 1920 included a pledge to support non-sectarian Christianity which beguiled many churchmen and satisfied the large numbers only generally interested in "religion" and "spirituality":

"We demand the freedom of all religious confessions in the State, insofar as they do not imperil its stability or offend against the ethical and moral sense of the German race. The Party, as

*Hitler's "jig" at Compiègne, 11 June 1940, following the French capitulation.*

such, adopts the standpoint of a *positives Christentum*, without binding itself confessionally to a particular creed." (Article 24)

The repudiation of any commitment to historical or concrete religious traditions or structures made it possible for the Nazi government to pretend to defend "religion" while in fact attacking any person or group in the churches which opposed Nazi ideology and practice. The chief struggle to defend the integrity of the Protestant churches was maintained by the Confessing Church (Barmen Declaration of May 1934) and allied "intact" churches in Hannover, Württemberg and Bavaria. The leading collaborateurs were organized in the *Deutsche Christen* movements. At the end of the war the Stuttgart Declaration of Guilt (October 1945) was issued by leading Protestant churchmen, and it provided a basis for speedy reconciliation with sister churches of the emerging World Council of Churches. However, it made no mention of the disaster that had overtaken the Jewish people.

The Roman Catholic Church became somewhat disillusioned when the Nazi government failed to keep the terms of the Concordat, and the encyclical *Mit brennender Sorge* of Pius XI questioned many of the ideas and actions of the Nazis (21 March 1937), although it made no mention of the plight of the Jews.

Although there were thousands of martyrs in both confessions, in the main the baptized millions apostatized and most church officials collaborated with the Nazis. Claus von Stauffenberg, who spearheaded the attack on Hitler on 20 July 1944, was a Roman Catholic; Dietrich Bonhoeffer was a Protestant ecumenical leader and theologian martyred 9 April 1945 whose writings have achieved great influence in the post-war period.

Documents now public make clear that Hitler planned the elimination of the church structures as soon as the war was over. The assault on the Jews, however, with antisemitism such a central part of Hitler's ideology and practice, began early and was carried through relentlessly. Trains were used to ship Jewish victims that were needed to carry ammunition. Even when the war was clearly lost, the antisemitic specialists and military moved in to finish off the Hungarian Jewry that until then had been spared.

# THE TWO CHINAS

SUN Yat-sen (1866–1925) was elected President of China (30 December 1911) with the overthrow of the Manchu dynasty. China participated in World War I on the side of the Allies but—like the USA—refused to sign the Versailles Treaty. During the 1920s the country was divided and ravaged by regional warlords. In 1927 conservatives in the Kuomintang party established a national government at Nanking under Chiang Kai-shek (1887–1975). In the same year Chiang married Sung Meiling, sister of Sun Yat-sen's widow, a beautiful and intelligent woman educated at Wellesley and active in the Methodist church. With the active encouragement of the Chiangs, Christianity spread rapidly throughout the republic.

In 1927–34 a number of Russian-style agricultural communes were established under the leadership of Mao Tse-tung (1893–1976) among the peasants of Kiangsi and Fukien. Forced out by the nationalist troops, they

*Mao Tse-tung, leader of the Chinese Revolution (1948).*

made a "Long March" (1934–36) into northern Shensi.

The Japanese invaded Manchuria in September 1931 and set up a puppet government under the Manchu pretender, Henry Pu-Yi, who had abdicated in 1912. They also landed at Shanghai

Border incidents since 1965

U. S. S. R.

Vladivostok

JAPAN

Tokyo

MONGOLIA

INNER MONGOLIA

1954 TO INNER MONGOLIA

Peking

N. KOREA

S. KOREA

SINKIANG UIGUR

Yenan

Nanking

Shanghai

1949 –The Communists under party charman Mao Tse-tung (b. 1893)- proclaim the People's Republic of China
1972–Communist China admitted to U.N.

Border skirmishes 1960's

PEOPLES REPUBLIC OF CHINA

Matsu Is.

Taipei

Full-scale border war erupts in late 1962 over disputed area 1963 — China withdraws

Chungking

The Long March 1934

Juichin

Invaded by China 1950-51

TIBET

disputed area

TAIWAN

Chiang Kai-shek (b. 1887) 1929-49 ruler of China and subsequent head of Chinese government in exile

PAKISTAN

KASHMIR

NEPAL

BHUTAN

Delhi

1947ff. — Disputed between India and Pakistan

INDIA

from Burma 1960

VIETNAM

Hanoi

Hong Kong

PHILIPPINES

1949 — Government of the Republic of China transferred to Taiwan

Manila

BURMA

LAOS

THAILAND

200   400 miles
200   400   600 km

THE TWO CHINAS

| | Communist China | | | Claimed by China |
| | Nationalist China | | | The Great Wall |
| | Other Communist states | | | The Long March (1934-36) |

and carved out an enclave. In 1937 the Nationalists and Communists effected an alliance for resistance to the Japanese, against which League of Nations resolutions were totally ineffective. Nanking was captured and given over to atrocities; the Japanese set up a puppet "Republic of China." Amoy, Kaifeng, Canton, Hankow and other major coastal cities fell. Chiang moved his government to the west, and with supplies provided by the United States over the "Burma Road" kept up resistance to the Japanese until World War II ended. He was accepted as a partner with Churchill and Roosevelt (Cairo Declaration of 1 December 1944) and China participated in launching the United Nations.

As the Japanese withdrew from north China, Mao and communist troops moved in. Civil war ensued, and an arbitration commission from the USA failed to settle it. The Kuomintang would not readmit communists, and the communists now saw a chance to capture power throughout China. The ruling Nationalist party lost credibility through internal corruption, inflation, profiteering, and failure to carry out long-overdue reforms. In early 1949 Chiang and the remaining Nationalist troops retreated to Formosa (Taiwan) and the Communist People's Republic of China was constituted (1 October 1949). For a number of years the USA prevented "red" China from joining the United Nations, on the basis that Chiang's was the legitimate government of the whole, but in 1971 agreed to replace the Nationalist representation with mainland China. In 1972 the American President visited China, meeting with Mao and Chou En-lai. In 1978 the USA recognized "The People's Republic" and withdrew its ambassador to Taiwan.

From 1949 to 1965 American aid to Taiwan totaled three billion dollars. The activity of missionary agencies was greatly expanded with the transfer of Nationalist government, and a number of Christian educational and medical institutions were also established.

The condition of Christianity in mainland China is much disputed, like the measure of success attained in Mao's "cultural revolution" of 1966–67. It is clear that the conflict between Russia and China, which came to the brink of war in 1969, had deep ideological roots. The government of mainland China remains the single major power ideologically Marxist. The repressive policies of Beijing toward "churches, cults and sects" give little cause for optimism in the religious sector. Neither was the slaughter of young democratic protesters at Tiananmen Square encouraging politically. In the conquest of Tibet to the south, mainland China has pursued openly genocidal policies. Following the incorporation of Hong Kong, threatening gestures have been made toward Taiwan. Nevertheless, China's vast supply of cheap labor combined with technological developments has encouraged other nations to anticipate mutually beneficial commerce.

## THE ARAB LEAGUE 1945 FF.

THE Arab League was founded in Cairo on 17 March 1945, and it became the chief instrument for promoting a romantic Arab nationalism and organizing diplomatic, economic and military action to destroy Israel. Only a small number of the peoples bracketed in the League are of Arab descent. The member nations are without exception new countries, formed in the twentieth century of fragments of the old Ottoman Empire or former European colonies. In member countries Islam is the established religion, in most of them the only religion tolerated. Conversion out of Islam incurs the death penalty. Most are governed by dictators—either old-fashioned feudal despotisms or military cliques of 20th-century style.

The military phase of the League's quest for identity has been expensive for Israel and diversionary for subject peoples. Only Egypt (1979) and Jordan (1994) have taken steps toward peace. In Israel itself, Arab terrorist groups have been heavily subsidized from the outside. Like the steps toward peace in Northern Ireland, the negotiations between the Palestinian Authority and the Israeli government are constantly jeopardized by terrorist attacks on civilians.

The chief cost in Christian lives has been the martyrdom at the hands of the fundamentalist Muslim regime in Khartoum of hundreds of thousands in southern Sudan.

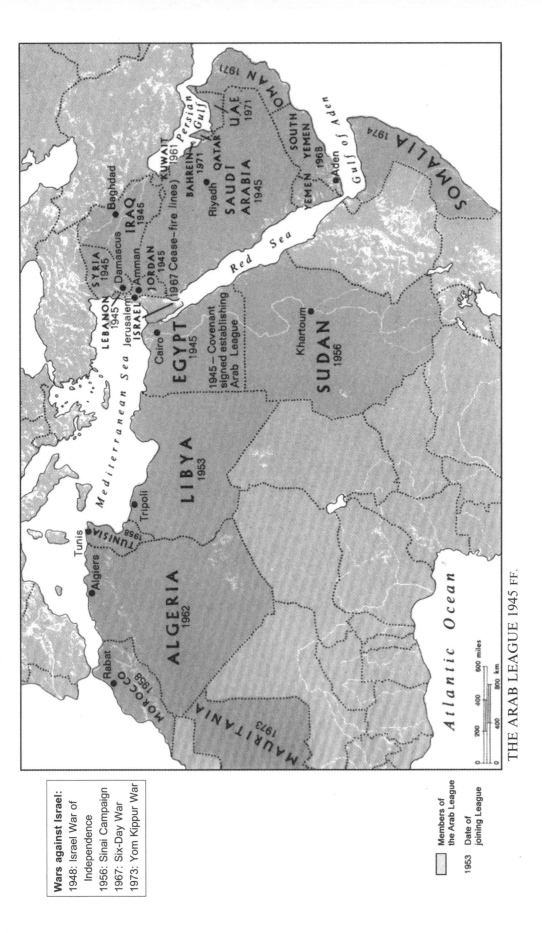

**Wars against Israel:**

1948: Israel War of
Independence
1956: Sinai Campaign
1967: Six-Day War
1973: Yom Kippur War

Members of
the Arab League

1953    Date of
joining League

THE ARAB LEAGUE 1945 FF.

Baghdad

IRAQ
1945

KUWAIT
1961

BAHREIN
1971

QATAR

UAE
1971

OMAN
1971

SOUTH
YEMEN
1968

Riyadh

SAUDI
ARABIA
1945

YEMEN
1945

Aden

Gulf of Aden

SOMALIA
1974

Persian
Gulf

SYRIA
1945

Damascus

Amman

JORDAN
1945

(1967 Cease-fire lines)

LEBANON
1945

Jerusalem

ISRAEL

Cairo

EGYPT
1945

1945 – Covenant
signed establishing
Arab league

Red   Sea

Khartoum

SUDAN
1956

Mediterranean Sea

LIBYA
1953

Tripoli

TUNISIA
1958

Tunis

Algiers

ALGERIA
1962

Rabat

MOROCCO
1958

MAURITANIA
1973

Atlantic Ocean

0   200   400   600 miles
0   400   800 km

313

*I will forge in the smithy of my soul the
uncreated conscience of my race.*

## THE TWO IRELANDS

— James Joyce

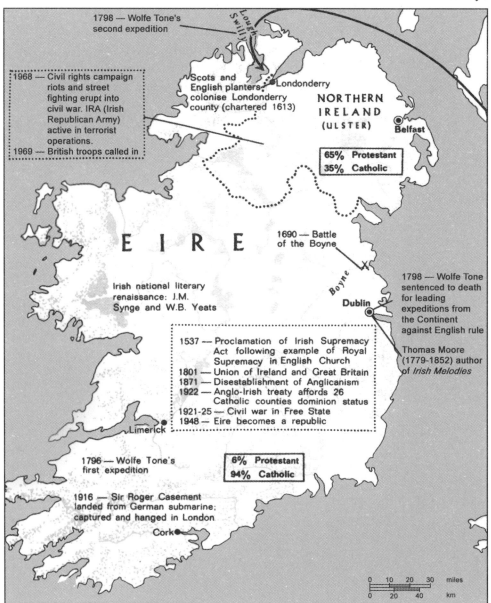

1798 — Wolfe Tone's
second expedition

1968 — Civil rights campaign
riots and street
fighting erupt into
civil war. IRA (Irish
Republican Army)
active in terrorist
operations.
1969 — British troops called in

Scots and
English planters
colonise Londonderry
county (chartered 1613)

Londonderry

NORTHERN
IRELAND
(ULSTER)

Belfast

65% Protestant
35% Catholic

E I R E

1690 — Battle
of the Boyne

Irish national literary
renaissance: J.M.
Synge and W.B. Yeats

Boyne

Dublin

1798 — Wolfe Tone
sentenced to death
for leading
expeditions from
the Continent
against English rule

Thomas Moore
(1779-1852) author
of *Irish Melodies*

1537 — Proclamation of Irish Supremacy
Act following example of Royal
Supremacy in English Church
1801 — Union of Ireland and Great Britain
1871 — Disestablishment of Anglicanism
1922 — Anglo-Irish treaty affords 26
Catholic counties dominion status
1921-25 — Civil war in Free State
1948 — Eire becomes a republic

Limerick

1796 — Wolfe Tone's
first expedition

6% Protestant
94% Catholic

1916 — Sir Roger Casement
landed from German submarine;
captured and hanged in London

Cork

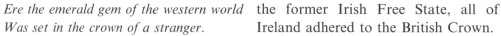

0  10  20  30  miles
0  20  40  km

*Ere the emerald gem of the western world
Was set in the crown of a stranger.*

— Thomas Moore, *Let Erin Remember
the Days of Old*

THE Norman conquest of England
(1066) was followed a century later
(1171) by a Norman conquest of Ireland. From that date until 1949, when
Eire was established in the south from

the former Irish Free State, all of
Ireland adhered to the British Crown.

English rule has not been unchallenged in Wales and Scotland. In Ireland its presence was additionally
unpopular for religious reasons, for
when the other three areas became
Protestant Ireland remained Roman
Catholic. Under James I (king: 1603–
25) extensive settlements of Scots Pres-

byterians were begun in the northern counties. When the Irish rose in support of the Stuart pretender, Oliver Cromwell personally directed the capture of Drogheda and Wexford (February 1649). The garrisons were slaughtered, and the conflict took on a new bitterness. In 1689 the Irish again rose in support of a Stuart pretender and were soundly defeated in the Battle of the Boyne (1 July 1690).

The push for Irish independence, which had never died out, flowered with the rise of nationalism and the literary renaissance associated with the names of W. B. Yeats, J. M. Synge, and James Joyce. On the current scene, with Eire independent, the conflict centers in Northern Ireland. Both Protestant and Roman Catholic extremist groups have taken sporadic recourse to violence.

In 1976 representatives of the interfaith "Mothers for Peace" received the Nobel Peace Prize, and in late 1999 their message was heard by the political parties. In November 1999, a joint regime—independent of British control and freed from Eire's claims to sovereignty—was initiated.

## STATE RELIGIONS AND IDEOLOGIES

*The members of the elite group are wholly identified with the movement: they have no profession and no private life independent from it. The sympathizers constitute a protective wall around the members of the movement and represent the outside world to them.*

— Hannah Arendt, *The Origins of Totalitarianism*

THE twentieth century has seen an unparalleled revolt of the old gods, once thought to be suppressed with the triumph of Christianity. With the spread of Christianity and the establishment of the structures and style of unitary Christendom, many of the old gods were laid away and others were baptized and incorporated into the Christian pantheon of saints. But Moloch was never buried: under the leadership of warlords and generals, the "Christian" nations have generation after generation sacrificed their youth. World War I, which brought to an end the century which began under the pious slogan of the Holy Alliance, destroyed much of the credibility of Christendom: many of the brightest leaders of Asia permanently lost their fascination with Christian civilization and Christianity. In World War II, *divus Augustus* and Thor and a host of lesser spirits emerged again from the abyss—and in the heart of Christendom.

The attempt was made in World War II to paint them over with Christian cosmetics. Thus Hitler proclaimed his Russian adventure to be a crusade to defend "the Christian west" against "atheistic Bolshevism," and even in Belgium, Spain and Italy volunteers responded. But Hitler's own anti-Christian program was too obvious to make his plea convincing to all. During the defense of Russia, Stalin found it pragmatic to resurrect the old slogans about "Holy Russia," exhume St. Vladimir and make a transitory peace with the Orthodox Church.

In the more intact sector of Christendom, the claim of governments to defend true religion had greater credibility. In one of his great speeches before the House of Commons Win-

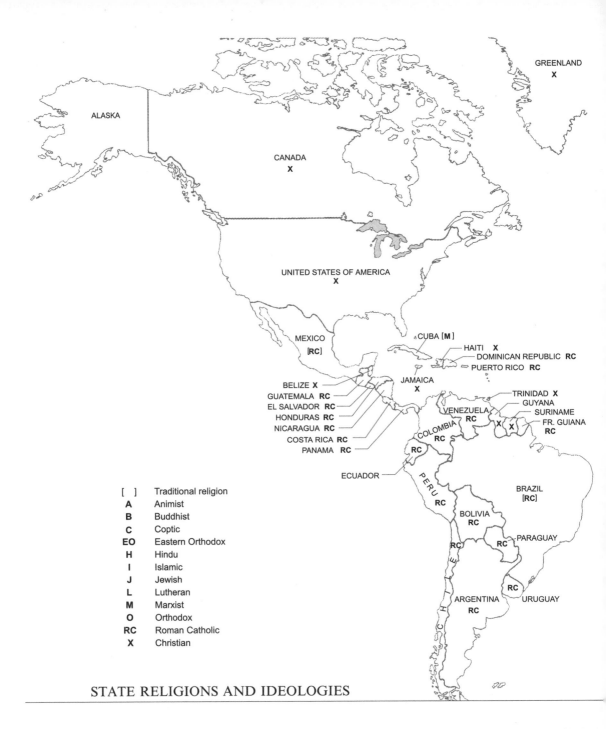

GREENLAND
**X**

ALASKA

CANADA
**X**

UNITED STATES OF AMERICA
**X**

MEXICO
**[RC]**

◦ CUBA [**M**]

HAITI **X**
DOMINICAN REPUBLIC **RC**
PUERTO RICO **RC**

BELIZE **X**
GUATEMALA **RC**
EL SALVADOR **RC**
HONDURAS **RC**
NICARAGUA **RC**
COSTA RICA **RC**
PANAMA **RC**

JAMAICA
**X**

TRINIDAD **X**
GUYANA
SURINAME
FR. GUIANA
**RC**

VENEZUELA
**RC**

**X** **X**

COLOMBIA
**RC**

ECUADOR

PERU
**RC**

BRAZIL
**[RC]**

BOLIVIA
**RC**

PARAGUAY
**RC**

**RC**

CHILE

ARGENTINA
**RC**

URUGUAY
**RC**

| [ ] | Traditional religion |
|---|---|
| **A** | Animist |
| **B** | Buddhist |
| **C** | Coptic |
| **EO** | Eastern Orthodox |
| **H** | Hindu |
| **I** | Islamic |
| **J** | Jewish |
| **L** | Lutheran |
| **M** | Marxist |
| **O** | Orthodox |
| **RC** | Roman Catholic |
| **X** | Christian |

## STATE RELIGIONS AND IDEOLOGIES

ston Churchill (1871–1947) called for a "defense of Christian civilization" against Nazism, and the well-known theologian John Baillie (1886–1960) wrote a small book defending the concept (*What is Christian Civilization?*). Franklin D. Roosevelt (1882–1945) and Charles De Gaulle (1890–1970) used similar language. Pius XII (pope: 1939–58) was for a time beguiled by the claim of Adolf Hitler to defend Christianity against Marxism, but his successor John XXIII (pope: 1958–63) opened the way for Roman Catholic dialogue with "the separated brethren," and with Marxists and atheists.

Most churches, including those of Germany, supported their national

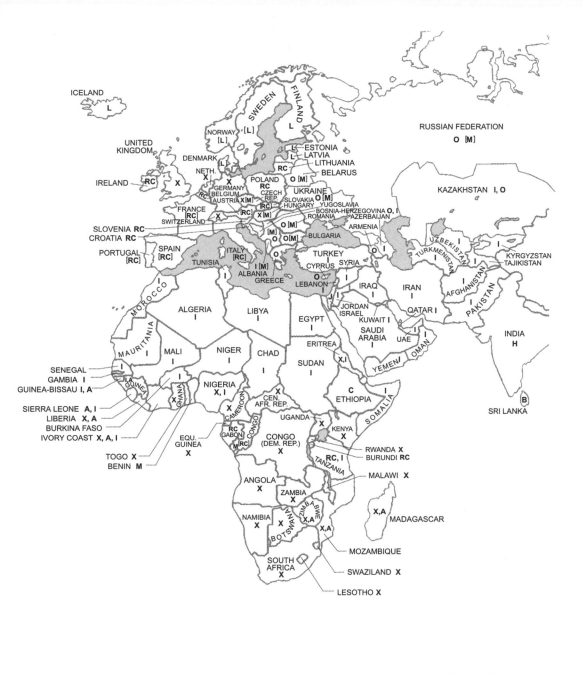

ICELAND
L

UNITED
KINGDOM
IRELAND RC
X

NORWAY [L]
[L]

SWEDEN

FINLAND
L

RUSSIAN FEDERATION
O [M]

DENMARK
[L]
NETH.
X
BELGIUM
GERMANY
RC
AUSTRIA X [M]
FRANCE
[RC]
SWITZERLAND
X
[RC]

ESTONIA
LATVIA
LITHUANIA
RC BELARUS
POLAND
RC
CZECH
REP.
SLOVAKIA O [M]
HUNGARY
YUGOSLAVIA
ROMANIA
BOSNIA-HERZEGOVINA O, I
AZERBAIJAN
ARMENIA

KAZAKHSTAN I, O

L
L

UKRAINE
O [M]

SLOVENIA RC
CROATIA RC

PORTUGAL
[RC]

SPAIN
[RC]

ITALY
[RC]

TUNISIA

[M]
O
O O[M]
BULGARIA

ALBANIA
GREECE
I [M]

TURKEY
CYPRUS
SYRIA
LEBANON

O
I
I

UZBEKISTAN
TURKMENISTAN
AFGHANISTAN

KYRGYZSTAN
TAJIKISTAN

PAKISTAN

MOROCCO

ALGERIA
I

LIBYA
I

EGYPT
I

IRAQ
I

JORDAN
ISRAEL
KUWAIT I
SAUDI
ARABIA I
UAE

IRAN
O

QATAR I
OMAN

INDIA
H

MAURITANIA
I

MALI
I

NIGER
I

CHAD
I

SUDAN
I

ERITREA
X, I

YEMEN

SENEGAL
GAMBIA I
GUINEA-BISSAU I, A
GUINEA

I

I

NIGERIA
X, I

GHANA
X

CAMEROON

CEN.
AFR. REP.

UGANDA
X

ETHIOPIA
C

KENYA
X

SOMALIA

SRI LANKA
B

SIERRA LEONE A, I
LIBERIA X, A
BURKINA FASO
IVORY COAST X, A, I

TOGO X
BENIN M

EQU.
GUINEA
X

GABON
RC
[RC]

CONGO
M

CONGO
(DEM. REP.)
X

RWANDA X
BURUNDI RC

TANZANIA
RC, I

ANGOLA
X

ZAMBIA
X

NAMIBIA
X

BOTSWANA
X

ZIMBABWE
X, A

X,A

MALAWI X

X,A MADAGASCAR

MOZAMBIQUE

SWAZILAND X

SOUTH
AFRICA
X

LESOTHO X

(continued →)

governments in World War II. Yet there was a conspicuous difference between World War I and II. In the First World War the churches simply identified the national cause with the cause of Christianity. In leading Germany into a two-front war in 1914 the Kaiser, who was also *summus episcopus* of the Prussian church, called upon the sons and daughters of the Reformation to do battle against the "unreformed" Catholics of France and the "schismatic" Orthodox of Russia. His soldiers carried on their personal equipment the old crusading slogan, "*Gott mit uns.*" American preachers presented arms and identified the crusade "to make the world safe for democ-

RUSSIAN FEDERATION
O [M]

MONGOLIA
B [M]

NORTH KOREA
M,A

JAPAN
B

CHINA
M

SOUTH KOREA
X,B

BHUTAN B

H

NEPAL

BANGLADESH

LAOS

TAIWAN
B

I

B

B

B

B

VIETNAM
M

PHILIPPINES
X

MYANMAR
THAILAND
CAMBODIA

B

SRI LANKA

MALAYSIA
I,A

I N D O N E S I A

I

TIMOR
I,A

AUSTRALIA
X

NEW ZEALAND
X

(← continued)

racy" with the claims of high religion. In World War II, even the German churches refused to ring church bells to celebrate military victories. In both Britain and America the churches supported the war effort with a good conscience but took great pains to distinguish between immediate political duties and ultimate Christian loyalties. In good part this was due to increased awareness that the fellowship of Christians is international, transcending any single national government's purview and program. To this the Preparatory Committee of the World Council of Churches contributed much, as did such forces as the Peace Aims Group in Britain and the Commission on the

Bases of a Just and Durable Peace in America.

A parallel test of the ability of high religion to distinguish between national and Christian purposes is provided by the treatment of conscientious objectors. Here England and America, largely due to the greatly respected status of the historic peace churches (Quakers, Mennonites, Brethren), had progressed much further by World War II than most other countries. When the Nazis drove the pacifist *Bruderhof* from its former settlement at Neuwied (1936), the members found refuge in England. Both England and America had legal provisions for alternative service by those conscientiously unwilling to bear arms. Since World War II, France and the German Federal Republic—but none of the Communist governments!—have joined those governments that count the cost of withheld military service less than the cost of suppressing a lively conscience.

There is more than a purely negative and pragmatic ground for challenging official religion or ideological establishments and asserting the integrity of the person who finds he must dissent from official policy. Even during dire national emergency, a government which stands on high ground will rather protect than harass or destroy hard-won liberties. John XXIII, in his great encyclical *Pacem in Terris* (10 April 1963), addressed "to all men of good-will," put the matter plainly:

"We see that every man has the right to life, to bodily integrity and to the means which are necessary and suitable for a proper development of life.... By the natural law every human being has the right to respect for his person, to his good reputation, the right to freedom in searching for truth and in

*John XXIII.*

expressing and in communicating his opinions.... And he has the right to be informed truthfully about public events."

Under John XXIII the Roman Catholic Church made great progress over the fortress mentality of *Quanta Cura* and the *Syllabus Errorum* (8 December 1864). The advance in understanding in Roman Catholicism signalized by Vatican II's Declaration on Religious Freedom owed much to the work of the American Jesuit, John Courtney Murray (1904–67).

Contemporary Protestant understanding, with its ecumenical vision, was also far beyond the record of persecution in Massachusetts Bay Colony in the seventeenth century, when both Roger Williams and Anne Hutchinson were driven into exile in the cause of freedom of conscience, and some Quakers were branded in the face, their ears cropped, or their nostrils slit for disagreeing with the religious establishment.

The "right to freedom in searching for truth and in expressing and communicating...opinions" was won with difficulty in the United States, where state churches flourished from 1607 to 1833. The major breakthrough occurred in Virginia, when the Great Bill of Religious Freedom was adopted after intense debate (1784–86). A few years later, the First Amendment was ratified with the adoption of the Federal Constitution (1789–91):

"Congress shall make no law respecting an establishment of religion, or prohibiting the free exercise thereof; or abridging the freedom of speech, or of the press; or the right of the people peaceably to assemble, and to petition the Government for a redress of grievances."

According to Constitutional authorities, the Bill of Rights is the cornerstone to the Federal Constitution, the First Amendment is the heart of the Bill of Rights, and of all rights reserved to the citizens freedom of religion is the most fundamental. The guarantee of freedom of religion is the most important and unique contribution of America to date to the theory and practice of government.

The protection of religious liberty carries two equally important provisions: government support of preferred religion is forbidden, and government repression of a disfavored religion is prevented. This is the watershed between "toleration" and "liberty," a distinction too little noted. In point of fact, in countries with traditional religious establishments which have progressed far in respect for human liberty, minority religious groups practice and teach uninhibited and undisturbed. The Netherlands, Germany, the Scandinavian countries, Switzerland, the United Kingdom—all are nations where state churches and governments generally have learned that persecution is morally wrong and religiously counterproductive. Yet flairups in the persecution of new religious movements are not unknown. In religious liberty, the positive principle of voluntary support is equally important, for the basic right is reserved to the citizen and is not a grant of government.

In the revolt of the pagan gods in the twentieth century, neither toleration nor liberty has been respected. As in all primitive societies, religion (or ideology) has functioned as the cement that holds a tribe or nation together. Under the "post-Christian" creeds and systems of the twentieth century, liberty has retrogressed. Nazism and Marxism are conspicuous illustrations, and there are others. Advocates of both systems have practiced the same controls familiar to students of coercive religions: dissenting minorities are persecuted and adherents of the official cult are preferred in employment, public office, and education. An official liturgy is used on public occasions, and a cult of shrines, heroes, symbols and recognition signs is elaborated. Theologically, a doctrine of man, an interpretation of history (including its periodization), and a style of life are taught which are fundamentally different from the Jewish and Christian understandings.

A respect for the human person and his integrity developed late in Christendom, and on large areas of the globe it has not yet appeared at all. In the world of Islam it is only recognized to a certain degree in Turkey, and not at all in the countries most attached to the older Muslim traditions. In those lands controlled by post-Christian ideologies, whether fascist or communist, the pretence of observing basic human rights is sometimes maintained, but it is without substance.

Although Religious Liberty is securely lodged in the list of basic human rights, and although most of the governments in the United Nations have signed pledges to abstain from persecution, the plight of the dissenter is still precarious. (See Appendix A for a list of countries with cases where the regimes have either recently persecuted or inhibited religious freedom.) The chief difference between contemporary and earlier persecutions is the slowly growing realization that the individual person as such has the right to protection at law in his exercise of faith commitments.

In brute statistics, more Christians have been martyred in the twentieth century than in the entire preceding two millennia. The martyrdoms have often been part of the phenomenon of genocide: since 1900, nearly four times as many people have been targeted and murdered *by their own governments* as perished in World Wars I and II and all the smaller civil and international wars of the period. As the murderous conflicts that have exploded in the ruins of the former Yugoslavia have demonstrated, low-grade religions continue to provide part of the cover for genocide.

With the collapse of state religions and ideologies in most of Europe, the "Christian" nations that were once the center of "Christendom" have become what theologians and missiologists call "post-Christian." Some state churches maintain a facade, with populations officially 99.2 percent Roman Catholic numbering c 11 percent in effective participation and 96 percent officially Lutheran numbering c 3.6 percent participating, but the general picture is clear: Europe is again, from a Christian point of view, needy missionary territory.

Countries recently limiting
religious liberty
(for list see Appendix A)

# B. RELIGIONS IN AMERICA

## AMERICAN REVIVALS OF RELIGION

As the American republic was launched, most of the colonies had a long experience of established churches and were in the process of shifting to the voluntary support of religion. The longest to hold out for establishment were New Hampshire (1817), Connecticut (1819) and Massachusetts (1834).

The introduction of the principle of voluntaryism came with the Great Awakening in the 1730s, with Frelinghuysen in New Jersey and Jonathan Edwards in Massachusetts the leading figures. Following the Great Awakening, the first round of revivals, dozens of independent congregations were formed of new converts, and the conviction slowly grew that the best religious profession expressed itself in voluntary participation and support rather than nominal adherence expressed through tax allotments.

The New England Standing Order was shattered in 1805 and 1819, and former defenders of the state church system (by then no longer persecuting) shifted with some reluctance to separation and voluntary membership. The 1805 event was the appointment of Hollis Ware—a liberal scholar—to the chair of New Testament at Harvard, after which the orthodox churchmen united to found the Andover Seminary. The 1819 event was the Dedham Case, which gave control of church property to the township rather than the congregations. Every parish within twenty miles of Boston was lost to the Unitarians. The orthodox were compelled to raise money to build new churches and launch new programs.

The changed attitude of Lyman Beecher (1775–1863), who had been a defender of the establishment, is typical:

"Unitarians will gain the victory if we are left without revivals, but they will perish by the breath of His mouth and the brightness of His coming if revivals prevail."

The Second Great Awakening in the Connecticut River Valley (1798–1810) and across the mountains in Kentucky ("Cane Ridge Revival," 1801–11) produced a host of missionary societies and new denominations.

Revivals were essential in the original thirteen states, for the people exited the churches en masse with the dismantling of the state churches. Church membership fell to its real percentage, then from 5 to 7 percent of the population, and it was not until 1926 that over half of the population again appeared on church rolls. Without revivals, the voluntary principle would have failed to prove itself.

Revivals were a natural development in the west, where there had never been state churches and local churches could only be formed where enough people responded to direct appeal. The camp meetings, which brought together hundreds and sometimes thousands of scattered families for days at a time after harvest, also served important cultural and political functions.

The master of the "new methods," who systematized the approach, was Charles G. Finney (1792–1875). Finney was a powerful preacher, a creative (if

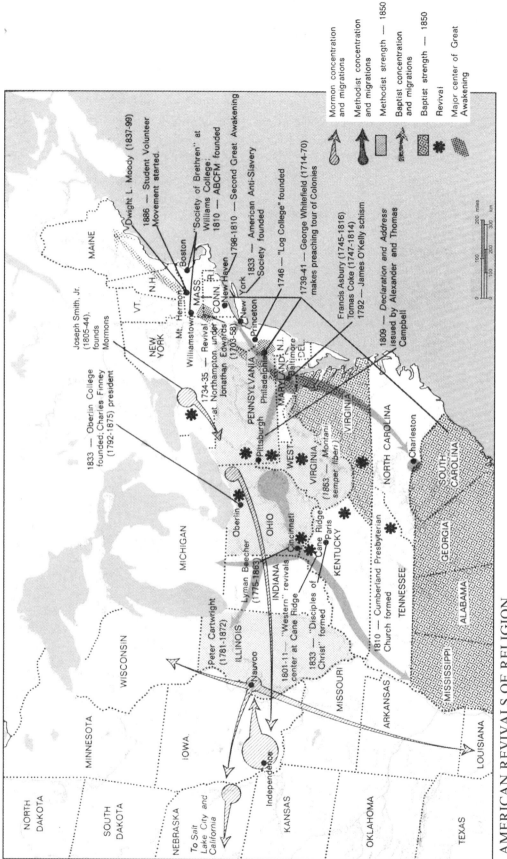

## AMERICAN REVIVALS OF RELIGION

**Legend:**
- Mormon concentration and migrations
- Methodist concentration and migrations
- Methodist strength — 1850
- Baptist concentration and migrations
- Baptist strength — 1850
- Revival
- Major center of Great Awakening

Dwight L. Moody (1837-99)

1886 — Student Volunteer Movement started.

"Society of Brethren" at Williams College:
1810 — ABCFM founded

1798-1810 — Second Great Awakening

1833 — American Anti-Slavery Society founded

1746 — "Log College" founded

1739-41 — George Whitefield (1714-70) makes preaching tour of Colonies

Francis Asbury (1745-1816)
Tomas Coke (1747-1814)
1792 — James O'Kelly schism

1809 — *Declaration and Address* issued by Alexander and Thomas Campbell

Joseph Smith, Jr. (1805-44), founds Mormons

1734-35 — Revival at Northampton under Jonathan Edwards (1703-58)

1833 — Oberlin College founded; Charles Finney (1792-1875) president

Peter Cartwright (1781-1872)

Lyman Beecher (1775-1863)

1801-11 — "Western" revivals center at Cane Ridge

1833 — "Disciples of Christ" formed

1810 — Cumberland Presbyterian Church formed

1863 — *Montani semper liberi*

To Salt Lake City and California

**Place names:**
MAINE, N.H., VT., MASS., R.I., CONN., NEW YORK, PENNSYLVANIA, NEW JERSEY, DEL., MARYLAND, WEST VIRGINIA, VIRGINIA, NORTH CAROLINA, SOUTH CAROLINA, GEORGIA, ALABAMA, MISSISSIPPI, TENNESSEE, KENTUCKY, OHIO, INDIANA, ILLINOIS, MICHIGAN, WISCONSIN, MINNESOTA, IOWA, MISSOURI, ARKANSAS, LOUISIANA, TEXAS, OKLAHOMA, KANSAS, NEBRASKA, SOUTH DAKOTA, NORTH DAKOTA

**Cities:** Boston, Mt. Hermon, Williamstown, New Haven, New York, Princeton, Philadelphia, Baltimore, Pittsburgh, Charleston, Oberlin, Cincinnati, Paris, Cane Ridge, Nauvoo, Independence

323

unorthodox) theologian, and his leadership was particularly important for bringing together revivalism and the anti-slavery impulse. As President of Oberlin College (1851–66), the first college to admit women and Negroes on an equal standing with male whites, he made the school a vital center of perfectionist theology and effective action against slavery.

## EARLY ACTIVITIES OF THE ABCFM

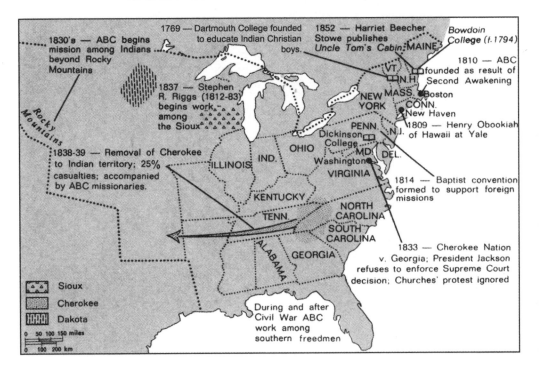

1830's — ABC begins mission among Indians beyond Rocky Mountains

1769 — Dartmouth College founded to educate Indian Christian boys.

1852 — Harriet Beecher Stowe publishes *Uncle Tom's Cabin.* MAINE

*Bowdoin College (f. 1794)*

1810 — ABC founded as result of Second Awakening

1837 — Stephen R. Riggs (1812-83) begins work among the Sioux

1838-39 — Removal of Cherokee to Indian territory; 25% casualties; accompanied by ABC missionaries.

1809 — Henry Obookiah of Hawaii at Yale

1814 — Baptist convention formed to support foreign missions

1833 — Cherokee Nation v. Georgia; President Jackson refuses to enforce Supreme Court decision; Churches' protest ignored

During and after Civil War ABC work among southern freedmen

Sioux
Cherokee
Dakota

0  50 100 150 miles
0  100  200 km

*We call the proceedings by the hard name of plunder. And we call upon the courts of Massachusetts to revoke these unrighteous decisions and put the Congregational churches of the state upon their original and proper basis.*

— Enoch Pond after the Dedham Case, 1819

PROFESSOR Kenneth Scott Latourette (1884–1968), whose *History of the Expansion of Christianity* is a classic, devoted three of his seven-volume survey to what he called "the Great Century of Christian Missions." During the nineteenth century Christianity became what it had always professed in principle to be: a universal, world-spanning faith. In this period, Christian missionaries went to more lands, the Bible and basic Christian literature were translated into msore languages and dialects, fellowships and churches were established in more areas, than ever before in its history. More missionary orders were founded in Roman Catholicism and missionary societies in Protestantism than ever before.

The first American missionary society was the American Board of Commissioners for Foreign Missions (f. 1810), and it was a product of the Great Awakening. A group of students at Williams College, taking refuge under a haystack during a storm, was moved to commitment to foreign mis-

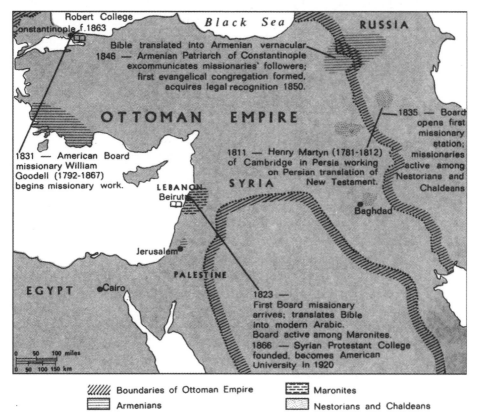

Robert College
Constantinople f.1863

*Black Sea*

RUSSIA

Bible translated into Armenian vernacular.
1846 — Armenian Patriarch of Constantinople
excommunicates missionaries' followers;
first evangelical congregation formed,
acquires legal recognition 1850.

OTTOMAN EMPIRE

1835 — Board
opens first
missionary
station;
missionaries
active among
Nestorians and
Chaldeans

1831 — American Board
missionary William
Goodell (1792-1867)
begins missionary work.

1811 — Henry Martyn (1781-1812)
of Cambridge in Persia working
on Persian translation of
New Testament.

SYRIA

LEBANON
Beirut

Baghdad

Jerusalem

PALESTINE

EGYPT    Cairo

1823 —
First Board missionary
arrives; translates Bible
into modern Arabic.
Board active among Maronites.
1866 — Syrian Protestant College
founded, becomes American
University in 1920

0  50  100 miles
0  50  100 150 km

////// Boundaries of Ottoman Empire        Maronites

        Armenians                          Nestorians and Chaldeans

sions (1806). The members organized themselves into a "Society of Brethren," meeting weekly to pray and to study together the implications of their decision. During school vacations they managed to secure invitations and scatter to the homes of key preachers in New England, discussing with their hosts the cause of missions. Later some of them went to the Andover Seminary, and there they picked up additional recruits, notably Adoniram Judson (1788–1850). By 1810 their cause was so far advanced that a group of ministers in Connecticut and Massachusetts organized the famous—and still functioning—"ABC."

The leading person of the group was Samuel J. Mills, Jr. (1783–1818), who stayed home to rally support while Judson and Luther Rice sailed for India. During the sea voyage, and traveling separately, Judson and Rice read their New Testaments and were converted to Baptist views. Their first letters home aroused consternation among the Congregational churches but led to the founding of the Baptist General Convention for Foreign Missions (1814). The ABC persisted, however.

The same persons who were at home active for foreign missions were also prominent in home missions. From 1801 to 1826 Congregationalists and Presbyterians cooperated in home missions in the Ohio and Mississippi River valleys ("Plan of Union"). Their work was augmented by the American Bible Society, American Tract Society, and numerous other free and interdenominational associations formed during the renaissance of voluntary religion.

Among the significant ventures

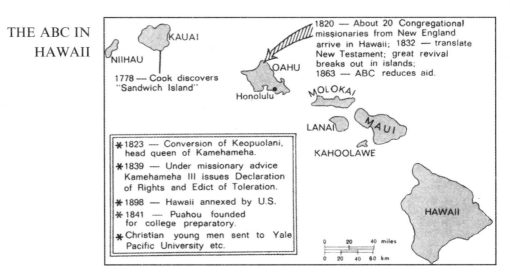

which carried on the tradition of the "Society of Brethren" were the "Yale Bands." "Societies of Inquiry" (into the claims of missions) spread rapidly among the eastern colleges following the Williams College event, both Yale and Princeton becoming major centers of recruitment for volunteers. Yale Bands went west to many states, having studied the Indian languages, agriculture, public school administration and other subjects relevant to creating a Christian civilization. In several states they founded the first colleges, in some they brought the legislatures to establish public school systems.

The Congregationalists were also prominent in missions to the Indians and freed slaves, operating chiefly through the ABC's sister organization, the American Missionary Association (f. 1846). Congregationalists took the lead in founding such outstanding institutions as the Hampton Institute, Atlanta University, and Fisk University.

# AMERICAN RELIGIOUS COMMUNITIES AND COMMUNES
## 19TH CENTURY

A common myth, assiduously cultivated by predatory political propagandists today, has it that the American frontiers were settled by rugged individualists. Quite the contrary is true: with the exception of a few mountain men, the survivors were those who traveled in organized wagon trains and settled in communities featuring mutual aid. The "individualists" came and prospered after the schools were founded, the lands surveyed and allocations made, rudimentary government put in force. The dominant theme of the nineteenth century was given by a bewildering variety of voluntary associations and intentional communities. With the breakup of old New England, not infrequently whole villages moved westward with their preachers, seeding the Puritan mores and style of life across the Great Plains to the west coast. Even the town square, which used to be such a familiar sight in the old Northwest Territory and on the prairies, shows the background in a certain understanding of social relationships.

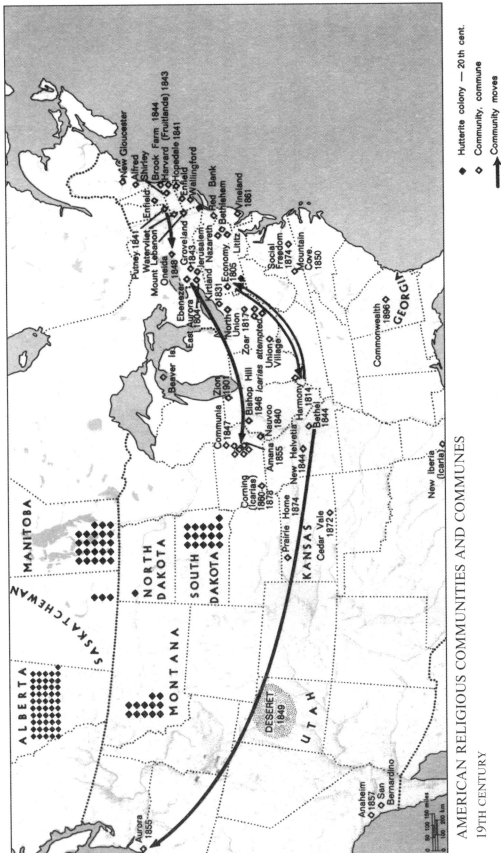

AMERICAN RELIGIOUS COMMUNITIES AND COMMUNES

19TH CENTURY

327

Even more striking were the dozens of religious communities and communes which dotted the landscape with intended models of the good society. The chief sources of communal settlements in America were Puritanism, Pietism, and Utopian Socialism; later, the Hutterites became prominent.

Representative Puritan communities were Brook Farm and Oneida. Brook Farm (1841–47) grew out of the religious discussion of the Hedge Club in Cambridge, Massachusetts. Among its illustrious associates were Nathaniel Hawthorne (1804–64), Bronson Alcott and Isaac Hecker (1819–88). Alcott's daughter, Louisa May, became famous for her children's stories. Oneida, founded by a Congregational minister, John Humphrey Noyes (1811–86), was at first highly successful. The colony manufactured the steel traps used in the booming beaver trade. Because of experiments with "complex marriage" and scientific birth control, Oneida was then attacked by the Presbyterian and Methodist clergy and broken up by law. The Shakers, whose nineteen settlements were for several generations successful celibate communes, and whose furniture and tools are still highly esteemed for their artistic and functional design, were also products of the New England culture. So too were the Mormons, the most successful of all the religious communes of New England background.

The contribution of revivalism to communalism should be noted. Many of the revivalists aroused their listeners to commitment to a new life but provided no guidance in the form it should take. Oneida, the Shakers, the Mormons—and a number of new denominations like the Seventh Day Adventists and Church of God (Anderson), whose first settlement practiced Christian communism modeled on the church at Jerusalem (Acts 4:32)—all harvested what revivalism had sown.

Ephrata (Penn.), founded by Johann Conrad Beissel (1691–1768) of the Seventh Day Baptists (German), was for a time the cultural center of the Pennsylvania Germans ("Dutch," from *Deutsch*). Graf Nikolaus Ludwig Zinzendorf (1700–60) also established Pietist colonies within Pennsylvania similar to the mother community in Herrnhut, Saxony. The followers of George Rapp (1757–1847) established highly successful communities at Economy (Penn.) and Harmony (Ind.).

Utopian Socialist colonies were numerous, and all of short duration. One mentor was Charles Fourier (1772–1837), a Frenchman who gained the support of such well-known Americans as Horace Greeley (a presidential candidate in 1872), Arthur Brisbane (famous New York editor), William Ellery Channing (Unitarian leader). Another was Etienne Cabet (1788–1856), whose "Icarias" were to exhibit *True Christianity* (the title of his book calling for settlers in America). These communes also splintered easily and died early.

*...to advance Learning and to perpetuate it to Posterity; dreading to leave an illiterate Ministry to the Churches, when our present Ministers shall lie in the Dust.*
— Founders of Harvard, 1636

UNTIL the Civil War, by far the largest number of colleges were founded by the Christian churches. For that matter, until 1890 eleven out of twelve high school graduates in America were products of private academies—most of them Christian foundations. For two centuries after the founding of Harvard (1636), 9/10 of all college presidents were clergymen.

During the colonial period and even later a number of private institutions received public funds for performing public purposes, and in spite of tax grants they were protected from political interference (Dartmouth College Case, 1819). After the Revolution several state universities were founded: Georgia (1785), North Carolina (1789), South Carolina (1801), Ohio (1804), etc. Thomas Jefferson regarded his role in the founding of the University of Virginia (1819) one of his three most important accomplishments. But until the Morrill Land Act of 1862, which made available to state colleges large grants of federal lands, the primary initiative lay with the churches. Even the foundings of state schools—e.g., the University of Michigan, f. 1817 by John Monteith (Presbyterian minister) and Gabriel Richard (Roman Catholic priest)—were frequently on Christian instance, and several of today's great state universities (e.g., Rutgers University, f. 1766) were originally church institutions and later transferred to state support.

Before the rise of public high schools, much of the work of the colleges was at secondary school level. It was, however, centered upon very clear objectives: to raise up clergy and laity schooled in Christian and humane values. The major academic degree was the *Magister Artium* (M.A.), a humanistic degree. The Ph.D., a degree signalizing competence in specialized

*Harvard University Tercentenary Crest, 1936.*

*Cotton Mather of Harvard.*

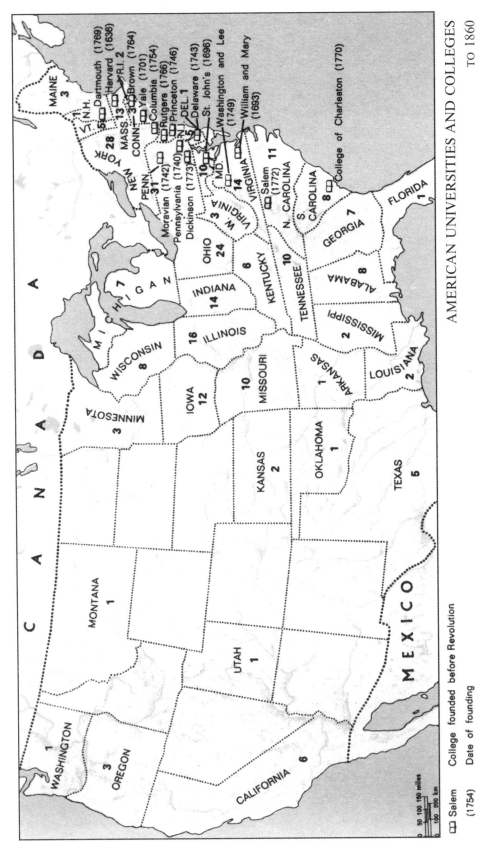

AMERICAN UNIVERSITIES AND COLLEGES
TO 1860

MAINE 3
N.H.
VT.
MASS. 13
CONN. 3
R.I. 2
N.Y. 28
NEW YORK 28
PENN. 31
N.J. 5
DEL. 1
MD. 10
VIRGINIA 14
W. VIRGINIA 3
N. CAROLINA 11
S. CAROLINA 8
GEORGIA 7
ALABAMA 8
FLORIDA 1
MISSISSIPPI 2
LOUISIANA 2
TENNESSEE 10
KENTUCKY 6
OHIO 24
INDIANA 14
ILLINOIS 16
WISCONSIN 8
MICHIGAN 7
MINNESOTA 3
IOWA 12
MISSOURI 10
ARKANSAS 1
KANSAS 2
OKLAHOMA 1
TEXAS 5
MONTANA 1
UTAH 1
WASHINGTON 1
OREGON 3
CALIFORNIA 6

Dartmouth (1769)
Harvard (1636)
Brown (1764)
Yale (1701)
Columbia (1754)
Rutgers (1766)
Princeton (1746)
Dickinson (1773)
Pennsylvania (1740)
Moravian (1742)
Delaware (1743)
St. John's (1696)
Washington and Lee (1749)
William and Mary (1693)
Salem (1772)
College of Charleston (1770)

C A N A D A
M E X I C O

□ Salem   College founded before Revolution
(1754)   Date of founding
8   Number of colleges in state
before the Civil War

0  50 100 150 miles
0  100 200 km

330

research, did not come into use in America until the 1870s, when leading universities were reorganized by men trained in Germany.

The elimination of Theology (or "Religion" as an intellectual discipline) from the campus dialogue, which was only being overcome in the 1960s and 1970s, resulted from two causes. First, the people of the great revival churches feared "secular," "profane," and "scientific" learning and preferred to have their sons and daughters educated in seminaries and/or Christian colleges far from "pagan" departments of learning. They supported the state colleges for training in industrial, agricultural and manual arts, but followed the example of Andover Seminary (f. 1808) in fleeing the perils of liberal scholarship and a scientifically oriented humanism. Second, the expansion of the state universities, reorganized on the von Humboldt design in the latter part of the nineteenth century, deleted the study of Theology and Religion because of a mistaken understanding of the logic of "the separation of church and state." The sectarian strife which marked the emergence of a multitude of new denominations also succeeded in convincing administrators it was wiser to keep religion at arm's length. Only with the Abington Township Case (1963), in which religious exercises in the public schools were declared unconstitutional but the study of religion was approved, did the tide turn. For long the typical professional center had been a "Department of Bible and Religion" in a Protestant college or a "Department of Theology" in a Roman Catholic school. After 1963 there was a landslide of foundings of departments of "Religion" or "Religious Studies" in state colleges and universities. The annual professional meeting (NABI: National Association of Biblical Instructors) jumped from c 70 in attendance to the current annual joint meetings of the American Academy of Religion and Society of Biblical Literature (SBL) numbering c 7,000.

In the first two centuries of higher learning in America, the split between the pursuit of wisdom and the attainment of technical competence had not yet appeared. As was reported of the founding of Harvard, the initiators acted "to advance Learning and to perpetuate it to Posterity; dreading to leave an illiterate Ministry to the Churches, when our present Ministers shall lie in the Dust." Yale (f. 1701) and Princeton (f. 1746) and King's College (Columbia, f. 1754) and many others had similar declarations at the beginning.

## THE AMERICAN CIVIL WAR 1861–65

*A compromise with rebellion is treason against God.*
— Detroit Annual Conference of the Methodist Episcopal Church, 1864

THE causes of "the War Between the States," as southern historians generally prefer to call it, were complex beyond the scope of the present writing.

In the political sense, the question was whether the United States was a union established by "the People of the United States" (as the Constitution opens) or a confederation of sovereign states. Since the war the process of centralization has proceeded apace,

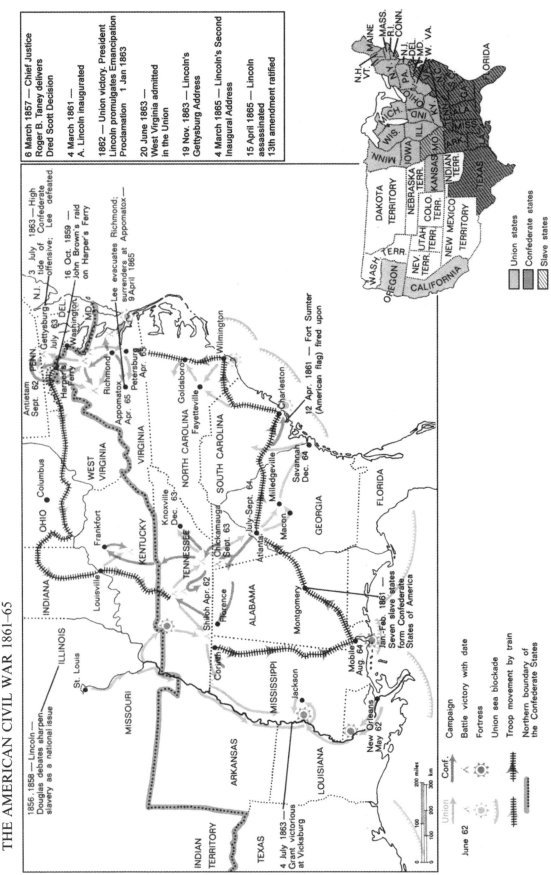

THE AMERICAN CIVIL WAR 1861–65

1856.1858 — Lincoln — Douglas debates sharpen slavery as a national issue

3 July 1863 — High tide of Confederate offensive; Lee defeated.

16 Oct. 1859 — John Brown's raid on Harper's Ferry

Antietam Sept. 62

Gettysburg July 63

Washington

Lee evacuates Richmond; surrenders at Appomatox— 9 April 1865

Harper's Ferry

Richmond

Appomatox Apr. 65

Petersburg Apr. 65

PENN.

N.J.

DEL.

MD.

Wilmington

OHIO

Columbus

WEST VIRGINIA

VIRGINIA

NORTH CAROLINA

Goldsboro

Fayetteville

Charleston

12 Apr. 1861 — Fort Sumter (American flag) fired upon

Frankfort

KENTUCKY

Knoxville Dec. 63

TENNESSEE

Chickamauga Sept. 63

SOUTH CAROLINA

July-Sept. 64

Milledgeville

Savannah Dec. 64

Louisville

INDIANA

ILLINOIS

St. Louis

MISSOURI

Shiloh Apr. 62

Florence

Corinth

ALABAMA

Atlanta

Macon

GEORGIA

Montgomery

FLORIDA

Jan.-Feb. 1861 — Seven slave states form Confederate States of America

MISSISSIPPI

Jackson

Mobile Aug. 64

New Orleans May 62

ARKANSAS

LOUISIANA

INDIAN TERRITORY

TEXAS

4 July 1863 — Grant victorious at Vicksburg

June 62

Conf.

Union

0   100   200

0   100   200   300 km

200 miles

Campaign

Battle victory with date

Fortress

Union sea blockade

Troop movement by train

Northern boundary of the Confederate States

6 March 1857 — Chief Justice Roger B. Taney delivers Dred Scott Decision

4 March 1861 — A. Lincoln inaugurated

1862 — Union victory. President Lincoln promulgates Emancipation Proclamation  1 Jan 1863

20 June 1863 — West Virginia admitted in the Union

19 Nov. 1863 — Lincoln's Gettysburg Address

4 March 1865 — Lincoln's Second Inaugural Address

15 April 1865 — Lincoln assassinated 13th amendment ratified

N.H.
VT.
MAINE
MASS.
R.I.
CONN.
N.Y.
N.J.
PA.
DEL.
MD.
W. VA.
FLORIDA

MICH.
WIS.
IOWA
ILL.
IND.
OHIO
KY.
TENN.
N.C.
S.C.
GA.
ALA.
MISS.
ARK.
LA.
TEXAS
MO.
KANSAS
INDIAN TERR.

MINN.
DAKOTA TERRITORY
NEBRASKA TERR.
COLO. TERR.
NEW MEXICO TERRITORY

WASH. TERR.
OREGON
NEV. TERR.
UTAH TERR.
CALIFORNIA

Union states

Confederate states

Slave states

with implications for religion as well as other phases of national life.

In the economic sense, the struggle was joined between an economy of independent farmers and tradesmen and a plantation system dominated by chattel slavery.

For the religious factor in the conflict, the most important force was the union of revivalism and abolitionism. The first anti-slavery testimony in America (1688) was written by Pastorius and circulated among Mennonites and Quakers in Philadelphia. With the work of Finney and other revivalists who were anti-slavery, the movement for abolition acquired a rapidly expanding base of public support.

The American Colonization Society was founded in 1817 to effect gradual emancipation and resettlement of freed slaves in Africa. Liberia was founded in consequence. The invention of the cotton gin made slavery profitable again, and the British navy's suppression of the slave trade (1833 ff.) put an end to the "triangular slave trade." In the states of the Old South, their soil ruined by years of tobacco planting, breeding slaves for the southwestern cotton states became a major industry. Harriet Beecher Stowe's *Uncle Tom's Cabin* (1852) shows the spirit of moral revolt which inspired the northern church people. In 1833 the American Anti-Slavery Society was founded: the colonization solution was abandoned. In 1837 Elijah P. Lovejoy was murdered in Alton, Illinois defending his abolitionist printing press. Peaceful solutions were giving out.

Methodists, Baptists and Presbyterians split over the slavery issue before the war started. The western part of Virginia—revivalist territory—split off and formed a new and free state in 1863, with the proud motto, *Montani Semper Liberi!*

With Abraham Lincoln's election (1860) and Southern secession, most of the leading professional officers served the southern states from which they had come. The Confederacy won the early victories, but by 1863 Lincoln had found a general who could use the Union's preponderance of equipment and raw manpower to overcome the superior professional competence of Robert E. Lee (1807–70) and his aides. The American Civil War was the first modern war—with machine guns, submarines, rifled artillery, ironclad ships, and open assault on civilian populations and targets. The bitter feelings it left behind dominated American politics for more than a century.

During the war the Emancipation Proclamation was issued (1 January 1863). With its conclusion, Constitutional amendments were adopted to secure the rights of the new black citizens. In 1876, however, the Republican Party bought the presidential victory of Hayes over Tilden in return for giving white organizations a free hand in restoring white supremacy in the Deep South. And in 1883 the Supreme Court ruled unconstitutional legislation to protect their civil rights— a decision as helpful to injustice and encouraging to violence as the Dred Scott decision of 1857. Not until Executive Order 8802 (1941), prohibiting racial discrimination in defense industries, and the Supreme Court decision of 5 May 1954, prohibiting discrimination in the schools, did the black citizens begin to regain basic rights.

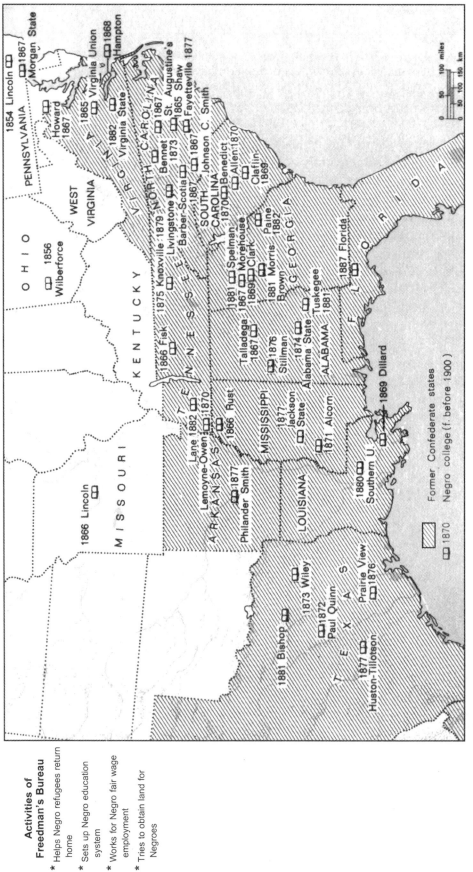

NEGRO HIGHER EDUCATION AFTER THE CIVIL WAR

**Activities of Freedman's Bureau**

* Helps Negro refugees return home

* Sets up Negro education system

* Works for Negro fair wage employment

* Tries to obtain land for Negroes

334

FOR seventy-one years that records were kept, 1952 was the first that went by without one or more lynchings. Nor was the cup of blood full. In 1963, Medgar Evers was shot in the back by an identified (and subsequently unpunished) murderer; Evers was NAACP organizer in Jackson, Mississippi. In September of the same year four little girls were murdered attending Sunday School in Birmingham, Alabama. In 1964, three student volunteers (Michael Schwerner, Andrew Goodman, James Chaney) registering black voters were tortured and killed in Mississippi. Their identified killers were not punished for murder.

That black citizens remained as nonviolent as they did over a century of unconstitutional denial of their rights and illegal, largely unpunished white terrorism has been in great part due to the quality of black community leadership. And although many preachers and community leaders have been self-educated, both the black churches and the Negro colleges have made massive contributions to the survival of America.

There were some thousands of freed slaves in the north before the Civil War. Frederick Douglass (1817–95), abolitionist orator and leader in the young Republican Party, whom Lincoln called "the most meritorious man of the nineteenth century," was one. A few colleges—notably Oberlin (f. 1833) and Berea (f. 1859)—admitted black students from the beginning. In 1854 the first Negro college—Ashmun Institute, now Lincoln University—was founded at Oxford, Pennsylvania. Wilberforce University, where the first black college president in America took office (Daniel A. Payne, 1811–93, a bishop of the AME Church), was founded in 1856 in Ohio. With emancipation, however, a mass problem of education was at hand. The total population of the United States in

*Long Island woman teaching freed slaves.*

*George Washington Carver, black scientist and educator.*

1868). The Congregationalists were especially active in founding Negro colleges, and they also recruited several hundred "New England schoolmarms" to teach in the new schools for black children.

The most influential black leader for more than a generation was Booker T. Washington (1856–1915), who opened Tuskegee Institute in 1881. He was convinced that black citizens could earn their place in society by becoming skilled workmen and hardworking citizens. In his school George Washington Carver (c 1864–1943), one of the greatest American chemists, developed a whole set of new agricultural products. Washington's Atlanta Exposition Address of 1895 won the approval of both white and black leaders.

The break from Washington's gradualism was led by W.E.B. DuBois (1868–1963), a Harvard-educated professor at Atlanta University. In 1905 he organized the militant "Niagara Movement," and in 1908 he split with Washington over support of the Republican Party. In 1910 he helped found the National Association for the Advancement of Colored People (NAACP), and became the first black member of the national staff.

1860 was c 31.5 million. The freed slaves were at least 3.5 million, chiefly in the south.

The Freedmen's Bureau was set up to assist in settlement and education. The Bureau dispensed c 15 million dollars before closing. General O. O. Howard, one of several of Lincoln's generals who devoted themselves to the education of the freed slaves, was in charge. Howard University carries his name. Another was General Samuel Chapman Armstrong, scion of a famous ABC missionary family in Hawaii, the first president of Hampton Institute (f.

## THE GROWTH OF ROMAN CATHOLICISM IN THE USA

*There is no conflict between the Catholic Church and America.*
— Archbishop John Ireland, 1884

By 1998, the Roman Catholic Church counted over 61 million adherents in the United States—four times the membership of the largest Protestant church. We are immediately thrown into the ambiguities attending religious statistics, however, for the Catholic count includes all who have ever been baptized while the largest Protestant church—the Southern Baptist Convention—reckons in its count only adult members. Nevertheless, remembering that of the population of c 3.6 million at the time of the American Revolution only c 20,000 were Roman Catholics, this is a remarkable development.

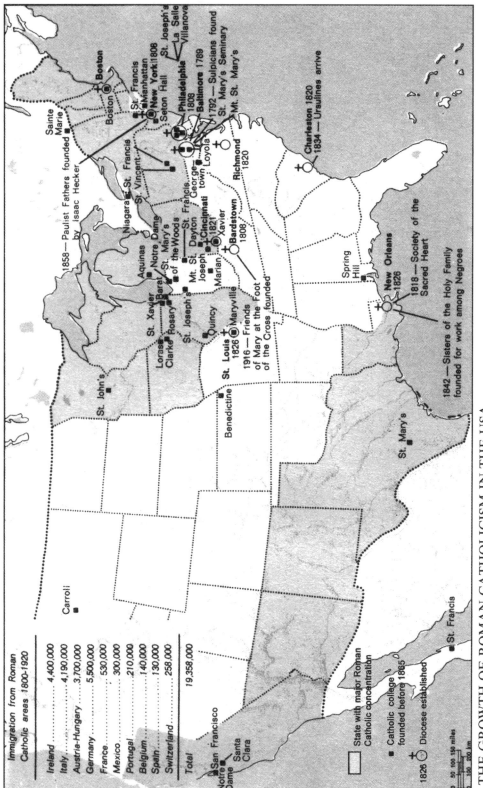

THE GROWTH OF ROMAN CATHOLICISM IN THE USA

Immigration from Roman
Catholic areas 1800-1920

| | |
|---|---|
| Ireland | 4,400,000 |
| Italy | 4,190,000 |
| Austria-Hungary | 3,700,000 |
| Germany | 5,500,000 |
| France | 530,000 |
| Mexico | 300,000 |
| Portugal | 210,000 |
| Belgium | 140,000 |
| Spain | 130,000 |
| Switzerland | 258,000 |
| Total | 19,358,000 |

State with major Roman
Catholic concentration

■ Catholic college
founded before 1865

1826 ⊕ Diocese established

0  50 100 150 miles
0   100  200 km

Boston
St. Francis
New York 1806
Manhattan
Seton Hall
St. Joseph's 1806
La Salle
Villanova
Philadelphia 1808
Baltimore 1789
1792 — Sulpicians found
St. Mary's Seminary
Mt. St. Mary's
Charleston 1820
1834 — Ursulines arrive
Sainte Marie
1858 — Paulist Fathers founded
by Isaac Hecker
Niagara
St. Francis
St. Vincent
Loyola
Richmond 1820
Notre Dame
St. Mary's
of the Woods
St. Francis
St. George
town
Cincinnati 1821
Aquinas
Barat
Dayton
Mt. St.
Joseph
Marian
Xavier
Bardstown 1808
St. Xavier
Lorass
Clarke
Rosary
St. Joseph's
Quincy
Maryville
1826
1916 — Friends
of Mary at the Foot
of the Cross founded
St. Louis
Benedictine
St. John's
Spring Hill
New Orleans 1826
1818 — Society of the
Sacred Heart
1842 — Sisters of the Holy Family
founded for work among Negroes
St. Mary's
Carroll
San Francisco
Santa Clara
Notre Dame
St. Francis

337

Roman Catholics were feared and disfranchised in most of the English colonies, and the Quebec Act (1774)—which sanctioned taxation to support Roman Catholicism in that province—was one of the chief causes of popular resentment against England. Puritan memories were still educated by Foxe's *Book of Martyrs*; they told the stories of martyrdoms under "Bloody Mary" (Mary Tudor, queen of England: 1553–58), and of how the Lord delivered His people in the destruction of the Spanish Armada (1588). They recalled how judgment had been visited on London after the Restoration of a Roman Catholic king (1660), in the Great Plague and the Great Fire of 1666.

The first great immigration of Roman Catholics came with the potato famine in 1847, during which a million and a half who remained in Ireland died of starvation. In the hierarchy, Irish gradually replaced the French who had held most of the important American posts since the early years of the French Empire in North America.

The second great immigration was German, taking place during the years of the Prussian rise to power among the German states. The *Kulturkampf* launched by Bismarck after the Infallibility Decree strengthened the appeal of America to Roman Catholics from Bavaria and the Rhineland. While the Irish fitted in as day laborers in the eastern cities, the Germans moved to the upper Midwest and became farmers. With Scandinavian immigration into the same area at about the same time, for decades every county in Wisconsin and Minnesota had either a Roman Catholic or a Lutheran majority.

By 1920 there were also 3.3 million Americans of Italian origin and c 3 million Poles. By 1970 there were c 9 million Americans of Spanish ancestry, some of them descendants from the early settlements in the Southwest and California, the majority immigrants from Mexico. Since the elimination (1956, 1965) of racial and national quotas for immigration, the numbers coming from traditionally Roman Catholic countries have grown exponentially.

Roman Catholic leadership in Rome was thoroughly reactionary during most of the nineteenth century, condemning all aspects of liberty and self-government (including "Americanism"). Thanks to the leadership of able men, the church in America was able to survive and surmount a bitter anti-foreignism which enlisted such distinguished spokesmen as Lyman Beecher and Samuel F. B. Morse (inventor of the telegraph). John Hughes (1797–1864) of New York, John England (1786–1842) of Charleston, and James Gibbons (1834–1921), a cardinal, led their flocks through the shoals of vestryism (church ownership and control at a local level), Know Nothingism and economic disadvantage, and also won from Rome the right of Catholics

*Samuel F. B. Morse.*

to participate fully in labor unions and other American institutions.

One of the most remarkable achievements of American Catholicism, unique to America, has been the building up by dedicated voluntary giving of a complete school system—elementary, secondary, and university. In recent years there has been a strong effort, in cooperation with Orthodox Jewish and Fundamentalist Protestant leaders, to get tax moneys for church schools.

With Vatican II (1962–65), Roman Catholicism entered into a new relationship with its sister churches in America. The encyclical "We Remember" (1998) signaled the opening of a new relationship with the Jewish community.

## ANTI-EVOLUTION LAWS IN THE USA

*I don't want my daughter or anybody's daughter to have to study a book that prints pictures of a monkey and a man on the same page.*
    — Governor Cameron Morrison of North Carolina

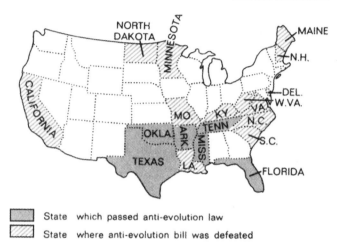

☐ State which passed anti-evolution law

▨ State where anti-evolution bill was defeated

IN the United States, social Darwinism gained wide acceptance—particularly in conservative economic circles. The philosophy of "survival of the fittest" pleased those of high social and economic status, and it severely modified the older Puritan tradition of mutual aid and stewardship of the commonweal.

In some religious circles, the teaching of evolution was considered a frontal assault on the biblical story of creation. Men like Lyman Abbot, Washington Gladden and Harry Emerson Fosdick attempted to correlate the theory of evolution with Christianity's message as a higher religion. But particularly among those who had pledged themselves to "The Fundamentals" (1910), evolution was considered a challenge to revealed truth about the origin and purpose of man. Campaigns were carried through a number of state legislatures to prohibit the teaching of evolution in the public schools. At Dayton, Tennessee, a schoolteacher was found guilty of breaking the anti-evolution law of that state. But the Scopes Trial (1925) attracted such attention that the Fundamentalists won the battle but lost the war.

The churches' embarrassment arose as much from misuse of state power to enforce religious doctrine as from the false definition of a conflict between "science" and "religion." The resurgence of Fundamentalism in some churches during the last decade has resulted in another push in some states to pass anti-evolution laws inhibiting public school instruction.

CHURCH growth today seems to be a function of lay initiative, and lay initiative seems to be most vigorous in those churches which have no strong hierarchies or judicatories. Church growth is also related to a strong sense of group identity, although this group identity may be manifested in different ways: church discipline, use of a foreign language (or esoteric idiom), unique interpretation of history, mutual aid. Those churches which feel that they are swimming against the stream appear to be most lively and most attractive to new members, while those which stood in the mainstream in the nineteenth century are definitely declining in their percentage of adherents in the total population.

One of the most rapidly growing churches has been the Lutheran Church, Missouri Synod, with 2.6 million members. Yet many of the churches of the Missouri Synod have only in the last half-century begun to use the English language, and many still have German-language services. The leader in the creation of the synod (f. 1847) was Carl F. W. Walther (1811–87). Under his leadership an extensive system of parochial schools was inaugurated. In 1872 a Lutheran Synodical Conference came into being which united several conservative

## THE LUTHERAN CHURCH, MISSOURI SYNOD

State where Synod is strong

## THE SOUTHERN BAPTIST CONVENTION

State with S. Baptist plurality

groups which stressed the responsibility and initiative of members of local congregations. In the 1960s the denomination was rent by a power struggle that led to division.

The largest Protestant denomination in America is the Southern Baptist Convention, although seriously damaged by a power struggle that reached its peak in the 1990s. Ostensibly the issue was "scriptural inerrancy." The Convention was formed (1845) during the controversies between north and south which preceded the American Civil War (1861–65). The Baptists were behind the Methodists in 1860, when one out of every five Protestants in

America belonged to the latter movement. But during the latter half of the nineteenth century and into the twentieth the Southern Baptists grew much more rapidly and today count over 15.6 million members, although the figure is uncertain because of divisions within state conventions. After the war and before the church struggle the SBC had more than doubled the number of its missionaries in the field. The intact SBC also have the largest seminary (Southwestern Baptist Theological Seminary at Fort Worth, Texas) as well as America's most prominent preacher: Billy Graham (b. 1918).

The Church of Christ, Scientist was founded by Mary Baker Eddy (1821–1910) in 1892. There are today c 3,500 churches and c 9,000 practitioners in the world. There are no clergy as such.

Among Jehovah's Witnesses, on the other hand, every adult member is a "minister" (a matter which brought them considerable difficulty under military conscription, education laws, and local ordinances until a dozen decisions of the U.S. Supreme Court defended their religious liberty). Some hundreds of thousands spend every spare hour, and take regular breaks of some weeks from their jobs, to distribute literature and visit from house to house in evangelistic work. Charles Taze Russell (1852–1916), a former Congregational minister, founded the movement as "International Bible Students" in 1872; the name "Jehovah's Witnesses" was taken in 1931. They were active in 63 countries in 1998. After great suffering and martyrdoms in the Nazi Third Reich, they are still subject to persecution in Russia and several western European countries.

The most successful communal society in America is the Church of Jesus Christ of Latterday Saints, commonly called "Mormons." With a strong work ethic and excellent mutual aid,

## THE CHURCH OF CHRIST, SCIENTIST

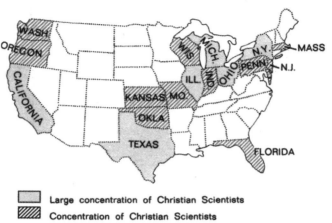

▨ Large concentration of Christian Scientists
▨ Concentration of Christian Scientists

## JEHOVAH'S WITNESSES

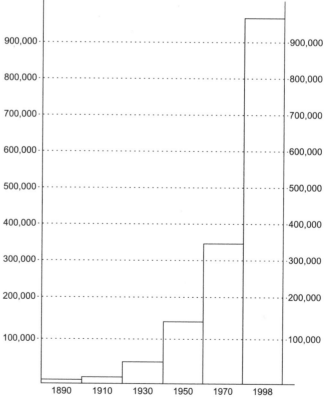

*Growth in membership of Jehovah's Witnesses in the U.S., 1880–1998.*

they survived persecution in the early decades and have developed a fine educational system and a vigorous program of missions. Since the war they have more than doubled their membership, with 4.8 million in the United States and over 10 million worldwide.

## THE CHURCH OF JESUS CHRIST OF LATTERDAY SAINTS (MORMONS)

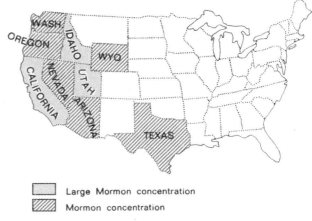

▨ Large Mormon concentration

▨ Mormon concentration

## BLACK RELIGION IN AMERICA

A common mistake is to suppose that the Negro churches are simply minority counterparts to white denominations. It is true that the first independent Afro-American churches arose in reaction to indignities suffered in white congregations, and they took the denominational names of their background. Thus Richard Allen 1760–1831) led his people out of a white church to found the "Mother Bethel" Church in Philadelphia in 1793; the African Methodist Episcopal (AME) Church held its first General Confer-

ence in 1816. And James Varick (1750–1827) led in founding the African Methodist Episcopal Zion (AME Zion) Church in New York in 1821. Among black Christians, whose percentage of church membership is as high as that in the white population, Baptist churches were early organized. The conventions themselves (National Baptist Convention of America—3.5 million members; National Baptist Convention USA, Inc.—8.2 million; Progressive National Baptist Convention—2.5 million; National Missionary Baptist Conven-

*Key to map (opposite).*

⌂
1  1787 — AME Church
2  1796 — AME Zion Church
3  1805 — Union American ME Church
4  1866 — African Union Meth. Protestant Church
5  1869 — Colored Cumberland Presb. Church
6  1870 — CME Church
7  1886 — United Holy Church
8  1895 — National Baptist Convention, Inc.
9  1896 — Church of Christ (Holiness)
10 1896 — Church of God and Saints of Christ
11 1901 — United Free Will Baptist Churches
12 1902 — Triumph the Church and Kingdom of God in Christ
13 1905 — Free Christian Zion Church of Christ
14 1907 — National Primitive Baptist Convention
15 1915 — National Baptist Convention
16 1916 — Apostolic Overcoming Church of God
17 1919 — Apostolic Faith, Inc.
18 1932 — Christ Church Union
19 1961 — Progressive National Baptist Convention

☫
1  1931 — Moorish Science Temple
2  1931 — Black Muslim Temple

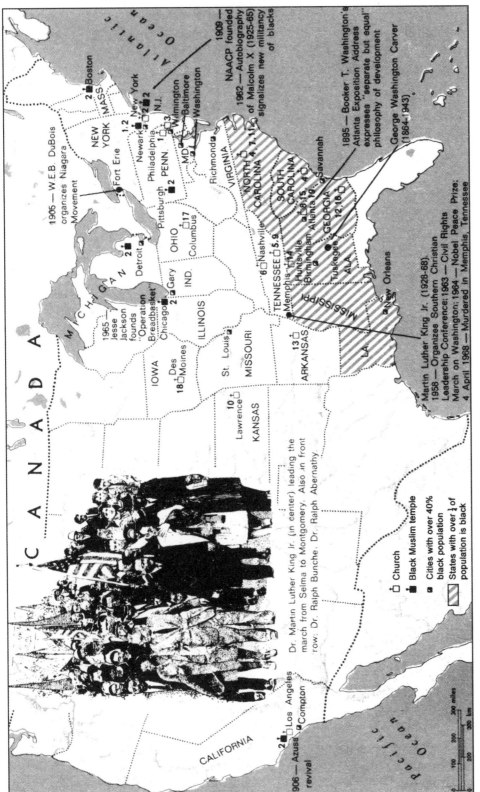

BLACK RELIGION IN AMERICA

tion—2.5 million) were organized later. Until the rise of the Pentecostal movement, four out of five black Christians in America were Baptists.

The first Afro-American foreign missionary effort was that of Lott Cary, who went to Liberia in 1821 for the Richmond (Va.) African Baptist Missionary Society (f. 1815).

Afro-American religion did not follow a parallel course to white churches, however, for with emancipation and the use of extra-legal and illegal means by the dominant society to force the freed slaves back into servitude, their churches became the only institution still controlled by the masses of black people. At the same time that most of the Protestant white churches were relaxing and giving up the function of Christian counter-cultures, and accepting the status of religious establishments (social, though not legal), the black congregations became the chief centers of black identity and (passive) resistance.

Booker T. Washington's gradualism was replaced by political and legal militancy which centered in the National Association for the Advancement of Colored People (NAACP), founded in 1910, and the National Urban League (f. 1911). The uniting of political initiative on a national level with the tremendous reserve strength of the black congregations provided the power base of the civil rights movement during and after World War II.

In 1942 the Congress of Racial Equality (CORE) was founded by James L. Farmer, Jr. and George Houser—a black and a white, both sons of Methodist ministers, both leaders in the Methodist youth movement. CORE and the Student Nonviolent Coordinating Committee (SNCC) were initially influenced by the philosophy of nonviolent direct action (NVDA), *satyagraha*, taught and practiced by Mohandas K. Gandhi (1869–1948) in South Africa and India. In 1957 the Southern Christian Leadership Conference (SCLC) was organized by Martin Luther King, Jr. (1929–68), a Baptist preacher who became the spokesman for black citizens' aspirations and liberal white citizens' hopes in America.

King was educated at Morehouse (one of the historic black colleges, in Georgia) and Crozer Theological Seminary (Baptist). He earned his Ph.D. at Boston University (Methodist). He thus carried high credentials, which won him and his movement the confidence and support of ecumenical, denominational, and educational agencies in the white society. In 1964 he received the Nobel Peace Prize. He never lost the capacity to use the language of the black congregations, however, and in repeated "freedom marches" he was backed by large numbers of ordinary black Christians. His message ("I have a dream") at the Lincoln Memorial (28 August 1963), during a march on Washington of more than 200,000 Americans, white as well as black, is considered by many to have been the high point of Christian preaching in twentieth-century America. Although after King's assassination clergymen like Ralph Abernathy carried on the SCLC, while Jesse Jackson and others have led the black churches to push America to fulfill its principles of social justice, more extreme black militants have collected in "the Nation of Islam." The assassination of Malcolm X in 1965 further radicalized young Afro-American males politically, who have the highest unemployment and prison percentages of any sector of the society.

*Can democracy suffer a hereditary minority to perpetuate itself as a permanent minority with its own distinctive culture, sanctioned by its own distinctive cult forms? They have no right in a democracy to remove their faith from the normal influences of the democratic process by insulating it behind the walls of a racial and cultural solidarity.*

— Charles Clayton Morrison in
*The Christian Century*, 9 June 1937

THE first Jews to reach the colonies were *Sephardim*, victims of the late crusade of Ferdinand and Isabella throughout the Iberian Peninsula and of the Portuguese recapture of Recife, Brazil, from the Dutch (1654). A generation later they founded Congregation Shearith Israel in New York. At the time of the American Revolution, there were hardly more than 2,000 Jews out of the 3.6 million in the colonies.

The first significant wave of immigration followed on the revolutions of 1848, especially with the enforcement of harsh antisemitic laws in Roman Catholic Bavaria. As *Ashkenazim* of the German area, they had teachers who were under the influence of the Enlightenment and the universities. Their thinking and practice moved toward assimilation. Schelling's friend Moses Mendelssohn (1729–86), who held to a rational and ethical Judaism but attained social eminence in Berlin, represented one option. Schleiermacher's friend David Mendel (Johann August Wilhelm Neander, 1789–1850), convert and church historian, represented another.

In America, Reform Judaism turned to the use of English in the liturgy and adopted in the Pittsburgh Platform (1885) a statement of belief that rejected the irrational and miraculous, outdated aspects of the Mosaic law, even the return to Palestine. The leader of the Americanization process, Isaac Mayer Wise (1819–1900), was also instrumental in founding the Union of American Hebrew Congregations

*The oldest synagogue in America: Touro Synagogue in Newport, Rhode Island.*

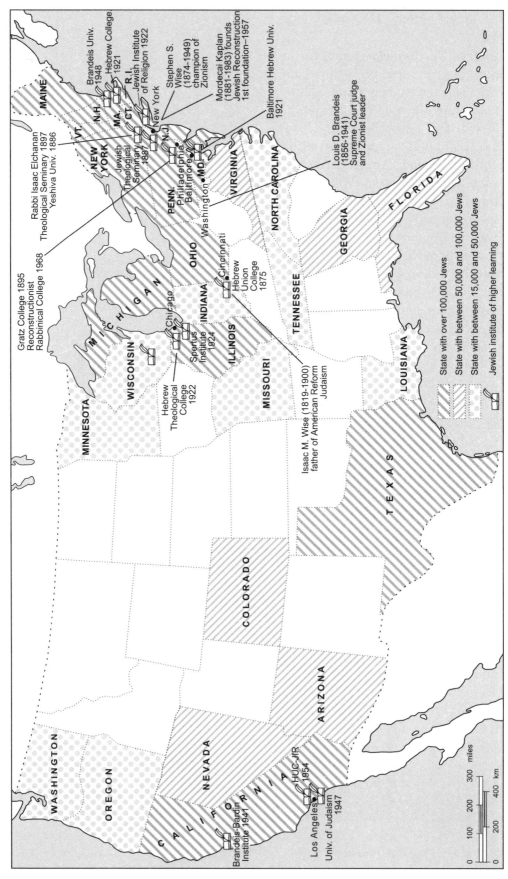

MAJOR JEWISH COMMUNITIES IN THE USA

(1873) and Hebrew Union College (1875).

Conservative Judaism emerged in reaction to the rapidity with which Reform leaders were abandoning landmarks of historic belief and practice. The Jewish Theological Seminary, New York (f. 1887) became the center of the movement, and under the leadership of Solomon Schechter (pres.: 1902–15) the institution rose to an eminence it has never subsequently yielded.

It was the flood of Jews from eastern Europe, which began c 1870, that turned the tide against assimilation and provided a base for Conservative Judaism. The religious leaders of these immigrants were not university men: they came up through the schools (yeshivas) of the Jewish ghetto, rich in oral tradition and study of the sacred writings. With the immigration of refugees from tsarist pogroms and other forms of persecution and oppression in Russia, Poland, and the Baltic states, two-thirds of American Jewry were traditional observants. Yeshiva University in New York (f. 1886) became the chief senior Orthodox educational institution.

Hitler's assault on European Jewry brought American Jewry together and energized cooperation in community service organizations, although overt political activity was slow in coming. Support for Israel has subsequently brought a renewed sense of identity, and Reform Judaism has also shifted to the Zionist position. In this change Stephen S. Wise (1874–1949) was a powerful force.

Today there are over 6 million in America who count themselves Jewish,

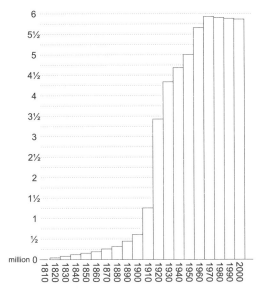

*Growth of Jewish population in America, 1810–2000.*

over one million without connection to organized Jewish religion—whether Orthodox, Conservative, Reform or Reconstructionist. Intermarriage has soared above 50 percent since 8 percent was noted in the 1940s. The birth rate is low, and a decline of 1.5 million is predicted by the year 2020. (Only in Israel is the Jewish birth rate climbing.)

On the one hand, just a half century after the Holocaust the Jewish communities—especially in Israel and North America—are showing the greatest intellectual, economic, political and cultural energy since the destruction of the Second Temple. On the other hand, survival tactics developed under centuries of persecution are proving disfunctional where the Jews of the diaspora are lodged in a free society. Alert communal leadership is working on ways to make adherence to Judaism, including conversion, attractive to outsiders.

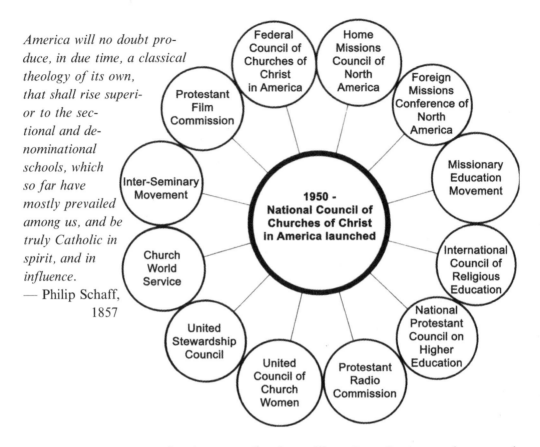

*America will no doubt produce, in due time, a classical theology of its own, that shall rise superior to the sectional and denominational schools, which so far have mostly prevailed among us, and be truly Catholic in spirit, and in influence.*
— Philip Schaff, 1857

Circles in diagram:
- Federal Council of Churches of Christ in America
- Home Missions Council of North America
- Foreign Missions Conference of North America
- Protestant Film Commission
- Missionary Education Movement
- Inter-Seminary Movement
- 1950 - National Council of Churches of Christ in America launched
- International Council of Religious Education
- Church World Service
- National Protestant Council on Higher Education
- United Stewardship Council
- United Council of Church Women
- Protestant Radio Commission

INTERCHURCH cooperation began early in America, in spite of recurring outbursts of sectarian conflict. In the early nineteenth century preachers of several denominations frequently cooperated in revivalist camp meetings. The Evangelical Alliance (f. 1846) had a strong following, with the great churchman and scholar Philip Schaff (1819–93) at the heart of the American section.

Ecumenism in America has from the beginning combined evangelism, missions, and social concern. Horace Bushnell (1802–76), author of *Christian Nurture*, Washington Gladden (1836–1918), author of *Social Salvation*, and Walter Rauschenbusch (1861–1918), author of *Christianity and the Social Crisis*, provided much of the theological base. Nor should we forget Josiah Strong (1847–1916), author of the bestselling *Our Country*, whose work in the Evangelical Alliance reached a high point in the World Parliament of Religions (Chicago, 1893). On this interfaith occasion Schaff but a few weeks before his death delivered a great address on ecumenism. During these sessions, too, Buddhism and Hinduism were effectively introduced to America.

In World War I, following an avowedly Christian president—a son of the parsonage and a Presbyterian (Woodrow Wilson)—the churches supported the great crusade in Europe with a good conscience. Wilson said that America entered the war (on Good Friday, 1917) "as a disinterested champion of right" and the Federal Council of Churches called upon the churches to do their part in winning "the war of righteousness."

The Federal Council organized the General Wartime Commission through which the Protestant denominations cooperated in various tasks, including support of the chaplains' work. Roman Catholics organized the National Catholic War Council, which after several metamorphoses became the U.S. Catholic Bishops' Conference of today.

During the 1920s the country suffered from a major religious depression, from which it emerged to face the challenges of the Great Depression and Nazism. American churchmen continued however to participate actively in world ecumenical organizations, including the Preparatory Committee of the World Council of Churches.

In the United States, a growing interdenominational amity led to major church unions such as the United Methodist Church (1939, 1968), the United Church of Christ (1957), the Presbyterian Church USA (1958, 1983) and the Evangelical Lutheran Church in America (1987).

The crisis of liberal Protestantism came with the rise of Hitler. A number of key personalities had emerged from World War I disillusioned with the slaughter of war, disappointed in America's failure to follow through in a responsible way with international cooperation, dejected by the obvious way in which the peace treaties were dictated by "power politics" rather than the high purposes proclaimed in the heat of conflict. One of them was Harry Emerson Fosdick (1878–1969), who became a fervent pacifist. A popular magazine survey in the late 1930s published pictures and short biographies of America's ten most respected preachers: nine of the ten were pacifists. The Fellowship of Reconciliation, a pacifist organization founded by Friedrich Siegmund-Schultze (1885–1969) and Henry Hodgkin (1877–1933) in 1914, was small but after the war influential in the churches.

The most powerful single voice to challenge that trend and to arouse the churches to the evils of Nazism and the plight of European Jewry was Reinhold Niebuhr (1892–1971). Niebuhr founded the Fellowship of Socialist Christians in 1930, and it became an influential center of neo-orthodox theological thinking, radical politics, and opposition to fascist and communist totalitarianism. During his years at Union Theological Seminary, where he was later joined by the German refugee theologian Paul Tillich (1886–1965), the institution became the most world-famous graduate school of religion in America, and during the Holocaust the major theological center of anti-Nazi thinking and action. The National Council celebrates its fiftieth anniversary at the turn of the millenium, with thirty-five Protestant, Anglican, Catholic and Orthodox member churches.

*Paul Tillich.*

# C. THE GREAT CENTURY OF CHRISTIAN MISSIONS

## NEW AMERICAN CHURCHES

THE nineteenth and twentieth centuries were a time of inter-church cooperation, but also a season of tremendous splitting and separation. Even the Peace Churches divided—the Friends (1827–28) between the followers of Elias Hicks and the Orthodox, while the Mennonites threw off more than twenty splinters. Separations from the small Church of the Brethren produced a Church of God (1848), the Old German Baptist Brethren (1881), the Brethren Church (1882), the Brethren (Ashland, Ohio—1926), and the Grace Conference Brethren (1939).

Splintering which occurred in the American denominations was not, therefore, exclusively a result of the revivals. Nonetheless, these revivals of religion—a recurring and uniquely American phenomenon for two centuries, imperative to win the masses back

*John Witherspoon.*

into the churches on a voluntary basis—did produce a whole series of new denominations. Splintering in the Congregational churches often produced communal experiments, attempts to create a model Puritan commonwealth in intentional communities. The most successful has been the Church of Jesus Christ of Latterday Saints ("Mormons").

The first major breakaways in Presbyterianism came during the Great Awakening, in which William Tennent, Sr. (c 1673–1746) and his three sons were active. In 1726 a seminary was founded by the elder Tennent, a "Log College" which eventually became Princeton University but was at the time an offense to those in the synod who demanded a clergy educated in recognized universities. In the split between the "New Side" and the "Old Side," the revivalists had the support of the laity. When the schism was healed, the college chose John Witherspoon (1723–94) of Scotland as President. Witherspoon was the only clergyman signatory of the Declaration of Independence. Not all disputes in the Presbyterian churches were healed so readily, however. After the Cane Ridge Revival, the Cumberland Presbytery was removed for revivalism and relaxation of traditional educational standards for the clergy: reunion waited until 1906.

A critical issue among the Baptists, in addition to the Civil War and the race question, was the issue of organized missionary work. There was from the

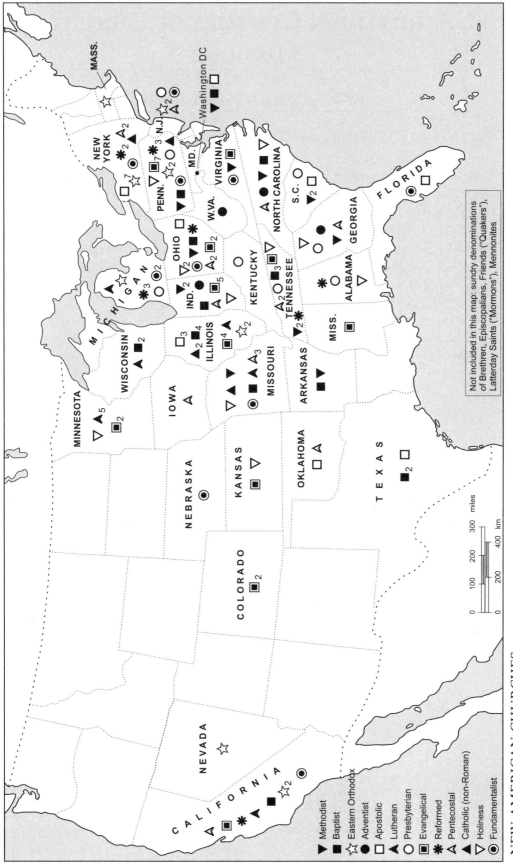

NEW AMERICAN CHURCHES

Not included in this map: sundry denominations of Brethren, Episcopalians, Friends ("Quakers"), Latterday Saints ("Mormons"), Mennonites

Methodist ▶
Baptist ■
Eastern Orthodox ☆
Adventist ●
Apostolic □
Lutheran ◀
Presbyterian ○
Evangelical ▣
Reformed ✳
Pentecostal △
Catholic (non-Roman) ◀
Holiness ▽
Fundamentalist ◉

beginning a difference between those who held a strong Calvinist doctrine of predestination and those who espoused evangelism and missions. Opposition to organized missions and other "unbiblical" efforts became strong among hyper-Calvinist Baptists, and c 1820 the Two-Seed-in-the-Spirit Predestinarian Baptists and in 1827 the Primitive Baptists were formed out of opposition to missions. Thirty years later an Anti-Missionary Baptist Convention was formed in the Mississippi Valley.

Among Methodists, after the sectional split (1844, with reunion only in 1939), the major issues were: 1) opposition to the power of the bishop, and 2) condemnation of the larger churches' surrender of membership standards. In 1830 the Methodist Protestants seceded from the Methodist Episcopal Church, again in opposition to episcopal power. The most fruitful source of division in the twentieth century has been the abandonment of membership standards. As a result of this slackening off, a number of vigorous new denominations were formed, including the Church of the Nazarene (f. 1908).

Many of the Pentecostal churches, which have had a phenomenal growth in recent decades, have a very strong emphasis upon such characteristic Wesleyan teachings as "Christian perfection" and "scriptural holiness." Whatever the form of words, the central question remains whether the church is one phase of the prevailing culture or an authentic counter-culture.

## THE RISE OF MODERN MISSIONS

*The Church exists by mission just as a fire exists by burning.* — Emil Brunner

WHEN Joseph I. Parker prepared his *Statistical Survey* and *Directory of World Missions* for the International Missionary Conference at Madras (1938), he discovered that two-thirds of all missionaries in the field were sent by the Free Churches. And of those who came from the established churches, the overwhelming majority had as background either Pietism (German, Swiss, Dutch and Scandinavian) or Wesleyanism (inside or outside the Church of England).

During the "Great Century of Christian Missions" (Kenneth Scott Latourette's phrase) the base of Christian outreach shifted from its foundation for hundreds of years: the military, political, and financial support of Christian rulers. The new base became the voluntary gifts of millions of ordinary church members, and the recruitment of tens of thousands of ordinary churchmen—chiefly young people, to go to the field.

When Gregory the Great sent Augustine of Canterbury as a missionary to Kent to re-establish the church, it was an act of high diplomacy. So was the sending of Bartholomäus Ziegenbalg (1682–1719) to Tranquebar, the first Protestant missions to Asia (see map, p.229), even though Ziegenbalg and his companion were products of Halle and had the new vision of missions. The Danish king hired and paid them. The birth of modern missions came when William Carey (1761-1834), an uneducated Baptist cobbler, became convinced of the imperative claim of the Great Commission (Mk. 16:15) upon his life. Carey taught himself Latin, Greek, Hebrew, Dutch, and French, and went out to India. For thirty years he taught Bengali, Sanskrit and Marathi at the new Fort William College in Calcutta, and he translated the entire Bible into Bengali (1809) and parts of it into twenty-four other languages and dialects. His work was supported in part by the Baptist Missionary Society (English), which he founded in 1792.

In America the beginning of modern missions dates from the students' "Society of Brethren" at Williams College and the founding of the American Board of Commissioners for Foreign Missions, 1810.

Throughout the nineteenth century, the main base of missions became those churches which had a strong belief in the participation of every member in the work of Christianity.

There was from the beginning opposition to missionary organization in some circles. However, on the other hand, and of much more lasting effect, many churches were founded to give primary emphasis to Christian missions: e.g., the Swedish Mission Covenant Church (f. 1877), the Christian and Missionary Alliance (f. 1897). A. B. Simpson (1844–1919), who founded the CMA, was also the founder of the first Bible Institute: Nyack Missionary College (f. 1882), of which there are now several hundred in the USA and Canada. The Bible Institutes or colleges are major centers for training ministers and missionaries.

In the course of missionary work, the advantages of inter-agency cooperation soon became apparent. Anglo-American Missionary Conferences began in 1854 and provided much of the impetus which led to the Edinburgh Conference: 1910. At the London Conference of 1888, delegates came from fifty-five societies in England and the colonies,

*J. Hudson Taylor.*

sixty-six societies in North America, eighteen societies in continental Europe. By 1900, at the New York Conference, 168 different societies were represented. In 1866 the Continental Missionary Conferences started meeting at Bremen; three years before that the Scandinavian Missions Conferences were launched. The first Scandinavian meetings were held on the initiative of the European branch of the Evangelical Alliance (Copenhagen, 1857; Lund, 1859; Christiania, 1861). In Scandinavian cooperation, a converted Jew—Christian H. Kalker (1803–86)—was for a generation the guiding spirit.

Among new agencies which expressed the broad and democratic basis of modern foreign missions and which made use of the most diverse talents, the China Inland Mission (CIM) was especially important. The CIM was a "faith mission," living on the free support of persons who responded according to their belief and substance. It became the largest single mission in China. The founder of the CIM (f. 1865) was J. Hudson Taylor (1832–1905).

The missionary agencies operated on

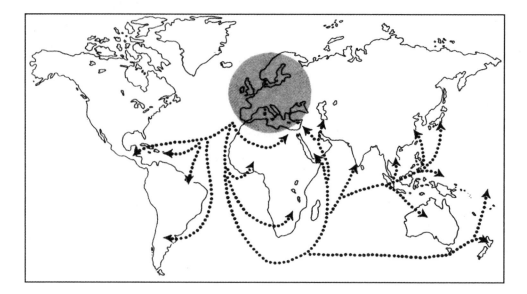

**AUSTRIA**
1829 — Leopold Foundation

**BELGIUM**
1857 — American College
Congregation of the Immaculate
Heart of Mary

**DENMARK**
1821 — Danish Missionary Society
"Folk Schools"

**ENGLAND**
London: 1826 — Beginning of Asbury Park
Conferences
1792 — Baptist Missionary Society
1795 — London Missionary Society
1799 — Church Missionary Society
1804 — British and Foreign Bible Society
1808 — London Missionary Society for the
Propogation of Christianity
among the Jews
1867 — Hebrew-Christian Alliance
Oxford: Universities Mission to Central Africa
Regions Beyond Missionary Union
Worldwide Evangelization Crusade

Society of St. Joseph

**FINLAND**
1859 — Finnish Missionary Society
Scandinavian Missionary Conferences:
1857 — Copenhagen
1859 — Lund
1861 — Christiania (Oslo)

**FRANCE**
Paris: 1822 — Paris Evangelical Missionary
Society

Paris: Societé des Missions Etrangers
1856 — Society of the Orient
1812 — Sisters of Providence of Portieux
1845 — Assumptionists
Sisterhood of Our Lady of Sion

**GERMANY**
Berlin: 1800 — Jänicke Mission School
1822 — Berlin Society for the Promotion
of Christianity among the Jews
1824 — Berlin Missionary Society
Bremen: 1836 — Bremen Missionary Society
1855 — Committee for German
Evangelical Missions:
1863 — Malmö
1885 — Gothenburg
1866 — Beginning of Continental
Missionary Conferences
Leipzig: 1848 — Leipzig Mission Institutum
Judaicum
Barmen: 1828 — Rhineland Mission
1836 — Gossner Mission
1836 — North German Missionary Society
Westphalia: 1836 — Kaiserswerth Deaconess
Association
Bavaria: 1841 — Neuendettelsau Mission
Hermannsburg: 1849 — Hermannsburg Missionary
Society
1882 — Neukirchen Mission
Liebenzell: 1899 — Liebenzell Mission
Tübingen: 1906 — Institute for Medical Missions

1838 — Ludwig Missionary Union
1875 — Society of the Divine Word

 **IRELAND**
1930 — Society of St. Patrick for Foreign Missions

 **ITALY**
1805 — Picpus Fathers
1816 — Society of Mary ("Marists")
1816 — Oblates of Immaculate Virgin Mary
1843 — Association of the Holy Childhood
1855 — Salesians of Don Bosco
1859 — American College
1862 — Congregatio pro Negotiis Ritus Orientalis
1887 — Society of St. Charles Borromeo
1917 — Missionary Union of the Clergy

**NETHERLANDS**
Zeist: 1793 — Herrnhuter Missions
1797 — Netherlands Missionary Society
1887 — Beginning of Dutch Missionary Conferences

.................................................................

Steyl: 1839 — Holy Ghost Fathers

**NORWAY**
1842 — Norwegian Mission

**SCOTLAND**
1796 — Scottish Missionary Society

**SWEDEN**
1835 — Swedish Missionary Society

**SWITZERLAND**
1780 — Basel Society for Christianity
1815 — Basel Mission
1830 — Swiss Evangelical Hebrew Mission
1900 — Swiss union for Missions to Muslims

1830 — Oblates of St. Francis de Sales

 Protestant

 Roman Catholic

*355*

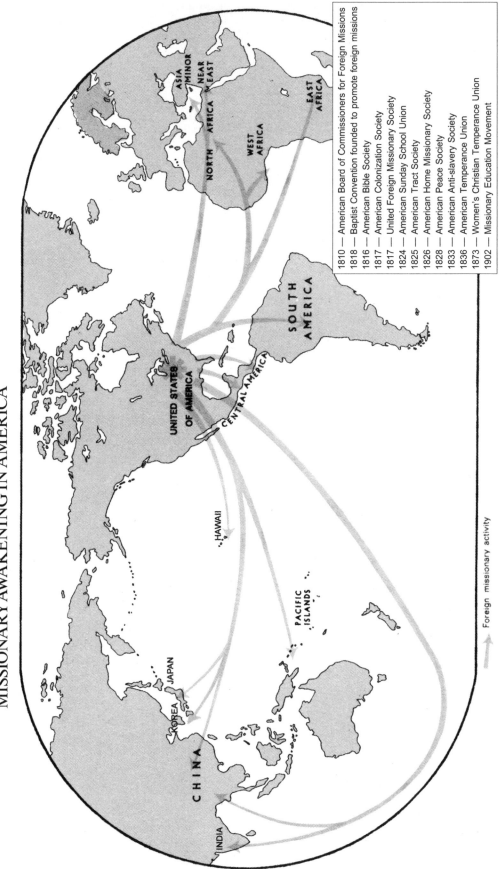

## MISSIONARY AWAKENING IN AMERICA

1810 — American Board of Commissioners for Foreign Missions
1818 — Baptist Convention founded to promote foreign missions
1816 — American Bible Society
1817 — American Colonization Society
1824 — United Foreign Missionary Society
1825 — American Sunday School Union
1826 — American Tract Society
1828 — American Home Missionary Society
1833 — American Peace Society
1836 — American Anti-slavery Society
1873 — American Temperance Union
1902 — Women's Christian Temperance Union
— Missionary Education Movement

→ Foreign missionary activity

ASIA MINOR
NEAR EAST
NORTH AFRICA
WEST AFRICA
EAST AFRICA
UNITED STATES OF AMERICA
CENTRAL AMERICA
SOUTH AMERICA
HAWAII
PACIFIC ISLANDS
CHINA
KOREA
JAPAN
INDIA

*Moody and Sankey at the Brooklyn Rink.*

a broad front. Almost all of them were active in the founding of colleges and other institutions. At one time 1/3 of all those in Who's Who in China had been educated in Protestant schools, and in 1931 nine-tenths of all trained nurses in China were Christians.

The United States became the chief launching pad for new Protestant missions and missionary personnel during the nineteenth century. In Roman Catholic missions, France was the greatest source of new orders and support. In the nineteenth century, c 160 new orders were established in the Roman Catholic Church, most of them devoted to home or foreign missions. Some of them, like the White Fathers— f. 1867 by Charles Lavigerie (1825– 92)—were made responsible for whole sectors of the church's mission.

The most important single event in America was the 1886 Student Conference at Northfield, Massachusetts, which set aside the "Mount Hermon Hundred" for the mission field. By 1920 over 20,000 young people had gone to the field under the impress of the Student Volunteer Movement (SVM).

One of the major changes during the "Great Century" was the growing participation of women in missionary work. At the opening of the century there were very few women, but by the end of the period they counted for slightly more than 50 percent of overseas staffs.

Important for the current encounter between the high religions is the fact that Christian missions produced a vigorous response in Islam, Hinduism and Buddhism. As early as 1828 the Brahmo Samaj was founded in an effort to resist Christian missionaries and to reform Hinduism. At the 1893 World Parliament of Religions, Swami Vivekenanda (1863–1902) presented Hinduism in a form which eventually won followers in the United States. The Vedanta Society which he founded in 1897 has several centers in major cities. In 1875 the Ahmadiya movement was founded at Lahore, sponsoring Muslim missions in Europe and North America. During the 1960s Zen Buddhism gained a wide following, especially among students, and even Soka Gakkai was reported to have over 60,000 adherents in the United States.

The "Great Century of Christian Missions" has for many now moved into the age of inter-religious dialogue, of which the *Journal of Ecumenical Studies* (f. 1963) is a significant instrument.

357

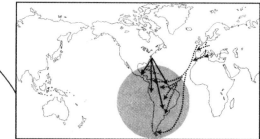

**ARGENTINA**

1836 — American Methodist Missionary in Buenos Aires

1853 — Nineteen Franciscan missionaries arrive

1858 — American Bible Society at work

**BOLIVIA**

1836 — Franciscan missionary group arrives from Europe

1901 — American Methodist mission

**BRAZIL**

Late 19th century — Pallotini, Society of the Divine Word, Italian Capuchins, Jesuits, French Dominicans, Belgian Benedictines, Holy Ghost Fathers, Italian Salesians and Franciscans at work

1819 — American Bible Society sends 500 Bibles for school use.

1835 — American Methodist mission

1892 — Help for Brazil Mission assisting Congregational Christians

**CHILE**

1836 — Group of Franciscan missionaries arrives from Europe

1855 — First Protestant church (Valparaiso)

**COLOMBIA**

1853 — Representative of American and Foreign Christian Union at work

1856 — Presbyterian mission begun at Bogotá

1902 — Augustinians, Capuchins and Jesuits at work

**CUBA**

1837–41 — Secularization of the properties of religious orders

**ECUADOR**

1860 — Franciscans renew work

1897 — Christian and Missionary Alliance mission begun

**FALKLAND ISLANDS**

1869 — Waite H. Stirling (1829–1923) made Anglican bishop

**GUATEMALA**

1852 — Papal Concordat

1882 — Protestant work begun in Guatemala City

1891 — Central American Mission at work

**MEXICO**

1865 — American and Foreign Christian Union at work in Monterey

1872 — Renewal of Roman Catholic missions by Josephites Latin America Missionary Conferences: Mexico City, 1888 and 1897

1895 — Priests from seminar of SS. Peter and Paul enter Baja, California

1900 — Jesuits renew missions to Indians

1902 — YMCA begins work

**NICARAGUA**

1849 — Moravians at work

**PANAMA**

1909 — Non-denominational Protestant work begins

**PARAGUAY**

1870 — Suicide of dictator F. S. Lopez

1903 — Protestant San Pedro Mission founded for work among Indians of the Chaco

1910 — Society of Divine Word sends missionaries

**PATAGONIA**

Patagonian Missionary Society founded by Alan Francis Gardner (1794–1851)

**PERU**

1822 — British and Foreign Bible Society agent in Peru

**VENEZUELA**

1835 — Independence of New Granada recognized by Pope

1887 — Agent of American Bible Society enters Venezuela

1894 — Beginning of Capuchin mission

1897 — Northern Presbyterian missionary in Caracas

# MISSIONS IN ASIA

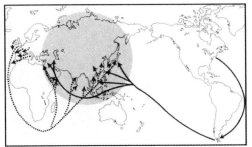

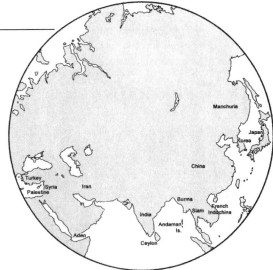

## ADEN
1885 — Free Church of Scotland
1889 — Arabian Mission (Dutch Reformed)

## ANDAMAN IS.
1885 — SPG

## BURMA (mod. MYANMAR)
1813 — Adoniram Judson (1788–1850)
1842 — Italian Oblates of Mary Immaculate

## CEYLON (mod. SRI LANKA)
1804 — London Missionary Society
1812 — English Baptists
1814 — English Wesleyans
1817 — CMS
c 1830 — Goa Oratorians
1847 — Oblates of Mary Immaculate

## CHINA
1807 — LMS
1830 — ABC
1831 — Lazarists
1834 — Jesuits
1857–58 — T'ai P'ing Rebellion
1870 — Tientsin anti-foreign outbreak
1900 — Boxer Rebellion; U.S. indemnity used for
scholarships for Chinese students
China Missionary Conference:
Shanghai — 1877; 1890; 1907

## FRENCH INDOCHINA (m0d. VIETNAM)
1833 — Decree vs. Christianity
1875 — Sisters of Providence of Portieux

## INDIA
1787 — CMS
1793 — William Carey arrives
1829 — Alexander Duff (1806–78)
1829 — John Wilson (1804–75) of Scottish Missionary
Society
1837 — Jesuits
1845 — Oblates of St. Francis de Sales
North India Missionary Conferences:
Calcutta 1855; Benares 1857; Lahore 1862
South India Missionary Conferences:
Ootacamund 1858; Bangalore 1879; Madras 1900
All-India Missionary Conferences:
Allahabad 1873; Calcutta 1882; Bombay 1892;
Madras 1902; Calcutta 1912

## IRAN
1833 — Basel Mission
1834 — ABC
c 1840 — Lazarists

## JAPAN
1859 — Paris Foreign Missionary Society (Roman Catholic)
1859 — Episcopal Mission (American)
1859 — American Presbyterians
1859 — Dutch Reformed Church Mission (American)
Japan Missionary Conferences:
Yokohama 1872; Tokyo 1878; Osaka 1883; Tokyo
1900

## KOREA
1865 — National Bible Society of Scotland
1909 — Bavarian Benedictines

## MANCHURIA
1875 — Sisters of Providence of Portieux

## PALESTINE (mod. ISRAEL)
1818 — ABC
1820 — London Missionary Society for Promoting
Christianity among the Jews
1840 — Michael Solomon Alexander appointed Bishop of
Jerusalem
1846–79 — Samuel Gobat, Bishop of Jerusalem
1847 — Pius IX appoints a Patriarch of Jerusalem
1851 — CMS
1878 — White Fathers

## SIAM (mod. THAILAND)
1828 — Netherlands Missionary Society
1831 — ABC
1840 — American Presbyterians

## SYRIA
1780 — Melchite Uniate Movement
1823 — ABC in Beirut
1831 — Jesuits
1860 — Massacres of the Maronites
1863 — ABC Syrian Protestant College incorporated

## TURKEY
1830 — Armenian Uniates
1831 — ABC
1856 — CMS

*359*

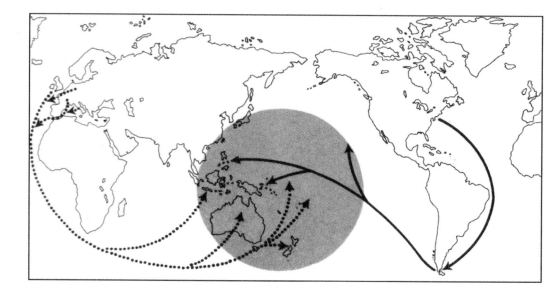

**AUSTRAL ISLANDS**
1820 — Christianity brought by native Protestants from
        Raiatea

**BISMARCK ARCHIPELAGO**
1874 — Australian Methodists

**CAROLINES**
Late 19th century — Spanish Capuchins
1852 — ABC, including Hawaiians

**CELEBES**
c 1890 — Dutch missionaries at work

**COOK ISLANDS**
1821 — Protestant work begins
1894 — Picpus Fathers

**DUTCH EAST INDIES (mod. INDONESIA)**
1797 — Netherlands Missionary Society
Malay Archipelago: c 1815 — Netherlands Bible Society

**FIJI**
1830 — Christianity brought by native Protestants from Tahiti
1835 — English Wesleyans
1842 — Marists
1857 — Chief Thakombau baptized

**FUTUNA IS.**
1837 — Marists

**GAMBIER IS.**
1834 — Picpus Fathers

**GILBERT IS.**
1857 — ABC

**HAWAII**
1820 — ABC party arrives
1823 — Widow of Kamehameha baptized
1828 — Picpus Fathers — Father Damien
**JAVA**
1814 — LMS
1847 — Netherlands Mennonite Missionary Society
Batavia: 1833 — ABC
1835 — Rhineland Missionary Society

**LESSER SUNDA IS.**
1864 — Jesuits

**LOYALTY IS.**
1834 — Christianity brought by native Protestants from
        Tonga

**MARIANAS**
1900 — ABC Mission in Guam

**MARQUESAS IS.**
1797 — LMS
1839 — Picpus Fathers

**MARSHALL IS.**
1857 — ABC

**MOLUCCAS**
1903 — Holy Heart of Jesus (Dutch) Mission

**NEW CALEDONIA**
1843 — Marists

**NEW GUINEA (PAPUA NEW GUINEA)**
1871 — LMS
1895 — Society of Divine Word

Hawaii

Marianas

Marshall Is.

Carolines

Sarawak

Moluccas

Bismarck Arch.

Gilbert Is.

Celebes

Sumatra

New Guinea

Dutch East Indies

Solomon Is.

Santa Cruz Is.

Marquesas Is.

Java

Lesser Sunda Is.

Rotuma

Wallis Is.

Samoan Is.

Tuamotu Arch.

New Hebrides

Fiji

Futuna Is.

Niue Is.

Cook Is.

Tahiti

New Caledonia

Loyalty Is.

Tonga Is.

Austral Is.

Gambier Is.

New Zealand

## NEW HEBRIDES
1839 — Christianity brought by native Protestants from Samoa
1842 — LMS

## NEW ZEALAND
1814 — First Worship Service among Maoris led by Samuel Marsden (CMS)

## NIUE IS.
1846 — Converted by native Protestants from Samoa

## ROTUMA
1839 — Christianity brought by native Protestants

## SAMOAN IS.
1830 — Christianity brought by native Methodists from Tonga
1845 — Marists

## SANTA CRUZ IS.
1878 – Anglican mission

## SARAWAK (MALAYSIA)
1847 — Anglican mission
1901 — Methodist mission of Chinese Christians

## SOLOMON IS.
1845 — Marists
1851 — Anglican mission

## SUMATRA
1859 — Jesuits

## TAHITI
1797 — Mission ship Duff lands (LMS)
1815 — Eimeo and Tahiti officially Christianized under chief Pomare II
1828 — Mamaia cult

## TONGA IS.
1822 — English Wesleyans
c 1880 — "Free Church" formed under King of Tonga

## TUAMOTO ARCHIPELAGO
1817 — Christianity brought by native Protestants from Tahiti

## WALLIS IS.
1834 — Christianity brought by native Protestants from Vavau
1837 — Marists

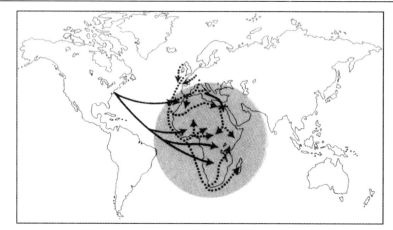

**ALGERIA**
1838 — Roman Catholic bishop appointed for Algiers
1867 — White Fathers founded by C. Lavigerie (1825–92),
Archbishop of Algiers

**ANGOLA**
1873 — Holy Ghost Fathers
1878 — English Baptists
1880 — ABC mission from America

**BRITISH SOMALILAND (mod. SOMALILAND)**
1892 — Capuchina

**CAMEROON**
1848 — English Baptists

**CONGO**
1878 — Holy Ghost Fathers
1878 — English Baptists
1878 — Livingstone Inland Mission
1885 — Christian and Missionary Alliance
1888 — Scheutvelders

**DAHOMEY (mod. BENIN)**
1861 — Society of African Missions

**EGYPT**
1741 — Coptic Patriarch of Jerusalem becomes Roman
Catholic
1825 — CMS mission
1854 — American Presbyterians — "The American Mission"

**ETHIOPIA**
1830 — CMS (including Samuel Gobat)
1839 — Italian Lazarists
1855 — Group from Pilgrim Mission of St. Christoma

**FERNANDO PO**
1841 — English Baptists

**FRENCH EQUATORIAL AFRICA (mod. CHAD)**
1842 — ABC
1849 — Sisters of the Immaculate Conception of Castres

**FRENCH GUINEA (mod. GUINEA-BISSAU)**
1855 — CMS
1878 — Holy Ghost Fathers

**GAMBIA**
1821 — English Wesleyans

**GOLD COAST (mod. GHANA)**
1752 — SPG
1828 — Basel Mission
1834 — English Wesleyans
1879 — Society of African Missions (Roman Catholic)

**IVORY COAST**
1895 — Society of African Missions (Roman Catholic)

**KENYA**
1862 — United Methodist Free Churches
1880s — CMS
1895 — Mill Hill Fathers
1902 — American Quakers
1913 — Kikuyu Conference

**LIBERIA**
1821 — American Baptist mission (Lott Carey)
1827 — Basel Mission
1833 — Methodist Episcopal Church (American)

**MADAGASCAR**
1818 — LMS
1836 — Bible published in Malagasy
1836–61 — Severe persecution under Rànavàlona I
1868 — Rànavàlona II baptized

**MAURITIUS**
1842 — Holy Ghost Fathers
1854 — Anglican bishopric established

**MOROCCO**
Spanish Franciscans
1880s — North Africa Mission
1908 — French Brothers Minor

**MOZAMBIQUE**
1881 — Jesuits renew work

**NIGERIA**
1840 — United Presbyterian Mission of Scotland
1842 — CMS
1842 — English Wesleyans
1850 — Southern Baptists (American)
1868 — Society of African Missions (Roman Catholic)

**NORTHERN RHODESIA (mod. ZAMBIA)**
1910 — English Wesleyans
1914 — South African General Mission

## NYASALAND (mod. MALAWI)
1876 — Universities' Mission to Central Africa
1876 — Livingstonia Mission (Church of Scotland)
1888 — Dutch Reformed mission from South Africa

## RÉUNION
1835 — Congregation of Holy Heart of Mary

## RWANDA
1907 — Bethel Mission Society
1927 — East Africa Revival

## SEYCHELLES
1863 — Capuchins of Savoy

## SENEGAL
1819 — Sisters of St. Joseph of Cluny
1833 — Holy Ghost Fathers
1862 — Paris Evangelical Missionary Society

## SIERRA LEONE
1806 — CMS
1811 — English Wesleyans
1864 — Holy Ghost Fathers

## SOUTH AFRICA
1799 — LMS (Robert Moffat [1795–1883])
1813 — W. Shaw, first British Wesleyan missionary in
    Kaffraria
1817 — Beginning of work of Moravian bishop Hans Peter
    Halbeck (1784–1840)
1829 — Rhineland Missionary Society
1834 — Berlin Missionary Society
1850 — Oblates put in charge of Roman Catholic work in
    Natal

1882 — Mariannhill, near Durban (Trappists)
1886 — South African Missionary Society
1916 — Lovedale School for Bantus founded, principal —
    James Stewart (1831–1905)

## SOUTHERN RHODESIA (mod. ZIMBABWE)
1854 — Moffat among the Matabele (LMS)
1879 — White Fathers at Lake Tanganyika

## SOUTH WEST AFRICA (mod. NAMIBIA)
1892 — Assigned to Oblates of Mary Immaculate

## SUDAN
1847 — Roman Catholic group arrives for missionary work
1880s — Rebellion of the Mahdi
1885 — Death of Charles G. Gordon at Khartoum
1913 — Sudan United Missions

## TOGO
1847 — North German Missionary Society
1860 — Society of African Missions (Roman Catholic)

## TUNISIA
1843 — Vicariate Apostolic for Tunis; College founded

## UGANDA
1874 — C. M. Stanley
1877 — CMS
1879 — White Fathers
1964 — Paul VI canonizes Ugandan Martyrs

## ZANZIBAR
1840s — CMS
1859 — Sisters of Mary

# D. The Ecumenical Movement

## THE YMCA AND YWCA

THE Young Men's Christian Association was founded in London in 1844 by George Williams (1821–1905). It became in two generations a worldwide laymen's movement, and the young leaders it produced joined with leaders of the Younger Churches of Africa and Asia to launch the modern ecumenical movement. The YWCA was founded in England in 1855.

The first student YMCAs were founded at the University of Michigan and the University of Virginia in 1858. The first college YWCA was at Illinois State College (Normal) in 1873. In 1877 Luther Wishard (1854–1925) became secretary of student work for the YMCA in the United States.

In 1886, under the leadership of Dwight L. Moody (1837–90), a conference was held at Northfield, Massachusetts, which profoundly influenced the future of missions and ecumenism. Moody had been president of the Chicago area YMCA for twenty years and was the leading (lay) evangelist of his day. He was accompanied by an associate, Ira David Sankey (1840–1908), a singer who did much to popularize gospel hymns in student circles and among the great numbers who responded to Moody's extensive preaching missions across England and America. Another of Moody's friends and associates was Henry Drummond (1851–97), whose books *Natural Law in the Spiritual World* and *The Ascent of Man* helped many to reconcile the apparently conflicting claims of Darwinism and religion, and whose lectures to students throughout the English-speaking world and in Germany were enormously influential. No association in Moody's career was more important for Christianity than the Northfield Conference of 1886, for during those days of Christian lectures, discussion and worship, the Student Volunteer Movement was launched.

Among the "Mount Hermon Hundred," who there pledged themselves to foreign missions, was John R. Mott (1865–1955), a layman who in the course of six decades (before the airplane changed travel) covered more miles for Christian causes than any other man in the faith's two millennia of existence. Nor was Moody's influence any less in England where, in spite of his own limited early education, he won the admiration and support of professors like the distinguished Old Testament scholar, George Adam Smith (1856–1942). One of Moody's greatest triumphs among students was in 1882, when he won the famous cricketer, C. T. Studd, and several friends ("the Cambridge Seven") to the cause of Christ. Studd (1862–1931) gave his life to missions, serving first in China with the China Inland Mission, then in India, and finally working in Africa from 1910 until his death. He founded the World Evangelization Crusade. His brother (also one of the "Seven") was the one who, on a student evangelism trip through American universities, brought John R. Mott to a personal decision.

In the popular mind the "Y" is associated with boys' clubs, basketball, swimming and physical culture. And it

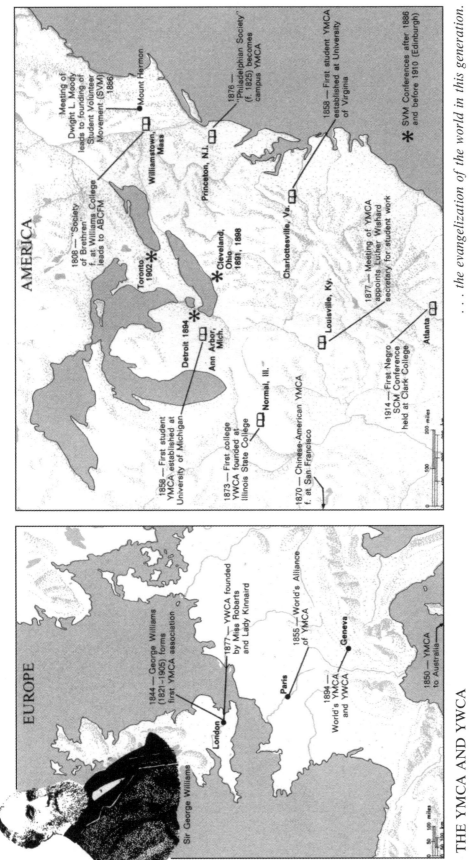

EUROPE

Sir George Williams

1844 — George Williams (1821-1905) forms first YMCA association

1877 — YWCA founded by Miss Roberts and Lady Kinnaird

London

1855 — World's Alliance of YMCA

Paris

1894 — World's YMCA and YWCA

Geneva

1850 — YMCA to Australia

AMERICA

Meeting of Dwight L. Moody leads to founding of Student Volunteer Movement (SVM) 1886

Mount Hermon

1876 — "Philadelphian Society" (f. 1825) becomes campus YMCA

Princeton, N.J.

1858 — First student YMCA established at University of Virginia

Charlottesville, Va.

* SVM Conferences after 1886 and before 1910 (Edinburgh)

1808 — "Society of Brethren" f. at Williams College leads to ABCFM

Williamstown, Mass

Toronto 1902 *

Cleveland, Ohio 1891, 1898 *

1858 — First student YMCA established at University of Michigan

Detroit 1894 *

Ann Arbor, Mich.

1873 — First college YWCA founded at Illinois State College

Normal, Ill.

1870 — Chinese-American YMCA f. at San Francisco

Louisville, Ky.

1877 — Meeting of YMCA appoints Luther Wishard secretary for student work

1914 — First Negro SCM Conference held at Clark College

Atlanta

THE YMCA AND YWCA

. . . the evangelization of the world in this generation.
— Motto of Student Volunteer Movement

365

has in fact since the beginning emphasized the importance of spiritual, mental and physical health. Because of its enormous popularity as a community center, the "Y" has also been imitated by others—notably the Young Men's Hebrew Association and the YWHA. But the "Y," in spite of its popular image, began with groups for prayer and Bible study and has consistently presented that emphasis for those who elected it. Furthermore, the "Y"—though open to associate membership of non-Christians—proclaimed its commitment to Jesus Christ as Lord and savior in its first international assembly ("Paris Platform," 1855), a formula which came to be widely used in the ecumenical movement.

The wider influence of the YMCA has been expressed in many institutional forms. One of its four chief program emphases has been continuing education, frequently in evening courses for working young men. A number of colleges and universities have grown out of this work (including Roosevelt University in Chicago). The emergency services of the "Y" in times of war have produced Special Services and expansion of the work of the chaplains. The work among refugees and war victims has been substantial in both World Wars. Symbolic is the fact that Henri Dunant (1828–1910), founder of the Red Cross and moving spirit in the first Geneva Convention (1864), was an active and avowed Christian layman of the YMCA.

## THE WORK OF JOHN R. MOTT (1865–1955)

*The layman must rise up and make Christianity what it was in the early days when every Christian was a missionary in the sense of spreading the faith.*

— John R. Mott

*John R. Mott.*

WHEN John R. Mott was asked to join the staff of the national YMCA for work among students, he agreed to do so with the understanding that he would not have to raise any money. In the course of his six decades of lay leadership, he raised more than 300 million dollars for Christian causes. Toward the end of his life, when many of the cooperative agencies to which he had devoted his energies were reaching maturity, he held representative posts in a number of international organizations:

Honorary President, World Council of Churches;

Honorary President, World's Alliance of the YMCAs;

Honorary Chairman, International Missionary Council;

Honorary Chairman, World's Student Christian Federation.

He was also long-time mentor and chief

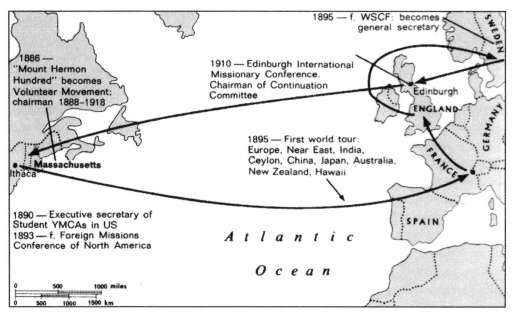

1895 — f. WSCF: becomes general secretary

1886 — "Mount Hermon Hundred" becomes Volunteer Movement; chairman 1888–1918

1910 — Edinburgh International Missionary Conference. Chairman of Continuation Committee

Edinburgh

ENGLAND

SWEDEN

GERMANY

FRANCE

Massachusetts
Ithaca

1895 — First world tour: Europe, Near East, India, Ceylon, China, Japan, Australia, New Zealand, Hawaii

SPAIN

1890 — Executive secretary of Student YMCAs in US
1893 — f. Foreign Missions Conference of North America

*Atlantic*

*Ocean*

0    500    1000 miles
0    500    1000    1500 km

THE WORK OF JOHN R. MOTT

officer of the Student Volunteer Movement, 1888–1920, until the founding of the International Missionary Council—in preparation for which he had helped to form more than seventy national councils. In 1946 he received the Nobel Peace Prize.

Mott, a Methodist, showed that peculiar combination of Pietism and administrative genius that European critics sometimes consider "typically American." He did not drink. He did not smoke. He once refused to accept as an executive secretary under his chairmanship a man who had left his wife to marry a younger woman. At the same time, he was tough in organizational matters and capable of traveling vast distances and meeting both day and night to achieve purposes he believed important. Most important of all, in the cause of Christ, was to unite the Christian forces which could help to build the Kingdom of God on earth.

After the founding of the World's Student Christian Federation (WSCF) at Vadstena Castle, Sweden, where he was elected chairman of the executive committee, Mott made the first of his many world trips.

After the first ecumenical conference at Edinburgh—in 1910—where he was elected chairman of the continuation committee, Mott traveled around the world again. On this trip he called twenty-one conferences, which resulted in the formation of the India National Christian Council, the National Christian Council of China, the General Council of Christian Missions in Korea, etc. Other world trips—e.g., in 1925–26, 1928–29—led to the creation of other national missionary councils or national Christian councils which laid global foundations for the eventual founding of the World Council of Churches.

Missionary historians called him the greatest Christian missionary since Paul. He was not just a gifted organizer: on one of his trips to Japan c 1500 young men professed Christian conversion through his speaking. Of his own constructive work, Mott said that his greatest contribution was the bringing

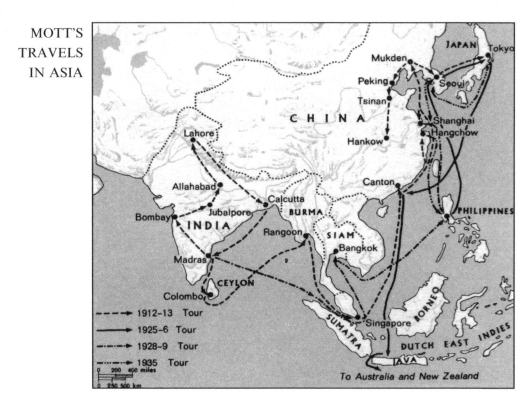

of national councils of churches into being. This very practical statement was typical of him, but it scarcely encompasses the enormous force of his personality or the great personal influence which he wielded upon all who—as Visser't Hooft's mother observed—came into the ecumenical "spider's net."

## THE WORLD'S STUDENT CHRISTIAN FEDERATION (F. 1895)

THE WSCF was founded in 1895, and most of the men who came to prominence in the ecumenical movement were trained in it or in one of its national constituent organizations. Of the later movements and conferences, W. A. Visser't Hooft (1900-85) had said that the WSCF was the place where all of the questions and issues first arose.

After the First World War a period of theological reappraisal set in among European churchmen, and it was early evident in magazine articles in *The Student World* and in the theological and Bible study units of the movement.

Key leaders at this time, besides the general secretary (W. A. Visser't Hooft), included Francis Pickens Miller (Southern Presbyterian layman, later professor, political leader in Virginia), Hanns Lilje (later leader in the "intact" church of Hanover during the *Kirchenkampf*, and in the Lutheran World Federation), Reinold von Thadden-Trieglaff (later leader in the Confessing Church, and also founder of *Kirchentag*), Pierre Maury (later leader in the Reformed Church of France), Reinhold Niebuhr (Professor at Union Theological Seminary, New York), Suzanne de Diétrich (later Associate

# THE WORLD'S STUDENT CHRISTIAN FEDERATION
## (F. 1895)

Christiania **1881** **1897** Uppsala

Vadstena Castle

**1895**

Nyborg Staand Copenhagen

**1** **1893**

**1909**

Oxford

**1925**

Sorø **1882** **5**

**2**

**1909** **1902**

Gross
Almorode

High Leigh

**1924**

Zeist

**1905**

Eisenach Castle

**1898**

Versailles

La Roche Dieu

**1900** **1938**

W. A. Visser't Hooft
1932—general secretary of WSCF;
gen. sec. of WCC for 27 years

**1920**

Geneva

Château de
Bossey

Beatenberg

**1946**

1940 — World
Student Relief
founded

**1911**

Constantinople

**6**

**1919-22**

Smyrna

CHINA

Peking

**1922**

JAPAN
Tokyo

**1907**

INDIA

Mysore

**1928**

SOUTH
AFRICA

**1**
**1896**

AUSTRALIA

**1**
**1904**

NEW
ZEALAND

**1**
**1904**

| | WSCF Ecumenical Conference |
|---|---|
| **1** | Student Christian Movement |
| **2** | German Student Christian Alliance |
| **3** | Norwegian Students' Missionary Union |
| **4** | Swedish Student Missionary Association |
| **5** | Academic Missionary Union |
| **6** | Mideast Christian Student Conferences |

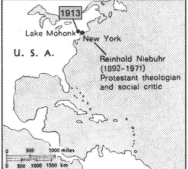

**1913**

Lake Mohonk New York

U. S. A.

Reinhold Niebuhr
(1892–1971)
Protestant theologian
and social critic

*W. A. Visser't Hooft.*

Director of the Ecumenical Institute, Château de Bossey), and William Temple (later Anglican archbishop).

During World War II Visser't Hooft was a major contact between Christian organizations and Jewish agencies, and also with Dietrich Bonhoeffer and others of the Christian resistance to Nazism in Germany.

John R. Mott was appointed general secretary of the WSCF from 1895 to 1920 and chairman from 1920 to 1928. True to his vision of a world movement, the 1907 Conference was held in Tokyo—the first Christian world conference to be held in the Orient. Among distinguished leaders who came into the ecumenical movement through the

Asian sector of the WSCF were C. Y. Chêng (1881–1940) of China, Daniel T. Niles (1908–70) of Ceylon, and Sarah Chakko (1905–54) of India.

Both the YMCA and the WSCF were concerned for the plight of students during World War I—both Asian students stranded in belligerent countries and also students caught in the war zones and in the German inflation of 1922–23. An Emergency Relief Committee was formed in London in 1919 and for several years following the war the money raised was virtually the only thing that kept some hundreds of students alive. The World Student Service (WSSF) grew out of this experience, and it did important work also in the years of the Depression, World War II, and post-war rehabilitation.

Although grounded in Christian profession of faith, with strong attention to the Bible and the recovery of Christian theology, the WSCF has operated on a broad front of human concerns: peace, racial justice, opposition to colonial exploitation of subject peoples. In this work it has not won the affection of the rulers of the Third Reich and other dictatorships, but it has raised up several generations of churchmen of broad vision and deep Christian compassion.

## ECUMENICS IN THE 19TH AND 20TH CENTURIES

*The divisions of Christendom may be a source of weakness in Christian countries, but in non-Christian lands they are a sin and a scandal.*

— Bishop V. S. Azariah, 1927

THE first great ecumenical conference was the International Missionary Con-

ference which was held in Edinburgh, Scotland, 1910. The administrative leaders were John R. Mott and Joseph H. Oldham (1874–1969). Mott had come up through the YMCA; Oldham was throughout his long life a leading statesman in foreign missions. It was among Christian minorities in Asia and

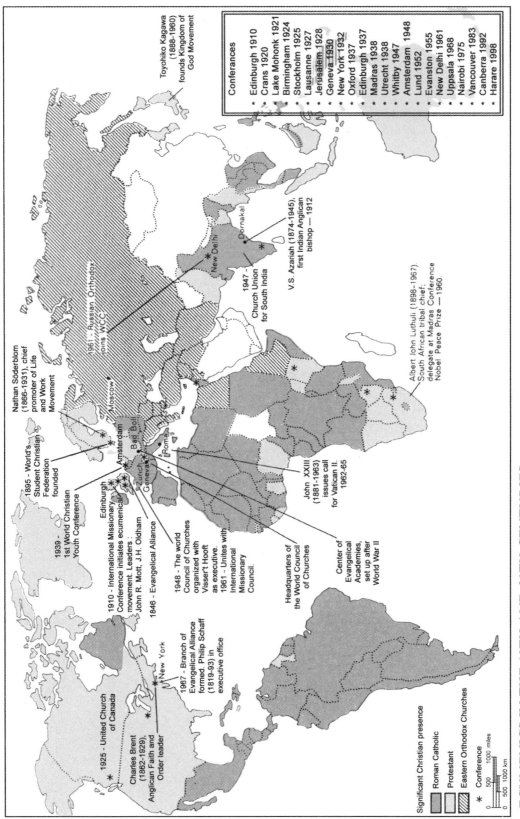

ECUMENICS IN THE 19TH AND 20TH CENTURIES

Significant Christian presence
- Roman Catholic
- Protestant
- Eastern Orthodox Churches
* Conference

0  500  1000 miles
0  500  1000 km

Conferences
* Edinburgh 1910
* Crans 1920
* Lake Mohonk 1921
* Birmingham 1924
* Stockholm 1925
* Lausanne 1927
* Jerusalem 1928
* Geneva 1930
* New York 1932
* Oxford 1937
* Edinburgh 1937
* Madras 1938
* Utrecht 1938
* Whitby 1947
* Amsterdam 1948
* Lund 1952
* Evanston 1955
* New Delhi 1961
* Uppsala 1968
* Nairobi 1975
* Vancouver 1983
* Canberra 1992
* Harare 1998

Toyohiko Kagawa (1888-1960) founds Kingdom of God Movement

Nathan Söderblom (1866-1931), chief promoter of Life and Work Movement

1895 - World's Student Christian Federation founded

1939 - 1st World Christian Youth Conference

1910 - International Missionary Conference initiates ecumenical movement. Leaders : John R. Mott; J.H. Oldham

1846 - Evangelical Alliance

1948 - The world Council of Churches organized with Visser't Hooft as executive.

1961 - Unites with International Missionary Council.

1967 - Branch of Evangelical Alliance formed. Philip Schaff (1819-93) in executive office

1925 - United Church of Canada

Charles Brent (1862-1929), Anglican Faith and Order leader

1961 - Russian Orthodox joins WCC

1947 - Church Union for South India

V.S. Azariah (1874-1945), first Indian Anglican bishop — 1912

Albert John Luthuli (1898-1967), South African tribal chief; delegate at Madras Conference Nobel Peace Prize — 1960

John XXIII (1881-1963) issues call for Vatican II; 1962-65

Headquarters of the World Council of Churches

Center of Evangelical Academies, set up after World War II

Moscow
New Delhi
Dornakal
Amsterdam
Bad Boll
Rome
Zurich
Geneva
Edinburgh
New York

371

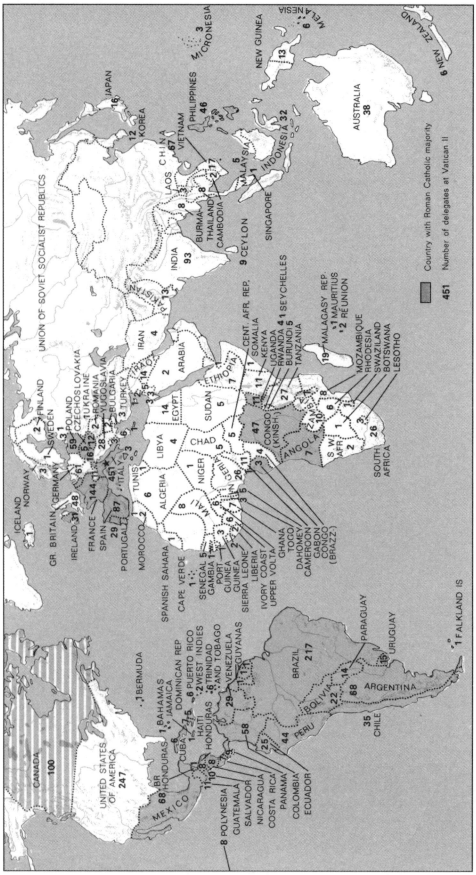

REPRESENTATION AT VATICAN II (1962–65)

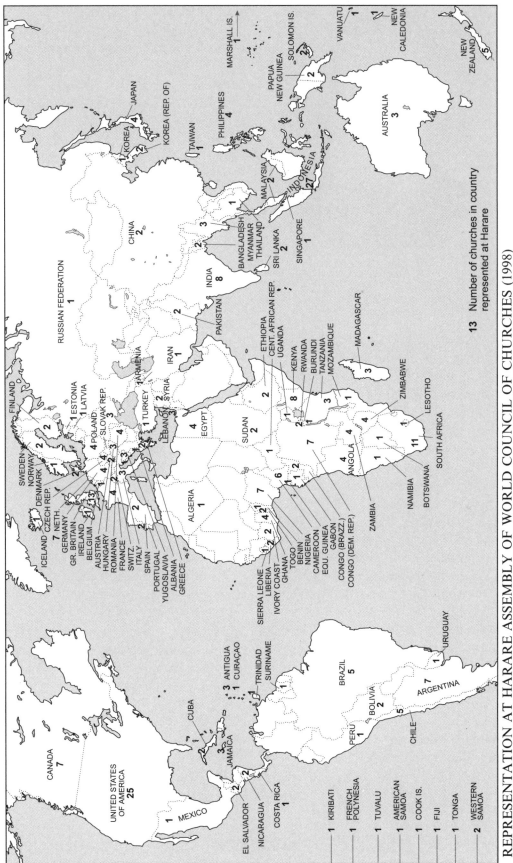

MARSHALL IS. 1

VANUATU 1
NEW CALEDONIA 1
NEW ZEALAND 5

SOLOMON IS. 2
PAPUA NEW GUINEA 2

AUSTRALIA 3

JAPAN 4
KOREA 4
KOREA (REP. OF) 3
TAIWAN 1
PHILIPPINES 4

MALAYSIA 2
INDONESIA 27

RUSSIAN FEDERATION 1
CHINA 2

BANGLADESH 1
MYANMAR 3
THAILAND 2
SRI LANKA 2
SINGAPORE 1

INDIA 8
PAKISTAN 2

IRAN 1
TURKEY 1
ARMENIA 1
SYRIA 2
LEBANON 3

EGYPT 4

ETHIOPIA 2
CENT. AFRICAN REP.
UGANDA

KENYA 8
RWANDA 2
BURUNDI 2
TANZANIA 3
MOZAMBIQUE 1
MADAGASCAR 3

SUDAN 2

ZIMBABWE 1
LESOTHO 1
SOUTH AFRICA 11

FINLAND 2
SWEDEN 2
NORWAY 2
DENMARK 1
ESTONIA 1
LATVIA 1
POLAND 4
SLOVAK REP. 3

ICELAND 1
CZECH REP. 7
GERMANY 11
GR. BRITAIN 13
IRELAND
BELGIUM
AUSTRIA 4
HUNGARY 4
ROMANIA 2
SWITZ. 3
FRANCE 3
SPAIN
PORTUGAL
ITALY 2
YUGOSLAVIA
ALBANIA
GREECE 2

NETH. 2

ALGERIA 1

SIERRA LEONE 1
LIBERIA 2
IVORY COAST 2
GHANA 1
TOGO 4
BENIN 2
NIGERIA 1
CAMEROON 6
EQU. GUINEA 1
GABON 1
CONGO (BRAZZ.) 7
CONGO (DEM. REP.) 7

ANGOLA 4
NAMIBIA 1
BOTSWANA
ZAMBIA 1

KIRIBATI 1
FRENCH POLYNESIA 1
TUVALU 1
AMERICAN SAMOA 1
COOK IS. 1
FIJI 1
TONGA 1
WESTERN SAMOA 2

CANADA 7
UNITED STATES OF AMERICA 25
MEXICO 1

CUBA 2
JAMAICA 3
ANTIGUA 3
CURAÇAO 1
TRINIDAD 1
SURINAME 1

EL SALVADOR 2
NICARAGUA 2
COSTA RICA 1

BRAZIL 5
PERU
BOLIVIA 2
CHILE 5
ARGENTINA 7
URUGUAY 1

**13** Number of churches in country represented at Harare

## REPRESENTATION AT HARARE ASSEMBLY OF WORLD COUNCIL OF CHURCHES (1998)

*John D. Rockefeller, Jr., Christian philanthropist, donor of the Ecumenical Institute near Geneva.*

Africa, divided by denominational differences at home base but facing great ethnic blocs of traditional religions (Hinduism, Buddhism, Confucianism, Islam), that the "sin of a divided church" first became a practical as well as theological issue.

The scandal of recurring war between "Christian" nations has also been an ecumenical reality, and has deepened ecumenism's devotion to peace. The momentum of Edinburgh was regained with difficulty before Crans (1920), because of the alienation of German members. The Preparatory Committee for the World Council of Churches (f. 1938), however, kept its international contacts alive throughout World War II and moved rapidly to found the Council (1948).

Following Edinburgh, three powerful movements developed: the International Missionary Council (f. 1921); the "Faith and Order" movement (f. 1920 in Geneva); the "Life and Work" movement (f. 1925 at Stockholm). All three were brought together in the World Council of Churches.

The man who steered the World Council through many difficult years was Willem A. Visser't Hooft, who began as an understudy of Mott in the World's Alliance of the YMCAs, served for ten years as Executive Secretary of the WSCF and from 1938 to 1968 as Executive Secretary of the WCC.

At Edinburgh all but a handful of delegates were white and Protestant. At the New Delhi Assembly (1961) the Council was joined by the Eastern Orthodox Churches of Russia, Romania, Bulgaria and Poland, and by ten independent African churches.

Roman Catholic participation in ecumenism was slow developing, in spite of the important unofficial contributions of a few men like Jacques Maritain (1882–1973) and Yves Congar, O.P. (b. 1904). *Mortalium Animos* (6 January 1928) condemned ecumenism as theological indifference. Churchmen were forbidden to attend the First Assembly (Amsterdam, 1948) as observers. With the accession of John XXIII (pope: 1958–63) and his appointment of Augustine Bea (1881–1968) to head up a new ecumenical office in the Vatican, Roman Catholic participation in the dialogue became very active. At Vatican II (1962–65) non-Roman observers were accorded full fraternal courtesies; Roman Catholic observers had attended Council meetings since Lund (1952).

In 1969 Paul VI (pope: 1963) visited the World Council office in Geneva, opening his greeting with the words, "My name is Peter," referring to Mt. 16:18. There are no immediate plans for the Roman Catholic Church to join the other denominations in the WCC.

# CHRISTIAN RENEWAL IN POST-WAR GERMANY

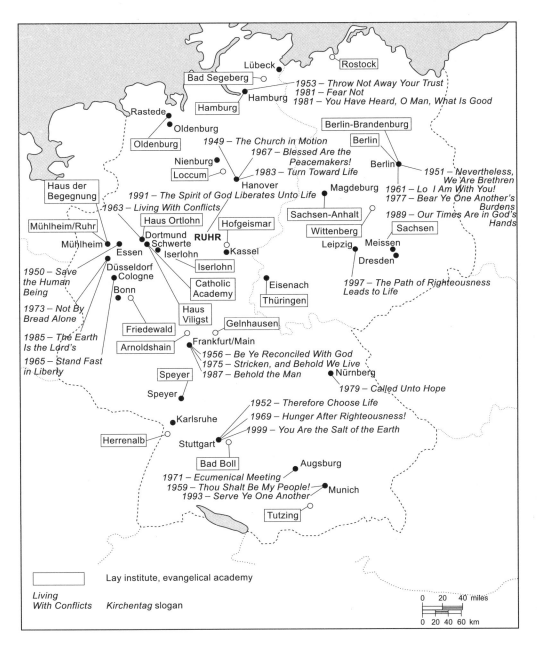

Lübeck
Rostock
Bad Segeberg
1953 – Throw Not Away Your Trust
1981 – Fear Not
Hamburg
1981 – You Have Heard, O Man, What Is Good
Hamburg

Berlin-Brandenburg
Rastede
Oldenburg
Berlin
1949 – The Church in Motion
Oldenburg
1967 – Blessed Are the
Peacemakers!
Berlin
Nienburg
1951 – Nevertheless,
Loccum
1983 – Turn Toward Life
We Are Brethren
Magdeburg
1961 – Lo I Am With You!
Haus der
Hanover
1977 – Bear Ye One Another's
Begegnung
1991 – The Spirit of God Liberates Unto Life
Burdens
1963 – Living With Conflicts
1989 – Our Times Are in God's
Sachsen-Anhalt
Hands
Haus Ortlohn
Hofgeismar
Mühlheim/Ruhr
Dortmund
RUHR
Wittenberg
Sachsen
Schwerte
Mühlheim
Leipzig
Meissen
Essen
Iserlohn
Kassel
Düsseldorf
Iserlohn
Dresden
1950 – Save
Cologne
the Human
Catholic
Eisenach
Being
Bonn
Academy
1997 – The Path of Righteousness
Thüringen
Leads to Life
1973 – Not By
Haus
Bread Alone
Viligst
Gelnhausen
Friedewald
1985 – The Earth
Is the Lord's
Arnoldshain
Frankfurt/Main
1965 – Stand Fast
1956 – Be Ye Reconciled With God
in Liberty
Speyer
1975 – Stricken, and Behold We Live
1987 – Behold the Man
Nürnberg
Speyer
1979 – Called Unto Hope
1952 – Therefore Choose Life
Karlsruhe
1969 – Hunger After Righteousness!
1999 – You Are the Salt of the Earth
Herrenalb
Stuttgart
Bad Boll
Augsburg
1971 – Ecumenical Meeting
1959 – Thou Shalt Be My People!
Munich
1993 – Serve Ye One Another
Tutzing

Lay institute, evangelical academy

*Living
With Conflicts*    *Kirchentag* slogan

0    20    40 miles

0   20  40   60 km

*Responsibility for the children is not an issue between parents and educational administrators, but between the parents and God.* — Otto Dibelius

WHEN the war ended, the men who had borne the heat of the day in resistance to Nazism were aware that the disaster would never have occurred except for the desertion of the Christian standard by large numbers of the baptized. A poorly trained and unformed *Laos*, clergy and laity, had followed blindly the resurrected heathen gods.

An Evangelical Academy, one of the fruits of the Church Struggle (*Kirchenkampf*) with Nazism, is an adult education center sponsored by the church. Several of the early initiators were men who were survivors of the Church

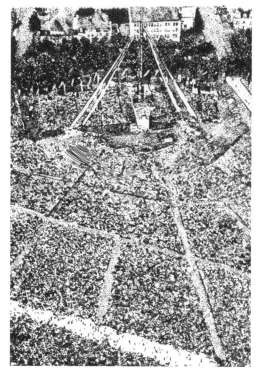

Kirchentag *at Munich, 1959.*

*Reinold von Thadden-Trieglaff, founder of the* Kirchentag.

Struggle. The first academy was opened at Bad Boll, east of Stuttgart, in September of 1945. The leader, and the most influential man in the history of the movement, was Eberhard Mueller (b. 1906). Mueller had been a student pastor and contact man between Theophil Wurm (1868–1953), bishop of the "intact" church of Württemberg, and the Confessing Church of the north. (The "intact" churches were the land churches of Hanover, Württemberg and Bavaria, where the church offices escaped capture by the Nazis and the resistance was not forced into extra-legal circumstances.) Others followed, and in 1947 a German Leaders' Conference was founded to provide a channel for consultation between staffs.

The purpose of an Academy is not unlike that of a university extension program in America, although the Academy intends to keep a place for Christian concern in planning for responsible action in society. A major stress is laid on dialogue, as a means to break the authoritarian structure of traditional decision-making in the clergy-dominated church (*Pastorenkirche*) and to bring laymen in key roles in society into full participation.

The second major form of Christian renewal in post-war Germany has been the *Kirchentag*, a mass movement of laymen. The *Kirchentag* was founded (Hanover, 1949) by Reinold von Thadden-Trieglaff (b. 1891), a leader in the WSCF before the Second World War and in the Confessing Church from the time of the Barmen Declaration (May 1934). Speakers at the launching of the *Kirchentag* included W. A. Visser't Hooft of the World Council of Churches (constit. 1948), Martin Niemöller (1892–1984), the famous pastor who was held for eight and a half years as a personal prisoner of the Führer, and Gustav Heinemann (1899–1976), a man of the Confessing Church, later President of the Federal Republic of Germany.

The *Kirchentag* met every year for a decade and thereafter alternated with the *Katholikentag* every other year. Hans Hermann Walz (b. 1914), previously executive of the Department of the Laity of the World Council of Churches and Associate Director of the Ecumenical Institute near Geneva, served for many years as Executive Director.

In 1961 Working Group VI was founded, concentrating on the problems of Christian/Jewish understanding. While conferences and published materials issued from Arnoldshain Evangelical Academy under the leadership of Martin Stöhr, the *Kirchentag* and the Academies became significant centers of energy in re-thinking Christian teaching and preaching about the Jewish people. Stöhr served later as President of the International Council of Christians and Jews.

## CHRISTIAN RENEWAL IN EUROPE

J. H. OLDHAM, the ecumenical statesman who was a partner to John R. Mott in the running of the 1910 Missionary Conference at Edinburgh, published the first important paper on "Work in the Modern World" used in ecumenical circles. It came out in 1937, in connection with the Oxford Conference on Church, Nation and State. In this writing he elaborated the theme which was to become important in all of the Evangelical Academies and Lay Institutes: the importance of articulating the layman's work in the world as an expression of Christian commitment.

In 1938 George MacLeod (b. 1895) founded the Iona Community. Iona has a structure of discipline which includes time spent rebuilding the ancient center of Celtic Christianity, as well as the sharing of income, work among industrial laborers in Glasgow, the reform of the church. MacLeod, a pacifist and Labour Party member, was later Moderator of the Church of Scotland. Iona has inspired a number of foundations, including Kirkridge (f. 1947 at Bangor, Pennsylvania).

In 1939 Hendrik Kraemer (1888–1965) founded Kerk en Wereld near Utrecht. Kraemer was already a famous missionary (in Indonesia) and author of the study book for the Madras Conference: *The Christian Message in a Non-Christian World* (1938).

The oldest of the non-German lay centers is Sigtuna, near Uppsala (Sweden), founded in 1917 by Manfred Björkquist. For a number of years the Director of Sigtuna's lay institute was Olov Hartman (b. 1906), a well-known poet and playwright.

In October of 1955 a European

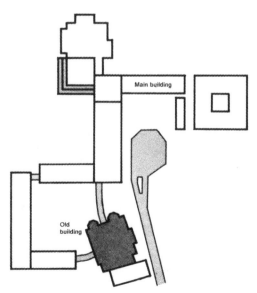

*Plan of Evangelical Academy at Bad Boll, Württemberg, Germany.*

CHRISTIAN RENEWAL IN EUROPE

Leaders' Conference of Evangelical Academies and Lay Institutes was founded during the tenth anniversary celebrations at Bad Boll. Meeting annually, this association has by a set of comity agreements led to the development of specializations in a number of centers—in agriculture, industrial organization, the use of mime and pantomime, etc. A good deal of attention has also been given to assisting the founding, staffing and financing of new Academy programs, as the movement spread to Asia in the 1950s, Africa in the 1960s, and by 1990 counted some ninety lay education centers in sixteen countries.

After 1958 the *Kirchentag* and the Academies shared the services of Mark Gibbs, an Anglican layman and writer (*God's Frozen People, God's Lively People*) whose work has been sponsored in part by the Audenshaw Foundation in England. Gibbs was the consultant to the ecumenical phase of Academy and *Kirchentag* work until his death, a post in which he succeeded Franklin H. Littell, an American

Methodist who was working in Europe for nearly a decade after the war. Littell founded the Ecumenical Commission of the *Kirchentag* in 1953 and was co-founder of the European Leaders' Conference in 1955. The *Kirchentag* is now regularly attended by several hundred non-Germans. The Academies have a steady stream of visitors and conference participants from overseas.

## CHRISTIAN RENEWAL IN THE USA

BOTH the *Kirchentag* and the Academies movement have arisen in the shadow of two World Wars, two totalitarian systems, a small (1923) and a great (1929 ff.) depression, and a far-reaching crisis in Christian belief. Although the implications of the Holocaust for Christendom have been faced by only a few scholars and churchmen and few denominations, the lessons of the Church Struggle (*Kirchenkampf*) are more widely known and discussed.

Until Vietnam, Christian life in America was still largely intact, morally and culturally secure in the nineteenth century harmony of "values," in which there is little disharmony between cultural, religious, social and political norms.

The Vietnam War brought a loss of innocence to America, alienating large numbers of people from their government—youth and students who protested its conduct, families of tens of thousands of fatalities, hundreds of thousands of veterans left with a sense of failure.

Beginning in the 1960s and continuing into the 1990s, the liberal "mainline" Protestant denominations lost members and public profile while conservative denominations and independents expanded exponentially. The journal *Christianity Today* prospered, *The Christian Century* held on, *Christianity and Crisis* withered and died. In spite of severe cuts in programs and personnel in the National Council of Churches and most member church offices, at the local level the lay leadership, participation and church attendance have remained strong in the continuing memberships.

The Roman Catholic Church in America now counts a membership four times as great as the largest Protestant church. During the same period as the liberal Protestant decline, several thousand priests and nuns returned to lay status. Parishes were closed or consolidated and parochial schools faced a major crisis in providing teachers, creating problems especially acute in the cities. At the turn of the millennium, however, vocations have been increasing in recruitment. Also, under the National Catholic Bishops' Conference the denomination has shown during the last generation a much higher profile in political affairs.

Not unlike developments in Europe, renewal movements in America have centered in small group work, retreat and conference centers, and mass appeals (including use of electronic media and the emergence of mega-churches).

Pioneering the work with fellowship groups or Christian cells in the 1940s was the Conference on Disciplined Life and Service, with an office at Lane Hall at the University of Michigan. The leadership included the well-known Quakers, Douglas Steere (1901–95) and Elton Trueblood (1900–94), and Methodists Harold Ehrensperger (edi-

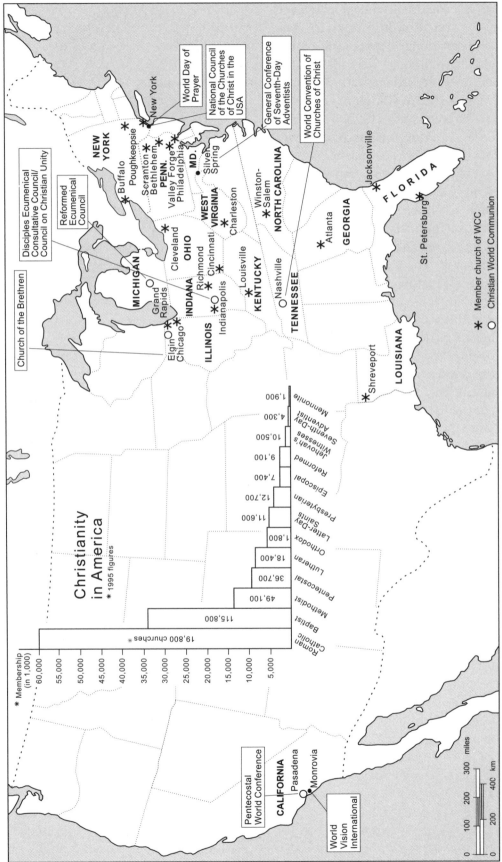

## Christianity in America

* 1995 figures

Membership (in 1,000)

| Denomination | Membership |
|---|---|
| Roman Catholic * 19,800 churches | 115,800 |
| Baptist | 115,800 |
| Methodist | 49,100 |
| Pentecostal | 36,700 |
| Lutheran | 18,400 |
| Orthodox | 1,800 |
| Latter-Day Saints | 11,600 |
| Presbyterian | 12,700 |
| Episcopal | 7,400 |
| Reformed | 9,100 |
| Jehovah's Witnesses | 10,500 |
| Seventh-Day Adventist | 4,300 |
| Mennonite | 1,900 |

Church of the Brethren

Disciples Ecumenical Consultative Council / Council on Christian Unity

Reformed Ecumenical Council

World Day of Prayer

National Council of the Churches of Christ in the USA

General Conference of Seventh-Day Adventists

World Convention of Churches of Christ

Pentecostal World Conference

World Vision International

* Member church of WCC
○ Christian World Communion

New York
Buffalo
Poughkeepsie
Scranton
Bethlehem
PENN.
Valley Forge
Philadelphia
NEW YORK
Silver Spring
MD.
Charleston
WEST VIRGINIA
Winston-Salem
NORTH CAROLINA
Jacksonville
FLORIDA
St. Petersburg
Atlanta
GEORGIA
Cleveland
OHIO
Richmond
Cincinnati
Louisville
KENTUCKY
Nashville
TENNESSEE
MICHIGAN
Grand Rapids
INDIANA
Indianapolis
Elgin
Chicago
ILLINOIS
LOUISIANA
Shreveport
CALIFORNIA
Pasadena
Monrovia

miles
0   100   200   300
0   200   400   km

CHRISTIAN RENEWAL IN THE USA

380

tor of the Christian student magazine *Motive*) and Franklin Littell. The major institutional expressions of the impulse at that time were the Yokefellow Institute (Richmond, Indiana) and Pendle Hill (Wallingford, Pennsylvania). A recent study (1998) by Robert Ruthnow of Princeton reports that 40 percent of Americans participate in small groups that meet regularly to cultivate the spiritual life in caring nurture.

Some intentional fellowships have gone on to establish permanent life communities. The Reba Place Fellowship in Evanston, Illinois, is one. Another is the community of East Harlem Protestant Parish, working in an interracial urban setting. The *Bruderhof* movement, which was founded by Eberhard Arnold (1883–1935) in Berlin in 1920, found refuge in England during the Hitler years in Germany, and since the war has grown to a dozen Christian communist communities in the United States. Today there are over a half million Americans living in communes, most of them of religious origin.

During the 1960s, effective mass meetings—comparable to small *Kirchentage*—were the Faith-in-Life Weeks conducted under the "Minnesota Project" by Loren Halvorsen of the American Lutheran Church. Involving Roman Catholics as well as other Protestants, and using all available media (movies followed by discussion, radio talk-in shows, issue-oriented

*Billy Graham.*

newspaper stories) in a week-long saturation approach, the Faith-in-Life Weeks confronted every spiritual issue and social problem.

Mass meetings have also become typical of the American megachurches, although none of them can compare in size with the Yoido Full Gospel Church in Seoul, Korea—with over 650,000 members, several hundred clergy, and several thousand lay groups ("house churches") for prayer and Bible study. The electronics media have also enabled individual preachers such as Billy Graham (b. 1918) and Pope John Paul II (b. Karol Wojtila, 1920) to reach millions. Popular TV ballad singers like Pat Boone (b. 1934) and Mark Heard (1952–92) have also given a new range to the Christian message.

Percentage of Christians
out of total population

| | |
|---|---|
| 10-25 | |
| 25-50 | |
| 50-75 | |
| over 75 | |

● National Council
  of Churches

## CHRISTIAN RENEWAL IN AFRICA

### TOTAL CHRISTIAN POPULATION (1999)

| | | |
|---|---|---|
| Angola: 12 million | Côte d'Ivoire: 3.6 million | Nigeria: 69 million |
| Benin: 1.8 million | Egypt: 10.5 million | Rwanda: 7.4 million |
| Botswana: 924,000 | Ethiopia: 32.2 million | Sierra Leone: 600,000 |
| Burkina Faso: 1.9 million | Gabon: 640,000 | South Africa: 40.7 million |
| Burundi: 6.9 million | Ghana: 15.8 million | Sudan: 4.5 million |
| Cameroon: 7.3 million | Kenya: 25.4 million | Swaziland: 790,000 |
| Central African Republic: 3 million | Lesotho: 1.9 million | Tanzania: 18 million |
| Chad: 2.4 million | Liberia: 1.3 million | Togo: 2.3 million |
| Congo: 2.5 million | Madagascar: 9.8 million | Uganda: 20.4 million |
| Congo, Democratic Republic of: 48 million | Malawi: 6.8 million | Zambia: 9.6 million |
| | Namibia: 1.3 million | Zimbabwe: 10.4 million |

AFRICA is one of the areas of greatest religious ferment in the world today. Many of the new nations have ecumenical agencies as well as vigorous independent churches. The Protestant Council for the Congo was founded in 1924, the Christian Council of the Gold Coast in 1929, the Christian Council of Kenya in 1943, etc. Some African churchmen played prominent parts in the ecumenical movement, including Chief Albert John Luthuli (1899–1967), a pacifist Christian who suffered greatly under the former totalitarian regime of South Africa. Luthuli received the Nobel Peace Prize in 1960.

*Albert Luthuli.*

Among ecumenical agencies founded since World War II have been several academies for lay training. They have sometimes survived with difficulty, having on occasion to stand against white racism, black nationalism, and attacks from Muslim and Marxist ideologues.

The spread of Christianity in Africa has been most rapid among peoples whose religious life was still at the level of Animism, most retarded among (northern) tribes that have already embraced Islam. Since Islam lays a light burden upon adherents—a Muslim is anyone who says the ritual prayer five times daily—and does not interfere with a fundamental social and economic practice like polygamy, it has spread widely in Africa in spite of the association of Arabs with the slave trade.

Spanish West Africa and Mauritania are virtually 100 percent Muslim. In the Maghreb nations—Morocco, Algeria, Tunisia and Libya—Christianity has made inroads only in the Kabyle tribe of Algeria. There has been little Christian advance, even in the form of indigenous churches, in such strongly Muslim areas as Gambia, Senegal, Guinea, Mali and Niger.

To the south, however, Christianity continues to make spectacular advances—especially in its Pentecostal expression and in independent movements. In South Africa and Zimbabwe the breakaway from control by white agencies is especially marked. The total of membership in independent African churches in Zimbabwe is more than 1.1 million and on the African continent, 35 million.

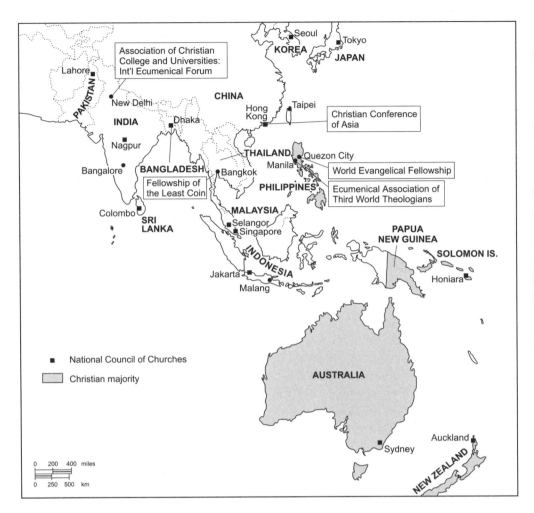

THE Association of Christian Institutes for Social Concern in Asia (ACISCA) brings into consultation and cooperation the key academies in that area of the world. The Christian Institute for the Study of Religion and Society at Bangalore (India) is world famous, and several other centers are well established.

As elsewhere in the world, programs and emphases vary widely. The Taipei Academy House (Taiwan) has regular conferences for doctors, managers and other vocational groups—along with a Lifeline Center (telephone counselling, suicide prevention). The Ecumenical Lay Center at Malang (Indonesia) specializes in a continuous Muslim-Christian dialogue.

Fraternal workers for academies in both Asia and Africa have been supplied by the German Evangelical Academies, and several of the European centers work in cooperation with the Ecumenical Institute near Geneva in providing training conferences for prospective lay institute workers in various parts of the world.

After 1952, under the leadership of Hendrik Kraemer (1888–1965), Suzanne de Diétrich (1891–1981) and Hans Hermann Walz (b. 1914), the Institute expanded its training courses and has greatly extended its influence among the Younger Churches.

TRADITIONALLY Roman Catholic, with even the writings of Erasmus and other Catholic reformers prohibited, the nations of Latin America always have had great difficulty in developing democratic cultures. During the nineteenth century colonial controls were cast off by new nations, but the great gap between the privileged few and the impoverished masses remained.

In the twentieth century, any signs of popular initiative have been brutally suppressed by dictators, using the armies against their own people: e.g., the Perons in the Argentine (1946–76), where many escaped Nazis were given refuge; Pinochet in Chile (1973–98), now facing trial for human rights violations; Stroessner in Paraguay (1954–89), and others. Only Costa Rica has removed the yoke of militarism and shown that with enlightened leadership another path is open.

In the past the church hierarchy has been closely tied to the heads of the great haciendas, while poverty, especially among the native Americans, has been desperate. Recently, however, there has emerged a school of creative Roman Catholic teachers of "Liberation Theology": Gustavo Gutiérrez (b. 1928) and Leonardo Boff (b. 1938) and others have proclaimed the Christian gospel in terms of "a preferential option for the poor." Initially an impulse from the universities, the center has shifted to common people gathered in "Base Communities" for prayer, Bible study, and dealing with social and political issues. Several dozen priests and at least two bishops have been martyred for confronting the exploitative power structures, the most famous being Archbishop Oscar Romero of San Salvador (1917–80).

Since World War II Protestantism has made enormous strides in Latin America, especially in its Pentecostal form. In Brazil, officially the largest Roman Catholic population in the world (c 120 million, or 70 percent), some 10 million are Protestant, and on any given Sunday surpass the Roman Catholic attendance at worship.

*The Christ of the Andes, erected in 1902 by Mateo Alonzo on the Argentinia-Chile border.*
*At foot of statue:*
*"These mountains shall crumble into dust before the peoples of the Argentine and Chile break the peace that they have sworn at the feet of Christ the Savior."*

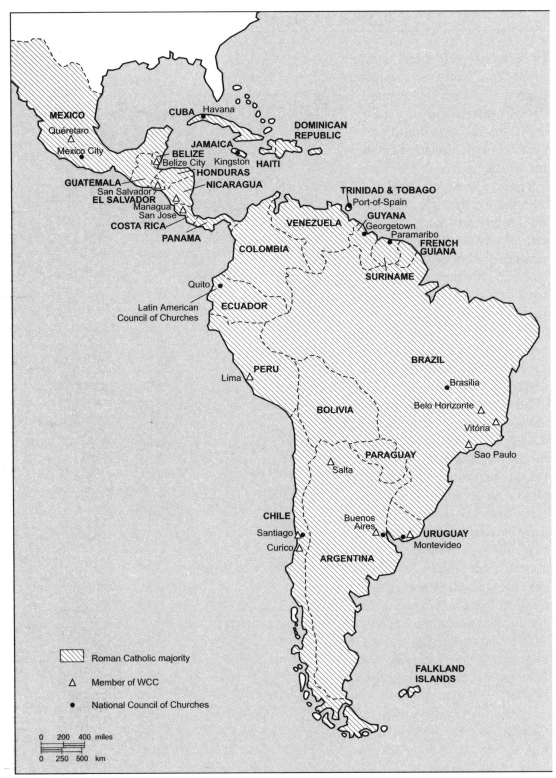

MEXICO
Querétaro
Mexico City

CUBA
Havana

DOMINICAN
REPUBLIC

JAMAICA
BELIZE
Belize City
Kingston
HAITI

GUATEMALA
San Salvador
EL SALVADOR
HONDURAS
NICARAGUA
Managua
San Jose
COSTA RICA
PANAMA

TRINIDAD & TOBAGO
Port-of-Spain

VENEZUELA
GUYANA
Georgetown
Paramaribo
FRENCH
GUIANA

COLOMBIA

SURINAME

Quito
ECUADOR
Latin American
Council of Churches

BRAZIL

PERU
Lima

Brasilia

Belo Horizonte

BOLIVIA

Vitória

Sao Paulo

PARAGUAY

Salta

CHILE
Santiago
Curico

Buenos
Aires
URUGUAY
Montevideo

ARGENTINA

FALKLAND
ISLANDS

Roman Catholic majority

△  Member of WCC

●  National Council of Churches

0    200   400 miles
0   250   500  km

CHRISTIAN RENEWAL IN LATIN AMERICA

386

IN spite of their small numbers, the historic "peace churches"—Friends, Mennonites and Brethren—have made major contributions to Christianity in America and to the world.

The Quaker leadership in colonial America was substantial, and not only in the famous colony of religious refugees, Pennsylvania. At one time there were no less than five colonial governors who were members of the Society of Friends. Among other things, the Quakers were noted for fair dealing with the Indians: the Charter Oak Treaty between William Penn (1644–1718) and the Indians was a model of its kind, a model unfortunately little followed by others. Quakers joined with some Congregationalists in a futile effort to protect the Cherokees from loss of their homelands in Georgia and the Carolinas (1833 ff.), and they were called upon by President Grant in his efforts to purge the Indian Service of unscrupulous officials who were cheating the Indians of their allotments (1871 ff.).

After the resignation of Quaker members from the Pennsylvania Assembly in 1756, they being unable in conscience to vote for guns and powder for the western frontier's battles with the Indians (and also too sensible to vote against the appropria-

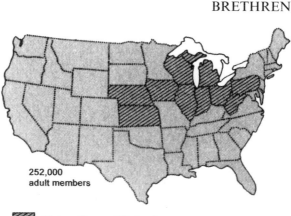

**BRETHREN**

252,000
adult members

▨ States with over 100 churches

**MENNONITES**

225,000
adult members

▨ States with over 50 churches

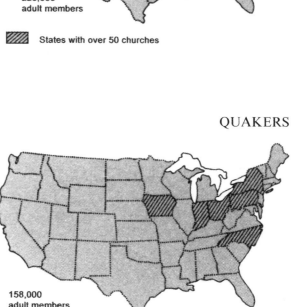

**QUAKERS**

158,000
adult members

▨ States with over 50 churches

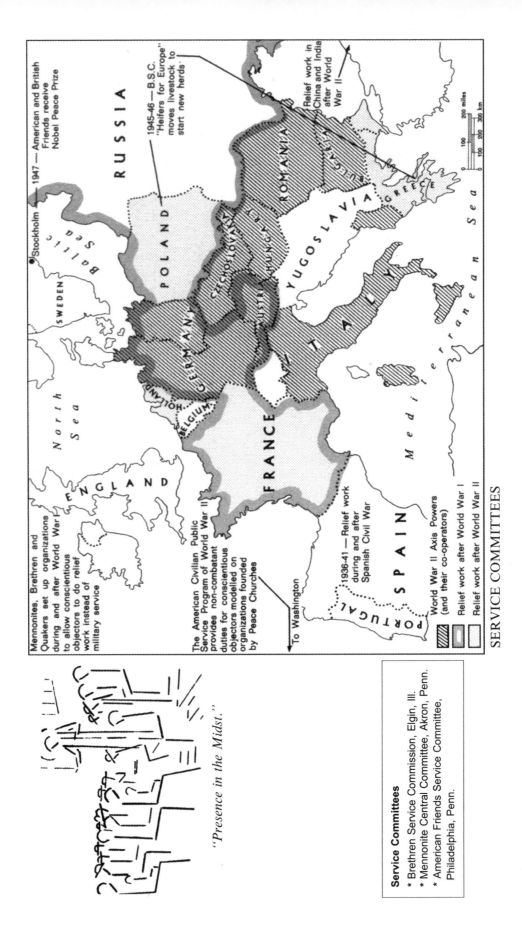

Mennonites, Brethren and Quakers set up organizations during and after World War I to allow conscientious objectors to do relief work instead of military service

1947 — American and British Friends receive Nobel Peace Prize

● Stockholm

1945-46 — B.S.C. "Heifers for Europe" moves livestock to start new herds

Relief work in China and India after World War II

The American Civilian Public Service Program of World War II provides non-combatant duties for conscientious objectors modelled on organizations founded by Peace Churches

To Washington

1936-41 — Relief work during and after Spanish Civil War

World War II Axis Powers (and their co-operators)

Relief work after World War I

Relief work after World War II

RUSSIA

SWEDEN

POLAND

GERMANY

CZECHOSLOVAKIA

AUSTRIA

HUNGARY

ROMANIA

BULGARIA

YUGOSLAVIA

GREECE

ITALY

HOLLAND

BELGIUM

FRANCE

SPAIN

PORTUGAL

ENGLAND

Baltic Sea

North Sea

Mediterranean Sea

200 miles
300 km

SERVICE COMMITTEES

*"Presence in the Midst."*

**Service Committees**

* Brethren Service Commission, Elgin, Ill.
* Mennonite Central Committee, Akron, Penn.
* American Friends Service Committee, Philadelphia, Penn.

388

*George Fox, founder of the Quaker movement.*

*Quaker President Herbert Hoover.*

tions), the role of the Friends in American public life has been more exemplary and humanitarian than political. Even the Quaker President Herbert C. Hoover (1874–1964) won his first public attention heading relief work in eastern Europe after World War I, and the relationship of Richard Nixon (1913–94) to his Quaker heritage was ambiguous at best. Nevertheless, the Friends have continued to exercise considerable political influence, especially on such matters as the status of conscientious objectors to war, congressional appropriations for refugee relief and overseas technical assistance, etc.

The Mennonites began to arrive in Pennsylvania in the year 1683. The "Dunkers" (Brethren) began to come in 1719. Founded by Alexander Mack (1679–1735), a radical Pietist, in Bad Schwarzenau (Germany), they also took little initial interest in voting, holding office, or other phases of the world's business.

In the modern period all three of the Peace Churches have had a renaissance of public activity. The American Friends Service Committee was organized in 1917 to develop alternative service programs for conscientious objectors and to raise money and send staff for relief work abroad. The Mennonite Central Committee was formed in 1920, and the Brethren Service Commission in 1940; they too were devoted to provision for opponents of war and violence and to extensive humanitarian work overseas. In 1947 the AFSC and the Friends Service Council (British) received the Nobel Peace Prize for their non-partisan relief work among the civilian victims of the two World Wars and the Spanish Civil War.

# E. New Perspectives

## UNUSUAL RELIGIOUS MOVEMENTS: USA

*The Constitution should contain a provision that every officer of the government who should refuse to extend the protection guaranteed in the Constitution should be subjected to capital punishment.*
— Joseph Smith III, 1843

THE three new religious movements most typically American were for several generations the Mormons, the Jehovah's Witnesses, and Christian Science.

The proper name for the Mormons is *The Church of Jesus Christ of Latterday Saints*, and it is commonly applied to the powerful movement which has grown out of the slender beginnings established at Salt Lake by Brigham Young (1801–77) in 1847. There is also

a Reorganized LDS Church, founded by Joseph Smith III (1832–1914), with headquarters in Independence, Missouri, which did not practice polygamy. There are half a dozen smaller splinters: the Temple Lot (f. 1844 at Bloomington, Illinois), the Church of Jesus Christ (Cutlerites)—founded 1853 at Clitherall, Minnesota, the Church of Jesus Christ (Bickertonites)—founded 1862 at Greenoak, Pennsylvania, and the House of David—founded 1903 at Benton Harbor, Michigan. One of the most esoteric of all was the Church of Jesus Christ (Strangites)—founded 1850 in Burlington, Wisconsin.

Two of the most important institutions of the largest branch are mutual aid and lay missions. Every member in good standing tithes ten percent to the church, a rule which has brought enormous wealth from mining in Nevada, real estate and the aviation industry in California, and oil in Texas. Every young man on reaching his majority is eligible for two years of missionary work at his own expense, a discipline which has spread Mormonism throughout Europe and the South Pacific. Today over half the LDS membership is outside the USA.

The *Jehovah's Witnesses* also count every member a "minister" and are known for their evangelism. They consider themselves a re-

*The Mormon Tabernacle, Brigham City, Utah.*

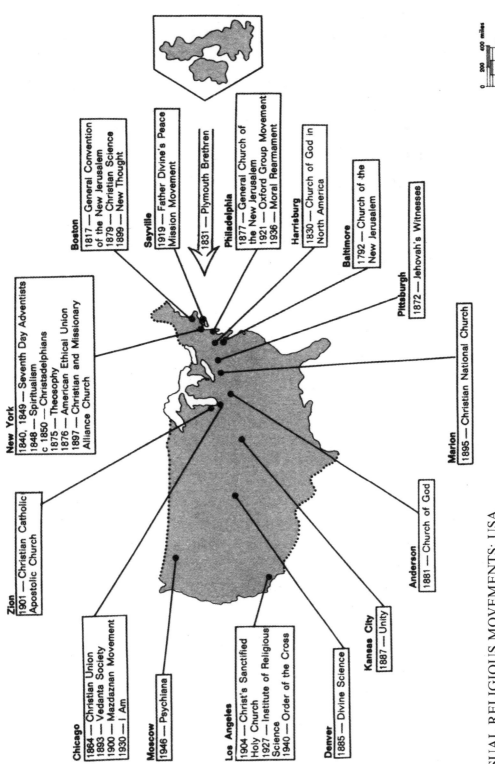

**Boston**
1817 — General Convention
of the New Jerusalem
1879 — Christian Science
1899 — New Thought

**Sayville**
1919 — Father Divine's Peace
Mission Movement

1831 — Plymouth Brethren

**Philadelphia**
1877 — General Church of
the New Jerusalem
1921 — Oxford Group Movement
1936 — Moral Rearmament

**Harrisburg**
1830 — Church of God in
North America

**Baltimore**
1792 — Church of the
New Jerusalem

**Pittsburgh**
1872 — Jehovah's Witnesses

**Marion**
1895 — Christian National Church

**New York**
1840, 1849 — Seventh Day Adventists
1848 — Spiritualism
c 1850 — Christadelphians
1875 — Theosophy
1876 — American Ethical Union
1897 — Christian and Missionary
Alliance Church

**Zion**
1901 — Christian Catholic
Apostolic Church

**Chicago**
1864 — Christian Union
1893 — Vedanta Society
1900 — Mazdaznan Movement
1930 — I Am

**Moscow**
1946 — Psychiana

**Los Angeles**
1904 — Christ's Sanctified
Holy Church
1927 — Institute of Religious
Science
1940 — Order of the Cross

**Denver**
1885 — Divine Science

**Kansas City**
1887 — Unity

**Anderson**
1881 — Church of God

UNUSUAL RELIGIOUS MOVEMENTS: USA

storation of New Testament Christianity and practice Christian communism modeled on the Church at Jerusalem (Acts 4:32) at their headquarters in Brooklyn.

The relationship of *Christian Science* to Phineas P. Quimby (1802–66) and "New Thought" is disputed. Mary Baker Eddy (1821–1910), the founder of the "Mother Church" in Boston, was healed by Quimby and for long praised his system. In 1875 she brought out the first edition of *Science and Health*, in 1883 she founded the monthly *Christian Science Journal*, in 1898 the weekly *Christian Science Sentinel*, and in 1908 one of the leading daily newspapers in America, *The Christian Science Monitor*. Although statistics are not public, Christian Science is today one of the wealthiest churches in America. An excellent set of schools functions near St. Louis, its highest level Principia College (f. 1910).

The many *Adventist* and *Pentecostal*

churches might be considered indigenous American movements, and they are certainly fruits of the great revivals. However, their basic teachings do not really deviate that much from the background of most American religion in Europe.

Of special interest is the emergence of the *Black Muslims* (see map, p. 343). Father Divine's Peace Mission (f. 1919) remained essentially Christian, and members were thus prevented from hating whites with a pure heart. The Black Muslims (f. 1931 in Detroit) have a system of thought and discipline which lends itself much more readily to black nationalism, Afro-American identity, and hatred of an oppressive white society and its structures. The "Nation of Islam" may prove to be one of the more important of indigenous American religious movements, although the Afro-American Christian churches remain very strong.

## UNUSUAL RELIGIOUS MOVEMENTS: GERMANY

FOR many years *Sektengeschichte* ("the history of sect movements") was one of the favorite studies in German universities. Professors and students of the established German churches (Roman Catholic, Lutheran, Reformed and United) were fascinated by the proliferation of "sects" and "cults" in the Anglo-Saxon world—especially in America. The Eisenach Convention of the German Protestants (1855) defined as a "sect" any religious body which was not included in the political and legal settlements at Augsburg (1555) or Westphalia (1648), which meant that for a long time Baptists and Methodists and other Free Churches were rated as "sects."

In recent years, specialists as well as churchmen have begun to distinguish between the Free Churches which also participate in the ecumenical movement and the "sects" which do not. The famous typology popularized by Ernst Troeltsch's *Social Teachings of the Christian Churches* (1912, English translation 1931), in which both "church" and "sect" types were held to have made contributions to church history, has also been widely used by American students.

Nothing can change the fact, however, that in the common meaning of language "church" is a plus word and "sect" is pejorative. There is also something bizarre about a usage which

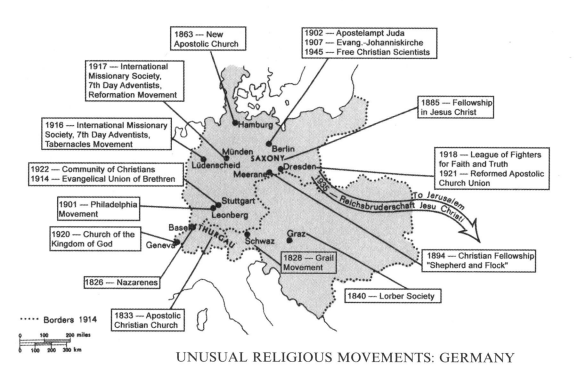

UNUSUAL RELIGIOUS MOVEMENTS: GERMANY

In the map:

1863 — New Apostolic Church

1902 — Apostelampt Juda
1907 — Evang.-Johanniskirche
1945 — Free Christian Scientists

1917 — International Missionary Society, 7th Day Adventists, Reformation Movement

1916 — International Missionary Society, 7th Day Adventists, Tabernacles Movement

1885 — Fellowship in Jesus Christ

1922 — Community of Christians
1914 — Evangelical Union of Brethren

1918 — League of Fighters for Faith and Truth
1921 — Reformed Apostolic Church Union

1901 — Philadelphia Movement

1920 — Church of the Kingdom of God

1826 — Nazarenes

1894 — Christian Fellowship "Shepherd and Flock"

1828 — Grail Movement

1840 — Lorber Society

1833 — Apostolic Christian Church

Borders 1914

0  100  200 miles
0  100  200  300 km

Hamburg, Münden, Lüdenscheid, Berlin, SAXONY, Dresden, Meerane, Stuttgart, Leonberg, Basel, THURGAU, Geneva, Schwaz, Graz, Reichsbruderschaft Jesu Christi, To Jerusalem

defines the Early Church as a "sect" because it was illegal and persecuted, the Christendom of the Constantinian settlement a "church" because it enjoyed legal and coercive power, and the indigenous Christian movements of Asia and Africa "sects" because they have broken away from control by boards and agencies in white Christendom. The better part of charity, as well as wisdom, would suggest that the term "sect" be allowed to lapse and some neutral terms, such as "unusual religious movements" or "New Religious Movements" (NRMs), take its place.

While scholars of the European state churches were assuming that the proliferation of new "sects and cults" was a peculiarly American distemper, a strong movement toward inter-church cooperation and union was flourishing in America, and a host of new religious movements was starting up in Germany. Some of these were products of broader movements, such as the Apostolic Christian Church (f. 1833)—a renewal movement among Swiss Mennonites, the Church of the Kingdom of God (f. 1920)—a splinter from the Jehovah's Witnesses, and the Free Christian Scientists (f. 1945). Others were indigenous to German Pietism, like the Lorber Society (f. 1840), the Fellowship in Jesus Christ (f. 1885), the Philadelphia Movement (f. 1901), and the Evangelical Union of Brethren (f. 1914).

One of the most influential movements, now called *Christengemeinschapt* ("Community of Christians"), began under the impulse of Rudolf Steiner (1861–1925). Originally known as Anthroposophy, and combining Hindu and Buddhist concepts with Christian in an esoteric cosmological philosophy, Steiner's movement was later consolidated into Christian congregations that deviate little from standard Christian practices. Perhaps the most important general contribution of the movement has been the founding of the excellent Waldorf Schools (high schools), which have now spread outside Germany.

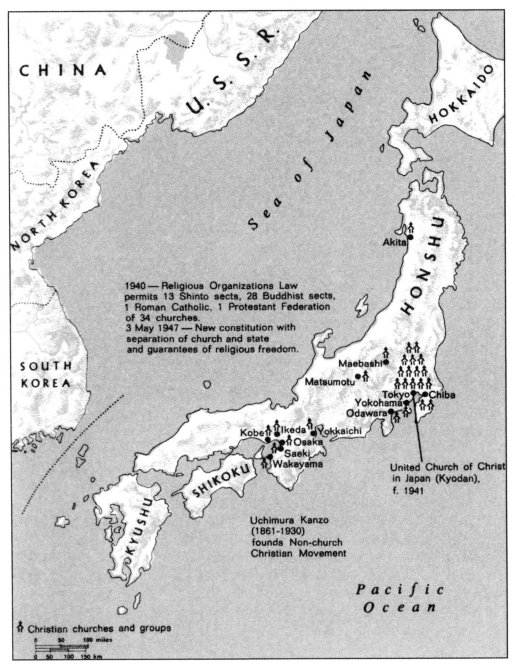

CHINA

U.S.S.R.

HOKKAIDO

NORTH KOREA

*Sea of Japan*

HONSHU

Akita

SOUTH KOREA

1940 — Religious Organizations Law permits 13 Shinto sects, 28 Buddhist sects, 1 Roman Catholic, 1 Protestant Federation of 34 churches.
3 May 1947 — New constitution with separation of church and state and guarantees of religious freedom.

Maebashi
Matsumotu
Tokyo●  ●Chiba
Yokohama
Odawara

United Church of Christ in Japan (Kyodan), f. 1941

Kobe  Ikeda  Yokkaichi
Osaka
Saeki
Wakayama

SHIKOKU

KYUSHU

Uchimura Kanzo (1861-1930) founds Non-church Christian Movement

*Pacific Ocean*

⛪ Christian churches and groups

0    50    100 miles
0  50  100  150 km

CHRISTIAN CHURCHES AND GROUPS

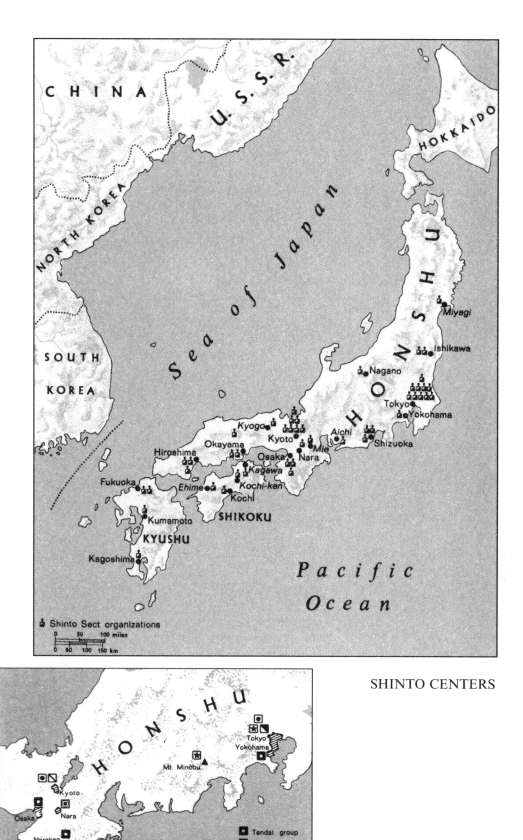

CHINA

U.S.S.R.

HOKKAIDO

NORTH KOREA

SOUTH KOREA

Sea of Japan

HONSHU

Miyagi

Ishikawa

Nagano

Tokyo

Yokohama

Kyogo

Kyoto

Aichi

Shizuoka

Okayama

Mie

Hiroshima

Osaka

Nara

Fukuoka

Kagawa

Ehime

Kochi-ken

Kochi

Kumamoto

SHIKOKU

KYUSHU

Kagoshima

Pacific
Ocean

Shinto Sect organizations

0       50      100 miles

0   50   100  150 km

SHINTO CENTERS

HONSHU

Tokyo

Yokohama

Mt. Minobu

Kyoto

Nara

Osaka

Naraken

◼ Tendai group
◪ Shingon group
◻ Pure Land group
◉ Zen group
✳ Nichiren group
◎ Nara group

0        20       40 miles

0   20   40   60 km

BUDDHIST GROUPS

395

# INDEPENDENT AFRICAN CHRISTIAN MOVEMENTS

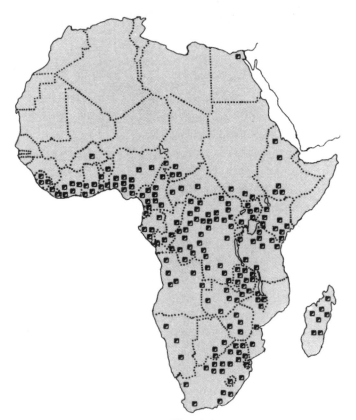

☑ African independent Christian movements

**Angola**
1949 — Red Star Cult
**Cabinda (enclave of Angola)**
1930 — Secession of prophet
Mayange

**Botswana**
Several Zionist churches

**Burundi**
1959 — Split from Society of Friends
1963 — Church of God

**Cameroon**
1888 — Native Baptist Church

**Central African Republic**
1956 — Comité Baptiste

**Congo**
1700 — Antonian sect
1872 — Kiyoka secession
1921 — Simon Kimbangu Church
1939 — Church of the Blacks

**Côte d'Ivoire (Ivory Coast)**
1913/15 — Revivals — Harris Church
1923 — Church of Ashes of Purification

**Dahomey (mod. Benin)**
1899 — Methodist schism

**Egypt**
1869 — Plymouth Movement

**Ethiopia**
1955 — Kambatta Evangelical Church
1966 — God's All Times Association

**Gabon**
Church of the Initiates

**Ghana**
1923 — Army of the Cross of Christ
Church
1939 — Apostolic Revelation Society

**Kenya**
1935 — African Orthodox Church
1942 — Africa Israel Church
1945 — African Brotherhood Church
1949 — African Christian Church and
Schools
1957 — Church of Christ in Africa
1963 — Legio Maria Church

**Lesotho**
1872 — First schism

**Liberia**
Church of the Lord

**Malagasy (mod. Madagascar)**
1894 — Eglise Protestante Malagache
1930 — Eglise Baptiste Biblique
1955 — Independent Reformed Church
1955 — Eglise du Réveil
1955 — Eglise du Réveil Spirituel
Malagache

**Malawi**
50 separatist churches
1900 — Providence Industrial Mission

**Nigeria**
1888 — Native Baptist Church
1891 — Untied Native Africa Church
1901 — Africa Church, Inc.
1925 — Cherubim and Seraphim
1930 — Church of the Lord
1931 — Christ Apostolic Church

**Rhodesia (mod. Zimbabwe)**
1932 — African Apostolic Church
1952 — Guta Ra Jehova

**Sierra Leone**
1819 — West Africa-Methodist Church

**South Africa**
1884 — Tembu Church
1892 — Ethiopian Church
1896 — Zulu Congregational Church
1898 — African Presbyterian Church
1904 — Ethiopian Catholic Church in
Zion
1910 — Church of Christ

1911 — Nazirite Baptist Church
1914 — Zion Christian Church
1917 — African Congregational Church
1933 Bantu Methodist Church

**South West Africa (mod. Namibia)**
1955 — Herero Church
Nama tribe split
1959 — 80% of Basters found
independent church

**Sudan**
1937 — Schism (Azunda tribe)

**Swaziland**
1904 — Methodist schism joined
A.M.E. Church

**Tanzania**
1953 — Church of the Holy Spirit
1956 — Tanganyika Africa Church

**Uganda**
1914 — Society of the One Almighty
God
1929 — African Greek Orthodox
Church

**Upper Volta (mod. Burkina Faso)**
1959 — Temple Apostolique

**Zambia**
1900 — Ethiopian Church
1908 — Church of the Watch Tower
1954 — Lumpa Church

CHRISTIANITY, with the exception of the ancient Coptic churches of Egypt and Ethiopia, entered Africa with European colonizers and missionaries. With the rise of self-consciousness in the late nineteenth century, various Christianized peoples had already begun to cut loose from agency controls and finances in Paris, London, and New York. During the recent years of rapid growth of Pentecostalism the expansion of independent Christian churches has been phenomenal.

Combined with the quest for folk-identity, the independents have made many of their gains through break-aways from white mission control as well as by reaching masses of the unbaptized. In Kenya, for example, the Church of Christ in Africa was formed of c 75,000 former Anglicans and the Legio Maria Church started with c 90,000 ex-Roman Catholics. In Ghana some 1.8 million members of independent churches are chiefly former Roman Catholics. In South Africa, the Bantu Independent Churches Union (f. 1937) brings together both breakaway churches and movements gathered by charismatic native prophets.

Many of the native African churches are "Zionist" in ideology and liturgy, owing a good deal to missionary work by followers of J. Alexander Dowie (1847–1907), founder of Zion (Illinois) in 1901. There may be seen a very strong sense of identification with the people, events and laws of the Old Testament. They take Old Testament names personally, and they name their centers—often communal and separatist—"Jerusalem," "Nazareth," "Bethel," etc. Isaiah Shembe (1870–1935), a Zulu prophet, founded the Nazirite movement (1911) and built a great center on a hilltop called "the Mountain of Moses." Some independent churches have cultivated contact with the Copts of Ethiopia, who have for centuries made extensive use of Old Testament ceremonial and food laws, observe Jewish festivals, and practice circumcision.

The first great native revivals were led in 1913–15 by William Wadé Harris on the Ivory Coast, against whom the colonial authorities took repressive action. The Harris Church now counts over 150,000 members. The largest independent church in Africa is the Church of Jesus Christ on Earth, f. 1921 by a prophet named Simon Kimbangu. This church is particularly interesting also because it has (1969)—although vigorously African and independent—joined the World Council of Churches. Based in Congo (former Zaire), which permits only four Christian denominations, it has given haven to some smaller independent churches and now totals 5 million members.

Although in some of the indigenous churches there has been contemporary controversy over native customs like polygamy, there is no evidence that the new churches are any more acculturated than churches in Europe or America. Quite the contrary: in the first flush of their movements, they are vigorously engaged in building counter-cultures—with extensive efforts in founding schools, organizing social welfare and mutual aid, supporting evangelism and missions.

Because of the extraordinary growth and energy of African churches, both traditional and independent, many Christian scholars have concluded that by the year 2020 Africa will count the majority of Christians in the world.

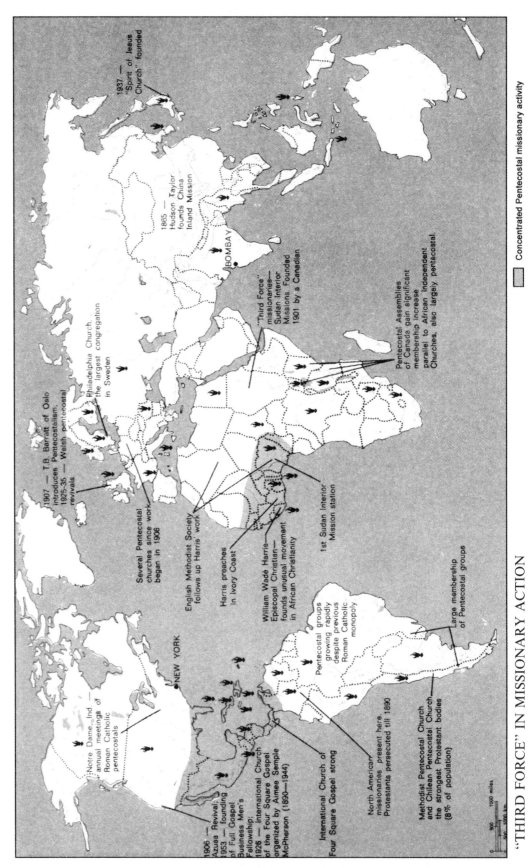

"THIRD FORCE" IN MISSIONARY ACTION

1937 —
"Spirit of Jesus
Church" founded

1865 —
Hudson Taylor
founds China
Inland Mission

BOMBAY

"Third Force"
missionaries—
Sudan Interior
Missions Founded
1901 by a Canadian

Pentecostal Assemblies
of Canada gain significant
membership increase
parallel to African Independent
Churches, also largely pentecostal.

Philadelphia Church,
the largest congregation
in Sweden

1907 — T.B. Barratt of Oslo
introduces Pentecostalism;
1925-35 — Welsh pentecostal
revivals

Several Pentecostal
churches since work
began in 1906

English Methodist Society
follows up Harris work

Harris preaches
in Ivory Coast

William Wade Harris
Episcopal Christian—
founds unusual movement
in African Christianity

1st Sudan Interior
Mission station

NEW YORK

Notre Dame, Ind.—
annual meetings of
Roman Catholic
pentecostals

1906 —
Azusa Revival;
1953 — founding
of Full Gospel
Business Men's
Fellowship;
1926 — International Church
of the Four Square Gospel
organized by Aimee Semple
McPherson (1890—1944)

International Church of
Four Square Gospel strong

Pentecostal
groups
growing rapidly
despite previous
Roman Catholic
monopoly

North American
missionaries present here.
Protestants persecuted till 1890

Methodist Pentecostal Church
and Chilean Pentecostal Church,
the strongest Protestant bodies
(8% of population)

Large membership
of Pentecostal groups

0  500  1000 miles
0  500  1000 km

☖ Concentrated Pentecostal missionary activity

☖ Major "Third Force" churches

398

IN post-war Japan, the "rush hour of the gods" (Neil McFarland's phrase) appears to be fairly evenly populated by the newly emerging Buddhist, Shinto and Christian movements. Moreover, in spite of the great influence of both Karl Barth (1886–1968) and Emil Brunner (1889–1966) upon post-war Christian theology in Japan, the popular bent in religion is eclectic. It is not at all uncommon for a family of religious turn of mind to participate in events and exercises in three or four of the new religious movements.

In Latin America, where there has also been a tremendous upsurge of religion in the last three decades, its doctrinal content is much more readily defined. This upsurge, whose growth in Latin America and Africa is so astounding that some scholars predict that after the turn of the century the majority of Christians will be from the "Third Force," Pentecostal in origin and style. Pentecostalism is strict in basic doctrine, although free in ecstatic expressions of the presence of the Holy Spirit. It derives in its modern expression from the Radical Reformation (see map, p. 147) and Revivalism (see map, p. 323). Pentecostals teach that the great church fell into disgrace and impotence when church leaders sought worldly prestige and church teachers sought pride of position through elaborate systems of philosophy. Before that "fall" the Christian fellowship was given great power of the Spirit—to prophesy, to speak in tongues, to perform miracles, to heal. With the restoration of primitive Christianity, these signs and wonders appear again.

In Brazil, the Assemblies of God now number over 4 million constituents. In Chile, the Methodist Pentecostals are more than 400,000. In areas like Congo-Kinshasa (former Zaire), Nigeria, Tanzania, Zimbabwe and South Africa, the "Third Force" in the expansion of Christianity has far surpassed Roman Catholicism or conventional Protestantism. Indeed, most of the new independent churches of Africa show the marks of this kind of Christianity.

Pentecostalism has also made large gains in Europe and America. The largest congregation in Sweden, once a traditional bulwark of state-church Lutheranism, is the Philadelphia Church in Stockholm (Pentecostal). In the United States, a number of rapidly growing denominations has arisen since the Latter Rain movement in Tennessee (c 1886) and the Azusa Revival (1906 in Los Angeles). The Full Gospel Business Men's Fellowship (f. 1953) has doubled and re-doubled its membership. The Fellowship's morning TV program is broadcast widely in the USA. Oral Roberts (b. 1918), one of the most successful of Pentecostal leaders, has built a great university at Tulsa, Oklahoma, with the support of "awakened" Christians.

Pentecostal influence has also reached far into the more traditional churches—Episcopal, Lutheran, Roman Catholic. Some 25,000 Roman Catholic Pentecostals have annually met in conference at the University of Notre Dame since June of 1973.

It is thus apparent that while organized cooperation and reunion seemed to be the shape of the future for Christianity during the first half of the twentieth century, the actual course of coming events now defies prediction.

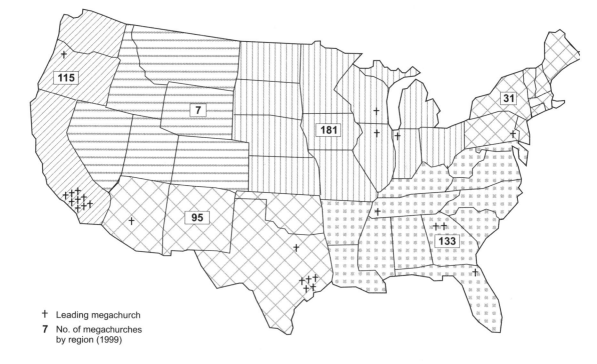

+ Leading megachurch
7 No. of megachurches by region (1999)

A remarkable phenomenon since the Second World War has been the tendency of some areas to develop huge congregations. These "mega-churches" have been especially successful in Korea and the United States. The largest single congregation in the world is the Yoido Full Gospel Church of Seoul, Korea, with c 750 clergy and c 650,000 members divided into several thousand house-churches for prayer and Bible study. According to Dr. John N. Vaughan, the leading specialist and writer on the development, Korea also has the largest Assembly of God, Baptist, Presbyterian and Methodist single congregations in the world.

In the United States, in 1990 the largest number of the 25 mega-churches were located in Los Angeles (9) and Houston (5), with the Chicago area and Atlanta sustaining two each. Of the twenty-five, ten are independent of denominational affiliation and six more are associated with a movement founded in the late 1960s ("Calvary Chapel"). Thus, while the total membership of most of the major Protestant denominations has been markedly declining for two decades, this new expression of non-liturgical, non-hierarchical, biblical and experiential Christianity has made tremendous growths. According to the most recent published report, there are now 465 non-Roman Catholic mega-churches in the United States.

Even after the collapse of the colonial state churches, and even though the federal and state constitutions no longer supported the myth, the popular notion of America as a Protestant nation persisted for well over a century. Newer immigrants, among whom Roman Catholics and Jews were in greatest number, found themselves at a grave disadvantage in education, employment, politics, and social mobility. At the lowest level, terrorist organizations such as the Ku Klux Klan (reorganized in 1915 to include anti-Catholic and antisemitic as well as anti-Negro planks) grew to power in many states. At a slightly higher level, Protestant champions of "Christian America" wrote pamphlets and preached against the foreign influences which were undermining the early Protestant and Anglo-Saxon traditions.

In 1928 the nativist forces reached a high point of malice and political effectiveness in helping to defeat Alfred E. Smith. Smith, the presidential candidate of the Democratic Party, was both Roman Catholic and "wet." Prohibition was a favorite crusade of the largest Protestant churches, in fact a substitute for the Social Gospel to many Methodists and Baptists, and it had been put into law by the Eighteenth Amendment and the Volstead Act (1919). In the 1928 campaign, Protestant nativism rode high.

Against this background a group of public-spirited Jews, Roman Catholics and Protestants founded the National Conference of Christians and Jews (NCCJ, f. 1928). The example of the NCCJ encouraged similarly organized "education for understanding" in the chaplaincy during the war and afterwards in the occupation of Germany.

Under American Military Government the first German Councils of Christian/Jewish cooperation were launched (1949), by 1999 reaching 79 in number. From a headquarters in Heppenheim councils were established in countries throughout Europe, including after 1989 several eastern countries; today the International Council of Christians and Jews (ICCJ) numbers more than 29 national members.

In the USA, the staff leader and moving spirit of the NCCJ for years was Everett J. Clinchey (b. 1896). In its first years the movement held convocations in thousands of schools and civil centers, at which a priest, minister and rabbi spoke and appealed to fellow-citizens to reject bigotry and learn appreciation of other traditions. The Religious News Service was begun, providing daily service to newspapers and magazine editors on developments in inter-religious conflict or cooperation.

During the war the military chaplains of several denominations and faiths cooperated closely (with the motto "Cooperation Without Compromise"), and that model powerfully influenced the American public's perception of right relationships between Protestants, Catholics and Jews in public life.

The NCCJ gave attention from the beginning to campus interfaith work. For many years only a few universities sponsored interfaith dialogue on campus: most, if they had religious work at all, maintained chaplains and chapel services in the tradition of the old Protestant establishment. When Cornell University set up Cornell United Religious Work (CURW) and the University of Iowa a School of Religion, both in 1923, the ventures were

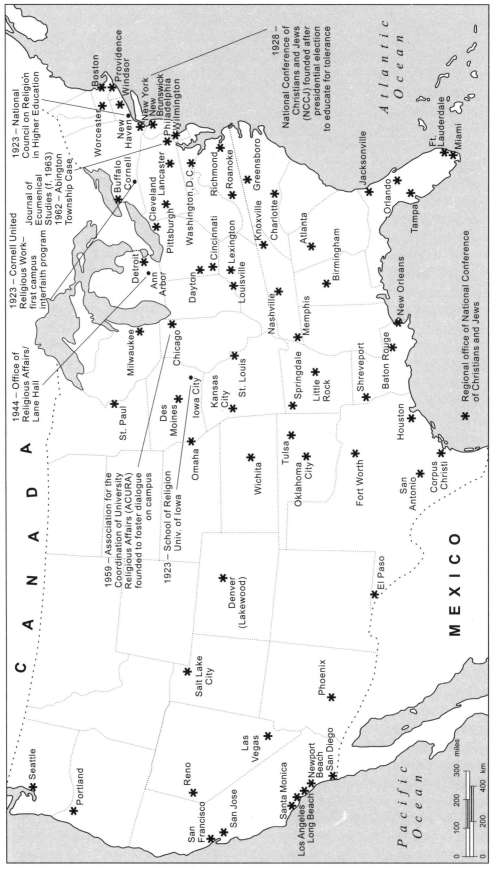

CENTERS OF INTERFAITH DIALOGUE

402

Map labels:

Atlantic Ocean

1928 – National Conference of Christians and Jews (NCCJ) founded after presidential election to educate for tolerance

1923 – National Council on Religion in Higher Education

Journal of Ecumenical Studies (f. 1963) 1962 – Abington Township Case,

1923 – Cornell United Religious Work– first campus interfaith program

1944 – Office of Religious Affairs/ Lane Hall

1959 – Association for the Coordination of University Religious Affairs (ACURA) founded to foster dialogue on campus

1923 – School of Religion Univ. of Iowa

Regional office of National Conference of Christians and Jews

CANADA

MEXICO

Pacific Ocean

Cities:

Boston, Providence, Windsor, Worcester, New Haven, New York, New Brunswick, Philadelphia, Wilmington, Buffalo, Cornell, Cleveland, Lancaster, Richmond, Roanoke, Greensboro, Jacksonville, Ft. Lauderdale, Miami, Orlando, Tampa, Pittsburgh, Washington, D.C., Cincinnati, Knoxville, Charlotte, Atlanta, Birmingham, Detroit, Ann Arbor, Dayton, Lexington, Louisville, Nashville, Memphis, New Orleans, Milwaukee, Chicago, St. Louis, Springdale, Little Rock, Shreveport, Baton Rouge, St. Paul, Des Moines, Iowa City, Kansas City, Tulsa, Oklahoma City, Fort Worth, Houston, San Antonio, Corpus Christi, Omaha, Wichita, El Paso, Denver (Lakewood), Salt Lake City, Phoenix, Seattle, Portland, Reno, Las Vegas, San Francisco, San Jose, Santa Monica, Los Angeles, Long Beach, Newport Beach, San Diego

Scale:
0 100 200 300 miles
0 200 400 km

## GERMAN COUNCILS OF CHRISTIANS AND JEWS

Schleswig-Holstein
Lübeck
Hamburg
Ostfriesland
Bremen Lüneburg
Oldenburg
Oldenburg-
Münsterland
Celle
Minden Hannover
Osnabrück
Münster
Hameln
Niedersachsen/
Ost
Berlin
Potsdam
Lippe
Paderborn
Göttingen
Kassel
Bonn
Görlitz
Fulda
Zwickau Dresden
Bad Nauheim
Gelnhausen
Trier
Bayreuth
Rhein-Neckar Unterfranken Bamberg
Saarland
Pfalz Heidelburg Franken Weiden
Karlsruhe
Stuttgart
Niederbayern
Freiburg
Augsburg u.
Schwaben
Oberschwaben
Munich
Regensburg
Konstanz

| | |
|---|---|
| 1 Aachen | 17 Koblenz |
| 2 Bad Kreuznach | 18 Köln |
| 3 Bielefeld | 19 Krefeld |
| 4 Darmstadt | 20 Limburg |
| 5 Dillenburg | 21 Main-Taunus-Kreis |
| 6 Dortmund | 22 Mainz |
| 7 Duisburg-Mülheim- | 23 Marburg |
| Oberhausen | 24 Moers |
| 8 Düsseldorf | 25 Mönchengladbach |
| 9 Essen | 26 Oberberg |
| 10 Frankfurt/M. | 27 Offenbach |
| 11 Gelsenkirchen | 28 Recklinghausen |
| 12 Gießen-Wetzlar | 29 Seligenstadt |
| 13 Hagen | 30 Siegerland |
| 14 Herford | 31 Wesel |
| 15 Hersfeld- | 32 Wetterau |
| Rotenburg | 33 Wiesbaden |
| 16 Hochtaunus | 34 Wuppertal |

● Seat of German Council (Bad Nauheim)

unique. In 1946 the University of Michigan established an Office of Religious Affairs, followed not long after by Ohio State University, the University of Minnesota, Kansas State University and others. Significantly, the strongest new centers arose in the great state universities of the Midwest, in an area where Protestantism had never been legally established.

In 1959 there was formed a professional Association of Coordinators of University Religious Affairs (ACU-RA), with c 200 personal and institutional memberships. In 1970 three significant centers of Christian/Jewish understanding were launched: the Annual Scholars' Conference on the Holocaust and the Churches, the Christian Study Group on Israel and the Jewish People, and the National Christian Leadership Conference for Israel.

The year 1963 was a major turning point. The Abington Township Case was decided by the U.S. Supreme Court, blocking sectarian religious exercises in the public schools but affirming the study of religions. In a few years several dozen Departments of Religion or Religious Studies were founded in state colleges and universities.

Interfaith dialogue and cooperation, so difficult in America before World War II, are now part of the culture. This has meant a decline in the high profile of the NCCJ, once pioneer in a difficult field. The work begun by the NCCJ is now spreading significantly, and with positive results toward understanding, throughout both western and eastern Europe. The German Councils have now become the center of energy for Christian/Jewish dialogue. The International Council of Christians and Jews has membership now reaching from Argentina and Australia to Uruguay and Venezuela (see Appendix B).

# F. DESTRUCTION AND RENEWAL

## CHRISTENDOM AND THE HOLOCAUST

GENOCIDAL antisemitism, to be distinguished from the earlier but still surviving *cultural* antisemitism and the even earlier *theological* antisemitism still taught and preached in many churches, centered in the use of anti-Jewish prejudice as a political tool. Unlike the layers of theological and cultural antisemitism (present also in the thought-world of Islam, which claims to supersede *both* Judaism and Christianity), modern genocidal antisemitism is intentional, calculated and aimed at achieving political power by attacking "the Jew."

The "Nazi Party Platform" (1920), unchanged even when the Party was attempting to gain public recognition as a legitimate democratic party after the failed coup attempt (1923), specifically excluded Jews from the German future ("Only a person with German blood, regardless of his religious adherence, can be a member of the community. No Jew may therefore be a member of the community."—Article 4). Adolf Hitler, the Austrian organizer of the NSDAP terrorist movement, who did not acquire German citizenship until 1932, preached a mystical message of ethnic cohesion (*Volksgemeinschaft*, national community of the folk or race).

When he came to power, a major component of Hitler's program was a physical culture emphasis that appealed to the young; it was accompanied by public campaigns against smoking and drinking. From time to time Germans were subtly reminded that the Führer was himself a vegetar-

*The burning of a synagogue on* Kristallnacht, *9–10 November 1938.*

ian and a bachelor, the only love of his abstemious life being service to the "Aryan" *Volk* (translated as people, nation, race). The victories of Jesse Owens and other black Americans in the 1936 Olympics were an offense compounded.

During the disintegration of the Weimar Republic, Nazi terrorism was expressed in street-fighting, assassinations, bombings of hostile media and opposition political offices. Just a week after Hitler became dictator a series of public attacks was made on Jewish businessmen. Professions and public office were closed to Jews. The Nürnberg Laws (15 September 1935) deprived Jews (including all persons with one Jewish grandparent) of all rights as citizens. In November of 1938 Jewish businesses and synagogues were pillaged and burned by mobs recruited by

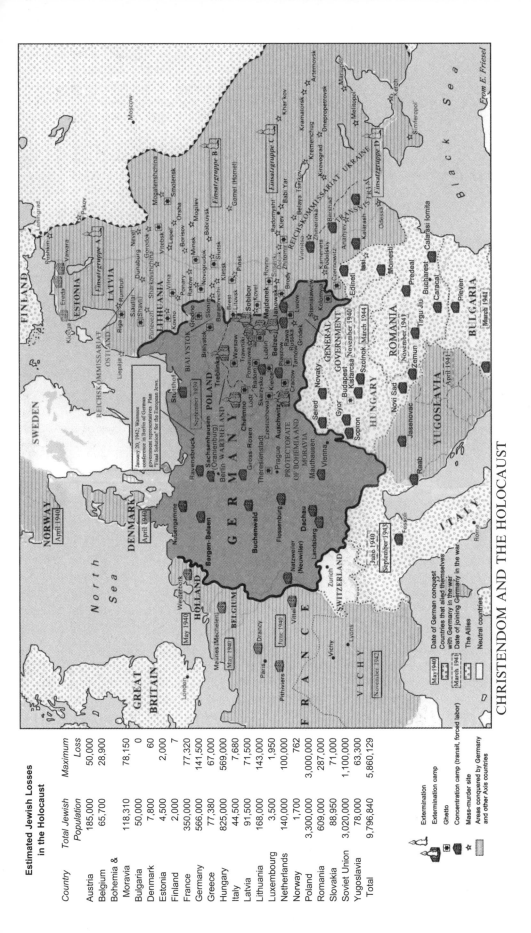

**Estimated Jewish Losses in the Holocaust**

| Country | Total Jewish Population | Maximum Loss |
|---|---|---|
| Austria | 185,000 | 50,000 |
| Belgium | 65,700 | 28,900 |
| Bohemia & Moravia | 118,310 | 78,150 |
| Bulgaria | 50,000 | 0 |
| Denmark | 7,800 | 60 |
| Estonia | 4,500 | 2,000 |
| Finland | 2,000 | 7 |
| France | 350,000 | 77,320 |
| Germany | 566,000 | 141,500 |
| Greece | 77,380 | 67,000 |
| Hungary | 825,000 | 569,000 |
| Italy | 44,500 | 7,680 |
| Latvia | 91,500 | 71,500 |
| Lithuania | 168,000 | 143,000 |
| Luxembourg | 3,500 | 1,950 |
| Netherlands | 140,000 | 100,000 |
| Norway | 1,700 | 762 |
| Poland | 3,300,000 | 3,000,000 |
| Romania | 609,000 | 287,000 |
| Slovakia | 88,950 | 71,000 |
| Soviet Union | 3,020,000 | 1,100,000 |
| Yugoslavia | 78,000 | 63,300 |
| Total | 9,796,840 | 5,860,129 |

Legend:

- Extermination
- Extermination camp
- Ghetto
- Concentration camp (transit, forced labor)
- Mass-murder site
- Areas conquered by Germany and other Axis countries

| May 1940 | Date of German conquest |
| | Countries that allied themselves with Germany in the war |
| March 1941 | Date of joining Germany in the war |
| | The Allies |
| | Neutral countries |

*From E. Friesel*

CHRISTENDOM AND THE HOLOCAUST

the Nazi Party. *Kristallnacht* was ostensibly in response to the killing of a second-level German diplomat by a distraught young Jewish refugee in Paris. In fact, the dates November 9, 10, 11 were chosen—in the mystical euphoria of Nazi political grandiloquence—to signal the canceling of the unhappy memories of previous events on those dates: German admission of defeat in World War I (1918) and Nazi street-fighters' defeat by loyal Munich police in 1923. The event also flaunted the Führer's contempt for the opinion of outsiders: he was certain that those governments that had responded with appeasement to his external aggressions (Rheinland, Austria, Czechoslovakia) would not protest his mistreatment of German citizens.

In 1941 the efficient gathering of European Jews into Death Camps was begun, and it was carried through to the end of the war even at cost of the military effort. The point at which the decision was reached to make the removal lethal is subject to dispute among competent scholars. Special Forces were assigned to kill Jews, accompanying the military units that invaded Poland after 1 September 1939. When Stalin and Hitler fell out and "Operation Barbarossa" struck eastward (22 June 1941), the killing of Jews expanded. Bureaucratically, the killing program was given a clear track at the Wannsee Conference (20 January 1942), where the several offices competing in the program were coordinated in a meeting of top officials chaired by Reinhard Heydrich. (A majority of those attending held the Ph.D.) Technologically, the program moved from first experiments using carbon monoxide in closed trucks to Death Camps such as Auschwitz, where thousands were daily dispatched using Zyklon B in sealed chambers. Rudolf Hoess's statement is representative: "I personally arranged on orders received from Himmler in May 1941 the gassing of two million persons between June–July 1941 and the end of 1943, during which time I was commandant of Auschwitz."

German Jews were far assimilated: patriotic Germans, they found it hard to leave before the doors closed to emigration and to immigration (Evian Conference, July 1938). They were, however, small in number in comparison with the millions in Poland and the western USSR who were trapped by the German invasion and abandoned by the Allied nations at the Bermuda Conference (April 1943). By then millions of Jews had already been murdered.

When Gerhard Riegner of the World Jewish Congress office in Geneva sent word to the United States (8 August 1942) of what was going on, Jewish leaders like Stephen S. Wise (1874–1949) attempted to get emergency rescue action. His appeal was greeted by some key churchmen as "Jewish propaganda" and the churches as a whole did nothing. The U.S. State Department, like the British Foreign Office heavily infected with antisemitism, also refused to make rescue of Jews a priority.

The destruction of European Jewry was the one permanent victory Hitler scored, and he did it with the active assistance or silent compliance of so-called Christian nations. Very few of the Christians, even of those martyred for opposition to Nazi ideology and politics, perceived at the time the significance for Christianity of the genocide of the Jews. This has remained, in fact, a matter of debate: whether the Holocaust was solely a caesura in the history of the Jewish people, or whether it also introduced the greatest credibility crisis in the history of Christianity. Certainly in recent decades the critical boundary line of Christian theology has been on the map of the post-Auschwitz encounter of Christians and Jews, and even more painfully the encounter of thinking Christians with the record of Christendom when verbal assault on "the Jews" metastasized into a genocidal assault on the Jewish people.

Along with the challenge to the churches to reconstruct Christian teaching and preaching, awareness of the Holocaust has also given the entire civilized world awareness of the crime of genocide. There were some categories of victims, especially Russian PoWs and "gypsies" (Romani and Sinti), who shared directly the fate of the targeted Jews. Since then the *Shoah*, a unique event, is related dialectically to the sufferings of other peoples—especially in the twentieth century.

Since 1900, four times as many people have been targeted and killed *by their own governments* as in World War I, World War II, and all the smaller wars and civil wars of the twentieth century. The century that

> **Definition of Genocide**
> - Killing members of the group;
> - Causing serious bodily or mental harm to members of the group;
> - Deliberately inflicting on the group conditions of life calculated to bring about its physical destruction in whole or in part;
> - Imposing measures intended to prevent births within the group;
> - Forcibly transferring children of the group to another group.

began with the slaughter of the Hereros in German Southwest Africa and the slaughter of the Armenians in the Ottoman Empire has produced an unrelenting litany of genocide: Cambodia, Tibet, Rwanda, Kosovo, East Timor....

The word "genocide" was invented by Raphael Lemkin (1901–59), a refugee from Hitler's Europe, and it was he who pressed hard to have the crime condemned at the first United Nations Assembly (San Francisco, 1946). He gathered support and continued to agitate on the responsibility of governments to repudiate genocide as an instrument of national policy and to punish those who commit the crime. By 1951 there was a critical mass of concerned regimes and the International Genocide Convention became part of the law of nations.

## MEMORY WORK AFTER THE HOLOCAUST

JEWISH memory work after the Holocaust was suffered in private, at first—in families and in congregations, when the lost were remembered as persons. With the founding of Yad Vashem in Jerusalem, and the fixing of a Day of Remembrance (*Yom Hashoah*), the struggle began to incorporate the story into the culture of the people. In due time, especially after the survivors' societies began to function, memorials

*Righteous of the Nations medal, Yad Vashem, Jerusalem.*

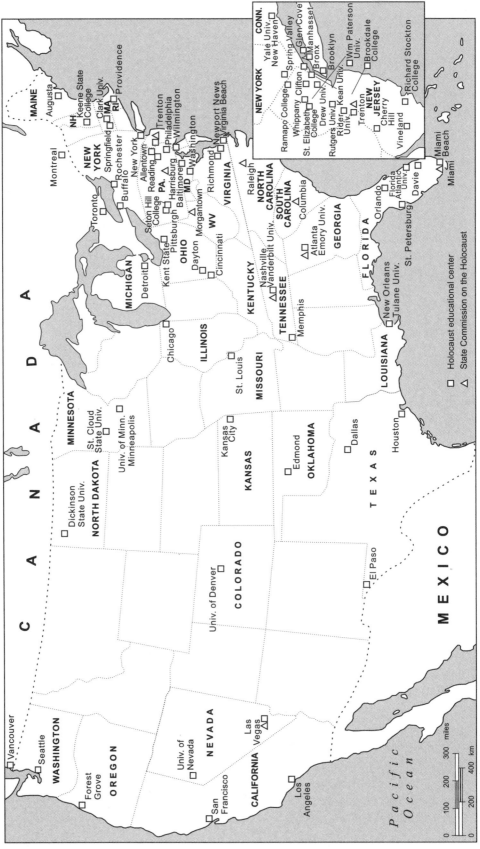

MEMORY WORK AFTER THE HOLOCAUST

**Inset (New York / New Jersey / Connecticut area):**

CONN.
Yale Univ.
New Haven
Spring Valley
Glen Cove
Manhasset
Bronx
Brooklyn
Wm Paterson Univ.
Brookdale College
Richard Stockton College
NEW YORK
Ramapo College
Whippany
Clifton
St. Elizabeth College
Drew Univ.
Rutgers Univ.
Kean Univ.
Rider Univ.
Trenton
NEW JERSEY
Cherry Hill
Vineland

**Main map labels:**

CANADA

MAINE
Augusta
NH
Keene State College
Clark Univ.
MA
RI
Providence
Montreal
NEW YORK
Springfield
Rochester
Buffalo
Toronto
New York
Allentown
Reading
Trenton
PA.
Harrisburg
Philadelphia
Wilmington
Seton Hill College
Pittsburgh
Baltimore
MD
Washington
Newport News
Virginia Beach
Richmond
VIRGINIA
Morgantown
WV
Dayton
Cincinnati
OHIO
Kent State
Detroit
MICHIGAN
Raleigh
NORTH CAROLINA
Columbia
SOUTH CAROLINA
Atlanta
Emory Univ.
GEORGIA
Nashville
Vanderbilt Univ.
KENTUCKY
TENNESSEE
Memphis
ILLINOIS
Chicago
St. Louis
MISSOURI
New Orleans
Tulane Univ.
LOUISIANA
FLORIDA
Orlando
Florida Atlantic
Davie
St. Petersburg
Miami Beach
Miami

MINNESOTA
St. Cloud State Univ.
Univ. of Minn.
Minneapolis
Dickinson State Univ.
NORTH DAKOTA
Kansas City
KANSAS
Edmond
OKLAHOMA
Dallas
Houston
T E X A S
El Paso
COLORADO
Univ. of Denver
MEXICO

WASHINGTON
Vancouver
Seattle
OREGON
Forest Grove
Univ. of Nevada
NEVADA
Las Vegas
CALIFORNIA
San Francisco
Los Angeles

Pacific Ocean

□ Holocaust educational center
△ State Commission on the Holocaust

miles
0   100   200   300
0   200   400 km

and Holocaust education centers were established in other countries. In America, the U.S. Holocaust Memorial Museum was dedicated in 1993, and the Simon Wiesenthal Center and over one hundred local and regional centers were founded. In 1975 there were but two in the United States—one founded by Yaffa Eliach in an Orthodox high school in Brooklyn and the other an interfaith institute founded by Franklin Littell in Philadelphia.

There is a growing awareness that the Holocaust is not only a Jewish tragedy, and a yet unresolved caesura in Christian credibility, but also the watershed event in the history of Western civilization. The Holocaust exposed the pathological underside of "Christendom." As the millennial year opened, the government of Sweden invited scholars and government representatives from forty-six countries to participate in an "International Forum on the Holocaust" in Stockholm (see Appendix C). There are widening rings of the post-Holocaust dialogue: Christian/Jewish (interfaith), academic, and intergovernmental.

The interfaith, international and interdisciplinary approach to Holocaust education began in 1970, with a conference on "The German Church Struggle and the Holocaust" at Wayne State University in Detroit, Michigan. The conference launched an Annual Scholars' Conference on the Holocaust and the Churches. It brought together for the first time Christians who were publishing and teaching about the ambiguous record of the churches during the German Third Reich and colleagues who had concentrated exclusively on the trauma of the Jewish people. Attendance was sparse during the early years, for few were working in either sector, but at the Thirtieth

*Memorial, sculpted by Boris Saktsier, of Janusz Korczak and the children of the ghetto, Yad Vashem.*

Anniversary of the Scholars' Conference (4–7 March 2000)—no longer confined to American, British, Israeli and German participants—c 500 registrants from twenty-five countries participated.

The Annual Scholars' Conference was founded by two Protestant academics who were also clergymen: Franklin Littell and Hubert Locke. Among those who gave it early impetus and have helped to build the annual sharing of research and interfaith dialogue are Elie Wiesel, Richard Rubenstein, Yehuda Bauer, John Conway, Burton Nelson and Richard Pierard.

The Conference has helped to launch parallel efforts to encourage Jews and Christians to do their memory work together. One of these is the "Remembering for the Future" series, with week-long community saturation programs and scholarly consultations in

Oxford/London: 1988, Berlin: 1994, and Oxford/London: 2000. Dr. Elisabeth Maxwell took the initiative in Britain and Dr. Erich Geldbach in Germany. A second spin-off has been a series of annual dialogues initiated by Abraham Peck, who was born in a DP camp, and Gottfried Wagner, author of *Wer mit dem Wolf nicht heult* and great-grandson of the composer (and antisemite). In the last decade there has been a considerable growth in the number of programs bringing together members of the second generation of survivors and perpetrators, to help each other in the healing process.

The work of remembering, re-thinking and re-working teaching after Auschwitz moves slowly forward—most slowly, perhaps, in the seminaries where the clergy are trained. Yet there are prophetic voices, a new generation of developing scholars, and a few notable official position papers.

In January of 1980, after several years of study in the parishes, the Synod of the Protestant Church of the Rheinland affirmed the most thorough-going program for reconstruction of Christian teaching and preaching in the shadow of the Holocaust. At the center of this initiative was Eberhard Bethge (b. 1909–2000), friend, biographer and editor of the famous martyr of the Church Struggle against Nazism, Dietrich Bonhoeffer. Major positions taken were these: "recognition of Christian co-responsibility and guilt for the Holocaust"; affirmation of the continuing existence of the Jewish people, and also the creation of the State of Israel, as signs of God's faithfulness; support for continuing Christian-Jewish dialogue and cooperation. A number of other German territorial churches have followed suit.

In April of 1998, after some years of work in committee, Pope John Paul II released through the office of Edward Cardinal Cassidy an authoritative teaching on the Holocaust: "We Remember." In this document Roman Catholics are called to remember "the catastrophe which befell the Jewish people"; to realize that the centuries of interaction between Christians and Jews has been largely negative; to reject "antisemitism, based on theories contrary to the constant teaching of the Church"; to "regret the errors and failures of those sons and daughters of the Church" who did not protest the Nazi assault and failed to give aid and succor to its targeted victims.

In speaking for the Christian faith in the post-Auschwitz world, the Church of the Rheinland and the Church of Rome have set landmarks of reappraisal and self-examination well ahead of most denominations. A current "Proposed Policy Statement" of the National Council of Churches of Christ in the USA sets today's Christian-Jewish relations within the context of the general society's religious pluralism. In contrast, a "Study Document" of the United Church of Canada, entitled "Bearing Faithful Witness," treats with resolute honesty the churches' role during the Holocaust and asks such pertinent questions as, "Do our Sunday morning services bear false witness against our Jewish neighbors today?" Many of the churches have not faced the problems of post-Auschwitz teaching and preaching at all.

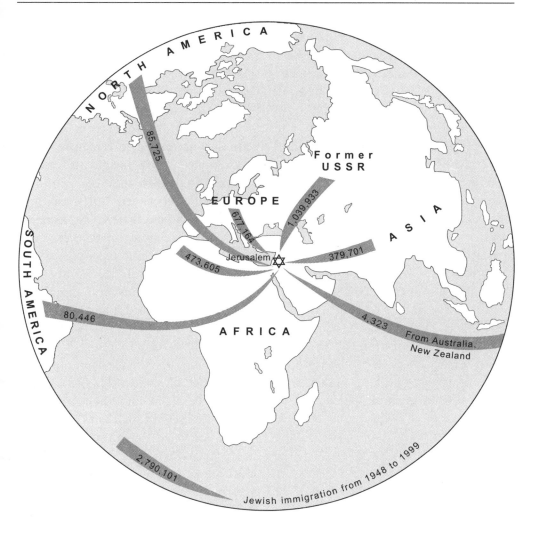

NORTH AMERICA
85,725

Former USSR
1,039,933

EUROPE
677,164

ASIA
379,701

Jerusalem ✡

473,605

SOUTH AMERICA
80,446

AFRICA

4,323
From Australia, New Zealand

2,790,101

Jewish immigration from 1948 to 1999

*The Christian community has never understood that Israel, so far as Jews are concerned, is a symbol in some sense analogous to the Christian symbol of resurrection: after death (Auschwitz), God miraculously raised His People to life (Israel) in the midst of the nations.*
— Alan T. Davies, *Antisemitism and the Christian Mind*

WHEN word was brought from the Reich of what was being done at Auschwitz and the other Death Camps, Jewish leaders tried desperately to arouse the churches. Neither the pope (Pius XII) nor the Protestant agencies gave any significant response. The Allied war leaders also rejected proposals that the railway approaches to Auschwitz be bombed. In France, the radical right praised Hitler's liquidation program and Pétain's Vichy collaborateurs assisted enthusiastically the roundup of French Jews.

Seeing the relentless consequences of centuries of theological, cultural, and political antisemitism in Christendom, even the most emancipated of Jewish leaders became convinced that Theodor Herzl (1860–1904) was right that only a national homeland could guarantee the survival of the Jews. The obvious solution was to actualize the promise made by the British govern-

*The ship* Exodus.

ment during World War I, before the dismemberment of the old Ottoman Empire. In the Balfour Declaration (2 November 1917) the pledge was made: "His majesty's Government views with favour the establishment in Palestine of a national home for the Jewish people...."

In 1933 Leo Baeck, Chief Rabbi in Berlin, declared that "the thousand-year history of German Jewry has come to an end." A comparatively few of the German Jews, accustomed to generations of status in enlightened German states, moved to the British Mandate of Palestine in time. Few made it through the British blockade during and immediately after the war. Some thousands of survivors were saved by Jewish rescue efforts after the war, in spite of continued post-war attacks on Jews in eastern Europe and a general opposition or indifference on the part of most western nations.

Following the War of Independence (1948) and subsequent military attacks on Israel, several hundred thousand Jews have emigrated from their ancient homes in Muslim North Africa to the ancient homeland of the Jewish people. In recent years large numbers have also come from Russia and Ethiopia.

In the history of the Jewish people, the return to the national homeland (including the achievement and defense of national existence in 1948 and a reunited Jerusalem in 1967) is reckoned an event as momentous as the Exodus from Egypt or even the First Return from Exile under Cyrus. In fact, Harry Truman, President of the United States who accorded diplomatic recognition of the new state when it was accredited by the United Nations, once said of his role in the event: "I am Cyrus!"

Using classical language, the path of the Jewish people from Auschwitz to Jerusalem is comparable to death and resurrection. The question left hanging is what the Holocaust and a restored Israel mean to Christians. The first event puts the credibility question to Christianity. The meaning of the second event has yet to be worked out in most churches in song, story, and prayer. For Protestants, the theological task was introduced by the January 1980 declaration of the Synod of the Church of the Rheinland: "Toward Renovation of the Relationship of Christians and Jews." For Roman Catholics, the encyclical of March 1998—"We Remember"—is definitive.

# Appendix A
# COUNTRIES RECENTLY LIMITING RELIGIOUS LIBERTY

Afghanistan
Algeria
Armenia
Austria
Azerbaijan
Bahrain
Bangladesh
Belarus
Belgium
Bhutan
Bosnia and Herzegovina
Brunei
Bulgaria
Burma
Burundi
Cameroon
Central African Republic
China
Colombia
Comoros
Congo, Democratic Republic of
Croatia
Cuba
Djibouti
Egypt
Equatorial Guinea
Eritrea
Estonia
Ethiopia
France
Germany
Greece
India
Indonesia
Iran
Iraq
Israel
Jordan
Kazakhstan

Kenya
Korea, Democratic People's
    Republic of (North Korea)
Kuwait
Kyrgyz Republic
Laos
Latvia
Lebanon
Lithuania
Malaysia
Maldives
Mauritania
Mexico
Moldova
Morocco
Nepal
Nicaragua
Nigeria
Pakistan
Peru
Romania
Russia
Saudi Arabia
Serbia-Montenegro
Singapore
Slovakia
Somalia
Sri Lanka
Sudan
Syria
Tunisia
Turkey
Turkmenistan
Ukraine
United Arab Emirates
United Kingdom
Uzbekistan
Vietnam
Yemen

# Appendix B

## MEMBERS OF THE INTERNATIONAL COUNCIL OF CHRISTIANS AND JEWS

Argentina — Buenos Aires
Australia — Kew/Victoria
Austria — Vienna
Belarus — Minsk
Belgium — Knokke-Heist
Brazil — Sao Paulo
Canada — Toronto
Chile — Santiago
Czech Republic — Prague
France — Paris
Germany — Bad Nauheim
Great Britain — London
Hungary — Budapest
Ireland — Bellinter/Meath

Israel — Jerusalem
Italy — Ancona
Luxembourg — Luxembourg
Netherlands — Weesp
New Zealand — Wellington
Poland — Warsaw
Russia — Moscow
Slovakia — Bratislava
Spain — Madrid
Sweden — Uppsala
Switzerland — Riehen
Ukraine — Kiev
United States — New York City
Uruguay — Montevideo

# Appendix C

## STOCKHOLM FORUM ON HOLOCAUST EDUCATION

Albania
Argentina
Australia
Austria
Belgium
Bosnia and
  Herzegovina
Brazil
Bulgaria
Canada
Croatia
Cyprus
Czech Republic
Denmark
Estonia
Finland

France
Germany
Greece
Holy See
Hungary
Ireland
Iceland
Israel
Italy
Latvia
Lithuania
Luxembourg
Macedonia
Moldova
Netherlands
Norway

Poland
Portugal
Romania
Russia
Slovak Republic
Slovenia
South Africa
Spain
Sweden
Switzerland
Turkey
Ukraine
United Kingdom
United States
Uruguay

# Appendix D
# MEMBERS OF THE WORLD COUNCIL OF CHURCHES

## AFRICA

### Algeria
Protestant Church of Algeria

### Angola
Evangelical Congregational Church in Angola
Evangelical Reformed Church of Angola
Evangelical Pentecostal Mission of Angola
United Evangelical Church, "Anglican Communion in Angola"

### Benin
Protestant Methodist Church of Benin

### Botswana
Church of the Province of Central Africa

### Burundi
Church of the Province of Burundi

### Cameroon
African Protestant Church
Evangelical Church of Cameroon
Native Baptist Church of Cameroon
Presbyterian Church in Cameroon
Presbyterian Church of Cameroon
Union of Baptist Churches of Cameroon

### Congo
Church of Christ in Congo — Evangelical Community
Evangelical Church of the Congo

### Congo, Democratic Republic of
Church of Christ — Light of the Holy Spirit
Church of Christ in Congo — Baptist Community of Western Congo
Church of Christ in Congo — Community of Disciples of Christ
Church of Christ in Congo — Mennonite Community
Church of Christ in Congo — Presbyterian Community
Church of Christ in Congo — Presbyterian Community of Kinshasa
Church of Jesus Christ on Earth by His Messenger Simon Kimbangu

### Côte d'Ivoire
Harrist Church (Côte d'Ivoire)
Protestant Methodist Church, Côte d'Ivoire

### Equatorial Guinea
Reformed Presbyterian Church of Equatorial Guinea

### Ethiopia
Ethiopian Evangelical Church
Ethiopian Orthodox Tewahedo Church

### Gabon
Evangelical Church of Gabon

### Ghana
Church of the Province of West Africa
Evangelical Presbyterian Church, Ghana
Methodist Church, Ghana
Presbyterian Church of Ghana

### Kenya
African Christian Church and Schools
African Church of the Holy Spirit
African Israel Church, Nineveh
Anglican Church of Kenya
Church of Christ in Congo
Kenya Evangelical Lutheran Church
Methodist Church in Kenya
Presbyterian Church of East Africa

### Lesotho
Lesotho Evangelical Church

### Liberia
Lutheran Church in Liberia
Presbytery of Liberia

### Madagascar
Church of Jesus Christ in Madagascar
Church of the Province of the Indian Ocean
Malagasy Lutheran Church

### Mozambique
Presbyterian Church of Mozambique

### Namibia
Evangelical Lutheran Church in the Republic of Namibia

*415*

**Nigeria**

Church of the Brethren in Nigeria
Church of the Lord (Aladura) Worldwide
Church of the Province of Nigeria
Methodist Church Nigeria
Nigerian Baptist Convention
Presbyterian Church of Nigeria
Reformed Church of Christ in Nigeria

**Rwanda**

Church of the Province of Rwanda
Presbyterian Church of Rwanda

**Sierra Leone**

Methodist Church, Sierra Leone

**South Africa**

Church of the Province of Southern Africa
Council of African Instituted Churches
Evangelical Lutheran Church in South Africa
Evangelical Presbyterian Church in South Africa
Presbyterian Church of Africa
Presbyterian Church of Southern Africa
Methodist Church South Africa
Moravian Church in Southern Africa
Reformed Presbyterian Church in Southern Africa
United Congregational Church of Southern Africa
Uniting Reformed Church in Southern Africa

**Sudan**

Episcopal Church of the Sudan
Presbyterian Church of the Sudan

**Tanzania**

Anglican Church of Tanzania
Evangelical Lutheran Church in Tanzania
Moravian Church in Tanzania

**Togo**

Evangelical Presbyterian Church of Togo
Methodist Church in Togo

**Uganda**

Church of the Province of Uganda

**Zambia, Chingola**

Church of Christ in Congo — Episcopal Baptist Community

Evangelical Lutheran Church in Congo
Reformed Church in Zambia
United Church of Zambia

**Zimbabwe**

Evangelical Lutheran Church in Zimbabwe
Methodist Church in Zimbabwe
Reformed Church in Zimbabwe
United Church of Christ in Zimbabwe

**ASIA**

**Australia**

Anglican Church of Australia
Churches of Christ in Australia
Uniting Church in Australia

**Bangladesh**

Bangladesh Baptist Sangha
Church of Bangladesh

**China**

China Christian Council
Hong Kong Council of the Church of Christ in China

**India**

Bengal-Orissa-Bihar Baptist Convention
Church of North India
Church of South India
Malankara Orthodox Syrian Church
Mar Thoma Syrian Church of Malabar
Methodist Church in India
Samavesam of Telugu Baptist Churches
United Evangelical Lutheran Churches in India

**Indonesia**

Batak Christian Community Church (GPKB)
Batak Protestant Christian Church (HKBP)
Christian Church in East Timor
Christian Church of Central Sulawesi (GKST)
Christian Church of Sumba (GKS)
Christian Evangelical Church in Minahasa (GMIM)
Christian Evangelical Church in Sangihe Talaud (GMIST)
Christian Protestant Angkola Church (GKPA)
Christian Protestant Church in Indonesia (GKPI)
East Java Christian Church (GKJW)
Evangelical Christian Church in Halmahera
Evangelical Christian Church in Irian Jaya
Indonesian Christian Church (GKI)

Indonesian Christian Church (HKI)
Javanese Christian Churches (GKJ)
Kalimantan Evangelical Church
Karo Batak Protestant Church (GBKP)
Nias Protestant Christian Church (BNKP)
Pasundan Christian Church (GKP)
Protestant Christian Church in Bali (GKPB)
Protestant Church in Indonesia (GPI)
Protestant Church in South-East Sulawesi
Protestant Church in the Moluccas (GPM)
Protestant Church in Western Indonesia
  (GPIB)
Protestant Evangelical Church in Timor
  (GMIT)
Simalungun Protestant Christian Church
  (GKPS)
Toraja Church

**Japan**

Holy Catholic Church in Japan
Korean Christian Church in Japan
Orthodox Church in Japan
United Church of Christ in Japan

**Korea**

Korean Methodist Church

**Korea, Republic of**

Presbyterian Church in the Republic of Korea
Presbyterian Church of Korea

**Malaysia**

Methodist Church in Malaysia
Protestant Church in Sabah

**Myanmar**

Church of the Province of Myanmar
Methodist Church, Upper Myanmar
Myanmar Baptist Convention

**New Zealand**

Anglican Church in Aotearoa, New Zealand
  and Polynesia
Associated Churches of Christ in New Zealand
Baptist Union of New Zealand
Methodist Church of New Zealand
Presbyterian Church of Aotearoa New Zeal-
  and

**Pakistan**

Church of Pakistan
Presbyterian Church of Pakistan

**Philippines**

Episcopal Church in the Philippines
Evangelical Methodist Church in the Philippines

Philippine Independent Church
United Church of Christ in the Philippines

**Singapore**

Methodist Church in Singapore

**Sri Lanka**

Church of Ceylon
Methodist Church, Sri Lanka

**Taiwan**

Presbyterian Church in Taiwan

**Thailand**

Church of Christ in Thailand


**CARIBBEAN**

**Antigua**

Church in the Province of the West Indies
Methodist Church in the Caribbean and the
  Americas
Moravian Church, Eastern West Indies Pro-
  vince

**Cuba**

Methodist Church in Cuba
Presbyterian Reformed Church in Cuba

**Curaçao**

United Protestant Church

**Jamaica**

Jamaica Baptist Union
Moravian Church in Jamaica
United Church in Jamaica

**Suriname**

Moravian Church in Suriname

**Trinidad**

Presbyterian Church in Trinidad


**EUROPE**

**Albania**

Orthodox Autocephalous Church of Albania

**Armenia**

Armenian Apostolic Church

**Austria**

Evangelical Church of the Augsburg and Helvetic Confessions in Austria
Old Catholic Church of Austria

**Belgium**

United Protestant Church of Belgium

**Czech Republic**

Czechoslovak Hussite Church
Evangelical Church of Czech Brethren
Orthodox Church of the Czech Lands and Slovakia
Silesian Evangelical Church of the Aubsburg Confession in the Czech Republic

**Denmark**

Baptist Union of Denmark
Evangelical Lutheran Church in Denmark

**Estonia**

Estonian Evangelical Lutheran Church

**Finland**

Evangelical Lutheran Church of Finland
Orthodox Church of Finland

**France**

Evangelical Church of the Augsburg Confession of Alsace and Lorraine
Evangelical Lutheran Church of France
Reformed Church of Alsace and Lorraine
Reformed Church of France

**Germany**

Catholic Diocese of the Old Catholics in Germany
Evangelical Church in Germany
Latvian Evangelical Lutheran Church Abroad
Mennonite Church

**Greece**

Church of Greece
Greek Evangelical Church

**Hungary**

Baptist Union of Hungary
Lutheran Church in Hungary
Reformed Church in Hungary

**Iceland**

Evangelical Lutheran Church of Iceland

**Ireland**

Church of Ireland

**Italy**

Evangelical Baptist Union of Italy
Evangelical Methodist Church of Italy
Waldensian Church

**Latvia**

Evangelical Lutheran Church of Latvia

**Netherlands**

European Continental Province of the Moravian Church (Netherlands)
Evangelical Lutheran Church in the Kingdom of the Netherlands
Mennonite Church in the Netherlands
Netherlands Reformed Church
Old Catholic Church of the Netherlands
Reformed Churches in the Netherlands
Remonstrant Brotherhood

**Norway**

Church of Norway

**Poland**

Autocephalous Orthodox Church in Poland
Evangelical Church of the Augsburg Confession in Poland
Old Catholic Mariavite Church in Poland
Polish Catholic Church in Poland

**Portugal**

Evangelical Presbyterian Church of Portugal
Lusitanian Catholic Apostolic Evangelical Church

**Romania**

Evangelical Church of the Augsburg Confession in Romania
Evangelical Synodal Presbyterian Church of the Augsburg Confession in Romania
Reformed Church in Romania
Romanian Orthodox Church

**Russian Federation**

Russian Orthodox Church

**Scotland**

Church of Scotland

**Slovak Republic**

Evangelical Church of the Augsburg Confession in the Slovak Republic
Orthodox Church of the Czech Lands and Slovakia
Reformed Christian Church in Slovakia

**Spain**

Spanish Evangelical Church
Spanish Reformed Episcopal Church

**Sweden**

Church of Sweden
Mission Covenant Church of Sweden

**Switzerland**

Old Catholic Church of Switzerland
Swiss Protestant Church Federation

**Turkey**

Ecumenical Patriarchate of Constantinople

**United Kingdom**

Baptist Union of Great Britain
Church in Wales
Church of England
Methodist Church
Methodist Church in Ireland
Moravian Church in Great Britain
Presbyterian Church of Wales
Scottish Congregational Church
Scottish Episcopal Church
Union of Welsh Independents
United Free Church of Scotland
United Reformed Church

**Yugoslavia, Federal Republic of**

Reformed Christian Church in Yugoslavia
Serbian Orthodox Church
Slovak Evangelical Church of the Augsburg Confession in Yugoslavia

**LATIN AMERICA**

**Argentina**

Anglican Church of the Southern Cone of America
Christian Biblical Church
Church of God
Church of the Disciples of Christ
Evangelical Church of the River Plate
Evangelical Methodist Church of Argentina
United Evangelical Lutheran Church

**Bolivia**

Bolivian Evangelical Lutheran Church
Evangelical Methodist Church in Bolivia

**Brazil**

Christian Reformed Church of Brazil
Episcopal Anglican Church of Brazil

Evangelical Church of Lutheran Confession in Brazil
Methodist Church in Brazil
United Presbyterian Church of Brazil

**Chile**

Evangelical Lutheran Church in Chile
Free Pentecostal Mission Church of Chile
Methodist Church of Chile
Pentecostal Church of Chile
Pentecostal Mission Church

**Costa Rica**

Evangelical Methodist Church of Costa Rica

**El Salvador**

Baptist Association of El Salvador
Salvadorean Lutheran Synod

**Mexico**

Methodist Church of Mexico

**Nicaragua**

Baptist Convention of Nicaragua
Moravian Church in Nicaragua

**Peru**

Methodist Church of Peru

**Uruguay**

Evangelical Methodist Church in Uruguay

**MIDDLE EAST**

Apostolic Catholic Assyrian Church of the East

**Cyprus**

Church of Cyprus

**Egypt**

Coptic Orthodox Church
Episcopal Church in Jerusalem and the Middle East
Greek Orthodox Patriarchate of Alexandria and All Africa
Synod of the Nile of the Evangelical Church

**Iran**

Synod of the Evangelical Church of Iran

**Israel**

Greek Orthodox Patriarchate of Jerusalem

**Lebanon**

Armenian Apostolic Church
National Evangelical Synod of Syria and Lebanon
Union of the Armenian Evangelical Churches in the Near East

**Syria**

Greek Orthodox Patriarchate of Antioch and All the East
Syrian Orthodox Patriarchate of Antioch and All the East

## NORTH AMERICA

**Canada**

Anglican Church of Canada
Canadian Yearly Meeting of the Religious Society of Friends
Christian Church (Disciples of Christ) in Canada
Estonian Evangelical Lutheran Church Abroad
Evangelical Lutheran Church in Canada
Presbyterian Church in Canada
United Church of Canada

**United States of America**

African Methodist Episcopal Church
African Methodist Episcopal Zion Church
American Baptists Churches in the USA
Christian Church (Disciples of Christ) in the USA
Christian Methodist Episcopal Church
Church of the Brethren
Episcopal Church
Evangelical Lutheran Church in America
Friends General Conference
Friends United Meeting
Hungarian Reformed Church in America
International Council of Community Churches
International Evangelical Church
Moravian Church in America (Northern Province)
Moravian Church in America (Southern Province)
National Baptist Convention of America
National Baptist Convention, USA, Inc.
Orthodox Church in America
Polish National Catholic Church of America
Presbyterian Church (USA)
Progressive National Baptist Convention, Inc.

Reformed Church in America
Religious Society of Friends
United Church of Christ
United Methodist Church

## PACIFIC

**American Samoa**

Congregational Christian Church in American Samoa

**Cook Islands**

Cook Islands Christian Church

**Fiji**

Methodist Church in Fiji

**French Polynesia**

Evangelical Church of French Polynesia

**Kiribati, Republic of**

Kiribati Protestant Church

**Marshall Islands**

United Church of Christ-Congregational in the Marshall Islands

**New Caledonia**

Evangelical Church in New Caledonia and the Loyalty Isles

**Papua New Guinea**

Evangelical Lutheran Church
United Church in Papua New Guinea

**Solomon Islands**

Church of the Province of Melanesia
United Church in the Solomon Islands

**Tonga**

Free Wesleyan Church of Tonga

**Tuvalu**

Tuvalu Christian Church

**Vanuatu**

Presbyterian Church of Vanuatu

**Western Samoa**

Congregational Christian Church in Samoa
Methodist Church in Samoa

# SELECTED PERSONS AND CONCEPTS

**Anabaptists** — 16th century radical Protestants who championed believers' baptism and the separation of church and state

**antisemitism** (the correct English translation of *Antisemitismus*) — a word invented by Wilhelm Marr of Hamburg to give pseudo-scientific tone to the modern and populist use of anti-Jewish propaganda and hatred as a political tool

**"Awakening"** — a term applied by historians to sundry movements of religious revival in America, e.g., "Great Awakening," "Second Great Awakening," and including "Cane Ridge Revival" and other surges of conversions and popular voluntary religion. The revivals were an important means of reclaiming the masses of people for the churches, from which they had exited before the state church system was abandoned and Religious Liberty embraced.

**Bolsheviks** — caucus that controlled the majority during the overthrow of the monarchy and institution of popular government in Russia (1917); terminated state church (Russian Orthodox); after civil war, established a dictatorship that lasted to 1989

**Byzantine** — related to Byzanz, the culture dominated by Orthodox Christianity and centered in Constantinople in the centuries between Constantine and the triumph of Islam in Asia Minor

**caesaro-papism** — a term applied to the control of the churches by secular rulers in the Eastern portions of Christendom. In the West, the struggle between kings and bishops, emperors and popes for control of the churches has continued for more than a millennium and a half.

**caliphate** — hereditary male rule, practiced by Hebrew Christians following James the brother of Jesus, by several branches of Islam, and by several Orthodox Jewish sects

**Carlsbad Decrees** (1819) — despotic decrees of the German states to suppress the influence of republican and national ideals among university students, proposed by reactionary Metternich of Austria and enforced by the King of Prussia

**Christendom** — the geographical area where after 325 CE the Christian religion was legally established and other religions persecuted; loosely, the Christian churches of the world

**concordat** — a treaty between a pope and a political regime, securing the rights and privileges of the Roman Catholic Church. The system of concordats was developed after the Congress of Vienna (1815), as the rise of nationalism and democracy threatened procedures and claims dating back to the Middle Ages.

**Constantine "the Great"** (274–337, Roman Emperor from 325) — Christian Emperor whose victories and rule ended the persecutions and united church and state in "Christendom," with disadvantages for other religions and discrimination against the Jews

**Crusades** — external military expeditions from 1096 to 1270 during which European armies recaptured Jerusalem and the Holy Land from the Muslims, losing them again; internally in the same period, persecution, pillaging and murder directed against "heretics" and Jewish enclaves in "Christendom"

**Darby, John Nelson** (1800–82) — leader in the Plymouth Brethren, whose numerous trips to America spread Dispensationalism (q.v.) widely, profoundly influencing larger Fundamentalist denominations

**death camps** — specifically, those collection centers set up by the German Third Reich to kill Jews (Treblinka, Sobibor, Belsec); loosely applied to *KZ* ("concentration camps") where numbers of prisoners died through brutality and lack of food and medicine

***Deutsche Christen*** — a German Protestant church caucus under Nazi control, which rejected the Jewish heritage of Christianity (see Marcion)

**Diaspora** — Jewish populations away from *Eretz Israel* ("the Land of Israel"), especially after the destruction of the Second Temple (70 CE)

***Didache*** — "the Teaching," probably from the 1st century CE — a manual of Christian discipline

**dispensation ("Dispensationalism")** — a certain period in a scheme of Christian history developed especially by John Nelson Darby (q.v.). The periodization gathers speed and intensity to accent a speculative description of the end-time.

***Donatio Constantini* ("Donation of Constantine")** — a forged document used to establish papal authority in political affairs during the Middle Ages; exposed as fraudulent by Lorenzo Valla in 1440

**Donatism** — a movement judged a "heresy" for its strong stand for discipline against the *lapsi* (q.v.). It also expressed a resistance of North African Christians against the expanding claims of the Latin Church and the Bishop of Rome.

***Endlösung*** — "Final Solution," a Nazi euphemism, with pseudo-scientific and political overtones, for the genocide of the Jews, later called SHOAH or "the Holocaust"

**Erastianism** — a theory of royal supremacy in making ecclesiastical appointments, favored by King Henry VIII in justifying his interventions in the staffing and policies of the Church in his realm; see caesaro-papism

**"first-order religious language"** — the language of a personal testimony or message, in theological discourse contrasting with references to third-party opinions or experience

**French Revolution** (1791–99) — political and social convulsion in France; temporarily eliminated the monarchy and asserted the Rights of Man and Citizens; ended in a period of despotism and aggressive wars (1800–15)

**gentiles** — in reference to outsiders, *goyyim*, those not belonging to the community (e.g., non-Jews, non-Mormons)

**Gnosticism** — a term applied to one or more speculative systems of knowledge that have influenced Judaism or Christianity

**Grundtvig, N.F.S.** (1783–1872) — leading statesman in the Lutheran Church of Denmark; prolific hymn-writer and champion of other cultural and national expressions of Christianity; moving spirit in the development of People's Colleges and the cooperative movement

**Hegira** (622 CE) — beginning event in the Muslim calendar, memorializing the escape of the Prophet Mohammed from Mecca to Medina

**Holocaust, the** — (Hebrew, *SHOAH*), the Nazi genocide of the Jews

**Iconoclasm** — hostility to prayers or votive offerings tendered to paintings or other physical representations of angels, saints or other spiritual entities; movements of austerity to remove such "icons" from churches and shrines; initiatives to purge the churches of "images," e.g., during the confrontation with a rising Islam and during the division of Christendom in the 16th century between Protestant and Roman Catholic churches

**"investiture controversy"** — during the struggle of many centuries in Western

Christendom as to whether ecclesiastical or political rulers should have major control of the churches, control of an appointment ("investiture") to a major see carried heavy financial, political and even military significance.

**Irenaeus** (c 125–c 202) — Bishop of Lyons; writing against the centrifugal force of several speculative systems upon Christianity, he developed the theory of a special succession of religious authority through bishops from earliest times

**Julian "the Apostate"** (Roman Emperor 361–63) — ruler who despised the Christians for exclusiveness ("intolerance") and accomplished a brief intermission in the union of church and state instituted by Constantine in 313 and 325

*Jus Naturale* ("Natural Law") — an approach to ethics through the interpretation of relationships in the natural world, fundamental to Greek systems of thought and especially important in Christian teachings since Thomas Aquinas (c 1225–74)

**Kierkegaard, Soren** (1813–55) — Danish literary figure and religious philosopher, of great influence upon 20th century "existentialism" and Dialectical Theology; author i.a. of "The Attack on Christendom"

**Kuyper, Abraham** (1837–1920) — Dutch Christian political philosopher; founder of the Anti-Revolutionary Party, of the Free University of Amsterdam, of the strict Calvinist Reformed Churches (*gereformeerde Kerken*); opponent of liberal and democratic movements

*Lapsi* ("the lapsed") — also called *traditores*, whence "traitors"; those Christians who during the persecution under Emperor Decius (d. 251) gave religious homage to his person. The question of their rehabilitation split the church at Rome and especially in North Africa.

**Logos Fathers** — early Christian teach-ers, trained in Greek philosophy, who identified Christ with the *Logos*, source of all human reason

**Manichaeism** — a heresy combining aesceticism and a radical dualism of soul and body, named for its early teacher, Mani (c 215–75). It was influenced by Zoroastrianism, the official state religion of Persia.

**Marcion of Sinope** (d. c 160) — early Christian layman who rejected the Hebrew Scriptures ("Old Testament"), OT references in the Christian "New Testament," and founded a splinter church

**Marx, Karl** (1818–30) — author of *The Communist Manifesto* (1848, with Friedrich Engels), *Capital* (1867), founder of "scientific socialism." His father a convert of convenience, he became an atheist and anti-clerical.

**Montanism** — an early heresy that heightened its adherents' excitement for the end-time or "the last things" and taught an austere morality and ethics

**Neo-Platonism** — a school of Greek philosophical thought that profoundly influenced Christianity, especially during the Renaissance and in radical Protestantism

**Oral Tradition** — the stories and lessons transmitted to the following generations in pre-literate societies, usually stored in the memories of persons trained and set aside from youth as "living libraries"; in literate societies, the layer of earlier popular cultural memories

**"perfectionist theology," perfectionism** — the teaching, generally associated with the teaching of John Wesley, the founder of Methodism, that through faith and the practice of disciplined living the Christian may find his way out of the darkness of sin into the sunshine of the New Humanity in Christ

**Pius IX** (1792–1878, pope from 1846) — reactionary pope, opposed to liberal, democratic and national political developments and institutions (e.g., popular suffrage, public schools); author of *Syllabus of Errors* (1864) against a list of 80 modern ideas, and of the dogma of Papal Infallibility (1870), which asserted final papal control of all matters of Roman Cathlic belief and practice

**primitivism** — as a type of historical interpretation, a teaching with a golden age in the past followed by a decline and fall. The typology was studied and explained to the wider circle of historians by Professor A. O. Lovejoy of Johns Hopkins University. Among religious groups, there is usually a consummation in an Age of Restitution

**Qumran** — the site of Jewish monastic communities on the Dead Sea (c 135 BCE–70 CE), today important as a depository for centuries of valuable ancient manuscripts ("Dead Sea Scrolls")

**Rabbinic Judaism** — the culture and teachings developed among the religious Jews in the Diaspora, after the destruction of the Second Temple and the separation of gentile Christianity from the Jewish people

**Ranke, Leopold von** (1795–1886) — early exponent of "the historical method," with special emphasis upon written primary sources and questioning the reliability of oral traditions

**Reformation, Magisterial** — established churches (chiefly Lutheran, Reformed and Anglican) that accepted the doctrinal changes of the 16th century Reformation, but continued the Constantinian (q.v.) union of church and state that characterized European Christendom

**Reformation, Radical** — sometimes called "the Left Wing of the Reformation"; churches that followed the doctrine of the 16th century reformers but rejected control by political regimes

*religio licita* — a religion, sect or cult permitted by the Roman Emperors

**Saravia, Adrianus** (1531–1613) — Dutch champion of the modern mandate of "the Great Commission" (Matt. 28:18–20, Mk. 16:15–16)

**secular** — post-Christendom social and political areas or institutions that have escaped the control of religion

**Septuagint** — the Greek translation and edition of the Hebrew scriptures completed in Alexandria during the 2d century BCE, but adding some books not in the Hebrew Old Testament ("the Apocrypha") and deleting some sections of Jeremiah and other books; commonly used by Christian teachers until Jerome's *Vulgate* returned to the original Hebrew language (translation into Latin completed c 404 CE)

**Tertullian** (c 160–c 220) — a layman and Church Father, important for writings that brought Latin forward in a church whose intellectuals had previously used Greek; also a key figure in Montanism (q.v.)

**Third Reich** — the historical period begun in 1933, according to Nazi mythologists, with the dictatorship of Adolf Hitler (1889–1945, dictator from 1933); to last one thousand years, succeeding the Holy Roman Empire and the imperium forged by Bismarck. Among the initiated, the myth also evoked the threefold historical periodization introduced by the Cistercian mystic Joachim of Fiore (1145?–1202?) into the spiritual and intellectual underworld of European culture.

**totalitarian, totalitarianism** — adjective and noun referring to a closed and unitary political or religious system

# INDEX

## PERSONS / PLACES / SUBJECTS

*Page numbers in italics refer to maps.*

## A

Aachen, Charlemagne's capital *70*, 74, *74*
Abbasid dynasty *68*, *82*, 83
Abdul Baha 284
Abelard, Peter *113*, 114
Abgar, King of Armenia 65
Abington Township Case 331, 403
Abolitionism, abolition of slavery
  Liberia 272
  William Wilberforce *279*
  Charles G. Finney 315
  and revivalism 333
  see Freedmen's Bureau
Abrabanel, Isaac *123*
Abraham, covenant with 1, 5
Abulafia, Abraham 122
Acre crusader center *101*, 102
Acton, J.E.E.D. 257
Adoptionism 29
  Felix of Urgel 72
Adrian VI (pope) 151
Adventists
  new churches in USA *351*
Afo-a-kom 269
Africa
  before European colonization 267, *268*, 269
  migrations in S. Africa *270*, 271–72
  under colonial rule 272, *273*, 275
  modern missions *362–63*
  Christian renewal *382*, 383
  independent Christian movements *396*, 397, 399
African Methodist Episcopal Church 342, *343*
African Methodist Episcopal Zionist Church 342, *343*
Afrikaners *270*
  see also Boers
Afro-Americans/Negroes
  see abolitionism
  see black religion
  see civil rights
Aglipayan Church 266, *267*
  see Old Catholic Church
Agricola, Johann 158, *158*
Ahmadiya movement *275*, 357
Aidan, monastic *63*
Ailly, Pierre d' 135, *137*, 143
Ain Jalut *116*, 117
Akbar (Emp. of India) 195

Alaric sack of Rome 49
Alaska *262*, 265
Albania under Ottoman Turks *138*
Albertus Magnus *113*, 114
Albigensi 98, 105
Alcalá de Henares *130*, 203
Alcuin *71*, 72, 74
Alembert, Jean d' *234*, 236
Aleppo *101*
Alesius, Alexander 185
Alexander the Great 18, 19, 20
  Empire *21*
Alexander I (tsar of Russia)
  Holy Alliance 241, *241*, 246, *246*
Alexander VI (pope) 151, *152*, *196*
Alexandria
  center of Hellenism 19
  Catechetical School of 33, *34*, 35
Alfred the Great 63, 80
Al-Ghazzali *116*, 117
Al-Hakim 221
Allen, Richard 342
Almohades 221
Almoravids *87*
Alsace-Lorraine
  in "Middle Kingdom" 72
Amalric of Bena *128*
Ambrose *50*, 51, 52
America
  effect of discovery on missionary theology 29
  English colonies 225, 225–27
American Academy of Religion 331
American Anti-Slavery Society 314, *323*, 333, *356*
American Bible Society *356*
American Board of Commissioners for Foreign Missions *323*, 324–26, *324–26*, 353, *356*
American Colonization Society 333, *356*
American Friends Service Committee *388*, 389
  Doukhobor resettlement 252
American Home Missionary Society *356*
American Missionary Association 326
American Peace Society *356*
American Revolution
  contrasted with French R. 237

American Sunday School Union *356*
American Temperance Union *356*
American Tract Society *356*
Amish 148, 149
Anabaptism, Anabaptists 147–49, 150, 173–74
  and Butzer 155
  separating OT and NT 190
  in the Netherlands 179
  see Hutterites
  see Mennonites
  see Swiss Brethren
Andover Seminary 322, 325
Andreae, Jacob 171
Angkor Wat 278
Anglicanism in American colonies 227, 263
Anglo-American Missionary Conferences 353
Animism 383
Anselm 112, *113*, 114
Anskar 75, *75*
Anthroposophy 393
Anticlericalism, anticlericals
  French Encyclopédistes 237
  Latin America 261
  tsarist Russia 245
Anti-evolution laws 339, *339*
Antioch
  school of *34*, 35
  Principality of 96, *101*
Antipope 133, *134*, 135
Antisemitism 191
  Justin Martyr 33
  John Chrysostom 52
  in the Crusades 95, 96, 98
  under Innocent III 105, *106*
  and the Black Death *118*, 119
  and false messiahs 122, *123*, 124
  in Spain *126*, 127
  16th–17th centuries 189–91, *190*
  repression of Jews 189–91
  in the Enlightenment 236
  in tsarist Russia *246*, 247
  in Papal States 254
  in post-Soviet Russia 301
  and genocide in Nazi Empire 310, 404, *405*, 406–07
Anti-Trinitarianism, in 16th century 173
Antony of Egypt *59*, 60
Apollinaris *32*, 47, *50*, 52
Apologists, the *32*, 33

Apostles, Twelve
  traditional missionary travels
    *28*, 29
"Apostolic," new churches in
  USA *351*
Apostolic Fathers 31
"Apostolic succession"
  Sweden 164
  England 181
  Old Catholics 256–58
Aquinas, Thomas
  see Thomas Aquinas
Arab League 312, *313*
Aragon 124, *125*
Archaeology 16
Arianism 44, 45, 47, 49, *50*, 52,
  53
Aristotle 18, 19, 22, 41
Arius
  at Antioch 35
  Christological dispute 44, *50*
  see Arianism
Armada, the Grand *205*, 205-06
Armenia, Armenians *21*, *325*
  Monophysites 48, *53*
  kingdom *101*
  revolts against Turks 281
  suffer genocidal attack from
    Muslims 284, *285*
Arminius, Jakob 172
Armstrong, Samuel Chapman
  336
Arndt, Ernst Moritz 240, 290
Arndt, Johann *231*
Arnold of Brescia *128*
Arnold, Eberhard 150
Arnold, Gottfried 231, *231*
Arnold, Thomas *279*, 293
Arras, Union of *178*
Asbury, Francis 264, *323*
Ashkenaz, Ashkenazim 120–
  22, 345
Ashmun, J. *273*
Asia
  colonial holdings in 274,
    *275*, 276
  modern missions 359, *359*
  lay training 384
Assisi *106*
Association for the
  Coordination of University
  Religious Affairs *402*, 403
Association of Christian
  Institutes for Social Concern
  in Asia 384
Astrology
  medallion with Zodiac
    symbols 36
Atatürk, Mustafa Kemal 282
Athanasius 40, 47, *50*
  Great Meteoron *61*
Athens
  at Paul's time *22*
  Christian center *32*
Attila the Hun 49, 55
  Empire *54*
Augsburg
  Interim *155*, 194
  Peace of Augsburg 190, 192,
    *193*, 194
  Augsburg Confession 154,

*154*, *193*
Augustine 50, *54*
  *City of God* 40–41, 52, 74
  persecution 40, 49
  Church Father 51, 52
Augustine of Canterbury 56, *63*
Auschwitz *405*, 406
Austerlitz, battle of *238*, 240
Australia missions *277*, 278
Austria
  Thirty Years' War *188*
  Napoleonic Wars *238*, 240,
    241, *241*
  in Holy Alliance *248*, 249–50
  loss of Hannover, Hessen-
    Nassau 244
  see Vienna
Averroës 84, 124
Avignon, papacy at *132*, 132–
  33, 135
Azariah, V. S. *371*
Azusa revival *343*, 399

**B**

Ba'al Shem Tov 124
Bab, "the Gateway" (Mirza Ali
  Mohammed) *283*, 283–84
Bach, Johann Sebastian *231*
Bacon, Roger *113*, 114
Bad Boll *371*, *375*, 376, 377, 378
Baeck, Leo 412
Baghdad
  Manichaean center *39*
  seat of Nestorian Catholicos
    65
  Abbasid capital *82*, 83
  center of Seljuk Empire *116*,
    117
  fall to Mongols *101*
Baha'i movement *283*, 283–84
Baha'u'llah, "the Splendor of
  God" (Mirza Husayn Ali)
  *283*, 284
Baillie, John 316
Balfour Declaration *282*, 412
Balkans
  Ottoman Turk
    conquests *138*
  independent movements 250
Baltic 107
  see Hanseatic League
  see Teutonic Knights
Bangalore: Christian Institute
  for the Study of Religion and
  Society 384
Bantu
  migrations *268*, *270*, 271
Baptism, adult 150, 295
Baptists
  in England 169, *181*
  in New England 263
  and revivalism 264, *323*
  Southern B. *340*, 340–41
  among Afro-Americans 342,
    344
  divisions in USA 350, *351*
Bar Kokhba 15
Bardstown *337*
Barmen, Synod of *306*, 309
Barnabites 212

Barth, Karl 399
Basel, Council of *134*, 135,
  136, 218
Basil 47, *50*
  monastic 61, *61*
Basilides *37*, 38
Basques 305
Basutos *270*, 272
Batak Church *277*
Baxter, Richard *181*, 183
Bayle, Pierre *234*
Bea, Augustin 374
Bede the Venerable 63, 74
Beecher, Lyman 264, 322, 338
Belgium
  Reformation 179
  in Africa *273*, 274
Belgrade
  captured by Turks 192
  staging area for attack on
    Vienna 219
Bellarmine, Robert 211
Benedict of Nursia 61, *62*
Bengel, J. A. *231*
Berkeley, George *234*
Berleburg *231*
Berlin
  university and national
    revival *233*, 240
Bernard of Clairvaux
  crusader preacher 96
  church reformer 102, *103*, 104
Bessarion, John *136*
Bethge, Eberhard 410
Beza, Theodore 29, *161*
  first Protestant psalter 202
Bible
  canon fixed 31
  interpretations at Alexandria
    and Antioch 36
  in Reformation 153, 167
  at Council of Trent 217
  King James Version (AV) 182
  and the scientific method *259*,
    260
Bible Institutes 353
Biblical Literature, Society of
  331
Bishop(s), growing authority of
  the 33, 35
Bismarck, Otto von 244
Björkquist, Manfred 377
Black Death, the *118*, 118–19
Black Muslims *343*, 392
Black religion 265, 335, 342–44
Bobbio, monastic center at *62*
Boehme, Jakob *188*, 189
Boers *270*, 271–72
Boff, Leonardo 385
Bogomili 98, 105
Bohemia
  Reformation and Counter-
    Reformation 187
  revolt against Habsburgs 194,
    *248*, 249
Boleslav V, King of Poland 121
Boleyn, Anne 166
Bolivar, Simon *261*
Bolivia 261
Bologna, university at *130*
Bonaventura *113*, 115

Bonhoeffer, Dietrich 310, 370
Boniface 62, 75, *75*
Boniface VIII (pope) 105
Bonn Reunion Conferences 256, 258
Booth, William *279*, 280
Borgia, Francis 211
Borneo *277*
Borromeo, Charles 212
Bosnia
  under Ottoman Turks *138*, 194
  see Bogomili
Bossey, Château de *369*, 370
Bossuet, Jacques *234*
Boxer Rebellion *275*, 276
Boyne, Battle of the *314*, 315
Brahe, Tycho *234*, 235
Brahmo Samaj *275*, 276, 357
Brandeis, Louis D. *346*
Brandhuber, Wolfgang 150
Brazil 261
Brent, Charles *371*
Brenz, Johannes 158, *158*, 159
Brest-Litovsk Treaty *299*, 300
Brès, Guido de 179
Brethren 149, *231*, 387
  peace testimony 319
  divisions 350
Brethren of the Common Life *142*, 142, 143
Brethren Service Commission *388*, 389
Briçonnet, Gillaume (Bishop of Meaux) 202
Britain, British Empire *292*
  North America 225–26
  South America 261
  South Africa 270, 271–72, *273*
  Asia 274, *275*, 276
  South Pacific *277*, 278
  see England
  see Ireland
  see Scotland
  see Wales
Brook Farm *327*, 328
Browne, Robert 169
*Bruderhof* 150, 319, 381
Brunner, Emil 352, 399
Buddhism
  in Mongol Empire 112
  Zen 357
  centers and sects in Japan *395*
Bufalo, Gaspare del 289
Bugenhagen, Johann 158, *158*, *163*, 164
Bulgar kingdom, Bulgars 73, *87*
Bulgaria
  under Ottoman Turks *138*
  independence 250
Bullinger, Heinrich *161*, 162
*Bundschuh*
  see peasants' revolts
Burgundy, the "middle kingdom" 72
Burke, Edmund 240, *279*
Burma, missions in *275*
Bushnell, Horace 348
Butzer, Martin 155, *155*, 158, *158*
  won by Luther 194
  in England *165*, 166

Byzantium *43*, 44, 56, *57*, *136*
  and Charlemagne 70
  and Muslim dynasties *82*
  in Italy *89*
  decline in 11th century 96
  during Crusades *99*, *106*

# C

Cabbala 122, 124
Cabet, Étienne 328
Cabot, John *198*, 199
Cabral, Pedro Alvaris *196*
Caesar
  Julius 23, 27
  Octavian 23
Caesarea, monastic center in *61*
Cairo
  caliphate 83, *101*
  oldest university 83
  sacked by Ottoman Turks 221
Cajetan 212
Calendar
  Easter and Passover 33
  Synod of Whitby 63
Caliph
  conquests of first four 68
  of Cordova 83
Callistus of Rome *34*, 35
Calvin, John 155, 157, *157*, *161*, 162, 202
Calvinism
  in England 170
  Synod of Dort *171*, 172
  in France 175, 176, 202, 203
  in the Netherlands *178*, 179
  in Scotland 185
  in Holy Roman Empire *188*
  in Transylvania 219
  and Cyril Lucaris 223
  and missions 352
  see Calvin, John
  see Geneva
  see Huguenots
Cambridge, Martin Butzer in 155
Camp meetings
  see revivalism
Campbell, Alexander 264, *323*
Campbell, Thomas *323*
Canaan *9*
Canada
  early voyages of discovery *198*, 199
  Doukhobors 252
  Hutterite colonies *327*
Cane Ridge Revival 264, 322, *323*
Canisius, Peter *210*, 211, 212
Canterbury, Archbishop of
  Augustine 56
  Dunstan 80
  Anselm 112
  in Reformation 167, 168
  Reginald Pole 217
  William Temple 370
Canute, King 93
Cape Town *270*
Cappadocia *21*
  Cappadocian Fathers 47, *50*

monasticism *61*
Cappel, Battle of *156*
Capuchins 170, 212
Carbonari *241*, 254
Carey, William *275*, 276, 352
Carlsbad Decrees *241*, 242
Carolingian Empire
  Charlemagne 70–73
  disintegration 86–88
Carpini, Joannes de Plano *109*
Carthage 24, 32, *43*, *50*, 51, *54*
Cartier, Jacques *198*, 199
Cartwright, Thomas 169
Carver, George Washington 336, *343*
Cary, Lott 344
Casimir III, King of Poland 121
Cassian, John
  monastic 61, *62*
Cassiodorus
  monastic 62, *62*
Castellio, Sebastian *147*, 173
Castile 125, *125*
Catechetical School
  see Alexandria
Catherine the Great 122
  Empire of *246*
  and Mennonites, Hutterites 251, *251*
Catherine of Aragon 166
Catherine of Siena *113*, 133
Catholic Apostolic Church *279*
Celtic Christianity 62, 63, *63*, 377
  Celtic cross 63
Celtis, Conradus *142*
Cerdo *37*
Ceylon *275*
Chakko, Sarah 370
Chalcedon, Council of 52, *53*
Chaldean Christians *325*
Chalmers, Thomas *279*
Champlain, Samuel de 199
Charlemagne 70–73, *74*
Charles Martel 68
Charles V (Emp.) 192, *193*, 194
  struggle with Protestants 160
  and the Netherlands 178
  wars with Francis I 202
  and African slave trade 271
Charles I, King of England 182
Charles II, King of England 183
Charter Oak Treaty 226, 228
Chateaubriand, Réne de 255
Chemnitz, Martin 171
Chêng, C. Y. 370
Cherokees, missions to *324*
Chiang Kai-shek 310, 311, *311*
Children's Crusade 96
Chile, Pentecostalism in *398*, 399
China 310–12
  and the Nestorians *65*
  medieval missions to 109, *109*
  M. Ricci 209, 211
  Jesuit convent in Macao 211
  missions in colonial era 274, *275*
China Inland Mission 276, 353
Chivalry
  legend of Roland 70

Chmielnicki, Bogdan
  antisemite  122, *190*
Christ of the Andes  385
Christendom
  Christian Roman
    Empire  40–42
  disintegration  49
  East/West schism  73, *87*
  split between Roman and
    Protestant parties  *170*, 194
  new alignments  171–72
  rebellion in 16th century 144*f*
  complicity in Holocaust  309
  disaster of World War I  315
  see Holy Roman Empire
Christian III, King of Denmark
  *163*, 164
Christian IV, King of Denmark
  *188*, 189
Christian and Missionary
  Alliance  353
Christian Science  341, *341*, 392
  see Eddy, Mary Baker
Christology  31, *32*, 33
  Nestorians, Monophysites  48
  see Chalcedon
  see *Deutsche Christen*
  see Marcion
Christus Pantocrator  72
Chrysostom, John  *50*, 52
Chungking  *311*
Church discipline  148, 189, 232
  in Radical Reformation  148,
    149
  Butzer and Calvin  155
Church lands  *137*
  in the Baltic  107
  during "Babylonian
    captivity"  *132*
  in England  *132*
  in Scandinavia  164
  in Germany  239
  in South America  261
  in Spain  305
Church Missionary Society  274
Church struggle  375–76, 379
  in Third Reich  *306*, 309–10
Churchill, Winston  315–16
Cisterian reform, Cîteaux  103,
  *103*, 104
Cities, rise of the  *128*, 129
Civil rights
  struggle of Afro-Americans
    333, *343*
Civil war
  in France  175–76
  in the Netherlands  178–80
  in England  181–83
  in Scotland  184–86
  Germany: Thirty Years' War
    187–89
  Spanish  *304*, 304–05
  American  331, *332*, 333
Clement of Alexandria  33,34,35
Clement of Rome  31
Clement V (pope)  *132*, 133
Clement VII (pope)  133, 151
Clermont  *95*
Clinchey, Everett J.  401
Clovis  51, *54*
  and the papacy  70

Cluniac reform, Cluny  *76*, 77
Codde, Petrus  257
Code Napoléon  239
Coleridge, Samuel Taylor  293
Colet, John  *142*, *165*, 167–68
Colleges (American)
  founded before 1860  329, *330*
  Negro colleges  *334*, 335
  Roman Catholic colleges  *337*
  Jewish institutes of higher
    learning  346
Colleges (Near East)  *282*, 325
Cologne, Dominican center  *130*
Colombia  261
Colonialism
  in Africa  272–74
  in Asia  274–76
  in South Pacific  277–78
Columba
  monastic  62, *63*
Columbanus
  monastic  62, *62*
Columbus, Christopher 195, *196*
Common Prayer, Book of  166
Communism, Christian
  Hutterite  150, 174
  in 19th century America  326,
    *327*, 328
Communism, Marxist 298–301,
  *299*
Comte, Auguste  *234*
Concentration camps
  in Boer War  272
  in Nazi Empire  *405*
Conciliarism  133, *134*, 135, 136
  ended at Council of Trent
    216–18
Concord, Formula and Book of
  *170*, 171, 172
Concordat, papal
  with Francis I  202
  with Franz Josef  250
  with Napoleon  252
  with Latin American
    nations  254
  with Mussolini  303
  with Hitler  308
Confederate States of America
  331, *332*, 333
Confessing Church (Germany)
  *306*, 376
Confessional  63
Confessions of faith
  Athanasius  44
  Chalcedon  53
  Reformation  153*f*
  Barmen  *306*, 309
Confirmation  149
  and Butzer  155
Congar, Yves  374
Congo (former Zaire)  273, *273*
  largest independent African
    church  397
Congregationalism,
  Congregationalists
  in New England  263, 322
  and missions  325, 326
  educating freed slaves  336
  see Independents
Congress of Racial Equality
  (CORE) 344

Connecticut River Valley  322
Conscientious objection  319
  see peace testimony
Conscription  239, 251
Constance, Council of  *134*, 135
Constantine (Emp.)  16, 42, *43*,
  44, 45
Constantinople  *43*, 44, 45, *46*
  Councils I, II, III  52, 53
  and the Crusades  95, 96, 97
  Latin patriarchate of  105
  fall of  138–39, *139*
Continental Missionary
  Conferences 353
Conversion
  in Pietism  231
Copenhagen, university in  164
Copernicus, Nicholas  213, *234*,
  235
Copts  48, *53*
  Jewish forms in Ethiopian
    church  269, 397
Cordova
  caliphate  *82*, 83
  cultural center  124
Cornell United Religious Work
  401, *402*
Corsica
  Vandal  *54*
  to Pisa  *89*
  to Aragon  124
Cortez, Hernando  *196*, 197
Councils of the church, early  *32*
Counter-culture  352
  see church discipline
  see communism, Christian
Counter-Reformation 209, *210*,
  212, 213
  antisemitism  190
Covenant
  Abraham  1
  Christian  1
  in Calvinism  170
  congregational  226
  in New England  263
Cracow
  captured by Mongols  109
  university of  121, *130*
Cranmer, Thomas  167, 168
Crete
  Minoan kingdom  9
  revolt against Turks  281
Crimean War  247
Cromwell, Oliver  *181*, 182, 183
  and Ireland  315
Crucifixion  10, 12
Crusades  94, *95*, 96–98
  capture of Jerusalem  *97*
  sack of Zara and
    Constantinople  96
  Crusader kingdoms  101, *116*
  Crusader fortresses  102, 107
  against Jews and
    heretics  105, *106*
  in the Baltic  107–08
  Spanish crusades  125
  and the explosion of
    learning  131
  motif in Loyola's vision of a
    new order  208
Cumberland Presbyterian

Church   *323*, 350
Cyprian   35
Cyprus
  home of Aphrodite   *21*
  Venetian colony   *101*
Cyril of Alexandria   53
Cyril of Thessalonica   *57*, 58
  and the Bulgars   73
Czechoslovakia
  sacrificed to Hitler   309
  see Bohemia
  see Prague

# D

Dakotas, mission to the   *324*
Damascus
  Christian center   *14*
  Muslim center   81, *82*
  emirate   *101*
Danes, the
  in England   *80*
Dante   *130*, 141
Danube valley   158
Darby, John Nelson   *279*, 280, 293
Dartmouth College Case   329
Darwin, Charles   *259*, 360
David, King   5
Dayaks   *277*
Dead Sea Scrolls   17
Death camps   *405*, 406
Decius (Emp.)   33, 35
Dedham Case   322
De Gaulle, Charles   316
Delmonte, Giovanni
  see Julius III
Demarcation, line of   *196*
Denmark
  Christianization of   *75*, 91
  and Bugenhagen   158, *163*
  Reformation   *163*, 164
  loss of Schleswig-Holstein   244
De Nobili, Robert   211, *229*
Descartes, René   *234*
*Deutsche Christen*   309
Deventer   *142*
Diaz, Bartholomew   *196*
Diderot, Denis   *234*, 236
Diétrich, Suzanne de   368, 384
Diocletion (Emp.)   24, 25, 35
Dionysius   34, 35
Disciples of Christ/
  Christian churches   264, *323*
Dispensationalism   293
Disraeli, Benjamin   280
Divine right of kings   181
Divine Word, Society of the   289
Divorce
  first Christian defense of   183
Docetism   *32*, 33
Döllinger, Ignatius von   *256*, 257, 258
Dome of the Rock, Jerusalem   69, *97*
Dominic   *106*
Dominicans   *106*
Donation of Constantine   16, 141
Donatism   40, 44, 49, *50*
  Synod of Arles   *43*

Dort, Synod of   *170*, 172
Dostoevski, Feodor M.   245, *246*
Douglass, Frederick   335
Doukhobors   252, *252*
Dowie, J. Alexander   397
Drake, Francis   197, 200
  repulse of the Grand Armada   *205*
Dred Scott Decision   333
Dreyfus Case   255
Drummond, Henry   *279*, 364
Druses   221
DuBois, W.E.B.   336, *343*
Dürer, Albrecht
  "Four Horsemen of the Apocalypse"   187
Dunant, Henri   366
Dunstan   80
Dupanloup, F.A.P.   257, 258
Dura-Europos   16, *21*
Durie, John   182, 183
Dwight, Timothy   264

# E

Early Church
  see primitive Christianity
Easter Synod   86
Eastern Orthodoxy   *138*, 138–39
  new churches in USA   *351*
Ebionites   29
Eckart, Meister   *113*, 115
Ecuador   261
Ecumenical cooperation,
  ecumenism   364, 370, *371*, 374
  O. Cromwell   183
  Pietism   230
  Old Prussian Union Church   *243*
  V. S. Soloviev   247
  Bonn Reunion Conferences   *256*, 258
  in USA   348–49
  and modern missions   353
  John R. Mott   366–68
  WSCF   367
  in Africa   383
Ecumenical Lay Center, Malang   384
Eddy, Mary Baker   341, 392
Edessa
  center of first Christianized nation   65
  Nestorian center   65, *65*
  County of   96, *101*
Edinburgh Conference   370
  John R. Mott   367
Edward the Confessor, King of England   93
Edward VI, King of England   166
Edwards, Jonathan   231, *232*, 323
Egypt   *9*, *21*, 37, *39*, 43, *59*, 68
  center of Islamic culture   117
Ehrensperger, Harold   379
Einsiedeln   *156*
Einstein, Albert   *234*, *306*
Eire
  see Ireland

El Aksa, Jerusalem   85, *97*
Electors
  see Holy Roman Empire
Elizabeth I, Queen of England   *165*, 167, 206
Emancipation Proclamation   333
Emperor
  title assumed in the West   70
Engels, Friedrich   296, *297*
England
  Roman conquest   26, *27*
  early monasticism   63, *63*
  Alfred the Great   80, *80*
  Norman conquest   92, 93
  fief of papacy   105
  lands in France, 14th century   *132*
  break from Rome   166
  voyages of discovery   *198*, 199
  Hundred Years' War   200
  Reformation   *165*, 165–69
  civil war   *181*, 181–83
  opposition to Holy Alliance   242
  Catholic Emancipation Act   254
  Imperial England   *279*, 279–80
  Christian revival   291, 293
England, John   338
English Revolution
  contrasted with French Revolution   237, 240
Enlightenment   2, *234*, 235–36, 294
  antisemitism   236
  enlightened despot   251
Ephesus   *32*
  Council of   48, 52, *53*
Ephrata   *227*, 328
Epicureans, Epicurus   *19*, 22
Episcopacy
  in England   181
  in Scotland   186
  see bishop
  see apostolic succession
Erasmus, Desiderius   *130*, 142, 143
Erikson, Leif   79, *90*
Essenes   7, 17, *37*
Étaples, Lefévre d'   *142*
  Christian humanist   202
Ethiopia
  monasticism in   64, *64*
  early contacts with Europe   268
  attacked by fascist Italy   303
Eucharist
  Radbertus of Corbie's treatise   72
  and Marburg Colloquy   156, 159
  at Trent   218
Europe
  missionary awakening   *354–55*
  evangelical academies and lay institutes   377–79, *378*
Eusebius of Caesarea   45, *50*
  baptizer of Constantine   45
Eusebius of Nicomedia   *50*
  at Antioch   35

patron of Ulfilas   45
Eutyches   48, 52–53
Evangelical
new churches in the USA   351
Evangelical Academies   375,
375–76, 377, 384
Evangelical Alliance   348
and missions
conferences   353
Evangelism   291, 293
Pietist motif   231, 291
Events, formative   3
Evolution   260, 339
Exile and return, the   7
"Exodus"   412
Extermination camps
see death camps

# F

"Faith and Order" movement
374
Faith-in-Life Weeks   381
"Fall of the church"   148, 150,
181, 399
False messiahs   122
Farel, Guillaume   161, 162,
202, 203
Fascism   246, 302
in Spain   304, 305
Father Divine's Peace Mission
392
Ferdinand of Aragon   125
Ferdinand (Emp.)   203
Ferdinand II (Emp.)   187, 188
Ferrara-Florence, Council of
136, 136, 217
Fellowship of Reconciliation
349
Feudalism
development   72, 86
and the church   132
Japanese shogunate   276
Fichte, J. G.   233, 240, 243, 290
Fiji   278
Finland, Reformation in   163
Finney, Charles G.   264, 293,
322, 323, 324
First Amendment (U.S.
Constitution)   263
Florence   141
cathedral   140
Fosdick, Harry Emerson   349
"Four Lands"   120, 121
Fourier, Charles   328
Fox, George   181, 227, 389
Foxe's Book of Martyrs   167,
338
France
early monasticism   62
political emergence   70
royal domain, 14th century
132
voyages of discovery   198, 199
Hundred Years' War   200
civil war   175, 175
loss of Alsace-Lorraine   244
in South America   261
in Africa   273
in Asia   275

in South Pacific   277
Christian renewal   288–89
Vichy governed area   306
new Roman Catholic orders
357
Francis of Assisi   106, 110
Francis I, King of France   200,
201, 202, 238
Franciscans
missionaries to Orient   109,
109
in the Americas   207
see Francis of Assisi
see Ochino, Bernardino
Franck, Sebastian   147, 173
Francke, August Hermann   228,
230, 231
Franco, Francisco   304, 305
Frank, Jacob   123, 124
Frankfurt am Main
P. J. Spener's work in   188
Frankfurt National Assembly
244, 258
Franklin, Benjamin   234, 237
Franz Josef I of Austria-
Hungary   249, 250
Frederick I (Emp.)/
"Barbarossa"   96, 98, 99, 100
Frederick II (Emp.)   96, 99,
100, 107
Frederick I, King of Denmark
163
Frederick William III   243
Free Churches
and missions   352
and "sects"   392
see religious liberty
see voluntaryism
Freedmen's Bureau   334, 336
Frelinghuysen, Theodore   232
French Revolution   237–40, 286
Friedrich Wilhelm IV (king of
Prussia)   244
Friends, Society of
origins in England   181
Pennsylvania   227–28
peace testimony   319
division   350
in USA   387, 387, 388, 389
Friends of Mary at the Foot of
the Cross   337
Frumentius   64, 64
Fulda
mission of Boniface   75
Full Gospel Business Men's
Fellowship   398, 399
Fundamentalism
"the Fundamentals"   339

# G

Galilee   11
Gallican Articles   252
Gandhi, Mohandas K.
in South Africa   272, 276
in India   227, 275
influence in USA   344
Garibaldi   254
Geldbach, Erich   410
General Council

see conciliarism
Geneva
and John Calvin   157, 157, 162
in Counter-Reformation   213
and Huguenots   177
Genghis Khan   116
Genoa
colonial and commercial
empire   89, 128, 136, 138
Genocide
of Armenians in Holy Muslim
Empire   284, 285
in Tibet   312
and martyrdom   321
of Jews in the Nazi Empire
310, 404, 405, 406–07
Genseric   47, 54
Gerhardt, Paul   188, 189
German Councils of Christians
and Jews   401, 403, 403
Germantown
founding of   227
Mennonite Church   228
Germany
Thirty Years' War   187–89
united under Prussia   244
Christian renewal in 19th
century   289–91
Nazi-Soviet Pact   299
Nazi Empire   307–10, 404–07
post-war Christian renewal
375, 375–77
unusual religious movements
392–93, 393
see Holy Roman Empire
see Prussia
Gerson, Jean   135, 137
Ghost Dance Religion   262, 265
Gibbon, Edward   30
Gibbons, James   266, 338
Gibbs, Mark   378
Gilbert, William S.   293
Giovanni de Marignolli   109
Giovanni of Verrazano   198
Gladden, Washington   138
Gladstone, William E.   279, 280
Glarus   156
Gnosticism   36–38
Nag Hammadi   16, 37, 38
Goa   229
"God-fearers"   15
Goethe, Johann Wolfgang
von   233, 233
"Göttingen Seven"   242
Götz von Berlichingen   146
"Golden Bull"
see Holy Roman Empire
"Golden Horde"
see Mongols
Gomar, Francis   172
Goodell, William   325
Graham, Billy   341, 381
Granada   125, 125
Great Awakening   231, 232,
232, 263, 264
and Presbyterianism   350
Great Schism of East and West
Patriarch Photius   73
Patriarch M. Cerularius   87
Innocent III's attempt at
reunion   105

"Great Schism" of the West 133, *134*, 135
Great Trek, the *270*, 271
Grebel, Conrad *147*, 148
Greece under Ottoman Turks *138*, 219
Gregory of Nazianzus 47, *50*
Gregory of Nyssa 47, *50*
Gregory "the Illuminator" 285
Gregory the Great (pope) *54*, 55, 58
Gregory VII (pope)/ Hildebrand *89*
  and Henry IV 79, 88, *89*
Gregory XI (pope) *132*, 133
Gregory XVI (pope) 254
Groote, Gerhard *113*, *142*, 143
Grotius, Hugo 172
Gruntvig, Nikolai *233*, 286
Guernica *304*
Gustavus Adolphus, King of Sweden in Thirty Years' War *188*, 189
Gustavus I Vasa, King of Sweden
  and Reformation *163*, 163-164
Gutenberg, Johann 131, *142*, 143
Gutiérrez, Gustavo 385

# H

Habsburg, house of 137
  Charles V 194, *201*
  in Thirty Years' War 187, *188*
  Austria-Hungary 249–50
Hadrian (Emp.) 25, *54*
  buildings in Athens *22*
  wall in Britain *27*
  Saalburg fortifications *26*
  desecration of Jerusalem 29, 46
Hagenau *193*
Hagia Sophia 45, 55
Haifa
  Baha'i world headquarters *283*
Halle *231*
  and first Protestant missions 228, 230
Haller, Berchtold *161*
Hamilton, Patrick *184*, 185
Hanseatic League 107, *128*, 129
Hardenberg, F. von *233*
Hardie, J. Keir *279*, 280
Harnack, Adolf von *234*, 240, 289
Harold, King of England *92*, 93
Harris, William Wadé 397
Hartman, Olov 377
Harun al-Rashid *82*, 85
Harvard University 225, 226, 329, 331
  Unitarian controversy 322
Hasidism 124
Hastings, Battle of 93
Hatt-i Humeyun 247, 281
Hawaii *262*, 277, *326*
  Henry Obookiah *324*
Hebrew Union College *346*
Hegel, G.W.F. *233*
Hegira 67

Heidelberg
  first German university *130*
  and Butzer *155*
Heinemann, Gustav 376
Hellenism 19, 20–22
Helwys, Thomas 169, *181*
Henry IV (Emp.) 88, *89*
Henry II, King of France 203
Henry VIII, King of England *165*, 165–66, 202
Henry of Lausanne *128*
Henry of Navarre, King of France *175*, 176, 203, *204*
Henry the Navigator, Prince 139, 195
Herder, J. G. 233, *233*, 236
Hermann von Wied 155
Herod the Great 10
  Herod's kingdom *11*
Herrmann, Wilhelm *234*
Herrnhut, Herrnhuter Brüdergemeine *231*, 290
  see Moravians
  see Zinzendorf
Herzegovina
  under Ottoman Turks 194
Herzl, Theodor 411
Hicks, Elias 350
Hippolytus *32*, 34, 35
History, theology of xi
  Augustine 40–41
  Joachim of Fiore 135
  Puritanism 170
  see primitivism
Hitler, Adolf 300, 305, 307, 308–10, 404, 406
Hodgkin, Henry 349
Hofmann, Melchior *147*
Hogarth's "Gin Lane" 280
Holland
  see Netherlands
Holocaust
  in Third Reich 404, *405*, 406
  meaning to Christianity 404, 406–07, 409, 412
  memory work 407, *408*, 409–10
Holocaust Annual Scholars' Conference 409
Holy Alliance *241*, 241–42
  and Prussia 242, *243*, 244
  and Russia 245, *246*, 247
  and Austria-Hungary 247, *248*, 249–50
Holy Muslim Empire 281, *282*
  massacre of Armenians 284, *285*
"Holy Places"
  Helena, mother of Constantine 43, 44, 46
  in 19th century diplomacy 281
Holy Roman Empire 78, 79, 87, *99*, *128*, *137*, 290
  Imperial cities *128*
  hereditary Electors 137
  Thirty Years' War *188*
  terminated *238*, 239
Holy Sepulchre, Church of the 48, *97*
Holy Synod 247
Hooker, Richard *165*, 169

Hooper, John 167, 168
Hoover, Herbert C. 389
Horns of Hittin *101*
Hosius of Cordova *43*, 45
Hospitalers (Knights of St. John) 94, 102, 151, *220*
Howard, O. O. 336
Hübmaier, Balthasar *150*
  antisemite 190, *190*
Hudson, Henry *198*, 199, 200
Hughes, John 266, 338
Hugo of St. Victor *113*, 115
Huguenots 175, *175*, 176, *177*
  and Philip II *204*
Humanism, Christian
  in northern Renaissance 143
  and Melanchthon 154
Hume, David *234*
Hung Hsiu-ch'üan *275*
Hungary
  conquered by Ottoman Turks 194, 219
  1848 revolt against Habsburgs *248*, 249
Huss, John *128*, 135
Hutchinson, Anne 226
Hutten, Ulrich von *144*, 144–45
Hutter, Jakob *147*, 150, *150*
Hutterite Brethren *147*, 148, 149, 150, *150*
  in Russia 251, *251*
  in North America *327*
Hymns
  Gregorian chant 56
  first Protestant psalter 202

# I

Iberian peninsula 127
  see Portugal, Spain
Ibn Batuta 269
Ibn Khaldun 117
Icaria *327*, 328
Iceland
  early Norse settlements *90*
  Reformation *163*, 164
Icons
  iconoclasm 53, 56, *57*
  Synod of Frankfurt 70
Idealism, idealistic philosophy 296
Ideology 296*f*
  polarization in Weimar Republic 308
  state religions 315–21, *316–18*
Ignatius of Antioch 33
Ilminski, N. I. *246*
Immaculate Conception *253*, 255
Imperial cities
  see Holy Roman Empire
"Independents"
  in England 169
Index of Forbidden Books 156, 157
India 195
  Nestorian Christians 65–66
  Portuguese explorations 195
  Robert De Nobili 211, *229*
  first Protestant missions 228
  missions and resistance *275*

see Thomas Christians
Indians, American
  in Spanish America  207
  revolt of Popa  *207*
  missions to  214, *215*, *262*, *324*
  Moravian Christian Indian
    villages 231
  religious resistance of Indians
    *262*, 264–65
  and Quakers  387
Indonesia  *275*, 276
  missions  *277*
Indulgences  133
Ingolstadt  *210*
Innocent III (pope)  105
Inquisition  157, 171
  introduced at Lateran IV  96
  in Spain  125, *125*, 203
  reorganized by Paul IV in
    Counter-Reformation  192
  in Spanish America  207
  in Papal States  254
"Intact" churches  376
Interfaith dialogue  401, *402*,
  403, 409–410
  International Council of
    Christians and Jews  401,
    403, 414
International Brigades  *304*, 305
International Church of the
  Four Square Gospel  *398*
International Missionary
  Council  367, 374
Investiture controversy  73, 79
Iona
  Celtic monastic center  62, *63*
  Iona Community  377
Iowa School of Religion  401
Iran
  persecution of Christians  *282*
Ireland
  early monasticism  *63*
  Eire and N. Ireland  *314*,
    314–15
Irenaeus  31, *32*
Irving, Edward  *279*
Isabella of Castile  125
  patroness of Columbus  195
Islam
  rise of  *68*, 69
  Mohammed  67, *67*, 69
  8th–9th century empires  81–
    85, *82*
  holdings in Italian area  *90*
  conversion of Bogomili  105
  Mongol attack  *116*, 117
  capture of Constantinople 138
  Mogul Empire in India  195
  in the Philippines  *267*
  in Africa  267, *268*, 274, 383
  Arab League  312, *313*
  state religion  *316–18*
  see Holy Muslim Empire
  see Lull, Ramon
Ismailites  *101*
Israel
  particularism and
    universalism  8
  victim of "Third World"
    ideology  301
  target of Arab League 312, *313*

restoration of  *411*, 411–12
Italy
  early monasticism  62
  in 11th century  89
  under Emp. Frederick I and
    II  98, 100
  French driven out  202, 241
  unification struggle  254
  in Africa  *273*
  Fascist Empire  *302*, 303
  see Papal States
Ivan the Great, ruler of Russia
  139
Ivan IV, Tsar of Russia  223

# J

Jackson, Jesse  *343*
Jacobites, Syrian  48, *48*, *53*
James I, King of England  181,
  182, 314
James II, King of England  183
Jamestown  200, *225*, 226
Janissaries
  organized by Ottoman Turks
    219
  liquidated by Mahmud II  281
Jansenism  257
Japan  274, 276
  missions  *275*
  empire in Asia  *275*
  empire in South Pacific  *277*,
    278
  Christian churches  *394*
  Shinto organizations  *395*
  Buddhist sects
    eclecticism  399
Java  *277*
Jefferson, Thomas  *234*, 237,
  263
Jehovah's Witnesses  341, 390
Jena, Battle of  *238*, 240
Jerome  *50*, 51, 52
  monastic  *59*, 61
Jerome of Prague  135
Jerusalem
  captured by Nebuchadnezzar
    7
  at Jesus' time  *12*
  Byzantine city  46, *47*
  Dome of the Rock  69
  captured by Crusaders  *95*,
    96, *97*
  Kingdom of  96, *101*
  Yad Vashem  307, *407*, 409
Jesuits (Society of Jesus)  199,
  209–13
  Ignatius Loyola  208–09
  in the Americas  214–16
  at the Council of Trent  217
Jesus  10, *11*
  his Jerusalem  *12*
  viewed as Messiah by early
    followers  13
Jewish Theological Seminary
  *346*, 347
Jews
  in middle ages  *120*, 121
  settlements in east Europe
    *120*, 121
  messianism  122, *123*

expulsion from Iberian
  peninsula  *126*, 127, 159
repression in Europe  189–91
return to England  182
individual conversions  233
in USA  345, *346*, 347
see antisemitism
see Israel
Joachim of Fiore  *89*, 135
Joan of Arc  200
Jogues, Isaac  *215*
Johannesburg  *270*
John VIII (Emp.)  *136*
John XXIII (pope)  316
  *Pacem in Terris*  319
  Vatican II  257, *371*, 374
John of the Cross  203
John of Damascus  *57*, 58
John Duns Scotus  *113*, 114
John of Luxembourg  137
John of Montecorvino  *109*,
  110
John Paul II (pope)  381, 410
John Scotus  73
Jonas, Justus  158, *158*
Joshua, leader of occupation of
  Canaan  5
*Journal of Ecumenical Studies*
  357
Juárez, Benito  261, *261*
Jud, Leo  *161*
Judaea  *11*
Judaism
  gentile fellow-travelers  15
  conversion of Khazars  66
Judson, Adoniram  325
Julian (Emp.)  30, 46
Julius II (pope)  151
Julius III (pope)  *217*
Julius Caesar  23, 24, 27
Justin Martyr  *32*, 33
Justinian (Emp.)  *43*, 55

# K

Kaaba stone  67
Kaffir Wars  272
Kagawa, Toyohiko  *371*
Kalker, Christian H.  353
Kalmar, Union of  163
Kant, Immanuel  *234*, 236
Kanzo Uchimura  *394*
Kaplan, Mordecai  *346*
Karlstadt, Andreas Bodenstein
  von  *147*
Kempis, Thomas á  *113*, 143
Kepler, Johannes  *234*, 235
Kerk en Wereid  377, *378*
Ketteler, Wilhelm E.  244, 291
Kharijites  81
Khazaria, Khazars  *66*, 67
  resist Muslim advance  *68*
Khubilai Khan  110
Kidderminster  *181*
Kierkegaard, Søren  286–87
Kiev
  monastic center  64
  Duke of Kiev  66
  center of Eastern
    Orthodoxy  91
Kimbangu, Simon  397

King, Martin Luther Jr. *343*, 344
Kingsley, Charles 293
Kipling, Rudyard *279*
*Kirchenkampf*
 see Church Struggle
*Kirchentag* 375, 376–77, 378, 379
Kirkridge 377
Knights of St. John
 see Hospitalers
Knights' War *144*, 144–45
Knox, John *184*, 185–86
Koran
 in Islam 69, 81
 translation into Latin 110
Korea 276
 missions *275*
 mega-churches 400
Korntal *231*
Kose Dagi, Battle of *116*
Kossuth, Louis 249
Kraemer Hendrik 377, 384
*Kristallnacht* 404, 406
Krüdener, Barbara von
 inspirer of Holy Alliance 241, 242
Kruschev, Nikita 301
Ku Klux Klan 401
*Kulturkampf* 244, 255, 338
Kuyper, Abraham 287
Kyodan *394*

# L

Labadie, Jean de *188*, *231*
Laity, lay leadership
 and church growth 340
 and Christian renewal 286*f*, 377
 YMCA/YWCA 364–66
 post-war Germany *375*, 375–77
 Europe 377–79, *378*
 USA 379–81
 Africa, Asia, South
 Pacific 383, 384
 active in Mormons, Jehovah's
 Witnesses 390
 see Radical Reformation
Lalibela, monolithic churches
 of 64, *64*
Lambert, Francis 159
Lammenais, Robert de 255
Lapsed Christians, status of 33
La Rochelle *175*
Las Casas, Bartolomé de 197, 216
Lasco, John à 213
Lateran Council, Fourth 105, *106*
Latimer, Hugh 167, 168
Latin America
 nationalism 260–61, *261*
 modern missions 358, *358*
 Christian renewal 385, *386*
Latourette, Kenneth Scott 324, 352
Latterday Saints, Church of
 Jesus Christ of 341–42, *342*, 350, 390

and revivalism *323*
and communalism *327*, 328
 Mormon Tabernacle 390
Laud, William *165*
 and Star Chamber 182
Lavigerie, Charles *273*, 289, 357
Law, William *232*
Laynez, James 211, *216*
Lee, Robert E. *332*, 333
Leibniz, Gottfried Wilhelm
 *234*, 235
Leipzig debate of Luther and
 Eck 153, *153*
Lemkin, Raphael 407
Lenin (Vladimir Ilyich Ulyanov)
 298, 300, 301
Leo the Great (pope) *54*, 55
Leo IX (pope) 86, 87, 141
Leo X (pope) 151
Leo XII (pope) 254
Leo XIII (pope) 255
Leo III (Emp.) 56
 repels Muslim invasions 57, *68*
Leopold II, King of Belgium
 273, *273*
Lepanto, Battle of *204*, 206, *220*
Lessing, Gotthold E. *234*, 236
Leyden, university of 179
"Liberation Theology" 385
Liberia *273*
"Life and Work" movement
 374
Lilje, Hanns 368
Lima 197, 207, *207*
Lincoln, Abraham 333
Lincoln University *334*, 335
Lindisfarne monastic center *63*
Lin Piao 301
Lithuania
 union with Poland *138*
Littell, Franklin H. 378, 381, 409
Liturgy
 Russian orthodoxy 245
 see hymns
Livingstone, David 271, *273*
Locke, Hubert 409
Locke, John 225, *234*, 235
"*Logos* Fathers" 20, *32*, 33
Lollards 167
Lombard League *99*, 129
London Missionary Society 278
Long March, the 310, *311*
Louis the Bavarian *132*, 133, *137*
Louix IX, King of France 97
Louis XIV, King of France 176, *177*, 237
Louisiana Purchase 239, *262*, 265
Loyola, Ignatius 208, *208*, 209, *210*
Lucaris, Cyril *222*, 223
Lucian of Antioch *34*, 35, 36
Ludwig-Missionsverein 289
Lützen, Battle of *188*
Lull, Ramon 110, *111*, 112
Luria, Isaac "Ashkenazi"
 ("Ari") *123*
Luther, Martin 153, *153*–54, 194

antisemitism 190, *190*
Lutheran Church, Missouri
 Synod 340, *340*
Lutheranism, Lutherans
 in Scandinavia *163*, 163–64
 in Hungary 219
 new churches in USA 340, *351*
 see Luther, Martin
 see Reformation
Luthuli , Albert John *371*, 383
Luxeuil monastic center *62*

# M

Maccabees 7
Macedonia *21*
Mack, Alexander *231*, 389
MacLeod, George 377
Madison, James 263
Magellan, Ferdinand *196*
Magna Carta *106*
Mahmud II 281
Maimonides 84, *116*
Malabar coast 229
 see Thomas Christians
Malaya *275*, 276, *277*
Malcolm X *343*
Malta
 withstands siege of Ottoman
 Turks *204*, *220*
Mandaeans *37*, 38
Mani 38, *39*
Manichaeism *37*, 38, *39*
Manning, Henry Edward 291
Mao Tse-tung
 in Marxist history 301
 Chinese Revolution 310, 311, *311*
Maoris 278
Mar Saba monastery *59*, 60
Marburg *130*
 university crest 130
 Colloquy 156, *158*, 158–60
Marcion 31, *32*, 36, *37*
Marcus Aurelius *19*, 20, 22, 26
Margaret d'Angoulême 202
Marianists 289
Marist Brothers 289
Maritain, Jacques 374
Marnix, Philip van 179
Maronites *325*
Marot, Clément 202
Marpeck, Pilgram *147*, 148
Marranos 127
Marsilius of Padua 133, 135, 137, *137*, 141
Martin of Tours, monastic
 founder 61, *62*
Martyn, Henry *325*
Martyrs
 Stephen 13
 early Christian *24*, 33, *34*, 35
 Anabaptist 147
 in England 168–69
 in former Soviet Union 300
 in Third Reich 310
Marx, Karl 296, *297*
Marxism 298–301
 *Communist Manifesto* 286, 298

state religion  *316–18*
Mary Stuart, "Queen of Scots"
  167, *184*, 185–86
Mary Tudor, Queen of England
  166–67
Maryland, first settlement of
  200
Masada  *11*
Mather, Cotton  329
Mathews, Shailer  *234*
Matteotti, Giacomo  303
Maurice of Saxony  194
Maurice, Frederick D.  293
Maury, Pierre  368
Maxwell, Elisabeth  410
Mayflower  *225*, 226
  see Pilgrim Fathers
McPherson, Aimee Semple  *398*
Meaux  *201*, 202
Mega-churches  379, 381, 400,
  *400*
Melanchthon, Philipp  154,
  *154*, 155, 158, *158*, 194
Melchiorites  *147*
Melitius of Lycopolis  44
Melville, Andrew  186
Membership standards  352
  see church discipline
Memmingen  *146*
Mendelssohn, Moses  *234*, 236,
  345
Menno Simons  *147*, 148, 149
Mennonites  148
  Germantown Church  *147*,
    149
  in Russia  251, *251*
  peace testimony  319
  divisions  350
  in USA  387, *388*, 389
  see Radical Reformation
Mennonite Central Committee
  *388*, 389
Mercenaries
  Swiss  160, 202
  in Spanish Civil War  305
Messianism, Jewish  122, *123*,
  124
Methodist Protestant Church
  352
Methodists
  revivalism  264, *323*
  divisions  *351*, 352
Methodius of Thessalonica  57,
  58
Metternich  242, 249
Mexico City  197
  capital of New Spain  207, *207*
Michael Cerularius (Patriarch)
  86, *87*
Michigan, University of
  campus YMCA  364
  Lane Hall Conferences  379
  interfaith center  403
Midhat Pasha  281
Milan
  Edict of  *43*
  Council of  50
  Renaissance city-state  140
  Counter-Reformation in  212
Miller, Francis Pickens  368
Millet system

Byzantine  138
Muslim  127, 221
Mills, Samuel J. Jr.  325
Milton, John  *181*, 182, 183
"Minnesota Project"  381
Mission Covenant Church  353
Missionaries of France, Society
  of  288
Missionary conferences  353
Missions
  Paul  *14*
  Twelve Apostles in
    tradition  *28*, 29
  Manichaean  *39*
  Ulfilas  *50*
  Celtic  *62*
  Frumentius  *64*
  Nestorian  65
  in northern Europe  *75*
  to "Cathay"  *109*, 110
  Hutterite  150
  in North America  199
  Jesuits  199, 209, 211
  in Spanish America  207
  Quaker  227
  Pietism  230, 231
  N. I. Ilminski  *246*
  in South America  *261*
  to American Indians  262, 264
  Protestant missions to
    Philippines, Puerto Rico
    266–67
  in Africa  *273*
  in Asia  *275*
  in South Pacific  *277*, 278
  in Ottoman Empire  *282*, 283
  modern principle of
    voluntaryism  295
  "Great Century"  324, 350f
  ABCFM  *324–26*
  Southern Baptists  341
  Afro-American missions  344
  modern missions  352–53,
    *354–56*, 357, *358–63*
  Mormon  390
  "Third Force"  *398*, 399
Missouri Synod  340, *340*
Mithraism  *21*
Moffat, Robert  271
Mogila, Peter  223
Mogul Empire  195, *229*
Mohács, Battle of  219, *220*
Mohammed  67, *67*, *68*, 69
Mohammed II (Sultan) 138, *138*
Molcho, Solomon  122
Monasteries, monasticism  51
  early  59–64
  Cluniac reform  *76*, 77
  Muslim  *68*
  Cistercian reform  *103*, 104
  dissolved by Henry VIII  *165*
  *startzi*  247
  see Dominicans
  see Franciscans
  see Jesuits
Mongols
  invasions  65, 109, *116*, 117
  kingdom  *65*
  empire  *109*
Monolithic churches  64
Monophysites  *48*, 53

Montanism
  Tertullian  *34*, 36, 53
  Ultramontanism  254
Monte Cassino monastic
  center  *62*
Montenegro
  under Ottoman Turks  *138*,
    194
  independence  250
Montesquieu (Charles Louis
  Joseph de Secondat)  237
Montserrat  208
  "Black Madonna"  208, 209
Moody, Dwight L.  293, *323*
  and YMCA  357, 364, *365*
Moore, Thomas  314, *314*
Moors  125, *152*
Moravia  150, *150*
Moravians  231, 232
More, Thomas  168
Moriscos  127, 205
Mormons
  see Latterday Saints, Church
  of Jesus Christ of
Morone, Giovanni  218, *218*
Morrill Land Act  329
Morrison, Robert  276
Morse, Samuel F. B.  *234*, 338
Moscow
  "Third Rome"  139, 223
  resists Napoleon  *238*
Moses
  illustration from Dura-
    Europos  6
  leads Exodus  5
Mosheim, Johann Lorenz von
  231, *231*
Mosque
  Dome of the Rock  69
  Abbasid mosque at Samarra
    83
  El Aksa  85
  at Cordova  124
"Mothers for Peace"  315
Mott, John R.  293, 366–68,
  *367*, *368*
  and YMCA  364, 366
  and WSCF  367, 370
Mount Hermon (Mass.)  *323*,
  357, 364, *365*
Mueller, Eberhard  376
Münster, Davidic Kingdom at
  *147*, 160, 174
Müntzer, Thomas  *146*, 174
Munich Agreement  309
Murray, John Courtney  319
Mussolini, Benito  *302*, 303,
  305
Mutual aid
  among Mormons  390
  see communism, Christian
  see Hutterites
Mysticism
  Muslim  81
  medieval Christian  115
  Jewish  122–24

N

Nag Hammadi  16, *37*, 38
Nanking  310, 311, *311*

Nantes, Edict of 175, *175*
  Revocation 175, 176, *177*
Naples
  under Philip II of Spain 205
Napoleon Bonaparte 237, *238*,
  239, 240, 241
  and the papacy 252, 254
Nasi, Don Joseph 221
National Association for the
  Advancement of Colored
  People (NAACP) 336, 344
National Catholic Bishops'
  Conference 379
National Conference of
  Christians and Jews 401,
  *402*, 403
National Council of the
  Churches of Christ 348–49
National Urban League 344
Nationalism
  Prussian revival 240
  Latin American 260, *261*
  Filipino 266
  Boer 272
Native American Church of
  North America *262*, 265
Nativism, native Americanism
  266, 338, 401
Navarre *125*
Nazarene, Church of the 352
Nazis
  antisemitism 191, 404
  intervention in Spanish Civil
    War *304*, 305
  Nazi Empire ("Third Reich")
    *306*, 308
  see Third Reich
Neander, Johann August
  Wilhelm (David Mendel)
  *233*, 345
Negro colleges *334*, 335–36
Neo-Platonism, Neo-Platonists
  *19*, 22
Nero 24, 25
Nestorianism, Nestorians 48,
  52, *53*, 65, 65–66
  and Mongols 111
  in India *229*
  Protestant missions
    among *325*
Nestorius 48, *53*
Netherlands
  civil war *178*, 178–80
  voyages of discovery *198*, 199
  independence movement 204,
    205
  in South America *261*
  in Asia *275*
  in South Pacific *277*
  see Renaissance, Northern
New England
  early settlements 200, 226
  breakup of established
    churches 263
New Spain *204*, 207
New Zealand, missionary work
  in *277*, 278
Newman, John Henry 257,
  258, *279*, 280, 291
Newport (R.I.)
  Touro synagogue *225*, 345

Newton, Isaac *234*, 235
Nicaea
  Council I *43*, 45
  Council II 53, 56, *57*, 58
  temporary capital during
    crusades 96
Nicholas I (pope) 73
Nicolas of Cusa *136*
Niebuhr, Reinhold 349, 368
Niemöller, Martin 376
Nigeria 273, *273*
Nightingale, Florence 281
Nikolsburg *150*
Nikon (Patriarch) *222*, 223, 224
Niles, Daniel T. 370
Ninety-five Theses 153
Nisibis, Nestorian center at 65,
  *65*
Noetus of Smyrna 31, *32*
"Non-intervention" *304*
Normans
  settlements in France 72
  rule in Italy *89*, 100
  conquest of England *92*, 93
  conquest of Ireland 314
Norsemen
  in England *80*, *92*, 93
  westward to America *90*, 91
Northampton, Mass. *232*
Norway
  Christianization of 91
  Reformation *163*, 164
Notre Dame (Ind.)
  Pentecostal Conferences *398*,
    399
Novatian 20, *32*, *34*, 35
Noyes, John Humphrey 328
Nürnberg Laws 404
  see antisemitism
Nyack Missionary College 353

## O

Oberlin College *323*, 324
Occam, William of 135, *137*
Ochino, Bernardino 143, *147*,
  170, 212
Ochrid monastic center 63, 64,
  73
Odoric of Pordenone *109*
Oecolampadius, Johann 158,
  *158*, 159, *161*
Old Believers *222*, 223
Old Catholic Church *256*,
  257–58
  Aglipayans 266, *267*
Old Testament
  and John Calvin 157
  see Marcion, *Deutsche
    Christen*
Oldham, Joseph H. 370, 377
Olivetan 203
Omayyad dynasty *68*, *82*, 83
  in Spain 124
Oneida *327*, 328
Opium Wars *275*, 276
Orange Free State 271, 272
Orders
  see Roman Catholic Church

Organic Articles 252
Origen *34*, 35, 36, *53*
Orosius 52
Orthodox churches
  see Eastern Orthodoxy
Osiander, Andreas 158, *158*
Otto the Great (Emp.) *78*, 79
Ottoman Empire *120*, 127,
  *136*, 192
  conquest of the Balkans *138*
  battle of Lepanto 205–06
  loss of the Balkans 250, 281
  in Africa *268*
  Mohammed VI 281
  see Holy Muslim Empire
Ottoman Turks
  see Turks
Owen, Robert *279*, 280
Oxford *130*
  university crest 131
  John Wesley 231–32
  see Wycliffe, John
Oxford movement *279*, 291

## P

Pachomius *59*, 60
Pacifism
  Fellowship of Reconciliation
    349
  see peace testimony
Padua *210*
Paine, Thomas *234*, 237
Palácky, Francis 249
Pale of Settlement *120*, 121,
  *246*
Palermo
  capital of Holy Roman
    Empire *99*
Palestine
  Roman province 10, *11*
  early monasticism *59*
  see Israel
Panama
  in Spanish Viceroyalty of
    Peru 207, *207*
Papacy
  emerges in West 46
  allied with Franks 70
  and feudalism 72
  under Roman families 77
  under Holy Roman
    Emperors *78*
  reform of elections 89
  and Crusades 94, *95*
  conflict with Emp. Frederick I
    and II 100
  at Avignon *132*, 132–33,
    *134*, 135
  and Louis the Bavarian 137
  see antipope
  see concordats
  see Papal States
Papal Infallibility 253, 255,
  256, 257, 258, 287
Papal States 71, 89, *99*, *106*
  in 14th century *132*
  at time of Alexander VI 151,
    *152*
  refuge for Jews from Spain
    190

during Holy Alliance 252, *253*, 254–55
Papua, missions in *277*
Paraguay 261
  Jesuit colonies *214*, 216
Paris
  Notre Dame Cathedral 115
  university 130, *130*, 135, 200
  Jesuit beginnings *208*, *210*
  Paris Commune 244, 298
Paris Evangelical Missionary Society 278
Paris Platform of the YMCA 366
Parish system 263
Parker, Matthew *165*, 167, 168
Parochial schools 339
Pascal, Blaise 213, *234*, 235
Pasteur, Louis *234*
Paul "the Apostle"
  missionary journeys *14*
  and Athens *22*
Paul of Samosata 31, *32*
Paul III (pope) 192, *216*
Paul IV (pope)/Caraffa 192, 212, *216*
  anti-Protestant 218
  antisemite *191*
Paul VI (pope) 167, 374
Paulicians 56
Paulist Fathers *337*
Paulus, Heinrich Eberhard Gottlob *234*
Payne, Daniel A. 335
Peace churches 319, 387, 389
  divisions 350
Peace testimony
  early Christian 26, 40
  "Truce of God" and "Peace of God" 94
  Radical Reformation 148, 150
  dissenting groups in Russia 251, 252
  churches in World War II 319
Peasants' revolts
  following the Black Death 118
  German peasants' wars 146, *146*
Peck, Abraham 410
Pelagius 50
Pendle Hill 381
Penitential discipline 63
Penn, William *225*, 226, *227*, 227–28, 263
Pennsburg 227
Pennsylvania *225*, *227*, 227–28, 263, 392
Pentecostalism, Pentecostals
  and Wesleyan perfectionism 352
  new churches in USA *351*
  in Africa 397
  in missions *398*, 399
Pepin "the Short" 70
Periodization xiv
  Augustine 40
  in Radical Reformation 148
  "Great Century" 350
  see history, theology of
  see primitivism
Perkins, William *165*, 169

Persecutions
  Roman persecutions of Christians 24, 25, 33, *34*, 35–36
  Christian persecution of dissenters 40, 49
  Pennsylvania, refuge from persecutions 227, *227*
  see antisemitism
  see Crusades
  see martyrs
Persia
  Empire 38, 53
  and the Nestorians 65
  see Iran
Peru
  fall of Inca Empire 197
  Spanish viceroyalty 207
Peter of Bruys *128*
Peter the Great, tsar of Russia *222*, 224
  Empire *246*, 247
Peter Lombard 112, *113*
Peter Martyr Vermigli 142, 166, 170
Peter the Venerable 110
Petrarch *130*, 141
Petri, Olavus *163*, 164
Pharisees 7
Philip IV, King of France
  robbing Templars 102
  quarrel with pope 105
  robbing Jews 119
  control of papacy 133
Philip II, King of Spain 167, 179, 203, *204*, *205*, 218
Philipp of Hesse 131, *158*, 158–60, 194
  and Butzer 155
  and Zwingli 156
Philippine Islands
  Spanish conquest *196*
  American conquest 266, *267*, *275*
Philo of Alexandria 10, *19*
Photius (Patriarch) 73
Phrygia *21*, *34*
Pietism 173, 189, 228, 229–33
  communes in USA *327*, 328
  and missions 352
  see Holy Alliance
Pilgrim Fathers 200, *225*
Pilgrimages, early Christian *54*
Pisa
  colonial and commercial empire *89*
  Council of *134*, 135
Pius IV (pope) 218
Pius VII (pope)
  prisoner of Napoleon 254
Pius IX (pope)
  see Vatican I
Pius XI (pope)
  *Mit brennender Sorge* 310
Pius XII (pope) 308, 316
Pizarro, Francisco *196*, 197
Plato 18, *19*, 22
Plymouth *225*, 226
  see Pilgrim Fathers
Plymouth Brethren *279*, 280
Pobedonostsev, C. P. *246*, 247

Pogroms *246*, 247
  see antisemitism
Poissy 175, *175*
Poland
  and Mongol invasion 109
  Jewish immigrants 122
  union with Lithuania *138*
  "Minor Church" 173
  Counter-Reformation 213
  divided by Soviets and Nazis 300
Pole, Reginald *216*, 217
Polo, Marco *109*, 110
Polycarp of Smyrna 33
Polygamy
  Philipp of Hesse 194
  at Münster 174
Pompeii 33
Port-Royal 213, 257
Portugal 127, 139
  voyages of discovery 195, *196*, 197
  under Philip II of Spain 206
  in South America *261*
  in Africa *268*, *273*
*Positives Christentum* 309
Prague *128*, 129
  university *130*
Predestination
  Gottschalk 72
Presbyterianism
  in conservative Puritanism 182, 183
  in Scottish Reformation 186
  in N. Ireland 314–15
  divisions in USA 350, *351*
"Presence in the Midst" — line drawing 388
Primitive Christianity
  Cistercian motif 104
  in Radical Reformation 147
  in Puritanism 170
  in Pietism 230
Primitivism
  cultural p. in Ibn Khaldun 117
  see Radical Reformation
Princeton 233
  and revivalism 350
Prohibition 401
Proletariat in Marxism 298
Prophet(s)
  Hebrew 6–7, 8
  Mohammed 67, *67*, 69
Protestant Church of the Rheinland 410
Protestantism,
  Protestants 153–57, 194
  Protestant missions to Spanish area 266, 267
  in Germany 289–90
  see Calvinism
  see Lutheranism
  see Radical Reformation
  see Reformation
Protocols of the Elders of Zion 247
Prussia
  humiliated by Napoleon 239–40
  Holy Alliance *243*, 244
Prussia, East

under Teutonic Knights 108, *108*
Puerto Rico 266, 267
Puritanism, Puritans 167, 169, 170, 173
  Millenary Petition 169, 181
  persecuted after the Restoration 182
  radical Puritans to New England 226
  within Anglicanism of southern colonies 263
  communes in USA *327*, 328
Putin, Vladimir 301

# Q

Quakers
  see Friends, Society of
Quebec Act 338
Quimby, Phineas P. 392
Qumran *11*, 17, *17*

# R

Radewyjns, Florentius *113*, 142
Radical Reformation 147–49, 171
  and Pentecostalism 399
Ranke, Leopold von 16
Rapp, George 328
Raritan valley *232*
Rationalism 230
Rauschenbusch, Walter 348
Ravenna, Byzantine exarchate at *57*
Red Cross 366
Reformation, Reformers 153–57, *153–57*
  in Switzerland 160–62
  in Scandinavia 163–64
  in England 165–69
  see Radical Reformation
Reformed
  new churches in USA *351*
Regensburg *193*
Reimarus, H. S. *234*, 236
Religion, *Religionswissenschaft* 236, 331
Religious liberty 321
  Hutterites 150
  in New England 226
  Pennsylvania 228
  in American colonies 263
  in Federal Constitution 320
  in Japan after World War II *394*
Religious News Service 401
Rembrandt *142*, 180
Renaissance, Italian 98, 140–41
Renaissance, Northern ("Christian") 142–43
Renan, Ernest *259*, 260
Resistance, duty of
  Huguenots 176
  see Bonhoeffer, Dietrich
  see Rutherford, Samuel

Restitution of the true church 148, 149
  Hutterite 150
  Jehovah's Witnesses 390, 392
  see Radical Reformation
Reuchlin, Johannes *142*, 143, 145
Reuveni, David 122, 123
Revivalism
  in America 263, 264, 322
  and communes 328
  and abolitionism 333
  and new denominations 350
  in Africa *396*, 397
  and Pentecostalism 399
Revolution(s), European
  of 1830, 1848, 1871 242, 244
  see American Revolution
  see English Revolution
  see French Revolution
  see Russian Revolution
Rhine Valley 158
Rhode Island 200, 263
Rhodes, fall of 151, *220*
Rhodes, Cecil 272, *273*
Ricci, Matteo 209, *210*
Rice, Luther 325
Richard I, King of England ("the Lion-Hearted") 96
Ridley, Nicholas 167, 168
Riga 107, *108*
Riggs, Stephen R. *324*
Rio Salado, Battle of 124
Ritschl, Albrecht *234*, 240, 289
Rizal, José *267*
Roberts, Oral 399
Robertson, Frederick W. 293
Robinson, John *181*
Rockefeller, John D. Jr. 374
Rolle, Richard *113*
Roman Catholic Church 287
  Council of Trent 171, 218
  in Latin America 261
  in USA 265–66, 336, *337*, 338–39, 379
  breakaways in Africa 397
Roman Empire *24*, *54*
  decline 55–56
Romania
  independence of Ottoman Turks 250
Romanov, Michael, tsar of Russia 223
Romanticism 233, *233*
Rome 23, 25, *32*, *34*
  conquest of Britain 26–27
  fall of Rome 41
  St. Peter's 140, *140*
Romero, Oscar (archbishop) 385
Roosevelt, Franklin D. 316
Rothmann, Bernt 174
Rousseau, Jean Jacques 233, *233*
Rugby *279*
Runic stone 91
Russell, Charles Taze 341
Russia
  division of Poland 122
  Ivan the Great 139

voyages of discovery in America *198*
  a European power 224
  Holy Alliance 245, *246*, 247
  Russian Revolution 298
  see Soviet Union
Russian Orthodoxy 139
  lapse of patriarchate under Peter 223
  in America 265
  in Soviet Union 300
  in post-Soviet Union 301
  see Eastern Orthodoxy
Rutherford, Samuel *184*, 186
Ruysbroeck, Jan *113*

# S

Saalburg 26
Sabas, founder of Mar Saba monastery *59*
Sabbatai Zevi *123*, 124
Sabellius *32*
Sacraments defined and numbered 217
Sadducees 7
Safed *123*
St. Bartholomew's Day Massacre *175*, 176, 177
  see Huguenots
Salaca, Battle of *87*
Saladin 96, *101*
Salazar, Domingo de 216
Salerno, university of *130*
Sales, Francis de 213
Salvation Army *279*, 280
Samaritans 7, *11*, 13
Samarkand *39*
San Martin, Jose de *261*
Sankey, Ira David 293, 357, 364
Saracens
  Charlemagne's campaigns against 70
Sarajevo *248*
Sardinia
  Vandal *54*
  Muslim *68*
  to Pisa and Genoa *89*
  to Aragon 124
Saturninus *37*, 38
Satyagraha Ashram *275*
Savonarola 151, *152*
Saxons
  Charlemagne's wars with 70
  in England *92*, 93
Scandinavia
  mission to 75, *75*
  Reformation 163, *163*, 164
  see Denmark
  see Finland
  see Iceland
  see Normans
  see Norway
  see Sweden
  see Varangians
Scandinavian Missions Conferences 353
Sceptics
  Greek philosophical school *19*

Schaff, Philip 348, *371*
Schechter, Solomon 347
Schelling, F.W.J. von *233, 243*
Schiller, J.C.F. *233*
Schlegel, Friedrich von *233*
Schleiermacher, F.D.E. *233*, 240
Schmalkald League 158, 160, *193*
Schwarz, C. F. 228
Schwarzenau *231*
Schweitzer, Albert 40n, *273*
Schwenckfeld, Caspar *147*, 173, 174
Science, scientific method *259*, 260
Scopes Trial 339
Scotland
 Mary Stuart 167, *184*, 186
 National Covenant, Solemn League and Covenant 182, 186
 civil war and Reformation *184*, 185-86
 in 19th century *279*
Second Great Awakening 263, 322
"Sects" 390*f*
Secularization 173, 230
 see church lands
Selim I and II 221
Selina, Countess of Huntingdon *232*
Seljuks
 see Turks
Sénanque, Abbey of *103*, 104
Seneca 18, *19*, 22
Sephardim
 see Jews
Sepoy Mutiny 274, *275*
Septimius Severus *24*, 25, 26
Serbia
 under Ottoman Turks *138*, 192, 219
 independence struggle 250
Serfdom 146
 Russian 245
 see feudalism
Servetus, Michael *147, 161*, 173
Service Committees 387, *387*, *388*, 389
Seven Years' War/ "French and Indian War" 226
Shakers 328
Shembe, Isaiah 397
Shi'ites 81
 persecuted by Selim II 221
Shinto centers in Japan *395*
*Shoah*
 see Holocaust
Shogi Effendi/"the Guardian" 284
"Shunning" *(Meidung)* 148
Sicily
 Muslim *68*
 Norman *89*
 under Emp. Ferdinand II 100
 papal fief 105
Sickingen, Franz von *144*, 145
Siegmund-Schultze, Friedrich 349

Sigismund II, King of Poland 213
Sigismund III, King of Sweden, King of Poland 213
Sigtuna 377
Simon Magus 36
Simpson, A. B. 353
Singapore *275*
Sioux, missions among the *324*
Sisters of the Holy Family *337*
Slavery 271
 introduced in Spanish America 197, *207*
 "triangular trade" *268*
 Assiento Treaty 271
 slave-ship 274
 American civil war *332*, 333
 see abolitionism
Slavs
 Slavonic literature 58
Smith, George Adam 364
Smith, Joseph Jr. *323*
Smith, Joseph III 390
Smuts, Jan Christian 272
Smyth, John 169, *181*
Sobieski, John (king of Poland) 219, *220*
Societies of Inquiry 326
Society of Brethren 325, 326, 353
Socinians *147*
 Sozzini, Lelio and Fausto 173
Socrates 18, 19, *19*
Söderblom, Nathan *371*
Soka Gakkai 357
Solomon
 King 6
 kingdom *9*
Soloviev, Vladimir S. *246*, 247
Sorbonne
 anti-Protestant center *201*, 202
Sorel, Georges 303
South Africa
 independent African churches *396*, 397
 see Boers
South German Brethren *147*, 148
 see Anabaptists
South Pacific
 colonialism in *277*, 277–78
 modern missions *360–61*
 lay training 384
Southern Baptist Convention 336, *340*, 340–41
Southern Christian Leadership Conference *343*, 344
Soviet Union
 Nazi-Soviet Pact *299*, 309
 in World War II 300–01
 intervention in Spanish Civil War *304*
Sozzini, Fausto and Lelio
 see Socinians
Spain 98
 tribal wanderings *54*
 Muslim conquest *68*
 Charlemagne's campaigns *71*
 unification of 124–25, *125*
 expulsion of Jews and Moors *126, 127*

voyages of discovery 194, *195*, 196
 the Grand Armada *204, 205*
 under Philip II 203, *204*
 conquests in America 197, 199, 207, *261*
 in Africa *273*
 Spanish Civil War 303, *304*, 304–05
Spanish-American War 266
Spener, Philipp Jakob *188*, 230, *231*
Speyer *153, 154*
Spinoza, Baruch *234*
Spiritualizer 173
Stalin, Josef 300, 301, 305
*Startzi* *246*, 247
Stauffenberg, Claus von 310
Steere, Douglas 379
Stein, Karl Freiherr von 240
Steiner, Rudolf 393
*Stetl* 121
Stockholm
 International Forum on the Holocaust 409, 414
Stöhr, Martin 377
Stoics, Stoicism *19*, 22
Stone, Barton W. 264
Stowe, Harriet Beecher 333
Strassburg
 Imperial city *128*
 M. Butzer 155, *155*
Strong, Josiah 266, 348
Studd, C. T. 364
Student Volunteer Movement 357, 364, 367
Stuttgart Declaration of Guilt 309
Suarez, Francisco de *210*, 211
Suez Canal 281
Sufism 81
Suleiman the Magnificent 192, 209, *220*, 221
Sullivan, Arthur S. 293
Sumatra *277*
Sun Yat-sen *275*, 310
Sunnis 81
Suso, Henry *113*, 115
Swarthmore Hall *181*
Sweden
 Christianization of 91
 Reformation 163, *163*
 in Russia 224
 Philadelphia congregation *398*, 399
Swiss Brethren *147*, 148, 162, 214
Switzerland *156*, 160, *161*
 Confessions of Faith 162
 Reformation 160, *161*, 162
 treaty with France 202
 Counter-Reformation 212
 U. Zwingli *156*
 see Zürich
 see Zwingli
Syllabus of Errors *253*, 255
Synagogue(s)
 of the diaspora 15
 at Capernaum 15
 at Newport, R.I. 345

# T

Tahiti 277, 278
T'ai P'ing Rebellion 275, 276
Taipei Academy House 384
Taiwan (Formosa) 275, 311, 312
Tamerlane
 and Nestorian Christianity 65
 conquests 110, *116*
Tatian *32*, 33
Tauler, Johann *113*, 115
Tausen, Hans *163*
Taylor, J. Hudson 276, 353
Tecumseh *262*, 265
Templars 94, 102
Temple, William 370
Tennent, William Sr. 350
Tennyson, Alfred *279*
Teresa of Ávila 203
Tertullian 20, *34*, 36
Teutonic Knights 102
 in the Baltic 107, *108*
 and Reformation 160
Thadden-Trieglaff, Reinold
 von 368, 376
Thailand (Siam)
 missions *275*
Theatines 212
Theodora, Empress 56
Theodoric 47
Theodosius (Roman Emp.) *43*, 49, *54*, 55
Theodosius II (Roman Emp.) 49, *54*, 55
"Third World" 301
"Thirty-Nine Articles" *165*, 169
Thirty Years' War 187–89
 Swiss independence
  recognized 160
Tholuck, F.A.G. *233*
Thomas Aquinas *113*, 114–15
 and Christendom 41
"Thomas Christians" *28*
Thomism
 see Thomas Aquinas
Thorlaksson, G. *163*, 164
Tillich, Paul *306*, 349
Timbuktu *268*, 269, 271
Tolerance, toleration
 Roman 30
 Constantine's grant at Milan
  42
 of Mongols 109
 of Philipp of Hesse 158
 of William the Silent 180
 of Akbar in India 195
 in Poland 219
 of Muslims 221
 Holy Muslim Empire 247, 281
 condemned by pope 252
 different from religious
  liberty 228, 320
Tolstoy, Leo 245, *246*, 252
Tone, Wolfe *314*
Torquemada, Tomás de *125*, 127, 203
Toulouse
 Albigensian center *106*
Tours

 monastic center *62*
 battle of 69
Tractarians *279*, 280, 291
Tradition
 and the Bible 217
Tranquebar *229*
Transvaal 271, 272
Transylvania 219
Trent, Council of 171, 209, 216–18, *216–18*
 Index of Forbidden Books 157
Tribal migrations *54*
Tripoli, County of 96, *101*
Troeltsch, Ernst 240, 289, 392
Trotsky, Leon 300, 301
Trueblood, Elton 379
Truman, Harry 412
Tübingen
 university reorganized 159
Turkey, republic of *282*, 283
Turks
 Seljuk empire 86, *116*, 117
 and crusader kingdoms *101*
 invasions of Europe 192, 219, *220*
 see Ottoman Empire
Tuskegee Institute *334*, 336
Tyndale, William *165*, 167
Tyrrell, George *259*, 260

# U

Uganda *273*, 274
Ulfilas 45, *50*
Union Theological
 Seminary 349
Unitarianism
 in Radical Reformation 127, 173
 in New England 263, 322
Uniates
 in India 66
 in Poland and Lithuania 223
U.S. Catholic Bishops'
 Conference 349
United States of America
 voyages of discovery *198*
 colonial holdings 263, *275*, 277
 revivals of religion 322, *323*
 missionary awakening 353, *356*
 unusual religious movements
  390, *391*, 392
Universities 98, 129, *130*, 131
 American foundings 329, *330*
Uppsala
 cathedral 164
Urban II (pope) 94
Urban VI (pope) 133, *134*
Utopian Socialism 296
 communes in America *327*, 328
Utrecht
 Willibrord 75
 Union of *178*, 256
 ecclesiastical reorganizations
  179, 257
 Old Catholic center *256*

# V

Vadianus, Joachim *161*
Valdés, Juan de 142, *147*, 170
Valentinus *37*, 38
Valla, Lorenzo 16, 141
Vandals
 kingdom in N. Africa 51, *54*
Varangians 91
Varick, James 342
Vatican I 255, *256*, 257
 see Papal Infallibility
Vatican II 257, 339, 374
 representation *372*
Vaughn, John N. 400
Vedanta Society 357
Venice
 commercial empire *89*, 102, *128*, *136*
 Renaissance city-state 140
 S. Giorgio Maggiore *140*
 wars with Ottoman Turks 219
Verdun, Treaty of 72, *87*
Vespucci, Amerigo *196*, 198
Vestries
 in American Anglicanism 263
Victoria (Queen of England)
 274, 280
Vienna
 First Siege of 192, *201*, 208
 Second Siege of 194, 219
 Congress of 242, 244, *253*, 254, 286
Vietnam *277*
 missions *275*
Viret, Pierre *161*
Virginia 200, *225*, 226, 333
 religious liberty 263
Visigoths
 in Spain 124
Visser't Hooft, W. A. 368, *369*, 374, 376
Vivekenanda 357
Voltaire (François-Marie
 Arouet) *234*, 236
Voluntaryism
 personal religious decision 44
 development in New England
  263
 and revivalism 264, 322

# W

Wagner, Gottfried 410
Wahhabis 221
Waldorf schools 393
Waldenses *175*, 182, *201*, 202, 203
Wales
 G. Whitefield *232*
Wallachia
 under Ottoman Turks *138*
Wallenstein, Albrecht Eusebius
 Wenzel von *188*, 189
Walther, Carl F. W. 340
Walz, Hans Hermann 377, 384
War
 see peace testimony
 see World War I
 see World War II

Wartburg *153*
Washington, Booker T. 336, *343*, 344
Waterloo, battle of *238*, 240
Weimar Republic 307–08
Wellhausen, Julius 289
Wesley, Charles 232, *232*
Wesley, John 231–32, *232*
Wesleyanism
    and missions 352
    see Methodists
Westminster Assembly *165*, *181*
    Westminster Confession 185
Westphalia, Treaties of 187, *188*, 189
    Switzerland 160
    Netherlands 180
Wetterau valley *231*
Whitby, Synod of 63
White Fathers *273*, 274, 357
Whitefield, George 232, *232*, *323*
Wichern, Johann Hinrich 244, 291
Wilberforce, William *279*, 293
Wilder, Robert P. 293
William the Conqueror *92*, 93
William of Orange, "the Silent" *178*, 179, 180
William III of Orange, and Mary (King and Queen of England) 183
William of Rubruquis *109*
Williams, George 364, *365*
Williams, Roger 200, 226, 263
Willibrord 62, *63*, 75
Wilson, Woodrow 348
Winthrop, John 226
Wise, Isaac M. 345, *346*
Wise, Stephen S. *346*, 347, 406
Wishard, Luther 364
Wishart, George *184*, 185
Witches 119
Witherspoon, John 350

Wittenberg *153*, *154*
Women in the church
    Empress Theodora 56
    opposition of J. Knox 185–86
    in modern missions 357
World Council of
    Churches 349, 374
    John R. Mott 367
    Harare Assembly *373*
    Membership 415–20
World Evangelization Crusade 364
World Parliament of Religions 348, 357
World Student Service 370
World War I
    assassination at Sarajevo 250
    German "war guilt" 307
    and the churches 317
    see Russian Revolution
    see Turkey
World War II
    in South Pacific *277*, 278
    in Europe *306*
    and the churches 318
World's Student Christian Federation 367, 368, *369*, 370
    John R. Mott 367
Worms 153, *153*, *193*
Wurm, Theophil 376
Wycliffe, John *128*, 135, 167

# X

Xavier, Francis 209, *210*, *229*
Ximénez de Cisneros, Francisco *125*, *130*, 203

# Y

Yad Vashem, Jerusalem 307, 407

"Yale Bands" 326
Yeshiva University *346*, 347
Yiddish 121
Yoido Full Gospel Church 400
Yokefellow Institute 381
Young, Brigham 390
Young Men's Christian Association 364, *365*, 366
Young Women's Christian Association 364, *365*
Young Turk movement 281

# Z

Zaire
    see Congo
Zara *95*
Zealots 7, 10
Zen Buddhism 357
Zentrum
    political parties, clerical 244
Ziegenbalg, Bartholomäus 228, *229*
Zinzendorf, Nikolaus Ludwig 231, *231*, *327*, 328
Zion, Illinois *327*
Zionism 411–12
"Zionist" churches 397
Zoroastrianism
    under Sassanids in Persia 65
Zosimus 30
Zürich
    and Zwingli 147, 156, *156*
    Anabaptists 147, 148
Zulu War *270*, 272
Zwickau prophets *147*
Zwingli, Ulrich 145, 147, 148, 156, *156*, 158, *158*
    Reformation in Switzerland *161*, 162
Zwolle *142*